HEROES AND HEROINES
OF FICTION

Modern Prose and Poetry

HEROES AND HEROINES
OF FICTION

MODERN PROSE AND POETRY

FAMOUS CHARACTERS AND FAMOUS
NAMES IN NOVELS, ROMANCES, POEMS
AND DRAMAS, CLASSIFIED, ANALYZED AND
CRITICISED, WITH SUPPLEMENTARY CITA-
TIONS FROM THE BEST AUTHORITIES

BY

WILLIAM S. WALSH

AUTHOR OF "CURIOSITIES OF POPULAR CUSTOMS," "HANDY BOOK OF LITERARY CURIOSITIES,"
" THE HANDY BOOK OF CURIOUS INFORMATION."

PHILADELPHIA AND LONDON
J. B. LIPPINCOTT COMPANY

REPUBLISHED BY GALE RESEARCH COMPANY, BOOK TOWER, DETROIT, 1966

Library of Congress Card Catalog Number: 66–29782

PRINTED IN UNITED STATES OF AMERICA

HEROES AND HEROINES OF FICTION

MODERN PROSE AND POETRY

A

Aaron, in *Titus Andronicus*, attributed to Shakespeare, a Moorish prisoner introduced into Act i, Sc. 1. Savage, uncouth and unnatural, cursing the day in which fate has restrained him from committing " some notorious ill," his subsequent conduct justifies the description he gives of himself.

Abaddon, in Milton's *Paradise Regained* (iv, 624) a personification of the Jewish hades. See vol. II.

Abadonna, the penitent fallen angel of Klopstock's *Messiah*. See vol. II.

Abberville, Lord, hero of a comedy, *The Fashionable Lover* (1780), by Richard Cumberland, a young nobleman who, under the guardianship of the nerveless and incompetent Dr. Druid, a Welsh antiquary, recklessly squanders his patrimony and becomes enmeshed in the toils of an unscrupulous woman of the town, Lucinda Bridgemore. He is saved from his evil courses by his father's executor, Mr. Mortimer, and his honest Scotch bailiff.

Abbot The, titular character in Scott's romance *The Abbot*. See GLENDENNING, EDWARD.

Abdael, in Dryden's *Absalom and Achitophel*, a character intended for General Monk, afterwards Duke of Albemarle, who was a loyal partisan of Charles II.

Abdaldar, in Robert Southey's oriental epic, *Thalaba the Destroyer* (1797), a magician chosen as the destroyer of Thalaba who died as he was on the point of stabbing Thalaba.

Abdallah, titular hero of *Abdallah or the Four-leaved Clover* (Fr. *Abdallah, ou le Trèfle à Quatre Feuilles*) an Arabian romance by Edouard Laboulaye (1859); English translation by Mary L. Booth (1868).

Abdallah, son of a Bedouin woman, widowed before his birth, is charged by an astrologer to seek the four-leaved clover, subsequently explained to be a mystic flower hastily snatched up by Eve at her expulsion from Eden. The leaves are respectively copper, silver, gold and diamond. The diamond leaf had dropped from Eve's trembling hand inside the garden; the others were scattered over the world. The deeds by which Abdallah seeks to win the successive leaves form the staple of the plot.

Abdallah, in Byron's poem, *The Bride of Abydos*, a brother of Giaffer, murdered by the latter.

Abdallah el Hadji (the Pilgrim), in Scott's romance, *The Talisman*, an ambassador from Saladin to Richard Cœur-de-Lion, who arranged all the preliminaries for the combat between Kenneth of Scotland (*q.v.*) and Conrade de Montserrat.

Abdelazer, hero of a tragedy, *Abdelazer, or the Moor's Revenge* (1677), which Mrs. Aphra Behn founded on *Lust's Dominion, or the Lascivious Queen*, an Elizabethan play falsely attributed to Marlowe. Mrs. Behn was, in turn, laid under contribution by Young in *The Revenge*.

Abdelazer is son of the King of Fez, who has been conquered and killed by the King of Spain. Devoting his life to revenge he begins by accepting the advances of the lascivious queen, proceeds to slay the king, his son, and then the queen herself, and is finally slain by the King's other son, Philip. The outlines of Young's Zanga (q.v.) are evidently borrowed from Abdelazer, but Zanga keeps true to his single aim of vengeance, while Abdelazer is furthermore swayed by ambition, jealousy, and lubricity.

Abdiel (Hebrew *abd*, servant, and *'el*, God), in Milton's *Paradise Lost*, the one seraph who refused to join Satan's rebellion against the Almighty in Heaven.

> Faithful found,
> Among the faithless, faithful only he;
> Among innumerable false unmoved,
> Unshaken, unseduced, unterrified,
> His loyalty he kept, his love, his zeal.
> *Paradise Lost*, Bk. v, 896.

Like Zophiel in the same poem he seems to have owed his introduction into the heavenly hierarchy to Milton himself. The name, indeed, may be found in I Chronicles v, 15, as the son of Guni, but thorough search has failed to reveal any mention of a seraph of this name in Biblical, Cabalistic or patriotic literature. As to the character itself Milton may have modelled it upon the herald angel Raphael in Vondel's choral drama of *Lucifer*. The lines quoted above apply equally well to Raphael as to Abdiel. In each case a single seraph opposes the enemy in his own palace, all undaunted by the hostile scorn of myriads. That this is no mere coincidence is shown by many other similarities between the Dutch drama and the English epic.

Abellino, hero of M. G. Lewis's tale, *The Bravo of Venice*, a bandit who for the furtherance of his schemes assumes staccato disguises as a beggar and winds up in glory as the husband of the Doge's niece. Lewis founded his tale on a German story by Zschokke, *Abællino the Great Bandit*, which was adapted for the American stage by William Dunlap (1801). Other plays were also based on Zschokke.

Abencerages. A powerful Moorish family whose quarrels with their rivals, the Zegris, hastened the fall of the kingdom of Granada in Spain. The love of Aben Hamad, an Abencerage, for the wife or sister of Boabdil, led, in 1485, to the slaughter of all the heads of the family in the Alhambra palace. This legend has been utilized by Chateaubriand in his romance of *The Last of the Abencerages* (1827). Aben Hamad, the hero, is accused of adultery with Queen Daxara and perishes with thirty-five other members of his family in a general massacre.

Aben-Ezra, Raphael, in Charles Kingsley's historical novel, *Hypatia*, a friend of the Prefect of Alexandria.

Abessa, in Spenser's *Faërie Queene* (1590), an impersonation in female form of abbeys, convents and monasteries. She is the daughter of Corceca ("blind-heart") and the paramour of Kirkrapine. Una on her lion, searching for the Red Cross Knight, called out to Abessa, who was so terrified at sight of the lion that she ran into the house of Blind Superstition. The lion, however, broke down the door. The allegory means that when Truth arrived the abbeys and convents became alarmed and barred her out. But that noble lion, Henry VIII, broke in as the royal advocate of the true faith.

Abhorson. An executioner introduced in *Measure for Measure* into a single scene (Act iv, Sc. 2), who has given much food for conjecture by his principal speech:

> Every true man's apparel fits your thief.

Abigail, a general name for a lady's maid or waiting maid among eighteenth century novelists, following in the wake of Beaumont and Fletcher, who bestowed it on the "waiting gentlewoman" in *The Scornful Lady*. Possibly Abigail Hill (Mrs. Masham), the waiting woman to Queen Anne, helped to popularize the name among her contemporaries. In the Old Testament (I Samuel xxv, 2, 42), Abigail waited on David during his flight from Saul when her husband Nabal refused to do so.

Abigail, heroine of Christopher Marlowe's *The Jew of Malta* (1591). When the house of Barabas, her father, is seized by the Christians and turned into a convent, she, at her father's command, becomes a nun in order to recoup the treasures concealed there. Her simulated conversion becomes real, she turns Christian in earnest, and Barabas goes mad, poisons her and ends by being precipitated into a boiling cauldron which he had prepared for a Turkish prince.

Abner, in Racine's tragedy of *Athalie,* the confidential friend of Joad. It is to him that the high priest addresses the famous line:

Je crains Dieu, Abner, et n'ai point autre crainte.
(I fear God, Abner, and have no other fear.)

Abou Ben Adhem, in Leigh Hunt's short poem of that name, learns from an angelic vision that " one who loves his fellow-man " stands first in the regards of the Almighty.

Abra, in Matthew Prior's historical and didactic poem *Solomon on the Vanity of the World* (1718), a concubine who captivates the weary and sated monarch by her obedience and fidelity. Two lines in Solomon's speech are specially famous as calling up in concise form an image of womanly devotion:

Abra was ready ere I called her name,
And though I called another, Abra came.
ii, 364.

Prior possibly borrowed the name from the mediæval romance of *Amadis of Gaul,* wherein the Sultan of Babylon has a sister, Abra, who secures his throne after he is slain by her lover, Lisuarte.

Abraham-Cupid, in *Romeo and Juliet* (Act ii, Sc. 1), is an expression which has given much trouble to the commentators. Upton conjectures it to be a printer's error for Adam Cupid, which he twists into an allusion to Adam Bell, the outlawed archer. Dyce, more plausibly, thinks that Abraham is merely a corruption of *auburn,* and supports his view by citing passages from old books where the corruption is unquestionable. Mr. R. G. White remarks, in confirmation of Dyce, that " Cupid is always represented by the old painters as auburn-haired."

Abram or **Abraham-men,** a cant term for a certain class of beggars of the sixteenth century. The anonymous *Fraternity of Vacabondes* (1575) supplies this definition:

An Abraham-man is he that walketh bare-armed and bare-legged, and feigneth himself mad, and carrieth a pack of wool, a stick with bacon on it, or such like toy and nameth himself Poor Tom.

Absalom, in Dryden's *Absalom and Achitophel* (1681), a political satire in verse, is intended for James, Duke of Monmouth, a natural son of Charles II by Lucy Waters. He resembles the Absalom of the Old Testament in his personal charms, his popularity with the masses and his unfilial behavior towards his putative father. See ACHITOPHEL.

Absent-minded Beggar. Kipling's jovial nickname for Tommy Atkins (the British soldier), in a poem of that name written at the beginning of the Boer war and printed in the *Daily Mail,* October 31, 1899.

Absolon, in *The Miller's Tale,* one of Chaucer's *Canterbury Tales* (1388), a pompous and conceited parish clerk, full of many small accomplishments of which he is inordinately vain. He is outwitted in his designs on Alison (*q.v.*), the young wife of an old carpenter, by his rival Nicholas.

Absolute, Sir Anthony, and **Captain Absolute,** father and son in Sheridan's comedy of *The Rivals* (1775). Sir Anthony is a boisterous, blustering, domineering old gentleman, firmly persuaded that he is the most amiable of beings and really hiding a warm heart under his fierce exterior. The son, though gallant and fine-mettled, is adroit enough to make his way by conciliation, strategy and dry humor. Under the name of Ensign Beverley he courts the heiress, Lydia Languish, and by this disguise precipitates a comedy of errors that are not cleared up until the end. Hazlitt thinks the

elder Absolute is a copy after Smollett's kind-hearted, high-spirited Matthew Bramble in *Humphrey Clinker*.
See ACRES, BOB.

Absolute Wisdom, a sobriquet
popularly bestowed upon Sir Matthew Wood (1768–1843). A staunch
supporter of Queen Caroline. On
the death of George III, he escorted
her from France to England and sat
by her side in an open landau when
she entered London (June 6, 1820).
He thus drew upon himself the shafts
of all the Tory wits and witlings of
the period.

Abudah, in James Ridley's *Tales
of the Geni* (1764), a wealthy merchant
of Bagdad. Nightly pestered by a
little old hag of hideous aspect, he is
driven by her threats to seek for
" the talisman of Oromanes," and
finds it after many terrible adventures
only to learn that it is an injunction
to love God and to obey His com-
mandments.

Like Abudah in the Arabian story, he is
always looking out for the Fury and knows
that the night will come and the inevitable
hag with it.—THACKERAY.

Acadia (Fr. *Acadie*, from the river
Shubencadie), the original name of
Nova Scotia given by the first French
settlers under De Monts, in 1604,
famous in literature as the scene of
Longfellow's *Evangeline*. After being
a subject of constant contention
between France and England, the
province was, by the treaty of Utrecht,
1713, ceded to England. But the
original settlers, French by blood,
remained French in feeling and in
language, a bar to Anglo-Saxon
colonizing and even a menace to
British security. In 1755 it was determined as a measure of safety to
expatriate the French Acadians. The
troops then in Nova Scotia were
enlisted New Englanders, under
Colonel John Winslow of Massachusetts. Acting by order of the
English governor, they gathered the
people together, drove them aboard
ship and distributed them among the
Atlantic colonies from Massachusetts
to Georgia. Parkman, in *Montcalm
and Wolfe* (1885), asserts that Long-

fellow and even Haliburton, the
historian of Nova Scotia, trusted for
their facts to Abbe Raynol, who never
saw the Acadians, and who " has
made an ideal picture of them, since
copied and improved in prose and
verse, until Acadia has become
Arcadia."

Acaste, in Molière's comedy *Le
Misanthrope*, a self-satisfied young
marquis, who easily consoles himself
when his suit is scorned by Celimene.

Achitophel, in Dryden's poetical
satire *Absalom and Achitophel*, is
meant for the Earl of Shaftesbury
(1621–1683). He was thus nicknamed by his contemporaries because
of the resemblance in character and
career between him and Achitophel
or Ahitophel, the treacherous friend
and counsellor of David, and the
fellow conspirator of Absalom (II
Samuel xv). The poem was written
at a critical juncture in public affairs
(see ABSALOM). Shaftesbury, who
had opposed the succession of the
Duke of York (afterwards James II)
to his brother Charles II and favored
that of the illegitimate Duke of
Monmouth, was then in the Tower
awaiting trial for high treason. Dryden, assuming that Shaftesbury had
nearly precipitated a civil war, found
in Achitophel's relation to Absalom
a Biblical parable sufficiently close
for his purpose.

Acrasia, in Spenser's *Faërie Queene*,
an enchantress personifying intemperance, who dwells in the Bower of
Bliss.

Acrates, in *The Purple Island*, an
allegorical poem by Phineas Fletcher,
the personification of Incontinence
and the father of Gluttony and
Drunkenness.

Acres, Bob, in Sheridan's comedy,
The Rivals (1775), is, with Captain
Absolute, one of the eponymic rivals
for the hand of Lydia Languish. An
ill-compounded mixture of the country squire and the London man about
town (a degenerate type of the first
and a pinchbeck imitation of the
second), he is redeemed from ignominy only by native kindliness and
good nature. He wears flashy clothes,

affects a bombastic swagger to cover his ludicrous cowardice and invents for himself a strange vocabulary of harmless profanity which he calls the oath sentimental or referential.

Acunha, Teresa d', in Scott's novel, *The Antiquary*, a Spanish servant of the Countess of Glenallan, who aided Edward Geraldin Neville in carrying off the new-born child of Eveline Neville. " If ever there was a fiend on earth in human form, that woman was one."

Ada, to whom Byron in *Childe Harold* addressed the invocation:

Ada! sole daughter of my house and heart.
Canto iii, Stanza 1.

was the Hon. Augusta Ada Byron, the poet's only legitimate child (1815–1852), who in 1835 married William King Noel, afterwards Earl of Lovelace. Unlike her father in feature and in the bent of her mind, which was towards mathematics rather than poetry, she inherited something of his mental vigor and intensity. Like him, too, she died in her thirty-seventh year. At her own request her coffin was placed by his in the vault at Hucknall Torkard. Thus it is evident that Byron realized his aspiration in Stanza cxvii of the same canto.

Yet, though dull Hate as duty should be taught,
I know that thou wilt love me,—though my name
Should be shut from thee, as a spell still fraught
With desolation, and a broken claim:
Though the grave closed between us,—'twere the same—
I know that thou wilt love me—though to drain
My blood from out thy being were an aim,
And an attainment,—all would be in vain,—
Still thou would'st love me, still that more than life retain.

Adah, the name which Lord Byron in *Cain, a Mystery*, bestows upon the wife of Cain, explaining that he does so because Adah is the first female name to be met with in the Old Testament (with the exception of Eve), being that of the wife of Lamech (Genesis iv, 19).

He paints her as a gentle wife and a devoted mother. It is curious that Rabbinical tradition gives her the very name that Byron stumbled on by accident. Adah's reputed grave is at Aboncais, a mountain in Arabia.

Adam, in Shakespeare's *As You Like It*, the aged family servant who casts his lot with Orlando when this, the younger of his masters, is exiled from court. He is a fine picture of healthy minded and generous old age. As he himself says:

My age is like a lusty winter
Frosty, but kindly.

There is a tradition—supported by two of Shakespeare's editors who sought for their facts in Stratford—that Shakespeare used to play this part. Oldys tells us that in his day he had met people who had known Shakespeare's brother in extreme old age.

All that could be recollected from him of his brother Will, was the faint general and almost lost ideas he had of having once seen him act a part in one of his own comedies wherein being to personate a decrepit old man, he wore a long beard, and appeared so weak and drooping and unable to walk, that he was forced to be supported and carried by another person to a table, at which he was seated among some company who were eating, and one of them sang a song.

This obviously refers to *As You Like It*, Act ii, Sc. 6 and 7.

Adam, in Arthur Hugh Clough's poem, *The Bothie of Tober-na-Vuolich* (1848), a nickname for the college tutor, probably intended as a portrait of the author himself.

The grave man, nicknamed Adam,
White-tied, clerical, silent, with antique square-cut waistcoat,
Formal, unchanged, of black cloth, but with sense and feeling beneath it.

Adamastor, " the spirit of the Cape " in Camoens' *Lusiad*, v (1569), a hideous monster guarding the Cape of Tempests—now known as the Cape of Good Hope—who appears to Vasco da Gama to warn him that he trespassed at his own risk on waters hitherto unvisited by man. The description of this monster has been greatly admired. These are the crucial lines:

An earthly paleness o'er his cheek was
 spread,
Erect arose his hairs of withered red;
Writhing to speak, his sable lips disclose,
Sharp and disjoined, his gnashing teeth's
 blue rows.
His haggard beard flowed quivering on the
 wind,
Revenge and horror in his mien combined;
His clouded front by withering lightnings
 scarred
The inward anguish of his soul declared.
His red eyes, glowing from their dusky caves,
Shot livid fires far-echoing o'er the waves;
His voice resounded, as the caverned shore
With hollow groan repeats the tempest's
 roar.
   "In me behold," he cried,
While dark-red sparkles from his eyeballs
 rolled,
"In me the Spirit of the Cape behold,
That rock by you the Cape of Tempests
 named,
By Neptune's rage, in horrid earthquakes
 framed,
When Jove's red bolts o'er Titan's offspring
 flamed.
With wide-stretched piles I guard the path-
less strand."

Adamida, a planet invented by
Klopstock in *The Messiah,* Bk. viii
(1771), to play an important part in
the crucifixion. It is described as a
spot whereon reside the unborn spirits
of saints and martyrs and other
humbler forms of true believers.
When the crucial moment occurs on
Calvary, Uriel, angel of the Sun, is
despatched by the Almighty with a
message to the planet (personified
for the occasion) that she should
place herself between the sun and
the earth in such fashion as to cause
a total eclipse. " Adamida, in obedience to the divine command, flew
amidst overwhelming storms, rushing
clouds, falling mountains, and swel-
ling seas. Uriel stood on the pole of
the star, but so lost in deep contemplation on Golgotha, that he heard
not the wild uproar. On coming to
the region of the sun, Adamida slack-
ened her course, and advancing before
the sun, covered its face and intercepted all its rays."

Adams, Parson Abraham, in Henry
Fielding's novel, *Joseph Andrews*
(1742), an eccentric and amiable
country curate, supposed to have
been drawn from the author's friend,
the Rev. William Young, who revised
Ainsworth's Latin Dictionary in 1752.
Deep read in books, he is utterly
ignorant of the world; easily duped,
and little disposed to anger on his
own account, he is yet a formidable
champion for the rights of others
especially the weak and the innocent.
Joseph Andrews in the novel calls
him " the best man I ever knew."
Sir Walter Scott considers the character " one of the richest productions
of the Muse of Fiction." Hazlitt
gives it the preference above all
Fielding's creations: " It is equally
true to nature, and more ideal than
any of the others. Its unsuspecting
simplicity makes it not only more
amiable, but doubly amusing, by
gratifying the sense of superior
sagacity in the reader. Our laughing
at him does not once lessen our
respect for him."

As to Parson Adams and his fist, and his
good heart, and his Æschylus which he
couldn't see to read, and his rejoicing at
being delivered from a ride in the carriage
with Mr. Peter Pounce, whom he had
erroneously complimented on the smallness
of his parochial means, let every body
rejoice that there has been a man in the
world called Henry Fielding to think of
such a character, and thousands of good
people sprinkled about that world to answer
for the truth of it; for had there not been,
what would have been its value? . . .
He is one of the simplest, but at the same
time manliest of men; is anxious to read a
man of the world his sermon on "vanity;"
preaches patience under affliction, and is
ready to lose his senses on the death of his
little boy; in short, has "every virtue under
heaven," except that of superiority to the
common failings of humanity, or of being
able to resist knocking a rascal down when
he insults the innocent. He is very poor,
and, agreeably to the notions of refinement
in those days, is treated by the rich as if
he were little better than a servant himself.
Even their stewards think it a condescension to treat him on equal terms.—LEIGH
HUNT.

Adam-zad, in Kipling's poem, *The
Truce of the Bear* (1898), a personification of Russia. The blind beggar
Matzun, eyeless, noseless, lipless, bids
the white men show no mercy when
they " go by the pass Muttiance to
shoot in the vale below." He tells
how after a long hunt " Adam-zad,
the bear that walks like a man," had
feigned exhaustion and begged for
mercy; how Matzun had restrained
his fire and how the bear tottering
nearer with a single blow—

From brow to jaw, the steel-shod paw,
It ripped my face away.

The poem was written at the time
Czar Nicholas II proposed the Peace
Congress and the disarmament of all
the powers.

Adicia, in Spenser's *Faërie Queene*
(1596) v. 8, wife of a soldan whom she
incites to distress Mercilla's kingdom.
Mercilla's ambassador, Samient, is
sent to arrange a peace; is ignominiously thrust out of doors, and two
knights are set upon her. Ill would
it have fared with the lady diplomat
but that the good knight Artegal
comes to the rescue, defeats the
assailants, and disarms Adicia of a
knife with which she rushes at Samient. Adicia is metamorphosed into
a tigress. The intended allegory is
aimed at Philip II of Spain, prefigured
by the soldan. Adicia is "papist"
bigotry; Mercilla, Queen Elizabeth;
and Samient is a composite of certain
ambassadors to Holland, who, seeking peace from Philip, were by him
detained as prisoners in defiance of
international law.

Adlerkron, Rupert Von, hero of a
novel, *Cyrilla* (1853), by the Baroness
Tautphoeus.

I happened to say that I thought Rupert
von Adlerkron at once the most heroic and
most lovable of modern imaginary heroes.
"But," I added, laughing, "you have much
to answer for in putting forth such an im-
possibly delightful ideal. How many girls
must have fallen hopelessly in love with
Rupert; and you know that your conscience
must make you say, with Iago, 'There is
no such man!'" I saw her glance at a
miniature which hung on the wall. It
represented an officer in Bavarian uniform,
with brown hair and mustache, and beautiful dark blue eyes. I knew it was her
husband's portrait, and ventured to say
that I had always imagined he must have
been something like Rupert.
"Well," she answered, with a sad smile,
"in his courage, and the equability and
brightness of his temperament, he was like
Rupert. In the forty-eight years we lived
together, I never had an angry word from
him."—*Baroness Tautphoeus,* an interview,
Atlantic Monthly, July, 1894.

Admirable Crichton (see CHRICH-
TON).

Adolphe, hero and title of a novel
(1816) by Benjamin Constant,
founded upon the author's liaison with
Madame de Stael. Adolphe is a
proud, reserved, sensitive and rather
feeble youth, a product of the age of
René and Werther; the victim alike
of culture and ennui—culture without
a purpose and ennui without a cause.
Partly urged by restless vanity,
partly in hopes of gaining an object
in life, he deliberately decides to fall
in love. He selects Ellenore, a Polish
lady, the acknowledged mistress of
the Count de P., who in her equivocal
position has borne herself with such
single-hearted devotion as to win a
certain position. He deliberately lays
siege to her, she struggles, and finally
succumbs to an overwhelming passion.
He, poor man, had contemplated only
a brief liaison but his sense of honor
will not allow him to desert Ellenore
after he wearies of her. He even gives
up his family, blasts all his worldly
prospects, and follows the lady to
Poland. At last she learns the truth;
it proves her death blow, leaving
Adolphe prostrated by suffering and
remorse.

Adon-Ai, in Lytton's romance
Zanoni, a mysterious spirit of love
and beauty apparently typifying pure
intellect.

Adonais, the name under which
Shelley laments his friend Keats
(1796–1821) in *Adonais, an Elegy on
the Death of John Keats* (1821). It
begins:

I weep for Adonais, he is dead!
Oh weep for Adonais! though our tears
Thaw not the frost which binds so dear a
head!

Shelley borrowed the name from
the title of an elegy on the death of
Adonis, written by Bion, a bucolic
poet who flourished about B.C. 280.
Bion's poem is called *Adonais.* This
is properly an adjective meaning
" of " or " belonging to Adonis,"
but Shelley has wrenched the word
from its original use and made it a
proper noun. As to his own poem,
Shelley was deeply stirred by the
opinion, since discredited, but then
very generally entertained, that
Keats's untimely death was the
result of a brutal criticism of *Endymion* in the *Quarterly Review.*
Shelley's lament is for the poet, not

the man (whom he barely knew), and for the loss that poetry, not Shelley himself, had sustained.

Adonbeck el Hakim, in Scott's historical romance, *The Talisman*, the name assumed by Saladin when he visited Sir Kenneth's squire as a doctor.

Adosinda, in Southey's epic *Roderick, the Last of the Goths* (1814), the daughter of the Gothic governor of Auria in Spain. Her husband and child having been massacred by the Moors, she dedicates herself to the work of liberating and avenging Spain. Being assigned to the captain of Alcahan's regiment, she murders him in his sleep and escapes by the assistance of Roderick in his disguise as a monk. In the great battle that resulted in the overthrow of the Moors (Canto iii) she gave the word of attack, " Victory and Vengeance! "

Adraste, hero of Molière's comedy, *Le Sicilien ou l'Amour Peintre* (1667), from whose disguise as an artist comes the sub-title of the piece.

Adrastus, in Tasso's *Jerusalem Delivered*, an Indian prince from the Ganges, an ally of the king of Egypt against the Christians. He rode an elephant and wore a serpent skin. In Book xx he is slain by Rinaldo. There is no historical basis for this character. Adrastus of Helvetia was the name of one of the Crusaders.

Adriana, in Shakespeare's *Comedy of Errors*, the wife of Antipholus of Ephesus.

Adriel, in Dryden's satirical poem *Absalom and Achitophel*, is intended for John Sheffield, Earl of Mulgrave (1649–1721), author of an *Essay on Poetry*:

Sharp-judging Adriel, the Muses' friend;
Himself a muse. In sanhedrim's debate
True to his prince, but not a slave to state;
Whom David's love with honours did adorn,
That from his disobedient son were torn.
Part i, 838, etc.

Ægeon, in Shakespeare's *Comedy of Errors*, a merchant of Syracuse. See ÆMILIA.

Ælla, hero of a tragedy of that name by Thomas Chatterton, the

most elaborate of the Rowley forgeries.

Æmilia, the lady Abbess in Shakespeare's *Comedy of Errors* (1593). A shipwreck had separated her from her husband, Ægeon, and her twin sons, both named Antipholus. At Ephesus, whither she was taken, she entered a convent and became abbess. One of her sons likewise settled in Ephesus, and, all unknown to her, was one of its wealthiest citizens. It happened that the other son and Ægeon simultaneously, but without knowledge of each other, arrived in Ephesus, occasioning many complications until the matter was set right at the duke's court, where the family were reunited.

Ætion, a character in Spenser's pastoral, *Colin Clout's Come Home Again* (1591), usually believed to be intended for Shakespeare:

And there, though last, not least, is Ætion:
A gentler shepherd may nowhere be found,
Whose Muse, full of high thought's invention,
Doth like himself heroically sound.

In similar vein Fuller speaks of the poet as " martial in the warlike sound of his surname, whence some may conjecture him of military extraction, *hasti-vibrans* or Shake-spear."— *Worthies of Warwickshire* (1662).

Fleay, Todd and others believe the name refers to Drayton, who published his *Idea* in 1593, and his *Idea's Mirrour* in 1594. " What more natural," asks Fleay, " than to indicate Drayton by Ætion, which is the synonym of Idea?"

The original Ætion (4th century B.C.) was a Greek painter famed for his picture of Alexander the Great's marriage.

Agape, in Edmund Spenser's *Faërie Queene*, a fairy who, having been delivered of triplets—Priamond, Diamond, and Triamond—visited the abyss of Demogorgon to consult the three fates as to what the future held for her sons. Clotho showed her that the threads of their lives were as thin as those spun by a spider. Agape begged the sisters at least to lengthen the life threads, but they could only be urged to a compromise:

When ye shred with fatal knife
His line which is the shortest of the three,
Eftsoon his life may pass into the next;
And when the next shall likewise ended be,
That both their lives may likewise be annext
Unto the third, that his may be so trebly
wext.
SPENSER: *Faërie Queene*, iv, 2 (1590).

Agatha, heroine of a poem of that name by George Eliot.

Aged P., *i.e.,* Aged Parent in Dickens's novel, *Great Expectations* (1860), the nickname under which Wemmick playfully alluded to his father, who lived with him at the castle at Walworth, was very deaf and very proud of his son.

Agnes, in Molière's comedy *L'École des Femmes* (The School for Wives), a typical ingenue, simple, ignorant and spotless, whose name has passed into the French language as a synonym for girlish innocence, real or pretended. Arnolphe, her guardian, has brought her up as his future wife on the theory that "extreme ignorance" is the only safeguard for maiden virtue and that all she needs to know is "to pray, to love me, to sew and to spin." She develops all the transparent simplicity of Miranda, although Shakespeare's more poetic theme imposed upon him a more imaginative treatment of a similar condition and character. Honest and openhearted, she is frankly inquisitive about matters she does not understand, pushes her ignorance to ridiculous extremes, rejoices with candid delight in the mere experience of being wooed, and is utterly unable to understand Arnolphe's sufferings. See ARNOLPHE, CELIMENE, PINCHWIFE.

Aguecheek, Sir Andrew, in Shakespeare's comedy, *Twelfth Night* (1599), a "straight-haired country squire" in love with Olivia. A shrill, fantastic figure, he is an embodiment of complacent fatuity, ever ready to retail maundering experiences that interest nobody and to verify his own character as "one whom many do call fool." In the duel scene with Viola, whom he imagines his rival with Olivia, Shakespeare has given the hint

which Sheridan utilized in Bob Acres. Viola is afraid of Aguecheek, but Aguecheek is still more afraid of her. Sir Toby Belch urges them both on; luckily the duel is interrupted.

Ah Sin, hero of Bret Harte's humorous poem known familiarly as *The Heathen Chinee*, but originally published under the title *Plain Language from Truthful James* (1870). There is much humor in the quiet undertone of incredulous surprise and outraged moral feeling with which the Pacific coast gambler discovers that the mild-looking coolie is as great a rogue and cheat as himself. With the assistance of Mark Twain, Bret Harte in 1880 produced a play entitled "Ah Sin."

Aiglon, L' (Fr. the eaglet), a name first given by Victor Hugo to Napoleon II, *i.e.,* the Duke of Reichstadt, son of Napoleon I and Marie Louise. Edmond Rostand took it as the title of a play (1900) of which this unfortunate lad is the hero. Brought up under the influence of Metternich at the Austrian court, every effort is made to keep him in ignorance of his father's achievements and of the possibilities that lie before him. In spite of this he learns all. He attempts flight, but his fellow conspirators are scattered on the field of Wagram and he himself is taken back to die in Vienna.

Aimwell, Thomas, Viscount, in *The Beaux Stratagem,* a comedy by George Farquhar. Aimwell is a bankrupt nobleman who joins his friend, Francis Archer, in redeeming their fortunes by stratagem. They appear in Lichfield as master and valet. Aimwell feigns to be ill and works on the sympathies of Lady Bountiful, who, true to her name and character, removes him to her own house. Here Dorinda, her daughter, falls in love with him and he wins her as his bride. Archer meanwhile prosecutes an intrigue with a married woman, the wife of Squire Sullen, reaping nothing but temporary amusement.

Airy, Sir George, in *The Busybody* (1709), a comedy by Mrs. Centlivre, a young gentleman, gay, generous and gallant, possessing a further virtue in an income of £4,000 a year, the wooer of Miranda.

Alastor, the tutelary spirit in Shelley's *Alastor, or the Spirit of Solitude,* who drives the hero, evidently meant for Shelley himself, far from the haunts of men in wild pursuit of an unattainable ideal that had been vaguely hinted to him in dreams. He crosses the Balkans and the steppes of southern Russia. Using his cloak as a sail, he drives a small boat up one of the rivers that flow down from the Caucasus, his hair turning gray all the time, and finally dies in a spot of apparently impossible geography. The title of the poem is said to have been suggested to Shelley by his friend T. L. Peacock, who "was amused," says Robert Buchanan, " to the day of his death by the fact that the public, and even the critics, persisted in assuming Alastor to be the name of the hero of the poem, whereas the Greek word 'Αλάστωρ signifies ' an evil genius,' and the evil genius depicted in the poem is the Spirit of Solitude."

Albert, in Knowles' drama, *The Beggar of Bethnal Green,* the assumed name of Lord Wilfrid.

Albion, in Dryden's opera of *Albion and Albinus* (1685), represents Charles II as Albinus represents his brother, the Duke of York, afterwards James II. While the opera was actually in rehearsal the original of Albion died. It was produced, Downes says, " on a very unlucky day, being the day the Duke of Monmouth landed in the west."

Albovine, hero of Sir William Davenant's *Albovine, King of the Lombards* (1629). He marries Rhodolinda, but shocks her on the wedding day by drinking out of the skull of her dead father. She intrigues with Paradine and incites him to slay the king. Paradine betrays the plot. Albovine fights a duel with Paradine and allows himself to be slain, whereupon the victor immolates Rhodolinda. The story is obviously taken with only a slight change of proper names from that of

Alboin and Rosmunda. See ROSMUNDA in vol. II.

Albumazar (the name is that of a famous Persian astronomer, 776-885), hero of a comedy so entitled (1606) which Thomas Tomkis founded upon *L'Astrologo* of G. B. Della Porta. Dryden, in a prologue written for a revival of this play (1668), accused Ben Jonson of having plagiarized his Alchemist from *Albumazar.* The plot of Tomkis's play turns upon the complications arising from the fact that Albumazar has metamorphosed Trincalo into Antonio. See SUBTLE.

Alceste, hero of Molière's comedy, *The Misanthrope,* a cynic whose originally generous, impulsive and sensitive nature, soured by contact with the coldness, artificiality and insincerity of conventional society, has encrusted itself behind an appearance of callous brutality. Alceste is the Hamlet of artificial eighteenth century France, a Hamlet drawn by an observer who keeps a keen eye upon the humorous possibilities of the character. Like Hamlet, too, his creator looked into his own heart to write. Alceste has much in common with Molière himself. Other originals have been suggested, especially the Duke de Montaussier, who in his native kindliness and acquired moroseness resembled both Molière and his hero. The duke, being informed that this portrait had been drawn by Molière, went to see the play and only said, " I have no ill will against Molière, for the original of Alceste, whoever it is, must be a fine character since the portrait is one."

Molière exhibited in his *Misanthrope* a pure and noble mind which had been sorely vexed by the sight of perfidy and malevolence disguised under the forms of politeness. He adopts a standard of good and evil directly opposed to that of the society which surrounded him. Courtesy seems to him to be a vice, and those stern virtues which are neglected by the fops and coquettes of Paris become too exclusively the objects of veneration. He is often to blame, he is often ridiculous, but he is always a good man.—MACAULAY *Essays, Comic Dramatists of the Restoration.*

Alcina, a personification of carnal licentiousness or sensuality. Bojardo introduces her into *Orlando Inna-morato* as a seductive fairy who carries off Astolfo. Ariosto, in *Orlando Furioso*, paints her in darker colors as a later Circe, living in an enchanted garden whither she decoys her lovers, and, after a brief season, converts them at her own will into trees, stones or brutes.

Alciphron, the chief character in *Alciphron or the Minute Philosopher* (1735), by Bishop George Berkeley, a dialogue on the model of Plato " written with the intention to expose the weakness of infidelity," and especially directed against the Earl of Shaftesbury. The original Alciphron was a Greek rhetorician who flourished about the second century A.D. His chief literary remains are three books of letters which profess to be written by peasants, fishermen, courtesans and parasites.

Alciphron, hero of *The Epicurean* (1837), a prose romance by Thomas Moore, a Greek youth brought up in the Epicurean school of philosophy who goes to Memphis in search of the priestly mysteries and there becomes enamoured of a young Christian girl, and the hero is thus introduced to " the secret religion " which he joins. This is a prose amplification of a poem of the same name by the same author.

Aldegonde, Lord St., in Benjamin Disraeli's novel *Lothair* (1870), a clever, witty and agreeable young nobleman into whose mouth the author puts some of his most successful epigrams. Though son and heir of a duke he is " a republican of the deepest dye " and is " opposed to all privileges and all orders of men except dukes, who were a necessity."

Bored with the emptiness of an existence which he knows not how to amend, a man who in other times might have ridden beside King Richard at Ascalon, or charged with the Black Prince at Poitiers, he lounges through life in good-humored weariness of amusements which will not amuse, and outrages conventionalism by his frank contempt for humbug. . . . A perfect specimen of a young English noble, who will not cant or lie; the wisest and truest when council or action is needed of him, yet with his fine qualities all running to waste in a world where there is no employment for them.

Alden, John (1599–1687), one of the Pilgrim Fathers, a cooper who came over in the *Mayflower*, settled at Duxbury, and married Priscilla Mullens. According to an accredited tradition, versified by Longfellow in *The Courtship of Miles Standish*, Alden was deputed by Captain Standish to win the maiden for him, but she gave John to understand that he had better woo for himself—and he took the hint. See STANDISH, MILES.

Aldiborontiphoscophornio, a courtier in Henry Carey's burlesque drama, *Chrononhotonthologos* (1734). Sir Walter Scott used to call James Ballantyne, the printer, this nickname, from his pomposity and formality of speech.

Aldrick, in Scott's *Peveril of the Peak*, the Jesuit confessor to the Countess of Derby.

Aleshine, Mrs. See LECKS, MRS.

Alexander the Great has figured in numerous modern dramas. The most notable examples in English literature are: (1) *Alexander and Campaspe* (1581), by John Lyly; (2) *The Rival Queens* (1677), by Nathaniel Lee; (3) *Alexander the Great in Little* (1837), a " grand tragi-comic operatic burlesque spectacle," by T. Dibdin.

Alfarata, an Indian maiden, heroine of one of the most popular songs ever produced in America—*The Blue Juniata*, by Mrs. Marion Dix Sullivan. The opening stanza runs thus:

> Wild roved an Indian girl,
>   Bright Alfarata,
> Where sweep the waters
>   Of the blue Juniata.
> Swift as an antelope,
>   Through the forest going,
> Loose were her jetty locks
>   In waving tresses flowing.

There is no great poetical merit in the lines, but they have a musical lilt which caught the public fancy. Every one sang them; girls and mares and boats and other things feminine were called Alfarata, and the name still survives in such corruptions as Alfareta, Alfaretta and Alfretta. The Juniata (or Choniata) River, which is formed by the union of three smaller streams that rise in the Allegheny

Mountains and unite near Hunting-don, Pennsylvania, to be lost in the Susquehanna, about a mile from Dun-cannon, was a former haunt of the Iro-quois Indians, who gave it its name.

Alice, heroine of Bulwer Lytton's novel, *Ernest Maltravers* (1837) and its sequel *Alice, or the Mysteries* (1838). She is the daughter of Darvil, a burglar; is educated by Maltravers, becomes his mistress, and bears him a daughter, who dies. They are separated for twenty years. Alice marries a banker named Templeton. The latter is raised to the peerage under the title of Vargrave. See MALTRAVERS, ERNEST.

Alice, the girl heroine of two fairy tales by " Louis Carroll " (C. L. Dodgson), which grew out of stories the author had told to his little friend Alice Liddell, daughter of Dean Liddell. *Alice's Adventures in Won-derland* (1865), tells of how she wan-dered in a dream through a strange country. *Through the Looking Glass and what Alice saw there* (1871) tell of further adventures in the Topsy-turvey land of which glimpses are presented in the ordinary mirror.

Alicia, in Nicholas Rowe's tragedy, *Jane Shore* (1713), the discarded mis-tress of Lord Hastings—" a laughing, toying, whimpering she "—who takes revenge on her rival Jane Shore by accusing her to the Duke of Gloster of luring Hastings from his allegiance to the lord protector. When her machinations end in the execution of Hastings, Alicia goes mad.

The king of Denmark went to see Mrs. Bellamy play "Alicia," and fell into a sound sleep. The angry lady had to say, "O thou false lord!" and she drew near to the slum-bering monarch, and shouted the words into the royal box. The king started, rubbed his eyes, and remarked that he would not have such a woman for his wife, though she had no end of kingdoms for a dowry.—*Cornhill Magazine* (1863).

Aliris, in Moore's *Lalla Rookh*, the real name of the Sultan of Lower Bucharia, who, under the disguise of the poet Feramors (*q.v.*), wooed and won Lalla Rookh.

Alison, in *The Miller's Tale*, one of Chaucer's *Canterbury Tales* (1588),

the young wife of John, an old car-penter, wealthy, miserly and easily duped. She is pursued by Absalon, the priggish parish clerk, but is her-self in love with her lodger Nicholas, who joins her in playing practical jokes upon her husband.

Allen, Benjamin, in Dickens's *Pickwick Papers* (1836), a medical student friend and room-mate of Bob Sawyer (*q.v.*), for whom he destines his sister Arabella, but the latter ran away and married Mr. Winkle with the connivance of Pickwick and Sam Weller.

Allen, Mr. and **Mrs.,** in Jane Austen's *Northanger Abbey*, the friends with whom Catherine Mor-land spends a season at Bath.

Mrs. Allen is sublime on her scale. A novelist who at the end of the eighteenth century could do Mrs. Allen, could do any-thing that she chose to do; and might be trusted never to attempt anything that she could not achieve.—GEORGE SAINTSBURY: *The English Novel*, page 194.

Allmers, Mr. and **Mrs.,** the chief characters in Henrik Ibsen's drama, *Little Eyolf* (1894). He is engaged in writing a book on *Human Respon-sibility*, while at his very hand his crippled son is perishing of neglect. He suddenly awakes to this, and simultaneously to the fact that his wife's jealousy has shifted from the book to the child. Her passion is so strong that it is evil. She cares noth-ing for the calm, deep tenderness of her husband. She will share him with nobody.

Allworthy, Squire, in Henry Field-ing's novel, *Tom Jones*, a man of scrupulous rectitude, great benevo-lence, philanthropy and public spirit, who shrank from any reward of money or fame. The character is drawn from Ralph Allen, the friend alike of Fielding and of Pope.

Let humble Allen with an awkward shame
Do good by stealth and blush to find it fame.
    POPE: *Epilogue to the Satires,*
                    Dialogue I, 136.

Allen, however, was not so humble as not to object to the epithet " low-born " which Pope had originally used, but which to please his friend he withdrew in the next edition in favor of " humble."

Allworthy, Mistress Bridget, in Fielding's novel, *The History of Tom Jones, A Foundling* (1750), the spinster sister of Squire Allworthy; eventually discovered to be the mother of Tom Jones. In the eighteenth century the term Mrs. or Mistress was applied to all ladies of mature years, whether married or single. Fielding concedes that Bridget was not remarkable for physical beauty. He continues:

"I would attempt to draw her picture, but that is done already by a more able master, Mr. Hogarth himself, to whom she sat many years ago and hath been lately exhibited by that gentleman in his print of *A Winter's Morning*, of which she was no improper emblem, and may be seen walking (for walk she does in the print) to Covent Garden Church, with a starved footboy behind, carrying her prayer book.—*Tom Jones*, Bk. i, Chap. xi.

It has been wondered why Fielding should have chosen to leave the stain of illegitimacy on the birth of his hero . . . but had Miss Bridget been privately married there could have been no adequate motive assigned for keeping the birth of the child a secret from a man so reasonable and compassionate as Allworthy.—*Encyclopædia Britannica*, article *Fielding*.

Alma (Latin, the soul), in Spenser's *Faërie Queene*, an allegorical character typifying the mind of man. She inhabits a castle emblematic of the human body.

But thousand enemies about us rave,
And with long siege us in this Castle hould:
Seven yeares this wize they us besieged have,
And many good Knights slaine that have us sought to save.
                              SPENSER.

The House of Temperaunce, in which
Doth sober *Alma* dwell,
Besieged of many foes, whom straunger Knights to flight compell.
                              SPENSER.

Alma is also the subject of a poem of the same name by Matthew Prior.

Almachide, the name under which Helorachis is Italianized in Alfieri's tragedy *Rosmunda*, the paramour of the titular heroine. See ROSMUNDA.

Almahide, hero of Madeleine de Scudery's historical romance (1660–1663), *Almahide or the Captive Queen*, which she derived from Perez de Hita's romance, *Historia de los Vandos*, dealing with the feuds of the Zegris and the Abencerrages in Granada. From Mdlle. de Scudery, Dryden drew the material for his tragedy, *The Conquest of Granada*.

Almahide, Queen of Granada and heroine of Dryden's drama, *Almanzor and Almahide, or the Conquest of Granada* (1672). During the lifetime of her husband Boabdelin, King of Granada, she resists the bold wooing of Almanzor, but becomes his consort after Boabdelin's death. She presents a picture of real female dignity against which the passion of love contends in vain.

Almanzor (Arabic, " The Invincible "), a title assumed by several Mussulman princes, notably by the second caliph of the Abbaside dynasty, Abou Giafar Abdallah, and by Mohammed, the great captain of the Moors in Spain.

The latter, under his assumed name, is the hero of Dryden's drama *Almanzor and Almahide, or the Conquest of Granada* (1670). He is represented as a prodigious warrior, an irrepressible lover, a bombastic self-appraiser. He persists in wooing Almahide, Queen of Granada, although she is the consort of Boabdelin. On the death of the king there is no longer any obstacle to the union of the titular characters. Dryden confesses of Almanzor that he derived " the first image from the Achilles of Homer; the next from Tasso's Rinaldo (who was a copy of the former), and the third from the Artaban of M. Calpranede, who had imitated both." Dryden complacently adds: " He is on a grand scale, not like the heroes of French romance." There is in fact much extravagance in the conception and much bombast in particular passages, but the impetus which enables the author to sustain the character through ten acts is remarkable. He was a favorite butt for caricature and is the undoubted original of Drawcansir in Buckingham's burlesque, *The Rehearsal* (1672).

It is not only the actual effects of Almanzor's valor which appear to us unnatural, but also the extraordinary principles and motives by which those exertions are guided. . . . The extravagance of sentiment is no less necessary than the extravagance of achievement to constitute a true knight errant; and such is Almanzor.—SIR WALTER SCOTT.

Blank verse is now, with one consent, allied
To Tragedy, and rarely quits her side.
Though mad Almanzor rhymed in Dryden's days,
No sing-song Hero rants in modern plays.
BYRON: *Hints from Horace*, l. 120.

Almeria, in William Congreve's drama, *The Mourning Bride* (1697), daughter of Manuel, King of Granada. Against her father's wishes she married Prince Alphonso, but the ship that was bearing her to her new home foundered at sea, and bride and groom were separated, only to meet again on the coast of Granada, whither Alphonso was brought as a captive. Under the assumed name of Osmyn he was cast into jail; escaped to head a successful invasion of Granada. He found King Manuel dead, assumed the crown and turned the "mourning bride" into a happy wife.

Almeyda, in Camoens' epic, *The Lusiad*, Canto x (1569), the Portuguese governor of India, who, fighting against the allied fleets of Cambaya and Egypt, had both legs shattered by chain shot. Refusing to let himself be carried to the rear, he insisted on being lashed to the mast, and in this condition waved his sword to cheer on the combatants until he expired from loss of blood.

Whirled by the cannons' rage, in shivers torn,
His thighs far scattered o'er the waves are borne;
Bound to the mast the God-like hero stands
Waves his proud sword and cheers his woful bands;
Though winds and seas their wonted aid deny
To yield he knows not, but he knows to die.

There was a story that, at the battle of New Orleans during the American Civil War, Admiral Farragut had himself lashed to the mast, but he always denied it.

Aloadin, in Southey's epic, *Thalaba* (Bk. vii), the possessor of an enchanted garden of impure delights to which he admitted only fools and his own enemies. Few who experienced its delights wished to return. Easily they yielded to the magician's demands that they should sign away their inheritances to him; whereupon Aloadin cut them off in the midst of their fancied bliss. The original forms Tale xxiv *Of the Suggestions of the Devil* in the *Gesta Romanorum*.

Alonzo the Brave, in M. G. Lewis's once famous ballad, *Alonzo the Brave and the Fair Imogine* (1795). A good knight and true who left his lady-love behind him when he went to the wars with a solemn pledge on both sides that each would be faithful until death. But Imogine became the bride of another and Alonzo's ghost, clad in complete steel, came and sat beside her during the wedding feast and she knew him not until he lifted up his vizor and showed a worm-infested skull. Then whisking her on his steed he carried her off to the grave. Many pantomimes, burlesques, and dramas have been founded on this theme, from *Alonzo and Imogine or the Bridal Spectre* (1801), a pantomimic romance by T. Dibdin, down to *Alonzo the Brave*, a burlesque by H. T. Craven.

Alph, an imaginary river which Coleridge, in his poem *Kubla Khan*, places in "Xanadu." The name was of his own invention, but was probably suggested by the Alpheus of classic myth.

In Xanadu did Kubla Khan
A stately pleasure-dome decree,
Where *Alph*, the sacred river, ran
Through caverns measureless to man,
Down to a sunless sea.

Alroy, David, a semi-legendary Jewish prince of the twelfth century whom Disraeli has made the hero of a historical romance in poetical prose, *The Wondrous Tale of Alroy*. After the Moslem conquest, Jerusalem had acknowledged the supremacy of the Caliphate, but the Jews of the east still retained a limited self-government under a governor of their own race who bore the title "Prince of the Captivity." The power of this prince always rose and fell in inverse proportion to that of the Caliphate, and the annals of the people tell of periods when the Prince of the Captivity enjoyed power and dignity scarcely less than those of the ancient kings of Judah. David Alroy was one of these princes at a time when the Caliphate was weakened. Four Seljuk sultans had divided the inheritance of the Prophet between them; but they, in their turn, had begun to languish from luxurious living, and therefore saw with concern the increasing power of the kings of Karasme.

On a slender basis of historical fact, Disraeli makes Alroy the temporary liberator of his people.

The psychological interest of the romance consists almost exclusively in the development of Alroy's character. He has scarcely come off victorious, and achieved his first task of liberating Israel, than the task itself seems insignificant to him, and he seeks for some greater object, for no one has been able to withstand him, and Western Asia lies at his feet. He will not be content with rebuilding Solomon's Temple; his ambition is not to be so easily satisfied; he.wants to found a great Asiatic empire. . . . This ambition occasions Alroy's fall. The Israelitish religious fanaticism, which raised him to victory, now turns against him with embitterment at the time when he is himself forgetting the projects and resolves of his youth by the side of a Mohammedan sultana in luxurious Bagdad. The King of Karasme assassinates him, and succeeds to his empire and his bride.—GEORGE BRANDES, *Lord Beaconsfield*.

Alsatia, the name given in the sixteenth century to Whitefriars, a London precinct formerly just outside of the city walls, where outlaws found immunity from arrest. It is famous in dramatic literature through Shadwell's comedy, *The Squire of Alsatia* (see BELFORD), and in fiction through Scott's description in *The Fortunes of Nigel*. Originally it had been the riverside monastery and gardens of a community of Carmelites (or White Friars), founded in the reign of Edward I and confiscated by Henry VIII. In the reign of Edward VI houses for persons of rank and wealth were erected here. The old monastery had possessed the right of sanctuary and this privilege of exemp-

tion affording immunity from arrest so far as debtors were concerned was continued to the district by James I in royal charter.

The result might have been foreseen. The prospect of immunity from arrest attracted so many bad characters that persons of respectability were driven out and their houses became the tenement of outlaws of both sexes.

In 1695 the nuisance of Alsatia had become so great that the Templars bricked up their eastern gateway. The Alsatians collected, killed one of the workmen, pulled down the wall, and when the sheriff of the city arrived they carried off his gold chain, which soon went to the melting pot.

Two years later a Captain Wynter was brought to the gallows for leading this riot. An act of Parliament finally suppressed the privileges of sanctuary in Whitefriars and similar spots in London. Warning was given that after a certain date the military would hunt out all the old rookeries of the precinct. There was a hasty flight of all the "copper captains" to France, Ireland and elsewhere. Since then practically all Alsatia has been rebuilt.

Altamont, Colonel Jack, sometimes known under other aliases—Johnny Armstrong or J. Amory—in Thackeray's novel *Pendennis*, the first husband of Lady Clavering and father of Blanche Amory. Convicted of forgery and sentenced to transportation, he had escaped from the convict colony and reappeared in London, where his wife, trusting to a report of his death, had married Sir Francis Clavering. For a time he subsists partly on dishonest winnings at the gaming table and partly by blackmailing the Claverings. Finally he is unmasked and forced to fly from England, but not without first revealing that his marriage to Lady Clavering was null and void through repeated bigamy before he had met her.

Althea, heroine of Richard Lovelace's poem, *To Althea in Prison*. See LUCASTA.

Altisidora, in Cervantes' *Don Quixote,* II, iii, 9, a maidservant of the duchess who in a spirit of mischief pretends to be in love with him and serenades him. He sings in response that he has no love for any one but Dulcinea, and while he is singing a string of cats are let into the room by a rope.

Alvan, Dr., hero of George Meredith's novel, *The Tragic Comedians,* which is founded on the love story of Frederick Lascelle.

Alving, Mrs., in Henrik Ibsen's domestic drama *Ghosts* (1881), a widow, mother of Oswald, the type of the new woman in revolt against the conventional lies of society as a result of her own bitter experience.

Mrs. Alving is not anybody in particular: she is a typical figure of the experienced, intelligent woman who, in passing from the first to the last quarter of the hour of history called the nineteenth century, has discovered how appallingly opportunities were wasted, morals perverted, and instincts corrupted, not only—sometimes not at all—by the vices she was taught to abhor in her youth, but by the virtues it was her pride and uprightness to maintain.—GEORGE BERNARD SHAW, *Dramatic Opinions.*

Alving, Oswald, in the same play, a victim of hereditary disease transmitted through his worthless and dissipated father. He has gone out into the world to make a name for himself but he, too, falls into evil courses and returns home to his mother to die of his own and his father's vices.

Alzire, heroine and title of a tragedy by Voltaire (1736). The scene is laid in Peru. Alzire is a captive who accepts the hand of Guzman, governor of Peru and conqueror of her country, under the impression that her betrothed lover Zamore has been slain. See ZAMORE.

Amanda. Under this name James Thomson, in a number of amatory verses, celebrated his passion, real or feigned, for a Miss Young, who eventually married Admiral Campbell. One little song won special popularity.

Unless with my Amanda blest,
  In vain I twine the woodbine bower:
Unless I deck her sweeter breast,
  In vain I rear the breathing flower:

Awakened by the genial year,
  In vain the birds around me sing,
In vain the freshening fields appear,
  Without my love there is no Spring.

Amanda, a character in Cibber's *Love's Last Shift* (1696), who reappears in its sequel Vanbrugh's *Relapse* (1697) and its rehabilitation by Sheridan, *A Trip to Scarborough* (1777). See LOVELESS.

The character of Amanda is interesting, especially in the momentary wavering and quick recovery of her virtue. This is the first homage that the theatre had paid, since the Restoration, to female chastity; and notwithstanding the vicious tone of the other characters in which Vanbrugh has gone as great lengths as any of his contemporaries, we perceive the beginning of a reaction in public spirit, which gradually reformed and elevated the moral standard of the stage.—HALLAM, *Literature of Europe.*

Amanda, heroine of Regina Maria Roche's romance, *The Children of the Abbey,* is the motherless daughter of the Earl of Dunreath. His second marriage results in her being cast aside by her father; she assumes a false name, becomes the innocent victim of slander, loses a will, refuses the hands of dukes and earls and finally with her brother's assistance overcomes her enemies and lives happily in the best society forever after.

Amarilli, heroine of *Il Pastor Fido* (*The Faithful Shepherd*), a pastoral drama (1585) by Giovanni Battista Guarini. She is a maiden in Arcadia, descended from Pan and betrothed to Silvio, who is reputed to be descended from Hercules. Because the union of these two semi-divine beings would avert a terrible calamity from her native province she remains faithful to Silvio though he cares nothing for her, and she herself is in love with Mirtillo, who through all tribulations remains faithful to her. It is finally revealed that Mirtillo is the real Silvio and the scion of Hercules.

Amarinth, Esme, in Robert S. Hichens' novel, *The Green Carnation* (1874), satirizing the æsthetic craze in England, is an evident portrait of Oscar Wilde, as Esme's disciple and admirer, Lord Reginald Hastings, is Wilde's friend, Lord Sholto Douglas,

son of the Marquis of Queensbury.
Amasis, in *The Ring of Amasis,* a
romance by E. R. Bulwer-Lytton
("Owen Meredith"), is a former
prince of Egypt whose mummy is
unearthed by Count Edmond R—,
together with a brilliant amethyst
ring and Amasis's story written on a
parchment scroll. From the latter
it appears that he was the younger
brother of Sethos, both sons of
Rameses IX. Sethos, being jealous,
allowed him to drown one day while
they were rowing together. Eventually Sethos lost his kingdom and
perished miserably. Edmond possesses himself of the fatal ring, and
the tragedy of the past is repeated in
his own life. He gives it to Juliet,
whom he loves, but who loves his
younger brother Felix. She loses the
ring; it is found by Felix, and he has
it upon his hand as he drowns before
his brother's eyes. Some time after
the catastrophe, Juliet, ignorant of
the truth, marries Edmond, who
becomes insane and dies.

Amaurot (Gr. *αμαυσος,* "shadowy"),
in Sir Thomas More's *Utopia,* the
chief city in his fanciful Utopia.

Amber Witch. See SCHWEIDLER,
MARY.

Amboyne, Dr., in Charles Reade's
novel, *Put Yourself in his Place* (1870),
a physician, philosopher, and peace-
maker whose pet phrase forms the
title of the book. He stoutly maintains that to get on with anybody you
must understand him and when you
understand him you will get on with
him. Probably the germ of this idea
lies in the French proverb, *Tout
comprendre est tout pardonner,* which
Reade may have found quoted in
Hazlitt's essays.

Put yourself in his or her or their place
is Dr. Amboyne's constant cry, and we need
hardly add that in his hands it leads to the
most satisfactory results. Guided by this
principle, he is always guessing at the
secrets of other people's behaviour; and,
as Mr. Reade arranges the conditions of the
problem of which Dr. Amboyne has to guess
the solution, we need hardly add that the
doctor's divinations come out with surprising correctness. We admit fully the wisdom
of the principle, and will only venture to
remark that the difficulty lies in its application.—*Saturday Review.*

Ambrose, in the *Noctes Ambrosianæ,* keeper of the (real) Edinburgh
tavern which was the scene of these
imaginary conversations. Seventy-
one in number, they appeared in
Blackwood's Magazine between the
years 1822 and 1835. Thirty-nine
were from the pen of Professor John
Wilson (1785–1854), and were republished, with notes, by Professor
Ferrier, in his edition of *Wilson's
Works* (1855–1858). The conversations were supposed to take place
between Christopher North (Wilson),
Tickler (Sym), the Ettrick Shepherd
(Hogg), and others, in the "blue
parlour" of a tavern, kept by one
Ambrose, and situated at the back
of Princes Street, close to the Register
Office, Edinburgh. Hence the title.
But, as Professor Ferrier says, a too
literal interpretation is not to be
given to the scene of these festivities.
"Ambrose's Hotel was, indeed, 'a
local habitation and a name,' and
many were the meetings which Professor Wilson and his friends had
within its walls. But the true Ambrose's must be looked for only in the
realms of the imagination. The
veritable scene of the *Ambrosian
Nights* existed nowhere but in their
author's brain." The following is
the running motto in the *Noctes:*

This is a distich by wise old Phocylides,
An ancient, who wrote crabbed Greek in no
    silly days:
Meaning "'Tis right for good wine-bibbing
    people,
Not to let the jug pace round the board like
    a cripple,
But gaily to chat while discussing their
    tipple."
An excellent rule of the hearty old cock 'tis—
And a very fit motto to put on our Noctes.

Ambrosio, hero of a romance by
Matthew Gregory Lewis, published
(1795) under the title *Ambrosio, or
the Monk;* now known more briefly as
The Monk. The extraordinary popularity of the book earned for its author
the sobriquet "Monk" Lewis. Ambrosio, surnamed the "Man of
Holiness," is abbot of the Capuchins
at Madrid. Self-righteousness, increased by his repute among the
people, puffs up his heart with the

pride that provokes a fall. An infernal spirit assuming female form and the name of Matilda tempts him, he succumbs, and one sin leads to another until finally he is exposed and condemned to death by the Inquisition. He sells his soul to Lucifer, gains his release from prison, but is dashed against a rock and dies. James Boarden renamed the characters in *Aurelio and Miranda*, a drama (1798) with a happy ending, founded on Lewis's novel.

Amelia, the first names of two kindred characters drawn by Fielding and Thackeray. See BOOTH, AMELIA, and SEDLEY, AMELIA.

Amlet, Richard (or Dick) in *The Confederacy* (1705), by Sir John Vanbrugh, a professional gambler, son of a wealthy but vulgar tradeswoman. " A notable instance," says Charles Lamb, " of the disadvantages to which this chimerical notion of affinity constituting a claim to acquaintance may subject the spirit of a gentleman."

Amoret, or **Amoretta,** in Spenser's *Faërie Queene*, Book iii, the type of wifely love and devotion. She was the twin sister of Belphœbe and daughter of Chrysogone. While mother and babes were deep in slumber Diana took Belphœbe to bring up and Venus took Amoret. Venus placed the child in charge of Psyche who reared her as tenderly as her own daughter Pleasure. On reaching maturity Amoret was removed to the court of the Faërie Queene and was wooed by many knights but gave her heart to Sir Scudamore; was abducted by Busirane, an enchanter, delivered from his toils by Britomart, and finally married Sir Scudamore.

Amory, Blanche (christened Betsy), in Thackeray's novel *Pendennis* (1848–1849), the daughter of Lady Clavering by her first husband, Colonel Altamont, alias J. Amory. Pretty, emotional, affected, untruthful, this young lady " had a sham enthusiasm, a sham hatred, a sham love, a sham taste, a sham grief, each of which flared and shone very vehemently for

an instant but subsided and gave place to the next sham emotion " (Chapter lxxiii). She engages herself to Pendennis, but to his great relief dismisses him when the wealthy Harry Foker proposes to her. Eventually Foker breaks with her and she declines upon a French nobleman of uncertain standing.

Jean Carlyle alludes to the original of Blanche in a letter dated 1851. "Not," she says "that the poor little —— is quite such a little devil as Thackeray, who has detested her from a child, has here represented, but the looks, the manners, the wiles, the larmes, and 'all that sort of thing' are a perfect likeness . . . She was the only legitimate child of a beautiful, young, improper female who was for a number of years ——'s mistress—she had had a husband, a swindler. His mother took the freak of patronizing this mistress and then of adopting the child and died, leaving her only £250 a year to support her in the luxurious habits to which she had been accustomed."

Amundeville, Lord Henry, in Byron's *Don Juan*, Books xiii and xiv, one of the English Privy Council who, with his wife, Lady Adeline, entertains Don Juan, Aurora Raby and others at his country seat. The lady is thus described in Canto xiii:

The fair most fatal Juan ever met,
  Although she was not evil nor meant
    ill. . . .
Chaste was she, to detraction's desperation,
  And wedded unto one she had loved well—
A man known in the councils of the nation,
  Cool, and quite English, imperturbable.

The description of the husband applies correctly enough to William Lamb (Lord Melbourne), and that of the lady may be the poetical perjury of a gentleman towards Byron's former flame, Lady Caroline Lamb.

Ana, or **Vrilya,** in Bulwer Lytton's novel, *The Coming Race* (1870), are imaginary beings inhabiting an imaginary subterranean world. They have outstripped man by many years in scientific acquirements, especially in the discovery of a force, *vril*, whereof all other forces are merely modifications. The discoverer of this Utopia is an American who tries to convert his hosts to the principles of democracy as he understands the word, but is told that they know all about democracy and have labelled it in their language Koombosh, or government of the ignorant.

Anacharsis the Younger, hero of an archæological romance by the Abbé Barthelemy, *Voyage du Jeune Anacharsis* (1779). A namesake and descendant of the Thracian King who was the friend and counselor of Solon (*circa* 600 B.C.), this Anacharsis settles in Athens during the reign of Alexander the Great, makes the acquaintance of Plato, Demosthenes, Xenophon, and other famous citizens of that period, and becomes an earnest student of all contemporary literature, history, and art, and an intelligent critic and commentator on the same.

Anacreon Moore, a sobriquet bestowed by Lord Byron upon Thomas Moore:

> In that heathenish heaven,
> Described by Mahomet and Anacreon
> Moore.

The allusion is to the fact that Moore had translated Anacreon and had imitated him in original poems.

Anastasius, hero of an oriental romance of that title (1819), by Thomas Hope, purporting to be " the Memoirs of a Greek, written at the close of the eighteenth century." To escape the consequences of his own profligacy and villainy Anastasius runs away from Chios, his birthplace, takes ship on a Venetian vessel which is captured by the Turks, resorts to all sorts of shifts such as jugglery, peddling, and medical quackery to earn his living in Constantinople; turns Mussulman and visits Egypt, Arabia, Sicily and Italy, and finally dies young, a worn-out adventurer.

Ancient Mariner, the otherwise unnamed hero of a poem, *The Rhyme of the Ancient Mariner* (1798), by Samuel Taylor Coleridge. An old, gray-bearded man, with a glittering eye, he stops a wedding guest on his way to the ceremony, first by a physical grasp, then, when that proves ineffectual, by a purely spiritual power. He pours out his story.

Wantonly, in Arctic seas, he had shot an albatross, a bird of good omen to sailors, and one, moreover, that loved him (l. 404), and the whole universe had seemed to shudder at the crime. The sun darkened, the wind was stilled; the ship lay " idle as a painted ship upon a painted ocean." Horrors accumulate; his comrades sicken and die; their places are taken by spectres. When finally the mariner is set free he is doomed to tell his story wherever he lands to the first comer. Many sources for the poem have been suggested: a passage in Shelvocke's Voyages which led Wordsworth to suggest the shooting of the albatross; the narrative of *The Strange and Dangerous Voyage of Captain Thomas Jones;* a friend's dream of a skeleton ship with figures in it. But these are all inadequate to account for or to explain a unique work of original genius.

The *Ancient Mariner* is perhaps the most wonderful of all poems. In reading it we seem rapt into that paradise revealed by Swedenborg, where music and colour and perfume were one, where you could see the hues and hear the harmonies of heaven. For absolute melody and splendour it were hardly rash to call it the first poem in the language. An exquisite instinct married to a subtle science of verse has made it the supreme model of music in our language.— *Swinburne.*

Andrea del Sarto (or The Tailor's Andrew), nickname of a famous painter of the Florentine school (1487–1531) who was the son of a tailor. He was also called the Faultless Painter from his mastery of technique. His love for his wife, Lucrezia del Fede, a wanton and a vixen, is one of the tragedies in the history of art. She was very beautiful; he used her as his model for the Madonna, and even in painting other women he made them resemble Lucrezia in type. Robert Browning's poem, *Andrea del Sarto,* in *Men and Women* (1855), was suggested by the painter's portrait of himself and his wife in the Pitti Palace at Florence.

"Faultless but soulless" is the verdict of art critics on Andrea's works. Why is this? Mr. Browning's poem tells us in no hesitating phrase that the secret lay in the fact that Andrea was an immoral man, an infatuated man, passionately demanding love from a woman who had neither heart nor intellect, a wife for whom he sacrificed his soul and the highest interests of his life.— EDWARD BERDOE, *The Browning Cyclopedia*, p. 16.

Andrews, Joseph, hero of Henry Fielding's novel, *The Adventures of Joseph Andrews and his friend Abraham Adams* (1742). It was begun simply as a burlesque upon Richardson's *Pamela* but the author grew serious before the close and presented an accurate picture of contemporary life and manners. It starts, however, with the true-born Briton's postulate that what is virtue in a woman is nonsense in a man. Joseph Andrews is the brother of Pamela and, like her, out at service. He obtains a position in the family of Lady Booby, a close relation of the mysteriously initiated Mr. B. of Richardson's novel. His adventures with Lady Booby closely resemble those of Pamela with Mr. B. (as likewise they resemble those of Joseph's biblical namesake and Mrs. Potiphar), but virtue triumphs, he retains his purity and remains true to Fanny, the honest, humble girl whom he loves and eventually marries. It turns out that she is the daughter of the family who had adopted him, while he himself is of more exalted rank and station.

Andrews, Pamela, in Richardson's novel, *Pamela, or Virtue Rewarded* (1741), a farmer's daughter, pure, refined, lovely and amiable. At the age of eighteen she becomes waiting-maid and half companion to a dowager lady of great fortune in Bedfordshire. The son of the family (mentioned only as Mr. B. in the letters that tell the story) conceives an ignoble passion for her; but does little towards achieving his design until the mother's death. Even then he is withheld by a grave doubt whether Pamela's social rank is such as would make her eligible as his mistress. This scruple overcome, he lays siege as one accustomed to conquest. Surprised at being rebuffed, he tries the effect of bribes—a handsome allow-

ance for herself and all sorts of good things for her parents—and then proceeds to the bolder alternative of abduction. Finding at last that he cannot seduce her, he marries her and reforms.

Andrews, Shamela, the name under which the heroine of Richardson's *Pamela* was ridiculed in a burlesque, *Apology for the Life of Mrs. Shamela Andrews. In which the many notorious Falsehoods and Misrepresentations of a Book called Pamela are exposed and refuted and all the matchless Arts of that young Politician set in a just and true light* (1741). This pamphlet purported to be from the pen of " Mr. Conny Keyber," a thin disguise for Colley Cibber, but Richardson imputed it to Henry Fielding, whose avowed burlesque, *Joseph Andrews*, came out a year later, and Austin Dobson (*Samuel Richardson*, pp. 43–45) thinks the imputation is at least plausible.

Andronicus, Titus, in a tragedy of that name wrongfully attributed to Shakespeare and printed in the First Folio (1623), a noble Roman general of an army sent against the Goths.

Angel, Miss, heroine and title of a novel (1875) by Miss Thackeray (Mrs. Richmond Ritchie), founded on the real story of Angelica Kaufman (1741–1807), a Swiss by birth who earned a great reputation in London as a portrait painter while Sir Joshua Reynolds was president of the Royal Academy. She is mentioned in one of Goldsmith's songs, frequently appears in Reynolds' journals (there is a legend that he was in love with her), corresponded with Klopstock and is admiringly alluded to by Goethe. Beautiful and rarely gifted, she was entrapped into a disastrous marriage with one " Count de Horn." He turned out to be a valet who had stolen the wardrobe and credentials of the real count. Cherbuliez has utilized the story in another form in *Samuel Brohl and Co.*

Angelica, heroine of Bojardo's *Orlando Innamorato* (1495) and of its sequel, the *Orlando Furioso* of Ariosto. She frequently appears in the works of their successors and imitators. Though there are some hints of a character of this sort in the early Carlovingian romances, she was practically an invention of Bojardo, whom Ariosto accepted and involved in fresh adventures. Daughter of Galaphron, the Saracen king of Cathay, she was dispatched to Paris for the purpose of disrupting Christendom by her beauty. Many of Charlemagne's paladins did fall in love with her to their own undoing. Chief among these was Orlando. Rinaldo, accidentally fortified against her wiles by drinking of the fountain of hatred, avoided and flouted her. She on her side had drunk of the complementary fountain of love and had incontinently become violently enamored of Rinaldo. Hence many amatory entanglements, not the least curious of which occurs when the conditions are reversed. Rinaldo drinking from the fountain of love and Angelica from the other exchange sentiments. In the end she married Medoro, whereupon Orlando went mad. His madness is the theme of Ariosto's poem.

Angelica, in Congreve's comedy, *Love for Love* (1695), the ward of Sir Sampson Legend and in love with Valentine, for whose sake she jilts her guardian. Angelica is supposed to represent Mrs. Bracegirdle; Valentine, the author himself, who was enamored of the actress, and was the rival of the dramatist, Rowe, in her affections.

Angelica, Princess, in Thackeray's burlesque juvenile story, *The Rose and the Ring.* The only child of King Valoroso, bad-tempered, selfish and really ugly, although she looks beautiful so long as she wears the magic ring which her cousin Giglio has given her, or the magic rose which Prince Bulbo has worn. In one period of recovered beauty she marries Bulbo and we are left to hope that the misfortunes which attended her at staccato intervals when she was ringless and roseless and therefore unbeautiful have taught her good sense and good nature.

Angiolina, in Byron's tragedy *Marino Faliero* (see FALIERO), the young wife of the septuagenarian Doge whom she seeks to dissuade from entering the conspiracy which results in his death.

Annie of Tharaw (Ger. *Angke von Tharaw*), subject of a song by Simon von Dach (*circa* 1630), who is highly praised throughout in a vein of bitter irony. The poet, it is said, smarting under the faithlessness of his lady love, sarcastically painted her as loyal, tender, gentle, the very reverse in short, of what she really was. In after life, it is added, he regretted this poetical revenge. The song seemed to haunt him even on his death bed. " Ah! " he exclaimed after each spasm of pain, " that was for the song of Angke von Tharaw! " Longfellow's translation admirably rendered the simple charm of the original. It is said that *Ann Hathaway,* a poem attributed to Shakespeare, is a similar ironical compliment to the poet's wife.

Anselmo, hero of a tale, *The Curious Impertinent,* which is included in Cervantes' *Don Quixote,* i, iv, 6 (1605). A noble cavalier of Florence, newly married to the beautiful Camilla, he foolishly persuades his friend Lothario to lay siege to her in the absolute certainty that she will surmount the test. Lothario reluctantly consents and succeeds all too well. At first the couple keep their secret but eventually they elope. Anselmo dies of grief; Lothario seeks death on the battlefield; Camilla ends her life in a convent.

Antipholus of Ephesus and **Antipholus of Syracuse,** in Shakespeare's *Comedy of Errors,* twin sons of Ægeon and Emilia.

Anton, Sir, in the Arthurian cycle was, according to Tennyson, the knight to whom Merlin confided King Arthur when an infant and who brought him up as his own son. Malory makes Sir Ector the prince's fosterfather.

Antonio, in J. F. Cooper's novel, *The Bravo,* an old fisherman.

Another very well-drawn character. The scene in which he is shrived by the Carmelite monk, in his boat, under the midnight moon, upon the Lagoons, is one of the finest we know of in the whole range of the literature of fiction, leaving upon the mind a lasting impression of solemn and pathetic beauty.— *Atlantic Monthly.*

Antonio, in Shakespeare's comedy, *Twelfth Night,* a sea-captain whose friendship for Sebastian and other loyal traits established the " old sea-dog " tradition in fiction and the drama.

Antony, hero of a tragedy of that name (1831) by Alexander Dumas. Obscure, illegitimate, a misanthrope, he loves Adele as passionately as he hates mankind. She loves him in return; he is too proud to offer her his hand; but after she has married Colonel d'Hervey he wins her by stratagem and violence. Dumas has told in his *Memoirs* how the idea came to him for the terrific dénouement: " One day I was strolling along the Boulevards when I stopped short all at once and said to myself— ' Suppose a man surprised by the husband of his mistress were to kill her, saying that she had resisted him, and was thus to save her honor.' " This is all very well. It has since been shown, however, that he had borrowed the situation from Emile Souvestre. We are further told that as the curtain fell on the last act shouts of terror and grief burst from the audience; they called for the author with " cries of fury." The whole audience was stupefied and confounded by the original and ingenious situation.

Dumas himself would have us believe that Antony is a portrait of himself, and of his own emotions at the time. The object of his passion was a lady whose husband was an officer absent on service. One day she received a letter from him announcing his return. "I thought I should go mad. I rushed to one of my friends, who was employed at the War Office. Three times the officer's leave of absence, duly signed and ready to be sent off, was torn up or burnt by this friend." This may be a piece of romance; but that such an idea should suggest itself shows how lamentably confused were the writer's notions of honor and morality.—PERCY FITZGERALD, *Life and Adventures of Dumas,* ii, 219.

Antony, Mark (83–30 B.C.), the nephew of Julius Cæsar, is a chief character in Shakespeare's play *Julius Cæsar,* and the hero of Shakespeare's *Antony and Cleopatra* (1608) and Dryden's *All for Love, or The World Well Lost* (1678). The first play deals with the conspiracy against Cæsar's life, Antony's oration over Cæsar's dead body, and his victory over the conspirators Brutus and Cassius at Philippi (B.C. 42). The second and the third plays deal with his love for Cleopatra, Queen of Egypt. Coleridge advises that Shakespeare's play be perused " in mental contrast with *Romeo and Juliet* as the love of passion and appetite as opposed to the love of affection and instinct," and adds: " If you would feel the judgment as well as the genius of Shakespeare in your heart's core compare this astonishing drama with Dryden's *All for Love.*"

Anville, Evelina, the heroine of *Evelina* (1778), a novel by Fanny Burney (Madame D'Arblay) depicting, as the sub-title indicates, the nature and behavior of *A Young Lady on her Entrance in the World.* She is a very girlish, amiable, genuine, unaffected young lady, and her social path is strewn with difficulty because she has certain vulgar city cousins, offspring of an avuncular mesalliance (see BRANGTONS), who complicate her relations with the finer world to which she belongs by instinct, breeding and hereditary right.

Before *The Vicar of Wakefield* there had been no English fiction in which the loveliness of family life had made itself felt; before *Evelina* the heart of girlhood had never been so fully opened in literature. There had been girls and girls, but none in whom the traits and actions of the girls familiar to their fathers, brothers and lovers were so fully recognized; and the contemporaneity instantly felt in *Evelina* has lasted to this day.—W. D. HOWELLS, *Heroines of Fiction,* vol. I, 14.

Aouda, in Jules Verne's romance, *Around the World in Eighty Days,* a young and beautiful Hindoo widow who is saved from suttee and eventually married by Phileas Fogg.

Apemantus, in Shakespeare's *Timon of Athens* (1600), a churlish Athenian philosopher, whose affected cynicism is strikingly contrasted with the profound misanthropy of Timon. Schlegel in his *Dramatic Art* especially praises " the incomparable scene " (iv, 3) where he visits Timon in the wilderness: " they have a sort of competition with each other in the trade of misanthropy."

Apollodorus, in W. E. Aytoun's burlesque, *Firmilian, a Spasmodic Tragedy* (1854), is meant for George Gilfinnan, a Scotch critic of more fervor than discrimination, who was especially loud in his applause of the " Spasmodic School " of poets. Carlyle had ever a good word for the compatriot, who was one of the first to welcome his *Sartor Resartus* as a work of genius. But Tennyson resented Gilfinnan's criticism of himself.

Apollyon, in Bunyan's *Pilgrim's Progress*, Part I, an evil spirit with whom Christian has a terrible encounter, from which he emerges victorious.

Aprile, in Robert Browning's poem *Paracelsus*, the Italian poet who forms a complement to the hero, living for love as Paracelsus lives for knowledge. Browning calls them " the two halves of a dissevered world." To a certain extent the portrait was influenced by Shelley.

Aquilina, a courtesan in Paris under the Restoration and Louis Philippe, who appears in several of Balzac's novels. Ostensibly a Piedmontese of obscure birth, she had borrowed her *nom de guerre* from Otway's *Venice Preserved*, which chance had thrown in her way. In *Melmuth Reconciled* she is the friend of Castanier Nucingen's cashier and has other intrigues. In *The Wild Ass's Skin* (*La Peau de Chagrin*) she is the companion of Rastignac and others at a famous orgy in Rue Joubert.

Aram, Eugene, hero of a novel of that name (1832) by Bulwer Lytton, founded on a celebrated case in English criminal annals. Eugene Aram (1704–1759), a schoolmaster of superior intelligence in Knaresborough, was the intimate friend of Daniel Clarke, a shoemaker who in 1745 mysteriously disappeared after having purchased a lot of goods on credit. Aram was suspected of being implicated with him in a conspiracy to defraud, was arrested, but discharged for lack of evidence. Fourteen years later he was again arrested, this time on the charge of murdering Clarke. A skeleton had been dug up near Knaresborough, Mrs. Aram had made some compromising admissions, and finally a man named Houseman confessed that he had been present at the murder of Clarke by Aram. The latter, despite a brilliant defence conducted by himself, was convicted on August 3, 1759. He confessed his guilt after condemnation. The night before his execution he composed a short poem in defence of suicide, opened a vein in his arm, but failed to cheat the gallows.

Bulwer represents his hero as an aspiring student who joins Houseman in the murder of Clarke only that he may obtain money to prosecute his own lofty speculations. Now Clarke was the assumed name of Geoffrey Lester. The murderer, all unwitting of this fact, takes up a new residence next door to the house in which live Lester's brother and son. The son conceives an unaccountable loathing for the mysterious stranger, which is increased on finding that his cousin Madeline Lester, whom he passionately loves, no less ardently loves Eugene. A series of clues, followed up one by one, reveals to young Lester, first the acknowledged facts of Aram's intimacy with his father, and then the hitherto unsuspected crime. He hastens to his uncle's and seizes the murderer when dressed to lead his bride to the altar. At the trial Aram makes a brilliant defence, but is convicted and later confesses, opens his veins in a slovenly fashion, is borne still breathing to the gallows, and expires while the hangman is fitting the noose.

Bulwer's novel has been imitated by the Russian Dostoviesky in a novel, *Crime and Punishment* (1866), where a student kills a miserly old hag with the intention of using her money for praiseworthy purposes. Thackeray has burlesqued Bulwer's hero in *George de Barnwall* (see BARNWALL). Thomas Hood has a gruesome ballad called *The Dream of Eugene Aram* (1845). W. G. Wills produced a tragedy (1873) in which Henry Irving played Aram.

Aramis, in Alexander Dumas' historical romance, *The Three Guardsmen,* one of the titular trio. See ARTAGNAN. Aramis, who has resigned the black coat of an abbé in order that as a layman he might resent an unbearable insult, combines a leaning towards piety and the church with all the airs of an accomplished gallant, full of delicate secrecies about his bonnes fortunes in detail but redolent of them in the gross.

There was a basis of fact to this portrait. The actual name of the original was Henry d'Aramitz. He was not a churchman, but the fact that he was the lay abbot of Aramitz, near Oleron, made him waver with some inconsistency between ostensible piety and ambition. He never held orders and history gives no sanction to any romantic love affair with the pretty Duchesse de Chevreuse. As a matter of fact, M. d'Aramitz married into the Bearn-Bonasse family and vanished into domesticity. His greatest exploit as recorded by Dumas is sheer invention. This is in *The Vicomte de Bragellone.* Aramis discovers the existence of a twin brother of Louis XIV who for reasons of state has been concealed ever since his birth. He conceives the stupendous idea of abducting the actual Louis and setting up his double, thus ensuring a king who will owe everything to himself. Even his personal safety will depend upon the secrecy and loyalty of Aramis, who dreams of being a second Richelieu—cardinal, prime minister, ruler of the state. After a splendid beginning the plot is frustrated by Floquet. Aramis and

Porthos fly. The latter meets a tragic death. Meanwhile the real Louis XIV puts his brother into prison as the Iron Mask.

Aranza, Duke of, in John Tobin's comedy *The Honeymoon* (1804), is the bridegroom of Juliana, a lady so haughty, arrogant and shrewish that Aranza feigned he was only a peasant, took her to a mean hut, and told her that she must perform all the household work. Juliana stormed and chafed for a period, but the firm will and the real love which Aranza masked under the pretence of severity finally conquered. Then the tamed and domesticated shrew was led by the duke to his castle and he revealed his real rank to her. The plot, it will be seen, has likeness in some points to the *Taming of the Shrew* (see PETRUCHIO), in others to the Lord of Burleigh (see BURLEIGH) and a curious likeness in unlikeness to the *Lady of Lyons.*

Arbaces, in John Fletcher's drama, *A King or no King* (1619), a mythical king of Iberia. Classical tradition mentions a prince of this name as the founder of the Median Empire. Byron recognizes him as the dethroner of Sandanapalus in the drama of that title. But in fiction at least the name has won its highest distinction from Bulwer's *Last Days of Pompeii,* where Arbaces is an Egyptian magician; a melodramatic compound of great wickedness with mighty intellectual powers, living in barbaric splendor and sensuality. Reckless of all restraints of conscience, holding, indeed, that as man had imposed those checks on the vulgar herd, so man can by superior wisdom raise himself above them, he establishes a dominion over the imagination and will-powers of others by his knowledge of the esoteric mysteries of Isis, whose priests are under his control and are made the instruments of his crimes.

Arbuton, Miles, leading character in W. D. Howells's *A Chance Acquaintance* (1873), a Boston aristocrat, wealthy, exclusive, narrow and cold. He has personal attractiveness of a certain sort enhanced by education and foreign travel, yet he remains a consummate snob whose blue blood freezes at any reference to the South End in his native city, and who finally betrays to the girl he truly loves that he is ashamed of her provincial ways. See ELLISON, KITTY.

Arcadia, an imaginary country in which Sir Philip Sidney lays the scene of his pastoral romance, *The Countess of Pembroke's Arcadia* (1590). Basilius, Prince of Arcadia, warned by an oracle of dubious meaning, retired from his court into a forest where he built two lodges, in one of which he lived with his queen, Gyneceia, and his younger daughter Philoclea, while in the other his elder daughter Pamela was placed under the care of a clown, Dametas.

Archer, Mr., in Thackeray's novel *Pendennis* (Chapter xxx), a literary bohemian who pulls the long bow. He is said to have been drawn from Tom Hill of the *Monthly Mirror*, who was also the Paul Pry (*q.v.*) in Poole's comedy of that name.

Archer, Francis, in *The Beaux Stratagem,* a comedy (1707) by George Farquhar, a gentleman who has come down in the world and acts as confidential servant to Aimwell, another broken-down adventurer.

The most successful conception is that of Archer, who pretends to be the valet of his friend the Beau, but carries on adventures on his own account. This became one of Garrick's most famous parts, and, indeed, the easy volubility of the pretended servant furnishes an admirable opportunity for a fine actor of light comedy.—A. W. WARD, *English Dramatic Literature,* vol. 3, p. 485.

Archer, Isabel, heroine of Henry James's international novel, *The Portrait of a Lady* (1882). A New Englander by birth. She becomes an heiress in old England through the testamentary dispositions of connections by marriage, and successively rejects Lord Warburton (because she cannot love him and wishes for larger maidenly experiences) and Caspar Goodwood, an earnest young New Englander (because she misses in him the romantic element that

craves), and finally marries Gilbert Ormonde, a man without rank or fortune but of exquisite taste, and, as it finally turns out, of abandoned morals. See CASAMASSIMA, PRINCESS.

Archimago or **Archimage,** in Spenser's *Faërie Queene,* Books i and ii, an enchanter typifying the principle of evil—in opposition to the Red Cross knight who represents holiness.

By his mighty science he could take
As many forms and shapes in seeming wise
As ever Proteus to himself could make:
Sometime a fowl, sometime a fish in lake,
Now like a fox, now like a dragon fell;
That of himself he oft for fear would quake,
And oft would fly away. Oh, who can tell
The hidden power of herbs, and might of
  magic spell?   *Faërie Queene,* I, ii, 10.

Assuming the guise of the Red Cross knight he deceived Una; under the guise of a hermit he deceived the knight himself.

Arden, Enoch, hero and title of a narrative poem (1864) by Tennyson. Enoch and Philip, the one a poor sailor lad, the other son of the wealthiest man in an English seacoast village, are playmates in boyhood of little Annie and rivals for her hand in early manhood. Enoch wins her. Shortly after marriage, poverty forces him to go on a long sea voyage. He is shipwrecked on an uninhabited island in the tropics and spends many years in Crusoe-like solitude. Rescued at last by a passing vessel, he returns home to find Annie married to Philip. Unwilling to disturb her happiness he does not reveal his identity until his death.

Enoch Arden is a true hero after the highest conception of a hero. He is as great as King Arthur—by his unconquerable will and by a conscious and deliberate bowing before love and duty.—H. A. TAINE, *English Literature.*

The story of Enoch Arden, as he has enhanced and presented it, is a rich and splendid composite of imagery and illustration. Yet how simple that story is in itself. A sailor who sells fish, breaks his leg, gets dismal, gives up selling fish, goes to sea, is wrecked on a desert island, stays there some years, on his return finds his wife married to a miller, speaks to a landlady on the subject and dies . . . It is true that he acts rightly, that he is very good. But such is human nature that it finds a little tameness in mere morality.—WALTER BAGEHOT, *Wordsworth, Tennyson and Browning* (1864).

Arden, Forest of (Celtic *Ard*, great, and *den*, a wooded valley), the scene of Shakespeare's comedy, *As You Like It*, is generally identified with a forest of that name in Warwickshire. Originally this covered nearly the whole shire, but by the eleventh century wide clearings had been made in it, and only poetical license could then figure the forest as a wood nymph touching Trent with one hand and Severn with the other. In Shakespeare's day it still contained enough thickets and sylvan retreats to make his Arden a faithful representation. Then as now, however, Shakespeare's fauna and flora were unknown there. Lions did not lash their tails there. To-day the forest has shrunk into a few stretches of woodland but still survives in certain village names: Henley-in-Arden, Weston-in-Arden, etc. Michael Drayton in his *Polyolbion*, xiii, gives a description of the Warwickshire forest which tallies substantially with Shakespeare's Arden. Nevertheless some commentators have held that Arden is the French forest of Ardennes.

Arden, Thomas, of Feversham, chief male character in an anonymous tragedy sometimes ascribed (falsely) to Shakespeare, founded on a real happening thus described in the original title page: *The Lamentable and True Tragedie of M. Arden of Feversham in Kent. Who was most wickedlye murdered, by the meanes of his disloyall and wanton wyfe, who for the love she bare to one Mosbie, hyred two desperate ruffians, Blackwill and Shakbag, to kill him* (1592). The crime happened in 1551. It is fully described in Holinshed's *Chronicle*, which is here closely followed. The first four acts are taken up with successive attempts upon the life of the unsuspecting Arden, who always escapes by some unlooked-for accident until finally stabbed in his own house at the beginning of Act v. The rest of the last act pictures the discovery and condemnation of the murderers. The dramatist makes no attempt to awaken sympathy or pity for Arden, who is painted in all his native avarice, cruelty, stupidity and insensate credulity.

Ardennes, Forest of, the *Arduenna Sylva* of Cæsar and Tacitus. It still exists, though in shrunken proportions, in northeast France between the Meuse and the Moselle, extending beyond the French border into Belgium. Lord Byron, in *Childe Harold*, describes the English army passing through the forest on their way to the battle of Waterloo.

And Ardennes waves above them her green
    leaves,
Dewy with Nature's tear-drops, as they
    pass—
Grieving, if aught inanimate e'er grieves,
Over the unreturning brave,—alas!
Ere evening to be trodden like the grass
Which *now* beneath them, but *above* shall
    grow
In its next verdure, when this fiery mass
Of living Valour, rolling on the foe
And burning with high Hope, shall moulder
    cold and low.   *Childe Harold*, iii, 27.

Malone and other commentators identify the Forest of Arden in *As You Like It* with Ardennes. But Furness holds it evident from the bits of description and the allusion to Robin Hood that Shakespeare meant to keep his audience at home, no matter in whatsoever foreign country the scene be laid.

Ardennes, Wild Boar of. See WILD BOAR OF ARDENNES.

Aresby, Captain, in Fanny Burney (Madame D'Arblay's) *Cecilia*, a captain in the militia full of affectations—" a most petrifying wretch."

Argantes, in Tasso's epic, *Jerusalem Delivered* (1575), one of the fiercest and bravest leaders of the infidel hosts against the Christians, standing second to Solyman. He was finally slain by Rinaldo, and Solyman by Tancred.

Argyle, Archibald, Marquis of, nicknamed Gramach (the "illfavored"), figures unfavorably in Scott's novel, *The Legend of Montrose*. Outgeneralled by Montrose, his army was completely routed at Inverlochy, while he himself incurred contempt by watching the battle from the safety of a galley on the loch.

Argyle, John, Duke of (1678–1743), appears in two of Scott's novels, *Rob Roy* and *The Heart of Midlothian.* He has little to do in the first but in the second he takes a prominent part as the courtier who introduces Jeanie Deans to Queen Caroline, a doubly irksome task because he was in ill favor with her majesty owing to his opposition to the seven measures proposed against Edinburgh after the Porteous Riot.

Ariel, in Shakespeare's comedy, *The Tempest* (1609), the favorite messenger of Prospero, an airy and fanciful creation who unites in himself the powers of all elemental spirits.

"At one time he appears as a sea elf, swimming and careering amid the waves; then as a fire spirit who sets the ship on fire and climbs like licking flame up the mast; then as a spirit of earth, buried for Prospero in the frozen veins of the ground. His ruling nature, however, as his name implies, is that of a sylph, a spirit of the air."—GERVINUS, *Shakespeare's Characters.*

Before Prospero's advent on the island, Ariel had been in the service of the witch Sycorax, but being too delicate for her " earthly and abhorred commands " he disobeyed her and she confined him in a cloven pine. Prospero set him free after twelve years' imprisonment.

Goethe in *Faust*, Part II, Act i, Sc. I, introduces Ariel as the leader of the elves in the intermezzo of the *Walpurgis Night.*

Ariel, the name which Shelley half sportively applied to himself. Leigh Hunt justifies the appellation. " If Coleridge," he says, " is the sweetest of our poets, Shelley is at once the most ethereal and gorgeous, the one who has clothed his thought in draperies of the most evanescent and most magnificent words and imagery. . . Shelley . . . might well call himself Ariel." There is a melancholy interest in the fact that when Shelley purchased the little fishing smack in which he eventually met his death he renamed it *The Ariel.*

Arius (280–336), a priest of the Early Church, the founder of the so-called Arian heresy, who refused to subscribe to the Nicean creed formu-lated at the Council at Nice, is the hero of a romance, *Arius the Libyan, an Idyl of the Primitive Church,* by Nathan Chapman Kouns.

Ark, Henry, one of the principal characters in Cooper's novel, *The Red Rover* (1827), lieutenant on the British man-of-war *Dart.* Disguised as a common sailor, under the name of Wilder he ships aboard the pirate craft of the "Red Rover" in order to betray that notorious freebooter to justice.

Armado, Don Adriano de, in Shakespeare's comedy, *Love's Labor's Lost* (1594), a fantastical Spaniard, a braggart and a pedant who supplies the farcical underplot by his wooing of Jaquenetta, a country girl, beloved also by the clown Costard. Costard offers to fight him in his shirt and Armado has to confess that he has no shirt. *The Pedant* in Act v, Sc. I, supplies a famous description of Don Armado:

His humor is lofty, his discourse peremptory: his tongue filed, his eye ambitious, his gait majestical, and his general behavior vain, ridiculous and thrasonical. . . . He draweth out the thread of his verbosity finer than the staple of his argument.

In him, as in the preposterous Holofernes (*q.v.*) and the pedantic curate Sir Nathaniel, the poet satirizes the euphuistic affectations introduced by John Lyly. But it is going too far to identify Armado with Lyly himself.

Armande, one of the titular " Learned Ladies " in Molière's comedy, *Les Femmes Savantes,* the prototype of the perennial blue stocking. She is differentiated from her mother Philaminte by adding a touch of prudery to her pedantry—feigning to put the pleasures of the mind above those of the senses while allowing us to suspect that her own thoughts dwell unduly and unpleasantly on more material things.

Armida, in Tasso's *Jerusalem Delivered,* a sorceress of the Circe type, daughter of Chariclea, the queen of Damascus, by the plebeian Arbilan. Satan sent her into the camp of Godfrey de Bouillon, where she seduced 50 Crusaders away from the siege of Jerusalem and later Rinaldo (*q.v.*), whom she conducted to a magnificent palace. Here he abandoned himself to a life of sinful luxury until rescued by Carlo and Ubaldo. She followed him but, having lost her power over him, went mad, burned her palace and exiled herself to Egypt. Here she offered to marry any one who would slay Rinaldo. She herself unsuccessfully aimed an arrow at him and then failed in an effort on her own life.

Armstrong, John, hero of Scott's tale, *Death of the Laird's Jock* (1827). He is known as " the Laird's Jock " even after his father's death leaves him the Laird of Mangerton. With his huge two-handed sword he was the unrivalled champion of the Border counties. When he became old and helpless he entrusted the sword to his son, but the English champion Foster won it away in fair combat and " with a cry of indignation, horror and despair " the Laird's Jock threw up his hands and fell dead.

Arnold, hero of Byron's dramatic poem, *The Deformed Transformed.* He is the hunchback son of Bertha, who hates him as he hates himself for his deformity. Weary of life, he is about to kill himself when a demon promises to turn him into any shape that pleases him, provided he will surrender his soul after twenty-four years of earthly experience. Arnold consents; the shades of the heroes of the past are summoned up in succession. Arnold chooses the body of Achilles for temporary tenantship, goes to Rome; joins the besieging army of Bourbon and enters the church of St. Peter's just in time to rescue Olympia. But the proud beauty, to escape being taken captive by him, leaps from the high altar to the pavement. Here the fragment comes to an end.

In this character Byron pictures the agonies that his own spirit had endured from morbid consciousness of the deformity in his feet. In the first line of the first scene Bertha cries, " Out, hunchback! " " I was born so, mother," returns Arnold. In his own *Life*, Moore quotes these lines and contrasts them with a passage in Byron's *Memorabilia*, recording his horror and humiliation when his mother, in one of her fits of passion, called him "a lame brat." Moore questions " whether that whole drama was not indebted for its origin to that single recollection." Byron acknowledges his indebtedness to a novel, *The Three Brothers* (1803), by Joshua Pickersgill, in which the hero, Arnauld, barters his soul to a demon for leave to inhabit for twenty-four years the body of some great and beautiful hero of antiquity. He chooses to be Julian.

Arnolphe, in Molière's comedy, *L'Ecole des Femmes* (*The School for Wives*), the representative of jealous middle age, a man of selfish purpose and rigid theories, ever suspicious and ever deceived, who has determined to train up a model wife for himself by keeping her mind undeveloped by learning and unpolluted by any knowledge of evil. In Agnes, a girl twenty years his junior, he fancies he has discovered the proper material, but she wofully disappoints him in the end. It is a little curious that both in this play and in its predecessor Molière's mind should have been occupied with the subject of mismated marriages just at the moment when he, a man of nearly forty, was about to marry a young girl of seventeen. The *Ecole des Maris* was first played in June, 1661, the *Ecole des Femmes* at the end of 1662. Half-way between, in February, 1662, he married Armande Bejart. See CELIMENE.

Was it Armande Bejart and the way of training her to be the best of wives and woman that occupied the mature lover; or was the temptation to laugh at himself and jeer away any doubts he might have,—or at least the faculty which can subsist even without genius, of seeing the ludicrous aspects in which his own position might appear to others,—the influence which kept him to this theme? The imagination can scarcely refuse to fancy some such reason for dwelling on such a subject.—OLIPHANT AND TRAVER, *Molière.*

Artagnan, Charles de Baatz, Seigneur d', the most famous of all the heroes of Alexander Dumas. In that great trilogy of historical romances— *The Three Musketeers, Twenty Years After*, and *The Vicomte de Bragelonne*—his career is traced from the time of his arrival in Paris, a lean and hungry Gascon stripling, with three crowns in his pocket, mounted on a raw-boned yellow pony, until his death as Comte d'Artagnan, Commander of the Musketeers and Marshal of France. The historical period covered by these novels extends from 1625 to 1665.

On his first day in Paris young d'Artagnan, fired with the ambition to enter Louis XIII's famous corps of musketeers, contrives to entangle himself in three duels with three of the most dreaded members of that body, known respectively as Athos, Porthos, and Aramis. His pluck, spirit and good humor win their hearty friendship. Thereafter all four, sharing alike in their fortune or misfortune, pass through stirring adventures in France and England. Though Dumas makes d'Artagnan the central figure of these romances— the man whose wit and courage and infinite resources always turn the tide when fortune seems to be blackest— he does not appeal to the reader as strongly as his fellows. There is a touch of worldly wisdom, an almost Yankee shrewdness—in fine, a Gascon keenness about d'Artagnan which robs him of the hearty sympathy we lavish upon the others. They fall into difficulties and are overwhelmed by disaster, and we breathe hard and wonder whether they will escape, and how. We never feel this delightful suspense in the case of d'Artagnan. We know that he is always sure to come out on top. He bears a charmed life. His author will not let him fall or fail. He can dispense with our sympathy.

Dumas's character is drawn largely from the genuine memoirs of Charles de Batz-Castlemore (1623–1673), who assumed the name d'Artagnan (his mother was a Montesquieu-d'Artagnan) when at the age of 17 he set out for Paris with a letter of introduction to Troisvilles, Commandant of the Musketeer Guard. He was warmly welcomed to Paris by his fellow countryman, Isaac de Portau, who had changed his name to Porthos, and through him made the acquaintance of the guardsmen who called themselves Athos and Aramis. On the very day of his enlistment he with his three companions fought and overcame four of Cardinal Richelieu's hirelings, whereupon Louis XIII gave the boy a special audience and presented him with fifty ducats and a cadet's commission. From then his advance was rapid. He retained Louis's friendship and gained that of Cardinal Mazarin. He married Mme. de Sainte Croix, widow of M. de Dumas, and fell as field marshal at the siege of Maastricht in the Low Countries in 1673.

Artaxaminous, in *Bombastes Furioso* (1810), a burlesque tragic opera by William B. Rhodes, the King of Utopia, married to Griskinissa whom he would divorce. See BOMBASTES.

Artegal, Sir (spelled Arthegal in the first three books), the impersonation of justice in Spenser's *Faërie Queene*. Son of Prince Gorlois of Cornwall, he marries Britomart (*q.v.*) in Book iii; but his career as an avenger and promoter of justice takes up all of Book v. In Canto i he delivers a Solomon-like decision concerning the ownership of a woman. In Canto ii he destroys the corrupt practices of bribery and toll. In Canto iii he exposes Braggadachio and his follower Trompart. In Canto iv he gave judgment as to the ownership of a chest of money found at sea. In Canto v he fell into the hands of Radigund, Queen of the Amazons, was released by Britomart in Canto vi, who killed Radigund in Canto vii. His last and greatest feat was the deliverance of Irena (Ireland) from Grantorto (great wrong) whom he slew in Canto xii, an obvious allusion to Desmond's rebellion in 1580. The character of Artegal is meant to represent Spenser's friend, Lord Grey, of Wilton, who was sent (1580) to Ireland as lord lieutenant with the poet as his secretary.

Artful Dodger. See DAWKINS, JOHN.

Arthur, King, the national hero of England, is the chief figure in Tennyson's *Idylls of the King*. In outline Tennyson follows the Arthurian romances as collated and harmonized by Sir Thomas Malory's *Morte* *d'Arthur.* But he makes some vital changes, notably in his characterization of Arthur. Malory indeed had dowered him with every virtue save one. He dared not so far antagonize the early historians and romances as to give him a stainless chastity. Tennyson does this and so eliminates the curse, the crucial element in the tragedy, and destroys its most appalling and at the same time most telling feature. It was Arthur's own sin of incest with his half-sister Margeuse (*q.v.*) that brought about the downfall of all his hopes and the destruction of the Round Table through its own impish issue, the treacherous Mordred.

In Tennyson's hands Arthur appears not only as the perfect ruler, the suppressor of anarchy, but also as—

> The great and gentle lord
> Who was as is the conscience of a saint
> Among his warring senses, to his knights.

When the subtle and malignant Vivien attempts to sneer at the king's blind confidence in Guinevere, Merlin cries out:

> Oh true and tender! Oh my liege and king!
> O selfless man and stainless gentleman!

Guinevere herself has no word of blame for the husband she has betrayed save only that he is blameless.

> He is all fault that has no fault at all.
> *Elaine.*

But in the poem which bears her name she laments too late that she had refused to understand him.

> I thought I could not breathe in that fine air.

In the same poem Arthur explains his purpose in organizing the Round Table and tells the repentant Geneviere how his enterprise had succeeded until her guilt and its consequences in the feud with Lancelot had brought in confusion and civil war and the invasion of the Saxon foe.

> To any one knowing his Maleore, knowing that Arthur's own sin was the cause of the breaking up of the Round Table, and Guinevere's the means only through which

that cause worked itself out—having felt Arthur's almost purposed refusal to see what was going on under his own eyes between his queen and Lancelot, so as to save a quarrel with his best knight, till it was forced on him; having watched with what a sense of relief as it were Arthur waited for his wife to be burnt on her second accusal—then for one so primed to come on Tennyson's representation of the king in perfect words, with tenderest pathos, rehearsing to his prostrate queen his own nobleness and her disgrace; the revulsion of feeling was too great; one was forced to say to the Flower of Kings, "if you really did this you were the Pecksniff of the period."— F. J. FURNIVAL.

Ascapart or **Ascupart,** in Drayton's *Polyolbion,* a giant thirty feet high who lifted up Sir Bevis, his wife Josian, his sword Morglay, and his steed Arundel and carried all of them away under his arm. Sir Bevis afterwards made Ascapart his slave to run beside his horse:

> Each man as Ascapart of strength to toss
> For quoits both Temple Bar and Charing Cross.

Ase, in Henrik Ibsen's drama *Peer Gynt* (1867), the mother of the titular hero. "This poem," said Ibsen, "contains much that has its origin in the circumstances of my own youth. My own mother—with the necessary exaggeration—served as the model for Ase." Her death forms a striking episode in Act iii.

Ashburton, Mary, heroine of Longfellow's romance of travel, *Hyperion* (1839), a young Englishwoman whom Paul Flemming meets when touring Europe in order to forget a domestic bereavement and with whom he falls in love. Though she esteems him, she rejects him, for she does not love him. The above outlines fit the story of Longfellow's courtship of Miss Fanny Ashburton, save that she was an American, from Boston. He met her in Switzerland four years after the death of his first wife. He was thirty-two; she was not yet twenty. She refused him, and he wrote *Hyperion* in the hope of winning her. He succeeded, although at first Miss Appleton was ill-pleased at thus becoming a centre of public attention. The marriage took place July 16, 1843. In a letter to Ferdinand Freligrath, November 24 of that year, Longfellow, after complaining of his eyes, continues, " But nevertheless, eyes or no eyes, engaged I was and married I am. I could see clearly enough for that—married to the very Mary Ashburton, whose name was Fanny Appleton and is Fanny Longfellow."

Ashton, Colonel Sholto Douglas, in Scott's novel, *The Bride of Lammermoor,* the elder brother of Lucy. Though he loves her, he bitterly resents her engagement to the Master of Ravenswood, is cruel to her, and openly insults her betrothed.

Ashton, Henry, Lucy's younger brother, a spoiled boy who unwittingly adds to his sister's unhappiness.

Ashton, Lucy, the titular " Bride of Lammermoor," Sir William's daughter, gentle, pliant and timid, easily controlled by the will of others. Betrayed into loving Ravenswood by the temporizing schemes of her father, she is " exasperated to frenzy by a long tract of unremitting persecution from her mother," at whose imperious will she throws over her betrothed and marries Frank Hayston, Laird of Bucklaw. Then the weak mind is broken and the animal stands at bay like a wild cat and breaks the toils that enmesh her, and Lucy dies a maiden in the bridal chamber, but not before, in a paroxysm of insane fury, she has stabbed and dangerously wounded the bridegroom.

Ashton, Sir William, Lucy's father. A parvenu who has risen to political importance during the great civil wars, he has established his own fortunes on the ruins of the Ravenswood family. His temporizing policy with regard to Ravenswood and his daughter prepares the way for the tragedy of her marriage to another.

Ashton, Lady, wife of Sir William. " In the haughtiness of a firmer character, higher birth, and more decided views of aggrandizement, the lady looked with some contempt on her husband," but was willing to join in any scheme that might advance the family fortunes. She hated Ravenswood and scrupled at no

means whereby she might shake her daughter's faith in his loyalty.

Aslauga, in La Motte Fougue's romance, *Aslauga's Knight* (1814), a spirit chosen by the knight Froda in preference to any earthly love. She appears to him in important moments in his career, and he dies fancying himself clasped in her arms and shrouded in her wonderful hair.

Asmodeus, the hell-born hero of de Sage's satirical romance, *Le Diable Boiteux,* translated into English by Smollet under the title, *The Devil on Two Sticks.* He expressly identifies himself with the Roman Cupid but is infinitely more cunning and bewildering. In one of the best known scenes of the book Asmodeus flies at night with Don Cleofas to the steeple of St. Salvador and, waving his hand, unroofs all the houses in the city, laying bare their interiors and exposing the various occupations of the inhabitants. See also vol. II.

Astarte, in Byron's tragedy, *Manfred,* a spirit in female form who intermittently visits the hero in his mountain solitude and always leaves him prostrated with grief. She is vaguely typical of remorse for some terrible sin of his past life wherein she has been an unwilling partner, but had singly paid the penalty. Murder? Incest?—these seem at least to be the Byronic implications. Lady Byron, according to Mrs. Stowe, read into them a confession of his guilty relations with Mrs. Augusta Leigh.

We think of Astarte as young, beautiful, innocent,—guilty, lost, murdered, pardoned; but still, in her permitted visit to earth, speaking in a voice of sorrow and with a countenance yet pale with mortal trouble. We had but a glimpse of her in her beauty and innocence, but at last she rises before us in all the mortal silence of a ghost, with fixed, glazed and passionless eyes, revealing death, judgment and eternity.—JOHN WILSON.

Astrea (Fr. *Astrée*), heroine of a once famous romance, *L'Astrée* (two volumes, 1609–1619), by Honoré d'Urfé. The period is the fourth century. The scene is the author's native province, Foreste, in France. Astrea is a beautiful shepherdess in

love with Celadon, who loves her,
but her jealous suspicions are awakened by evil-minded rivals. Hence
a succession of evils. Celadon, attempting suicide, is saved by the
Princess Galatea, who carries him to
her court. The maiden's grief at his
disappearance worries her parents
into the grave. Astrea, all unwitting,
falls in with Celadon disguised as a
Druidess, becomes his companion but
abandons him when she discovers the
deception. Again Celadon attempts
suicide—this time in the Fountain of
Truth which is fatal only to liars and
hypocrites. Astrea accepts the test
when he survives, begs forgiveness
for her doubts, and a reconciliation
makes everybody happy.

Astrophel, the name which Sir
Philip Sidney assumed for himself in
writing the love sonnets to Stella,
i.e., Lady Penelope Rich (see STELLA).
The process by which he evolved the
name is a curious one. Having
abridged Philip Sidney to Phil. Sid.,
he anagrammatized it into Philisides.
Refining still further, he translated
Sid. (the abridgment of *Sidus,* Latin
for " Star ") into Astron (Greek for
star), and treating Phil. as if it were
abbreviated from Philos, " loved," he
constructed for himself another pseudonym, the poetical Astrophil, *i.e.,*
" beloved by a star," or, if you prefer,
" love star "—" star of love." Lady
Rich being the bright particular star
when he worshipped and whose love
he craved, he designated her, in
conformity with his own assumed
name, Stella. (See *Atlantic Monthly,*
November, 1858, vol. 2, p. 676.)
Hence Philip Sidney was the lover or
the beloved of a star, or both, while
Penelope Rich was the star.

Astynome. See CHRISEIS.

Atala, heroine of a romance, *Atala,
or the Loves of Two Savages in the
Desert* (1801), by Francois Réné de
Chateaubriand. The scene is laid in
North America. Atala is a maiden
of the Natchez tribe, European on
her father's side and a Christian.
She falls in love with Chactas, a
young Indian captive, liberates him
and flies with him into the wilder-

ness. After weeks of wandering
through forest and prairie the couple
reach a missionary station. Atala
had been vowed to celibacy by her
mother. When she finds herself on
the verge of yielding to passion she
poisons herself and dies.

Atalantis, The New, an imaginary
island described in a romance by Mrs.
de la Rivière Manly, *Secret Memoirs
and Manners of Several Persons of
Quality of Both Sexes from the New
Atlantis, an Island in the Mediterranean* (1617). The New Atlantis
is really England and the book is a
scandalous chronicle of crimes ascribed to the Whig statesmen and
other public characters who helped
to bring about the Revolution of 1688.

Ataliba, in the drama *Pizarro,* attributed to R. B. Sheridan, the name
given to the historical Atahualpa, an
Indian chief from Ecuador who invaded Peru but was defeated and
slain (November 16, 1532) by the
Incas and their ally Pizarro.

Atar Gul, hero of a romance of that
name by Eugene Sue, a negro domestic in one of the French West Indies,
who has the esteem and confidence
of his master and the entire neighborhood, yet pursues for years a deliberate plan to destroy the family he
serves. When his plans have all succeeded he tortures the deathbed of
his master, a hopeless paralytic, by
revealing the truth, and gloating over
the impotent wrath and horror of
the man who had loved and trusted
him. After the master's death Atar
Gul is awarded the Monthyon prize
for virtue in recognition of his supposed devotion and self-sacrifice.
There may be a finishing touch of
cynicism in the man's very name
which, in Persian, means Ottar of
Roses (*cf.* Byron):

She snatched the urn wherein was mixed
The Persian Atar-gul's perfume.
Bride of Abydos, Canto i, x.

Athalie, heroine of a tragedy (1691)
of that name by Racine, founded
upon the Old Testament story of
Athaliah (2 Kings xi; 2 Chronicles
xxii, xxiii) who dreamed that she was

stabbed by a child robed in priestly vestment; she recognized its lineaments in Joash, the only surviving member of a royal line, and thenceforth bent all her energies to accomplish his ruin. He escaped through the devotion of his followers and eventually mounted the throne of his ancestors.

Athelstane, thane of Coningsburgh, in Scott's romance, *Ivanhoe,* is the rival of the titular hero for the affections of Rowena. She prefers Ivanhoe, but his father and her guardian, Cedric, favors Athelstane, as legitimate heir to the Saxon monarchy which Cedric is plotting to restore. Athelstane, though vain of his descent, " stout of heart and strong of person," is so " slow, irresolute, procrastinating and unenterprising" that he has earned the nickname of " the unready." He has no stomach for plots that entail hurried journeys and indigestions.

Athens, Maid of, title and subject of a lyric by Lord Byron. It was addressed to Theresa Macri, the eldest of three daughters of a Greek lady, Theodora Macri, with whom Byron and Hobhouse lodged during the ten weeks they spent in Athens, 1809–1810. Byron wooed her in Greek fashion, giving himself a wound across his breast with a dagger in order to attest his sincerity. Teresa, it has been said, received the attention as her due and failed to be impressed. On the other hand, her daughter, Madame Caroline Black, in some letters recently discovered by Cambourogen, librarian of the Athens library, asserts that the " Maid " was honestly *éprise,* and that until her later days she had dreams of the poet appearing to her to upbraid her for giving herself in marriage to another. Madame Black adds that Byron wrote to Teresa when he embarked at Missolonghi and that she was on the point of making a journey thither to consecrate her old-time adorer to the cause of Greece when the end came. See DUDU.

Athos, in Alexander Dumas' historical romances, *The Three Guards-*

3

men, *Twenty Years After,* and *The Vicomte de Bragelonne,* was one of the trio of guardsmen with whom d'Artagnan affiliates himself on his arrival in Paris. A gallant and chivalric figure, he bears with him all the languor and the mystery of some secret sorrow. He hates women and loves the winecup, yet is ever a gentleman in his conduct towards both. In real life Athos was the *nom de guerre* of Armand de Sillegue, member of an ancient family which has given many a notable fighting man to French history. The real Athos was slain in a duel.

Atkins, Tommy, a nickname for the English soldier, which has been popularized by the London music halls, and especially by Kipling in his *Barrack-room Ballads.* One explanation states that the name was first found in a model roster issued by the War Office for the guidance of company sergeants in making out their returns, that in a certain random set of names the necessity of an alphabetical arrangement was exhibited by placing there Richard Roe and John Dow, soldiers, in the initial order of surnames. The first of these model entries being " Atkins, Thomas," it was not long before Thomas Atkins was picked to represent the model soldier.

Mr. Kipling, in his capacity of interpreter, and by means of his *Barrack-room Ballads,* made the nation appreciate and understand its soldiers infinitely better than they had ever done before. Indeed, it is not too much to say that by means of this process of interpretation he changed the attitude of the nation. But though many thousands of people read how—

"It's Tommy this an' Tommy that, an'
'chuck him out, the brute;'
But it's 'saviour of his country' when the
guns begin to shoot,"

the change was for the most part wrought indirectly. When you let fly into a whole heap of balls, all are moved and affected, though only one or two feel the impact direct. It is enough if the poet touches those who can influence the rest.

Atossa, in Pope's *Moral Essays,* Epistle ii, a satirical portrait sometimes identified with Sarah, Duchess of Marlborough, but more probably meant for the Duchess of Bucking-

ham. Both these ladies were great
friends of Lady Mary Wortley Montagu, who in the same poem figures
as Sappho. The original Atossa of
classic fame was a daughter of Cyrus
and the queen successively of Cam-
byses and Darius Hystaspis. By the
latter she became the mother of
Xerxes. Herodotus speaks of her as
a follower of Sappho.

But what are these to great Atossa's mind?
Scarce once herself, by turns all womankind.
          POPE, *Moral Essays*, Ep. ii.

Atticus, an epithet applied by the
Latins to a person distinguished for
wit, eloquence or learning—from
Attica, the seat of Greek culture.
Hence Pope borrowed the name in his
savage attack upon Addison later in-
corporated into the *Epistle to Dr.
Arbuthnot* (1735). The portrait ends
with the couplet which Dr. Quincey
has attacked as being intrinsically
illogical:

Who but must laugh if such a man there be?
Who would not weep if Atticus were he?

Hazlitt considers the whole passage
to be " the finest piece of personal
satire in Pope." Macaulay praises
" the brilliant and energetic lines
which everybody knows by heart or
ought to know by heart" but complains of their injustice. He concedes
that one charge is probably not without foundation:

Addison was, we are inclined to believe,
too fond of presiding over a circle of humble
friends. Of the other imputations which
these famous lines are intended to convey,
scarcely one has ever been proved to be
just, and some are certainly false. That
Addison was not in the habit of "damning
with faint praise" appears from innumerable
passages in his writings, and from none more
than from those in which he mentions Pope.
And it is not merely unjust, but ridiculous,
to describe a man who made the fortune of
almost every one of his intimate friends, as
"so obliging that he ne'er obliged."

See also COURTHOPE, *Life of Pope*,
Chapter viii.

Aubert, Therese, heroine and title
of a historical romance (1819) by
Charles Nodier. Her lover is a
sympathizer with the Royalists during the French Revolution. He disguises himself in female attire and is
befriended by Therese, who for a
time is ignorant of his sex.

Auburn, Sweet, the scene of Goldsmith's poem, *The Deserted Village.*
It is not to be found on the map.
There is indeed an Auburn in Wiltshire but it is not Goldsmith's.
Macaulay complains that Auburn is
an English village in its prosperity
but an Irish in its decay, and that
by thus confusing the rural life of the
two countries the poet had been so
untrue to fact as to injure his poem
as a work of art. Goldsmith claimed
to have taken " all possible pains "
to be certain of his facts, declaring
that his account of the village's decline is based upon personal observation of conditions in England " for
these four or five years back." But
there is no doubt that, perhaps unconsciously, he drew upon his memories of his own native village of
Lissoy, in Ireland, and wove them
into his descriptions of an imaginary
English town.

Auchester, Charles, in Elizabeth
Sara Sheppard's novel of that name
(1853), a brilliant young Jew who
from earliest childhood finds his
greatest delight in hearing and studying music and pouring out his soul
in melody. When introduced he is a
child in an old English town living
quietly with his mother and sister.
Going to the Cecilia school in Germany to carry on his studies he falls
under the influence of a musical
genius, Seraphael, who is drawn
from Mendelssohn, and a great
singer, Clara Bennette, who is probably meant for Jenny Lind. The
novel was originally published under
the punning pseudonym of E.
Berger.

Audley, Lady, heroine of a novel,
Lady Audley's Secret (1862), by
Mary Elizabeth Braddon, a golden-
haired murderess who is driven to
crime in order to protect her honor
and suffers agonies of repentance in
consequence. See FLOYD, AURORA.

Audrey, a reduced form of Ethel-
dritha or Etheldrida, as in St. Audrey,
from whose name comes also the
word " tawdrey." In Shakespeare's

comedy *As You Like It* this is the name of an awkward and simple-minded country girl whom Touchstone wins away from William. " A little thing but mine own " is Touchstone's description of her.

Augusta, a title given by the Romans to London (Londinium Augusta) and to other cities in honor of the Emperor Augustus. London is not infrequently thus referred to by the poets of the seventeenth and eighteenth centuries.

> Close to the walls which fair Augusta bind.
> DRYDEN, *MacFlecknoe,* l, 64.

In his opera *Albion and Albinus* (1685) Dryden introduces Augusta upon the stage as a personification of London.

Augusta, whom Byron addresses in *Stanzas to Augusta* and *Epistle to Augusta* (1816), is his half-sister, the Honorable Augusta Byron (1783–1851), daughter of Captain John Byron by his first wife, Amelia D'Arcy, Baroness Conyers. Augusta married (1807) her first cousin, Colonel George Leigh. There are numerous references to this Byron's only sister scattered through *Childe Harold* and others of his longer poems. In fact she was the good genius of his life. The sentiment with which she inspired him was probably the purest and most ennobling he ever felt, despite the fact that Byron's wife, through the medium of Mrs. Stowe, and, more recently, Byron's grandson, the Earl of Lovelace, have sought to cast suspicion on it. In *Cain* and in *Manfred* these ill-advised relatives misread allusions to incest as veiled poetical confessions of actual crime.

Augustina, the heroine of the historic siege of Saragossa as Joseph Palafox was its hero. That Spanish city was invested (June 15, 1808) by the French army during the Peninsular war, and, after extraordinary heroism on both sides, surrendered with all the honors of war on February 20, 1809.

Augustina, a mere girl, was a peddler of cool drinks in the beleag-uered city. From beginning to the end she was ever in the heat of the conflict, her courage and resource heartening the defenders in the darkest hours of those bloody months. She won the name of La Artillera from having snatched the match from the hands of a dying gunner and discharged the piece at the besiegers. She died in Cuerta, Spain, in 1857 at a very advanced age. It was Byron who gave her the name of the Maid of Saragossa. When he was in Seville in July–August, 1809, he used to see her as she walked daily on the prado wearing the medals and orders decreed to her by the junta. In the stanzas dedicated to her in *Childe Harold* he adds a touch of fanciful romance to her story by making the slain gunner her lover:

> Ye who shall marvel when you hear her tale,
> Oh, had you known her in her softer hour,
> Marked her black eye that mocks her coal-black veil.
> Heard her light, lively tones in lady's bower,
> Seen her long locks that foil the painter's power,
> Her fairy form, with more than female grace,
> Scarce would you deem that Saragossa's tower
> Beheld her smile in Danger's Gorgon face,
> Thin the closed ranks and lead in Glory's fearful chase.
>
> Her lover sinks—she sheds no ill-timed tear;
> Her chief is slain—she fills his fatal post;
> Her fellows flee—she checks their base career;
> The foe retires—she leads the sallying host;
> Who can appease her like a lover's ghost?
> Who can avenge so well a leader's fall?
> What maid retrieve when man's flushed hope is lost?
> Who hang so fiercely on the flying Gaul?
> Foiled by a woman's hand, before a battered wall?   *Canto i.*

Auld Ane, a provincial name for the devil in Scotland and in northern England, indicating that he can only appear in the shape of an old man, especially if taken in connection with other nicknames for the same personage: Auld Clootie (probably an allusion to his cloven feet), Auld Hangie, Auld Hornie (from his horns), Auld Nick.

> O thou, whatever title suit thee,
> Auld Hornie, Satan, Nick, or Clootie
> Hear me, Auld Hangie, for a wee,
> And let poor damned bodies be.
> BURNS.

Auld Reekie, a nickname for Edinburgh, an allusion either to its smoky appearance as seen from a distance or the filth of its streets revealed by a nearer inspection. It is fair to add that the designation is ill-desired to-day. But in 1850 the *London Review* complained that the quarter of the city to which it was most applicable " presents, even to this day, the spectacle of the most flagrant violation of the most elementary rules for the preservation of public health and the maintenance of domestic decency."

Aunt, Mr. F's, in Charles Dickens's novel, *Little Dorrit,* " an amazing little old woman with a face like a staring wooden doll, too cheap for expression, and a stiff yellow wig, pushed unevenly on the top of her head." She was characterized by extreme severity and grim taciturnity, sometimes interrupted by a propensity to offer remarks in a deep, warning voice traceable to no association of ideas." Among the most famous of these irrelevant remarks is the one she flung at her particular detestation, Arthur Clennam: " There's milestones on the Dover Road." A further remarkable thing about her was that she " had no name but Mr. F's aunt." She was sometimes alluded to as Flora's Legacy, because Flora had inherited her from her late husband.

Ausonia, a poetical name for Italy from the Ausones or Ausonii who were early settlers on the western coast of what was later Campania.

The soft Ausonia's monumental reign.
CAMPBELL, *Gertrude of Wyoming,* ii, 25.

Autocrat of the Breakfast Table, the hero of a book of that name (1857–58) by O. W. Holmes, so called because he monopolizes the conversation at a Boston boarding house. The epigraph on the title page, " Every man his own Boswell," favors the popular idea that Dr. Holmes was chronicling his own imaginary conversations. The successors, respectively, *The Professor* and *The Poet at the Breakfast Table* (1859 and 1872),

carry on the same or a very similar personality under different masks, though in the latter book the main speaker is not " The Poet " but " The Master," a title derived from his degree as Master of Arts, but also appropriate on account of the air of authority with which he lays down the law.

Autolycus, in Shakespeare's comedy, *The Winter's Tale,* a travelling pedler, and incidentally a thief, self-described as " a snapper up of unconsidered trifles " (Act iv, Sc. 3), who feels, and half persuades his hearers, that there is nothing criminal in his rogueries, for heaven is his accomplice:—" If I had a mind to be honest, I see Fortune would not suffer me; she drops booties into my mouth." Shakespeare took the name from the master thief of classical antiquity, the son of Hermes (Mercury) and Chione. Thus his rogue said, " My father named me Autolycus, who was littered under Mercury."

That, at the close of his dramatic life, after all the trouble he had passed through, Shakespeare had yet the youngness of heart to bubble out into this merry rogue, the incarnation of fun and rascality, and let him sail off successful and unharmed, is wonderful.—F. J. FURNIVAL.

Automathes, hero of one of the many imitations that followed in the wake of *Robinson Crusoe,* a philosophical fiction (1745) by John Kirby, entitled: *The Capacity and Extent of the Human Understanding, exemplified in the extraordinary case of Automathes, a young nobleman, who was accidentally left in his infancy upon a desolate island, and continued nineteen years in that solitary state, separate from all human society.*

Automathes, son of a shipwrecked exile living alone from infancy on a desert island, grows to manhood, a self-taught though speechless philosopher. The author was indebted not only to Defoe's masterpiece but also to the Arabian romance, *Hai Eben Yokhdan,* which he might have read in the Latin version of Pocock.

Avenel, Lady Alice, in Scott's historical romance, *The Monastery,* widow of Walter, Baron of Avenel, and mother of Mary, who eventually marries Halbert Glendenning. Mary is described as by nature " mild, pensive and contemplative." In *The Abbot* she reappears as the Lady of Avenel who finds the family castle so gloomy in her husband's many absences that she welcomes with effusion the advent of her spirited page, Roland Græme.

Avisa, the subject of a series of poems, *Willobie and his Avisa, or the True Picture of a Modest Maid and of a Chaste and Constant Wife,* which was first published in 1594 and reprinted in 1880 by Rev. A. B. Grosart. She is described as a young woman of lowly origin, of delicate beauty, and constant both as a maiden and a wife against the attacks of many lovers of high degree. At last came Henry Willobie, the reputed author of the poems, who applied for assistance " unto his familiar friend W. S. who not long before had tried the courtesy of the like passion and was now newly recovered of the like infection." The context shows that W. S. not only was prominent as a love poet but that he was connected, probably as an actor, with the stage. Hence the inference that W. S. was no less a person than William Shakespeare.

At last a perfect copy of the much-discussed *Avisa* has been discovered; at last it has been very carefully and exhaustively edited by one of the most learned of our Elizabethan critics, with the careful collation of all collateral and illustrative literature; and the result is that some one, we know not who, being in love with the hostess of a country tavern, appealed to Shakespeare for assistance in prosecuting his suit, and that Shakespeare teased and bantered him in humorous malice. This is interesting, and the record of it is valuable; but it brings us so near to the person of the great poet, and at the same time reveals to us so extremely little of his nature, that we are almost like the boy in Mr. Sala's novel who was so much hurt by the pennies which the lady threw in his face that he forebore to thank her.—*Saturday Review,* April 3, 1880.

Axel, in Daudet's *Kings in Exile* (1880), is a thinly disguised portrait of the Prince of Orange.

Ayesha, heroine of an Oriental romance, *Ayesha, the Maid of Kars*

(1834), by James Morier. She is the reputed daughter of a rich old Turk in Kars. Lord Ormond, a young travelling Englishman, sees and falls in love with her. His efforts to gain acquaintance lead to his imprisonment. He escapes to the stronghold of Cara Bey, a noted robber. The latter is himself fired with unholy passion by Ormond's description of Ayesha's charms. He casts the Englishman into an oubliette, makes a midnight foray upon Kars and carries off the maiden. Meanwhile Ormond has succeeded in communicating with the Russian commander on the neighboring frontier. The commander surprises the castle, captures Cara Bey and his gang, and releases Ormond and Ayesha. The latter turns out to be a daughter of Sir Edward Wortley, is converted to Christianity, and marries Ormond.

Aylmer, Rose, subject and title of an eight-lined poem by Walter Savage Landor (1800) which seems destined to outlive all his other works in prose or verse. Rose Whitworth Aylmer was an English maiden whom Landor had known in his youth and who died at Calcutta in her twentieth year on March 2, 1800. In 1909 the stanzas were engraved upon her tomb through the intervention of Lady Graves Sawle, whose mother was Rose Aylmer's half-sister.

Aymer, prior of Jorvaulx Abbey in Scott's romance, *Ivanhoe,* " a free and jovial priest who loves the wine-cup and the bugle-horn better than bell and book." It was his denunciation of Rebecca as " a witch of Endor " that led the Grand Master to deal with her "as the Christian law and our own high office warrant."

Azo, in Lord Byron's narrative poem, *Parisina* (1816), the wronged husband of the titular heroine. He wreaks a terrible vengeance upon the lady and her paramour (see PARISINA). Byron found the story in Gibbon's *Antiquities of the House of Brunswick,* where it is told of Nicholas III, Marquis of Este. " The name of Azo," he says, " is substituted for Nicholas as more metrical."

B

B. Under the title and initial of " Mr. B." and under that alone (the novel being composed in a series of imaginary letters) the reader is made acquainted with the chief male character in Richardson's *Pamela, or Virtue Rewarded* (1740). The heroine is a servant girl in his family whom he pursues dishonorably. She indignantly rejects him and leaves the house. Mr. B. follows her; passion is transformed into love; he overlooks the difference of station and marries her. Fielding in his novel *Joseph Andrews* (1742), originally begun as a burlesque of *Pamela*, suggests a solution of the mysterious initial by supplying Mr. B. with a sister, Lady Booby. It may be noted that in some later editions of *Pamela* an endeavor has been made to neutralize this outrage by revealing " Mr. B." as Mr. Boothby.

Bab, Lady, in Rev. J. Townley's farce, *High Life below Stairs* (1763), a maid-servant, who, following the custom of the servants' quarters, adopts and is known by the name of her mistress. She is addressed as " your ladyship," affects aristocratic airs, reads only one book " which is Shikspur," and anticipates Mrs. Malaprop by such verbal felicities as " downright hottenpots " applied behind their backs to gentlemen who call upon her mistress.

Baba, in Byron's *Don Juan*, the chief eunuch at the court of Sultana Guebeyas.

Babbie, in J. M. Barrie's novel, *The Little Minister* (1896), the name assumed by the wilful and winsome heroine when she disguises herself as a gypsy woman. She wishes to escape from her betrothed, Lord Rintoul, and almost before she knows it finds herself caught by Gavin Dishart, the exemplary " Little Minister " of Thrums, who himself falls an easy victim to her brilliant and unconventional ways.

Babley, Richard, in Dickens' *David Copperfield*, a harmless lunatic generally called Mr. Dick. See DICK.

Baboon (*i.e.*, **Bourbon**), **Lewis,** in Arbuthnot's political satire, *The History of John Bull* (1712), a caricature of Louis XIV and hence, by extension, of the French people, as John Bull is of the English. He is thus described by his creator:

Sometimes you would see this **Lewis** Baboon behind his counter selling broadcloth, sometimes measuring linen; next day he would be dealing in mercery ware; high heads, ribbons, gloves, fans and lace he understood to a nicety; nay, he would descend to the selling of tapes, garters and shoe-buckles. When shop was shut up, he would go about the neighborhood, and earn half a crown by teaching the young men and maidens to dance. By these means he had acquired immense riches, which he used to squander away at backsword, quarter-staff and cudgel play, in which he took great pleasure.

Backbite, Sir Benjamin, in Sheridan's comedy, *The School for Scandal* (1777), a jealous, conceited, cynical and censorious gentleman, a would-be poet and wit, highly esteemed as such among the foolish who consorted with him, but publishing nothing, because as he pretended " 'twas very vulgar to print," and, moreover, he found that he could obtain a wider circulation " by giving copies in confidence to friends."

Bacon, Roger (1214–1292), a mediæval English monk and experimenter in natural science who, like other pioneers in the middle ages, was reputed to be a magician and as such has passed into popular folklore. His feats were commemorated in a pamphlet entitled *The Famous Historie of Frier Bacon, containing the wonderful things that he did in his Life, also the Manner of his Death, with the Lives and Deaths of the Two Conjurors, Bungye and Vandermast*, and they form the comic element in Robert Greene's comedy, *Friar Bacon and Friar Bungay* (1594).

The play is worth editing; it is **Greene's** masterpiece, and the masterpiece of one who was an early rival of Shakespeare must be interesting. There is an interest in its treatment of the story of Bacon, the great student degraded by popular superstition to the level of a vulgar conjurer, and raised again by the imagination of a poet to be the friend of kings and the prophet of great-ness for his country. There is a charm, moreover, in the genuinely English atmosphere which Greene contrives to throw over his piece—in the Suffolk meads and in the schools and streets of Oxford, in the English Edward and the "fair maid of Fressingfield."

Saturday Review.

Badebec, in Rabelais' comic romance, *Pantagruel*, ii, 2 (1533), the wife of Gargantua and the mother of Pantagruel, who died in giving him birth—no great marvel when it is recorded that he came into the world accompanied by 81 sellers of salt, each leading a mule by a halter, 9 dromedaries laden with ham and smoked tongues; 7 camels, laden with eels, and 25 wagons full of leeks, garlic, onions and shallots.

Badger, Bayham, in Dickens's novel, *Bleak House* (1853), a physician at Chelsea under whom Richard Carstone pursues his medical studies. He is described as a pink, fresh-faced, crisp-looking gentleman with a weak voice, white teeth, light hair and surprised eyes. Proud of being Mrs. Badger's "third," he is continually dragging in allusions to her first and second husbands, Captain Swosser and Professor Dingo.

Badman, Mr., the titular hero of John Bunyan's allegorical tale, *The Life and Death of Mr. Badman.* As Badman is the very opposite of Christian in the *Pilgrim's Progress*, so his path leads to hell and not to heaven.

Bagarag, Shibli, in George Meredith's oriental fantasy, *The Shaving of Shagpat*, a whimsical youth who, after many remarkable adventures, becomes a barber and shaves Shagpat.

Bagot, William, in Du Maurier's *Trilby.* See BILLEE, LITTLE.

Bagstock, Major Joe, in Dickens's *Dombey and Son* (1846), a retired military officer, blue-faced, red-nosed and apoplectic, who cherishes a partly concealed passion for Miss Tox and a consequent jealousy of Mr. Dombey. He is fond of alluding to himself by affectionate diminutives and nicknames: " Old J. B.," " Old Joe," " Rough and Tough Old Joe," etc.

Bailey, Tom, hero of the *Story of a Bad Boy*, by Thomas Bailey Aldrich

(1869), which is largely autobiographical. Tom is only comparatively a bad boy and his badness is thrown into comic relief by the puritanic austerity of the quaint New England town where he lived whose " inhabitants were, many of them, pure Christians every day of the seven except the seventh." This town, called Rivermouth in the story, is evidently Portsmouth, N. H.

Baillie, Gabriel, in Scott's novel, *Guy Mannering* (1815), the nephew of Meg Merrilies, known among the gypsies as Gabriel Faa, and among his own people in Liddesdale as Tod Gabbie or Hunter Gabbie. Pressed into naval service under Captain Pritchard in the *Shark*, he deserted in order to warn Dirk Hatteraick of the *Shark's* approach. It was he who, under the compelling influence of his Aunt Meg, gave conclusive testimony as to the identity of Vanbeest Brown with the missing heir of Mannering.

Bajazet, surnamed The Thunderbolt (in Rowe's tragedy, *Tamerlane*, 1702), the Sultan of Turkey, fierce, reckless, indomitable, who is captured by Tamerlane (*q.v.*).

Balaam, Sir, in Pope's *Moral Essays*, iii. A " citizen of sober fame " and a " plain good man " so long as he remained in obscurity, he was ruined by becoming wealthy, a knight and a courtier. Finally, accepting a bribe from France, he was hanged for treason. The character has never been identified.

Balafré, Le (the Man with a Scar), the nickname in real life of Henry, son of the second Duke of Guise, whose face had been slashed by a sword at the battle of Dermans (1575), and, in Scott's *Quentin Durward*, that of Ludovic Lesly.

Balaustion, in Robert Browning's *Balaustion's Adventure* (1871) and *Aristophanes' Apology, including a Transcript from Euripides, being the Last Adventure of Balaustion* (1875), a pure invention of Browning. The daughter of a Rhodian father and an Athenian mother, she casts in her lot with Athens when, under the disastrous failure of the Sicilian expedition, the allies of that city were deserting for Sparta. Balaustion witnesses the disgrace of the former city and the triumph of the latter, makes friends with Euripides, and through the power of her womanhood extorts from the ribald Aristophanes a plea for his art in answer to a mute reproach of Euripides and a direct charge from herself.

Balder, in Sydney Dobell's poetical tragedy of that name (1854), a morbid young poet who qualifies himself for what he conceives to be his mission in life by murdering his wife and child and putting into literary form the agonies which he and they have experienced. W. E. Aytoun has burlesqued the character in *Firmilian, a Spasmodic Tragedy.*

Balderston, Caleb, in Scott's novel, *The Bride of Lammermoor,* the only male servant who retained his loyalty to the Ravenswoods in their misfortunes and who remained in their employ without expectation of reward. The queer shifts to which he is put to conceal the bareness of the domestic larder and the wealth of language under which he seeks to divert attention from all appearances of indigence are diverting enough at first but eventually weary the reader by multitudinous repetition. Nevertheless he has passed into literature as the type of the faithful servitor— a composite in humble station of Abdiel and Munchausen.

Of all our author's fools and bores, he is the most pertinacious, the most intrusive, and, from the nature of his one monotonous note, the least pardonable in his intrusion. His silly buffoonery is always marring, with gross absurdities and degrading associations, some scene of tenderness or dignity.—SENIOR.

Balfour, John, of Burley, or **Kinloch,** in Scott's historical romance, *Old Mortality,* a leader in the Covenanters' army. He occasionally hides his identity under the *nom de guerre* of Quintin Mackell of Irongray. Daring in design, precipitate and violent in execution, and going to the very extremity of the most rigid recusancy, he even justifies the murder of Archbishop Sharpe in which he took part. " My conduct is open to men and

angels," he says to Harry Morton. " The deed was not done in a corner; I am here in arms to avow it, and care not where, or by whom, I am called on to do so; whether in the council, the field of battle, the place of execution, or the day of the last great trial."

Balibari, Chevalier de, the name assumed by Cornelius Barry, uncle to Redmond Barrie, the titular hero of *The Memoirs of Barry Lyndon, Esq.* (1844). The Chevalier is a professional gambler and adventurer, who, under pretence of a diplomatic appointment, goes from one European capital to another running a private faro bank for callow youth and imbecile maturity. He makes Barry his partner and his tool. Ever a devoted Roman Catholic, the Chevalier in his broken old age retires to a convent.

Baliol, Mistress Martha Bethune, of Baliol Lodging, Canongate, Edinburgh, a lady " of quality and fortune " who is sketched at some length in the introduction to Scott's romance *The Fair Maid of Perth.* At death she is represented as leaving to her cousin Chrystal Croftangry the material for the Chronicles of the Canongate. Sir Walter notes that in this lady he " designed to shadow out in its leading points the interesting character of a dear friend," Mrs. Murray Keith, who died in 1831. " The author had, on many occasions, been indebted to her vivid memory for the *substratum* of his Scottish fictions." *The Highland Widow* is given " very much as the excellent old lady used to tell the story."

Balisardo, in Ariosto's *Orlando Furioso,* a sword owned by Ruggiero, made by Falerina, a sorceress, for the express purpose of slaying Orlando, so true and keen that it would cut even magic substances.

Balnibarbi, in Swift's *Gulliver's Travels,* a portion of the fabulous island of Laputa, inhabited by inventors and projectors.

Balthasar or **Balthazar,** in Shakespeare's plays, a frequent name for a servant or valet. Thus **Romeo,**

Portia, and also Don Pedro in *Much Ado about Nothing* have attendants so called. Portia assumes the name of Dr. Balthasar when she appears in court disguised as a lawyer.

Balthazar, in the *Comedy of Errors,* a merchant who appears only in Act iii, Sc. 1.

Balue, John of, Cardinal and Bishop of Auxerre (1420–1491), a historical character introduced by Scott in his romance, *Quentin Durward.* In the fiction as in fact he is a trusted counsellor of Louis XI of France, a man of obscure origin whose head had been turned by sudden elevation to clerical rank and political influence. His downfall came when in a moment of wounded vanity he yielded to the advances of Crèvecoeur and so worked upon the "peculiar foibles" of his royal master as to induce him to visit the Duke of Burgundy in Peronne. After the disastrous issue of that episode he was confined for eleven years in an iron cage of his own invention.

Balwhidder, Rev. Micah, in John Galt's novel, *Annals of the Parish* (1821), a Presbyterian minister prejudiced, narrow minded and conventional, but full of the milk of human kindness and the cream of Scotch piety, with just enough of the acid of humor to flavor but not curdle.

Banister, in Shakespeare's *Henry VIII,* a servant who had murdered his master, Henry, Duke of Buckingham. He appears only in Act ii, Sc. 1.

Bantam, Angelo. Cyrus, Esq., M. C., in Chapter xxxv of the *Pickwick Papers* (1836), by Charles Dickens, grand master of the ceremonies at the ball which Mr. Pickwick attends at Bath. The original of his house has been identified as No. 12 Queen Square, Bath.

Bantam, Lord, the eponymic hero of a novel (1871) by Edward Jenkins, attacking the domestic arrangements of the upper classes in England and the theories of social and religious reformers of a more advanced type than the author's.

Baptista, in *The Taming of the Shrew,* a rich gentleman of Padua, the father of Katherine and Bianca. His full name is Baptista Minola.

Barabas, titular hero of Christopher Marlowe's tragedy, *The Jew of Malta* (1586). Maddened by Christian persecutors, who treat him like a beast, he hates them like a beast. His daughter has two Christian suitors and by forged letters he causes them to slay each other. In despair she takes the veil. He poisons her and the whole nunnery, invents an infernal machine to blow up the Turkish garrison, plots to cast the Turkish commander into a well and falls into it himself, and finally is boiled alive in a cauldron prepared by English law for poisoners, howling and remorseless, regretting only that he had not done evil enough.

Dyce opines that Shakespeare was probably acquainted with Marlowe's tragedy. "But," he adds, "that he caught from it more than a few trifling hints for the *Merchant of Venice* will be allowed by no one who has carefully compared the character of Shylock with that of Barabas." On the other hand A. W. Ward, while admitting the marked difference between the two characters, affirms that the two plays are written in essentially the same spirit. It is, he thinks, the invention of modern players and commentators that Shakespeare consciously intended to arouse sympathy with the Jew; and the fact of such sympathy being aroused is due to the "unconscious tact with which the poet humanized the character." In both plays the view is that fraud is the sign of the Jew's tribe; and that counter-fraud, though accompanied with violence, on the part of a Christian is commendable. It seems an inevitable conclusion that in the *Merchant of Venice* no pity was intended to be felt for Shylock; but Barabas, as Mr. Ward points out, was meant to excite ridicule as well as dislike, and the character, which after the beginning of the play degenerates into a caricature, has little affinity with humanity, while Shylock is throughout human and real. See SHYLOCK.

Barataria, in Cervantes' romance, *Don Quixote* (1615), an island city over which Sancho Panza was appointed perpetual governor. It contained about 1000 inhabitants. " They gave him to understand that it was called the island of Barataria, either because Barataria was really the name of the place, or because he obtained the government of it at so cheap a rate. On his arrival near the gates of the town, the municipal officers came out to receive him. Presently after, with certain ridiculous ceremonies, they presented him with the keys of the town, and constituted him perpetual governor of the island of Barataria." The honor was an empty one. Sancho's very table was presided over by Dr. Pedro Rezio de Aguero, who had every dish whisked away before he could touch it, sometimes because it heated the blood and sometimes because it chilled it, but always on some ridiculous pretext.

Bardell, Mrs. Martha, in Dickens's *Pickwick Papers* (1836), the relict and sole executrix of a deceased custom-house officer, landlady of " Apartments for Single Gentlemen " in Goswell Street, where Mr. Pickwick for a period was her star lodger. She was a comely woman, of bustling manners and agreeable appearance with " a natural genius for cooking, improved by study and long practice into an exquisite talent." Mr. Pickwick's will was law in her house; he had little to grumble at in his apartments, which, though on a limited scale, were neat and comfortable. Unfortunately she either misunderstood or deliberately plotted to misunderstand his intentions, and one day was found fainting in his arms by his friends—the result of an innocent remark which she had construed as a proposal. Hence a breach of promise case trumped up and by the unprincipled lawyers Dodson and Fogg. The trial occurs in Chapter xxxiv. The character is said to have been founded on a Mrs. Ann Ellis, " who kept an eating house near Doctors' Commons."

Bardolph, in both parts of *King Henry IV* and in *The Merry Wives of Windsor*, is a corporal in Sir John Falstaff's company. In *Henry V* he has been promoted to lieutenant.

Bareacres, Countess of, in Thackeray's *Vanity Fair*, the poor and proud wife of George, Earl of Bareacres. She snubs Becky Sharp in Brussels just before the battle of Waterloo, goes down to her knees to her to beg for her horses to escape from the city, and later tries once again to snub Becky at Gaunt House, but this time finds she has caught a tartar. She had previously appeared in *Jeames' Diary* as " a grand and hawfile pusnage with a Roming nose." Her husband, briefly sketched in *Vanity Fair* as a gentleman with " not much pride and a large appetite," flits anachronistically through the pages of that novel and of *Pendennis* (Chap. ii) and *The Newcomes* (ix).

Barker, Lemuel, the chief character in a novel, *The Minister's Charge* (1887), by W. D. Howells, a self-imagined poet who takes too seriously the praises bestowed upon his verses by the amiably unveracious Mr. Sewell, leaves his rustic home for Boston and meets with many disappointments before he finds his level.

A young New England rustic who goes to Boston and falls into temptation, but no temptation of the grosser sort in which a true follower of the realists would delight to wallow. The truth is that Mr. Howells, though he professes to be a realist and to describe life as it is, is not one. He paints the life around him as he chooses to see it. He fits his human beings for presentation in the pages of a family magazine and in novels which may be read by every young girl. He impresses us as a sincere and pure-minded gentleman who arranges his groups, carefully chosen, each member with his working clothes on, and then photographs them.— *Catholic World.*

Barker, Peter, hero of a once famous novel, *The Bachelor of the Albany* (1874), by Marmion W. Savage. A thoroughly humorous creation.

Barkis, Mr., in Dickens's *David Copperfield*, the Yarmouth carrier, a silent, shy man, who marries Clara Peggotty, declaring his intentions by sending through David the laconic message, " Barkis is willin'." He is said to have been drawn from one Barker, whom Dickens knew at Blunderston.

Barlass, Kate, a sobriquet given to Catherine Douglas. When King James I, of Scotland, was pursued by conspirators he sought refuge in the Black Friars' monastery at Perth. To keep out the murderers Catherine thrust her arm through the door-staples. The door was forced, Catharine fell back with a shattered arm, and the king was murdered in the sanctuary where he had taken refuge. In honor of her deed Catherine received the famous sobriquet. Dante Gabriel Rossetti made this episode the subject of his ballad, *The King's Tragedy* (1880). Catherine in her old age is supposed to tell the story.

Barleycorn, Sir John, a humorous personification of ale and all other liquors made from barley. The jest is very old; it may be found in a fifteenth century tract, *The Arraigning and Indicting of Sir John Barley corn, knt.,* and in a ballad preserved in *The English Dancing Master* (1651). The poem has been slightly revamped by Burns.

Barlow, Billy, hero of an English comic song popular in the early nineteenth century. In 1855 Robert Brough adopted his name as that of the pretended author of the *Barlow Papers,* writing on current topics in various forms of verse, but never proceeding for long without some harking back to the refrain of the original song:

> Now isn't it hard upon Billy Barlow.
> O dear ragged-y O,
> Now isn't it hard upon Billy Barlow.

Barlow, Mr., in Thomas Day's juvenile story, *Sandford and Merton,* the didactic tutor of the two boys who never loses an opportunity for advice or instruction. Dickens has an essay, " Mr. Barlow " (*Uncommercial Traveller,* xxxii), in which he presents a parallel case—an irrepressible instructive monomaniac, who knows everything and knows that he knows it.

Barlow, Rev. William, the titular hero of an opera, *The Vicar of Bray* (1882), by Grundy and Solomon. Joe Barlow and his wife Alice are characters in H. J. Byron's comedy, *A Hundred Thousand Pounds* (1866).

Barnabas, Parson, in Fielding's *Joseph Andrews* (1742), a vain and weak though not unworthy clergyman. Very dictatorial, mightily impressed with his own dignity and importance, he especially prides himself on his knowledge of the law and on the excellence of his sermons: " three bishops had said that they were the best that ever were written, and were even better than Tillotson's discourses, though he was a good writer and said things very well."

Barnaby, Mrs., heroine of Frances Trollope's novel, *Widow Barnaby* (1838), a fussy, good-natured, vulgar woman whose chief aim in life is to marry again. This object she accomplishes in a sequel, *Widow Barnaby Married* (1840), and subsequent experiences in the United States are recorded in a third book, *The Barnabys in America* (1843), which repeats the unfavorable verdict on transatlantic manners already expressed in the same author's *Domestic Manners of the Americans* (1832).

Barnacle Family, in Dickens's *Little Dorrit,* " a very high family and a very large family." Nine of them figure in the novel: Lord Decimus Barnacle, " a cabinet Minister; " Mr. Tite Barnacle, " a permanent. official at the circumlocution office; " Mrs. Tite Barnacle, nee Stiltstalking; Clarence Barnacle, a son of Mr. Tite Barnacle, " had a youthful aspect, and the fluffiest little whisker perhaps that ever was seen; " the Misses Barnacle, daughters of Mr. Tite Barnacle, " double loaded with accomplishments and ready to go off; " Ferdinand Barnacle, private secretary to Lord Decimus Barnacle, and William Barnacle, member of Parliament.

Barnardine, in Shakespeare's *Measure for Measure,* is described in the cast as " a dissolute prisoner." Though introduced into but two short scenes in Acts iii and v he makes an ineffaceable impression. Hazlitt praises the character as " one of the finest (and that's saying a bold word) in all Shakespeare. He is what he is by nature and not by circumstance ' careless, reckless and fearless of past, present, and to come.' "

Barnhelm, Minna von, titular heroine of a drama by Gotthold Ephraim Lessing (1767). She is the betrothed of a Prussian officer in the Seven Years' War, Major von Tellheim, who being disgraced and degraded on a false charge of embezzlement, renounces her hand. Vainly she vows unaltered love. She is an heiress, and he will not be beholden to her generosity. But he learns that for his sake she has been disinherited by her wealthy uncle. Then he begs her to renew the engagement. As she seems about to yield, a letter arrives. Tellheim's innocence has been established; his rank and pay restored; he is even assured of speedy promotion. Minna, assuming the rôle her lover had dropped, now refuses in her poverty to take advantage of his generosity. While Tellheim is still pleading, her uncle arrives, and it then transpires that the story of the disinheritance had been invented by Minna in order to win back her lover. As the first German drama dealing with national characters and contemporary events, it exerted a wide and salutary influence in Germany. It was translated or, rather, paraphrased into French as *Les Amans Généreux,* and into English (1786), by James Johnstone as the *Disbanded Officer,* and was the parent of numerous soldier dramas which flooded the European stage during the last half of the eighteenth century.

Barnwell, George, hero of a famous English ballad of unknown authorship and uncertain date, but probably issued in the later sixteenth century: *An Excellent Ballad of George Barnwell, an Apprentice of London who Thrice robbed his Master and Murdered his Uncle in Ludlow.* Originally innocent and industrious, he falls into the toils of Sarah Millwood, a courtesan, who instigates him to rob

and murder, and then threatens to inform upon him. He flies beyond seas, writes a letter of confession to the Lord Mayor of London implicating Sarah; she is executed, and Barnwell himself suffers capital punishment in Polonia for some fresh crime. His posthumous celebrity, won through the ballad, was very greatly increased when George Lillo made him the subject of a tragedy (1731), and during the latter half of the eighteenth century he became the hero of songs, novels and pantomimes which deviated still further than Lillo's play from the original ballad. Finally Thackeray apotheosized him under the more aristocratic name of George de Barnwell (*q.v.*).

Barnwell, George de, hero of a burlesque in Thackeray's *Novels by Eminent Hands,* which originally appeared in the London *Punch* as *Punch's Prize Novelists* (1847). This, the first in the series, is facetiously attributed to " Sir E. L. B. L. Bart." and purports to give three specimen chapters of a romance whose scene is laid in London at " an indefinite period of time between Queen Anne and George II," and in which George de Barnwell, like Bulwer's Eugene Aram, murders his uncle from the highest and noblest motives, the desire to rid the world of a monster who had no sympathy with the Beautiful and the Ideal and to use his wealth in relieving poverty, in aiding science, and in uplifting art. There was a real George Barnwall (*q.v.*), who figured in the criminal annals of England.

Barry, Mrs., Barry Lyndon's mother in Thackeray's novel of Barry Lyndon, an energetic, thrifty and handsome Irish lady who is proud of her son's successful rascality and his rich bride, though she eventually resents his assumption of superiority.

Barry, Redmond, the real name of Barry Lyndon. See LYNDON, BARRY.

Barsisa, a Santon or Mohammedan saint, whose story, as told by Addison, in No. 148 of the *Guardian,* furnished Lewis with the germ of his novel, *The Monk.* Addison took the story from the *Turkish Tales*. Barsisa, after a life of great sanctity, was in his old age tempted by the devil to offer violence to a beautiful princess who had been confided to his care. To conceal his crime he was driven to murder her, and when the murder was discovered he sold himself to Satan in a vain effort to purchase his freedom.

Barstowe, Captain, in Scott's *Peveril of the Peak*, the name assumed by a Jesuit named Fenwicke who gives Julian Peveril a treasonable letter from the Countess of Derby to be delivered in London. His plans are frustrated by Fenella.

Bart, Lily, heroine of *The House of Mirth* (1906), a novel by Mrs. Edith Wharton. A beautiful, elegant, highstrung woman whom fate has thrown into fashionable society in New York City without money enough properly to maintain her position. This is how she appears in Chapter i to the eyes of Lawrence Sheldon who is destined to be her lover:

He had a confused sense that she must have cost a great deal to make, that a great many dull and ugly people must in some mysterious way have been sacrificed to produce her. He was aware that the qualities distinguishing her from the rest of her sex were chiefly external, as though a fine glaze of beauty and fastidiousness had been applied to vulgar clay. Yet the analogy left him unsatisfied, for a coarse texture will not take a high finish, and was it not possible that the material was fine, but that circumstance had fashioned it into a futile shape?

Barthole, Dr., in Beaumarchais' comedies, *Le Mariage de Figaro* and *Le Barbier de Seville*, a jealous, suspicious and exacting tutor.

Barton, Amos, principal male character in George Eliot's story, *The Sad Fortunes of the Rev. Amos Barton*, collected in the volume, *Scenes of Clerical Life*.

Barton is a poor country clergyman little liked by his parish, always at odds with his vestry, shabbily dressed, ever thinking of the little mouths at home which he finds it hard to fill or of his invalid wife, wasting away before the bloom of youth is passed but every moment growing sweeter in his eyes as the final parting draws irrevocably nearer.

The sad fortunes of the Rev. Amos Barton are fortunes which clever storytellers with a turn for pathos, from Goldsmith downwards, have found of very good account—the fortunes of a hapless clergyman in daily contention with the problem how upon £80 a year to support a wife and six children in ecclesiastical gentility.—LESLIE STEPHEN.

Barton, Sir Andrew, hero and title of a ballad, probably written in Queen Elizabeth's reign, which versified the story of that famous Scotch admiral (died 1511). Aroused by his depredations against English merchant ships, the Earl of Surrey sent his two sons out to sea to retaliate, and in the engagement that followed (August 2, 1511) Sir Andrew was killed.

Barton, Mary, heroine of the novel of that name (1848) by Mrs. E. C. Gaskell, is the daughter of a weaver in Manchester. When the factory shuts down during the troubles of 1842 her mother and her little brother die from privation and she is left alone to tend to her father. Embittered by reverses John Barton has become a Chartist and is involved in a plot to assassinate a young millowner. Jem Neilson, whom Mary loves, is arrested on suspicion and Mary devotes herself to the task of clearing Neilson without exposing her father.

Bashville, in George Bernard Shaw's novel, *Cashel Byron's Profession,* a footman in the service of Lydia Carew, an orphan heiress and a beauty for whom he cherishes a daring but unrequited affection. R. L. Stevenson delighted in this character, as may be seen in a letter first published in the preface to the revised edition of the novel (1902) where he wishes that the author " only knew how I had enjoyed the chivalry of Bashville—O Bashville! *j'en chortle!* (which is finely polyglot)."

Basile, in Beaumarchais' comedies, *The Marriage of Figaro* (1775) and *The Barber of Seville*, a miser, a bigot and a slanderer. His favorite formula is " Calumniate, calumniate; some of it will stick."

Basilisco, in the anonymous comedy, *Soliman and Persida* (1592), a boastful but cowardly knight. When the newly knighted Bastard in *King John* (Act i, Sc. 2) is called by his mother a " most untoward knave" he humorously reproves her

Knight, knight, good mother, Basilisco-like, What, I am dubbed, I have it on my shoulder.

Basilius, in Sir Philip Sidney's romance, *The Arcadia,* the king of that imaginary region.

Bassanio, in Shakespeare's comedy, *The Merchant of Venice* (1598), " a kinsman and friend to Antonio," and suitor to Portia. His success in choosing the right one among three caskets wins him her hand. It was for Bassanio that Antonio entered into his strange compact with Shylock (*q.v.*). One of the most colorless of all Shakespeare's characters, he seems hardly deserving of Antonio's affection or Portia's love.

Bassett, Octavia, heroine of *A Fair Barbarian* (1881), a novel by Mrs. Frances Hodgson Burnett. A nineteen-year-old girl from Nevada, she comes to visit her aunt, Miss Rhoda Bassett, in the English village of Slowbridge. Her innocent abandon outrages the chill proprieties of the elder ladies, raises secret jealousies among the younger ones and excites open admiration from the bucks and beaux who flock around her, half ashamed of their own devotion.

Bastard of Orleans (Fr. Bâtard d'Orléans). A nickname given to Jeane Dunois (1403–1468), a natural son of Louis, Duke of Orleans, the brother of King Charles VI. He fought against the English by the side of Joan of Arc and contributed largely to their expulsion from France after the death of that heroine. He figures in Shakespeare's *I Henry VI,* in Mark Twain's and generally in all novels and plays concerning Joan of Arc (*q.v.*).

Bates, Charley, generally called Master Bates in *Oliver Twist* (1837), by Charles Dickens, one of Fagin's pupils in the art of pocket picking. His dexterity is almost equal to that of the Artful Dodger. See DAWKINS, JOHN.

Bates, Miss, in Jane Austen's novel, *Emma* (1815), a worthy old maid, happy in eking out a narrow income and caring for a failing mother. Though conceded to be the village bore, " a great talker on little matters, full of trivial communications and harmless gossip," she was yet universally popular from her effusive goodness of heart. " She was a happy woman and a woman no one named without good-will. It was her own contented temper that worked such wonders. She loved everybody, was interested in everybody's happiness." Goldwin Smith opines that " the hand which drew Miss Bates, though it could not have drawn Lady Macbeth, could have drawn Dame Quickly, or the nurse in *Romeo and Juliet.*"

Bath, Major, in Henry Fielding's novel, *Amelia* (1751), a vain but kindly and high-minded gentleman, fellow prisoner with Captain Booth who strives to conceal his poverty under a lofty bearing and magniloquent speech. George Colman the younger has imitated this character in Lieutenant Worthington, hero of his comedy, *The Poor Gentleman* (1802).

Bathsheba, in the Old Testament, was the wife of Uriah. David had the husband treacherously put out of the way in order to enjoy the embraces of his wife. Bathsheba became the mother of Solomon. In Dryden's satirical poem, *Absalom and Achitophel,* the name Bathsheba is given to Louise de Keroual, the French mistress of Charles II, whom he bestowed in marriage on one of his minions, making him Duke of Portsmouth.

Battle, Ben, a " soldier bold " in Thomas Hood's punning ballad, *Faithless Nelly Gray,* who is forsaken by his eponymic love after he has lost all his limbs in the service of his country.

Battle, Sarah, in Charles Lamb's *Mrs. Battle on Whist,* one of the *Essays of Elia,* was in real life Sarah Burney, *née* Payne, the wife of

Madame D'Arblay's brother and the mother of Lamb's great friend, Martin Burney. All Mrs. Battle required, it will be remembered, was "a clear fire, a clean hearth, and the rigor of the game."

Bayes, the chief character in *The Rehearsal* (1671), a burlesque by George Villiers, Duke of Buckingham, intended to ridicule the extravagance of the "heroic" plays during the Restoration. The founder of this school, Sir William Davenant, was living when the piece was begun. He was poet laureate, *i.e.*, wearer of the bays, whence Bayes. The play was so long in hand that Davenant died (1668) before it was produced; Dryden succeeded him as laureate and the character of Bayes was passed on to him. Some of Davenant's characteristics, *e.g.*, his broken nose, were retained, but the "hum and buzz," the rhodomontade were even more applicable to Dryden than to Davenant, and the profuse quotations from Dryden's plays emphasized the likeness. Dryden retaliated by making Buckingham the Zimri (*q.v.*) of *Absalom and Achitophel.* Bayes is represented as the author of a mock tragedy under rehearsal, and takes both himself and his play in a grotesquely serious spirit. He is vain, foolish and irritable, obsequious to the great and tyrannous to his subordinates.

Sheridan recast *The Rehearsal* into *The Critic, or a Tragedy Rehearsed* (1779), and remodelled Bayes into Sir Fretful Plagiary (*q.v.*).

Bayham, Frederick, in Thackeray's novel, *The Newcomes,* appearing incidentally also in *The Adventures of Philip,* Chapter x, a good-natured, rollicking, magniloquent Bohemian attached to the staff of the *Pall Mall Gazette.* He alludes to himself familiarly as F. B. and is known to most of his friends by those initials. The character is said to have been drawn from one of Thackeray's Bohemian acquaintances, William Proctor, who among other points of resemblance always spoke of himself in the third person as William.

Baynes, Charlotte, in Thackeray's novel, *The Adventures of Philip,* the loyal, faithful and devoted girl with whom Philip Firmin is in love and whom he marries despite all opposition from her family. She is introduced in Chapter xvi with the following description: "A tall young lady in a brown silk dress and rich curling ringlets falling upon her fair young neck—beautiful brown curling ringlets, *vous comprenez,* not wisps of moistened hair, and a broad clear forehead, and two honest eyes shining below it, and cheeks not pale as they were yesterday; and lips redder still. Indeed, never was a pleasanter picture of health and good-humor."

Baynes, General Charles, in Thackeray's novel *Philip,* father to Charlotte, a brave man in action, but timorous and weak in common life, especially in presence of his wife, who rules him with vigor and acrimony.

Bazan, Don Cæsar de, hero and title of a French drama (July, 1844) by Dumanoir and D'Ennery which has been freely imitated, adapted or burlesqued by English playwrights. The first English version by à Beckett and Mark Lemon (October, 1844) retained the French title and followed the original more closely than its half-dozen successors. This is the version prepared for Lester Wallack in London and reproduced by him in New York in 1849. Fechter's version dates from 1861. John Brougham brought out the first burlesque, *Don Cæsar de Bassoon,* in 1845.

Bazaroff, in Tourgenief's novel, *Fathers and Sons,* a young student of advanced opinions despising the gentler graces exemplified in the young nobleman Kirsanoff. His views clash not only with the world at large but also with his own circle and there is a deep pathos in the confused efforts of his father to understand the son's new ideas and the young man's vain attempts to convert the father.

Bazaroff dies, not on the scaffold as his early career might seem to foreshadow, but of blood poisoning contracted while dissecting a corpse. Having given up his wild dreams and conquered his fierce passions he has returned, resolved to practise medicine and play the part of a useful citizen. Just when one might hope all from so strong a character he dies a victim to blind chance.

Beatrice, heroine of Shakespeare's comedy, *Much Ado about Nothing* (1600). Niece to Leonato, governor of Messina, she and Benedick (*q.v.*) clash at their first meeting but fall in love as the result of a stratagem ingeniously contrived by their friends.

The extraordinary success of this play in Shakespeare's own day, and ever since, in England, is to be ascribed more particularly to the parts of Benedick and Beatrice, two humorsome beings, who incessantly attack each other with all the resources of raillery. Avowed rebels to love, they are both entangled in its net by a merry plot of their friends to make them believe that each is the object of the secret passion of the other. —SCHLEGEL, *Trans.*

In Beatrice, high intellect and high animal spirits meet, and excite each other like fire and air. In her wit (which is brilliant without being imaginative) there is a touch of insolence, not infrequent in women when the wit predominates over reflection and imagination. In her temper, too, there is a slight infusion of the termagant; and her satirical humor plays with such an unrespective levity over all subjects alike that it required a profound knowledge of women to bring such a character within the pale of our sympathy. But Beatrice, though wilful, is not wayward; she is volatile, not unfeeling. She has not only an exuberance of wit and gayety, but of heart, and soul, and energy of spirit.—MRS. JAMESON.

Beaucaire, Monsieur, hero and title of a historical romance (1900) by Booth Tarkington, a pretended French barber at Bath during the Beau Nash regime who falls in love with an aristocratic Englishwoman. He eventually turns out to be Louis Philippe de Valois, cousin of Louis Philippe of France, who had escaped to England to avoid a projected marriage with the Princesse de Bourbon-Conti.

Beauchamp, Nevil, titular hero of George Meredith's novel, *Beauchamp's Career*, a gallant English naval officer of high birth who, after serving in the Crimea and elsewhere, comes home a radical reformer. He falls under the influence of Dr.

Shrapnel, a kindly man hated and feared as a revolutionist by Whig and Tory respectabilities. Beauchamp runs for Parliament but is beaten by the corrupt constituency of Bevesham (probably Southampton) and takes to lecturing and writing for the people. He marries Jennie Denham after courting two other women and is eventually drowned in rescuing a boy. His political career was in part suggested by that of Admiral Maxse, to whom in 1862 Meredith "affectionately inscribed "a volume of poems.

Beaujeu, Monsieur de, in Scott's novel, *The Fortunes of Nigel*, owner of an ordinary to which Lord Dalgarno introduced Nigel—" the well-known and general referee in all matters affecting the mysteries of Passage, Hazard, In and In, Penneck, and Verquire, and what not. Why, Beaujeu is King of the Cardpack, and Duke of the Dice-box! "

Beaumanoir, Sir Lucas de, in Scott's historical romance, *Ivanhoe*, the Grand Master of the Templars, a bigoted ascetic who loyally devotes himself to the purification of his order but is unscrupulous as to means. He is especially vindictive towards Rebecca whom he looks upon as a Delilah, a "foul witch who hath flung her enchantments over a brother of the Holy Temple," *i.e.*, Bois Guilbert.

Beaumelle, in Massinger and Field's *Fatal Dowry* (1632), the betrothed of Charalois (*q.v.*), who detects her in an intrigue with Novall and slays both. In 1703 Rowe made the *Fatal Dowry* the basis of his *Fair Penitent* and changed the heroine's name to Calista (*q.v.*).

When Beaumelle falls a victim to the seductions of a contemptible fribble her guilt remains so wholly without excuse or "motive" as to find no atonement, in a dramatic sense, even in her repentance and death.—A. W. WARD, *English Dramatic Literature.*

Bebé, heroine of a novel, *Two Little Wooden Shoes* (1874), by Ouida; an innocent little girl of Brabant petted by a rich painter who leaves her to her peasant lover. Hearing that he has fallen ill, she walks to Paris to offer him loving succor, but finds him sunk in debauchery, flies home and dies.

Bede, Adam, the titular hero of George Eliot's novel, *Adam Bede*, a village carpenter of strenuous life and high ideals, who was closely patterned after the author's father. We are told that an old friend of Robert Evans had the story read to him, and sat up for hours to listen to descriptions which he recognized, exclaiming at intervals, " That's Robert; that's Robert to the life!"

She loves to paint persons whose lot in life is insignificant, but whose spirit is high. Nowhere has she accomplished this with so much effect as in Adam Bede. Adam is the complete realisation of Carlyle's peasant-saint—perhaps we ought to say artisan-saint. In other respects also the conception bears the mark of Carlyle, notably in the dignity with which honest work is clothed. A bishop once said that probably Adam Bede was the nearest portraiture of what the human life of Christ in Nazareth was like that is possible to human art—and it would be difficult to offer a higher compliment to George Eliot's genius.—SIR LESLIE STEPHEN.

My chief complaint with Adam Bede, himself, is that he is too good. He is meant, I conceive, to be every inch a man; but, to my mind, there are several inches wanting. He lacks spontaneity and sensibility; he is too stiff backed. He lacks that supreme quality without which a man can never be interesting to men—the capacity to be tempted.—HENRY JAMES, *Views and Reviews*, p. 20.

Beefington, Milor, in Canning's burlesque, *The Rovers, or the Double Arrangement*, first published in the *Anti-Jacobin*. An English nobleman exiled by John before the signing of Magna Charta, he reads all about the episode in the daily paper when he arrives in Paris.

Beetle, in Rudyard Kipling's *Stalky and Co.*, a supposed portrait of the author in his schooldays. See STALKY, YOUR UNCLE.

Belarius, in *The Tragedy of Cymbeline* (1605), a nobleman and soldier in the army of Cymbeline, King of Britain, who being suspected of treacherous dealings with the Romans is banished and lives twenty years in a cave in the wilds of Wales. Mean-

while he has stolen the king's infant sons, Guiderius and Arviragus, and brought them up to manhood in ignorance of their origin, and away from all their kind. Cymbeline is vanquished and captured in a battle between Romans and Britons. Belarius comes to his rescue, releases the king, but he himself falls into captivity.

Belch, Sir Toby, in Shakespeare's comedy, *Twelfth Night* (1614), uncle of Olivia, the wealthy Countess of Illyria, and a dependent on her bounty. He is an old-fashioned roysterer whose drunken and boisterous wit appealed to Shakespeare's audience and still possesses a historic interest as showing what our ancestors considered humor. Even Hazlitt says, " We have a friendship for Sir Toby." One noteworthy phrase is credited to him: "Dost thou think, because thou art virtuous, there shall be no more cakes and ale ?"

Bel Demonio (It. The Beautiful Demon), in John Broughman's drama of that name (1863), the name assumed by Angelo when he puts himself at the head of a band of Zingari to enforce his claim upon the hand of Lena. He is thought to be a plebeian but he turns out to be of noble birth, and he wins his bride after gallant and desperate struggles. The play is founded upon L'Abbaye de Castro.

Belford, Young, titular hero of *The Squire of Alsatia* (1688), a comedy by Thomas Shadwell which borrows some of its incidents from the *Adelphi* of Terence and the *Truculentus* of Plautus, but is mainly founded on the traditions of the Whitefriars sanctuary in London known popularly as Alsatia (*q.v.*). Belford, enticed into the clutches of the rascally denizens, makes common cause with them under the nickname of " The Squire of Alsatia " against his own father, Sir William Belford, and other would-be rescuers; beats back the officers of the law summoned by Sir William, and even takes him a prisoner. In the end Sir William is rescued by a younger son and the " squire " is borne away from Alsatia, repents, and is forgiven.

4

Belinda, heroine of Pope's mock-heroic poem, *The Rape of the Lock* (1712), which De Quincey calls "the most exquisite monument of playful fancy that universal literature affords." In real life her name was Arabella Fermor. She was the lady to whom Pope had already addressed the famous lines:

If to her share some female errors fall,
Look on her face and you'll forget them all.

Pope dedicates the poem to Mistress Fermor, having written it in the hope of patching up a quarrel between her and Lord Petre that had broken the friendship between them and threatened to disrupt two families. His lordship, in a freak of gallantry, had abused a lover's privilege by cutting off a lock of her hair. She resented this liberty. Pope undertakes to answer the questions thus put in the introduction:

"Say, what strange motive, Goddess, could compel
A well bred lord to assault a gentle belle?
O say what stranger cause, yet unexplored,
Could make a gentle belle reject a lord?"

and he embellishes the story with invocations, apostrophes, the intervention of supernatural beings and the rest of the epic mechanism. See BERENICE.

Belinda Harvey. See HARVEY, BELINDA.

Beline, in Molière's comedy, *Le Malade Imaginaire*, the second wife of Argan, the treacherous and self-seeking stepmother of his children, who abets and encourages his follies in the hope that his death may leave her free to despoil his estate.

Belisarius, the greatest of Justinian's generals (obit. 565), is the hero of Marmontel's historical romance, *Belisaire*, which utilizes some famous traditions now discredited. According to authentic history Belisarius, after overthrowing the Vandal kingdom in Africa and the Gothic kingdom in Italy, was in 563 accused of a conspiracy against the life of Justinian. He was imprisoned for a year in his own palace and then restored to favor. Marmontel follows the pathetic legend that he was dis-

graced, blinded, and reduced to beg for a living in the streets of Constantinople, with a label around his head *Date obolus Belisarii* ("Give an obolus to Belisarius").

Bell, Bessy, in Allan Ramsay's ballad of *Bessie Bell and Mary Gray*, the daughter of a country gentleman near Perth who, when the plague broke out in 1666, retired with her friend Mary Gray to a romantic spot called Burn Braes. Here their needs were supplied by a young man who was in love with both of them. Unfortunately he caught the infection, communicated it to the ladies, and all three died.

Bell, Helen Laura, generally known as Laura, the heroine of *Pendennis*, who eventually marries Arthur, her cousin. As Mrs. Arthur Pendennis she also appears incidentally in *The Newcomes* and *Philip*. She is modest, amiable and nobly generous, coming to the aid of Helen Pendennis with her own money when Arthur has been extravagant. Brought up with Arthur and more or less attached to him from infancy, her love for the heroic is momentarily captured by Warrington and might have grown into a strong passion had he not checked it by the story of his unfortunate secret marriage.

Pendennis, so the story goes, was based upon a true anecdote of Brighton life, told to Thackeray by the Misses Smith (daughters of Horace, part author of *Rejected Addresses*) when he told them he had to produce the first number of a novel in a few days and had no idea how to start one. In gratitude he christened his heroine Laura after a younger sister, Mrs. Round. When Pendennis was finished the original Laura was very angry, or at least pretended to be very angry. "I'll never speak to you again, Mr. Thackeray," she declared; "you know I meant to marry Bluebeard" (Lady Rockminster's name for George Warrington). It may perhaps be remarked that it is rather curious that Thackeray should have christened his heroine Laura Bell, for that was the name of a demi-mondaine of the day, so notorious that it is inconceivable that such a man about town as the author should not have heard of her.—LEWIS MELVILLE, *Thackeray's Originals* in *Some Aspects of Thackeray* (1911).

Bellair, in Etherege's comedy of *The Man of Mode* (1676), is supposed to be a bit of self-portraiture.

Bellair, Count, a French officer held prisoner at Lichfield, in Farquhar's comedy of *The Beaux Stratagem* (1707).

Bellario, in Beaumont and Fletcher's *Philaster*, the name assumed by Euphrasia (*q.v.*) when she disguises herself as a page.

Bellario, Doctor, in Shakespeare's *Merchant of Venice*, a learned lawyer cousin to Portia who, when she disguises herself to plead in court, gives her a letter to the Doge that aids her in her stratagem. He never appears on the scene.

Bellaston, Lady, in Fielding's novel, *Tom Jones* (1750), a profligate woman of wealth and fashion from whom Tom Jones accepts a degrading maintenance during an impecunious period of youth.

Suppose we were to describe the doings of such a person as Mr. Lovelace, or my *Lady Bellaston* . . . ? How the pure and outraged Nineteenth Century would blush, scream, run out of the room, call away the young ladies, and order Mr. Mudie never to send one of that odious author's books again!—THACKERAY, *English Humorists.*

Belle Dame sans Merci, La, heroine of a poem of that name, once supposed to be a translation by Chaucer of a dialogue, by Alain Chartier, "between a gentleman and a gentlewoman, who finding no mercy at her hand dieth for sorrow." A ballad by John Keats, *La Belle Dame sans Merci* (1819), evidently takes its title from the earlier poem, but it invests the cruel lady with a hint of mystic and magic qualities quite foreign from the original and more in keeping with Spenser's Phædria (*Faërie Queene*, ii, 6.3, 14.7).

Bellefontaine, Benedict, in Longfellow's poem, *Evangeline* (1849), a wealthy farmer of Grandpré, the father of Evangeline. When his fellow Acadians were driven into exile by the British, Benedict died of a broken heart as he was about to embark and was buried on the seashore.

Bellenden, Edith, heroine of Scott's historical romance, *Old Mortality*. The granddaughter of Lady Margaret, she is engaged to Lord Evandale, though in love with Henry Morton. When Henry was in danger she saved his life through the influence of Evandale, whom she subsequently married. On the death of Evandale, she married Morton.

Bellenden, Lady Margaret, in Scott's *Old Mortality*, an old Tory lady, "life-rentrix of the barony of Tillietudlem," uncompromisingly devoted to the Jacobite cause. During the great civil wars under Charles I she had lost her husband and two sons but felt that she had received her reward after the Restoration, for Charles II "had actually breakfasted at the Tower of Tillietudlem; an incident which formed from that moment an important era in the life of Lady Margaret." She is constantly dragging in references to this story to the boredom of her friends and, it must be confessed, to the eventual weariness of the reader.

Belloni Sandra, in George Meredith's novel of that name (1864) and its sequel *Vittoria* (1866), a noble Italian lady, an incarnate genius, surrounded by commonplace sentimentalists and formalists. In the sequel she breaks away from her circle, and her public career as Vittoria, the great singer, takes us to the revolutionary Italy of 1848.

Belphœbe, in Spenser's *Faërie Queene*, a huntress divinely fair and most divinely chaste, who is a sort of complement to Gloriana (*q.v.*) in the same poem—being intended as a likeness of Queen Elizabeth, the woman, as Gloriana represents the sovereign in her royal state.

Flattery more highly seasoned may have been offered her [Queen Elizabeth], but none more delicate and graceful than that contained in the finished portrait of Belphœbe. She represents that pure and high-spirited maidenhood which the ancients embodied in Diana; and, like her, the forest is her dwelling-place, and the chase her favorite pastime. The breezes have imparted to her their own fleetness, and the swaying foliage its graceful movement. . . . She is passionless and pure, self-sustained and self dependent, "in maiden meditation fancy free," and shines with a cold lunar light, and not the warm glow of day. The author has mingled the elements of her nature so skillfully that the result is nothing harsh, unnatural, or unfeminine; and has so combined the lofty and the ideal with the graceful and attractive, that we behold in her a creature . . .

"Too fair for worship, too divine for love"
GEO. S. HILLARD.

Belsize, the Honorable Charles, familiarly known as Jack, and later rising to the peerage, as Lord Highgate, one of Lord Kew's gay set in Thackeray's novel, *The Newcomes.* He and Lady Clara Pullen had been in love from early youth, but poverty separated them. She became the unhappy wife of Sir Barnes Newcome and eloped with " Jack " when he succeeded to his father's titles and property.

Belted Will, a nickname bestowed upon Lord William Howard (1563-1640), warden of the western marches.

His Bilboa blade, by Marchmen felt,
Hung in a broad and studded belt;
Hence in rude phrase the Borderers still
Called noble Howard "Belted Will."
SIR W. SCOTT.

Belvawney, hero of W. S. Gilbert's comedy, *Engaged* (1877), an amorous young gentleman who has connected himself with matrimonial intentions, express or implied, to three women.

Belvawney, Miss, in Charles Dickens's *Nicholas Nickleby* (Chap. xlviii), a member of Mr. Crummles's theatrical company who seldom aspired to speaking parts, but usually went on as a page in white silk hose to stand with one leg bent and contemplate the audience.

Belvidera, the heroine of Thomas Otway's tragedy, *Venice Preserved* (1682), daughter of Priuli, a senator, and wife of Jaffier (*q.v.*).

Like Shakespeare he had conceived genuine women—Monimia, above all Belvidera, who, like Imogen, has given herself wholly, and is lost in an abyss of adoration for him she has chosen, who can but love, obey, weep, suffer, and who dies like a flower plucked from the stalk, when her arms are torn from the neck around which she has locked them.—TAINE, *English Literature,* vol. II, bk. iii.

The great attraction is in the character of Belvidera and when that part is represented by such as we remember to have seen,

no tragedy is honored by such a tribute not of tears alone, but of more agony than many would seek to endure.—HENRY HALLAM. *Introduction to the Literature of Europe,* 1837-39.

Bendish, George, hero of Maurice Hewlett's novel, *Bendish, a Study in Prodigality* (1913), is obviously patterned after Lord Byron.

Bendish, the protagonist of the book, is a poet, a sentimentalist, a man of clear cut, statuesque features, rejoicing in the "marble pallor" which is said to appeal to certain romantic souls as the finest type of masculine beauty. Moreover, his baptismal name is George, he belongs to the English aristocracy, and he lived in the early part of the last century. All this seems to point to one inevitable conclusion; but, alas! Bendish was not lame—and so, perhaps, Mr. Hewlett does not intend him as a study of Lord Byron any more than he intends his Gervase Poore as a full length portrait of the poet Shelley.—*N. Y. Times.*

Benedick, in Shakespeare's comedy, *Much Ado about Nothing* (1600), a young lord of Padua who as wit, soldier and scholar achieves the fully rounded combination whereof Biron in *Love's Labor's Lost* was a prophecy. One may imagine that here was Shakespeare's conception of himself at maturity, as Biron adumbrated him in his salad days. The name Benedick has passed into colloquial use as a synonym for a married man. He who began as a railer against women and a bachelor by unassailable conviction proves recreant to his professions and in Act v, Sc. 4, is thus greeted by Don Pedro, " How dost thou, Benedick, the married man? "

The chief force of Shakespeare in the play comes out in the characters of Benedick and Beatrice. They have not a touch of misanthropy, nor of sentimentality, but are thoroughly healthy and hearty human creatures; at first a little too much self pleased, but framed by and by to be entirely pleased with one another . . . The trick which is played upon the lovers to bring them together is one of those frauds practised upon self-love which appear in several of the comedies of this period. But neither is an egotist except in a superficial way. Beatrice is filled with generous indignation against the wrongers of her cousin, and she inspires Benedick to become (not without a touch of humorous self consciousness) champion of the cause.—E. DOWDEN, *Shakespeare Primer.*

Bennet, Elizabeth, heroine of Jane Austen's novel, *Pride and Prejudice* (1813), a bright, witty, fresh, original and amiable girl, considerate of others but quite capable of asserting herself when occasion demands. She was a deserved favorite with her creator. "I must confess that I think her as delightful a creature as ever appeared in print," says Miss Austen in a letter to a friend. Mr. George Saintsbury frankly avowed that he would like to have married her.

Bennet, Lydia, in *Pride and Prejudice,* the youngest of the Bennett sisters, a spoiled child, a silly flirt, pretty but wilful, who makes a disreputable elopement with a young officer named Wickham. Darcy pursues the couple and reinstates them in the eyes of the world.

Bennet, Mr., in Jane Austen's novel, *Pride and Prejudice* (1813), an amiable, peace-loving and mildly cynical English gentleman, thoroughly in sympathy with his second daughter Elizabeth, but openly bored by his four other girls; and though equally out of harmony with their mother—a querulous, ambitious, narrow-minded, matchmaking matron—ever yielding with humorous acquiescence to her domineering disposition.

Bennet, Mrs., in *Pride and Prejudice,* the most determined of matchmaking mammas with a fatal readiness to discuss the affairs of her family with anybody who will listen to her.

Benson, in George Meredith's novel, *The Ordeal of Richard Feverel,* a butler at Raynham Abbey, the seat of Richard's father. He shares his master's mistrust for women and is beaten by Richard Feverel for spying on him and Lucy Desborough.

Benvolio, in *Romeo and Juliet* (1598), a quarrelsome member of the Montague family, deeply attached to his cousin Romeo. "Thou!" says Mercutio, another cousin, "why thou wilt quarrel with a man that hath a hair more, or a hair less, in his beard than thou hast: thou wilt quarrel with a man for cracking nuts,

having no other reason but because thou hast hazel eyes" (Act iii, Sc. 1).

Beppo, hero and title of a narrative poem (1818) by Lord Byron. Taken prisoner by the Turks, he turns Mussulman, but finally escapes, returns to his home in Venice; at a masked ball finds his wife Laura flirting with a strange cavalier but forgives her and takes her back. Beppo (more properly Beppe) is diminutive for Giuseppe (Joseph) and so might be translated Joe. Pope Pius X, who by birth and baptism was Giuseppe Sarto, was affectionately known to his own family as Beppe, even when he had reached the papacy. The sources of Byron's poem were a Venetian scandal "in high life" of recent occurrence.

Berengaria of Navarre, queen consort of Richard Cœur-de-Lion, is introduced by Scott into his historical romance, *The Talisman.* He describes her as a beautiful and fascinating woman who "affected, or at least practised a little childish petulance and wilfulness of manner" and was only too fond of "idle frolics that ill comported with royal dignity and sometimes brought her into serious difficulty." See KENNETH OF SCOTLAND.

Berenger, Eveline, heroine of Scott's historical romance, *The Betrothed,* who is engaged to Sir Hugo de Lacy but is in love with his nephew, Sir Damian de Lucy. Nevertheless, when Sir Hugo is absent in the Crusades she faithfully kept her troth with him until his return, when he relinquished her to his nephew.

Berger, E., a pseudonym of Eliza Sheppard used in her first published novel, *Charles Auchester* (1853).

That name of hers is not the most attractive in the tongue, but all must love it who love her; for, if any theory of transmission be true, does she not owe something of her own oneness with Nature, of her intimacy with its depths, of her love of fields and flowers and skies, to that ancestry who won the name as, like the princely Hebrew boy, they tended the flocks upon the hills, under sunlight and starlight and in every wind that blew? Never was there a more characteristic device than this signature of "E. Berger;" and nobody learned anything by it.—*Atlantic Monthly.*

Bergerac, Cyrano de, French poet and dramatist, contemporary of Molière, who is said to have plagiarized from him a famous scene in *The Rogueries of Scapin.*

He is the hero of Edmond Rostand's play named after him (1897). The size of his nose is exaggerated for dramatic purposes, and he is represented as being extremely sensitive to any mocking allusion. Hence he is involved in street fights in which he performs wonders of strength and skill. Desperately in love with his kinswoman, Roxane, a beautiful precieuse, he yet aids Christian de Neuvillette, a handsome but rather dull gallant, to win her hand by writing his love letters for him and prompting him with pretty phrases when Christian plays Romeo to her Juliet on a dark night. He arranges a stolen marriage between the pair and, after Christian's death on the field of battle, continues to be the platonic friend of the widow until his own imminent death unseals his lips.

Berinthia, in Vanbrugh's *Relapse* (1697), and Sheridan's modernized and condensed version of the same comedy *A Trip to Scarborough* (1777), is a brilliant and coquettish young widow in love with Colonel Townly but flirting desperately with Loveless as he in turn flirts with Amanda, Berinthia's cousin, and wife of Loveless, each in order to play upon the other's jealousy.

Berkeley, Old Woman of, heroine of Southey's ballad of that name versified from Olaus Magnus. A wicked old woman, she sends on her deathbed for her son, the monk, and her daughter, the nun, and asks that they shall place her when dead in a great stone coffin fastened to the ground with strong iron bands. Fifty priests and fifty choristers shall pray and sing over her for three days while the bell tolled unceasingly. The first night passed with little disturbance; on the second the lights burned blue and yells were heard outside the church; on the third the devil in person broke into the church and carried off the body on his black horse.

Berlichingen, Goetz von, or **Gottfried of the Iron Hand,** a historical character (1480–1562) whom Goethe has made the titular hero of an historical drama.

Goetz, a German burgrave, took a prominent part in the wars for civic independence against the electors of Brandenberg and Bavaria, losing his right hand at the siege of Landshut (1505). The iron hand which replaced it (his own invention) is still exhibited in Jaxthausen, his birthplace.

Bernardo, in *Hamlet,* an officer on guard with Marcellus at Elsinore. They are the first mortals to whom the Ghost makes his appearance. They report to Horatio.

Bernstein, Baroness, in Thackeray's novel of *The Virginians,* the Beatrix Esmond (*q.v.*) of *Henry Esmond,* now grown old, retaining little of her former beauty but still brilliant, lively and loquacious, possessor of a tongue that can be amusing or venomous as she chooses. She has passed through many notorious adventures and has survived two husbands, Bishop Tusher and the Baron de Bernstein.

Berry, Mrs. The old nurse of Richard Feverel in George Meredith's novel of that name who later befriends Lucy Desborough when she has become Richard's wife.

Bertram, Count of Rousillon, the unworthy hero of Shakespeare's comedy, *All's Well That Ends Well;* the recalcitrant husband of Helena, who lures him back to her by stratagem.

I cannot reconcile my heart to Bertram; a man noble without generosity, and young without truth; who married Helen as a coward, and leaves her as a profligate; when she is dead by his unkindness, sneaks home to a second marriage, is accused by a woman he has wronged, defends himself by falsehood and is dismissed to happiness.— SAMUEL JOHNSON, *General Observations on Shakespeare's Plays* (1768).

Johnson expresses a cordial aversion for Count Bertram, and regrets he should have been allowed to come off at last with no other punishment than a temporary shame, nay, even be rewarded with the unmerited possession of a virtuous wife. But does not the poet point out the true way of the world, which never makes much of man's injustice to woman, if so-called family honour is preserved.—A. W. SCHLEGEL.

Bertram, Edmund, hero of Jane Austen's novel, *Mansfield Park* (1814), and the most agreeable of all her clerical types. He is cultivated, right-minded, kindly, but not over brilliant. Miss Austen herself acknowledged that he was very far from being what she knew an English gentleman often was. He devotes half a dozen years to drawing the timid Fanny Price out of her shell, directs her taste in reading, interests himself in her pursuits, makes her by degrees a lovable and charming companion and (after following for a period the false lights held out by Mary Cranford) ends by marrying her.

Bertram, Harry, hero of Walter Scott's romance, *Guy Mannering,* son of Godfrey Bertram and legitimate heir to Ellangowan. Kidnapped in his infancy he is brought up under the name of Vanbeest Brown (*q.v.*). Meg Merrilies is the first person to recognize him and he is eventually restored to his own and enabled to marry Julia Mannering, daughter of Colonel Guy Mannering, under whom he has served in India. Julia described him in these words:

His good-humour, lively conversation, and open gallantry suit my plan of life, as well as his athletic form, handsome features, and high spirit, would accord with a character of chivalry.

These qualities are but inadequately brought out in the narrative and, like most of Scott's heroes, he can only be accepted on trust. See WAVERLEY, EDWARD.

Bertrand, the cowardly and imbecile accomplice of Robert Macaire in some of the plays and burlesques founded on that clever scoundrel's adventures, though in the original production of *L'Auberge des Adrets* he is known as Jacques Strop.

Bertuccio, in Tom Taylor's *The Fool's Revenge* (1859), an adaptation of Victor Hugo's *Le Roi d'Amuse,* is the name of the titular " fool." See TRIBOULET and RIGOLETTO.

Bess, Bessie or **Bessy,** a familiar diminutive for Elizabeth, used either in affection or contempt. Thus Good Queen Bess is the term by which her countrymen have expressed their love and loyalty for Queen Elizabeth (born 1533; reigned 1558–1603), while Bess o' Bedlam is the contemptuous term for any female lunatic vagrant, her male counterpart being Tom o' Bedlam.

Bess, heroine of Sheridan Knowles' drama, *The Beggar's Daughter of Bethnal Green* (1828), who is called Bessy in other dramatic versions of the ballad, and Bessee in the original.

Bessie, heroine of *Curfew Shall Not Ring To-night,* narrative poem by Rosa Hartwicke Thorpe. See HERIOT, BLANCHE.

Bessus, in John Fletcher's comedy, *King or no King,* a cowardly, swaggering army captain of close literary kindred with Boabdil and Parolles. Like Boabdil he excels in shifty excuses. Having received a challenge he writes back that he cannot accept the honor for thirteen weeks as he already has 212 duels on hand.

The story which Clarendon tells of that affair [the panic of the royal troops at Naseby] reminds us of the excuses by which Bessus and Bobadil explain their cudgelings. —MACAULAY.

Beverley, in Edward Moore's domestic tragedy, *The Gamester* (1753), a well-meaning, weak-willed, womanish man who lets himself be duped by the transparent villainy of Stukeley, loses his all at play, loses likewise his sister's fortune, and then takes his own life.

He is but a poor creature who at no time enlists the sympathies of his audience. His passion for play is without the enthusiasm that might have gained for it some measure of respect. The spectator can only feel contempt for a man who so readily permits himself to be duped and endures his misfortunes with so little fortitude. Still, Beverley is permitted one of these agonizing death-scenes which have always been dear to tragedians. —HAZLITT.

Beverley, Mrs., wife of the above, full of unwise devotion and impolitic patience, who lets her husband drift on to his ruin without the angry word that might have saved him.

Beverley, Charlotte, sister of Beverley, an amiable girl with occasional bursts of justifiable wrath, who rises nobly to the occasion when she finds her brother has gambled away her fortune as well as his own.

Beverley, Cecilia, heroine of a novel by Frances Burney, *Cecilia, or Memoirs of an Heiress* (1782). Left an orphan with a fortune and no restriction save that her husband must take her name, Cecilia goes to London and is introduced to society by one of her guardians (Mr. Harrel) and his wife. That gentleman plunders her, and commits suicide, and she transfers her visit to another guardian, whose son Mortimer Delville is deeply in love with her, but because he considers her an inferior in birth and station and also because he objects to change his name to Beverley hesitates long before he proposes marriage to her.

Beverley, Ensign. A name which Captain Absolute, in Sheridan's *The Rivals* (1775), assumes in his courtship of Lydia Languish—the better to impress the romantic fancy of the lady and to mislead other characters who might oppose his suit. This masquerade is a fruitful source of comic misunderstandings which are not fully cleared up until the last act.

Bevis, in Scott's romance, *Woodstock*, the favorite mastiff or bloodhound of Sir Harry Lee. He was "as tractable as he was strong and bold," regularly followed him to church and "in old time had saved his master by his fidelity." In old age he found his only joy in lying by Sir Henry's feet in the summer or by the fire in winter licking his withered hand or his shrivelled cheek from time to time. Sir Walter notes that "Bevis, the gallant hound, one of the handsomest and most active of the ancient Highland deerhounds, had his prototype in a dog called Maida, the gift of the late Chief of Glengarry to the author. A beautiful sketch of him was made by Edwin Landseer and afterwards engraved."

Bezaliel, in Dryden's poetical satire, *Absalom and Achitophel*, an accomplished and scholarly gentle-

man, is meant for the Marquis of Worcester, afterwards Duke of Beaufort. Dryden probably took the name with but slight alteration from that of Bezaleel (*Heb.*, "in the shadow of God"), the artificer who executed the works of art in the tabernacle.

Bezonian (It. *bisogno*, "need" or "business"), an Elizabethan name for either needy or needed persons, but in both cases denoting a low or mercenary type and especially a raw recruit. Thus Pistol asks of Justice Shallow, when the latter claims to be "under the King in some authority:

Under which king, bezonian? Speak or die.
II Henry IV, v, iii, 115.

The word is often but erroneously printed with a capital as if it were a proper noun.

Bianca (It., the feminine of Bianco, white).
1. In Shakespeare's *Taming of the Shrew* the gentle and well-mannered younger sister of Katharine, a striking contrast to "Kate the Curst." Afterwards married to Lucentio.
2. In *Othello* a woman of Cyprus with whom Cassio has an intrigue.
3. In Middleton's *Women Cusare Women*, a Venetian beauty, wife of Leontio, tempted to become the Duke's mistress.
4. In Ford's *Love's Sacrifice*.
5. The heroine of *The Fair Maid of the Inn*, by Massinger Rowley and Fletcher.
6. In Dean Milman's tragedy, *Fazio*, the jealous wife of the hero, who ruins him by false accusations and then, failing to save him by confession, goes mad and dies.

Bianca, heroine and spokeswoman of Mrs. Browning's poem, *Bianca among the Nightingales*, a devoted Italian Ariadne mourning for an English Theseus in his own country, a passionate utterance of sorrow and of unreasoning indignation against the northern climate and landscape. One may take it that the poet is here vicariously or dramatically expressing her own antipathy against the native land she had forsaken for Italy.

Bickerstaff, Esq., Astrologer, Isaac, the pseudonym of Sir Richard Steele as editor of the *Tatler* (April 12, 1709–January 2, 1711). The name was already famous when he assumed it. Swift had invented it as that of the imaginary author of a satirical pamphlet against John Partridge, astrologer and almanac-maker. The last name he had found upon a blacksmith's sign; the first he had added as a humorous conjunction. Yet half a century later a real Isaac Bickerstaff (1735–1785) won sounder laurels for the name as the author of many successful dramas.

Swift's Bickerstaff announced in his pamphlet that he would give no vague oracles, such as Partridge's, but would foretell events in a plain, straightforward manner. He began by predicting the death of Partridge himself at a given day and hour. On the day after the specified time a circumstantial narrative appeared recounting the fulfilment of the prediction. Partridge was foolish enough to answer with a protest that he was still living, whereupon Bickerstaff issued a Vindication gravely arguing that the astrologer *was* dead, in spite of his assertions to the contrary. The joke was taken up by all the town wits. Rowe, Steele, Addison, and Prior contributed to it in various amusing ways; Congreve, in a pamphlet issued under Partridge's name, made the poor astrologer complain of the discomforts Squire Bickerstaff had exposed him to, so that he could not leave his door without being twitted for sneaking about without paying his funeral expenses; the Stationers' Company was induced to apply for an injunction against the continued publication of almanacs put forth under the name of a dead man; and it was even said that the Portuguese Inquisition had been taken in and had condemned Mr. Bickerstaff's predictions to the flames. When Steele started his *Tatler* the popularity of the name of Bickerstaff induced him to assume it as that of the pretended editor of that periodical.

Big-Endians, in Swift's *Gulliver's Travels*, a religious party in Lilliput, the bitter opponents of the Little-Endians on the question whether the big or the little end of an egg should be broken in eating. The Little-Endians being in power, the others are denounced as heretics. Under the name Big-Endian the Catholics are satirized; their opponents represent the Church of England.

Biglow, Hosea, the feigned author of *The Biglow Papers* (first series, 1848; second series, 1867), by James Russell Lowell. See WILBUR, REV. HOMER.

Billee, Little, the nickname given to William Bagot, the hero of George Du Maurier's novel, *Trilby* (1894), an amiable, generous, imaginative English art student in Paris whose boyish love for the titular heroine comes to a tragic end even before the death of both. The portrait is sketched from Frederick Walker (1840–1875), famous artist and illustrator, whose early death blighted a brilliant promise. The nickname was borrowed from a grotesque ballad by Thackeray, which he was fond of chanting on social occasions and which he had imitated from an old Breton folk-song beginning:

Il etait un petit navire (*bis*)
Qui n'avait ja ja jamais navigué (*bis*)

The song is given in full in *Melusine*, vol. i, p. 463.

Binnie, James, of the Indian Civil Service in Thackeray's novel, *The Newcomes*, a jolly, hard-headed, kind-hearted Scotch bachelor, who shares an apartment in London with Colonel Newcome.

Birch, Harvey, the titular "spy" in James Fenimore Cooper's novel, *The Spy*. With heart and mind devoted to the patriot cause, and with no hope or wish for reward, he allows himself to be suspected of being a British spy at the risk of being maltreated or shot by his own comrades, in order the better to carry on his true task of spying on the enemy and revealing their weaknesses to Washington. See HARPER.

Biron, in Shakespeare's *Love's Labor's Lost* (1594), "a merry, madcap lord" in attendance on Ferdinand, King of Navarre. He is in love with Rosaline, and the raillery exchanged between them anticipates the more elaborate wit combats between Benedick and Beatrice in *Much Ado about Nothing*. The name was originally spelt Berowne and not altered until the second folio. From line 249 of Act iv, Sc. 3, where it rhymes with " moon," one may infer that it was pronounced Beroon. It is conjectured that contemporary events in France influenced Shakespeare in his choice of names for this play. When it was produced, Henry IV of Navarre was king, and two of his most strenuous supporters were Biron and Longaville.

The relation in which Biron stood to the English people between 1589 and 1598 would fully account for the distinction thus conferred upon him. Of all the leaders on Navarre's side he was best known to Englishmen. Almost invariably the English contingent served under him, and every one of those five years added something to the English knowledge of his character (Sidney Lee).

Rosaline's description of Biron is famous:

> A merrier man,
> Within the limit of becoming mirth,
> I never spent an hour's talk withal.
> His eye begets occasion for his wit,
> Which his fair tongue (conceits expositor)
> Delivers in such apt and gracious words,
> That aged ears play truant at his tales,
> And younger hearers are quite ravished.
> So sweet and voluble is his discourse.
> Act ii, Sc. 1.

In this character, which is never quite in touch with, never quite on a perfect level of understanding with, the other persons of the play, we see, perhaps, a reflex of Shakespeare himself, when he has just become able to stand aside from and estimate the first period of his poetry.—WALTER PATER.

Biron, Charles De Gontault, Duke of. A historical character (1562–1602) whose last name Shakespeare is supposed to have borrowed for one of his characters (see above) and who is the acknowledged hero of two tragedies by George Chapman, *The Conspiracy of Duke Biron* and *The*

Tragedy of Biron, both produced in 1605. The Duke was an admiral and marshal of France; governor of Burgundy in 1595; ambassador to the Court of St. James in 1601, and the trusted friend of Henry IV until 1602, where he was detected in treasonably plotting with Savoy and Spain for the dismemberment of France and his own elevation to the sovereignty of Burgundy. Recalled to Paris, he was thrown into the Bastille and executed.

Birotteau, Cæsar, titular hero of Balzac's novel, *Greatness and Decline of Cæsar Birotteau*, a perfumer in the Rue St. Honoré, Paris. Affiliating himself with the militant royalists he becomes captain and then major of a battalion in the National Guard and deputy mayor of the Eleventh arrondissement. In 1818 he was made a Chevalier of the Legion of Honor. To celebrate the event he gave a grand ball which necessitated elaborate changes in his apartments. Unlucky speculations and extravagant living completely ruined him within a year and he had to file a petition in bankruptcy. Within three years he had settled with all his creditors, but he died soon after his solemn rehabilitation by the courts.

Bisarre, in Farquhar's comedy, *The Inconstant* (1702), a brilliant, volatile, unconventional young woman, fully realizing the meaning of the French word Bizarre from which her name is modified. Her flirtations with Duretete continually involve him in awkward situations.

Blackacre, Widow, in Wycherley's comedy, *The Plain-Dealer*.

The Widow Blackacre, beyond all comparison Wycherley's best comic character, is the Countess in Racine's *Plaidleurs* talking the jargon of English, instead of French, chicane.—MACAULAY, *Comic Dramatists of the Restoration in Essays*.

Black Beauty, a high-bred, gentle horse who is supposed to tell his own story in *Black Beauty, his Grooms and Companions*, by Anna Sewall. Through the breaking of his knees by a drunken groom he passes from kind treatment in a rich man's mews to hard knocks and exhausting work in a livery stable. After being a cab-horse, a cart-horse, and then a cab-horse again, he is bought by a farmer who recognizes that he comes from good stock and nurses him back to health and strength. Restored to something like his former condition he is purchased by a family of ladies whose coachman is an old friend of his and the end of him is peace.

Black Dwarf, titular hero of Scott's romance, *The Black Dwarf,* also known as " Elshender the Recluse," " Canny Elshie," " the Wise Wight of Mucklestane Moor," or " the Solitary," but in reality he is Sir Edward Mauley (*q.v.*).

In real life the Black Dwarf was David Ritchie (1740–1811), whom Scott visited in the summer of 1797 and reproduced from memory nineteen years later. David, known familiarly as Bowed Davie or Davie o' the Wuddus (Woodhouse), was just such an extraordinary being as Elshie, a sort of truncated giant with remarkably strong arms, but legs so diminutive and deformed that he stood only 3½ feet high. He was a man of humble birth, however, and his motive for retiring from the world was not blighted love but simple dread of ridicule. His first cottage in Peeblesshire was built by his own hands on grounds belonging to the farm of Woodhouse. Scott has described it accurately. "David Ritchie," says Professor Ferguson, "was a man of powerful capacity and original ideas, whose mind was thrown off its just bias by a predominant degree of self-love and self-opinion, galled by the sense of ridicule and contempt, and avenging itself upon society, in idea at least, by a gloomy misanthropy." See W. S. CROCKETT, *The Scott Originals,* p. 143.

Blackstick, Fairy, in Thackeray's Christmas extravaganza, *The Rose and the Ring* (1854), a mysterious female sprite with an ebony wand, fairy godmother at large in Paflagonia and Crim Tartary who gives a magic rose to Bulbo's mother, and a magic ring to Giglio's mother.

The writer cannot, alas! lay claim to the personal qualities for which Blackstick was so remarkable, although she can fully appreciate the illustrious lady's serious composure, her austere presence of mind, her courageous outspokenness and orderly grasp of events. Blackstick belongs to the utilitarian school of Miss Edgeworth and Mrs. Barbauld. The lighter elegances of the Mrs. Chapones and the Laura Matildas of the day she put aside. Neither had she anything to do with your tripping, fanciful, moonlight sprites and fairies, who waste so much valuable time and strength by dancing on the green, and sitting up till cockcrow; but a wide and most interesting field of fresh interest remains, which was specially her own domain. —LADY ANNE THACKERAY RITCHIE, Introduction to *The Blackstick Papers.*

Blair, Adam, hero of a novel by John G. Lockhart, *Some Passages in the Life of Mr. Adam Blair, Minister of the Gospel at Cross Meiktree* (1822).

Plunged into affliction by the loss of his wife, Adam is visited by the latter's bosom friend, Mrs. Campbell, who has left her husband abroad. A mutual love springs up, of which neither is conscious until Mrs. Campbell is ordered home to the Highland tower of her husband. After bearing his solitude for some time, Blair returns her visit, arrives at night, is rapturously welcomed, drinks copiously of wine, gazes with her on the moonlit sea, is again pressed to the winecup, and finds himself next morning and is found by the servants clasped in her embraces. Horror-struck, he flies to the desert, repelling her prayers to accompany him with the wildest execrations. His contrition brings on frenzy and fever, he is carried back to her tower, is nursed by her during his delirium, and recovers to find that she has caught the fever and died. He then journeys homeward, proclaims his fall to the presbytery, resigns his parish, and becomes a day-laborer in his former parish. After ten years of penitence and contrition, his neighbors voluntarily restore him to his pastorate.

Blake, Goody, in Wordsworth's poem, *Goody Blake and Harry Gill, a True Story,* a poor old woman driven by necessity to pilfer a few sticks of wood from the grounds of her neighbor Gill. He makes her surrender them whereupon she invokes upon him the curse that he may never " more be warm." The curse is heard. Ever after " his teeth they chatter, chatter still."

Blancove, Edward, in George Meredith's novel, *Rhoda Fleming,* the seducer of Rhoda's sister Dahlia, who inflicts a still greater wrong by marrying her under pressure, when she is in love with another and he with her. Witty, selfish, half cynical to begin with, he is somehow overwhelmed by a moral revolution which leaves him devoted and, indeed, for the moment pious. " This youth," says another of the characters, " is one of great Nature's tom-fools, an elegant young gentleman outwardly of the very large class who are simply the engines of their appetites, and to the philosophic eye still run wild in woods."

Blane, Niel, in Scott's romance, *Old Mortality*, the town piper and, by virtue of his marriage to the jolly widow of a publican, the landlord of the Howf. After his wife's death he initiated their daughter Nelly " in those cares which had been faithfully performed by his wife."

Blas, Gil, hero of a picaresque romance, *The Adventures of Gil Blas de Santillane* (1715), by Alain René Le Sage. Gil Blas, brought up by his uncle, Canon Gil Perez, starts out as a raw lad to seek his fortunes and gradually wins his way from the condition of a valet to that of a secretary, and from the service of private gentleman to that of the Prime Minister of Spain. This career brings him in contact with people of almost every condition, whom he sees as they are and not as they claim to be, and the suggestion at every step is that there is no such thing in the world as substance, that all is a show and a very bad one. Doctors are little better than murderers, lawyers are licensed robbers, the clergy do not practise what they preach. The very ministers of state are panderers and parasites, revenging themselves for slights received from royalty by an overbearing demeanor towards their inferiors. Lastly, the king is but a wretched puppet in the hands of his ministers, pretending to govern the country but actually passing his life in signing his name to papers he never reads and in gossiping over frivolous scandals that do not really concern him.

Gil Blas . . . is naturally disposed towards honesty, though with a mind unfortunately too ductile to resist the temptations

of opportunity or example. He is constitutionally timid, and yet occasionally capable of doing brave actions; shrewd and intelligent, but apt to be deceived by his own vanity; with wit enough to make us laugh with him at others, and follies enough to turn the jest frequently against himself. Generous, good-natured, and humane, he has virtues sufficient to make us love him, and, as to respect, it is the last thing which he asks at his reader's hand.—SIR W. SCOTT.

Blatant Beast, in Spenser's *Faërie Queene*, a huge, bellowing monster typical of slander or calumny. It had 100 tongues and a sting. Sir Artegal goes in pursuit of it in Canto v and Sir Calidore resumes the pursuit in Canto vi. But, as Macaulay says, not one in a hundred readers perseveres to the end of the poem. " Very few and very weary are those who are in at the death of the Blatant Beast." Now, as a matter of fact the Beast does not die. It is pursued and taken, but not killed, by Calidore. Indeed, for aught anybody may learn from the poem, it may be still roaming the earth:

Then was this monster by the mastering might
Of doughty Calidore suppressed and tamed,
That never more he might endamage wight
With his vile tongue which many had defamed,
And many causeless caused to be blamed.
So did he eke long after this remain
Until that (whether wicked fate so framed
Or fault of men) he broke his iron chain
And got into the world at liberty again.
                    Book vi, Canto 12.

Blefuscu, in Swift's *Gulliver's Travels*, an imaginary island " situated to the northeast side of Lilliput, from whence it is parted only by a channel of eight hundred yards wide." Ruled over by an emperor, it is peopled, like Lilliput, by pygmies.

Blefuscu is France, and the ingratitude of the Lilliputian court, which forces Gulliver to take shelter there rather than have his eyes put out, is an indirect reproach upon that of England, and a vindication of the flight of Ormond and Bolingbroke to Paris. —SIR W. SCOTT, *Life of Swift.*

Blessed Damozel, subject and title of a poem (1850) by Dante Gabriel Rossetti. The damozel, one of the blessed or saved in heaven, leans out yearningly towards her betrothed on earth. Hall Caine tells us that the poem grew out of Rossetti's youthful love for Poe's *Raven.* " I saw," Rossetti said to Caine," that Poe had done the utmost it was possible to do with the grief of the lover on earth, so I determined to reverse the conditions, and give utterance to the groaning of the loved one in heaven."

Blifil, in Fielding's novel, *The History of Tom Jones, a Foundling,* a consummate scoundrel and hypocrite, introduced as a foil to the openhearted yet erring hero. Pretending to be a friend to the latter he assumes over him an air of superior morality, but is eventually detected as a libertine, a hypocrite, a liar and a swindler. The only indication as to his Christian name is in a note signed " W. Blifil " in Book VII, Chap. ii.

Blifil is perhaps the only case (for Johnathan Wild is a satire, not a history or, as M. Taine fancies, a tract) in which Fielding seems to lose his unvarying coolness of judgment, and the explanation is obvious. The one fault to which he is, so to speak, unjust is hypocrisy. Hypocrisy cannot indeed be painted too black, but it should not be made impossible. When Fielding has to deal with such a character he for once loses his self-command, and, like inferior writers, begins to be angry with his creatures. Instead of analyzing and explaining he simply leaves us in presence of a moral anomaly.—SIR LESLIE STEPHEN, *Hours in a Library—Fielding.*

Blondel de Nesle, the famous troubadour minstrel beloved by Richard, Cœur de Leon. He discovered the prison in which his royal master was immured and helped to plot his escape. Blondel appears in Scott's historical romance, *The Talisman.* He entertains the king and his court encamped before Jerusalem.

Blood, Lydia, heroine of Howells' novel, *The Lady of the Aroostook* (1879), who earns the nickname as the only female passenger aboard the *Aroostook,* a sailing vessel bound for Venice.

A rare and charming personation, a heroine who is distinctly and honestly countrified without a tinge of vulgarity and who, though taking but a modest part in the conversation of which the book is full, never for a moment loses her individuality or incurs the reproach of tameness.—*N. Y. Nation.*

Blood, Colonel Thomas, a historical character (1628–1680) introduced into Scott's novel, *Peveril of the Peak,* as an emissary of the second Duke of Buckingham. The Duke himself thus describes him to Jerningham:

There goes a scoundrel after my own heart, a robber from his cradle, a murderer since he could hold a knife, a profound hypocrite in religion, and a worse and deeper hypocrite in honour—would sell his soul to the devil to accomplish any villainy, and would cut the throat of his brother, did he dare to give the villainy he had so acted its right name.

His most notorious exploit was the theft of the crown from the Tower.

Blougram, Sylvester, the hero and spokesman of *Bishop Blougram's Apology* in Robert Browning's volume of miscellaneous poems, *Men and Women* (1885).

He is a sceptical churchman whose emotions still cling to the faith on which his intellect has relaxed its hold. Talking over the walnuts and raisins to Gigadibs, the literary man, he expounds his theory of life. He doubts indeed, but he is too true a sceptic to be certain even of his doubt. He accepts the honors and emoluments of a Church whose doctrines offend his reason, for who can assure him that his reason is right in taking offence? So long as that "plaguy hundredth chance" remains that they may be true, is it not the part of wisdom to accept them and teach them—to strangle the doubts which for aught he knows may be hell-born? He is living in comfort, in honor, in peace of mind; he is venerated by his co-religionists; his titles earn him the respect of the worldly; he is even an object of flattering curiosity and interest to those higher minds who think him a hypocrite and affect to despise him. Why should he throw aside all the good things of the present, the chances of better things in the future, for the sake of a sincerity which might look pretty in poetry but for which there is no real need and no place in this world? The true philosophy is not to strive after the impossible *ought to be,* but to find out what *is,* and to make that as fair as you can. This philosophy may not be a very lofty one, but in the very moderation of its ideals and the certainty of their attainment is it not, he asks, preferable to the Gigadibs theory, which aims at the highest and attains nothing?

Blouzelind or **Blouzelinda**, in the first pastoral of John Gay's *Shepherd's Week* (1714), a shepherdess in love with Lobbin Clout. The name varies according to the exigencies of metre and is spelled indiscriminately with a *u* or a *w*. Its uncouthness was evidently designed as part of Gay's plan to ridicule the Delias and Aramintas of pseudo-pastoral poetry. " Thou wilt not," says Gay, " find my shepherdesses idly piping on their reeds, but milking the kine, tying up the sheaves, or, if the hogs are astray, driving them into the sties." Blouzelinda is painted as an ignorant, unkempt, frolicsome lass but to her lover she is perfection:

My Blouzelinda is the blithest lass,
Than primrose sweeter, or the clover-
grass . . .
My Blouzelind's than gilliflower more fair,
Than daisie, marygold, or kingcup rare.
. . . . .
Sweet is my toil when Blowzelind is near,
Of her bereft 'tis winter all the year . . .
Come, Blowzelinda, ease thy swain's desire,
My summer's shadow, and my winter's fire.

Scott borrows the name with a further change to Blowselinda for an inmate of Whitefriars (alternatively known as Bonstrops) whose room was suggested as a refuge for Nigel when he sought sanctuary in Alsatia.

Bludsoe, Jim, in John Hay's poem of that name (*Pike County Ballads*), was in real life Oliver Fairchild, engineer of the steamer *Fashion*, plying between Memphis and St. Louis, who beached his burning ship and sacrificed himself to save passengers and crew exactly as Hay narrates. The poet had known Fairchild personally in his boyhood days. Mark Twain found fault with the ballad on the score that no engineer could perform the feat ascribed to him.

Bludyer, Mr., in Thackeray's novel, *Pendennis* (1850), a " slashing " book

reviewer who " had a certain notoriety in his profession and reputation for savage humor. He smashed and trampled down the poor spring flowers with no more mercy than a bull would have on a parterre; and having cut up the volume to his heart's content, went and sold it at a bookstall, and purchased a pint of brandy with the proceeds of the volume " (Chap. xxxv). He also makes brief appearances in *Men's Wives, the Ravenswood* (1843), and *Reading a Poem* (1841).

Bluff, Captain Noll. In Congreve's comedy, *The Old Bachelor*, a braggadocio and a coward.

Those ancients, as Noll Bluff might say,
Were pretty fellows in their day.
SIR W. SCOTT.

Blumine, the " Rose Goddess " in Carlyle's *Sartor Resartus* (1833–1834), chapter *Romance*, with whom Teufelsdröckh was in love. Apparently she is a composite figure made up from Jean Welsh whom Carlyle married, Margaret Gordon, his first love, and Kitty Kirkpatrick, to whose cousin, Charles Buller, he was tutor.

On his own confession "Sartor" was "not to be trusted in details," albeit many of the dramatic situations in the book were personal experience idealised. Blumine, the Rose-Goddess, was "unhappily dependent and insolvent; living, perhaps, on the not too gracious bounty of moneyed relations." This was Margaret Gordon. Blumine was "young, hazel-eyed, beautiful, and someone's cousin; high-born and of high spirit." This was in part Kitty Kirkpatrick, in part Jane Welsh. All three entered in turn into Carlyle's colour-scheme. Doubtless Kitty Kirkpatrick, as well as Margaret Gordon and Jane Welsh, made Carlyle "immortal by a kiss." No biographical evidence, however, exists for any such tragic rejection and parting as that described in anticlimax in *Romance*, except in the story of young Carlyle's abortive love for Margaret Gordon, when, after the kiss had made Teufelsdröckh immortal, "thick curtains of night rushed over his soul, as rose the immeasurable crash of doom; and through the ruins as of a shivered universe was the falling, falling, towards the abyss."—J. M. SLOAN in *T. P.'s Weekly*, January 13, 1911.

Blushington, Edward, hero of the comic drama, *The Bashful Man* (1857), by W. T. Moncrief. He is so shy that he cannot muster up courage to propose marriage to Dinah

Friendly, despite all her coquettish advances, until the pyschologic moment arrives when he is flushed by wine.

Bly, Nelly, in Grundy and Solomon's operetta, *The Vicar of Bray* (1882), a ballet girl beloved by Thomas Merton. The name was assumed as a pseudonym by a New York female journalist who especially signalized herself in 1890 by making a tour of the world to beat the record of Phileas Fogg in *Eighty Days Around the World.*

Boatswain, a dog belonging to Lord Byron—

Who was born at Newfoundland May, 1803, And died at Newstead Abbey Nov. 18, 1808.

So says the prose inscription on the monument which Byron raised to his memory in the garden of Newstead which further informs us that he "had all the Virtues of Man without his Vices." A poetical inscription following the prose concludes with this couplet:

To mark a friend's remains, these stones arise;
I never knew but one,—and here he lies.

Byron thus announced the death of this favorite to Hodgson: "Boatswain is dead!—he expired in a state of madness on the 18th after suffering much, yet retaining all the gentleness of his nature to the last; never attempting to do the least injury to any one near him. I have now lost everything except old Murray." In a will executed in 1811 he desired to be buried in a vault with his dog and Joe Murray.

Bob, Son of Battle, hero and title of a novel (1898) by Alfred Ollivant, who must thus be credited with the invention of the novelistic dog. Horses have often figured in fiction. So indeed have dogs, but only in a subordinate way. Ouida's *Puck,* for example, is the narrator of the story in which he plays a small part, but he is an impossible dog in a wild romance while Bob is a real dog whose adventures are severely realistic. "Owd Bob," as he is sometimes nicknamed, is the last of the renowned "gray

dogs of Kenmuir," a fine and sagacious breed of Shepherds in which the dalesman took great pride. He behaves with lofty and pathetic dignity when his rival and enemy, "Red Wull," the tailless Tyke, is caught red-fanged in the commission of the one capital crime of the sheep-dog.

Bobadil, Captain, in Ben Jonson's comedy, *Every Man in his Humor* (1599), a braggadoccio, bully and coward, "a man of big words and little heart," whose bluster dupes many into the belief that he is a valiant soldier of great achievement. "He is," says Hazlitt, "the real hero of the piece. His extravagant affectation, his blustering and cowardice, are an entertaining medley, and his final defeat and exposure, though exceedingly humorous, are the most affecting part of the story." Barry Cornwall deemed him worthy to march in the same regiment with Bessus, Pistol, Parolles and the Copper Captain (see these entries).

It is not generally known that the original of Ben Jonson's "Bobadil" was an officer of high rank in the army of the Duke of Alva, whom the haughty Philip II sent to subdue the Netherlands. After the battle of Giesen, near Mons, in 1570, Strada informs us, in his *Historia de Bello Belgico,* that to fill Spain with the news, the Duke of Alva, as haughty in ostentation as in action, sent Captain Bobadilla to the king, to congratulate his majesty upon the victory won by his arms and influence. The ostentation of the message, and still more of the person who bore it, was the origin of the name being applied to any vain-glorious boaster.—*Spence's Anecdotes.*

Bobadil, especially, is one of Ben's masterpieces. He is the most colossal coward and braggart of the comic stage. He can swear by nothing less terrible than "by the body of Cæsar," or "by the foot of Pharaoh," when his oath is not something more terrific still, namely, "by my valor!" Every schoolboy knows the celebrated passage in which the boasting captain offers to settle the affairs of Europe by associating with himself twenty other Bobadils, as cunning i' the fence as himself, and challenging an army of forty thousand men, twenty at a time, and killing the whole in a certain number of days. Leaving out the cowardice, we may say there was something of Bobadil in Jonson himself; and it may be shrewdly suspected that his conceit of destroying an army in this fashion came into his head in the exultation of feeling which followed his own successful exploit, in the presence of both armies, when he was a soldier in

Flanders. Old John Dennis described genius "as a furious joy and pride of school at the conception of an extraordinary hint." Ben had this "furious joy and pride," not only in the conception of extraordinary hints, but in the doing of extraordinary things.— *Atlantic Monthly*, October, 1867.

Bodach Glas (Glas is the Gaelic for Gray, and Bodach, from the Saxon Bode, means a messenger), in Scott's novel of *Waverley*, a ghostly bearer of evil tidings, who appeared to the head of the MacIvor family whenever any calamity was at hand (see especially Chapter lix, where Fergus MacIvor is warned of his coming doom). A superstition of this kind was a common one in the great Scottish families. Thus the family of Rothmurchan had the Bodach an Dun, or Ghost of the Hill, and the Kincardines, the Spectre of the Bloody Hand. Gartinbeg Castle was haunted by Bodach Gartin and Tullochgorum by Mauch Moulach, or the Girl with the Hairy Left Hand.

Bodwinkle, in Laurence Oliphant's novel, *Piccadilly* (1870), a cockney promoter who launches more or less shady companies in London. Having pursued wealth as an end through years of toil, he and his wife perceive, as their mental horizon expands, that it may be used as the stepping stone to social distinction. Through the agency of Spiffington Goldby's they reach a position where they are tolerated: first, because they spend thousands in dinners, concerts and balls, and secondly, because they look for no equivalent beyond a few crumbs of contemptuous notice.

Boffin, Nicodemus, in Dickens's novel, *Our Mutual Friend* (1864), the foreman of old John Harmon, dustman and miser, who as the latter's residuary legatee comes in for £100,-ooo until the discovery of Harmon's son. Hence Boffin is sometimes known as the " Golden Dustman." He is described as " a broad, round-shouldered, one-sided old fellow, whose face was of the rhinoceros build, with over-lapping ears." He is generous and kindly and a model of integrity. His prototype is said to have been one Henry Dodd, a

contractor of City Wharf, New North Road, Hoxton.

Bolingbroke, Henry, Duke of Hereford, in Shakespeare's historical drama, *Richard II*, reappears as the king in the three parts of *Henry IV* by the same author.

Bolingbroke, who pushes Richard from the throne, is a man framed for such material success as waits on personal ambition. He is not, like his son Henry V, filled with high enthusiasm and sacred force derived from the powers of heaven and earth. All Bolingbroke's strength and craft are his own. His is a resolute gaze which sees his object far off, and he has persistency and energy of will to carry him off without faltering. He is not cruel, but shrinks from no deed that is useful to his purpose because the deed is cruel.—E. DOWDEN, *Shakespeare Primer*.

Bolton, Fanny, in *The History of Pendennis*, by Thackeray, the daughter of the portress of Shepherd's Inn, pretty, foolish and sentimental, who falls desperately in love with Arthur. She adorns him with all the heroic virtues, and he for a time is stimulated into a temporary passion which he conquers before it has done harm to any one.

Boltrope, in J. Fenimore Cooper's romance of the sea, *The Pilot*. The author considered this a finer bit of character painting than Long Tom Coffin in the same novel.

We cannot assent to this comparative estimate; but we admit that Boltrope has not had full justice done to him in popular judgment. It is but a slight sketch, but it is extremely well done. His death is a bit of manly and genuine pathos; and in his conversations with the chaplain there is here and there a touch of true humor, which we value the more because humor was certainly not one of the author's best gifts.— *Atlantic Monthly*, January, 1862.

Bolus, Benjamin, hero of a farce by Munden the comedian, *Benjamin Bolus or the Newcastle Apothecary*, which was performed at the Haymarket for his benefit August 8, 1797. It is founded upon a comic poem by George Colman, in *Broad Grins*, a collection of miscellaneous tales in verse first published (1797) under the title, *My Nightcap and Slippers*.

Bombastes Furioso, in a burlesque tragic opera of that name (1810), by William Barnes Rhodes, a general commanding the army of Artaxaminous, King of Utopia. The monarch wishes to divorce his Queen Griskinissa for Distaffina, the betrothed of Bombastes, and wooes her with the offer of half a crown, which she accepts. Bombastes goes mad and among other exploits hangs his boots upon a tree, with this defiant legend:

Who dares this pair of boots displace
Must meet Bombastes face to face.

Artaxaminous accepts the challenge, cuts down the boots and is slain by Bombastes. More men are killed, and at the end the dead all rise again and join in a dance, promising the audience to die again tomorrow. The farce is a travesty on *Orlando Furioso* (*q.v.*), the mad hero of which hangs up his armor on a tree with the legend:

Orlando's arms let none displace,
Or meet Orlando face to face.

Bonduca (an alternate name for Boadicea), heroine and title of a tragedy (1611) by Beaumont and Fletcher. Like the tragedies of *Boadicea* by Hopkins and Glover, *Bonduca* is founded on Tacitus, *Annals*, xiv, 29. Caractacus is here called Caratach. The play was re-cast by J. R. Planché and revived (1837) under the title of *Caractacus*.

Bon Gaultier, the pretended author of the *Bon Gaultier Ballads* which originally appeared in *Tait's Magazine* (1842–1844) and were the joint authorship of William Edmonston Aytoun and Theodore Martin. The name comes from Rabelais—" A moy n'est que honneur et gloire d'estre dict et réputé Bon Gaultier et bon compaignon; en ce nom, suis bien venu en toutes bonnes compaignies de Pantagruélistes." The Bon Gaultier of the ballads was at once made welcome in all good companies of people who liked vigorous and racy humor. Some too fastidious persons have been very angry with the authors for a supposed irreverence in these parodies. Mr. Martin protested that parody is a veiled compliment, and that it was precisely the poets whom they most admired that they imitated most frequently.

" This was not certainly from any want of reverence, but rather out of the fulness of our admiration, just as the excess of a lover's fondness runs over into raillery of the very qualities that are dearest to his heart."

Boniface, in Scott's historic romance, *The Monastery*, is Lord Abbot of St. Mary's; in its sequel, *The Abbot*, he has retired to private life under the name of Blinkhoodie as the proprietor of a large garden at Kinross. Good-natured, easy-going and charitable, he had sought the seclusion of the cloister for quiet, but the turmoil of the times had deprived him of his rest as Abbot, and even in retirement he was " dragged into matters where both heading and hangings are like to be the issue." At the end he sighs, " A weary life I have had for one to whom peace was ever the dearest blessing! "

Boniface, Will, in Farquhar's comedy, *The Beaux Stratagem* (1707), landlord of the inn at Lichfield, in league with the highwaymen, but of so sleek and jolly an exterior that he is a great favorite with all customers. His pet expression " as the saying is " he lugs into his talk with ludicrous irrelevance, as " Does your master stay in town as the saying is? " and " I'm old Will Boniface, pretty well known along this road, as the saying is." The popularity of this character has caused the name Boniface to be a generic one for a publican or tavern keeper.

Bonnard, Sylvestre, hero of Anatole France's novel, *The Crime of Sylvestre Bonnard*. A learned, simple-minded, kindly gentleman, an archæologist and a member of the Institute, Bonnard's " crime " was that of abducting a minor, a young girl in whom he is platonically interested, from a wretched school near Paris where she is cruelly maltreated. He escapes penal prosecution only by the accident that Jeanne's guardian had already decamped with the money of all his clients. Hence Jeanne becomes naturally and legally the ward of her good old friend.

Bonnivard, Francis, a historical character (1495–1570), who has had undeserved dignity thrust upon him in Byron's poem, *The Prisoner of Chillon.* Instead of losing one brother by fire, two in the field, and two by death in the dungeon, the fact is that there is no evidence that he had any brothers at all, and none that his father died for his faith. Byron himself acknowledges that he was unacquainted with the history of Bonnivard when he wrote the poem. He subsequently wrote a sonnet to his hero, in which he represents him as a high-minded patriot appealing " from tyranny to God," and this character has sometimes been ascribed to him by historians. In plain truth, there was little of the heroic about Bonnivard. He was simply a good-natured scatter-brain, whose high animal spirits and graceless wit were continually getting him into trouble; and he seems to have employed the six years of his imprisonment chiefly in making immoral verses.

Bontemps, Roger, an ideal personification of cheery content and unshakable optimism current among the French peasantry whom Beranger immortalized in one of his most famous songs (1814). The opening stanza is thus translated by William Young:

> To show our hypochondriacs,
>   In days the most forlorn,
> A pattern set before their eyes,
>   Roger Bontemps was born.
> To live obscurely at his will,
>   To keep aloof from strife,—
> Hurrah for fat Roger Bontemps!
>   This is his rule of life.

Booth, Amelia, titular heroine of Fielding's novel, *Amelia* (1751), the ever-loving, ever-amiable and ever-forgiving wife of the graceless Captain Booth. This new type of wifehood was not greatly relished either by the belles or the beaux of Fielding's age. Elizabeth Carter tells us that they pronounced her history " sad stuff," though Miss Carter herself does not seem to concur in the verdict. Fielding felt the weight of public disapproval. With semi-defiant humor he acknowledged as much in the *Covent Garden Journal,* which he edited. He

brings the novel before his own " Court of Censorial Enquiry," and lets Amelia's accusers speak, but he disdains to plead her cause against them. " If you, Mr. Censor, are yourself a Parent, you will view me with Compassion when I declare I am the Father of this poor Girl the Prisoner at the Bar; nay, when I go farther, and avow, that of all my Offspring she is my favourite Child.' He explains what models he has followed, and then continues, " I do not think my Child is entirely free from Faults. I know nothing human that is so; but surely she does not deserve the Rancour with which she hath been treated by the Public."

Nor was she (Lady Mary Wortley Montagu) a stranger to that beloved first wife whose picture he drew in his Amelia, where as she said even the glowing language he knew how to employ did not do more than justice to the amiable qualities of the original or to her beauty, although this had suffered a little from the accident related in the novel—a frightful overturn which destroyed the gristle of her nose.—LADY LOUISA STUART, *Letters and Works of Lady M. W. Montagu* (1837).

Fielding's wife, whether she had "a broken nose" or not, must have been an angel. It is she who sat for Sophia Western and Amelia Booth, the kindest, the dearest, the most charming and lenient of women.— ANDREW LANG.

Booth, Captain, the not too heroic hero of Fielding's novel *Amelia.* He is brave enough and in a man-of-the-world way possesses even a rudimentary sense of honor, but he is a prodigal and a profligate whose easy good-nature is held in leash by none of the sterner virtues. When first introduced he is in prison for participation in a street quarrel. He has a mistress there, Miss Matthews, a frail beauty who has murdered her seducer. But he is really in love with his wife whose purity, virtue and devotion eventually rescue him from vice and jail. Fielding sat for his own portrait in this character and utilized many of his own experiences, adventures and misadventures in the story of his career.

Amelia, whose portrait Fielding drew from that of his second wife, has indeed been always a favorite character with readers; but the same cannot be said about her husband Booth, who, we may suppose, was meant to represent Fielding himself. If so the likeness he drew is certainly not a flattering one. Thackeray preferred Captain Booth to Tom Jones, because he thought much more humbly of himself than Jones did, and went down on his knees and owned his weaknesses, but most will be inclined to agree with Scott, who declares that we have not the same sympathy for the ungrateful and dissolute conduct of Booth which we yield to the youthful follies of Jones.—H. J. NICHOL.

Boots, an otherwise unnamed character in Dickens's Christmas story, *Boots at The Holly Tree Inn,* who in his own vernacular tells the story of two eloping children.

Sam Weller is the great type of this class, and it may be said of him as of his fellow Boots of the Holly Tree Inn that one of the greatest charms about them is that we cannot tell whether they are really like or unlike what living Boots could be. The picture is full of those traits of keen personal observation, of minute inspection, of trifling eccentricities and peculiarities which have lent so much life and vigor to Mr. Dickens's writing. The language, too, and the characteristic expressions smack of the trade and of the life to which the Boots are supposed to belong. But all this is only a clothing under which the novelist conceals himself. There are no Sam Wellers in real life. The Boots of a real Holly Tree Inn, if he uses the phrases that his imaginary representative adopts, uses them sparingly and accidentally. The Boots of the tale is all Boots and talks his language from beginning to end. The author is never lost sight of, and we feel that art has collected together what nature separates by long intervals, and has exaggerated with a grotesque unity what nature leaves simple, undefined and incomplete.—*Saturday Review,* v, 636.

Boots, Bonny, a nickname reappearing in various Elizabethan ballads and evidently referring to some court favorite. His skill in dancing and singing are specially noted. Hence he is sometimes identified with one Hale or Hales whose singing is known to have pleased the Queen, but more frequently with the Earl of Essex, whose courtly graces included these accomplishments. Essex was beheaded in February, 1601, and in that year was published *The Triumphs of Oriana,* a collection of pieces in honor of Elizabeth, wherein Bonny Boots is mourned as recently dead.

Boots, Major Wellington de, in Stirling Coyne's comedy, *Everybody's Friend* (1859).

In order to amplify the part of the

Major for one of its greatest exponents, John Sleeper Clarke, the play was rewritten and, under the title of *The Widow Hunt,* produced at the Haymarket in 1867.

Borkman, John Gabriel, hero and title of a drama by Henrik Ibsen (1896), " a man of the most energetic imagination whose illusions feed on his misfortunes, and whose conception of his own power grows hyberbolical and Napoleonic in his solitude and impotence." So says George Bernard Shaw in *Dramatic Opinions,* and the same authority adds that Borkman " meets the fate of a vehement dreamer who has for thirteen years been deprived of that daily contact with reality and responsibility without which genius inevitably produces unearthliness and insanity."

Bothwell, Francis Stewart, Earl of, known as the Bastard Earl (d. 1624), appears in Scott's romance, *The Fortunes of Nigel.* Following hard on the heels of the young king James I when fleeing in his night gear down a turret stair, a prick of the Earl's sword in the nether extremities is said to have confirmed His Majesty's aversion to cold steel. The incident has a historical basis.

Bothwell, Sergeant, in Walter Scott's historical romance, *Old Mortality* (1816), an officer in Claverhouse's regiment of Life Guards who fights Charles II. Francis Stewart is his real name, but as the illegitimate descendant of the last Earl of Bothwell (himself known as the Bastard Earl) he assumes the titular pseudonym. Gallant, licentious, boastful, arrogant, he died at Drumelog " hoping nothing, believing nothing and fearing nothing."

Bottom, Nick, in *A Midsummer Night's Dream,* a weaver full of fantastic vanity, self-assurance, impudence and ignorance. The name is a weaver's term for a bobbin or spindle full of yarn. See TITANIA.

Bottom, in his broad-blown self-importance, his all but impenetrable self-satisfaction, stands a head and shoulders higher in absurdity than any other comic character in Shakespeare's early plays. He is the admitted king of his company, the cock of his walk—and he has a consciousness that his gifts are more than equal to his opportunities. When the ass's head is on his shoulders it seems hardly a disguise, so naturally does the human-asinine seem to come to Bottom; he might have been for twelve months Titania's long-eared lover, so easily do his new honors sit upon him.— E. DOWDEN, *Shakespeare Primer.*

Bountiful, Lady, in Farquhar's comedy, *The Beaux Stratagem* (1705), the widow of Sir Charles Bountiful whose gracious mood it is to look after the sick in the parish and relieve the necessities of the deserving poor. As her nephew says in Act i, Sc. 1, "My Lady Bountiful is one of the best of women. Her late husband, Sir Charles Bountiful, left her with £1000 a year; and I believe she lays out one-half on't in charitable uses for the good of her neighbors. In short she has cured more people in and about Lichfield within ten years than the doctors have killed in twenty, and that's a bold word."

Bourgh, Lady Catherine de, in Jane Austen's novel, *Pride and Prejudice* (1813), a great lady but vulgar, in the way that some great ladies can be vulgar. Insolent, inquisitive, overbearing, she is properly set down by the witty Elizabeth Bennet in a memorable scene in "the prettyish kind of little shrubbery" where they walk together.

Bourke, Chevalier, in R. L. Stevenson's *The Master of Ballantrae.*

It is not very easy to understand the Chevalier Bourke, that Barry Lyndon, with no head and a good heart, that creature of a bewildered, kindly conscience; but it is easy to like him. How admirable is his undeflected belief in and affection for the Master! How excellent and how Irish he is, when he buffoons himself out of his perils with the pirates!—ANDREW LANG, *Essays in Little.*

Boursoufle, Comte de, hero of a pretended posthumous play by Voltaire, produced in Paris in 1862, which, after fooling critics and public, was discovered to be an adaptation of Vanbrugh's *Relapse.* Boursoufle, of course, is Lord Foppington transferred to the boulevards.

Bovary, Emma, heroine of *Madame Bovary* (1857), a realistic novel by Gustave Flaubert. A farmer's daughter, married to a village apothecary, but educated above her station, she seeks to relieve ennui by two successive intrigues, plunges hopelessly into debt, and, when her lovers refuse to aid her, poisons herself. Her devoted husband, his eyes opened at last, dies of grief.

Emma's character is pitilessly dissected. Morally irresponsible, she has no object in life but self-gratification. Her father's farm was dull and she left it; her husband's house proves as dull; she takes a vindictive pleasure in betraying him. Her child is but a transient amusement. Even in her love, when aroused at last, there is nothing noble or generous.

Bowling, Lieutenant, in Smollett's novel, *Roderick Random,* the hero's maternal uncle. In him Smollett seized at once and fixed forever the eighteenth century type of seaman— rough as a polar bear, brave, simple, kindly, and out of his element everywhere except afloat. Bowling has left his mark in many a novel and drama of the sea. He carries the habit of professional speech at least as far as the limits of art will allow. Sea life and war and the hardening habits of the service have made him indifferent to that social softening down which, without amending hearts, refines manners.

Bowling, Tom, hero and title of *A Tale of the Sea* (1839), by Captain Frederick Chamier, a composite portrait drawn partly from Nelson's flag-captain Hardy and partly from Richard Bowen, captain of the frigate *Terpsichore,* who fell in the attack on Santa Cruz, July 24, 1797—

than whom a more enterprising, able and gallant officer does not grace his majesty's naval service.—*Nelson's Dispatches,* ii, 423.

Bows, Mr., in Thackeray's novel, *Pendennis,* a fiddler with a crippled body, a lively imagination, and intense feelings. He cherishes a far-off hopeless passion for Miss Fotheringay whom he has taught how to act, and has a paternal affection for Fanny Bolton, his pupil in music.

Box and Cox, the heroes of a farce of that name (1847), by J. Maddison Morton, which, according to F. C.

Burnand (*London Times*, October 18, 1889), is " the best farce for three characters in the English language."
It is founded upon a *comédie-vaudeville* by Labiche and Lefranc entitled *Frisette*, produced at the Palais-Royal, Paris, April 28, 1846.

Boynton, Dr., in William D. Howells's novel, *The Undiscovered Country* (1880), a country doctor who has gone daft on spiritual manifestations. Half fanatic, half self-deceiver, he has brought up his daughter Egeria, a delicate, high-strung, nervous girl, as a medium. Failing to take Boston by storm, the pair find refuge in a Shaker community.

Dr. Boynton is a fervent believer in spiritualism—or, rather, an ardent hankerer after fervent belief in it. But, not being exactly an idiot, he has observed the quackery which generally prevails on the subject, and has drawn the bright conclusion that a certain amount of slipperiness is inseparable from the mediumistic temperament. He accordingly mixes himself up with some very doubtful people, whom he allows, in his own words, to "assist the Spirits." The spirits are of course assisted to their hearts' content, and when Dr. Boynton finds out how far the assistance has gone he is in a paroxysm of rage, grief, and despair, being indeed, as his confederate justly calls him, " a new sort of fool." He is always going through these alterations of eager belief in having found the clue, and of frantic disappointment when it fails him.—*Saturday Review*.

Boynton, Egeria, the daughter of the above.

Egeria Boynton is an unhappy young woman, not very brilliant, who is passionately fond of her father, and deeply disgusted at the charlatanism which she is forced into partaking; but who, nevertheless, owing to filial affection and a nervous temperament, allows herself to be mesmerized and materialized or immaterialized— we really cannot undertake to use the jargon correctly—and thus to bamboozle others, to ruin her own health, and to confirm her father in his self-deluding folly.—*Saturday Review*.

Boythorn, Laurence, in Dickens' novel, *Bleak House* (1853), a friend of Mr. Jarndyce, robust-minded, loud-voiced, self-assertive, combative, but intrinsically noble, kindly and affectionate. The character was generally recognized as a study of the external traits of Walter Savage

Landor, and was good-naturedly accepted as such by Landor himself.

The chivalry, the sincerity, the vehemence, the extravagance, the grace of manner, the boisterous laughter, the childish love of pets—every salient trait of Landor in the spirit or the flesh is reproduced in this life-like study. The tendency to exaggerate the expression of every momentary impulse, which is such a humorous feature in this character, must be taken into account in any judgment passed upon the failings of his prototype . . . His worst exhibitions of temper, like those of a child, generally excite too much laughter to leave room for anger.—*The Contemporary Review*.

Bracegirdle, Anne (1674–1748), one of the most famous of English actresses, figures under her own name in John Oxenford's *Tragedy Queen*, and is the supposed original of two stage characters which she "created" —Angelica in Congreve's *Love for Love* and Lavinia in Rowe's *Fair Penitent*.

It was even the fashion for the gay and young to have a taste or *tendre* for Mrs. Bracegirdle. She inspired the best authors to write for her and two of these (Rowe and Congreve), when they gave her a lover in the play, seemed palpably to plead their own passion and make their private court to her in fictitious characters.—COLLEY CIBBER, *Apology*.

Bradwardine, Baron of, in Thackeray's *Book of Snobs*, ii. He is described as " the most famous man in Haggisland " and an admirer of Georgius IV who, " coming on board the royal yacht and finding a glass out of which Georgius had drunk, put it into his coat pocket as an inestimable relic and went ashore in his boat again. But the Baron sat down upon the glass and broke it, cut his coat-tails very much, and the inestimable relic was lost to the world forever." The Baron is meant, of course, for Sir Walter Scott and the story is retold in Thackeray's lecture on George IV with proper credit.

Bradwardine, Cosmo Comyne, Baron of, in the romance, *Waverley* (1814), one of Scott's most successful comic characters, " the very model of the old Scottish cavalier," says the author," with all his excellencies and peculiarities." He is a scholar, of the Scotch pedantic sort; full of anecdotes, almost always curious and informing, yet whimsical from prejudice and pedantry; and full also of the pride of race and position.

Bradwardine's prototype was Alexander Stewart of Invernahyle, on whose valour and magnanimity at Preston-pans the plot of Waverley is made to turn. To Invernahyle Scott owed much of his knowledge of Highland life and scenery. He was "that friend of my childhood who first introduced me to the Highlands, their traditions and manners, "and whose visits to Scott's household brought delight to his children in later life." To this picturesque figure fighting his battles over again with all the garrulousness of a veteran campaigner, "much of the inspiration of Waverley was no doubt due." "Inverness had been out with Marr and with Charlie." He died at an advanced age in 1795. But there were features in Bradwardine—such as his scholarship and pedantry—which Invernahyle did not possess, and these seem to have been borrowed from Lord Forbes of Pitsligo (1678–1762), "patriot, outlaw, scholar, saint" who at the age of 65 took active part in the Jacobite rising of 1745.—See CROCKETT, *The Scott Originals.*

What could be more delightful, more loving in its fun, more whimsical in its quaint conception, and, at the same time, more completely true to nature, than the Baron of Bradwardine, a knight and gentleman every inch of him—with his wisdom, his learning, his vanity, and gravest solemn foolishness? "I had a great deal of fun in the accomplishment of this task," says Scott, with the gleam of enjoyment in his eyes. He, too, liked it as much as his audience. To him, as to every true humorist, his Baron was dear—there is moisture beyond the laughter in his eye, rising half from the heartiness of the laugh, half from a tender affection below.—*Blackwood's Magazine,* August, 1871.

Braggadochio (which orthographically is Spenser's attempt to transliterate the Italian *braggadoccio*), in the *Faërie Queene,* an empty boaster who succeds for a period in making his way by sheer bluff, but is eventually exposed and stripped of his borrowed plumes. His early career is related in Book iii, 8 and 10; his downfall occurs in v, 3. A caricature of Philip II of Spain may be intended; but in a more general way Braggadochio, like Ariosto's Rodomont, is a satire on intemperance of speech and is to some extent reminiscent of the earlier character.

Brainworm, in Ben Jonson's *Every Man in his Humor* (1598), a servant to Ola Knowell, whose versatility and adaptiveness enabled him to appear in various disguises under as many aliases.

Brainworm is a particularly dry and abstruse character. We neither know his business nor his motives; his plots are as intricate as they are useless, and the ignorance of those he imposes upon is wonderful. This is the impression in reading it. Yet from the bustle and activity of this character on the stage, the changes of dress, the variety of affected tones and gypsy jargon, and the limping, distorted gestures it is a very amusing exhibition.—WILLIAM HAZLITT.

Bramble, Matthew, a testy but kindly valetudinarian, a sort of Roderick Random grown old and much improved by age, who is the projector of the family tour described in the (misnamed) *Expedition of Humphrey Clinker* (1771), a novel by Tobias Smollett. Not until one-fourth of the journey has been accomplished is Humphrey Clinker taken on as a postilion—Bramble being himself the chief character in the book. He takes with him his spinster sister Tabitha, her maid Winifred Jenkins, and the party enjoys or suffers a series of comic adventures and misadventures not dissimilar to those that had already been described in Christopher Anstey's *New Bath Guide.*

Brand, the hero of Ibsen's drama of that name (1866), a peasant priest who from his rural parsonage—perched midway between the precipice and the fjord—hurls defiance against the world and its prejudices, conventions, time-serving and hypocrisies. Perhaps he hardly knows what he wants save that it must be a total upheaval of present conditions that shall bring men closer to God. An avalanche brought down upon him by his own wrath finally buries him in the ruins of the Ice-church. "Brand is myself in my best moments," wrote Ibsen. Nevertheless other like-minded men undoubtedly furnished hints for this character, notably Pastor Gustav Adolf Lammers, who dwelt in the parish of Skien until his troubled and rebellious mind forced him to give up his flock and found the Free Apostolic Christian Communion, and the eminent

Danish philosopher, Sören Kierke-gaard (1813–1855).

The difference between these two proto-types of Brand was largely a matter of exter-nal estimate on the part of Ibsen. Lammers was not a closet philosopher, whereas Kierkegaard was, and therefore, should people absolutely need to have a model for Brand, they had best take the former.—MONTROSE J. MOSES, *Henrik Ibsen*, p. 168.

Brand, Agnes, sister of the above. She is supposed to have been drawn from Thea Brunn, whom Ibsen met in 1864 with her widowed mother, Frau Lina Brunn. Thea was a sensi-tive, self-sacrificing person who even-tually died as a result of nervous strain attendant upon the death of her brothers.

External interpretation always irritated Ibsen. When Laura Kieler, the authoress, sent him her novel, *Brand's Daughters*, in which Brand's teachings were applied prac-tically to life, wearied with so much dis-cussion, Ibsen wrote to her from Dresden in June, 1870, that his poem was an æsthetic work and not a system of philosophy. He had experienced, not only observed, the things he treated of; and, impelled by an overpowering necessity of putting his thoughts into form, he had done so; now he cared not whether his book demolished or built up.—MONTROSE J. MOSES, *Henrik Ibsen*, p. 201.

Brand, Ethan, hero and title of a tale in N. Hawthorne's *Mosses from an Old Manse* (1846).

He was then (1840) beginning to revolve one of the two great romance themes that preoccupied his whole after-life, neither of which he was destined to write. This was the idea of the Unpardonable Sin; the other was the conception of the Deathless Man. The only essay we have towards the embodi-ment of the first vision is the short fragment published in *Mosses from an Old Manse*, called *Ethan Brand*. The other was attempted in various forms, of which *Sep-timius, Dr. Grimshawe's Secret*, and *The Dolliver Romance*, all posthumously pub-lished, are the most important.—JULIAN HAWTHORNE, *Hawthorne and His Circle*.

Brandon, William, in Bulwer-Lytton's *Paul Clifford* (1830), the father of the eponymic hero. See CLIFFORD, PAUL.

William Brandon is the lawyer who always plays an important part in melo-dramatic fiction. Directly we are intro-duced to him and find that he has an icy smile, a serpent eye—that his features are "steeped in sarcasm," that he is usually cold and self-possessed, but that he some-times walks about his room at night and mutters "Ha!—I have it—yet methinks, 'twere well;—but—but—this is weakness" —we know perfectly well what is coming; we see as in a glass, that he has committed a great crime, and that he is secretly tor-tured by remorse; we are sure that he is laying plans that will come to nothing, and that he is destined to an untimely end.—*Westminster Review*, March, 1865.

Branghtons, The, in FannyBurney's novel, *Evelina*, a set of vulgar cousins related to the heroine through Mme. Duval (*q.v.*), who compromise her position in the finer world to which she by instinct and breeding belongs. Though horribly ashamed of them, they remain all unconscious of her shame, for she is incapable of wound-ing them even to free herself from torment.

The family consists of a father—Madame Duval's nephew—a silver-smith on Snow Hill, a man of fair but cockneyfied intelligence who despises everybody not born and bred in London. His son Thomas is "weaker in his understanding and more gay in his temper, but his gaiety is that of a foolish, overgrown schoolboy whose mirth consists in noise and disturbance." He disdains his father and ridicules his sisters, who despise him in return. The elder daughter, Miss Biddy, is not ill-look-ing, but proud, ill-tempered, and con-ceited. "She hates the city though without knowing why, for it is easy to discover she has lived nowhere else." The younger sister, Polly, is "rather pretty, very foolish, very ignorant, very giddy and very good-natured." This family, after the fashion of eighteenth century trades-people, live over their shop in the city and rent some of the rooms. Poor Evelina, after she has been pestered with the attentions of the under-bred Mr. Smith, and threatened by Madame Duval with young Brangh-tons as a husband, reaches the full measure of her mortifications at KensingtonGardens, where in a soak-ing shower her cousins contrive to borrow Lord Orville's coach in her name, although against her will. As a result the coach is badly injured in taking these discreditable connections to Snow Hill.

Brass, Miss Sally, in Dickens's *The Old Curiosity Shop*, sister and partner of Sampson, who shares his evil traits and physically is his counterpart in petticoats.

Brass, Sampson, brother of the above, a vulgar, unscrupulous, untidy and servile attorney.

Brassbound, Captain, hero of G. B. Shaw's comedy, *Captain Brassbound's Conversion*, an impossible pirate in an imaginary Morocco, bound on a mission of private punishment which appears to him a God-given duty, and apparently invented for the purpose of emphasizing the idiosyncrasies of the heroine, Lady Cicely Waynefleet (*q.v.*).

The pirate Brassbound orders his life upon the principle that, as Bacon puts it, "revenge is a sort of wild justice." He is imbued with mediæval concepts of right and wrong. In opposition to him he discovers his opposite,—a cool, tactful, unsentimental woman of the world, disarming all opposition through her Tolstoyism. With sympathetic interest she soon wins from Brassbound the secret of his life, and with quiet and delicious satire, opens his eyes to the pettiness of his mock-heroics, the absurdity of the melodramatic point of view—the code of the Kentucky feud, the Italian vendetta. The revulsion in Brassbound is instant and complete.—ARCHIBALD HENDERSON, *George Bernard Shaw*, p. 324.

Brattle, Carry, in Anthony Trollope's novel, *The Vicar of Bullhampton*.

We gather from the preface that Mr. Trollope has a moral design in his book. "I have introduced in *The Vicar of Bullhampton* the character of a girl whom I will call—for want of a truer word that shall not in its truth be offensive—a castaway. I have endeavoured to endow her with qualities that may create sympathy, and I have brought her back at last from degradation at least to decency." In the pursuit of his aim Mr. Trollope cannot be reproached with making vice attractive. He tells us that Carry is pretty and that a certain early charm had won the good will of the vicar and his wife; but a less taking wrongdoer seldom demands our pity. We suppose she was led astray at first by her affections, though we are not told so, but her cool indifference whether the man she is afterwards engaged to is hanged or not shows that they were well under control by the end of the story. And her father and brother, who share the vicar's regard, are as sour a pair as we ever knew time spent

upon. Old Brattle is perhaps the best character as a work of art, the writer's mind has been most present in him; but no clownish rustic of fiction was ever a more ungracious piece of realism.—*Saturday Review*.

Breck, Alan, more properly Alan Breck Stewart, the most picturesque and forceful character in R. L. Stevenson's romances, *Kidnapped* (1886), and its sequel, *David Balfour* (1893).

As to Alan Breck, with his valor and vanity, his good heart, his good conceit of himself, his fantastic loyalty, he is absolutely worthy of the hand that drew Callum Beg and the Dougal creature.—ANDREW LANG, *Essays in Little*.

Breen, Grace, heroine of Howells's novel, *Dr. Breen's Practice* (1881). Having had an unfortunate love affair, in which she had been badly treated by her lover, she has adopted the practice of medicine much as other women enter convents or go out as missionaries.

Dr. Breen . . . represents what Mr. Howells seems to think the modern form of Puritanism, this ancient faith taking in her a moral rather than a religious form, and making her conscience sensitive as regards all her relations with fellow creatures to a degree unknown in parts of the world unaffected by Puritan traditions.—*N. Y. Nation*.

Breitmann, Hans, hero of the *Breitmann Ballads* by Charles Godfrey Leland, first collected into book form in 1868. He is a genial caricature of the German immigrant in Pennsylvania, drunk with the new world as with new wine, and rioting in the expression of purely Deutsch nature and half-Deutsch ideas through the broken English of the half-Americanized German fellow citizen. He made his first appearance in *Hans Breitmann's Party* in 1856.

Breitmann is one of the battered types of the men of '48—a person whose education more than his heart has in every way led him to entire scepticism or indifference, and one whose Lutheranism does not go beyond Wein, Weib und Gesang. Beneath his unlimited faith in pleasure lie natural shrewdness, an excellent early education, and certain principles of honesty and good fellowship, which are all the more clearly defined from his moral looseness in details identified in the Anglo-Saxon mind with total depravity.—*Author's Preface to the English edition*, 1871.

Brent, John, titular hero of a novel (1862) by Theodore Winthrop. A generous, noble-minded man of adventurous disposition, he accompanies Richard Wade, an unsuccessful gold miner in California, on a ride across the plains to his family in the east.

Brentford, Two Kings of, a couple of burlesque monarchs introduced into *The Rehearsal* (1671), a famous farce written by George Villiers, Duke of Buckingham, with the assistance of Butler Sprat and others (see BAYES). They are represented as inseparable; as dancing or singing together; walking hand in hand, and generally as living on terms of the greatest affection and intimacy. Bayes (Act i, Sc. 1) explains: " Look you, sirs, the chief hinge of this play . . . is that I suppose two kings at Brentford, for I love to write familiarly." A certain Colonel Henry Howard wrote a play, *The United Kingdom*, which had two kings in it. Though it failed on the stage and was never printed, Buckingham is supposed to have had this drama in mind when he set up two kings in Brentford. A more likely theory is that they are caricatures of Boabdelin and Abdalla, the two contending kings in Dryden's tragedy , *The Conquest of Granada.*

Bretherton, Isabel, the heroine of Mrs. Humphry Ward's first novel, *Miss Bretherton* (1884), is obviously drawn from Mary Anderson, the American actress, who had recently taken London by storm, yet failed to satisfy the critics. The motif underlying the story is the insufficiency of natural gifts, and the fatal consequences of the world's too easy acceptance of them. Mrs. Ward virtually asks: How shall an exceptional natural endowment of physical perfection, with no inheritance of cultivation from the past, no accumulation of personal thought and experience, reach the heights of artistic excellence? Will Undine find a soul?

Brewster, Margaret, heroine of Whittier's poem, *In the Old South Church* (1878). The poet has closely followed historical fact. Margaret Brewster was a Quaker enthusiast who one Sunday in July, 1677, appeared before the Puritan congregation of Old South Meeting House in Boston clad only in a sackcloth gown, her head ash-besprinkled, her hair dishevelled, her face besmeared with soot. Judge Sewall, an eyewitness, tells us that this apparition " occasioned the greatest and most amazing uproar that ever I saw." Margaret was seized and sentenced to be whipped at the cart's tail up and down the town.

Brick, Jefferson, in Dickens's *Martin Chuzzlewit*, the War Correspondent of the *Rowdy Journal*. A small gentleman, very juvenile in appearance, snub-nosed, and of an unwholesome pallor. He and his employer are quite sure that Europe trembles at his name.

Jefferson Brick, the American editor, twitted me with the multifarious patented anomalies of overgrown, worthless Dukes, Bishops of Durham, etc., which poor English society at present labors under, and is made a solecism by.—CARLYLE.

Bridge of Sighs (It., *Ponte dei Sospiri*), the popular name for a picturesque bridge in Venice which spans the Rio canal and connects the court-room in the Doge's palace with the state prisons. Prisoners have to pass over it on their way to and from the hall of judgment. As Mr. Howells says, the name arose from " that opulence of compassion which enables the Italians to pity even rascality in difficulties." No really romantic episode in the history of Venice can be associated with it (except the story of Antonio Foscarini), for it was not built until the end of the sixteenth century and the criminals who have passed across it have been almost exclusively murderers and thieves and other members of the proletariat of crime. Yet Byron himself was deluded into adopting and promulgating this pathetic fallacy in the lines in *Childe Harold:*

I stood in Venice on the Bridge of Sighs,
A prison and a palace on each hand.

Hood borrowed the name and bestowed it on London Bridge in his poem, *The Bridge of Sighs*. For that London Bridge as the " jumping off place " for suicides was in Hood's mind is highly probable. An old London proverb ran: " London Bridge was made for wise men to go over and fools to go under." Nevertheless Walter Thornbury, in his *Haunted London*, thinks Waterloo Bridge was the place intended, and he had consulted the younger Tom Hood.

Bridlegoose, Judge, the name under which the translators of Rabelais's *Pantagruel* English the name Brid'oison.

Bridoison, Taiel de, familiarly known as Juge Bridoie, in Rabelais's satirical romance *Pantagruel*, iii, 39 (1545), a judicial luminary who decided all cases that came before him by throwing a couple of dice. Nothing can be more naïve than his self-satisfied explanation that this is the best way of getting through the calendar. In this character Rabelais is said to have caricatured Guillaume Poyet (1474–1548) Chancellor of France under Francis I.

Brid'oison, Judge, in Beaumarchais' comedy *The Marriage of Figaro* (1784), an absurd jurist imitated from the famous character in *Pantagruel*, who loves formality and red tape and hides his ignorance of the spirit of the law by clinging desperately to the letter.

Brierly, Bob, hero of Tom Taylor's comedy, *The Ticket of Leave Man* (1863), which embodies the misfortunes of a young English rustic. Falling into bad company he unwittingly circulates a forged note and is transported. He leaves Portland by virtue of a ticket of leave. In vain he tries to begin life again. At last he is killed in a struggle with a burglar against whom he would protect the property of a city gentleman from whose service he had been dismissed, not for any fault, but simply on account of his unfortunate antecedents.

Brigard, Gilberte, the heroine of *Frou-frou*, a drama by Meilhac and Halévy, who receives the titular nickname from the perpetual rustling of her silk dresses. See FROU-FROU.

Briggs, Mr., a blundering amateur sportsman, the artistic conception of John Leech, whose misadventures with rod and gun and horse and hounds were depicted serially in the London *Punch* and kept all England laughing for years. Of Leech himself it is told that he was an ardent rather than a successful sportsman, and had so little confidence in his horsemanship that he once insisted on buying a broken-winded horse because it was sure not to carry him far if it bolted.

Britomart, in Spenser's *Faerie Queene* (1590), the representative of chastity, to whom Book iii is largely devoted. Daughter of King Ryence of Wales, she fell in love with Sir Artegal, whose features she saw reflected while gazing into a magic mirror. With Glauce, her nurse, she starts out fully armored in search of him. Her adventures allegorize the triumphs of chastity over temptation. Malacasta (lust), not knowing her sex, tried to seduce her in Castle Joyous, but she fled from that palace of luxury: Marinel forbade her to pass his cave but she knocked him over with one blow from her spear. In her next appearance as the Squire of Dames she does great deeds for ladies in distress, capping them with the deliverance of Amoret (wifely love) from the enchanter Busirane. In Book v, 6, she meets Sir Artegal, and after tilting with him discloses herself for a woman; he, removing his helmet, is instantly recognized by her as the object of her long search.

Brobdingnag (usually misspelled Brobdignag), an imaginary country described in Swift's *Gulliver's Travels*, inhabited by giants " as tall as an ordinary steeple " who are both amused and amazed by the insignificant stature of Lemuel Gulliver and by the account he gives them of his own country.

Brook, Master, in Shakespeare's comedy, *The Merry Wives of Windsor* (1601), the name assumed by Ford when Sir John Falstaff lays siege to his wife in order the better to turn the tables on the fat knight. In the Folio of 1623 the assumed name is Broome and not Brook. See FORD.

Brooke, Celia, in George Eliot's novel, *Middlemarch* (1871–1872), a sort of foil to her superior sister Dorothea. The latter says of her that she never did anything naughty since she was born, and she really never goes contrary to the normal sense of what is amiable and dutiful in woman. Less clever than Dorothea, she has more worldy wisdom; not feeling it her duty to reform or subvert the world, she can take her place in it naturally. Serenely happy in a happy home she does her best to help and alleviate the suffering within her reach.

Brooke, Dorothea, the principal female character in George Eliot's *Middlemarch* (1871–1872)—a sort of modern St. Theresa lost in a provincial environment, feeling out vaguely for some worthy outlet of her energies, aspiring to reform the world but quite ignorant of the means, idealizing the bloodless pedant Casaubon and marrying him only to wake to bitter delusion, and putting up at last with the gay trifler, Will Ladislaw, whom she marries after Casaubon's death.

Dorothea, brought up with Mr. Brooke in place of a parent, is to be a Theresa struggling under "dim lights and entangled circumstances." She is related, of course, both to Maggie and to Romola, though she is not in danger of absolute asphyxiation in a dense bucolic atmosphere, or of martyrdom in the violent struggles of hostile creeds. Her danger is rather that of being too easily acclimatised in a comfortable state of things, where there is sufficient cultivation and no particular demand for St. Theresas.—LESLIE STEPHEN, *George Eliot.*

She is described as a shortsighted girl, disliking lapdogs, but fond of a horse; with beautiful profile, beautiful bearing, and particularly beautiful and frequently ungloved hands; with perfect sincerity of delight, and as perfect straightforwardness and transparency of expression, though she cannot always make others understand her. —*Quarterly Review.*

Brooke, Squire, in George Eliot's novel, *Middlemarch* (1873), the bachelor uncle, Squire of Tipton Grange in Loamshire, with whom Celia and Dorothea reside. He is described as " a man of nearly sixty, of acquiescent temper, miscellaneous opinions, and uncertain vote." His conversation is of the same miscellaneous character as his opinions. The " scrappy slovenliness " with which he jerks out his disjointed talk is highly comical. He indulges a goodhumored illusion that he is a kind of undeveloped universal genius, a Crichton in posse who could have beaten his listeners at their own favorite weapons if he had cared to take the pains. Indeed his natural zeal for knowledge would have " carried him over the hedge," as he observes, " but I saw it wouldn't do — I pulled up; I pulled up in time."

Browdie, John, in Dickens's novel, *Nicholas Nickleby* (1838), a Yorkshire corn factor, a big, brawny, brusque but kindly man, talking the local dialect with a quaint infusion of his own verbal idiosyncrasies. When Nicholas meets him he is courting his future wife, 'Tilda Price, and he blurts out his uncalled for jealousy toward the spruce newcomer in noisy fashion. Once pacified, he is transformed into an exuberant friend of both Nickleby and Smike, and co-operates with the former in breaking up Dotheboys Hall. The original of this character is said to have been John S. Broodie, of Broodiswood, in Yorkshire, to whom Dickens bore a letter of introduction when he was getting local color for his novel. There is some kinship between Dickens's Browdie and Scott's Dandie Dinmont, which may not be altogether accidental.

Brown, Jessie, heroine of a poem, *The Relief of Lucknow,* by Robert S. Lowell. Shut up in the Hindoo city, beleaguered by Sepoy mutineers, Jessie Brown, a Scotch servant, is the first to hear the piping of the pibrochs that announce the arrival of British relief. In great joy she cries out:

The Highlanders! Oh, dinna ye hear
  The slogan far awa?
The McGregors? Ah, I ken it weel;
  It is the grandest of them a'.

Boucicault introduced the same
incident in his drama *Jessie Brown*
(1862). Both poet and dramatist
found it current in papers contemporary with the raising of the siege. But
it was a pure invention of a French
journalist. It was accepted for fact,
was copied as such into the English
papers, and will very likely live forever in history, though it was cate-
gorically denied by the Calcutta
correspondent of the London *Non-
conformist*. (See *Notes and Queries*,
VII, iii, 480, and II, v, 147, 425; also
Illustrated American, June 14, 1890.)

Brown, Matilda, more affectionately known as Miss Mattie, the
principal female character in Mrs.
Gaskell's *Cranford* (1853).

Her gentleness of heart and depth of
affection, her conscientious and dignified
sense of right, her perpetual shelter under
the precepts and counsels of beloved ones
who have gone before—invest the character
with an interest which is unique when her
weakness of intellect and narrowness of
training are also considered.—*Athenæum.*

Brown, Tom (*i.e.*, **Thomas**), hero
of two famous tales by Thomas
Hughes: *Tom Brown's School-days*
(1857) and *Tom Brown at Oxford*
(1861), illustrating respectively public
school and collegiate life in England.
A typical English boy of the higher
middle classes, with the wholesome
British virtues of pluck, honesty, and
a love of fair play,—he enters the
lowest form at Rugby and develops
from a homesick, timid lad into a big,
brawny fellow, a football hero and the
head of the school, and so passes on
to Oxford where he continues his
career on the same robust lines. In
the main " Tom " Hughes may have
drawn " Tom " Brown from himself;
but his schoolfellow, Rev. Augustus
Orlebar (1824–1913), was generally
recognized as the hero of the famous
fight with " Slugger " Williams which
set all Rugby rejoicing.

Brown, " Lieutenant " Vanbeest,
in Scott's novel, *Guy Mannering*, the
mate of Dirk Hatteraick's smuggling
vessel who brings up the kidnapped
Harry Bertram as his son and gives
him his name. He is fatally wounded
during the smugglers' attack on
Woodbourne. Glossin, finding that
the pseudo " Vanbeest Brown " is
really the heir to Ellangowan, tries
to ruin his cause by identifying him
with the smuggler.

Brummell, Beau, hero and title of
a drama by Clyde Fitch. The subject had previously been treated less
successfully by Blanchard Jerrold in
Beau Brummell, the King of Calais
(1859).

Brute, Sir John and **Lady,** leading
characters in Vanbrugh's comedy,
The Provoked Wife.

Sir John Brute is Vanbrugh's masterpiece.
Caricature though he be, there are many
touches of nature about him. He is the
beau inverted, the man of fashion crossed
with the churl. And he is fully conscious
of his dignity. " Who do you call a drunken
fellow, you slut, you?" he asks his wife.
"I'm a man of quality; the king has made
me a knight." His cry is "Liberty and
property, and old England, Huzza!" He
stands out in high relief by the side of Lady
Brute and Belinda who speak with the
accent of every day.—FELIX E. SCHELLING,
Cambridge History of English Literature,
viii, 183.

Buck, the canine hero of Jack
London's novel, *The Call of the Wild*
(1903), a St. Bernard shepherd dog
who feels the ancestral past surging
through blood and brain. Behind
him were the shades of all manner of
dogs and half wolves and wolves
dictating his moods and directing his
actions. " Deep in the forest a call
was sounding and as often as he
heard this call, mysteriously thrilling
and luring he felt compelled to turn
his back upon the fire and the beaten
earth around it, and to plunge into
the forest and on and on, he knew not
where or how."

Bucket, Inspector, the detective
officer in Dickens's *Bleak House.*

Neither Chaucer nor Molière has ever
breathed life into a child of his genius more
worthy and more sure of immortality.
Blathers and Duff, the Bow-Street runners,
will always hold a place in all men's affectionate remembrance, while gratitude
cherishes and admiration embalms the
name of Conkey Chickweed; but they are
faint and pale precursors of the incompar-

able Mr. Bucket. It is a crowning feather in the cap of Mr. Wilkie Collins that he alone should have been able to give us, in the person of Sergeant Cuff, a second detective officer worthy to be named in the same day with that matchless master of them all.—SWINBURNE, *Charles Dickens.*

Buckingham, George Villiers, the first Duke of, and his son, the second Duke, who bore the same name, both appear in the *Waverley Novels.* The first, " the omnipotent favorite both of the King [James I] and of the Prince of Wales "—called " Steenie " by the king from a fancied resemblance to the Italian pictures of Stephen the martyr—is a prominent character in *The Fortunes of Nigel* (1822). The second figures both in *Woodstock* (1826), where he is one of the gallants of Charles II's " wandering court," and in *Peveril of the Peak* (1823), where he continues to be " the most licentious and most gay " amid " the gay and the licentious of the laughing court of Charles." Dryden, in *Absalom and Achitophel* (1681), had caricatured this second Duke under the name of Zimri (*q.v.*), and Macaulay complains that Walter Scott, following too closely on the lines laid down by Dryden, has produced only a personified epigram. " Admiring, as every judicious reader must admire, the keen and vigorous lines in which Dryden satirized the Duke of Buckingham, Sir Walter attempted to make a Duke of Buckingham to suit them, a real living Zimri, and he produced not a man but the most grotesque of all monsters."

Bulba Taras, hero and title of a gruesome story (1839) of Cossack life in the fifteenth century by Nikolai F. Gogol. Taras is a strange compound of savagery and devotion. One of his sons Andrii turns traitor against the Cossacks, and Taras slays him. Another, Ostap, is captured and taken to Warsaw where he is tortured to death, Taras himself, in disguise, being a witness to the execution. Thereafter he is devoured by a mad passion for vengeance. He raises an army and pitilessly slays, burns and plunders, shouting always " This is a

mass for Ostap! " He is captured— one man against thirty—and burned to death, but in the midst of his last agonies he shouts a warning which saves his Cossack adherents.

Bull, John, a humorous personification of the English people, made his first appearance in John Arbuthnot's *History of John Bull* (1712), designed to ridicule the Duke of Marlborough (satirized as Hocus) and turn the nation against the French war. He is described as in the main an honest, plain-dealing fellow and of a very unconstant temper, " very apt to quarrel with his best friends especially if they pretended to govern him; if you flattered him you might lead him like a child. John's temper depended very much upon the air; his spirits rose and fell with the weather glass. John was quick and understood his business very well; but no man alive was more careless in looking into his accounts, or more cheated by partners, apprentices and servants. This was occasioned by his being a boon companion, loving his bottle and his diversion, for, to say truth, no man kept a better house than John, nor spent his money more generously." See also JOHN BULL in vol. II.

Bumble, Mr., in Dickens's *Oliver Twist* (1837), the beadle at the workhouse where Oliver was born, mean and cowardly and puffed up with the insolence of office. His courtship of Mrs. Corney, matron of the workhouse, his marriage to her, his failure to bully her into submission and eventual reduction to a figure-head in his own household, give point to his famous epigram when accused of theft. Pleading that " it was all Mrs. Bumble; she would do it," he is told " the law supposes that your wife acts under your direction." " If the law supposes that," said Mr. Bumble, squeezing his hat emphatically in both hands, " the law is a ass, a idiot. If that's the eye of the law, the law's a bachelor; and the worst I wish the law is, that his eye may be opened by experience—by experience."

Bumppo, Natty (*i.e.*, **Nathaniel**), the real name of a famous character who figures under various pseudonyms (the Deerslayer, Hawkeye, Leatherstocking and the Pathfinder) in a series of novels of frontier life in America by James Fenimore Cooper. These novels are known collectively as the *Leather stocking* series from Natty's most popular nickname. In the chronological order of incident, he appears in the following sequence: *The Deerslayer* (1841), which portrays his youth and early adventures; *The Last of the Mohicans* (1826), showing him in the prime of life, taking part in the romantic incidents of the old French war of 1756–1757; *The Pathfinder* (1840), describing his hopeless love for Mabel Dunham; *The Pioneers*, in which he is an old man of seventy back again in the regions near Lake Otsego where he had spent his boyhood; and *The Prairie* (1826), where he makes his last appearance as an octogenarian trapper on the upper Missouri, driven west by the inroads of civilization.

Of all the children of his brain, Natty Bumppo is the most universal favorite—and herein the popular judgment is assuredly right. He is an original conception—and not more happily conceived than skilfully executed. It was a hazardous undertaking to present the character backwards, and let us see the closing scenes of his life first—like a Hebrew Bible, of which the beginning is at the end; but the author's genius has triumphed over the perils of the task, and given us a delineation as consistent and symmetrical as it is striking and vigorous. Ignorant of books, simple and credulous, guileless himself, and suspecting no evil in others, with moderate intellectual powers, he commands our admiration and respect by his courage, his love of nature, his skill in woodland lore, his unerring moral sense, his strong affections, and the veins of poetry that run through his rugged nature like seams of gold in quartz.—*Atlantic Monthly.*

Buncle, John, hero of a novel by John Amory, *The Life of John Buncle, Esq.* (1766), a sort of innocent Bluebeard who marries seven wives and loses them all through no fault of his own, but with no diminution of his habitual vivacity. To stumble upon a fine country house, to find in it a lady of exquisite beauty and amazing intellectual qualifications, to marry her offhand and bury her in the next page, is Buncle's regular practice. Though his amours are all decorous he can be wild enough in other ways. He loses in one night's gambling " all the thousands he had gained by his several wives." He once drank for a day and a night, with a party all naked, except that they had on breeches, shoes, and stockings; and in that time he consumed so much burgundy that " the sweat ran of a red colour down his body." He was so bewildered by his potations that, on riding out for a little air, he leapt his horse into a frightful quarry and was only saved by descending into a deep pool. " This is a fact," he adds, " whatever my critics may say of the thing. All I can say to it is, my hour was not come."

Bungay, in Thackeray's *Pendennis*, a publisher who issues Arthur's novel and is financially interested in a proposed weekly, *The Pall Mall Gazette*. He is a caricature of Colburn, proprietor of the *New Monthly Magazine*. Colburn had decided against the publication of *Vanity Fair* when Thackeray submitted the earlier chapters to him.

Bungay or **Bongay, Friar,** in English folklore, a sort of familiar of Friar Bacon (who because of his experiments in natural science was held to be a magician in league with the powers of hell) and a co-practitioner of the Black Art. He appears in this character in Robert Greene's comedy, *Friar Bacon and Friar Bungay* (1594). After many astonishing exploits the piece concludes with the carrying off of one of their pupils on the back of a demon.

Bunsby, Captain Jack, in Dickens's *Dombey and Son* (1846), owner of the *Cautious Clara* and a great friend of Captain Cuttle, who looks up to him as " a philosopher and quite an oracle." With all his caution and prudence he is entrapped into an unwilling marriage by his landlady, Mrs. MacStinger. The captain had a very red face adorned with " one stationery and one revolving eye;" he wears " a rapt and imperturbable manner" and seems to be "always on the lookout for something in the extreme distance."

Burchell, Mr., in Goldsmith's novel *The Vicar of Wakefield*, the name under which Sir William Thornhill (*q.v.*) prefers to be known when he goes around as an incognito benefactor—a righter of the wrongs of the poor and oppressed.

Burgundy, Charles the Bold, Duke of (1433–1437), one of the greatest princes of Europe, whose mind was set upon extending the dominions of his house in every direction, but who came to grief at the siege of Nancy, appears as an important character in two of Walter Scott's novels, *Quentin Durward* and *Anne of Gierstein*.

Burke, Thomas, known familiarly as Tom, the hero of Charles Lever's historical romance, *Tom Burke of Ours* (1844). The orphaned son of an Irish gentleman, he gets mixed up when little more than a child in an Irish plot against the government, is arrested, contrives to escape, and flees to France, where he enters the *école militaire* and is given a commission by Napoleon himself. Subsequently he is unjustly suspected of complicity in the Chouan conspiracy in which Georges Cadoual loses his life, takes his trial with the leaders, and is saved only by the intercession of personages in high places. This is an historical novel of the old school, in which an obscure Irishman mixes in the best society, is always on the spot at the right moment, and is invariably in the confidence of his generals. Napoleon—the Napoleon of fiction, tender at one moment, cruel at the next—figures largely in the tale, and Tom is frequently in his presence, on one occasion actually saves his life, and at the end meets him by accident at Fontainebleau on the eve of his abdication.

Burleigh, Lord of, in Tennyson's ballad of that title, a landscape painter who wooes and weds a simple village maiden and after the ceremony takes her to a magnificent country seat, where numerous attendants bow down before him and informs her that all she sees is hers and his—for he is the Lord of Burleigh, the greatest man in all the country. But "the burden of a greatness to which she was not born" proved too much for the little country girl, and in a few years she faded away and died.

Tennyson has founded his poem on a slender basis of fact. Henry Cecil, heir to the Earldom of Exeter, unhappily married to Emma Vernon of Hanbury and oppressed with debts, retired to the village of Bolas Common in Shropshire where he assumed the incognito of Mr. Jones. Here he fell in love with a country girl, whose unromantic name was Sarah Hoggins. Despite the difference in their ages—for she was fifteen and he was thirty-five—he married her as soon as he could obtain a divorce. He lived with his wife several years in Bolas, until his uncle, the Earl of Exeter, discovered his retreat and invited the young people to come and live with him at Burleigh Hall, the family seat. On the death of the uncle Cecil became Earl, and, subsequently, Marquis of Exeter. The "fading" of Sarah appears to have been a slow one, for she left three children.

It is a curious coincidence that the story of how a lover of apparently low degree discovers himself after marriage to be both noble and wealthy is a common one in the ballad literature of all countries. The Scotch alone have four well-known versions: *Donald of the Isles, Earl Richmond, Lizie Lindsay, Huntingtower.*

Burley, John, in Bulwer-Lytton's *My Novel*, an impoverished ne'er-do-well, a literary hack, never sober, never solvent, but always genial, always witty, preserving through a wild and dissipated life something of the innocence and freshness of his childhood, and, on his death-bed, like Falstaff, babbling of green fields.

Burns, Helen, in Charlotte Brontë's *Jane Eyre*, the school-fellow of the heroine at Lowood school, a gentle, patient, long-suffering girl who finally succumbs to the cruel treatment of

Mrs. Scatcherd. She is drawn from Charlotte's sister Maria who was carried out dying from the school at Cowan's Bridge near Leeds, " as exact a transcript," says Mrs. Gaskell, " as Charlotte's wonderful power of reproducing character could give." Mrs. Gaskell adds that Charlotte's heart " beat, to the latest day on which we met, with unavailing indignation at the worrying and cruelty to which her gentle, patient, dying sister " was subjected by the original of Mrs. Scatcherd.

Busiris, hero and title of a bloody and bombastic tragedy (1718) by Edward Young. Busiris, king of Egypt, has murdered his predecessor on the throne and in turn is plotted against by Memnon. In the end he dies of wounds received in conflict, his wife Myris is torn to pieces by the mob and his son Myron is slain by Memnon. A story told of this monarch by Herodotus (ii, 59–61) is typical of his rough and ready humor. It is thus versified by Ovid in the *Art of Love:*

'Tis said that Egypt for nine years was dry:
Nor Nile did floods, nor heaven did rain supply.
A foreigner at length informed the king '
That slaughtered guests would kindly moisture bring.
The king replied "On thee the lot shall fall;
Be thou, my guest, the sacrifice for all."

In *Paradise Lost,* i, 306, Milton identifies Busiris with the Pharaoh drowned in the Red Sea.

Bussy, D'Ambois, hero and title of a tragedy (1607) by George Chapman, and of its sequel, *The Revenge of Bussy D'Ambois* (1613). It is founded on fact; D'Ambois was a gentleman of the court of Henry III of France whose love for a married lady resulted in his assassination.

Chapman, the writer who in fulness and fire of thought approaches most nearly to Shakespeare, is an ardent worshipper of pure energy of character. His Bussy D'Ambois cannot be turned from his purpose even by the warnings of the ghost of his accomplice, and a mysterious spirit summoned expressly to give advice. Pure, undiluted energy, stern force of will, delight in danger for its own sake, contempt for all laws but the self-imposed—those are the cardinal virtues and challenge our sympathies even when they lead the possessor to destruction.—LESLIE STEPHEN: *Hours in a Library,* iii, 26.

Buttercup, Little, in Gilbert and Sullivan's comic opera *H. M. S. Pinafore* (1877), the bumboat woman, responsible for having changed at nurse the two babes who grow up respectively to be Ralph Rackstraw and the Captain of the *Pinafore.* An earlier study in the same stratum of life was Poll Pineapple in the *Bumboat Woman's Story,* one of Gilbert's *Bab Ballads,* who dressed herself in seaman's clothes and sailed with Lieutenant Belaye in the *Hot Cross Bun.* One day the lieutenant announced that he had just married her, when all the crew fainted. For it turned out that all were females who had disguised themselves to follow the fascinating lieutenant.

Buzfuz, Sergeant, in the *Pickwick Papers* (1836), by Charles Dickens, a pleader retained by Dodson and Fogg for the plaintiff in the famous breach-of-promise case, Bardell v. Pickwick. He is a capital caricature of the blatant and boisterous forensic orator and the brutal and insolent cross-examiner, and is said to have been studied from Sergeant Bompas, a London criminal lawyer of much celebrity in his day.

Byron, Cashel, the pugilist hero of George Bernard Shaw's novel, *Cashel Byron's Profession.* The son of an English actress, he ran away from school, worked his passage to Australia, made his mark (in more senses than one) in the eye of the antipodean public, and returned to England to find a patron and backer in Lord Worthington, an enthusiastic supporter of the manly art of self-defence. Installed in a cottage on Lydia Carew's estate, he is given out to be an invalid, but in reality is in strict training for a prize-fight. The situation is developed with perfect disregard for conventionality and constant resort to the unexpected until it reaches its impossible yet logical conclusion, Lydia, for all her cleverness, being the last to penetrate Cashel Byron's disguise, and, when recognition is forced upon her, defying the traditions of her caste with imperturbable equanimity.

Byron, Miss Harriet, in Richardson's *Sir Charles Grandison* (1754), an orphan of great personal charms (enhanced by the possession of a comfortable fortune of £15,000) who falls in love at first sight with the titular hero and eventually marries him, despite the rival claims of the Lady Clementina.

C

Cabestainy, William, hero of a lay sung by Thiebault in Scott's *Anne of Geierstein.* Cabestainy was a troubadour who had an intrigue with Margaret, wife of Baron Raymond de Roussillon. The baron assassinated him and ordered his heart to be dressed and served to the lady. She declared that after food so precious " no coarser morsal should ever after cross her lips." The story may be found in Boccaccio's *Decameron.*

Cadenus (an anagram of *decanus,* " dean "), the name which Dean Swift gives himself in the poem *Cadenus and Vanessa* (1726). See VANESSA.

Cadurcis, Lord, in Disraeli's *Venitia,* a poet and an active political intriguer during the period subsequent to the coalition ministry of Lord North. He is drawn from Lord Byron, as his friend Marmion Herbert is drawn from Shelley, but there is a purposed confusion between fact and fiction. Venitia is the daughter of Herbert and the wife of Cadurcis.

Cadwallader, Rev. Mr., in George Eliot's novel, *Middlemarch* (1872), the rector of the parish, a provokingly amiable man. " He even spoke well of his bishop." A little more acerbity is conceded to Mrs. Cadwallader, his wife, a bright bit of worldly commonsense who distributes epigrams among her provincial acquaintances, quite like a well-educated Mrs. Poyser.

Cadwallon, in Scott's romance, *The Betrothed,* the chief bard of Gwenwyn, a Welsh prince. Swearing revenge after his master was slain by Hugo de Lacy, he assumes the name and guise of Renault Vidal, a minstrel, accompanies Sir Hugo to the crusade and seeks to compass his death.

Cæsar, Julius (B.C. 100–44), the greatest of all the Romans, dictator and undisputed master of the Roman world from the defeat of the Pompeian army at Thapsus, April 6, B.C. 46, until his own assassination by Brutus and other conspirators on March 15, 44 B.C. He is a prominent character in many English and European plays of which preëminently the chief is Shakespeare's *Life and Death of Julius Cæsar* (1601). Shakespeare does scant justice to the splendid abilities and noble nature of the dictator. He follows in outline the story told by P utarch but almost as a burlesque might follow the outlines of a heroic drama. His Julius Cæsar is little more than a glorified Parolles, a bombastic Braggadochio who saves the play from failure by his lucky removal in Act iii, Sc. 1. George Bernard Shaw echoes a favorite opinion when he boldly says that " it is impossible for even the most judicially minded critic to look without a revulsion of indignant contempt at this travestying of a great man as a silly braggart, whilst the pitiful gang of mischief-makers who destroyed him are lauded as statesmen and patriots. Mr. Shaw adds: " There is not a single sentence uttered by Shakespeare's Julius Cæsar that is, I will not say worthy of him, but even worthy of an average Tammany boss."

Shaw avowed that he wrote his own *Cæsar and Cleopatra* (1898) " to give Shakespeare a lead."

" Shakespeare's Cæsar is the *reductio ad absurdum* of the real Julius Cæsar." Mr. Shaw once remarked to me: " My Cæsar is a simple return to nature and history."— ARCHIBALD HENDERSON: *George Bernard Shaw,* p. 332.

Cæsar, in fact, is the one blot on the play, and I wonder that Shakespeare did not recognise the fiasco. There is an obvious

6

reason why we cannot accept Cæsar as he is here presented. He appears merely as a subordinate figure, with very little time to disport himself on the stage. Our notion of the real Cæsar is a notion of such awe, he looms so largely over us, that we could not possibly be illuded by a stage-figure of him unless it were a central and dominant figure, elaborately created. Also, we think of Cæsar always as a man of enormous power, a conqueror, a bender of wills; whereas here he is presented as a purely passive figure in the hands of fate and of a few men who disliked him. Historically this presentment of him is right enough, but dramatically it is no good at all. Had Shakespeare shown him to us first in all the majesty of his will, then the coming of his doom would move us. We should echo the warnings of Calpurnia, and, with the soothsayer, clutch at his toga as he passes to the Senate. But, as we hardly see him except under the immediate shadow of his doom, our imagination is unstirred: we do not see Cæsar, but only a stage-puppet, a transparent ghost.—MAX BEERBOHM: *Saturday Review*, September 15, 1900.

Cain, the son of Adam and and slayer of his brother Abel (Genesis, Chap. iv), is the hero of Byron's *Cain, a Mystery* (1821). It is called " a mystery," Byron explains, in conformity with the title annexed by mediæval authors to dramas dealing with Biblical subjects. Byron assumes with Cuvier that the world had been destroyed several times before the creation of man. His attempt to re-state the metaphysical or theological problem of the origin of evil raised a storm of remonstrance. The " parsons preached at it from Kentish Town to Pisa." " Even," says Byron, " the very highest authority in the land, King George IV, expressed his disapprobation of the blasphemy and licentiousness of Lord Byron's writings! " Better judges thought differently. Scott, to whom the Mystery was dedicated, said that the author " had matched Milton on his own ground." Shelley declared that " it was a revelation never before communicated to man." Campbell's summary of the central theme is concise and clear. " Cain," says Campbell, " disdains the limited existence allotted to him; he has a rooted horror of death, attended with a vehement curiosity as to its nature; and he nourished a sullen anger against his parents, to whose misconduct he

ascribes his degraded state. Added to this, he has an insatiable thirst for knowledge beyond the bounds prescribed to mortality; and this part of the poem bears a strong resemblance to *Manfred*, whose counterpart indeed, in the main points of character, Cain seems to be."

Caius, Dr., in Shakespeare's comedy, *The Merry Wives of Windsor*, an irascible French physician whose clipped English is amusing. A suitor to Anne Page, he sends a challenge to his imagined rival, Parson Evans.

Calantha, heroine of John Ford's tragedy, *The Broken Heart* (1633). Daughter of the King of Laconia (Sparta), she is wooed and won by Ithocles through the initiative of his sister Penthea. While presiding over the court revels she hears in quick succession of the death of her father, of the starving of Penthea, and finally of the murder of Ithocles, who has been lured into a chair with secret springs and there stabbed by Orgilus. She finishes the dance as though nothing had happened; in the next scene places a ring upon the finger of the dead Ithocles, and, brokenhearted, falls dead.

I do not know where to find, in any play, a castrophe so grand, so solemn and so surprising as this. The fortitude of the Spartan boy who let a beast gnaw out his bowels till he died, without expressing a groan, is a faint bodily image of this delaceration of the spirit and exenteration of the inmost mind, which Calantha, with a holy violence against her nature, keeps closely covered till the last duties of a wife and queen are fulfilled.— CHARLES LAMB.

Caledonia, the ancient Latin name of Scotland, which still survives in poetry and semi-jest.

O Caledonia, stern and wild,
Meet nurse for a poetic child!
SIR WALTER SCOTT.

Calendau, hero and title of a narrative poem (1867) by Frédéric Mistral, a poor fisherman in Cassis Provence who falls in love with a strange lady recently come to the neighborhood. He learns that she is the virgin bride of an outlaw, Count Severan, whom she had unwittingly married and abandoned on learning the truth. He seeks the count and his bandit crew in the castle of Aiglun, challenges him to mortal combat, but is disarmed and cast into a dungeon. Through one of the outlawed women, who had fallen in love with him, Calendau is released and flies to the rescue of his lady, knowing too well that Severan is in pursuit of her. He arrives just in time to hold the bandits at bay until the people rush to the assistance of the lover and his lady. Severan is killed and Calendau married his widow.

Caliban, in Shakespeare's comedy, *The Tempest,* a misshapen monster curiously anticipating the " missing link " between man and beast which caused a good deal of semi-scientific mirth in the early days of the Darwinian controversy. The name is a metathesis or verbal reconstruction of cannibal. He is represented as the " freckled whelp " of Sycorax, a loathsome hag who had been banished to Prospero's island from her native Argier (Algiers). Robert Browning has a poem *Caliban upon Setebos, or Natural Theology in the Island,* which is an ingenious attempt to enter into the mind of this monster and picture his concept of a Diety. See SETEBOS.

It was this character of whom Charles I and some of his ministers expressed such fervent admiration; and among other circumstances most justly they admired the new language almost with which he is endowed for the purpose of expressing his fiendish and yet carnal thoughts of hatred to his master. Caliban is evidently not meant for scorn, but for abomination mixed with fear and partial respect. He is purposely brought into contrast with the drunken Trinculo and Stephano, with an advantageous resul. He is much more intellectual than either, uses a more elevated language not disfigured by vulgarisms, and is not liable to the low passion for plunder as they are. He is mortal, doubtless, as his "dam" (for Shakespeare will not call her mother) Sycorax. But he inherits from her such qualities of power as a witch could be supposed to bequeath. He trembles indeed before Prospero; but that is, as we are to understand, through the moral superiority of Prospero in Christian wisdom; for when he finds himself in the presence of dissolute and unprincipled men, he rises at once into the dignity of intellectual power. —DE QUINCEY.

Calidore, Sir, in Spenser's *Faërie Queene,* Books v and vi, the type of chivalry and courtesy, evidently modeled after Sir Philip Sydney. In Canto xii of Book v he begins his quest of the Blatant Beast (*q.v.*) which had escaped from Sir Artegal. His first exploit is to make Lady Briana remit her discourteous toll of " the locks of ladies and the beards of knights " (vi, 1). Falling in love with Pastorella, a shepherdess, he assumes shepherd's guise and helps her tend his sheep until she is carried off by bandits, when he dons again helmet and spear, rescues the lady, leaves her to be cared for at Belgard Castle, and resumes his quest for the Blatant Beast. After a terrible fight with the monster he succeeds in chaining and muzzling it and drags it after him. But it breaks loose again as it had done before.

Sir Calidore was a favorite character with Keats who made him the hero of a fragment entitled *Calidore,* where, after an elaborate preparation for a " tale of chivalry " and a description of the " ambitious heat of the aspiring boy," Calidore succeeds in doing nothing but help two ladies to descend from their palfreys.

Calista, heroine of Nicholas Rowe's *Fair Penitent* (1703) and wife of Altamont. Detected in an intrigue with Lothario, the latter is slain by Altamont, and Calista stabs herself.

The character of Calista is quite in the *bravura* style of Massinger. She is a heroine, a virago, fair, a woman of high spirit and violent resolutions, anything but a penitent. She dies, indeed, at last, not from remorse for her vices, but because she can no longer gratify them.—HAZLITT.

Callista, heroine of Cardinal Newman's historical romance, *Callist:: a Sketch of the Third Century* (1855). A beautiful Greek girl, a sculptress, who sings like a Muse, dances like a Grace and recites like Minerva, she is beloved by Agellius, a Christian; is herself converted through the agency of Cyprian, who gives her the Gospel of St. Luke; suffers martyrdom and is canonized, her death proving the revival of the church at Sicca where she died. Agellius, who becomes a bishop after her death, is likewise martyred and sainted.

Callum Beg, Little, a page in the service of Fergus McIvor in Scott's novel *Waverley* (1814), passionately devoted to his master, but "a spirit naturally turned to daring evil and determined by the circumstances of his situation to a particular kind of mischief." Though ready to protect Edward Waverley's life when he deems him the friend of Fergus, he is equally willing to take it in his master's supposed interest.

Calmady, Sir Richard, in the novel of that name (1901) by Lucas Malet, was born a beautiful, healthy child save for one terrible deformity—the lower part of each leg is missing, the feet being attached at the point where the knees should be.

Lucas Malet has done her best to make Sir Richard Calmady repulsively attractive. But we cannot all be expected to love him because he is horrible, as Helen does. Physical deformity in real life excites pity; deformity invented for the novel or the stage excites only disgust. In the last generation there was an Irish member of parliament who had neither legs nor arms. He rode and drove. People forgot his deformity, or took it for granted, though they admired his pluck and skill. If his biography had been written, it would have been futile affectation to ignore his defects. Sir Richard Calmady's leglessness is never for an instant forgotten. That is the difference, the Aristotelian and the real difference between history and art.—*Blackwood's Magazine.*

Calvo, Baldassare, in George Eliot's novel, *Romola*, the adopted father of Tito Melemma. Tito abandons him when he falls into the hands of pirates, appropriates his goods, and is hounded to his death by the vindictive Baldassare.

Camille, heroine of a famous American adaptation of a famous French play. The latter was *The Lady of the Camelias* (*La Dame aux Camélias*) by Alexander Dumas, Fils. It ran for 200 nights in Paris, a marvellous success in 1852. Among its auditors was an American actress, Miss Jane Lander Davenport, who procured a copy of the play, paraphrased it under the title *Camille, or*

the Fate of a Coquette, and produced it in New York, October 9, 1853, with herself in the title part. Three years later (January 22, 1857) Matilda Heron appeared as Camille in a new version made by James Mortimer, and she and her play held possession of the American stage for an unprecedented period, to be followed by Clara Morris in 1874 with almost equal éclat. See GAUTHIER, MARGUERITE, and DU PLESSIS, MADELEINE.

Camillo, in Shakespeare's comedy, *A Winter's Tale*, a lord of Sicilia. See POLIXENES.

Camiola, heroine of Massinger's drama, *The Maid of Honor* (1637) represented as a lady of wealth, spirit and beauty in love with Bertoldo, whose ransom she pays only to meet with ingratitude.

Camiola, the Maid of Honor, deserves this appellation though perhaps the poet impaired the nobleness of her presence and of her actions by two superfluous additions: the violence of her refusal of an unwelcome, boisterous wooer—whose bodily defects she criticises in a strain approaching, though by no means equalling, the invectives which the passionate Donusa hurls at the head of the unfortunate basha of Aleppo when he comes to court her—and the cautious contract (taken from the source of the play) by which Bertoldo, to liberate whom Camiola spent a fortune, is placed under an obligation to marry her.—EMIL KOPEL: *Cambridge Library of Literature.*

Camors, hero of a novel, *M. de Camors* (1867), by Octave Feuillet. His father, a suicide, bequeathes him a letter of solemn warning and advice embodying certain precepts learned too late to save himself from ruin. "Recognize," said this cynical aristocrat, "that there is no such thing as vice or virtue. ᴮe absolutely and consistently selfish. Cast off all natural ties, instincts, affections and sympathies, as so many shackles on your liberty." The son deliberately fashions his life on these principles, works hard, amasses a fortune, indulges in elegant dissipation, seduces his cousin, whose husband dies on discovering her shame, and at last, weary of his mistress, writhing under the scorn of his wife, whom he had married for convenience, but whom too late he learns to appreciate, sick of the world and of his own life he dies unrepentant and hopeless.

Campaigner, The Old, in Thackeray's novel, *The Newcomes*, nickname given to Mrs. Mackenzie (*q.v.*) the mother of Rosa.

Camus, in Milton's *Lycidas*, a personification of the Cam, the stream on which Cambridge is situated. He is thus described:

Next, Camus, reverend sire, went footing slow,
His mantle hairy and his bonnet sedge,
Inwrought with figures dim, and on the edge
Like to that sanguine flower inscribed with woe.
"Ah, who hath reft," quoth he, "my dearest pledge."

Commenting on this passage Masson says: "He comes attired in a mantle of the hairy river-weed that floats on the Cam; his bonnet is of the sedge of that river, which exhibits peculiar markings, something like the *ià, ià* (alas! alas!) which the Greek detected on the leaves of the hyacinth, in token of the sad death of the Spartan youth from whose blood the flower had sprung."

Candida, heroine and title of a comedy by George Bernard Shaw. A practical, prosaic English matron, free from all "emotional slop," she remains true to her commonplace husband, James Morrell, for "natural reasons, not for conventional ethical ones." She loves him; she is not carried away by the ecstasies of the brilliant and erratic Eugene Marchbanks (evidently drawn from the poet Shelley) who wishes her to fly with him. As to the latter she "makes a man of him by showing him his own strength—that David must do without poor Uriah's wife." The quoted passages are from a letter written by the dramatist to James Huneker. See ARCHIBALD HENDERSON: *George Bernard Shaw*, p. 346.

The wife is asked to decide between two men, one a strenuous, self-confident popular preacher, her husband, the other a wild and weak young poet, logically futile and physically timid, her lover, and she chooses the former because he has more weakness and more need of her. Even among the plain

and ringing paradoxes of the Shaw play this is one of the best reversals or turnovers ever effected.—G. K. CHESTERTON: *George Bernard Shaw*, p. 120.

Candide, hero and title of a satirical romance (1758) by Voltaire, a young man of ingenuous mind and excellent principles brought up in the castle of Baron von Thunder-ten-tronch by the celebrated Dr. Pangloss (*q.v.*), whose theory is that everything is for the best in this best of all possible worlds. The Baron kicks Candide out of the castle because he loves and is caught kissing the fair and fat Cunegonde, daughter of the house, and Candide wanders from place to place in this best of all possible worlds, everywhere receiving fresh buffets from fortune, until at last, after all sorts of mishaps, he and his Cunegonde and Dr. Pangloss are reunited in Turkey upon a modest farm where Candide sententiously announces his own philosophy of life: "Il faut cultiver son jardin" ("one must cultivate one's garden"). Goethe put the same idea in another form: "Do the duty that lies nearest you."

Candour, Mrs., in Sheridan's comedy, *The School for Scandal* (1777), a typical female slanderer and backbiter.

The name of Mrs. Candour has become one of those formidable bywords which have more power in putting folly and ill-nature out of countenance than whole volumes of the wisest remonstrance and reasoning.— THOMAS MOORE, *Life of R. B. Sheridan.*

Cantwell, Dr., the English Tartuffe. He is the leading character in Isaac Bickerstaff's comedy, *The Hypocrite* (1768), which is founded on Molière's *Tartuffe.* Meek in appearance, saintly by mealy-mouthed profession, he makes his garb of holiness a cloak for sensuality and greed until he overreaches himself by his treachery toward Lady Lambert and her daughter and is arrested as a swindler. The character has none of the finesse or plausibility of Molière's hero. "He is a sturdy beggar and no more," complains Hazlitt; "he is not an impostor but a bully. There is not in anything that he says or does, in his looks, words, or actions, the least reason that Sir John Lambert should admit him into his house or friendship." Bickerstaffe's comedy, instead of coming directly from the French, was adapted from Cibber's adaptation, *The Non-juror* (1717). See MAWWORM.

Canty, Tom, in Mark Twain's romance, *The Prince and the Pauper* (1881), a young beggar who is the physical double of Edward, Prince of Wales, son of Henry VIII. In a boyish freak the prince and he change clothes, the attendants fail to comprehend the situation, Edward is driven out to wander in the streets of London, while Tom is installed in his place. All the pauper's vagaries and solecisms are ascribed to a sudden derangement of the prince's mind, and the mistake is not cleared up until Tom is on the point of being crowned as Edward VI. The real prince turns up at the Cathedral and proclaims his rights just as the crown is being placed on the head of Tom, who insists on changing places with the beggarly claimant, though the courtiers are loath to believe that Tom is not the prince. There is a likeness in the plot to the medieval legend of King Robert of Sicily.

Caponsacchi, Giuseppe, in Browning's poem, *The Ring and the Book,* the chivalrous priest, canon of Arezzo, who aided Pompilia in her flight to Rome from the tyranny of Count Guido. All Rome is divided on the question whether he was or was not, her lover.

Capulets, in Shakespeare's tragedy, *Romeo and Juliet,* a noble family in Verona at feud with the Montagues. Romeo was a Montague, Juliet a Capulet, hence the bloody abyss that separated the lovers. The Italian names which Shakespeare remodelled to his own use were Capelletti and Montecchi or Monticoli, two rival families whose jealousies disturbed the peace of Verona in the last half of the thirteenth and first half of the fourteenth century. The familiar expression—"the tomb of the Capulets," was invented by Burke, who

first used it in a letter to Matthew Smith. Shakespeare makes the head of the Capulets a man of mingled mirth and wrath, jovial with his friends, irascible and vindictive to his enemies. Lady Capulet shares his pride and his hates, but has no laughter in her make-up.

The Lady Capulet comes sweeping by with her train of velvet, her black hood, her fan and her rosary—the very beau-ideal of a proud Italian matron of the fifteenth century, whose offer to poison Romeo in revenge for the death of Tybalt stamps her with one very characteristic trait of the age and country. Yet she loves her daughter, and there is a touch of remorseful tenderness in her lamentation over her which adds to our impression of the timid softness of Juliet and the harsh subjection in which she has been kept.—MRS. JAMESON: *Heroines of Shakespeare's Plays.*

Careless, in Sheridan's comedy, *The School for Scandal* (1777), one of the boon companions of Charles Surface. Ned Careless, in Colley Cibber's *Double Dealer* (1700), makes love to Lady Plyant. Another Careless in Cibber's *Double Gallant* is described as "a fellow that's wise enough to be but half in love, and makes his whole life a studied idleness." The hero of Cibber's *Careless Husband* is Sir Charles Easy (*q.v.*).

Cargill, Rev. Josiah, in Scott's novel, *St. Ronans' Well,* the minister of St. Ronans, a mild, melancholy, absented man—pitied, blamed, loved or laughed at alternately by his parishioners. "All the neighborhood," we are told, "acknowledged Mr. Cargill's serious and devout discharge of his ministerial duties; and the poorer parishioners forgave his innocent peculiarities in consideration of his unbounded charity."

Carker, James, in Dickens's *Dombey and Son* (1846), a plausible villain, business manager to Mr. Dombey, who elopes with Dombey's wife and is killed in a railway accident. His chief physical peculiarity is a set of teeth whose glistening whiteness and regularity are "quite distressing." He showed his teeth whenever he spoke and smiled so wide a smile that "there was something in it like the snarl of a cat." Enjoying the confidence of his employer he speculates on his own account and amasses a fortune. A sharp contrast to this whited sepulchre with his hypocritical subservience to his employer is James's brother John, who having robbed the firm in his thoughtless youth and been forgiven makes restitution by years of faithful service. The sister, Harriet Carker, is a gentle and beautiful girl who marries Mr. Morfin.

Carlisle, Lady, in Browning's tragedy, *Strafford*, a nonhistorical personage whom the poet introduces in order to add a love element. He himself acknowledges that " the character of Lady Carlisle in the play is wholly imaginary.

Carne, Caryl, in Richard D. Blackmore's semi-historical novel, *Springhaven* (1887). A native of the English village of Springhaven, he is only half English by descent and all French in sympathy. Hence he is selected by Napoleon to prepare the way for his intended descent upon the English coast in 1805.

Carne owns a worthless estate and ruined castle close by Springhaven, and through him general misery and particular tragedy fall upon the little town. He is as cold-blooded and ruthless a traitor as ever sold his birthright, as picturesque a villain as ever served novelist a good turn.—*N. Y. Nation*, May 19, 1887.

Caroline, consort of George II, figures in Walter Scott's novel, *The Heart of Midlothian*, as Queen Regent during George's absence on the continent in 1736—the time of the Porteous riots. She is painted as accomplished, proud but just, ready at repairing any false step and loving " the real possession of power rather than the show of it." Though her relations with the Duke of Argyle were strained, she received his protégée, Jeanie Deans, and granted her petition.

Carpathian Wizard, so Milton styles Proteus in the song sung by Sabrina in *Comus:*

And the Carpathian wizard's hook.

He was reputed to dwell in a cave in the island of Carpathus, and he

had a hook because he was the shepherd of the sea calves.

Carson, Kit, is the hero of Joaquin Miller's poem, *Kit Carson's Ride.* Kit is supposed to tell the story of how on his wedding day he and his bride, and Revels his friend, were compelled to flee before a prairie fire, how they got entangled in a herd of affrighted buffaloes, how Revels dropped dead, how the bride succumbed, and how he himself was borne senseless into safety.

Christopher Carson (1809-68), better known as Kit, was a famous trapper and mountain guide in the Rocky Mountains and the adjacent territories.

Carstone, Richard, in Dickens's *Bleak House* (1853), is, with his cousin Ada Clare (later his wife), a ward in Chancery. Though naturally of a carefree and sanguine disposition, he is driven to melancholy and death by the collapse of his expectations when the Jarndyce case is finally closed and the whole estate is found to have been swallowed up in costs.

Carter, George Fairfax, hero of F. Hopkinson Smith's novel, *Colonel Carter, of Cartersville* (1896), an unreconstructed Virginia gentleman.

We have all met many Virginia types in print, but this one has a distinct difference from the rest in that he is brought down to date and is beheld floating in rosy stream clouds of railroad schemes. The impossibility of adjusting the street-raiment of commerce to the untrammelled spirit of a Southern chevalier leads to a hundred comicalities, which are never far from the pathetic and which are excellently told.—*N. Y. Nation*, June 11, 1891.

Carton, Sidney, principal character in Dickens' historical romance of the French Revolution, *A Tale of Two Cities* (1859). A young lawyer, he has wasted his talents in bohemian dissipation. His one redeeming trait is his pure and unselfish love for Lucie Manette, who marries Charles Darnay. Taking advantage of his resemblance to Darnay he substitutes himself for the latter in prison. As he rides to his death none but the little sewing girl in the tumbril with him knows his secret. Mounting the guillotine he has a vision of the Paris and France of the future. In his heart is the serenity of triumph: " It is a far, far better thing that I do than I have ever done; it is a far, far better rest that I go to than I have ever known."

Carvel, Richard, hero and title of a novel (1899), by Winston Churchill, whose scene is laid on both sides of the Atlantic before and during the Revolutionary period. Richard has been brought up by his grandfather, Lionel Carvel of Carvel Hall, Maryland, as the heir to the family estates. His fiery advocacy of the cause of the colonists makes it easy for an uncle, Grafton Carvel, to plot against him in the interests of Grafton's son Philip. Richard is kidnapped and smuggled aboard the pirate slaver *Black Moll;* the slaver is captured by John Paul, afterwards known as John Paul Jones. Paul and Richard become great friends and are thrown into the society of the most important personages in London. On the outbreak of the war Carvel enlists under Paul Jones and is in the great naval fight between the *Bonhomme Richard* and the *Serapis.* Peace restores him to his own and he marries Dorothy Manners with whom he has been in love from childhood.

Casabianca, titular hero of a short poem (1798) by Mrs. Felicia Hemans, founded upon a historical episode. He was a ten-year-old lad at the time he so stoutly met his death. His father, Louis Casabianca, was captain of the *Orient,* the flagship of the fleet that conveyed Napoleon and his troops to Egypt for his Nile campaign. At the battle of Aboukir, when the fleet was attacked by the English, Admiral Brueys was killed, and the command devolved upon Captain Casabianca. The *Orient* was struck and took fire, but he remained to the last, and went down with his ship. His ten-year-old son refused to leave the ship, and also perished.

Of course it was an act of sublime obedience in Casabianca to remain where his father had told him, to perish in the flames,

and in a child such an action was not only magnificent, but perfectly intelligible. But had he possessed the mental flexibility which comes with maturer years, he would probably have perceived that the tremendous change in the state of things on board the *Orient,* since his father's order was given, virtually cancelled that order, and restored to him his freedom of action. When the order was given the vessel was intact and in good fighting condition, and it was presumably for some useful strategic purpose that he was stationed at his post. His father was alive to direct the movements which the occasion required. . . .

The last thing his father would have desired was that he should stay to perish in the final explosion. Instead of indulging in that series of appeals to the wind which our poetess has emphasized with so much pathos, he should have flung himself into the waves, and endeavoured to save a life so precious to his family and to France.— *Saturday Review,* August, 22, 1874.

Casamassima, Princess, in Henry James's novel of that name (1887), is the Miss Isabella Light of Roderick Hudson, come to London with her beauty and splendor to forget her hated husband in semi-sincere sympathy with cockney socialists and semi-personal love-making with two of the handsomest among them.

Casaubon, Edward, in George Eliot's novel of English provincial life, *Middlemarch* (1871–1872), the first husband of Dorothea Brooke (*q.v.*), a dull, dry, dreary pedant, lean of person, with blinking eyes, white moles and formal phrases. He has labored for years over a *Key to all Mythologies* and in his pursuit of gods and goddesses has lost all clue to his fellow-men; in his burrowings into the past has loosened all hold upon the pleasures of the present. Solid Sir James Chettam remarks that he is a man with no good red blood in his veins. " No," retorts Mrs. Cadwallader. "Somebody put a drop under a magnifying glass and it was all semicolons and parentheses." Determined to correct the error of overstudiousness by marrying a young and beautiful wife he finds her in Dorothea who takes him at his own valuation but is speedily disillusionized. The situation is not without precedent in real life—one remembers Madame de Stael, when a prodigy of fifteen, gravely proposing to her parents that she should marry Gibbon, as fat a specimen of distinguished middle life as Casaubon was a lean one. Mark Pattison has been suggested as the possible original for this character and it is a curious coincidence that in 1875 he wrote a biography of Isaac Casaubon.

Mr. F. W. H. Myers tells the story of how one day George Eliot and her husband were making good-humored fun over the mistaken effusiveness of a friend who insisted on assuming that Mr. Casaubon was a portrait of Mr. Lewes and on condoling with the sad experiences which had taught the gifted authoress of *Middlemarch* to depict that gloomy man. "And there was, indeed, something ludicrous," says Mr. Myers, "in the contrast between the dreary pedant of the novel and the good-natured self-content of the living savant who stood acting his vivid anecdotes before our eyes." "But from whom, then," said a friend, turning to Mrs. Lewes, "did you draw Casaubon?" With a humorous solemnity which was quite in earnest, however, she pointed to her own heart.—WALSH: *Handy Book of Literary Curiosities*, p. 951.

Cass, Godfrey, in George Eliot's novel, *Silas Marner* (1861), the father of the little girl whom Marner adopts; whom Cass himself had disowned, and who disowns him later when he would fain reclaim her to comfort his childless age.

Cassio, Michael, in Shakespeare's tragedy, *Othello*, the hero's lieutenant, a young and handsome Florentine, introduced in i, 2. Iago, hating him for that he has been promoted above himself, implicates him in his plot against Desdemona.

Cassius, Caius, one of the conspirators against Cæsar (B.C. 44), married to Brutus's sister Junia, is introduced in Shakespeare's drama, *Julius Cæsar*, i, 2. His death occurs in iv, 3. He is keen, practical, prompt, energetic, severe and inexorable; his hatred of tyranny is mingled with envy of the man whose life he had once saved and for whose physical powers he feels contempt, and yet who seems about to " bestride the narrow world like a Colossus." A keen politician, he knows the special means to employ in influencing each of the confederates.

Castara (from Latin *casta*, fem. of *castus*, chaste, or perhaps *casta ara*,

sacred altar), a poetical name under which William Habington (1605–1654) celebrated the praises of Lucy, daughter of Lord Powis, whom he married.

Castlewood, Francis Esmond, fourth Viscount Castlewood, in Thackeray's novel, *Henry Esmond*, the Lord Castlewood of the story, patron of Henry and first husband of Lady Rachel. A good-natured profligate who neglects his wife and children, and gambles away his substance, he is killed in a duel with Lord Mohun, whose uninvited attentions to his wife he resents.

Castlewood, Rachel, Viscountess, the wife and later widow of the fourth Viscount, a principal character in Thackeray's *Henry Esmond*, the Lady Castlewood of the story, who eventually marries the hero, though she is seven years his senior. As the aged, white-haired but still lovely Rachel Esmond she reappears in *The Virginians*.

She is drawn from Mrs. Jane Octavia Brookfield, wife of Rev. William Brookfield (who himself figures in a *Punch* sketch, *The Curate's Walk*, as Rev. Frank Whitestock), with whom Thackeray kept up a correspondence that has found its way into print. Mrs. Brookfield survived her husband by twenty years.

"Had she been inclined to change her state and move in a higher and more exclusive sphere," write her biographers, "she had several opportunities for re-marrying, but her love for her children made her consider them, and she concluded to devote the rest of her life to them. She did not as a widow remain in retirement," but continued to enliven the company of her old friends, and graciously welcomed the new, "always surprised and pleased that she was still sought out and noticed."

"The distance of time," says Hannay, "at which the action of *Esmond* goes on, seems to have acted on Thackeray's imagination like a stimulant, for there is not only more romance, but more sentiment in *Esmond* than in his other fictions. That the hero, after having been the lover of Beatrix, should become the husband of her mother, jars on the feelings of some of his admirers. But it would be well worth their while to study, phase by phase, the admirable delicacy with which Henry Esmond's attachment is made to grow, and the exquisite art by which the final result is hinted at."

Caterina, the heroine of Meyer-beer's opera, *L'Etoile du Nord* (The Star of the North), founded upon the historical love of Catherine for her imperial husband, the faithless Czar Peter. This part was a favorite with Adelina Patti, because no other offered her more variety.

Those who wish to see and hear Mdme. Patti in as many costumes and as many characters as possible cannot do better than witness the performance of *L'Etoile du Nord*, with Mdme. Patti assuming turn by turn in that work the part of a waiting-maid at an inn, a fortune-telling gypsy, a young recruit, a sentinel, a young lady clothed in melancholy and white muslin, and finally a princess, sound as to body and mind and decked in robes of regal splendour.—*Pall Mall Gazette.*

Catesby, Monsignor, in Disraeli's *Lothair* (1871), the handsome, subtle and clever Roman Catholic dignitary who almost succeeds in converting Lothair to the Roman communion. In real life Monsignor Capel, from whom the portrait is drawn, did bring the Marquis of Bute, the original of Lothair, into the fold.

Cardinal Grandison is mainly founded upon Cardinal Manning with just a soupçon of his predecessor in the See of Westminster, Cardinal Wiseman. Monsignor Catesby is drawn direct from Monsignor Capel. In neither case did Disraeli take any pains to conceal the fact of portraiture. The models are unmistakably revealed. Indeed by a slip of the pen or of the types "Capel," instead of "Catesby," was printed in the third volume of the first edition.

Mgr. Capel never took umbrage at the notoriety he had acquired through *Lothair*. On the contrary, he revelled in it. It was his great stock in trade for a while, and finally it proved his temporary ruin. Folks, and especially the women folks, were more interested in Catesby than in Capel, and their worship of the real man was largely compounded of admiration for the fictitious character.—*N. Y. Times.*

Cathay (a corruption of the Tartar word Khitai), an ancient name for China said to have been introduced into Europe by Marco Polo, the Venetian traveller.

Better fifty years of Europe than a cycle of Cathay.
                TENNYSON: *Locksley Hall.*

Caudle, Mrs. Margaret, the mono-logist in *The Curtain Lectures*, by Douglas Jerrold. The full-blown flower of nagging womanhood, she has delivered for nearly thirty years a nightly lecture between the hours of 11 P.M. and 7 A.M. to her husband, Joe Caudle, usually in rebuke of some dereliction of duty on his part. Jer-rold used with good effect a new trick of humor whereby the reader is left to infer what the hen-pecked, sleepy husband had to offer in his attempted defence, from the acerbity of the conjugal retort and a fresh access of grumbling. The term " curtain lec-ture " sometimes credited to Jerrold is at least as old as Dryden:

Besides what endless brawls by wives are bred
The curtain lecture makes a mournful bed.

Caxton, Austin, in Bulwer Lytton's novel, *The Caxtons* (1849), and its sequels, *My Novel* (1853) and *What Will He Do with It?* (1858), a book-worm of vast learning and dreamy moods, neglectful of his own affairs, who yet can be waked up to unex-pected worldly wisdom in the manage-ment of other people's affairs. He is engaged on a great book, *The History of Human Error.*

Caxton, Pisistratus, son of the above, a bit of a prig but manly, good-hearted, sensible, who returns from Australia with funds to launch his father's magnum opus. His uncle, Captain Roland Caxton, is a narrow-minded man of robust honor and courage, full of sentimental affection for the ruined ancestral tower and its barren acres. Herbert Caxton, Roland's son, of gypsy blood on his mother's side, early turned against his father by maternal complaints, goes through life a pariah, but even-tually works out his own salvation, repents and enters the army. Not seeking death, but knowing that death alone can redeem his errors, he meets it bravely when it comes during a great victory.

Cecilia, heroine of Madame D'Ar-blay's novel of that name (1782).

Cedric of Rotherwood, in Scott's historical romance *Ivanhoe*, a Saxon thane, proud, fierce, jealous and irrit-able, who cherishes the dream of restoring the independence of his race with single-hearted enthusiasm. He disinherits his only son Wilfrid for seeking Rowena, whom he had destined for Athelstane.

Celadon, a shepherd in love with *Astree* (see ASTREA) in D'Urfy's prose pastoral of that name; hence a stock name for a lover in dramatic literature and pastoral poetry. Dryden confers the name upon the hero of his comedy, *Secret Love, or the Maiden Queen,* a witty, inconstant gallant who marries the like-minded Florimel on the understanding that neither shall interfere with the other.

In Thomson's *The Seasons: Summer* (1627), Celadon is a shepherd betrothed to Amelia. A lightning flash strikes her dead in his arms.

Besides its purely literary use the name is used in France as a common noun, a synonym for a constant and usually a platonic lover. Thus Gautier: "Sais tu que voilà tantot cinq mois cinq éternités, que je suis le celadon en pied de Mme. Rosette?"

Celestial City, in Bunyan's *Pilgrim's Progress,* the object of Christian's pilgrimage—the heavenly Jerusalem whose glories are described in the Apocalypse. Hawthorne, in his *Mosses from an Old Manse,* has an exquisite satire entitled *The Celestial City, or a Modern Pilgrim's Progress* in which the luxurious " progress " of the latter-day Christian is compared with the trials and tribulations of his predecessor.

Celestial Empire, in Europe and America, a popular and semi-humorous name for China roughly translating the Chinese Tien Chan (Heavenly Dynasty), meaning the kingdom ruled over by a heaven-appointed dynasty.

Celia, the name given by Thomas Carew, an English poet of the seventeenth century, to his lady-love, whose real name is unknown.

Celia, in Shakespeare's *As You Like It,* a cousin of Rosalind and her companion in the forest under the name of Aliena.

As You Like It would be one of those works which prove, as Landor said, long since the falsehood of the stale axiom that no work of man's can be perfect were it not for that unlucky slip of the brush which has left so ugly a little smear in one corner of the canvas as the betrothal of Oliver to Celia; though with all reverence to a great name and a noble memory I can hardly think that matters were much mended in George Sand's adaptation of the play by the transference of her hand to Jaques.— SWINBURNE: *A Study of Shakespeare* (1880).

Celimene, in Molière's comedy, *Le Misanthrope* (1666), a heartless flirt with whom Alceste is in love, until he discovers her worthlessness and flings her away. There is another Celimene in Molière's *Les Precieuses Ridicules,* but she has little or nothing to do with either action or dialogue. The Celimene of the *Misanthrope,* on the other hand, both by word and deed adds the last drop to the bitterness that brims the cup of the disillusioned Alceste. As Agnes is drawn from the childwife whom Molière had taken to his heart at forty, so Celimene is drawn from the abandoned but beautiful deceiver into whom that wife had matured in his latter days.

It is said that this strange and passionate play, so wonderfully different in tone from all those productions which we think of most when we name Molière, was the expression of his own wounded and outraged feelings. When betrayed by his wife and separated from her, he yet had to undergo the extraordinary ordeal of meeting the beautiful creature whom he loved and loathed, as man can love and loathe an unfaithful woman—on the stage and acting with her in that sombre travesty of their own spoiled existence, he the melancholy, proud Alceste, and she the brilliant, false Celimene.— OLIPHANT AND TARVER: *Molière.*

Cenci, Beatrice (1577-1599), in real life was one of a dozen infamous children of an infamous Roman, Francesco Cenci (1549-1598), the illegitimate son of a priest and a miser of great wealth. Harsh and tyrannical to all his family, he treated Beatrice with especial cruelty on discovering her intrigue with one of his stewards. There is no evidence that he outraged her, as legend avers. Finally Beatrice, with her stepmother Lucrezia, a friend of the family named Monsignor Guerra and two of her brothers, Giacomo and Bernardo, instigated the assassination of the father by hired bravos. Olimpio, one of these bravos, was probably Francesco's lover. Guerra escaped; the other conspirators were arrested and confessed the crime, though Beatrice denied everything until repeated tortures broke her spirit. Beatrice and Lucretia were beheaded, Giacomo was subjected to a cruel death, but Bernardo, on account of youth, was sentenced only to imprisonment.

Legend has amplified vulgar fact into lurid romance. Beatrice has been painted as the innocent victim of an unnatural father, joining with other members of her family in parricide only that she might escape from a life of incest. Francesco has been painted as a monster of crime and domestic tyranny. Such is the story presented by Shelley in his poetical tragedy, *The Cenci* (1819); by F. D. Guerrazzi in a prose romance, *Beatrice Cenci* (1872); and by numerous others. A famous portrait in the Barbcrini Palace at Rome, long attributed to Guido Reni, won for Beatrice the title of "The Beautiful Parricide." Later researches prove that she was not beautiful and that the portrait was not of her, nor was it painted by Guido Reni. See *Edinburgh Review*, January, 1879.

Cerdon, in Butler's satiric poem, *Hudibras*, i, 2, the boldest leader of the rabble which overwhelms Sir Hudibras at the bearbaiting. He is said to have been drawn from Colonel Hewson, a one-eyed soldier, cobbler and preacher, unwearied in his denunciations of bearbaiting and other worldly amusements.

Chadband, the Reverend Mr., in Dickens's novel, *Bleak House* (1853), a bland and hypocritical clergyman, attached to no particular denomination, who is fond of describing himself as a vessel, and affects contempt for carnal things, but is shamelessly devoted to the fleshpots and their possessors or distributers.

Chanticleer (Old Fr. Chantecler, from *chanter*, sing, and *cler*, clear), the name of the cock in the epic, *Reynard the Fox*. Chaucer took the same name for the barnyard hero of *The Nun Prieste's Tale* in his *Canterbury Tales*. More recently (1907) Edmond Rostand made Chanticleer the titular hero of a play which may be indebted for here and there a hint to Chaucer but is more evidently built around an epigram by Mrs. Poyser in George Eliot's *Adam Bede*. " He is velly like a cock that thinks the sun has risen a' purpose to hear him crow."

Cf. also the exquisite lines about the lark which John Lyly introduces into his comedy, *Alexander and Campaspe*.

How at heaven's gate she clapt her wings,
The morn not waking till she sings.

Character, A. Subject of a poem in Tennyson's *Juvenilia*. He has been identified by Hallam Tennyson with one Sunderland, "a very plausible, parliament-like and self-satisfied speaker at the Union Debating Society " in Cambridge University. Grant Duff, in *Notes from a Diary*, says that Sunderland was " a most extraordinary and brilliant person who lost his reason, and ended, I have been told, in believing himself the Almighty.

Charicles, hero and title of a classical romance (1830) by W. A. Becker, written to illustrate the manners and customs of Greece under Macedonian domination. Charicles is introduced as travelling (B.C. 329) from Argos to Corinth on his way to Athens. In the latter city he meets, wooes and marries Cleobule, a virgin widow of barely sixteen, to whom the aged Polycles, her husband only in name, leaves all his wealth.

Charles XII of Sweden. He is the hero of a historical drama (1828) by J. R. Planché, and of a historical sketch by Voltaire which, though admirably written, has some of the characteristics of romance. In *The Vanity of Human Wishes* (1749), a poetical satire, Dr. Johnson give a rapid sketch of his career, concluding with the famous couplet:

He left the name at which the world grew
pale
To point a moral or adorn a tale.

Charlotte, heroine of George Lillo's domestic tragedy, *Fatal Curiosity* (1736), the betrothed of young Wilmot (*q.v.*). She remains faithful to his memory after his supposed loss at sea and is the only one to recognize him on his return.

Charmian, in Shakespeare's *Antony and Cleopatra*, an amiable nonentity attendant on Cleopatra, who acts as a foil to that fiery queen. After Cleopatra's death she applied one of the asps to her own arm and fell dead when the Roman soldiers entered the room.

Charyllis, in Spenser's pastoral poem, *Colin Clout's Come Home Again* (1594), is readily identified with Anne, Lady Compton, fifth of the six daughters of Sir John Spenser of Althorpe, whom Spenser had already complimented by dedicating to her his satirical fable, *Mother Hubbard's Tale.* Spenser claims kinship with her in these lines:

No less praiseworthy are the sisters three,
The honor of the noble family
Of which I meanest boast myself to be;
Phyllis, Charyllis and sweet Amaryllis;
Phyllis the fair is eldest of the three,
The next to her is bountiful Charyllis.

Chastelard, hero of Swinburne's tragedy of that name, was a historical character, a gentleman of Dauphiny, who fell in love with Mary, Queen of Scots, was discovered in her bedroom and expiated his crime or his misfortune on the scaffold.

Chastelard himself, though drawn with complete delicacy and finish, is in truth only a subordinate person in the play, and is almost commonplace in comparison with his mistress. Mr. Swinburne presumed that the figure of a passionate lover, full of gracious courtesy and gentle knightly virtues and unbounded devotion, was so familiar as to be scarcely worthy the foremost place on his canvas. This is assigned to the beautiful, inhuman, bright Mary Stuart, whose character he has conceived with inexhaustible subtlety and depth, and represented with a rarely equalled perfection of light and colour and fire.—*Saturday Review.*

Chattan, Clan, in Scott's novel, *The Fair Maid of Perth*, a Highland clan whose rivalry with Clan Quhele tore the country to pieces. At the suggestion of King Robert III, a meeting was arranged on the North Inch of Perth between thirty picked warriors of each clan. After a terrific combat only twelve of the original combatants survived.

Chauvin, in Scribe's *Soldat Laboureux*, a veteran of the Napoleonic wars, with unbounded admiration for his former chief and blind idolatry of all that pertains to him.

Cheeryble, Brothers (Charles and Edwin), in Dickens's novel, *Nicholas Nickleby* (1838), twin brothers, partners in business, the benefactors and employers of Nicholas. In their large-hearted generosity and noble charity they are said to have been modelled on the Brothers Grant, cotton-mill owners of Manchester, England. In the original preface Dickens said that they were copied from life and that "their liberal charity, their singleness of heart, their nobleness of nature, and their unbounded benevolence are no creations of the author's brain." In a later edition he added:

If I were to attempt to sum up the hundreds of letters from all sorts of people, in all sorts of latitudes and climates, to which this unlucky paragraph has since given rise, I should get into an arithmetical difficulty from which I should not readily extricate myself. Suffice it to say that I believe the applications for loans, gifts, and offices of profit that I have been requested to forward to the originals of the Brothers Cheeryble (with whom I never exchanged any communication in my life) would have exhausted the combined patronage of all the Lord Chancellors since the accession of the House of Brunswick, and would have broken the rest of the Bank of England.

Cheese, Rev. Cream, in G. W. Curtis's Satire, *The Potiphar Papers* (1856), a high church Episcopalian clergyman, finnicky, effeminate, ultra refined and deeply versed in all the trivialities of religion, who gravely advises Mrs. Potiphar as to the color of the cover of her prayer book.

Cherubim, Don, the titular hero in Le Sage's novel, *The Bachelor of Salamanca*, who is interested in all varieties of life and character.

Chester, Emily, heroine and title of a novel by A. Moncure Seemuller (1864). It is Emily's misfortune to become in her early life an object of passionate devotion to a man for whom she feels intellectual sympathy, but physical repulsion. At a time of weakness and prostration she marries him but, with renewed strength, this feeling of repulsion returns with added force and continues until her death.

Chester, Sir John, in Dickens's *Barnaby Rudge* (1841), an elegant gentleman, punctiliously polite but heartless and unprincipled, evidently modelled upon the Lord Chesterfield of history. He seeks unsuccessfully to break off a match between his son Edward and Emma Havedale and is killed in a duel with that lady's father, Geoffrey Havedale.

Chettam, Sir James, in George Eliot's novel, *Middlemarch*, an easygoing, amiable baronet, the lover and eventually the husband of Celia Brooke.

Cheyne, Harvey N., hero of *Captains Courageous, a Story of the Grand Banks*, by Rudyard Kipling (1897). A selfish young brute, the spoiled child of an American millionaire, Harvey is washed overboard from a big Atlantic liner and is rescued by a Gloucester fishing schooner. Disko Troop, the skipper, scoffs at the boy's tale of his father's wealth and importance and sets him to hard work on the schooner. The change from a petted hot-air life to the rough and tumble of his new environment proves the saving of Harvey. When the season's end restores him to his parents he has become docile, self-reliant, well disciplined and physically fit.

Chickweed, Conkey, sometimes known as " Nosey," in Dickens's *Oliver Twist*, a thief who for a long time evaded detection by helping the police to chase innocent men.

Childe Harold. See HAROLD, CHILDE.

Chillingly, Kenelm, hero of Bulwer-Lytton's novel, *Kenelm Chillingly, His Adventures and Opinions* (1873), is the long-prayed-for heir to a noble family, whom he early alarms by his precocity and singularity. After graduating from Cambridge he leaves home in search of adventures, but periodically returns there and is ever welcome to his family and society, which is attracted by his charm, piqued by his eccentricities, and worshipful of his wealth and rank. With the temperament of the idealist Kenelm possesses a face and figure of unusual beauty, perfect health. and considerable skill in athletic exercises.

Chillingworth, Roger, in Hawthorne's *The Scarlet Letter* (1850), a physician, husband to Hester Prynne. Of cold, intellectual temperament, he is proud, cunning and vindictive. Finding that his wife has wronged him, and suspecting the Rev. Arthur Dimmesdale as her accomplice, he attaches himself to the latter, ostensibly to watch over his health, but in reality to detect his secret and gloat over his tortures.

Chingachcook, an Indian chief, called, by the French, *Le Gros Serpent* (the Big Serpent), who is prominent as a friend of Natty Bumpo in four of Cooper's novels: *The Deerslayer, The Pathfinder, The Last of' the Mohicans,* and *The Pioneer.*

> Chingachcook, with Uncas to supplement' him, is the ideal Indian—grave, silent, acute, self-contained, sufficiently lofty-minded to take in the greatness of the Indian's past, and sufficiently far-sighted to see the hopelessness of his future—with nobility of soul enough to grasp the white man's virtues, and with inherited wildness enough to keep him true to the instincts of his own race. Probably at his first appearance, in *The Pioneers,* this hero was a study from life. Afterward, when Cooper began to present him in youth and manhood, the character was idealized; but the ideal is a noble one, worthy to stand for the heights of the savage nature—a god-send to the later romancers, who have never been able to escape from him. Chingachcook appears at his best, perhaps, but under another name, in *The Last of the Mohicans.*—*The Native Element in Fiction. American Century,* vol. 28.

Chowne, Parson Stoyle, in Blackmore's novel, *The Maid of Sker,* a man of family, a clergyman and a justice of the peace, but withal a boor and bully, the terror of his parish, who kidnaps the two grandchildren of Sir Philip Bampfylde. Chowne has been identified with John Froude, Vicar of Knowstone.

> One of the worst specimens of his class was the Rev. John Froude, Vicar of Knowstone, the original of Parson Chowne . . .

He came of gentle birth, was soured and cheated in his younger days, and then his hand was turned against every man, and he ruled the countryside with the power of a malignant fiend. Froude had at his beck and call a set of young farmers and grooms who, controlled by fear or for sake of reward, were ever ready to do his bidding. The novelist tells of a race of naked savages who lived not far from the rectory, and were sent on errands of vengeance and to terrify the neighbourhood. Chowne fed them with the refuse of his hounds' food and entirely controlled them, treating them much in the same way as he did his dogs. But this part of the story is imaginary. It was said that if he had turned his talents to good account he might even have been a bishop if he had chosen. For this, says the author of *The Maid of Sker*, he possessed some qualifications, "for his choicest pleasure was found in tormenting his fellow-parsons."—P. H. DITCHFIELD: *The Old-Time Parson*, p. 299.

Crichton, Admirable, the familiar name for James Crichton (1551–1573), a Scotch youth of extraordinary beauty, brilliancy and versatility. As a boy of distinguished birth, he was the fellow pupil, under private tutors, of James VI of Scotland, who become James I of England. Later he was educated at Perth and at Edinburgh. At seventeen his intellect was fully developed, and he was reported to be master of Latin, Greek, Hebrew, Chaldaic, Italian, Spanish, French, Flemish, German, Scottish and English. His memory was such that he could repeat, without an error, whatever he had once heard. He was no less skilled in athletic than in scholarly directions. As a fencer, none could rival him, and his horsemanship was most accomplished. Nor did any troublesome modesty obscure his attainments. He is said to have given proof of his precocity at Paris by issuing placards announcing that in six weeks he would present himself at the College of Navarre to answer orally in any one of twelve languages whatever question might be proposed to him "in any science—liberal art, discipline or faculty, whether practical or theoretical." After acquitting himself admirably before the crowded audience that assembled in answer to this challenge, he was victorious next day in a spectacular tilting match at the Louvre. Crichton himself later wrote

a satiric comedy and played the principal parts therein. He was a handsome youth, save for a deforming red mark on his right cheek, and as graceful as he was learned. Like all such prodigies, though, he died young, being only two and twenty when he passed away at Mantua in the height of his career.

He is the hero of a novel by Harrison Ainsworth which was dramatized in 1837; of a drama (1820) in which Kean made a hit by his imitations of actors and exploits in fencing, music, etc., and of a "fantasy" by J. M. Barrie (1902).

Christabel, heroine of a poetical fragment of that name (1816), a weird tale of mystic and haunting melody by S. T. Coleridge. Christabel, the gentle and pious daughter of Sir Leoline, is induced by a gentle but powerful spell to introduce into her father's castle a lady, "beautiful exceedingly," who calls herself Lady Geraldine, but is evidently of diabolical origin. The fragment breaks off before the secret of her identity is revealed.

The poem is a romance of Christianity, a legend of sainthood. The heroine is not only the lovely but the holy Christabel. For no fault of hers, but rather for her virtues, are the powers of evil raised against her; and one of the most subtle and wonderful touches of truth in the tale is the ignorance of her innocence—her want of any knowledge or experience which can explain to her what the evil is, or how to deal with it. The witch Geraldine has all the foul wisdom of her wickedness to help her—her sorceries, her supernatural knowledge, her spells and cunning. But Christabel has nothing but her purity, and stands defenceless as a lamb, not even knowing where the danger is to come from; exposed at every point in her simplicity, and paralysed, not instructed, by the first gleam of bewildering acquaintance with evil.—*Blackwood's Magazine.*

Christian, hero of Bunyan's allegory, *The Pilgrim's Progress from this world to that which is to come* (1678). Awakened to the consciousness of sin, Christian flees alone from the City of Destruction, after having vainly sought to make his wife and children accompany him.

This concludes Part I. In Part II

his wife and family travel the same path. See CHRISTIANA.

> The Pilgrim, though in a Puritan dress, is a genuine man. His experience is so truly human experience that Christians of every persuasion can identify themselves with him; and even those who regard Christianity itself as but a natural outgrowth of the conscience and intellect, and yet desire to live nobly and make the best of themselves, can recognize familiar footprints in every step of Christian's journey.— J. A. FROUDE.

Christian II, King of Illyria, in Daudet's *Kings in Exile* (1880), is a portrait of Francis II, the last king of Naples, who lost his throne in 1860. He is painted as an easy-going, pleasure-loving youth, without self-respect or enthusiasm, who much prefers the easy joys he finds in Paris to the cares of ruling a remote kingdom. His queen is exactly the opposite. She earnestly desires that her husband or her son may be restored to the throne of his ancestors. She believes fully in the divine right of kings. She chafes under exile. Though indifferent to her husband, save as the possible occupant of a throne, her life is spent not so much in forgiving as in trying to hide and condone his villainies.

Christian, Edward, alias **Dick Ganlesse** and **Simon Canter,** in Scott's novel, *Peveril of the Peak* (1823), a conspirator false to everybody. Educated as a Puritan he retained the confidence of his people by a resourceful hypocrisy while acting as " a sagacious, artful and cool-headed instrument of Buckingham, the father of Fenella, whom he had trained as an instrument of his fiendish vengeance. Scott, in the introduction written in 1831, explains that he is a mere creature of the imagination, though he makes him the brother to a historic character, William Christian. Unfortunately he learned too late that William did have a brother of the name of Edward. " As I was not aware," says Scott, " that such a person had existed, I could hardly be said to have traduced his character."

Christian, Colonel William, in Scott's novel, *Peveril of the Peak,* brother of Edward. For many years he sacrifices his own Puritanical conscience in the interest of the Roman Catholic Countess of Derby, but finally revolts and yields up the Isle of Man to the Parliamentary army. When the Restoration replaces the Countess in the sovereignty of the island he is shot as a traitor.

Christiana, in the second part of Bunyan's *Pilgrim's Progress* (1684), who, under the guidance of Mr. Great Heart, sets out with her children to rejoin her husband when she hears of his safe arrival in the Celestial City.

Chrononhotonthologos, a pompous character in a burlesque tragedy of the same name by Henry Carey.

Chrysal, the feigned author of *Chrysal, or Adventures of a Guinea* (1760), a satirical novel by Charles Johnstone. Chrysal, *i.e., Golden,* is the spirit inhabiting a guinea and tells its own tale, which necessarily included the adventures of those into whose possession it comes for the time being.

Chucks, in Captain Marryat's novel of naval life afloat and ashore, *Peter Simple* (1833), the boatswain under Captain Savage.

> We have not the least doubt that there were originals for most of his characters, serious and comic, including the ever-delightful Chucks, and his brother warrant officer, the carpenter, who held that everything taking place around him had taken place just 27,672 years before, and would take place just 27,672 years afterwards. A man-of-war, in days when men-of-war were sometimes a whole year without casting anchor, contained as many queer animals as Noah's Ark.—*Pall Mall Budget.*

Chuzzlewit, Jonas, Martin's cousin, who with Mr. Seth Pecksniff plots his undoing, is a sly, cunning, ignorant young man whose rule of life is, " Do other men for they would do you." He is detected in an unsuccessful attempt to poison his own father who dies of a broken heart, murders Montague Tigg, who had blackmailed him in connection with the poisoning, and when arrested poisons himself on the way to prison.

Jonas Chuzzlewit has his place of eminence forever among the most memorable types of living and breathing wickedness that ever were stamped and branded with immortality by the indignant genius of a great and unrelenting master. Neither Vantrin nor Thénardier has more of evil and of deathless life in him.—SWINBURNE: *Charles Dickens*, p. 30.

Chuzzlewit, Martin, hero of a novel of that name (1843) by Charles Dickens. Being cast off by a grandfather bearing the same name, because of his love for Mary Graham, he emigrates to the United States and invests his little all in a real estate deal in Eden, a place described in the advertisements as justifying its name, but which turns out on reaching it to be simply a dozen log cabins situated in a malarious swamp. He returns to England completely disillusioned with America and the Americans.

Cinq-Mars, Henri, Marquis de (1620–1642), a French courtier who began life as a protégé of Cardinal Richelieu (*q.v.*), but turned against him because Richelieu discountenanced his love for Maria de Gonzaga; was detected in a conspiracy, and, with his friend and fellow plotter, De Thou, was beheaded at Lyons. He is the hero of a historical novel by Alfred de Vigny: *Cinq-Mars, ou une Conjuration sous Louis XIII* (1826) and of an opera by Gounod founded on the novel (1877).

Circumlocution Office, a term invented by Dickens in *Little Dorrit* (1855) to satirize the red tape and consequent waste of time and money in British public offices. " It was equally impossible to do the plainest right and to undo the plainest wrong, without the express authority of the Circumlocution Office. If another Gunpowder Plot had been discovered half an hour before the lighting of the match, nobody would have been justified in saving the Parliament until there had been a score of boards, half a bushel of minutes, several sacks of official memoranda, and a family vault full of ungrammatical correspondence on the part of the Circumlocution Office." In short, " what-

ever was required to be done, the Circumlocution Office was beforehand with all the public departments in the art of perceiving—HOW NOT TO DO IT." (Chapter xxvii.)

Citizen of the World, the epithet which Goldsmith bestows upon the imaginary author of the letters published collectively in 1762 under that title. He is a philosophical Chinaman tarrying in London, who writes home to his friends in the Orient his observations on occidental morals, manners and customs. The epithet had already been applied by one of the characters in *Sir Charles Grandison* (1754) to the hero of that novel.

The phrase, "a Citizen of the World," is as old as Bacon's *Essays*; but it is interesting to find it in Richardson only a few years before Goldsmith made it the title of his collected *Chinese Letters*. Sir Charles Grandison, says Lucy Selby, "is, in the noblest sense, a Citizen of the World."—AUSTIN DOBSON: *Samuel Richardson*, p. 163.

Claes, Balthazar, in Balzac's novel of *La Recherche de l'Absolu* (1834), translated into English as *The Alkahest*, is a wealthy chemist at the opening of the nineteenth century, the head of the leading family in the Flemish town of Douai. His life dream is to solve the mystery of matter—the secret of the Absolute. Sacrificing everything in his devotion to chemical analysis he dies heartbroken and defeated, a tragic figure, touching in its pathos and dignified even in its fall.

Clarchen, heroine of Goethe's historical tragedy, *Egmont*, a bright, winsome and loyal girl, devoted to the titular hero, from whom Scott has borrowed some of the traits of his Amy Robsart.

Clare, Angel, in Thomas Hardy's novel, *Tess of the D'Urbevilles*, the younger son of Rev. James Clare, Vicar of Emminister. Intended for the church, he develops free-thinking tendencies, though retaining a bigoted belief in social conventions. He marries Tess but cannot forgive her past nor her unintentional concealment of the facts and leaves her on the wedding night, a wife only in name.

Clarence George, Duke, son of the Duke of York, introduced in Shakespeare's *III Henry VI* and also in *Richard III*, where his imprisonment in the Tower ends in secret murder (i, 4). His ghost appears to Richard (v, 3). His unstable character deserves the Shakespearean epithets "false, fleeting, perjured Clarence."

Clari, heroine of an opera by J. Howard Payne and Sir Henry Bishop entitled *Clari, or the Maid of Milan* (1823). The Duke of Milan, with evil intentions, induces Clari to leave her home under promise of marriage; she is warned by a play acted before her and escapes. The Duke repeats his offer with intentions now of the most unexceptionable; she believes him, returns, and they are married. This opera is only famous in dramatic history because the melody of *Home Sweet Home* occurs in it.

Claridge, David, the hero of Sir Gilbert Parker's novel of Anglo-Egyptian life, *The Weavers*.

David Claridge was, however, a creature of the imagination. It has been said that he was drawn from General Gordon. I am not conscious of having taken Gordon for David's prototype, though as I was saturated with all that had been written about Gordon there is no doubt that something of that great man may have found its way into the character of David Claridge. The true origin of David Claridge, however, may be found in a short story called "All the World's Mad," in "Donovan Pasha," which was originally published by Lady Randolph Churchill in an ambitious defunct magazine called the *Anglo-Saxon Review*. The truth is that David Claridge had his origin in a fairly close understanding of and interest in Quaker life. I had Quaker relatives through the marriage of a connection of my mother, and the original Ben Claridge, the uncle of David, is still alive, a very old man, but who appealed to me in my boyhood days, and who wore the broad brim and the straight preacher-like coat of the old-fashioned Quaker. The grandmother of my wife was also a Quaker, and used the "thee" and "thou" until the day of her death.—Sir G. Parker.

Clarinda, the name given by Robert Burns to his friend, Mrs. Agnes McLehose. He first met her (December, 1787) at a tea party in Edinburgh. A married woman of about his own age, she and her two children had been deserted by an unworthy husband. Handsome in person, lively and easy in manners, of a poetical turn of mind, with some wit and not too high a degree of refinement or delicacy, she was exactly the woman to fascinate Burns. The pair took an immediate fancy to each other. Mrs. McLehose asked him to her house, but an accident prevented his keeping the appointment. He sent a letter of excuse and so began the famous *Letters to Clarinda*. Burns first adopted the signature Sylvander in the third of his letters. Begun half in jest the correspondence soon grew warm on both sides. The sportive acquaintance ripened unaware into a genuine passion. But it does not seem to have cost Burns any heartbreak to sever the connection on his marriage with Jean Armor in 1791. With Clarinda it was otherwise. In her private journal, written 40 years afterwards, she alludes to December 6 as a day she can never forget, as it was on that date she parted with Robert Burns "never more to meet in this world. Oh! may we meet in heaven!"

Clarke, Micah, hero and title of a novel by Conan Doyle.

Claude, hero of Arthur Hugh Clough's rhymed novelette, *Amours de Voyage* (1849). Claude is in love with Mary Trevellyn, but, as the motto on the title page says, "*Il doutait de tout, même de l'amour*" ("He doubted everything, even love"). He allows his fancy to roam everywhere at will, and settle nowhere; he shrinks from action and declines into a gentle gloom.

Claudio, in Shakespeare's comedy, *Measure for Measure*, a young lord of Florence, brother to Isabella, who urges her to sacrifice her virtue to Angelo in order to save him from imprisonment and impending death.

A very ill-conditioned, self-righteous young fop who is saved from punishment by the virtues of others and the necessities of the plot. It is a comfort to have Antonio speak his mind on him and on his like.

What, man! I know them, yea,
And what they weigh even to the utmost scruple

Scambling, out facing, fashion mongering boys
That lie and cog and flout, deprave and slander

WALTER RALEIGH: *Shakespeare.*

Claudius, King of Denmark, in Shakespeare's tragedy, *Hamlet, Prince of Denmark,* is the uncle and stepfather of the prince and has achieved the throne by murdering his own brother. In the original story by Saxo Grammaticus he is called Fengo.

Clavering, Sir Francis, in Thackeray's novel, *Pendennis,* a baronet who dissipates his money in gambling and profligacy, marries a wealthy widow, Mrs. Amory, facetiously dubbed the Begum, who is no widow, for her first husband, a forger, reputed dead, turns up to blackmail Sir Francis (see ALTAMONT, COLONEL JACK). Lady Clavering is the mother of Blanche Amory (*q.v.*) and herself a good-natured, kindly, ill-educated vulgarian.

Clavijo, hero and title of a drama (1774) by Goethe, founded on the real story of Don José Clavijo y Foxardo (1730–1806), a Spanish official who seduced a sister of Beaumarchais and was called to account by the latter. Failing to receive satisfaction Beaumarchais, a friendless stranger, fought his way to the king's presence. His own eloquence did the rest. Clavijo was dismissed in disgrace. On these incidents Beaumarchais himself founded his drama of *Eugenie.* While Beaumarchais naturally painted Clavijo as a villain, Goethe presents him as an amiable, generous but reckless youth who is led by passion and circumstances into unpremeditated wrong.

Clay, Robert, hero of Richard Harding Davis's novel, *Soldiers of Fortune* (1897), a young engineer who takes charge of a mine in "Olancho," South America, and is involved in a revolution.

Cleishbotham, Jedediah, the feigned editor, as Peter Pattieson is the feigned author, of Scott's *Tales of My Landlord.* He figures in the Introduction to *The Black Dwarf* as a pompous pedant, fond of many-syllabled words, the schoolmaster and parish clerk of Gandercleugh. Pattieson is his assistant teacher. Jedediah's wife, Dorothea, figures briefly as a Scotch Xantippe.

Clélie, heroine of a historical romance by Madelein: de Scudery, *Clélie, Histoire Romaine* (10 vols., 1654–1660). She is the daughter of a noble Roman who has taken refuge from the tyrant Tarquin in Carthage. There Clélie's hand is sought by three lovers, but she favors Aronce, son of Lars Porsena of Clusium. The rape of Lucrece and the expulsion of Tarquin and all his brood are worked into a plot that shifts from Carthage to Capua, to Perusia, Lake Thrasimine, Ardea and Rome. Lee's play, Lucius Junius Brutus, was taken from Clélie. See CLOELIA.

Clelie, in Molière's comedy, *L'Etourdi* (1653), a young slave girl who, in violation of all historic probability, is held on French soil by Trufuldin. Lélie, the blunderer, loves her; so does his friend Leandre. Unhappily for Lélie he has not the money to ransom her. Mascarille, his valet, proposes to carry her off. He suggests a dozen different plans; all are frustrated by the well-meaning density of Lélie (*q.v.*).

Clemenceau, Pierre, hero of *L'Affaire Clemenceau* (1866), a novel by Alexander Dumas Fils. In its earlier chapters it is partly autobiographical. Like the author, Paul is an illegitimate child and suffers agonies of shame and humiliation when old enough to realize his position. He becomes a famous sculptor and falls into the nets of an adventuress—a pseudo countess from Spain and her daughter Inez. He marries the girl to find out too late that, with all her calculated naivetés, she is a harlot at heart. After a vain struggle between unconquerable love and righteous wrath he ends by killing her.

Clementina, Lady (whose full name, rarely used in the narrative, is the Signorina Clementina della Porretta), an Italian lady, in Richardson's novel, *Sir Charles Grandison* (1754), beauti-

Cleofas — 100 — **Cleves**

ful, accomplished, amiable, but mentally ill-balanced. Engaged to be married to the titular hero, she is distracted between her love for him and her attachment to the Catholic religion. Religious devotion prevails, she renounces him to enter a convent, but goes insane and flees to England pursued by her family and by a new lover, the Count of Belvedere. Finding Sir Charles has just been married to Harriet Byron, she regains her self-control and it is understood that she eventually became the Countess of Belvedere.

In a letter to a correspondent Richardson hints at certain prematrimonial love-affairs, among them one with "a violent Roman Catholic lady of a fine fortune, a zealous professor; whose terms were (all her fortune in her own power—a very apron-string tenure!) two years' probation, and her confessor's report in favour of his being a true proselyte at the end of them." Mrs. Barbauld surmises that this lady may have given the first hint of Clementina.

Cleofas, Don, hero of Le Sage's novel, *Le Diable Boiteux*, known in English as *The Devil on Two Sticks*, a high mettled, chivalric young Spaniard who takes the fiend Asmodeus (*q.v.*) as his mentor and guide.

Cleopatra, Queen of Egypt, sister and wife of Ptolomy Dionysius. She was driven from her throne but re-established by Julius Cæsar in B.C. 47. After Cæsar's death she captivated Mark Antony so that he repudiated his own wife Octavia to live with her until he fell in battle at Actium. Thereupon Cleopatra poisoned herself with an asp. She is the heroine of numerous dramas in many languages, notably French tragedies named after her: *Cleopatra* by E. Jodelle (1550), Jean Mairet (1630), Isaac de Benserade (1670), J. F. Marmontel (1750), and Madame de Girardin (1847); an Italian tragedy by Vittorio Alfieri (1773); and in English a tragedy called *Cleopatra* (1599) by Samuel Daniel; Shakespeare's *Antony and Cleopatra* (1608), Dryden's *All for Love, or the World Well Lost* (1682), and G. B. Shaw's *Cæsar and Cleopatra* (1898).

According to Plutarch Cleopatra's beauty was not "unmatchable of other women," but Shakespeare makes her peerless among them, transcending the artist's ideal as much as that transcends mortal womanhood. He agrees, however, in making beauty the least part of her spell. Though we never forget it we think most, when she is present, of her other charms whose infinite variety age cannot wither nor custom stale.

Upon Cleopatra the genius of Shakespeare has been lavished. She is the most wonderful of his creation of women, formed of the greatest number of elements—apparently conflicting elements, yet united by the mystery of life. To heap up together all that is most unsubstantial, frivolous, vain, contemptible and variable, till the worthlessness be lost in the magnitude, and a sense of the sublime spring from the very elements of littleness: to do this belonged only to Shakespeare, that worker of miracles.— E. DOWDEN: *Shakespeare's Primer.*

Cleveland, Captain Clement, the titular hero of Scott's novel, *The Pirate* (1822), "the daring leader of the bold band whose name was as terrible as a tornado." He differs from Byron's Corsair in a nearer kinship to average humanity.

Clèves, The Princess of. Heroine and title of a historical novel (Fr., *La Princesse de Clèves*), by the Countess Marie de La Fayette (1677). "One of the classics of French literature," says George W. Saintsbury, and adds: "Its scene is laid at the court of Henry II and there is a certain historical basis, but the principal personages are drawn from the author's own experience, herself being the heroine, her husband the Prince of Clèves, and Rochefoulcauld the Duc de Nemours, while other characters are identified with Louis XIV and his courtiers by industrious compilers of keys." Married to a husband whom she respects but does not love, beloved by a younger man whom she, too, loves in secret, the princess flees from temptation into the country. There the Duc de Nemours overhears her confession to her own husband that she loves another and is afraid of him. One night the duke is seen climbing the wall of the princess's garden in a mad desire to catch a distant glimpse of her. The facts are misrepresented to the prince, who dies of a broken heart. Even now the princess refuses to marry her ducal lover—partly because she holds him responsible, in a measure, for her husband's death, and partly because his love is so essential to her happiness that she dare not risk its loss in the coolness that might succeed to marriage.

Clifford, Paul, titular hero of a novel (1830) by Bulwer-Lytton, a child of unknown parents, who after a misspent but not a guilty youth is thrown into prison on the false charge of stealing a watch from Brandon, a lawyer. He becomes corrupted there, escapes with the rascal who corrupted him, and turns highwayman. His exploits finally land him again in jail. Brandon, now a judge, sentences him to death though he has irrefutable evidence that the culprit is his own son, and himself falls dead of heart disease. Clifford escapes to America.

Clinker, Humphrey, a character who gives his name to Smollett's novel, *The Expedition of Humphrey Clinker* (1771), but is really of small importance to the plot and does not make his appearance until a full quarter of the story has been told, when he takes the place of a postilion discharged from the service of Mr. Matthew Bramble. He is described as " a shabby country fellow " who " seemed to be about twenty years of age, of a middle size, with bandy legs, stooping shoulders, high forehead, sandy locks, pinkish eyes, flat nose and long chin; but his complexion was of a sickly yellow, his looks denoted famine, and the rags that he wore could hardly conceal what decency requires to be covered." He improves rapidly under the patronage of his new master and it eventually turns out that he is that gentleman's illegitimate son.

Clio, in classic mythology the Muse of history (see MUSES), usually rep-

resented with a half-open parchment roll in her hand. Addison used one or other of the four letters in her name in signing his contributions to the *Spectator*. Hence he is supposed to have had this muse in his mind, and he himself was sometimes called Clio by his contemporaries. A contrary theory has, however, been hazarded, that the initial affixes refer to the places where the essays were composed *i.e.*, Chelsea, London, Islington and the Office.

When panting virtue her last efforts made
You brought your Clio to the Virgin's aid.
SOMERVILLE: *Epistle to Addison.*

Clonbrony, Lady, in Maria Edgeworth's novel, *The Absentee*, is the wife of Lord Clonbrony, one of the Irish landed gentry. They forsake their homes and their duties in order to cut a splash in London society. Unfitted to her new career, Lady Clonbrony submits to humiliations, rebuffs and sacrifices in the vain hope of final triumph. She pretends she is not Irish and even affects a contempt for her native land, but being unable to conquer her brogue she is sometimes forced to hold her tongue and thus appear more foolish than she really is, and at others to caricature the English pronunciation, and thus betray the fact that she is not English. In vain also she struggles to school her free, good-natured Irish manner into the cold, sober, stiff deportment she deems to be English.

Clonbrony, Lord, the titular *Absentee* in Maria Edgeworth's Anglo-Irish novel of that name (1812). Yielding to the importunities of his wife, he takes her away from Ireland to London in order to cut a figure in fashionable society. Oblivious of the state of the unfortunate tenants who suffer by his absenteeism, yet feeling lost in his new surroundings and unable to adjust himself to new conditions he sinks into the vices of gaming and betting.

Clorinda, in Tasso's epic poem, *Jerusalem Delivered* (1675), the heroine of the pagan army, an Amazonian maid of great martial courage and of many noble traits. She was the daughter of a Christian, Senapus of Ethiopia, but because she was born white her mother changed her for a black child, and Clorinda was taken by the eunuch Arsetes to Egypt. There she was brought up a pagan. She appeared in full armor before King Aladine to sue for the lovers, and the king, granting her plea, welcomed her among the defenders of Jerusalem. Though herself impervious to sexual passion she inspires love in many men, including Tancred, the leader of the Christian forces. Finding himself engaged in battle with her and deeming her a man, he breaks her helmet, discovers her to be the maiden of his love, and refuses to continue the fight. Later she sets fire to one of Godfrey's engines of war, is pursued to the walls of Jerusalem by Tancred, and, again unrecognized, is this time slain—to his own eternal sorrow. But she dies not before he can give her the sacred rites of baptism and a dream consoles him with the assurance that she is among the blessed in Paradise.

Cloten, in Shakespeare's comedy *Cymbeline* (1605), the rejected lover of Imogen, subsequently slain by Guiderius.

The character of Cloten, the conceited, booby lord and rejected lover of Imogen, though not very agreeable in itself, and at present obsolete, is drawn with much humour and quaint extravagance. The description which Imogen gives of his unwelcome addresses to her—"Whose love-suit hath been to me as fearful as a siege" —is enough to cure the most ridiculous lover of his folly. It is remarkable that though Cloten makes so poor a figure in love, he is described as assuming an air of consequence as the Queen's son in a council of state, and with all the absurdity of his person and manners, is not without shrewdness in his observations. So true is it that folly is as often owing to a want of proper sentiments as to a want of understanding!— HAZLITT: *Characters of Shakespeare's Plays.*

Miss Seward, in one of her letters, assures us that, singular as the character of Cloten may appear, it is the exact prototype of a person whom she once knew. "The unmeaning frown of the countenance, the shuffling gait, the burst of voice, the bustling insignificance, the fever-and-ague fits of valor, the forward tetchiness, the unprincipled malice, and—what is most curious—

those occasional gleams of good sense, amidst the floating clouds of folly which generally darkened and confused the man's brain, and which, in the character of Cloten, we are apt to impute to a violation of unity in character; but, in the sometime Captain C——n, I saw the portrait of Cloten was not out of nature."

Clout, Colin, or **Colyn Cloute.** Title and pretended author of a poetical satire by John Skelton (1460–1529), which is a vigorous pre-Reformation attack upon the Catholic clergy, their alleged self-indulgence and disregard for their flock, their lack of piety and learning. It ends with these lines:

> And if ye stand in doubte,
> Who brought this rhyme aboute
> My name is Colyn Cloute.

The surname is clearly suited to the ostensibly dull-witted clown of the satire, while the Colin is modified from Colas (Claus), short for Nicholas, which was a typical proper name because of the popularity of the saint who bore it.

From John Skelton the pseudonym was adopted by several Elizabethan poets, notably Edmund Spenser, who called himself Colin Clout not only in *Colin Clout's Come Home Again* (1595), but in all his pastoral poems.

Colin Clout is also a character in Gay's pastoral, *The Shepherd's Week.*

Clumsy, Miss Hoyden, daughter of Sir Tunbelly Clumsy (see below), a lively, high-spirited, innocent but ill-educated girl who falls in love with Tom Fashion (*q.v.*) when he personates her betrothed lover, Lord Foppington.

Clumsy, Sir Tunbelly, father of Miss Hoyden in Vanbrugh's *The Relapse* (1697) and in Sheridan's rifacimento of that comedy, *A Trip to Scarborough* (1777). A justice of the peace, a cringing toady to the aristocracy, but harsh, brutal and meanspirited to his equals and inferiors, a lineal ancestor of Squire Western.

The ancestor in a direct line of Squire Western. That he bears a close resemblance to nature need not be admitted. That he is an excellent piece of fooling cannot be denied. He holds siege in his country house, asks at the approach of a stranger if the blunderbuss is primed, and, when he and his servants at last appear on the scene, they come armed with "guns, clubs, pitchforks and scythes." PROF. FELIX E. SCHELLING: *Cambridge History of English Literature,* viii, 183.

Clutterbuck, Cuthbert, the feigned editor of Scott's novels, *The Monastery* and *the Abbot* and also of *The Fortunes of Nigel.* The "Prefatory Letter" to *Peveril of the Peak* is addressed to him in a serio-comic vein. He is represented as a retired captain living in Kennaquhair and guarding himself against ennui by a devotion to the lighter and trivial branches of antiquarian study.

Codlingsby, hero and title of a burlesque "novel" by W. M. Thackeray. See CONINGSBY.

Coelebs (*Lat.,* a bachelor), the hero of Hannah More's novel, *Coelebs in Search of a Wife* (1808). A young gentleman of fortune and family in the north of England, he sets out to find a bride. His departed mother had warned him that "the education of the present race of females is not very favorable to domestic happiness." His father had left a dying injunction that he should take the advice of an old friend named Stanley. After brief and unsatisfactory experiences with the fashionable world in London, Coelebs makes his way to Stanley Grove, and there finds the threefold ideals of his father, mother and himself realized in Lucilla, one of the three daughters of the house.

Mrs. Clifford tells me that Mrs. Hannah More was lately at Dawlish and excited more curiosity there, and engrossed more attention, than any of the distinguished personages who were there, not excepting the Prince of Orange. The gentleman from whom she drew Coelebs was there, but most of those who saw him did him the justice to declare that he was a much more agreeable man than Coelebs. If you have any curiosity to know his name I can tell you that—young Mr. Harford of Blaise Castle.—MARIA EDGEWORTH to MRS. RUXTON, January, 1810.

Coffin, Long Tom, in Cooper's novel, *The Pilot,* one of the most famous of all sailors in fiction. Born "while the boat was crossing Nantucket shoals," he loves the sea as "his native soil." He has been a whaler before he has been a man-of-war's man and his favorite weapon continues to be a harpoon.

Long Tom Coffin may be described as Leatherstocking suffered a sea-change—with a harpoon instead of a rifle, and a pea-jacket instead of a hunting-shirt. In both the same primitive elements may be discerned: the same limited intellectual range combined with professional or technical skill; the same generous affections and unerring moral instincts; the same religious feeling, taking the form at times of fatalism or superstition. Long Tom's love of the sea is like Leatherstocking's love of the woods; the former's dislike of the land is like the latter's dislike of the clearings. Cooper himself, as we are told by his daughter, was less satisfied, in his last years, with Long Tom Coffin than most of his readers—and, of the two characters, considered that of Boltrope the better piece of workmanship.—*Atlantic Monthly,* January, 1862.

Colambre, Lord, in Maria Edgeworth's novel, *The Absentee,* the son of Lord Clonbrony. While his parents are away in London he visits in disguise the family estates, which have been left in charge of a rapacious agent, who feels secure in his master's absence and in that master's indifference to all but the money result of his estate. The scene in which Lord Colambre discovers himself to his tenantry and to their oppressor Macaulay pronounces the best thing written of its kind since the opening of the twenty-second book of the *Odyssey.* No mean authority and no mean praise!

Coldstream, Sir Charles, in Charles Matthews' farce *Used Up,* the blasé hero who sees nothing in the world to admire or esteem.

Collins, Mr., in Miss Austen's novel, *Pride and Prejudice,* a clergyman, solemn, conceited, priggish, self-satisfied, a toady to the great, abundantly humorous in his total lack of humor. He courts Elizabeth Bennett, and when rejected marries Charlotte Lucas.

Mr. Collins has been justly described as the representative under a somewhat altered form of the servile domestic chaplain of the seventeenth century. He was a possible character in Jane Austen's day. Perhaps a vestige of him might be found even now.— GOLDWIN SMITH, *Life of Jane Austen,* p. 84.

Colville, Theodore, the middle-aged hero of W. D. Howells' informational novel, *Indian Summer* (1886), whose engagement to the twenty-year-old Imogene Graham convinces him of the emptiness of his claim to youth. His honesty of purpose, which accomplishes its aims less straightforwardly than its owner intends, his goodness of heart, his tireless amiability of spirit, and his habit of taking life with all earnestness, yet with a drollery which gives to all living a pleasant savor, help him out of what had once threatened to be a serious dilemma. Like Henry Esmond he ends by marrying his intended mother-in-law.

Conachar, the foster child of the White Doe, the name under which Eachin Maclan is apprenticed to Simon Glover in Scott's *Fair Maid of Perth.*

To me one of the most remarkable figures he ever drew was that of Conachar. Nothing could be more difficult than to provoke at once pity, contempt and sympathy for a coward. Yet he has successfully achieved this feat; and as far as I can recollect it is the sole instance in English literature where such an attempt was ever made. More than this, he has drawn two cowards in this remarkable novel—each quite different from the other and contrasted with remarkable skill—the comic, swaggering, good-natured, fussy little coward, Oliver Proudfute, who provokes a perpetual smile; and the sullen, irritable, proud and revengeful coward Conachar, whom we cannot but pity while we despise him.—W. W. STORY: *Conversations in a Studio* (1890).

Coningsby, Harry, hero of Disraeli's political novel, *Coningsby or the New Generation* (1844). The name may have been borrowed from that of a well known statesman of Queen Anne's day (Thomas Earl Coningsby 1656–1729) the portrait is drawn to same extent from Disraeli's contemporary and friend (George Sidney Smythe 1818–1857 afterwards Viscount Strangford and Baron Penshurst) and in larger degree from himself. Thackeray satirized both the novel and the hero (whom he obviously identified with Disraeli) in *Codlingsby,* one of his *Novels by Eminent Hands* republished in America as *Punch's Prize Novelists.*

Coningsby is the impersonation of Young England, and in him the author intends that we should see the beginning, growth, and manhood of that school of perfect statesmen.—*North British Review.*

He paints his own portrait in this book in the most splendid fashion. It is the queerest of the whole queer gallery of likenesses: he appears as the greatest philosopher, the greatest poet, the greatest horseman, the greatest statesman, the greatest roué in the world; with all the qualities of Pitt and Byron and Burke, and the great Mr. Widdicomb of Batty's amphitheatre. Perhaps one is reminded of the last named famous individual more than of any other.—W. M. THACKERAY in *The Pictorial Times,* May 25, 1844, quoted in T. P. O'Connor's *Lord Beaconsfield,* p. 240.

Connell, Father, the chief character in a novel of that name by Michael and John Banim. An old Catholic priest whose simple virtues kin him to the Dr. Primrose of Goldsmith, he befriends a poor vagrant boy, Neddy Fennell, whose adventures form the staple of the narrative.

Conrad, hero of Byron's poem, *The Corsair* (1814), a pirate chief living on the Pirate's Isle with Medora, his wife. Hearing that the Sultan Seyd meditated an attack on his stronghold, he set sail secretly for the Sultan's dominions, and while his fleet was employed in setting fire to the Moslem ships he entered the palace in disguise as a dervish, but was detected and cast into a dungeon. Gulnare, the queen of the harem and the most beautiful of Seyd's slaves, released him, confessed her love for him, assassinated Seyd, and fled in page's costume with Conrad. But when the latter found that Medora had died during his absence he forsook the island with Gulnare and disappeared. We are allowed to infer that he reappears as Lara in the poem of that name (*q.v.*). Gulnare still attends him as a disguised page under the name of Kaled.

Conroy, Gabriel, in Bret Harte's novel of that name (1876), is the brother of the heroine, Grace Conroy, and himself an important factor in the plot, though the hero is more properly Arthur Poinsett, travelling under the name of Philip Ashley who woos and wins the heroine.

Constance of Brittany, in Shakespeare's historical play *King John*, the mother of Arthur, Duke of Bretagne, and widow of Geoffrey Plantagenet. In real life she was twice married after Geoffrey's death and died in 1201—before John gained possession of Arthur.

Constantin, The Abbé, in Ludovic Halevy's novel of that name (1882), is a generous, genial, self-sacrificing priest, curé for thirty years of the little village of Longueral.

Consuelo, heroine of a romance of that name (1844) and of its sequel, *The Countess of Rudolstadt* (1846), by George Sand. She is introduced as a waif in the streets of Venice, a child musician, barefooted and meagrely clad, earning her bread with voice and guitar in the cafés. She has all the freedom of the lowest social class and all the knowledge acquired unaware by children bred in the open; she lives in her garret unguarded and unguided save by her own instincts of right. Even the youthful depravity of her betrothed, Anzoleto, is kept in check by her fierce innocence. Her musical gifts attract the attention of Porpora, an old maestro, who educates her and supplies the funds for her triumphal debút as an opera singer. He takes her on a tour through the capitals of Europe and sends her up to his friends, the Rudolstadts, for a vacation. They are an old Catholic family of eccentric ways. The eldest son, Albert, Count de Rudolstadt, falls in love with her and marries her on his deathbed. Wife and widow all in one day, but still a virgin, she renounces her title to return to the theatre. In the end it turns out that Albert was buried in a deathlike trance. He reappears under the incognito of Liverani.

Copper, Captain, in Beaumont and Fletcher's *Rule a Wife and Have a Wife* (1640), the nickname given to Michael Perez, a loud-mouthed Spanish soldier of great but unfounded pretensions to wealth and fashion. He marries Estifania, an intriguing servant girl, under the idea that she is an heiress, and when both are dis-

appointed and his jewels turn out to be counterfeit, she hurls at him the taunt from which his nickname is derived:

Your clothes are parallel to these, all coun-
    terfeits.
Put these and them on, you're a man of
    copper,
A copper, copper captain.

Copperfield, David, hero of a novel of that name (1849–1850) by Charles Dickens, which is to some extent autobiographical, especially in the earlier scenes. David is a timid and imaginative lad whose widowed mother marries Mr. Murdstone. The latter proves cruel both as husband and stepfather. David's mother dies, David himself is put to the lowest kind of work at the warehouse of Murdstone and Grinby, wine merchants, and in a shoe-blacking establishment. He runs away to his father's aunt, Miss Betsy Trotwood, is kindly received by that eccentric spinster, in due course becomes a newspaper reporter and then an author, marries Dora Spenlow, " the childwife," who dies just as her pretty childishness is beginning to pall upon David's matured taste, and he is left free to marry his real love, Agnes Wickfield. Among Copperfield's friends and acquaintances are the humble Peggottys, the humorsome Micawbers, the irridescent James Steerforth, and the good and reliable Tommy Traddles (see these entries).

Coquette, in William Black's novel, *A Daughter of Heth* (1871), is a nickname given to Catherine Cassilés, daughter of a Scotch father and a French mother, who, after the latter's death, is entrusted to her uncle, minister of Airlie. Her unselfish eagerness to harmonize herself with her dour surroundings succeeds at last, but only at the cost of her own life. The account of her refining influence upon the disorderly household and rough children of the Scotch clergyman is full of pathos and humor.

Cordelia, in Shakespeare's tragedy, *King Lear*, the youngest daughter of that monarch, who, though she refuses to join in their hypocritical professions, is the only one that truly loves him. Disinherited and banished she returns in Act iii with an army to restore her father, but is defeated, captured and put to death in prison. Lear, in a last outburst, kills the slave who hanged her and dies upon her body.

Spenser (*Faërie Queene*, II, x, 27) first used the form Cordelia, which Shakespeare followed.

If Lear be the grandest of Shakespeare's tragedies, Cordelia, in herself as a human being, governed by the purest and holiest impulses and motives, approaches near to perfection and, in her adaptation as a dramatic personage to a determinate plan of action, may be pronounced altogether perfect.—MRS. JAMESON: *Characteristics of Women.*

In Holinshed's Chronicle, Cordelia survives her misfortunes, regains her kingdom, and comforts the declining years of her father, but Shakespeare, before reaching the close of his play, had wound up the tragedy to such a pitch that a happy ending would have come as an anticlimax. "A deeper peace than the peace of old age by the fireside was needed to compose that heartrending tragedy."—WALTER RALEIGH: *Shakespeare*, 1907.

Corey, Bromfield, in W. D. Howells's novel, *The Rise of Silas Lapham*, an amiable Boston aristocrat; a connoisseur in art and a dilettante artist; full of pleasant whims and mild unconventionalities, while essentially conservative at heart; well bred, well groomed, looking on life with a cynical wit that includes himself and all he stands for in its gentle iconoclasm.

Corey, Giles. Hero and title of one of Longfellow's *New England Tragedies*, and of a historical drama by Mary Wilkins Freeman.

In real life Giles was one of the unfortunates put to death in Salem, Massachusetts, during the witchcraft trials. An old man of eighty, he confronted his persecutors unflinchingly and let himself be crushed to death under huge weights without a sign of weakening, his fortitude winning for him the title of The Man of Iron. His ghost, it is rumored, occasionally reappeared on the site of his martyrdom, these visits boding little good to the city of Salem. See an anonymous contemporary ballad preserved in Drake's *New England Legends*, p. 186.

Corinne, heroine of a novel of that name by Madame de Staël, a young woman whose lover proves faithless and who pines away and dies under pathetic circumstances.

Coriolanus, in Roman legend the surname of Cnaeus or Caius Marcius. He appears to have flourished in the fifth century B.C. and is represented as the champion of the patricians, the conqueror of the Volscian city of Corioli, whence his surname, and finally as the leader of the Volscians against Rome. Shakespeare makes him the hero of a tragedy, *Coriolanus* (1608), founded on North's Plutarch, with a slight shifting of names in the female characters. Plutarch gives the name of Volumnia to the wife of Coriolanus; Shakespeare transfers it to his mother, called Veturia by Plutarch.

Coriolanus is by nature of a kindly and generous disposition, but he inherits the aristocratic tradition, and his kindness strictly limits itself to the circle which includes those of his own rank and class. For his mother he has a veneration approaching to worship; he is content to be a subordinate under Cominius; for the old Menenius he has an almost filial regard, but the people are "slaves," "curs," "minions." His haughtiness becomes towering, because his personal pride which in itself is great, is built up over a solid and high-reared pride of class. When he is banished his bitterness arises, not only from his sense of the contemptible nature of the adversaries to whom he is forced to yield, but from the additional sense that he has been deserted by his own class, "the dastard nobles."— E. DOWDEN, *Shakespeare Primer.*

Corny, King, in Maria Edgeworth's novel of Irish life, *Osmond*, the nickname popularly given to Cornelius O'Shane, cousin to Osmond and self-styled "King of the Black Islands," from his estate. Hasty and violent at intervals, he is essentially kind, warm-hearted and affectionate. His frank and unsuspecting nature makes him adored by all his tenantry, none of whom would harm their king.

Besides being one of the most delightful creations in romantic literature, he is an instructive study toward the comprehension of the Irish character. Macaulay pointed out, in speaking of the aboriginal aristocracy of Ireland, that Miss Edgeworth's King Corny belongs to a later and much more civilized generation, but added that "whoever has studied that admirable portrait can form some notion of what King Corny's great-grandfather must have been like."—HELEN ZIMMERN.

Corombona, Vittoria, heroine of Webster's tragedy, *The White Devil* (1612). She fascinates the Duke of Bracchiano and spurs him on to the murder of his duchess and her own husband. Accused of these crimes, she conducts her own defence so as to baffle the judges, retires to a convent, from which Bracchiano releases her in order to marry her, and after Bracchiano's death by poison is herself stabbed by her brother Flaminio because she had not procured his advancement by Bracchiano. Webster has departed from the facts of history as related by French and Italian authors, who are in substantial accord with one another. See ACCORANBONI, VITTORIA.

Correze, hero of Ouida's *Moths,* an operatic tenor who captures the world by the charms of his voice which are equalled only by the chivalry of his conduct. He is in love with Vere and she with him, but he respects her and plays Mentor to her, warns her against wicked mamma, advises her to keep herself unspotted from the world, fights her husband because he neglects her and makes love to her only after she has been unrighteously divorced.

Correze is not an ordinary tenor, he sustains with perfect ease what would generally be regarded as the enormous strain of conducting himself when off the stage with the same lofty ideality that characterizes his behavior in tights and before the footlights. After he meets Vere, grand-duchesses throw themselves at his feet in vain; he oozes exalted didacticism in the intervals of singing the highest order of music, and if it were not for his almost holy devotion we feel, instinctively, Vere would be in great peril among the gins and pitfalls of the world. As it is, she comes out unscathed, though divorced, and safe in his arms though bereft of public respect.—*N. Y. Nation,* March 25, 1880.

Corsican Brothers. See FRANCHI.

Costard, in Shakespeare's *Love's Labor's Lost* (1594), a clown who apes the stilted language of the Eliza-

bethan courtiers and misapplies it in a fashion that reveals him as one of the earlier literary ancestors of Mrs. Malaprop. Such a word as *honorificabilitudinitatibus* has special charms for him.

Costigan, Captain J. Chesterfield, familiarly known as Cos. in Thackeray's *Pendennis,* an ex-army officer; Irish, jovial; humorous in himself and exciting the humor of others; drunken and disreputable, but careful of the good repute of his daughter Emily. He encourages her to accept the respectful advances of Arthur Pendennis until he is convinced by Major Pendennis that the boy has no prospects, then he cheerfully breaks the engagement. Several prototypes for this character have been suggested, the most likely being the father of Miss Eliza O'Neill, the actress, concerning whom some stories are told in Moore's *Diary* that must at least have proved suggestive to Thackeray. But he insisted that he never met Costigan in the flesh until long after the publication of *Pendennis.*

In the novel of *Pendennis,* written ten years ago, there is an account of a certain Costigan, whom I had invented (as I suppose authors invent their personages out of scraps, heel-taps, odds and ends of characters). I was smoking in a tavern parlor one night, and this Costigan came into the room alive—the very man:—the most remarkable resemblance of the printed sketches of the man, of the rude drawings in which I had depicted him. He had the same little coat, the same battered hat, cocked on one eye, the same twinkle in that eye. "Sir," said I, knowing him to be an old friend whom I had met in unknown regions, "sir," I said, "may I offer you a glass of brandy-and-water?" "*Bedad, ye may,*" says he, "*and I'll sing ye a song tu.*" Of course he spoke with an Irish brogue. Of course he had been in the army. In ten minutes he pulled out an Army Agent's account, whereon his name was written. A few months after we read of him in a police court. How had I come to know him, to divine him? Nothing shall convince me that I have not seen that man in the world of spirits. In the world of spirits and water I know I did; but that is a mere quibble of words. I was not surprised when he spoke in an Irish brogue. I had had cognizance of him before, somehow.—THACKERAY: *Roundabout Papers, De Finibus.*

Costigan, Emily, in Thackeray's *Pendennis.* See FOTHERINGAY, MISS.

Courtenay, Miles, in *King Noanett*, F. J. Stimson's romance of colonial America (1896), a dashing and chivalrous young Irishman of the royalist party, who, with Blampfylde Moore Carew, is captured by Cromwell's soldiers and shipped off to the colonies. Each, unknown to the other, is in love with Mistress St. Aubyn. The character of Courtenay is said to have been modelled upon that of John Boyle O'Reilly, with whom the author had often talked over the plan of the work.

Courtly, Sir Hartley, in Dion Boucicault's comedy, *London Assurance*, an elderly fop devoted to fashion and engaged to a young heiress, Grace Harkaway. She ends by rejecting him for his son Charles, a typical specimen of metropolitan coolness, cheek, and " assurance " whom Sir Harcourt blindly imagines to be a shy, studious and retiring boy.

Coverley, Sir Roger de, in the *Spectator*, by Steele and Addison, a member of the imaginary club under whose directions it was feigned that the paper was issued. He is a country gentleman of kindly heart, whimsical ways, and exquisite courtesy, who is adored by his family, worshipped by his servants, and beloved by all his acquaintances. The first sketch of this character, as of all the other members of the pretended club, was by Sir Richard Steele, but the details were filled out by Addison and it was Addison who finally killed him off in No. 517, because he thought that Steele had slurred the good knight's dignity by making him converse too familiarly with a street walker.

What would Sir Roger de Coverley be without his follies and his charming little brain-cracks? If the good knight did not call out to the people sleeping in church, and say "Amen" with such a delightful pomposity; if he did not make a speech in the assize court *apropos des bottes*, and merely to show his dignity to Mr. Spectator; if he did not mistake Madam Doll Tearsheet for a lady of quality in Temple Garden; if he were wiser than he is; if he had not his humour to salt his life, and were but a mere English gentleman and game-preserver,— of what worth were he to us? We love him for his vanities as much as his virtues. What is ridiculous is delightful in him; we are so fond of him because we laugh at him so."—THACKERAY: *The English Humorists.*

Who is there that can forget, or be insensible to, the inimitable, nameless graces, and various traits of nature and of old English character in it,—to his unpretending virtues and amiable weaknesses,— to his modesty, generosity, hospitality, and eccentric whims,—to the respect of his neighbors and the affection of his domestics, —to his wayward, hopeless, secret passion for his fair enemy, the widow, in which there is more of real romance and true delicacy than in a thousand tales of knighterrantry (we perceive the hectic flush of his cheek, the faltering of his tongue in speaking of her bewitching airs and the "whiteness of her hand")—to the havoc he makes among the game in his neighborhood,—to his speech from the bench, to show the *Spectator* what is thought of him in the country,—to his unwillingness to be put up as a sign-post, and his having his own likeness turned into the Saracen's head,—to his gentle reproof of the baggage of a gypsy that tells him "he has a widow in his line of life,"—to his doubts as to the existence of witchcraft, and protection of reputed witches,—to his account of the family pictures, and his choice of a chaplain,—to his falling asleep at church, and his reproof of John Williams, as soon as he recovered from his nap, for talking in sermon-time?— HAZLITT.

Crabshaw, Timothy, in Smollett's *Adventures of Sir Launcelot Greaves*, the servant of Sir Launcelot's squire.

Crane, Ichabod, in Washington Irving's short story, *The Legend of Sleepy Hollow*, in *The Sketchbook*, an awkward and credulous country schoolmaster, rival of a Dutch farmer, a "burly, roaring, roystering blade" named Brom Van Brunt, for the hand of Katherina Van Tassel, but put out of the running by a practical joke.

The cognomen of *Crane* was not inapplicable to his person. He was tall, but exceedingly lank, with narrow shoulders, long arms and legs, hands that dangled a mile out of his sleeves, feet that might have served for shovels, and his whole frame most loosely hung together. His head was small, and flat at top, with huge ears, large, green, glassy eyes, and a long, snipe nose, so that it looked like a weather-cock perched upon his spindle neck, to tell which way the wind blew. To see him striding along the profile of a hill on a windy day, with his clothes bagging and fluttering about him, one might have mistaken him for the genius of famine descending upon the earth, or some scarecrow eloped from a corn-field.—W. IRVING.

There is a story in the Legends of Rubezahl by Musaeus, wherein a headless horseman is introduced similar to the one described by Washington Irving, who very likely borrowed the most amusing feature of his *Legend of Sleepy Hollow* from that author.—*American Notes and Queries*, vol. i, p. 180.

Cratchit, Bob, in Dickens's extravaganza, *A Christmas Carol*, the ill-paid clerk of Scrooge, unselfish, kindly, living cheerfully in a four-room house with a large family on fifteen bob a week—" he pocketed on Saturdays but fifteen copies of his Christian name." His youngest child, known as Tiny Tim, is a cripple whose favorite phrase is, " God bless us all of us! "

Crawley, Rev. Josiah, Vicar of Hogglestock in Anthony Trollope's *The Last Chronicle of Barset* (1867), a poor country clergyman, scholarly, upright and fiercely pious, but unpleasantly strict and stern and driven almost insane from wounded pride and the pressure of biting ills which come from household want. He is accused of having stolen a check; the facts tell against him; even his best friends fear that, maddened by debts and duns, he may have committed the crime; and his wife, heroically patient and loving, half thinks he must be mad when he cannot tell even her how he got it.

Crawley, Sir Pitt, " of Great Gaunt Street and Queen's Crawley, Hants," a vulgar, miserly, ill-bred and ill-educated gentleman and an M.P. in Thackeray's novel, *Vanity Fair*. Though an aristocrat by birth, all his tastes are for low life. He is introduced in Chapter vii as " a man in drab breeches and gaiters, with a dirty old coat, a foul old neckcloth lashed round his bristly neck, a shining bald head, a leering red face, a pair of twinkling grey eyes, and a mouth perpetually on the grin." We are further told (Chap. ix) that the whole baronetage, peerage, common-age of England did not contain a more cunning, mean, selfish, foolish, and disreputable old man—a man who could not spell and did not care to read—who had the habits and the cunning of a boar; whose aim in life was pettifogging; who never had a

taste, or emotion, or enjoyment, but what was sordid and foul; and yet, he had rank, and honors and power somehow; and was a dignitary of the land and a pillar of the state."

Charles Kingsley used to tell a good story of a lady who confided to Thackeray that she liked *Vanity Fair* exceedingly. "The characters are so natural," she said, "all but the baronet, Sir Pitt Crawley, and surely he is overdrawn; it is impossible to find such coarseness in his rank of life." "That character," the author smilingly replied, "is almost the only exact portrait in the book." The identity of the prototype was not revealed for many years, but it has recently been asserted that the character was sketched from a former Lord Rolle. "Sir Pitt's letters to Becky were very badly spelt and written," remarks the gentleman who puts forward this theory, "and I may say that I have in my possession a letter written by Sir Robert Brownrigg to His Royal Highness the Duke of York when Commander-in-Chief of the British army, complaining that a report received from Lord Rolle, as Lord-Lieutenant of his county, was so badly written that he could not decipher it."—LEWIS MELVILLE.

Crawley, Pitt, in Thackeray's *Vanity Fair*, eldest son of Sir Pitt (see above) and brother to Rawdon, but widely differentiated from either. He is neat, prim, precise and proper; and of pronounced evangelical views until it no longer pays him to profess them. At Eton he was called "Miss Crawley." He inherited money, married money, and was careful in hoarding it.

Crawley, Captain Rawdon, in Thackeray's *Vanity Fair*, is the son of Sir Pitt Crawley and the husband of Rebecca Sharp, a dragoon of good height and good looks with a great voice and meagre brains, a haw-haw manner, a hectoring yet not unamiable disposition, prodigal in giving but too improvident to be honest with his tradespeople. Becky for a period showed him how to live on nothing a year, but he detected her in an intrigue with Lord Steyne, thrashed that nobleman, and left his wife.

Crayon, Geoffrey, Esq. The pseudonym under which Washington Irving published *The Sketchbook*, and which he occasionally returned to in his miscellaneous sketches.

Cressid, Creseide, or **Cressida,** in mediæval and modern literature the fickle flame of Troilus whose infidelity has kinned her to Faustina and Messalina and made her name a byword. She is unknown to Grecian myth, but may plausibly be identified with Briseis of the *Iliad*, the more so that like Briseis she was said to be the daughter of a Trojan priest Calchas. Under the cognate name of Briseida she made her first appearance in mediæval poetry as the heroine of a tale by Benoist de St. Maure, a trouvère of the twelfth century, and her second in Guido delle Colonne's *Historia Trojana.* From Guido, the story passed to Boccaccio, who substituted the modern name, and thence was adopted into English literature in the *Troilus and Creseide* of Chaucer (1380) and the *Troilus and Cressida* of Shakespeare (1609). See TROILUS.

Shakespeare's treatment of Chaucer's heroine Cressida is a shock to any lover of the early poet's work. To have the beautiful Cressida,—hesitating, palpitating like the nightingale before her sin, driven by force of hard circumstances which she could not control into unfaithfulness to her love,— to have this Cressida whom Chaucer spared for very ruth, set before us as a mere shameless wanton, making eyes at all the men she sees and showing her looseness in the movement of every limb, is a terrible blow.— F. J. FURNIVALL: *The Leopold Shakespeare* (1877).

Crochet, Squire, in Peacock's satirical novel, *Crotchet Castle*, a retired man of business who withdraws into the country and gathers around him a company of eccentrics—all caricatures of famous men of the day.

Crocodile, Lady Kitty, in Samuel Foote's comedy *A Trip to Calais* (1777), a caricature of Elizabeth Chudleigh, so-called Duchess of Kingston, who after the Duke's death was tried for bigamy. The House of Lords found her guilty of having inveigled the Duke into a marriage while she was lawfully the wife of the Earl of Bristol, but she succeeded in escaping punishment by pleading the benefit of the peerage. Her entirely logical argument was that if she were not the wife of the Duke she was the wife of the earl and entitled to the privileges of her rank. Abandoning England for the continent she continued her brilliant but scandalous career at many royal courts, finally opening a *salon* in Paris which was frequented by persons of rank and talent. Thackeray is thought to have had her career in mind when he drew his Beatrix Esmond, especially in her final avatar as Baroness Bernstein.

Croftangry, Chrystal, the feigned editor of Scott's *Chronicles of the Canongate.* According to Lockhart he was drawn from Sir Walter's father, " the fretful patient at the deathbed " being a living picture.

Crowe, Captain, in Smollett's novel, *Adventures of Sir Launcelot Greaves* (1760), the attendant squire upon the Quixotic hero when he starts out to reform the world. The former commander of a merchant ship in the Mediterranean trade, innocently ignorant of life ashore, he was admirably fitted to play the part of a modern Sancho Panza. Smollett thus describes him:

He was an excellent seaman—brave, active, friendly in his way, and scrupulously honest, but as little acquainted with the world as a sucking child; whimsical, impatient, and so impetuous that he could not help breaking in upon the conversation whatever it might be, with repeated interruptions that seemed to burst upon him by involuntary impulse. When he himself attempted to speak, he never finished his period, but made such a number of abrupt transitions that his discourse seemed to be an unconnected series of unfinished sentences.

Croye, Isabelle, Countess de, in Scott's historical romance, *Quentin Durward* (1823), a ward of Charles the Bold, Duke of Burgundy, who fled to the court of Louis XI in France to escape from a distasteful marriage. See DURWARD, QUENTIN.

Crummles, Mr. Vincent, in Dickens's novel, *Nicholas Nickleby*, actor-manager of a company of strolling players which is joined by Nicholas and Smike. He is an eccentric but not unkindly gentleman, humorously discoursing the jargon of his trade. His family consists of a wife, a tragedy queen full of benevolence, a son Percy and two daughters, the younger of whom, Ninetta, is known on the playbills as the Infant Phenomenon (*q.v.*).

Mr. Crummles and the whole of his theatrical business is an admirable case of that first and most splendid quality in Dickens—I mean the art of making something which we call pompous and dull, becoming in literature pompous and delightful.—G. K. CHESTERTON: *Appreciations of Dickens.*

Cruncher, Jerry, in Dickens's *Tale of Two Cities,* an odd-job man at Telson's bank in London and also a resurrection man. His wife, a pious woman, is distressed at the nature of his nocturnal occupation, and, remonstrance being useless, falls to prayers and supplications to heaven on bended knee. Cruncher, though no believer, has a vague alarm at her " flopping against him " and resorts to curses and even violence in self-defence.

Crusoe, Robinson, hero of a novel by Daniel Defoe, *The Life and Strange, Surprising Adventures of Robinson Crusoe of York, Mariner* (1719), and of its sequel, *The Further Adventures of Robinson Crusoe* (1719). Robinson runs away to sea in his boyhood; is captured by the corsairs; lives for a period in Brazil; sets sail from San Salvador for the coast of Africa, is shipwrecked and washed ashore (the only survivor) on an uninhabited island in the Caribbean Sea near the mouth of the Orinoco River. There he lives for twenty-eight years in a solitude that was broken only toward the last by the presence of a fugitive savage whom he named Friday (*q.v.*). Finally, both he and Friday were rescued by savages. In theme rather than in incident the story bears some resemblance to that of Alexander Selkirk (*q.v.*), whose narrative of an enforced stay upon Juan Fernandez had appeared in 1712 and whom Defoe had seen and conversed with. Selkirk, however, was only one of many instances of mariners being wrecked or purposely abandoned in an uninhabited island, and the situation was

ready for any master genius who could profit by it. Defoe himself, in his *Serious Reflections during the Life of Robinson Crusoe* (1720), assures us that the book had an allegorical meaning—" a kind of type of what the dangers and vicissitudes and surprising escapes of his own life had been."

[Defoe] was essentially a bluff, masculine, matter-of-fact man, and he tells his story in a matter-of-fact way. Prosaic accuracy of detail serves him perhaps better than heroics. The man he paints is a sturdy, plain-minded seaman, who sets himself to solve the problem of how to live under conditions which would have overwhelmed a more sensitive mind. It is the indomitable courage of Crusoe which charms us. He is typically Anglo-Saxon in his stolid endurance of fate, his practical grasp of circumstances, his ingenuity, his fertility of resource, his determination to make the best of his unfortunate situation. He behaves after the manner of his race. Having by chance become the monarch of a desert island, he sets himself to govern it to the best of his ability, and to arrange his life with decent orderliness.—W. J. DAWSON: *Makers of English Fiction.*

Crusoe's Island. Until recently it has been imagined that because Daniel Defoe owed the idea of his *Robinson Crusoe* to conversations held with Alexander Selkirk, who had been shipwrecked on the island of Juan Fernandez, therefore that was the island on which his own hero repeated the experiences of Selkirk. But Juan Fernandez is located in the Pacific Ocean off the coast of Chili. All Crusoe's statements show that he was wrecked in the Atlantic Ocean on an island near the mouth of the Orinoco River. This island is now positively identified as Tobago, which is situated off the coast of Venezuela, a few miles from Trinidad.

Cunegonde, heroine of Voltaire's satirical tale, *Candide.* See also KUNIGUNDE.

Cunizza, heroine of Robert Browning's poem, *Sordello,* who is called Palma until her true name is revealed at the close of the poem. She was a historical character, sister of Ezzelino III. Dante places her in *Paradise,* ix, 32. Sordello had an intrigue with her while she was married to her first husband (DANTE: *Purgatory,* vi).

D

Dale, Laetitia, in George Meredith's novel, *The Egoist*, a romantic girl whose father, a half pay officer, rents a cottage on Sir Willoughby Patterne's estate. She adores Sir Willoughby and he basks in her adoration until longer acquaintance opens her eyes to his true character. See PATTERNE and MIDDLETON, CLARA.

Dale, Lily, heroine of Anthony Trollope's novel, *The Small House at Allington* (1864).

One of the characters which readers of my novels have liked the best. In the love with which she has been greeted I have hardly joined with much enthusiasm, feeling that she is something of a French prig. She became first engaged to a snob who jilted her; and then, though in truth she loved another man who was hardly good enough, she could not extricate herself sufficiently from the collapse of her first great misfortune to be able to make up her mind to be wife of one whom, though she loved him, she did not altogether reverence. Prig as she was, she made her way into the hearts of many readers, both young and old; so that from that time to this, I have been continually honored with letters; the purport of which has always been to beg me to marry Lily Dale to Johnny Eames.

Dalgarno, Lord Malcolm of, in Scott's historical romance, *The Fortunes of Nigel* (1822), a profligate young nobleman, son of the Scotch Earl of Huntinglen. Pretending friendship for the inexperienced Nigel, he lures him into evil resorts and gives him ruinous advice. When his true character is exposed by Lady Hermione, whom he had seduced, he bears his disgrace with calm effrontery, going through the forms of marriage with the lady only to secure the means of burning her house to ashes.

Dalgetty, Rittmaster Dugald, in Scott's historical novel, *A Legend of Montrose* (1819), the Laird of Drumthwacket, a soldier of fortune who lets out his sword to the highest bidder, and after sundry exploits is retained in the service of the Earl of Menteith. Brave and always ready of resource he is a vainglorious braggart and an amusing pedant. The original of Dalgetty was probably Munro, member of a band of Scotch and English auxiliaries in the island

of Swinemunde in 1630, who wrote the story of the campaign.

The general idea of the character is familiar to our comic dramatists after the Restoration, and may be said in some measure to be compounded of Captain Fluellen and Bobadil; but the ludicrous combination of the *soldado* with the divinity student of Mareschal College is entirely original.—JEFFREY.

Dugald is a garrulous pedant and may be styled one of Scott's bores, but he never bores us, whether he sets forth his simple reasons for serving with the king's army and not with the Covenanters; or criticises the various services of Europe; or lectures on the propriety of fortifying the sconce of Drumsnab; or faces Argyll in Inverary or masters him in the dungeon; or wheedles the Presbyterian chaplain; or mocks the bows and arrows of his allies, the Children of the Mist; or does deeds of derring-do at Inverlochy, or swaggers about in the fresh glories of his title of Knight Banneret.—ANDREW LANG: *Sir Walter Scott.*

There is good warrant for the character of Dalgetty. The name itself was borrowed from that old acquaintance of Scott's boyhood, Captain Dalgetty of Prestonpans, "who had fought in all the German wars, but found very few to listen to his tales of military feats." "He formed," says Scott, "a sort of alliance with me, and I used invariably to attend him for the pleasure of hearing these communications." The real antecedents, however, out of which grew the Dalgetty as we knew him, are to be found in the memoirs of the Scottish mercenaries of the period. Two in particular were used by Scott, both of them written, he remarks, very much in the humour of the doughty captain, the Memoirs of Lieutenant Colonel Robert Munro and of Sir James Turner.—W. S. CROCKETT: *The Scott Originals*, p. 273.

D'Amville, in *The Atheist's Tragedy* (1611), by Cyril Tourneur, a man of good abilities and originally good disposition who becomes a human fiend through unbelief in revealed religion, is hurried on from crime to crime and finally kills himself by accident. D'Amville himself (the name may have been meant to suggest Damn Villain) attributes his atheism to the impression made upon him by the worthlessness of his brother's Puritan chaplain. When his accomplice in a midnight murder is terrified by a storm of thunder and lightning he calmly philosophises on the origin of such phenomena. He justifies even incest by the general liberty which nature allows to her creatures. His reason is finally overthrown by the death of his younger son, and the collapse of all his schemes.

Dantes, Edmond, hero of Alexander Dumas' romance, *The Count of Monte Christo.*

A young sailor in Marseilles in 1815 just before the "Hundred Days," Edmond has won the captainship of the merchantman *Pharaon* and the promised hand of Catalan Mercedes. He has two disappointed rivals; one covets the ship, the other the girl. They trump up a charge that he is a Bonapartist emissary carrying letters between Ella and the mainland. He is sentenced to life imprisonment in the Chateau d'If, which faces the Mediterranean. There he digs a secret passage to the room of a fellow prisoner, the Abbé, a Catholic priest and a supposed madman, who confides to him the secret of a buried treasure on the barren island of Monte Christo. With his knowledge Dantes escapes. He unearths the treasure and bursts upon astonished Paris as the mysterious millionaire Count of Monte Christo. He devotes the remainder of his life to dazzling the world at large, rewarding his friends and punishing one by one the enemies who had been responsible for his captivity.

Dapper, a clerk in *The Alchemist,* a comedy by Ben Jonson. Face and Subtle swindle him by feigning that the Queen of the Fairies is his aunt.

This reminds us of the extreme doting attachment which the queen of the fairies is represented to have taken for Dapper.—Sir W. Scott.

Dapple, the name of Sancho's ass, in Cervantes's romance of *Don Quixote.*

Darby and **Joan,** hero and heroine of a ballad, *The Happy Old Couple,* which has been attributed to Matthew Prior but probably antedates him. Another claimant has been put forward in the person of Henry Woodfall, the printer. According to Timberley, Woodfall was an apprentice of John Darby, a printer of Bartholomew Close, who died in 1730, and

whose devotion to his wife Joan was notorious in the locality. This "happy couple," in their simple contentment and dislike for change, present some analogies to the Philemon and Baucis of classic myth.

Darcy, Fitz William, hero of Jane Austen's novel, *Pride and Prejudice,* a young country gentleman of wealth and family, dignified and courtly, quite conscious of his superior station in life but still dowered with many excellent qualities, including that of loyal devotion to the heroine, Elizabeth **Bennet.** She in her part is at first strongly prejudiced against the pride which she eventually succeeds in humbling and bringing to her feet.

Philip Darcy is Pride; Elizabeth Bennet is Prejudice; and the plot is the struggle of their mutual attraction against their mutual repulsion, ending in love and marriage. Elizabeth has been playfully pronounced a charming being by her creatress, who perhaps made her partly in her own image. She is not supremely beautiful, but has force and charm of character, excellent sense and a lively wit.—Goldwin Smith.

Darling, Dolly, heroine of Richard Blackmore's novel, *Springhaven* (1887), with whom Blythe Scudamore is in love.

A very charming maiden, and just as romantic and silly as a charming, idle maiden may be without harm or shame. No real man could escape being Dolly's slave; if Mr. Blackmore had had her alive, in his study, he would never have dared to treat her so harshly as he does. He takes a mean advantage of the fact that Dolly is either dead or old enough to be past mischief. He sneers at her little vanities, makes much ado about her little deceits, and finally throws on her shapely shoulders the whole burden of her father's death.—*N. Y. Nation,* May 19, 1887.

Darnay, Charles, Marquis St. Evremonde in Dickens's *Tale of Two Cities,* the lover and afterwards the husband of Lucie Manette. He is the physical double of Sydney Carton (*q.v.*). The latter takes advantage of this resemblance to sacrifice himself in his stead.

Darnel, Aurelia, in Smollett's novel, *Sir Launcelot Greaves,* is described by Sir Walter Scott (*British Novelists*) as "by far the most feminine, and, at the same time, lady-like person to whom the author has introduced us."

8

Darrel, the titular hero of Irving A. Bacheller's novel, *Darrel of the Blessed Isles* (1903), an old clock-tinker and a philosopher familiar with Shakespeare Milton and the Bible, from whose perusal he has drawn wisdom, charity and contentment. The Blessed Isles of the title refer to the land of poetry and imagination in which Darrel's mind continually dwells.

Darrell, William, the Lord of Littlecote, hero of a ballad introduced by Sir Walter Scott into the fifth canto of *Rokeby*. It is founded on a legend current in Queen Elizabeth's time and attached to Littlecote Hall in Wiltshire. A nurse taken blind-folded to the hall, assists at the birth of a child, and witnesses the unnatural father throw it to its death in a blazing fire. Despite all efforts to muffle her both going and coming, she secured a clue and denounced the murderer. Scott tones down the horror of the story. A gray friar is sent for to shrive a dying woman; he is conducted to the mansion with his eyes bandaged, performs his sacred function to one in apparent health, and next day the countryside mourns the sudden death of the mistress of Littlecote Hall. Hubert Hall, in *Society in the Elizabethan Age*, has rescued Wild Darrell from much of the slander which pollutes his name. See *American Notes and Queries*, March 25, 1889.

Dartle, Rosa, in Dickens's *David Copperfield*, companion to Mrs. Steerforth and hopelessly in love with her son James. " She had black hair and eager eyes," writes Copperfield, " and was thin and had a scar upon her lip. I concluded in my own mind that she was thirty and wished to be married. She was a little dilapidated like a house with having been so long to let: her thinness seemed to be the effect of some wasting fire within her which found a vent in her gaunt eyes." The scar was the work of Steerforth when a child. It is the index to Miss Dartle's susceptibilities and owns some allegiance to the hand that caused it.

Dashwood, Elinor, the heroine of Jane Austen's *Sense and Sensibility,* who represents the " sense " in the title as Marianne represents the " sensibility." This clever and amiable pair are the stepsisters of John Dashwood, a meanly avaricious man, ever fearful lest his income should be encroached upon by them. He is married to a selfish, scheming wife. A painful disillusion shows Marianne Dashwood that if a girl is gifted with sensitive or romantic feelings she had better keep them under control and disguise them from the public gaze; and finally, after her brief period of romance is over, she puts up very quietly with a husband of forty.

Dass, Durga, in the story of *Gemini,* in Rudyard Kipling's volume, *In Black and White,* is one of twins, Ram Dass being the other. Through a remarkable resemblance between the two, Durga is the victim of a comedy of errors which enables his brother to fleece him out of all his possessions.

David, King of Israel, whose story is told in I and II Samuel and in I Chronicles, is a favorite character in the literature and drama of mediæval and later Christendom. Following the Old Testament writers he is represented as in youth standing high in the favor of the Almighty: " the Lord hath sought him a man after his own heart " (I Samuel xiii 14), though in maturity he falls away by grievous sin, is chastened by retributory affliction and restored to favor by sincere repentance.

David and Goliath (1630) a narrative poem by Michael Drayton, shows the young shepherd in his mighty youth.

David and Bethsabe (1598), a drama by George Peele, represents the entire episode of Uriah's wife, from David's first meeting with her to his bitter repentance. Abraham Cowley wrote an epic in 4 books, *Davideis, A Sacred Poem of the Troubles of David.* A more ambitious but less successful effort is *Davideis, or the Life of David, King of Israel* (1712), by Thomas Elwood. *A Song to David* (1763), written by Christopher Smart while confined as a lunatic, is a wild but splendid rhapsody.

Davidson, Joshua, hero of a novel by Mrs. E. Lynn Linton, *The True History of Joshua Davidson, Christian Communist* (1872), a young English workingman who is really an avatar of Christ reincarnated in modern times and painfully adjusting himself to a nineteenth century environment.

Daw, Marjorie, heroine of T. B. Aldrich's short story of that name (*Atlantic Monthly*, April, 1873), which leads up by a climax to an unforeseen conclusion that makes a fool of the reader to his own delight.

Dawkins, John (nicknamed the Artful Dodger), in Charles Dickens's novel, *Oliver Twist*, a young pickpocket in the service of Fagin, the Jew. He meets Oliver fleeing to London, gives him something to eat and introduces him to Fagin's den. Although an adept in thieving and all knavery, the Dodger is finally caught in attempting to pick a pocket and is sentenced to transportation for life.

Deadeye Dick, in Gilbert and Sullivan's comic operetta, *H. M. S. Pinafore,* an excellent burlesque of the traditionary villain of the forecastle.

Deadwood Dick, nickname of Robert Dickey (1840–1912) whose actual adventures formed the basis for many of the " dime novels " which fed the imaginations of a callow youth in 1860–1880. He was a scout under Gen. George Crook in the days when the red man of the plains was making his last stand against the invading white. He served under Gen. Alfred H. Terry during a part of that commander's campaigns in the foothills of the Rocky Mountains. He became successively an Indian agent, a United States marshal, a trapper and a fur merchant and, having made a fortune, lost it and died poor.

He fought Indians for a good many years, and his hair-breadth escapes and his well-known courage made him dear to the writers, who loved to describe the hero dashing madly across the prairie through a flight of arrows and a hail of bullets and eluding his pursuers. He was one of that dying and dead galaxy of heroes of the old west that included Kit Carson, Buffalo Bill, Bat Masterson and others of the noted Indian and gun fighters who passed with the red man, the cow camps and the buffalo. In picturesqueness he was not equaled even by the skin-shirted, wide-hatted Cody. If the dime-novel writer could have created an ideal character in the flesh Deadwood Dick would have been that character.— *Obituary in Utica Globe.*

Deans, Davie, in Scott's novel, *The Heart of Midlothian,* a poor cowfeeder at Edinburgh, affectionately known as Douce Davie, full of whims and follies, but rigid and unbending in his adherence to what seemed to him the only righteous course, and a staunch Presbyterian. He is the father of Jeanie and Effie.

The very pearl of belated Covenanters. He is "lifted" straight from that honest, brave, absurd Peter or Patrick Walker who suffered torture as a mere boy during the Restoration and lived well into the eighteenth century, compiling his biographies of covenanting characters, such as Cameron and Peden. Walker was to them what Izaak Walton was to the great divines of the Church of England in his long and well-contented day. How true Davie Deans is to his model the reader may discover in Mr. Harry Fleming's *Saints of the Covenant,* a reprint of Walker's biographies with notes. —ANDREW LANG: *Sir Walter Scott.*

Deans, Effie (Euphemia), daughter of Davie by his second wife, a pretty, vain, foolish girl who is betrayed by George Staunton and imprisoned for child murder. After her half-sister Jeanie has procured her pardon, she marries Staunton and, having blazed for some years in the fashionable world as Lady Staunton, retired in her widowhood to severe seclusion in a convent.

Deans, Jeanie, daughter of Davie by his first wife, who saves her half-sister Effie by walking from Edinburgh to London to plead her cause with Queen Caroline.

The prototype in real life of Jeanie Deans was Helen Walker (1712–1791) the daughter of a small farmer in the parish of Irongray, Dumfriesshire. The very day of her sister's condemnation she got a petition drawn up and afterwards walked the whole distance to London barefoot. There with the help of John, Duke of Argyle, she secured a pardon. One of the last acts of Scott's life was to raise a tombstone to her memory in Irongray churchyard.

Jeanie Deans, to our thinking, is the cream and perfection of Scott's work. A creature absolutely pure, absolutely truthful, yet of a tenderness, a forbearance, and long-suffering beyond the power of man, willing to die rather than lie, but resolute that the truth her nature has forced her to speak shall not be used for harm if her very life can prevent it. There is not one scene in which this high valour of the heart, this absolute goodness, fails her; nor is there one in which she departs ever so little from the lowliness of her beginning. She is as little daunted by the Duke and the Queen as she is by the other difficulties which she has met and surmounted with that tremulous timidity of courage which belongs to nerves highly strung; nay, she has even a certain modest pleasure in the society of these potentates, her simple soul meeting them with awe, yet with absolute frankness; making no commonplace attempt at equality.—*Blackwood's Magazine*, August, 1871, p. 250.

Debree, Walter, hero of a tale, *The New Priest of Conception Bay* (1858), by Robert Lowell. A Protestant clergyman, he is converted to Catholicism and takes orders as a priest, but repenting, determines to return to his fold and his wife; is overtaken by a snowstorm and perishes. His lifeless body is taken to his wife. The story, which is poetical and pathetic, is ruined by the fact that a married man cannot take orders in the Catholic church unless his wife does the same.

Dedlock, Sir Leicester, Bar't, in Dickens's novel, *Bleak House* (1853), a generous and high-minded aristocrat intensely conscious of his rank and jealous of his family honor, married to Lady Honoria, a beautiful and stately woman of inferior rank. Under a cold exterior she hides an ever-present consciousness of a wretched episode in her past when, engaged but not married to a gay rake named Captain Hawdon, she became the mother of the girl now known as Esther Summerson. Finding that her secret is on the eve of discovery she flees from her home and dies at the gate of a squalid graveyard where the father of her child is buried.

Dedlow, George, hero of a story,

The Case of George Dedlow (1900), by Dr. S. Weir Mitchell. He is represented as a soldier who had all his limbs amputated and nearly lost his sense of identity. The case was widely accepted as genuine, and author and publishers were embarrassed by receiving subscriptions from sympathetic readers.

Deerslayer, in Cooper's novel of that name, a nickname for Natty Bumppo. See BUMPPO.

Deever, Danny, subject of a poem of that name in Rudyard Kipling's *Barrack-Room Ballads*. Danny Deever is hanged in the presence of his regiment for having shot a sleeping comrade.

Defarge, Madame Thérèse, in *A Tale of Two Cities* (1859), by Charles Dickens, a terrible old woman who sits quietly knitting all day long, but is an eager and watchful accomplice of her husband, the wineseller Ernest Defarge, ringleader of the Revolutionists in the suburb of St. Antoine in Paris.

Delectable Mountains, in Bunyan's *Pilgrim's Progress* (1678), a range of hills whose summits commanded a view of the Celestial City, the object of the Pilgrim's quest. The suggestion came from the Old Testament: "When the morning was up, they had him to the top of the house, and bid him look south. So he did and behold at a great distance he saw a most pleasant mountainous country, beautified with woods, vineyards, fruits of all sorts, flowers also with springs and fountains very delectable to behold" (Isaiah xxxiii, 16, 17). Christian, with his companion Hopeful, climbs to the top of the mountains. Finding shepherds there feeding their flocks, they ask "whose delectable mountains are these and whose be the sheep that feed upon them?" The shepherds answer, "These mountains are Emanuel's lambs and they are within sight of his city and the sheep are his, and he laid down his life for them."

Delia, a name sometimes given to Diana, from her birthplace Delos, just as her fellow-citizen Apollo is styled Delius. Virgil has called a shepherdess in the Eclogues by this name and it is frequently used in amatory and pastoral poetry as the generic name for a sweetheart. Among the cases of real women who have been thus designated by adoring poets the following are the best known:

1. The ladylove of the Roman Theocritus whose real name is conjectured to have been Plania (from *planus*), for which the Greek δηλια is an equivalent, both words signifying plain, clear, manifest.

2. The Miss Dashwood celebrated in James Hammond's Elegies. She rejected his suit and died unmarried in 1779.

3. William Shenstone addressed his love poetry, including his *Pastoral Ballad*, to a lady whose real name has been effectively hidden under this title.

4. William Cowper wrote a number of verses to Delia, whom it is easy to identify as his cousin Theodora. She was in love with him, but her father, Ashley Cowper, forbade the union, nominally on the ground of consanguinity, really, as Southey thinks, because he saw that the poet was unfit for business and not likely to be able to support a wife. Theodora remained unmarried and never forgot her lover. She preserved his letters till her death at an extreme old age. Her sister, Lady Hesketh, was subsequently one of Cowper's most intimate friends.

5. Samuel Daniels addressed his sonnets to a lady whom he calls Delia, and who is understood to have refused him for a wealthier lover.

Delobelle, Desirée, in Daudet's novel, *Fromont Jeune et Risler Aîné,* a deformed girl, daughter of a pretentious imbecile actor. She is poor, stunted, laborious, toiling at a small industry; she is in love, is rejected, she tries to drown herself, she dies. "The sequence of ideas," says Andrew Lang, " is in Dickens's vein; but read the tale and I think you will see how little the thing is overdone, how simple and unforced it is, compared with analogous persons

and scenes in the work of the English master."—*Essays in Little,* p. 124.

DeLonge. See LONGE, DE.

Delorme, Marion, heroine and title of a tragedy by Victor Hugo. Written in June, 1829, its production was not permitted until August 31, 1831. Marion was a historical character, a courtesan who flourished under Louis XIII. She is introduced as repentant—purified and ennobled by deep love for Didier, an obscure youth, naturally generous but soured by contact with the world. He knows nothing of her past but adores her as the one true and lovely being in the world. She is doubly tortured by her inability to explain why she cannot marry him. Didier resents the freedom with which the Marquis de Saverny treats the lady, his former mistress. A duel is interrupted by Richelieu's guards. Saverny escapes by feigning death. Didier is arrested, but with Marion's assistance scales the walls of his jail. Disguised as Spaniards the couple join a troupe of players. One day they are recognized by Saverny in the audience. He reveals Marion's true character to Didier who, horror-stricken, makes no resistance when a moment later he is arrested for murder. But Saverny comes forward, throws off his disguise and proves that Didier never murdered him. Both, however, are arrested for duelling. Marion pleads for her lover's life first with the king, then with Laffermas, who had made the arrest. He agrees to spare Didier if she will gratify his lust. She yields but the sacrifice is in vain. Didier refused the pardon so dearly purchased. He and Saverny perish together on the scaffold.

Delville, Mr., in Fanny Burney's novel *Cecilia* (1782), one of the guardians of the heroine, a purse proud and haughty gentleman, magnificent and ostentatious in his manner of living, and cultivating an air of affable condescension toward his inferiors.

Demetrius, in Shakespeare's *Midsummer Night's Dream*, in love with Hermia.

Democritus, in Greek history, the " Laughing Philosopher " of Abdera, so-called from his avowed determination to laugh at the follies rather than weep at the miseries of mankind. Robert Burton took the pseudonym of Democritus Junior for his *Anatomy of Melancholy*, and the name is inscribed on his monument in Christ Church Cathedral.

Dempster, Janet, heroine of George Eliot's *Janet's Repentance*. Married to a brutal drunkard she takes refuge in drink against his ill-usage, and is rescued through the kind offices of the Rev. Edgar Tryan.

Dence, Jael, in Charles Reade's novel, *Put Yourself in his Place*, a daughter of the people, strong bodied and strong minded, the maid and companion of Grace Carden, herself loving Henry Little, to whom Miss Carden is engaged, yet risking her own life in a terrible emergency to save him for her mistress.

Denham, Ruth, titular heroine of the *Queen of Sheba* by T. B. Aldrich, receives that sobriquet because in the earlier chapters, when suffering from temporary aberration of mind, she fancies herself the Biblical character. A contributor to *The Atlantic Monthly* October, 1895, calls attention to a similar delusion cherished a century previous by a lunatic in Hallowell, Maine. According to the annals of that town she used to wander about the country " in a happy mood " with " an air of command." One day in 1764 this Queen of Sheba made her way in court to the judge's bench—no one daring to oppose her— and calmly took her seat near the presiding judge. Her removal by a sheriff was not easily effected, but with no sacrifice of dignity on her part.

Denise, titular heroine of a problem play (1886) by Alexander Dumas, fils. She is the daughter of excellent parents, the Brissots, who are befriended by the Comte André de Bardannes, and she herself is companion to André's sister Marthe. André loves her—a fact which he confides to Mme. de Thauzette, a woman of the world, formerly his mistress—and he would propose for Denise but that he has reason to suspect that she is not what she seems. In truth, she has been the mistress of Mme. de Thauzette's unworthy son Fernand; a child, since dead, was born of the *liaison*, and the problem is whether André should or should not marry a woman with a past of this sort.

Dennis, Father, in *The Mutiny of the Mavericks* and other short stories by Rudyard Kipling, the popular Roman Catholic chaplain of the Mavericks, an Irish regiment stationed in India. He could blare like a bull on occasion, but had been known to tuck up his cassock and take part in a rush—usually finding that some saint had furnished him with a revolver for the emergency.

Deronda, Daniel, titular hero of a novel by George Eliot, evidently her ideal of youthful manhood. " You could not have seen his face thoroughly meeting yours," she says, " without believing that human creatures have done nobly in times past and might do more nobly in time to come." He has satisfied a few male critics (George William Curtis and Edward Dowden, for example, hailed him with enthusiasm), but repelled most men and practically all women. Sir Leslie Stephen calls him " not merely a feminine but, one is inclined to say, a school-girl's hero. He is so sensitive and scrupulously delicate that he will not soil his hands by joining in the rough play of ordinary political and social reformers." Young ladies in real life (probably because they resent this essential femininity) have never cared for him, but in the novel they fall at his feet. To Gwendolen this seraphic person becomes an " outer conscience." She begins " a new existence," but it seems " inseparable from Deronda," and she longs that his presence may be permanent. Happily she does not dare to love him, and hopes only to be bound to him by a " spiritual tie." That is just as well, because he is in love with Myra, a young Jewess, whom he has rescued from suicide in the Thames. Through her family he makes the discovery that he himself is a Jew by birth, and so solves many mysteries.

George Eliot, in later years, came to know several representatives in the younger generation of the class to which Deronda belonged. She speaks, for example, with great warmth of Henry Sidgwick. His friends, she remarks, by their own account, always "expected him to act according to a higher standard" than they would attribute to any one else or adopt for themselves. She sent Deronda to Cambridge soon after she had written this, and took great care to give an accurate account of the incidents of Canbridge life. I have always fancied— though without any evidence—that some touches in Deronda were drawn from one of her friends, Edmund Gurney, a man of remarkable charm of character, and as good-looking as Deronda. In the Cambridge atmosphere of Deronda's days there was, I think, a certain element of rough common-sense which might have knocked some of her hero's nonsense out of him. But, in any case, one is sensible that George Eliot, if she is thinking of real life at all, has come to see through a romantic haze which deprives the portrait of reality.— SIR LESLIE STEPHEN: *George Eliot*, p. 191.

Desborough, Colonel, in Scott's novel, *Woodstock*. One of the Commissioners sent by Parliament to dispose of Woodstock Palace and Park as national property.

Desborough, Lucy, in George Meredith's novel, *The Ordeal of Richard Feverel*, a maiden wooed and secretly married by Richard. Sir Austin, the father, learning of the marriage, keeps the couple apart in accordance with his famous "system" with the usual disastrous results.

Deschapelles, Pauline, heroine of *The Lady of Lyons*, a drama by Bulwer-Lytton. See MELNOTTE, CLAUDE.

Desdemona, heroine of Shakespeare's tragedy *Othello* (1611). She is the daughter of Brabantio, a Venetian senator, whom she alienates by her marriage with the Moorish general of the Venetian forces, Othello (*q.v.*). The story is derived from Giovanni Giraldi Cinthio's *Hecatommithi*, III, vii. Desdemona is the only name mentioned in Cinthio's

story. He writes of the Moor, the Lieutenant, the Ancient or Ensign, and his wife, "a handsome and discreet woman," without assigning them any names whatever.

It is so difficult for even the very greatest poets to give any vivid force of living interest to a figure of passive endurance that perhaps the only instance of perfect triumph over this difficulty is to be found in the character of Desdemona. Shakespeare alone could have made her as interesting as Imogen or Cordelia; though these have so much to do and dare, and she after her first appearance has simply to suffer.—SWINBURNE: *The Age of Shakespeare*.

Desgenais, in Alfred de Musset's *Confessions of a Child of the Age*, a gentlemanly roué who preaches a cynical morality, an enlightened selfishness, a sort of Franklin-like respect for honesty as the best policy. His name and some of his characteristics were borrowed by Theodore Burrière in *Les Filles de Marbre* (1853), known in this country as *The Marble Heart* and in *The Parisians of the Decadence*. He reappears under other names in other plays by Barrière and has been copied and imitated by other dramatists and novelists. See CAMORS, M. DE.

Barrière has broadened and coarsened the outlines of the original so that his Desgenais has come to be accepted as a type of the class whereof Musset's Desgenais is merely an individual. A modern Diogenes who has realized by practice what is so hard to learn by precept, the hollowness and vanity of vice, his cynicism is sheer contempt for the folly of a world which will continue to be wicked against its own interests. He knows that his own experiences cannot be utilized for the benefit of others, that wisdom can be learned only at the cost of singed and mutilated wings, and the sarcasms which he pours into heedless ears acquire increased bitterness from his knowledge of their uselessness.

Despair, Giant, in Bunyan's *Pilgrim's Progress* (1678), a redoubtable monster who lived with his wife Diffidence in Doubting Castle— obviously an allegory of the doubt, distrust and despair that waylay the pilgrim on his heavenward path. The giant, finding Christian and Hopeful asleep on his grounds, takes them captive and locks them up in a dungeon. Here they languish from Wednesday to Saturday "without one bit of bread or drop of drink or ray of light." Further, acting on the advice of Diffidence, the giant beats them soundly with a crab-tree cudgel. On Saturday night Christian remembers that he has in his bosom a key called "Promise," wherewith he opens the door of the prison house and escapes with his companion.

Deuceace, Hon. Algernon Percy, a black-leg of good family, fifth and youngest son of the Earl of Crabs, whose story is told by Thackeray in *The Amours of Mr. Deuceace*, and who flits through the pages of other novels and stories, *i.e.*, *The Shabby Genteel Story*, *Vanity Fair*, *Pendennis* and *The Ravenswing*. In the *Amours* Mr. Deuceace conspires with Mr. Blewett to fleece rich young Mr. Dawkins, and after relieving the latter of £4,700 refuses to divide the swag either with his accomplice or with his own father. Hence the Earl allows him to fall into a misconception which leads Algernon to propose to the heiress Matilda Griffin, who forfeits her wealth when she marries without her step-mother's consent. The character has its grim original in Thackeray's own experience. Sir Theodore Martin tells how at Spa, the novelist once pointed out to him a seedy-looking gambler. "That was the original of my Deuceace," he explained, and then went on to tell how this man and a companion, knowing that Thackeray would have money when he came of age, had once fleeced him out of £1,500 at écarté. "I have not seen him," he added, "since the day he drove me down in his cabriolet to my broker's in the City, where I sold out my patrimony and handed it over to him."

Deukalion, Prince, hero of a lyrical drama of that name by Bayard Taylor (1878). Deukalion is the Greek Noah who is here made the typical man, as Pyrrha is the typical woman. They wander over earth from the primitive ages, sharing the advance from barbarism to classical paganism; experiencing successively the Catholic and Protestant forms of Christianity; always awaiting the consummation of their nuptials, and that final perfection which shall come only with the freest and purest religion, the highest culture,—the serene faith and absolute knowledge to which Science directs them, revealing a power which governs all, and whispering a pledge of spiritual immortality.

Diaforus, Thomas (father and son of the same name), two characters in Molière's comedy, *Le Malade Imaginaire* (1673), introduced to burlesque the medical science of the period. They are fanatically wedded to Æsculapian antiquity, dealing in empty words and in Greek and Latin formulas.

In all Molière's comedies there are no two figures of a more amusing veracity and of a more irresistible humor than the Diaforus pair; the father inflated with sonorous solemnity and the son stuffed with barren learning.—BRANDER MATTHEWS: *Molière*.

Diarmid, John, in Mrs. Oliphant's novel, *The Minister's Wife* (1869), a Scotch enthusiast who, having lived "a wicked, sensual, evil life," is converted at the revival in the parish of Loch Diarmid and rushes into religion "as he had rushed into dissipation, from the same passionate thirst for excitement." See MAC-FARLANE, AILIE.

Diavolo, Fra (It. *Brother Devil*), a nickname given to Michele Pezza (1760–1806), a native of Calabria, a robber and a Bourbon partisan leader who was hanged at Naples, but whose fame is kept green by popular songs and traditions and especially by the fact that he is the hero of Scribe and Auber's opera, *Fra Diavolo*, which was produced at Paris in 1830 but had little historical connection with the original.

Dick, Mr., in Dickens's *David Copperfield*, the name by which Richard Babley elects to be called—a slightly crazed but harmless old gentleman, florid and greyheaded, who resides with Miss Betsy Trotwood. His daily task is the writing of his own "Memorial," but he is obsessed by the idea of King Charles's head, which is continually obtruding itself into the narrative, "and then it was thrown aside and another one begun."

Diddler, Jeremy, in Kenney's farce, *Raising the Wind*, an ingenious swindler, ever needy, ever seedy, and ever contriving by some shift or other, by jest or song or stratagem, to borrow money or obtain credit that will tide him over until to-morrow.

Diggory, in Goldsmith's comedy *She Stoops to Conquer*, an extemporized butler to the Hardcastles, "taken from the barn to make a show at the side-table." He is awkward and garrulous, but effusively anxious to please.

Do we not owe an eternal debt of gratitude to honest Diggory for telling us about Old Grouse in the gun room—that immortal joke at which thousands and thousands of people have roared witty laughter, though they never any one of them could tell what the story was about?—WILLIAM BLACK: *Goldsmith*.

Dimmesdale, Arthur, in Hawthorne's romance, *The Scarlet Letter*, the guilty partner of Hester Prynne in the adultery that literally lays the letter A upon her breast and figuratively sears it into the heart of Dimmesdale. Finally, unable to bear any longer the tortures of concealment he publicly proclaims his crime and dies. See PRYNNE, HESTER, and CHILLINGWORTH.

The Puritan clergyman, reverenced as a saint by all his flock, conscious of a sin which, once revealed, will crush him to the earth, watched with a malignant purpose by the husband whom he has injured, unable to sum up the moral courage to tear off the veil and make the only atonement in his power, is undoubtedly a striking figure, powerfully conceived and most delicately described.—LESLIE STEPHEN.

Dinah, Aunt, in Sterne's novel, *Tristram Shandy*, aunt to Mr. Walter Shandy; also a character in *Uncle Tom's Cabin*.

Dinmont, Dandie (*i.e.*, Andrew), in Scott's novel, *Guy Mannering*, a shrewd, humorous, eccentric and kindly store-farmer at Charlie's Hope, "cunning like the patriarchs of old in that which belongeth to flocks and herds."

Dandie Dinmont is beyond all question, we think, the best rustic portrait that has ever yet been exhibited to the public—the most honorable to rustics, and the most creditable to the heart as well as the genius of the artist—the truest to nature, the most interesting and the most complete in all its lineaments.—FRANCIS JEFFREY: *Essays*.

In his lifetime it does not appear to have been suggested that Elliot was Dandie's original. It was otherwise with James Davidson of Hyndlee, who carried the name of Dandie with him to the grave. Yet Scott and Davidson never met until more than a year after the novel had established the man's celebrity all over the border. "I have been at the Spring Circuit" wrote Scott to Terry," and there I was introduced to a man whom I never saw in my life before— the genuine Dandie Dinmont. Dandie is himself modest, and says 'he believes it's only the dougs that is in the buik and no himsel'. In truth I knew nothing of the man except his odd humor of having only two names for twenty dogs." Shortreed— one of Davidson's intimates—would no doubt tell Scott about the Hyndlee terriers. —W. S. CROCKETT: *The Scott Originals*, p. 60.

Diomedes, in Shakespeare's *Troilus and Cressida*, a Greek general for whose love Cressida deserts Troilus. The rivals fight in v, 6.

Diver, Colonel, in Dickens's *Martin Chuzzlewit* (Chap. xv), the editor of the *New York Rowdy Journal*.

Dixie or **Dixie's land,** a name now popularly applied to an imaginary Utopia or negro lubberland vaguely located somewhere in the southern portion of the United States. Thus the famous song, *Dixie*, has the line:

Oh 'way down south in Dixie.

The song was written (1859) by D. D. Emmett for Bryant's Negro Minstrels in Mechanic's Hall, New York, was insensibly appropriated by the South, and became one of the favorite Confederate battle songs during the war. Yet, strangely enough, the term Dixie, which antedated the song by at least half a century, is said to have been originally applied to Manhattan Island. Here in ancient days one Dixie or Dixy owned a large number of slaves. The growth of the emancipation sentiment constrained him to transfer his slaves to safer quarters in the south, but they and their descendants looked back upon their original home with ever-increasing regret as the illusions of memory settled down upon it, until Dixie's land or Dixie became synonymous with an ideal locality combining ease and comfort with every material basis of happiness.

Djabel, in Robert Browning's tragedy, *The Return of the Druses*, a man of many virtues and great force of character. Out of patriotic love for his people, the Druses, a semi-Mahommedan sect from Syria who have taken refuge under the knights of Rhodes but found their trust abused, he deliberately pretends to be the incarnate God Hakeem, and seeks to lead them out of bondage. When the imposture is revealed he stabs himself.

Dobbin, William, in Thackeray's *Vanity Fair*, the awkward and adoring fag of George Osborne at Dr. Swishtail's famous school; his doggedly patient, lifetime friend, and, after his death the equally patient friend and suitor of George's widow Amelia, who discovers his worth after a dozen years of selfless devotion on his part.

Doboobie, Dr. Demetrius, in Scott's historical romance, *Kenilworth*, the bold, adventurous practitioner in physic from whom Wayland Smith obtained his knowledge of the healing art.

Dodd, David, in Charles Reade's novel, *Love Me Little, Love Me Long* (1859), the mate, later the captain, of an East Indiaman, a model of all manly qualities of body and mind but whose clumsiness and awkwardness on shore make him frequently ridiculous. He wins the vacillating Lucy Fountain by rescuing her from imminent peril when out sailing with a rival, thus convincing her of the strength, skill and courage he is capable of when in his proper element and away from the drawing rooms. Dodd reappears in *Hard Cash* (1864), as the father of the heroine Julia. He is bringing home to her and to her mother the hard cash of the title, £14,000 in bills and notes, which survives awful sea risks to be deposited triumphantly in a Barkington Bank. He has hardly got out on the street again when he hears that the bank is on the brink of failure. He rushes back, has a struggle with a fraudulent banker who refuses to return the deposit and loses his reason by apoplexy. Immured in a private madhouse he escapes when it burns down, gets on board a frigate as " Silly Billy Thompson " (for he has forgotten his own name and history), jumps overboard to rescue a youngster; narrowly misses being buried alive in a resultant fit of catalepsy; recovers his reason as a result of the shock; regains his £14,000 and is restored to wife and daughter.

Dodd, Julia, daughter of David and heroine of *Hard Cash*, by Charles Reade, a mixture of vehemence and sweetness, a young creature brimmed with the blissfulness of being.

Dodds, The, an Anglo-Irish family in Charles J. Lever's novel, *The Dodd Family Abroad*, written to satirize the ignorance, prejudice and self-assertiveness of British travellers on the Continent. Mr. Dodd is a fairly sensible man temporarily thrown off his balance by the complete change of surroundings. Mrs. Dodd is a silly woman who dearly loves a lord which weakness she shares with her son James, a dissipated dandy, and her daughter Mary Anne. It is a relief to turn to the other daughter, Catherine, agreeable, sensible, refined, tender—Lever's favorite female character, said to have been drawn from his wife.

Dodge, Esq., Steadfast, in Cooper's novels, *Homeward Bound* and *Home as Found*, an American journalist—a thoroughpaced demagogue at home and a servile tuft hunter abroad—who is an abstract of all the vanity, vulgarity and mean-spiritedness which Cooper despised in the American parvenu. The correspondence that Dodge has sent to the home newspapers during his European tour, and which he reads to his fellow-passengers on the homeward voyage, is an evident fling at N. P. Willis and his *Pencillings by the Way*.

Dodo, nickname of the heroine of Edward F. Benson's novel, *Dodo, a Detail of To-day* (1893), which was contemporaneously recognized as a thinly veiled sketch of Miss Emma Alice Tennant (familiarly known as Margot), who in 1895 married England's future Prime Minister, Mr. Asquith. A character in the story says of her: " She makes me feel as if I were sitting under a flaming gas-burner which was beating on what nature designed to be my brain-cover." And Dodo says: " The first time a man sees me he usually thinks I'm charming and sympathetic and lively. But it turns out I've got a bad temper, that I smoke and swear and only amuse myself."

A cruel and cynical commentary upon this brilliant woman's life was uttered by William Watson in a poem, *The Vampire*, beginning,

> She is not old, she is not young,
> The woman with the serpent tongue.

Dods, Meg, in Scott's novel, *St. Ronan's Well*, the landlady and despotic ruler of the Cleikum Inn at St. Ronan's Old Town. Her excellent cuisine and her well-chosen wines attracted customers whom she either patronized or sent about their business if they would not accept her domination. She said of herself that her bark was worse than her bite; " but what teeth," asks her creator, " could have matched a tongue, which, when in full career, is vouched to have been heard from the Kirk to the Castle of St. Ronan's." With the increased prosperity of the rival inn her humor became more capricious, but to her old and valued friends she could still make her inn " the neatest and most comfortable, old-fashioned house in Scotland."

Dodson and Fogg, in *The Pickwick Papers* (1836), by Charles Dickens, a firm of legal sharks who engage in speculation to prosecute Mrs. Bardell's breach of promise suit against Mr. Pickwick.

Doe, John, a sham plaintiff in actions of ejectment tolerated by a fiction of the law. and usually associated with a sham defendant in Richard Roe.

Doeg, in the Old Testament (I Samuel xxi, 7), was the chief of Saul's herdsmen " having charge of the mules." Under this name, Dryden, in the second part of *Absalom and Achitophel*, satirized Elkanah Settle, a poetaster who for a period was held to be no contemptible rival by Dryden's political enemies.

Dogberry, in Shakespeare's comedy, *Much Ado about Nothing* (Act iv, Sc. 2), a city official full of loquacious vanity and fond of large words whose sound he appreciates without fully grasping their meaning, a masculine anticipation, in short, of Sheridan's Mrs. Malaprop. " Write me down an ass! " he cries in rueful reprisal at an uncomplimentary epithet from Conrade.

Even at stupidity and pretension this Shakespeare does not laugh other than genially. Dogberry and Verges tickle our very hearts; and we dismiss them covered with explosions of laughter; but we like the poor fellows only the better for our laughing; and hope they will get on well there and continue Presidents of the City Watch. Such laughter, like sunshine on the deep sea, is very beautiful to me.—CARLYLE: *The Hero as Poet*, in *Heroes and Hero-worship*.

The character of Dogberry, says Aubrey, was studied from a live original. "The humor of the constable in *A Midsummer Night's Dream*" (Aubrey was no sure guide among the plays) "he happened to take at Grendon in Bucks, which is the road from London to Stratford, and there was living that constable about 1642, when I first came to Oxon." However this may be, that constable was living in many another place and was adorned, not created, by Shakespeare's imagination. — WALTER RALEIGH: *Shakespeare in English Men of Letters* series, p. 48.

Doister, Ralph Roister, hero and title of the first regular comedy in English (circa 1550), partly founded on the *Eunuchus* of Terence. The only copy known of, and that lacking a title page, was discovered in 1818. The discovery of the author's name, Nicholas Udall, was made by John Payne Collier in 1825. Its leading motive is the courtship of Dame Custance by the hero, who falls a victim to the wiles of Matthew Merigreek and, after being sadly discomfited, at last joins in with the humour of the others, and consents to the union of the dame with Gawin Goodlucke, a merchant, to whom she is already betrothed. Rafe Roister is a character in Fulwel's *Like Will to Like,* and a " roister-doister " was used proverbially for a hare-brained fellow. The word " roister " is evidently from the French " rustre," a ruffian, and recalls the " rustarii," or French freebooters, of the eleventh century.

Dolls, Mr., in Dickens's novel, *Our Mutual Friend.* See WREN, JENNIE.

Doltaire, the moving spirit in Sir Gilbert Parker's romance, *The Seats of the Mighty.* The scene is laid in and around Quebec during the war between the English and the French which resulted in the capture of that city (1789) by James Wolfe, and the eventual transfer of all Canada to the British. Doltaire, a dashing, handsome, masterful Frenchman, a favorite of Madame de Pompadour, is sent over to Quebec by that left-handed Queen of France to possess himself of certain papers in the hands of Captain Robert Moray, held as a hostage by the French in Quebec. He finds in Moray a rival for Alixe Duvarney, with whom he himself falls in love and receives a new incentive in fierce jealousy that maddens his imperious mind. Doltaire and Alixe are mere fictions. Robert Moray (*q.v.*) is drawn from a historical character.

Dombey, Edith, second wife of Mr. Paul Dombey (*q.v.*), daughter of Mrs. Skewton and widow of Colonel Granger. Handsome, haughty, self-willed, marrying only for money, she rebels against the cold arrogance of her husband and goes through the form of an elopement with John Carker, content to wear the appearance of an adulteress if by so doing she can avenge herself upon her husband and simultaneously upon Carker, who for some time has made

her an object of vulgar and nauseating pursuit.

Dombey, Florence, daughter of Paul Dombey, a loving and lovable girl whom her father cannot forgive because she was not born a boy, whom he drives out of his house after her stepmother's elopement, holding her to be a fellow conspirator against him, and who pours coals of fire upon his head in his broken age.

Dombey, Paul, in Dickens's *Dombey and Son,* Mr. Dombey's son and heir, a delicate and pretty child, thoughtful beyond his years, whose early death powerfully affected contemporary readers, as may be seen from the extract.

Oh my dear, dear Dickens! What a No. 5 you have now given us! I have so cried and sobbed over it last night, and again this morning, and felt my heart purified by those tears, and blessed and loved you for making me shed them; and I never can bless and love you enough. Since the divine Nelly was found dead on her humble couch, beneath the snow and the ivy, there has been nothing like the actual dying of that sweet Paul, in the summer sunshine of that lofty room. . . . Every trait so true and so touching—and yet lightened by the fearless innocence which goes playfully to the brink of the grave, and that pure affection which bears the unstained spirit, on its soft and lambent flash, at once to its source in eternity.—FRANCIS, LORD JEFFREY, *Letter to Charles Dickens,* January 31.

Paul Dombey was inspired by the pathetic personality of a favorite nephew, Henry Burnett, a cripple who died in his tenth year. Notwithstanding his affliction he was one of the happiest and brightest of children with an ever-active mind and a passion for Bible reading.—F. G. KITTON, *The Novels of Charles Dickens.*

Dombey, Mr. Paul, in Dickens's novel, *Dombey and Son,* a wealthy London merchant, starched, pompous, self-satisfied. Wrapped up in his mercantile ambitions, he cares only for little Paul, who enables him to retain the words " and Son " in the firm name. The loss of the mother affected him little; he married again and was as coldly cruel to his second wife as he had been to his first. She elopes and he keenly feels the disgrace but is otherwise unmoved. His son's death breaks his heart; he loses interest in his business, and the great house which he had inherited goes down in bankruptcy. In his later days he repents and is reconciled to his daughter Florence.

Dominic, Father or **Friar,** titular hero of Dryden's comedy, *The Spanish Friar* (1681). Macaulay calls him the best comic character of Dryden, and assigns his origin to the hypocritical confessor in Machiavelli's comedy, the *Mandragola*. He is thus described in Act ii, Sc. 3: " He is a huge, fat, religious gentleman . . . big enough to be a pope. His gills are as rosy as a turkey-cock's. His big belly walks in state before him, like a harbinger, and his gouty legs come limping after it. Never was such a tun of devotion seen."

Donatello, Count, in Hawthorne's romance, *The Marble Faun* (called *Transformation* in England), is the Italian lover of the American Miriam. He bears a singular resemblance to the Faun of Praxiteles, and the author tantalizingly plays with a doubt whether, if the breeze should lift his clustering locks a little higher, his ears sould stand revealed as human or animal. His character corresponds to his appearance. Morally irresponsible but humanly conscious, he is an Adam before the fall, the trusted friend and playmate of nature until brought into personal contact with sin and suffering. See MIRIAM.

It is a triumph of art that a being whose nature trembles on the very verge of the grotesque should walk through Hawthorne's pages with such undeviating grace. Let him show but the extremest tip of one of his furry ears—or were they not furry?—and he would be irretrievably lost. Mr. Darwin or Barnum would claim him as their own and he would pass from the world of poetry into the dissecting room or the showman's booth. In the Roman dreamland he is in little danger of such prying curiosity, though even there he can only be kept out of harm's way by the admirable skill of his creator.—LESLIE STEPHEN: *Hours in a Library.*

Donnithorne, Arthur, in George Eliot's *Adam Bede,* the seducer of Hetty Sorrel, a vain, affectionate, frank-hearted, susceptible and self-indulgent young gentleman who owed no one a grudge and would have been delighted to see everybody happy around him, especially if they recognized that a large part of their happiness came from the handsome young landlord.

Doola, Namgay, hero and title of a short story in Rudyard Kipling's *Life's Handicaps,* a red-headed, half-breed son of a Hindoo woman and her orientalised husband, Thimla Dhula (Tim Doolan), who refuses to pay taxes and otherwise betrays the secret of his Irish parentage. Thereupon the teller of the story advises the native king to raise Namgay Doola to a position of honor in the army, since he came of a race that never could be coerced into paying rent or taxes, but which would do heroic work if flattered and humored.

Dooley, Mr., a fictitious humorist through whom Finley Peter Dunne, his creator, voices in burlesque form his protests against the shams and conventions of the hour. Dooley, an Irishman by birth, an American by adoption, presides' over a saloon in Archey Road, Chicago, where he amuses himself by shooting folly as it flies with shafts dipped in vinegar and honey. His favorite interlocutor is Mr. Hennessy, and he also lends a ready ear to the questions of Mr. McKenna, his neighbor.

Doone, Lorna, titular heroine of a novel (1871), by R. D. Blackmore, the only girl in a fierce family of aristocratic outlaws who, smarting under wrongs suffered from the government, have retired to a valley in Exmoor, whence they periodically emerge to plunder the countryside. As a mere child she rescues the four-teen-year-old John Ridd from capture by the band. Seven years later, now developed into the tallest and stoutest youth on Exmoor, he seeks Lorna again. He hates the Doones, who killed his father, but he loves Lorna, whom he remembers as the fairest, daintiest child he had ever seen, becomes her protector against her own people, and eventually wins her hand.

Dora, in Dickens's *David Copperfield.* See SPENLOW, DORA.

Dora, heroine and title of a poetical idyll by Alfred Tennyson, founded upon a story in Miss Milford's *Our Village.*

Dorante, hero of Pierre Corneille's comedy, *The Liar* (Fr. *Le Menteur,* 1643), a young gentleman who has been studying law at Poitiers and comes to Paris to see the sights. His guide and adviser is the valet Cliton, who in vain seeks to stem or interrupt the stream of lies which Dorante pours out in his anxiety to impress women and impose upon friends and relatives.

Dorante, in Molière's farce, *Les Facheux,* a noisy, blustering, swearing huntsman. The play is a gallery of caricatures of typical titled bores in the court of Louis XIV, and this portrait is said to have been added by royal suggestion as a hit at the *grand veneur,* the master of the hounds.

In the comedy of *Les Facheux* which is one of the finest of M. Molière's, the huntsman who is introduced is M. de Soyecourt. It was the king who gave him this subject, upon leaving, after the first representation of this piece at M. Fouquet's. His Majesty, seeing M. de Soyecourt pass, said to Molière: "There is a great original that you have not copied," and all the hunting terms are said to have been dictated by the king himself.—MÈNAGE: *Menagiana.*

Dorax, in Dryden's tragedy, *Don Sebastian* (1690), the name assumed by Don Alonzo of Alcazar, when he deserted Sebastian, King of Portugal, and went over to the Emperor of Barbary.

Dorax is indeed the *chef d'œuvre* of Dryden's tragic characters and perhaps the only one in which he has applied his great knowledge of human kind to actual delineation. It is highly dramatic because formed of those complex feelings which may readily lead either to virtue or vice, and which the poet can manage so as to surprise the spectator without transgressing consistency. The Zanga of Young, a part of great theatrical effect, has been compounded of this character and that of Iago.—HALLAM, *Review of Scott's Dryden, Edinburgh Review,* vol. 13, p. 125.

Doricourt, the betrothed lover of Letitia Hardy in Mrs. Cowley's comedy, *The Belle's Stratagem.* Though a fashionable man about town and something of a rake, he keeps his plighted word even when he fancies that he loves another, and is rewarded by finding that it is the same. For explanation of this paradox see HARDY, LETITIA.

Dorimant, in Sir George Etherege's comedy, *The Man of Mode or Sir Fopling Flutter* (1676). A man of rank and fashion and an unscrupulous rake, his wit, shrewdness and strategy make him a brilliant foil to the rather foolish hero. Evidently intended to be a model fine gentleman, he is as evidently drawn from John Wilmot, Earl of Rochester, the tinselled darling of contemporary London society. In later English literature the name was used to signify any loose and unprincipled, but witty, modish, and agreeable young man.

Dorothea, heroine of Goethe's pastoral in hexameter verse, *Hermann and Dorothea* (1797) whose scene is laid in Germany at the period of the French Revolution. Hermann, son of the leading burgher of a peaceful village in Southern Germany, is sent to minister to a band of refugees from the Upper Rhine districts. Struck with the beauty and goodness of Dorothea, one of the exiles, he wrings from his father a reluctant permission to woo her. All ignorant of her destiny, Dorothea comes into the household as a servant. Misunderstandings arise, Dorothea takes alarm, and begs leave to return to her own people. Tearfully she paints her forlorn condition and naively confesses that from the first her heart had gone out to Hermann, and she had hoped that some day she might be deemed worthy of becoming his bride. Everything is cleared up, reconciliation follows, and Dorothea is betrothed to Hermann.

Dorrit, Amy, heroine of Dickens's novel, *Little Dorrit* (1856). Born and brought up in the Marshalsea prison, Bermondsey, where her family were immured for years owing to the imprisonment of her father for debt, she has hardly reached the age of fourteen before she has begun to do needlework for scanty wages. The prisoners worshipped her, the men in Bermondsey took off their hats when she appeared in the streets. When the family are restored to freedom and to comparative wealth she is the only one who does not become arrogant and selfish under the new conditions. She and Arthur Clennan fall in love and, when the troubles incident to family opposition are all over, she elects to be married in the Marshalsea.

Little Dorrit might be less untruly than unkindly described as Little Nell grown big or, in Milton's phrase, "writ large." But on that very account she is a more credible and therefore a more really and rationally pathetic figure.—A. C. SWINBURNE, *Charles Dickens Qua. Rev.*, 196, 29.

Dorrit, William, in Dickens's *Little Dorrit*, a weak, shy man, father of Amy, whose term as a debtor is so long that he comes to be known as the Father of the Marshalsea. On becoming heir to a large estate he is released.

The Father of the Marshalsea is so pitiably worthy of pity as well as of scorn that it would have seemed impossible to heighten or to deepen the contempt or the compassion of the reader, but when he falls from adversity to prosperity he succeeds in soaring down and sinking up to a more tragicomic ignominy of more aspiring degradation. And his end is magnificent.—SWINBURNE: *Charles Dickens*, p. 47.

Dory, John, title and hero of an old ballad, frequently alluded to by the dramatists of the sixteenth and seventeenth centuries. John O'Keefe adopted the name for one of the characters in his comedy, *Wild Oats, or the Strolling Gentleman.*

Dot, the pet name of Mrs. Mary Peerybingle, the carrier's wife in *The Cricket on the Hearth*, a Christmas story by Dickens. The story has been dramatized by Boucicault.

Dotheboys Hall (*i.e.*, Hall where the boys are done), the name of a Yorkshire school in Dickens's *Nicholas Nickleby* (1838), kept by Mr. Wackford Squeers (*q.v.*), under whom Nicholas for a time was assistant. This caricature of the abuses in the country boarding-school system was efficacious in causing a complete reform. See also SMIKE.

The original of Dotheboys Hall is still in existence at Bowes, some five miles from Barnard Castle. The King's Head Inn at Barnard Castle is spoken of in Nicholas Nickleby by Newmann Noggs.—*Notes and Queries*, April 2, 1875.

Doubting Castle, in Bunyan's *Pilgrim's Progress*, the abode of Giant Despair (*q.v.*).

Douglas, a family famous not only in Scotch history but in Scotch poetry and romance. After Bruce, Baliol and the Soulis had passed away, the Douglases, descendants of Sholto Dhu Glass, "the dark grey man," rose to unrivalled power. As Scott says in his *Tales of a Grandfather*, they often cast their coronet into the scale against the Crown, and as Andrew Lang shows in his *History of Scotland*, too often their ambition was fatal to their country. But, as King Robert said at council in the Dominican Convent at Perth, the broad breast of Douglas had been Scotland's best bulwark. In Scott's eyes their patriotism and martial renown covered a multitude of sins. As the hero of *Castle Dangerous* (1831), he takes "the good Sir James," brother-in-law of Bruce, who "loved better to hear the lark sing than the mouse squeak."

Sir James was the first of the Black Douglases. It is he whose very name was such a terror to his southron foes that English mothers would frighten or pacify unruly children by threatening to deliver them over to the Black Douglas.

Hush ye, hush ye, little pet ye;
Hush ye, hush ye, do not fret ye;
The Black Douglas shall not get thee.
Nursery Song quoted by SCOTT in
Tales of a Grandfather, i, 6.

Next in chronological order comes Archibald the Grim, in *The Fair Maid of Perth* (1828), an incarnation of all the pride and terror of the race, whose will was iron and whose word was law.

The Red Douglases rose on the fall of the Black, their representative in the Waverley series is the Regent Morton (James Douglas, Earl of Morton); loose in his loves, unscrupulous in his methods, greedy of the gold he scattered, and boundless in the ambition which brought him to the block. He is the most significant figure in the two romances that deal with Mary, Queen of Scots—*The Monastery* (1820) and *The Abbot* (1820)—where he is drawn as the embodiment of wise and beneficial statescraft in times made difficult by the strife of factions and the unruly spirits of the barons with whom he had to deal—as the man who, had he been born without the bar sinister, would have been the most illustrious monarch of the unhappy Stewart line. Douglas, in John Home's tragedy of that name. See NORVAL, YOUNG.

Douglas, Archibald, Earl of Douglas, appears in Shakespeare's *I Henry IV.* The ally of the Percys when they rebelled against Henry IV, he kills Lord Strafford and Sir Walter Blunt, mistaking them for the king, at the battle of Shrewsbury (July 23, 1403). When finally he meets the king, Prince Hal comes to his father's rescue and Douglas is put to flight.

Douglas, Ellen, heroine of Scott's narrative poem, *The Lady of the Lake.*

It is no profound study of an ideal woman, but it is a true Highland girl, frankest, most courageous and most stainless of human creatures. In her simplicity there is at once a gleam of frolic and a possibility of all the stateliness which becomes a lady of the far-famed Douglas blood—*Blackwood Magazine*, July, 1871.

Dowlas, Dick, in George Colman the Younger's comedy, *The Heir at Law,* son of Daniel Dowlas, an old Gospert shopkeeper, who, on account of the supposed loss of the son of Lord Duberly, succeeds to a peerage and an estate of £15,000 a year. See PANGLOSS, DR.

Dowling, Captain. "A great drunkard," who figures in Crabbe's *Borough.*

Drake, Francis, the famous English voyager and privateer, is the hero of *Drake, an English Epic,* by Alfred Noyes.

Francis Drake—the *deus ex machina,* as it were, of the Armada tragedy, clothed with terrors not of this world by the panic of his enemies—is a theme pre-eminently suited for epic treatment; while tales of mutiny and torture, of fabulous treasure, and forlorn hopes crowned with almost supernatural success, provide a wealth of stirring episode that contrasts effectively with the beautiful love-idyll of the hero and Bess of Sydenham. Nevertheless, through all, clearly discernible at intervals more or less frequent, is a sense of effort, culminating in a Twelfth—and final—Book which verges on the perfunctory.—*London Athenæum.*

Drapier, M. B. (a suppositious Irish trader), the pseudonym under which Swift wrote his *Drapier Letters* (1724), a series of epistles directed against the introduction of "Wood's half-pence" into Ireland. Copper coin having become scarce there, William Wood of Wolverhampton had received from the English government a patent to supply the demand to the amount of £80,000 by coining half-pence and farthings for fourteen years. Swift denounced the patent because it had been obtained surreptitiously through the Duchess of Kendal, the mistress of George I, to whom Wood had pledged a share in the profits; because it had passed without consultation with either the Lord Lieutenant or the privy council of Ireland, and also and especially because it surrendered to an obscure individual the right of exercising one of the highest privileges of the Crown. Swift succeeded in raising a storm of indignation in Ireland that made King George quail; Wood was compelled to withdraw his patent, and his copper coinage was totally suppressed.

Dravot, Daniel, hero of a short story, *The Man Who Would Be King,* in Rudyard Kipling's *Phantom Rickshaw.* A shrewd adventurer, he aspires to be ruler of Kafristan. With Peachey Carnehan as his servant, he gains unlimited power over the native tribes. They deem him a god, give him and Carnehan each a gold crown and divide the empire between them. Finally Dravot demands a wife; the girl puts his godship to a test by biting him; seeing the blood betrays him as a mere human being, he is put to death and Carnehan is tortured and banished. J. M. Barrie pronounces this the author's masterpiece: "Positively, it is the most audacious thing in fiction, and yet it reads as true as Robinson Crusoe."

Drawcansir, in *The Rehearsal,* the Duke of Buckingham's burlesque, is a noisy braggart meant especially as a caricature of the Almanzor of Dryden's *Conquest of Granada.* As described by Mr. Bayes, his author, he is " a great fierce hero, that frights his mistress, snubs up kings, baffles armies and does what he will without regard to good manners, justice or numbers " (*The Rehearsal*, Act iv, Sc. 1). So popular was the play that Drawcansir passed into a synonym for a braggadocio.

If some Drawcansir you aspire to draw,
Present him raving, and above all law:
BYRON: *Hints from Horace*, l. 173.

Henry Fielding assumed the name of " Sir Alexander Drawcansir " in the editorship of the *Covent Garden Journal.*

Dred, hero of Mrs. Harriet Beecher Stowe's novel of that name (1856), a runaway negro living in the Dismal Swamp.

Dreeme, Cecil, in Theodore Winthrop's novel of that title (1872), the name assumed by Clara Denman when she dons male apparel and passes herself off as a man.

Dromio of Ephesus and **Dromio of Syracuse,** in Shakespeare's *Comedy of Errors,* twin brothers, servants respectively of the twin Antipholuses, the suffix names being taken from the cities in which the two pairs of master and servant respectively settled after the family's dispersal by shipwreck. The first Dromio is a simpleton, but he of Syracuse is a merry rogue described by his master as:

A trusty villain, sir, that very oft
When I am dull with care and melancholy
Lightens my humor with his merry jests.

Drood, Edwin, hero of Dickens's novel, *The Mystery of Edwin Drood* (1870), which mystery was left unsolved by the death of the author while the story was still running in monthly parts. *Once a Week,* February 18, 1871, first chronicled the fact that the name, though nothing else, was suggested by that of Dickens's neighbor, Edwin Trood, the keeper of a public house near Gad's Hill.

Drugger, Abel, in Ben Jonson's comedy, *The Alchemist* (1610), a simple-minded tobacco dealer who applies to Subtle, the alchemist, for advice on the minutest points—how to set his shelves so as to secure good

luck, on what days he might trust his customers, what days were unpropitious, etc. This was one of Garrick's favorite parts. Noticing his performance, Hannah More writes (1776): " I should have thought it as possible for Milton to have written *Hudibras* and Butler *Paradise Lost* as for one man to have played Hamlet and Drugger with so much excellence. There is a story that a young lady who had fallen in love with Garrick as Hamlet was cured by seeing him in Abel Drugger. On this hint Robertson constructed his play *David Garrick.*

Dryasdust, The Rev. Dr., a pretended assistant in the preparation of the *Waverley* novels, first introduced in Scott's *Antiquary* as a correspondent of Johnathan Oldbuck. Ivanhoe is dedicated to this " grave antiquary; " the introductory epistle to *Nigel* is addressed to him; he is feigned to be the editor of *Peveril of the Peak* and the writer of the conclusion to *Redgauntlet.* The name, which is admirably self-descriptive, has passed into literary and colloquial use as a synonym for a musty and dreary pedant.

Truth is the Prussian Dryasdust, otherwise an honest fellow, excels all other Dryasdusts yet known. I have often sorrowfully felt as if there were not in Nature, for darkness, dreariness, immethodic platitude anything comparable to him.—CARLYLE.

Dryfoos, in William D. Howells's novel, *A Hazard of New Fortunes,* a Pennsylvania German who has made a fortune and comes to New York to spend it. With the aid of Fulkerson, a pushing westerner, as manager, he establishes a journal entitled *Every Other Week,* of which Basil March becomes editor. He is vulgar, ignorant and coarse. His daughters, despite some superficial culture, inherit his nature, their one devouring desire being to enter " society." Not so the son of the family, Conrad, whose sympathies are all with the laboring classes, the unfortunate and the downtrodden of the metropolis. Conrad is killed by a chance shot during a strike of street-car drivers and conductors while he is trying to shield their open sympathizer, Lindau.

Duchess, The, in Browning's poem, *The Flight of the Duchess*, is married to a pompous and narrow-minded duke whose chief ambition is to reproduce Middle Age customs in elaborate detail. One day he brings home a sunny-haired and sunny-hearted bride from a convent. He and his austere mother, by indifference and repression, do their best to crush her spirit. She dejectedly declines to take part in a carefully arranged mediæval hunting party. To rebuke her by a sense of contrast the duke sends in to her an aged gypsy crone, squalid and wretched looking. The crone is really a gypsy queen. She assumes her royal aspect before the duchess, holds out to her a vista of the free life that awaits her if she will join the gypsies, or of a greater joy in giving her " wondrous self" to "a stronger nature's sway." The duchess flees with the crone and is never seen again.

Dudu, in Byron's *Don Juan* (1824), one of three beauties in the harem of a Turkish Sultan, into which Juan, disguised as a woman, has been hurriedly smuggled by order of the Sultana. The others are Lolah and Katinka. All three are drawn from the daughters of Theodora Macri, an Athenian lady with whom Byron lodged in 1809–1810. He thus alludes to them in a letter to his former tutor Professor Fry: " I came near forgetting to tell you that I am dying of love for three sisters who inhabit the same house with me; three Greeks, sisters, Theresa, Mariana and Katinga. These are the names of these divinities; the eldest isn't fifteen." To Moore and to Murray, his publisher, he likewise thinks it important enough to make known his amorous inclinations toward these three astonishing Greek maidens.

It was Theresa, the eldest (Dudu), whom Childe Harold addressed as the "Maid of Athens" (see ATHENS, MAID OF) in a passionate song of farewell.

Lolah was dusk as India and as warm;
Katinka was a Georgian, white and red,
With great blue eyes, a lovely hand and arm,
And feet so small they scarce seemed made to tread,
But rather skim the earth; while Dudu's form
Looked more adapted to be put to bed,
Being somewhat large, and languishing, and lazy,
Yet of a beauty that would drive you crazy.

A kind of sleepy Venus seemed Dudu
Yet very fit to "murder sleep" in those
Who gazed upon her cheek's transcendent hue,
Her Attic forehead, and her Phidian nose:
Few angles were there in her form, 't is true,
Thinner she might have been, and yet scarce lose;
Yet, after all, 't would puzzle to say where
It would not spoil some separate charm to pare.

Don Juan, Canto vi.

Duessa (Lat. *duo,* two, and *essa,* a feminine termination), in Spenser's *Faërie Queene,* Book i, the double-minded counterpart to the single-souled Una. She represents the papacy in a general way but, more specifically, the threatening figure of Mary, Queen of Scots, whose succession to Elizabeth would have meant the restoration of the Roman Catholic faith in England. She lures the Red Cross Knight to the palace of Lucifera where Orgoglio (Pride) casts him into a dungeon, after which he marries Duessa. For the bridal ceremony Orgoglio arrays her in gorgeous apparel with a triple crown (or tiara) upon her head and sets her on a monster beast with seven heads (see *Revelation,*). Arthur comes to the rescue of the Red Cross Knight, slays Orgoglio, wounds the beast, releases the knight and strips Duessa of her finery, whereupon she flees into the wilderness to hide her shame. This part of Spenser's poem is taken in almost literal translation from Ariosto's *Orlando Furioso,* where the loathly lady is called Alcina.

Duke, " living in exile," in Shakespeare's comedy *As You Like It,* a philosophical potentate who finds " good in everything " even when suffering wrong at the hands of an evil brother.

And the comfortable old Duke, symbolical of the British villa dweller, who likes to find "sermons in stones and good in everything," and then to have a good dinner! This unvenerable impostor, expanding on his mixed diet of pious twaddle and venison, rouses my worst passions. Even when Shakespeare, in his efforts to be a social philosopher, does rise for an instant to the level of a sixth-rate Kingsley, his solemn self-complacency infuriates me. And yet, so wonderful is his art, that it is not easy to disentangle what is unbearable from what is irresistible.—G. B. SHAW: *Dramatic Opinions and Essays.*

Dulcinea del Toboso, in Cervantes' *Don Quixote* (1605), the lady whom the Don, in true knight-errant fashion, selects as the object of his love. " Her name," we are told, " was Aldonza Lorenzo, and her he pitched upon to be the lady of his thoughts; then casting about for a name which should have some affinity with her own, and yet incline toward that of a great lady and princess, he resolved to call her Dulcinea del Toboso (for she was born at that place), a name to his thinking, harmonious, uncommon and significant." She was merely a fresh-colored country wench, but the Don describes her thus: " Her flowing hair is of gold, her forehead the Elysian Fields, her eyebrows two celestial arches, her eyes a pair of glorious suns, her cheeks two beds of roses, her lips two coral portals that guard her teeth of oriental pearl, her neck is alabaster, her hands are polished ivory and her bosom whiter than the new fallen snow." Sancho, in Part I, iii, 11, views her very differently.

Dulness, " daughter of Chaos and Eternal Night," is a personification celebrated in Pope's satirical poem, *The Dunciad* (1728–1742), as a goddess and queen. She selects a favorite to reign over her kingdom. In the early issues the choice fell upon Theobald (1688–1744), who had severely criticized Pope's edition of Shakespeare—to the marked improvement of subsequent editions. In 1743 Pope substituted Colley Cibber for Theobald, a still greater mistake, for Cibber was one of the most brilliant men of his day. Having selected her favorite, Dulness transports him to the Elysian shades and unfolds before him a vision of her triumphs—past,

present and future. The last book represents her coming in triumph to establish her universal dominion.

Dumain, in Shakespeare's *Love's Labor's Lost,* a French lord in attendance on the King of Navarre thus described:

For he hath wit to make an ill shape good
And shape to win grace though he had no wit.

Act i, Sc. i.

Dumbie, Jock, laird of Dumbiedykes after the death of his greedy, grasping father, is a bashful young Scotchman in Sir Walter Scott's *Heart of Midlothian,* " a tall, gawky, silly-looking boy," who falls in love with Jeanie Deans. For many years his admiration contents itself with " pertinaciously gazing on her with great stupid greenish eyes."

The railway mishap which occurred on Friday last at Irongray, near Dumfries, reminds us," writes a correspondent, "that Jeanie Deans lies buried in the parish churchyard. Jeanie Deans in real life was Helen Walker, but the scenes in which she is associated in *The Heart of Midlothian* are laid in and around Edinburgh, and tradition still points out her cottage near Duddingston, where the young laird of Dumbiedykes, after his father's death, in the old man's tarnished laced hat and coat, used to sit silent with an empty tobacco pipe in his mouth, glaring at Jeanie for an hour at a time, deluding himself that he was making love to her."—*London Globe,* 1911.

Duncan, King of Scotland, who succeeded to the throne about 1034 and was assassinated through the treachery of Macbeth, Mormaer of Moray, in 1040, appears in Shakespeare's tragedy, *Macbeth,* as a just and gentle ruler whose virtues emphasize " the deep damnation of his taking off." This character is given to him in Hollinshed's *Chronicles,* from whom Shakespeare derived his story, but earlier historians describe him as unjust and weak. The circumstances of the murder are not as Hollinshed gives them; they are taken from the historian's account of the assassination of King Duff (967) by Donwald and his wife in their castle at Fores.

Dunces, King of the, in Alexander Pope's mock-heroic epic, *The Dunciad*

(1728), was originally Lewis Theobald, the Shakespearean editor and critic. Colley Cibber, however, incurred the enmity of Pope by burlesquing the farce, *Three Hours after Marriage*, and he eventually displaced Theobald as the hero of the satire. The choice of Theobald was sufficiently unjust—he was a man of more than average parts; but the substitution of Cibber was absurd, as he was one of the liveliest wits of the day, an excellent actor, a successful dramatist, and a failure only as a poet.

Dundreary, Lord, in Tom Taylor's comedy, *Our American Cousin*, a typical English " swell " of the titled classes, courteous and well bred though carrying himself with aristocratic nonchalance, foppish, indolent, absurd, with a befogged brain that is ever employed in ingenious misinterpretations of the obvious. Originally the part was an insignificant one, containing only forty-seven lines, but when it was entrusted to E. A. Sothern he continuously added new jokes and new business until in his version Dundreary eventually overshadowed Asa Trenchard, the " American Cousin," and became the chief feature in the play.

Dunn, Davenport, hero of a novel of that name (1859) by C. J. Lever, a clever commercial swindler whose operations involve the fortunes of princes and who is eventually " done" by his rival, Grog Davis.

Dupin, C. Auguste, an amateur detective introduced into three of Poe's tales—*The Murders in the Rue Morgue, The Mystery of Marie Roget,* and *The Purloined Letter*—in all of which he is represented as rendering important services to the Parisian police by unravelling apparently insoluble mysteries. According to a letter published (1879) in the *New York World* and signed F. D. C., the character was drawn after a real person, one C. Auguste Dupont, a man of acute analytical powers, who was frequently called in to aid the police in the manner Poe describes. The *Murders in the Rue Morgue*, indeed, is very largely founded upon

facts, which F. D. C. claims to have supplied to Poe, having learned them from Dupont himself, with whom he was very closely associated during a sojourn of seven years in Paris. " Dupont," he adds, " merely laughed when he saw his name disguised in Charles Baudelaire's translation, nor did he ever take offence at the liberty I had taken in sending to Poe the true facts of the solution of the mystery—facts which in their results were, of course, well known to the police authorities, although not in their details. Dupont had done more work for the police than ever came to Poe's knowledge: if Poe had not used the name under so thin a disguise he might have learned more, and perhaps would have written better and more astounding and analytical tales."

Duplessis, Marie, the name in real life of the Parisian courtesan who became the Marguerite Gauthier (*q.v.*) of Dumas's *LaDame aux Camelias* and the Violetta Valery of *La Traviata*.

D'Urberville, Alec, in Hardy's *Tess of the D'Urbervilles* (1891), the seducer of the heroine. " Despite the touches of barbarism in his contours there was a singular force in the gentleman's face, and his bold, rolling eye." When Tess flees from the household in which he is the son and heir and she a mere servant, Alec experiences a brief fit of reform. He takes to field preaching, and during his consequent wanderings he again meets Tess. She has been abandoned by her husband, Angel Clare. By misrepresenting Angel's feelings and intentions Alec persuades her to accompany him to Sandbourne, and she ends by slaying her double betrayer.

Durbeyfield, Tess, heroine of Hardy's novel, *Tess of the D'Urbervilles*. Her father fancies himself a member of the leading county family, the D'Urbervilles. On the basis of this supposed relationship she applies for a position; is engaged through the influence of the elder son Alec, a debauched youth, who plans to seduce her and succeeds. A child is born and dies. Eight years later she marries Angel Clare, who abandons her on the wedding night when she reveals to him her past. From being a victim of the natural vices of man she thus becomes a victim also of his conventional virtues. Both Alec and Angel eventually seek to regain her but Alec acts treacherously in regard to Angel and she kills him.

Durgin, Jeff, in Howells's novel, *The Landlord of the Lion Inn* (1897), is the titular landlord, described from his surly boyhood to his college days at Harvard; and then to manhood and marriage with a woman of superior station and culture.

He was superior to most men in beauty, force, will, temper; about scholarship he was indifferent; the only equality he cared for was social equality, and, before he had been a year at college, he saw and knew he could never get that. His vanity was hurt, but he was not disheartened or in any way discredited to himself. He made no struggle for the recognized unattainable, but he felt that there was a memorable day coming, soon or late, when he should get even with some one of the persons who represented this unattainable.—*N. Y. Nation.*

Durrie, James, in R. L. Stevenson's romance, *The Master of Ballantrae* (1889), is the titular " Master." He is for the Pretender; Henry, his brother, is for King George. Alison Græme loves James, but when he is reported dead she makes a loveless marriage with Henry. James returns to make trouble between Alison and Henry, who endures the double persecution with patience and fortitude. The brothers at last meet in a duel. The Master feigns death and is buried by his Hindoo attendant, Secundra Dass, who has merely put him in a state of suspended animation. In digging him up again Secundra is interrupted by the arrival of Henry. James lives just long enough to open his eyes,—at which vital sign his

brother falls dead. Both are buried in one grave in the western wilderness.

The Master of Ballantrae is stamped with a magnificent unity of conception, but the story illuminates that conception by a series of scattered episodes. That lurid embodiment of fascinating evil, part vampire, par-Mephistopheles, whose grand manner and heroic abilities might have made him a great and good man, but for "the malady of not wanting," is the light and meaning of the whole book. Innocent and benevolent lives are thrown in his way that he may mock or distort or shatter them. Stevenson never came nearer than in this character to the sublime of power.—WALTER RALEIGH: *Robert Louis Stevenson,* 1895.

Durward, Quentin, hero and title of a historical romance (1823) by Sir Walter Scott. A nephew of Ludovic Lesly (Le Balafré), he enrolls himself in the Scottish Guard of Louis XI of France, saves the King's life in a boarhunt, wins the love of the Countess of Croye, and finally marries her. As Monseigneur de la Croye he reappears in the same author's *Anne of Geirstein,* where he serves under Charles the Bold, Duke of Burgundy.

Duval, Madame, in Fanny Burney's novel *Evelina* (1778), the terrible grandmother through whom the heroine is related to the vulgar Brangtons (*q.v.*). An English servant girl, she had eloped with Evelina's grandfather and led him many years of hapless marriage in France. After his death and that of her second husband Duval, she returns to London just as Evelina is entering the fashionable world there, and becomes the low comedy and low tragedy of the novel.

She is not only very awful herself, with a French bourgeois vulgarity thickly overlaying her English servile vulgarity, but she is surrounded by Evelina's city cousins, who have a cockney vulgarity of their own, and for whom she claims the girl's affection, together with her duty to herself.—W. D. HOWELLS: *Heroines of Fiction.*

E

East Lynne, in the novel of that name by Mrs Henry Wood, the ancestral home of the Vane family. See VANE, LADY ISABEL.

Easy, Sir Charles, in Colley Cibber's comedy, *The Careless Husband* (1704), a profligate fine gentleman yet so lazy, even in his amours, that " he would rather lose the woman of his pursuit than go through any trouble in securing or keeping her." He leaves his love letters scattered about; he even forgets to lock his door against imminent detection; and, as a consequence, his wife knows all though she forgives all, until finally her patience and constancy win him back to her.

Easy, Jack, hero of a romance of the sea, *Mr. Midshipman Easy,* by Captain Frederick Marryat (1836), is the spoiled son of a so-called philosopher. He cruises about the world, has misfortunes, and at last good luck and a happy life.

Ebony, a familiar name for *Blackwood's Magazine* and for its proprietor, William Blackwood (1777–1834). It was first used in the *Chaldee MS,* an article that appeared in the number for October, 1817, in which Blackwood is introduced in these terms:— " And I looked, and behold a man clothed in plain apparel stood in the door of his house; and I saw his name, and the number of his name; and his name was as it had been the colour of ebony."

Eccles, Robert, in George Meredith's novel, *Rhoda Fleming.*

There is a great deal that is lovable about Robert Eccles despite his weakness for drink and his general reckless conduct. Something in him reminds one of Mr. Jefferson's able delineation of Rip Van Winkle; and if the novel had appeared later, Mr. Meredith might possibly have been told that he had taken the clever American actor as a model. Jonathan Eccles plays a subordinate part, but he never comes upon the stage without impressing the reader with his life-like reality.—*London Morning Post,* October 18, 1865.

Edgar, in Shakespeare's *King Lear,* the legitimate son and heir of Gloucester. Plotted against by his elder but illegitimate brother, he flies (ii, 1), feigns madness (ii, 3; iii, 4-6; iv, 1), and is restored to his place in the last act. His unsuspicious honesty and simplicity make him at first an easy prey to his brother's schemes, but his patience and fortitude win out at last.

Chiefly interesting to that part of an audience which likes to be called upon to sympathize with virtue in distress and to have its curiosity excited by seeing a noble-

man in the guise of a beggar . . . He is a very good young man; but like many other good young men he is not interesting in himself—he is only the occasion of our interest in others. The drama neither rests upon hint nor moves by his means; and yet without him it would halt.—RICHARD GRANT WHITE, *Atlantic Monthly,* July, 1880.

Edmund, in Shakespeare's tragedy, *King Lear* (1605), the natural son of the Duke of Gloucester, who succeeds in disinheriting his younger brother Edgar, the legitimate issue. Both Goneril and Regan are in love with him, and the latter on her husband's death designs to marry him, but is poisoned by the jealous Goneril.

Edmund suggests Iago; but with other minor differences—differences of person and of manner—there is this great unlikeness between them: Edmund is not spontaneously malicious; he is only supremely selfish and utterly unscrupulous. For he, too, has a comprehensible reason for his base and cruel actions. It was not his fault that he was illegitimate. He was no less his father's son than Edgar was; and yet he found himself with a branded stigma upon his name. This is not even a palliation of his villainy; but it is a motive for it that may be understood. Iago's villainy is the outcome of pure malignity of nature.—RICHARD GRANT WHITE.

Edward IV, King of England (1442–1483), appears in Shakespeare's historical dramas *Henry VI* (Parts II and III) and in *Richard III.* In *II Henry IV* he appears only in v, 1, as Edward, son of the Duke of York. In *III Henry IV* he is introduced in Scene I as Earl of March. On the death of his father at Wakefield (i, 4) he becomes Duke of York and claimant to the throne. Defeating the Lancastrians he was proclaimed King in London and secured his throne by his victory, May 4, 1471, at Tewksbury (v, 4). The profligate character attributed to him by Shakespeare is historical.

Edwin, hero of a ballad by Oliver Goldsmith introduced into the *Vicar of Wakefield* (1766) and there called *The Hermit,* but more generally known as *Edwin and Angelina.*

In reply to the accusation that he had borrowed from Percy, Goldsmith wrote: " I do not think there is any resemblance between the two pieces in question. If there be any, his ballad is taken from mine. I read it to Mr. Percy some years ago, and he told me, with his usual good humor, the next time I saw him, that he had taken my plan to form the fragments of Shakespeare into a ballad of his own."

Edwin, hero of Henry Taylor's *Edwin the Fair, an Historical Drama* (1842) which follows pretty closely the facts in the brief reign of the Saxon Edwin, his luckless marriage to his cousin Elgiva, the annulment of that marriage through the influence of Dunstan, the imprisonment of Edwin and his release by his partisans, the death of Elgiva at the hands of some of Dunstan's adherents, the defeat and death of Edwin, and the terrible onslaught of the Danes which overwhelms Dunstan's party in the flush of victory while they are celebrating their victory over Edwin. The best drawn character is Dunstan, who, whether he be the Dunstan of history or not, is at least natural and consistent.

Eglamour, in Shakespeare's comedy, *The Two Gentlemen of Verona* (1594), a character who aids in Silvia's escape from her father's court.

Egmont, Lamoral, Count of (1522–1568), a Flemish general and popular leader, who fought under Charles V and subsequently, though himself a Catholic, opposed the proselytizing schemes of Philip II and was treacherously seized and executed in company with the Count of Hoorn. He is the hero of Goethe's tragedy *Egmont* (1788).

For the exceptional popularity of *Egmont* a single sentence from Mr. G. H. Lewes's *Life of Goethe* sufficiently accounts: "As a tragedy, criticism makes sad work with it; but when all is said, the reader thinks of Egmont and Clärchen, and flings criticism to the dogs." That Clärchen has secured for her lover his position with the general multitude there is no doubt, though, strange to say, the connexion between this prettiest of plebeian sinners and her aristocratic adorer has drawn upon Goethe more censure than anything else in the piece. Schiller, who criticized *Egmont* shortly after its publication, and before his intimacy with its author began, could not sufficiently lament the departure from history which made of the Flemish patriot the protector of a damsel of low degree, instead of being,

as he actually was, a respectable paterfamilias, with a devoted wife of lofty birth and eleven children. Moral propriety and historical truth were both hit with one recklessly flung stone.—*Saturday Review.*

Elaine. In the Arthurian cycle of romances there are several ladies of this name, chief among whom stands " the lily maid of Astolat " who fell in love with Lancelot and, learning who he was and that he was bound to celibacy, pined away and died. In a juvenile poem Tennyson celebrated her as *The Lady of Shalott;* later he included her story in his *Idylls of the King.* Following the version of Sir Thomas Malory, in the prose *Morte d'Arthur,* iii, 123 (1470), Tennyson makes it her dying request that her body shall be placed in a barge and thus conveyed by a dumb servitor down the Thames to King Arthur's palace. A letter addressed to the king tells the story of her love and he orders it to be blazoned on her tomb.

Eleanor, heroine of Mrs. Ward's novel of that name. See MANISTY, EDWARD.

Elena, heroine of *On the Eve,* a novel by Ivan Tourgenief, a pure and emotional girl, whose eyes are opened through love to the full comprehension of life. Her passion for Insgrov develops womanhood in her virgin soul and sweeps all before it to a tragic consummation.

Elizabeth, heroine of a romance, *Elizabeth ou les Exilés en Siberie* (1806), by Mme. Sophie R. Cottin, founded on the true story of Prascovie Lepourloff.

Elizabeth, the 18-year-old daughter of Polish parents exiled to Siberia, determined to seek the Czar in person and implore his pardon. She sets out, accompanied by an old priest who is on his way westward, but he dies before the journey is half done. She continues bravely on alone, crossing forests and rivers, triumphing over all dangers, until at last she reaches Moscow. Her story comes to the ears of the Emperor Alexander on his coronation day in 1801, he admits her to his presence, and grants her request. The same story has been told by Xavier de Maistre under the title *La Jeune Sibérienne.*

Elizabeth, in *Elizabeth and Her German Garden* (published anonymously in 1898 but now known to be by Marie Annette, Countess von Arnim, *née* Beauchamp), is, like her creator, an English woman married to a German aristocrat. The latter is humorously styled " The Man of Wrath." Elizabeth, wearied of the empty splendors of city life, persuades her husband to retire to an old family estate in the country and redeem it from decay. In the course of the narrative Elizabeth reveals herself as a vivacious and brilliant woman full of life and energy, of enthusiasm for nature; of delighted and delightful insight into human foibles. Further glimpses of the same character are afforded in sequels: *The Adventures of Elizabeth in Rugen* (1904).

Elizabeth, daughter of the king of Hungary, and heroine of Charles Kingsley's dramatic poem, *The Saint's Tragedy.* She is intended, says the author, as " a type of two great mental struggles of the Middle age; first, of that between Scriptural or unconscious, and Popish, or conscious, purity; in a word, between innocence and prudery; next, of the struggle between healthy human affection and the Manichæan contempt with which a celibate clergy would have all men regard the name of husband, wife, and parent. To exhibit this latter falsehood in its miserable consequences is the main object of my poem."

Elizabeth, heroine of Miss Thackeray's *Story of Elizabeth.* See GILMOUR, ELIZABETH.

Elizabeth, Queen (1533–1603), appears in many romances and dramas, but in none more effectively than in Sir Walter Scott's *Kenilworth.* According to this authority she had a character " strangely compounded of the strongest masculine sense, with those foibles which are chiefly supposed proper to the female sex. Her subjects had the full benefit of her virtues, which far predominated over her weaknesses; but her courtiers, and those about her person, had often to sustain sudden and embarrassing turns of caprice, and the sallies of a temper which was both jealous and despotic." To the Earl of Leicester she showed " all those light and changeable gales of caprice and humour, which thwart or favour the progress of a lover in the favour of his mistress, and she, too, a mistress who was ever and anon becoming fearful lest she should forget the dignity or compromise the authority of the Queen, while she indulged the affections of a woman." Yet, when by his own confession Leicester was " doubly false," and " doubly forsworn," she forgave him, and saw in him, after the Countess's tragic death, " the object rather of compassion than resentment."

Ellida, heroine of Ibsen's drama, *The Lady from the Sea* (*Fruen fra Havet*). Ellida the lady from the sea, before her marriage with Dr. Wangel has been engaged to a stranger, a seafaring person, who exercised a kind of hypnotic influence over her. Although he has long ago disappeared from her part of the country, the mere thought of him continues to have a power over her. With horror she discovers that even after her marriage she remains under his influence. When he returns to claim her she is on the point of leaving her home and her husband to follow him. But the kindness and love of Dr. Wangel, and the respect he shows for her own independence and liberty as an individual, even with regard to her sickly infatuation, liberate her at last from the stranger's influence. In the decisive moment she elects to remain with her husband.

Ellinor, in Miss Edgeworth's novel, *Ennui* (1809), an old Irish nurse, " the most delectable personage," thinks Francis Jeffrey (*Essays,* p. 516), " in the whole tale . . . The devoted affection, infantine simplicity, and strange, pathetic eloquence of this half-savage, kind-hearted creature afford Miss Edgeworth occasion for many most original and characteristic representations."

Elliot, Anne, heroine of Jane Austen's novel, *Persuasion* (1818). Tender, suffering and sensitive, she is the most interesting of Jane Austen's women next to the blooming and joyous Emma Woodhouse.

Of Anne Elliot [Miss Austen] wrote to a friend: "You may *perhaps* like her, as she is almost too good for me." She is too good for most of us but not the less charming, and even the brilliancy of Elizabeth Bennett pales a little before the refined womanliness of this delightful English lady . . . There can be no sort of question as to the absolute bliss of Anne Elliot and Captain Wentworth, who is another of those pleasant, manly naval officers whom Miss Austen, drawing no doubt from material in her own family circles, depicts so delightfully.— AUSTIN DOBSON.

Dear Anne Elliot!—sweet, impulsive, womanly, tender-hearted—one can almost hear her voice, pleading the cause of all true women. . . . Her words seem to ring in our ears after they have been spoken. Anne Elliot must have been Jane Austen herself, speaking for the last time. There is something so true, so womanly, about her, that it is impossible not to love her. She is the bright-eyed heroine of the earlier novels, matured, chastened, cultivated, to whom fidelity has brought only greater depth and sweetness instead of bitterness and pain.— LADY ANNE THACKERAY RITCHIE: *Jane Austen, Cornhill Magazine.*

Elliot, Sir Walter, of Kellynch Hall, in *Persuasion*, father of Anne and one of Jane Austen's most amusing bores, vain and pompous and ever mastered by appearances. Having to let Kellynch he is properly condescending over the business, but is kind enough to admit that his tenant, Admiral Croft, is the best looking sailor he ever saw, and even goes so far as to say that if his own man had the arranging of the Admiral's hair he should not be at all ashamed to be seen with him.

Ellison, Kitty, heroine of *A Chance Acquaintance*, by W. D. Howells (1873). A western girl, she has had none of the advantages of fashionable finishing schools, but has been reared among sensible people, who attended to the homely duties of life and had only time to spare for heartfelt interest in Abolitionism. From the glimpse we get of her past it is easy to see how well it encouraged the independence and individuality of her character and the humor which rarely fails her. See ARBURTON, MILES.

With Kitty Mr. Howells has been remarkably successful; he has drawn a really charming girl and how difficult and rare a thing that is to do every novel reader can testify. All her part in the love-making, her innocence, her readiness to be pleased, her kindness toward Arburton's foibles, her sensitive dignity, her charming humor, belong to a real human being, not to the familiar lay figure.—*N. Y. Nation.*

Eloisa, the heroine and the feigned writer of Pope's *Epistle from Eloisa to Abelard,* in which the lady, immured in her convent, pours out her passion for her lost love. Hallam holds that Pope has done injustice to Heloisa's character, in putting into her mouth sentiments proper only to an improper woman. Her refusal to marry Abelard arose, not from an abstract predilection for the name of mistress above that of wife, but from her disinterested affection, which would not deprive him of the prospect of ecclesiastical dignities, to which his genius and renown might lead him. As to Abelard (*q.v.*) he would willingly have repaired by marriage the injury that he had done her.

Elsie, the heroine of Longfellow's dramatic poem of *The Golden Legend,* in love with Prince Henry von Aue. See AUE, in volume II.

Elsmere, Robert, hero of a novel so entitled (1888) by Mrs. Humphrey Ward. A young, sensitive clergyman, fresh from the old world environment of Oxford, he marries Catherine Leyburn, a woman of sternly orthodox mind, who loves him but can neither understand nor sympathize with him when he finds that he must renounce the conventional conception of Christianity for a more liberal faith, better fitted, as he thinks, to the needs of the age. Heartbroken by his apostacy, Catherine nevertheless accompanies him to London, where he works among the poor on the east side, and founds a new brotherhood of Christians. In the introduction to *The Case of Richard Meynell* (*McClure's Magazine,* 1913) Mrs. Ward says that "Elsmere is a figure of pure imagination, inspired and colored as all such figures are, by the actual human experience amid which he was conceived. In the picture of the Squire those who knew Mark Pattison at Lincoln College may have recognized a few of his more obvious traits."

Squire Wendover is the friend whose opinions on the question of evidence as applied to the story of Christ have great weight with Elsmere. See CASAUBON, GREY, HENRY, and LANGHAM.

Elton, Mrs., in Jane Austen's novel, *Emma*, the finished type of a feminine bore.

Whether she is irritating poor Emma as she dines at Hartfield in lace and pearls, patronizing sweet, patient Jane Fairfax, exploring at Box Hill, or officiating at Mr. Knightley's strawberry party with a little basket and a pick riband, she is always intolerable. Mrs. Elton goads even Jane into a bitterness and an eloquence very rare in Miss Austen's heroines; she is worse still with her underbred chaff upon Jane's engagement.

Elvira, in Dryden's drama, *The Spanish Friar* (1680), the wife of Gomez, a rich old banker. She is assisted by Friar Dominick in an intrigue with Colonel Lorenzo, who turns out to be her own brother.

Emanuel, Paul, in Charlotte Brontë's *Villette*, the principal of the Brussels school in which Lucy Snowe obtains employment as a teacher. He is drawn after M. Héger, proprietor of the school where the author herself was a teacher.

Charlotte Brontë's genius was ardently impatient of the actual; it cared only for its own. At the least hint from experience it was off. A glance, a gesture of M. Héger's was enough to fire it to the conception of Paul Emanuel. He had only to say a kind word to her, to leave a book or a box of bonbons in her desk (if he did leave bonbons) for Charlotte's fire to work on him. She had only to say to herself, "This little man is adorable in friendship. I wonder what he would be like in love," and she saw that he would be something, though not altogether, like Paul Emanuel. She had only to feel a pang of half-humorous, half-remorseful affection for him, and she felt what Lucy felt like in her love-sick agony. As for Madame Héger, Madame's purely episodic jealousy, her habits of surveillance, her small inscrutabilities of behavior, became the fury, the perfidy, the treachery of Madame Beck. For treachery and perfidy and agony and passion were what Charlotte wanted for *Villette*.—MAY SINCLAIR, *The Three Brontës*.

Emile, hero of a didactic romance, *Emile ou de l'Education* (1762), by Jean Jacques Rousseau.

The book opens with discussions of a system of education which might develop first the perfect man and then the perfect woman. The process is next shown in actual operation; the perfect man is developed in Emile, the perfect woman in Sophie. They meet and fall in love. The perfect tutor superintends their marriage. The couple live happy among woods and fields, but in an evil hour they decide upon a visit to Paris. The artificial atmosphere of society stifles their better natures, they succumb to the corruptions of the city, fall away and are separated. Afterwards Emile being wrecked on a desert island, finds a priestess there who is no other than the lost Sophia and they are reunited. Restored to their pristine virtue they renounce the conventional world and in the bosom of nature they live happy ever after. A famous episode in the book is the *Confessions of a Savoyard Vicar*.

Emilia, in Shakespeare's *Othello*, the wife of Iago, whom he suspects of undue intimacy with the Moor.

Emilia, the heroine of Chaucer's *Knight's Tale* and all other versions of the story of Palamon and Arcite (see PALAMON). A beautiful lady of high birth she was beloved by both knights and was won by Palamon. Shakespeare gives the name to an attendant on Hermione in *A Winter's Tale;* but has made it specially notable as the name of Iago's wife in the tragedy of *Othello*, introduced in ii, 1. She reveals her husband's perfidy and he stabs her.

Emily, Little, in Dickens's *David Copperfield*, the niece of Daniel Peggotty. David meets her when they are both children and falls in love with her infantile graces. Later she is engaged to Ham Peggotty, but elopes with the fascinating Steerforth, who speedily tires of her. Peggotty sets out on a long search for her and her seducer, learns of the seducer's death, finds her and brings her home. See PEGGOTTY.

Enid. See GERAINT.

Enobarbus, in Shakespeare's tragedy, *Antony and Cleopatra*, a friend of Antony, bluff roughspoken, clearsighted.

Enobarbus, who sees through every wile and guile of the queen, is as it were a chorus to the play, a looker-on at the game; he stands clear of the golden haze which makes up the atmosphere around Cleopatra; and yet he is not a mere critic or commentator. . . . Enobarbus himself is under the influence of the charm of Antony, and slays himself because he has wronged his master. —DOWDEN.

Epicene, in Ben Jonson's comedy, *Epicene, or the Silent Woman* (1610), is introduced to Morose by his prodigal nephew Delphine as a silent woman who will make him the wife he seeks. For Morose is a selfish egotist, hating all noise and all sound save that of his own voice. In the midst of the wedding festivities, which Delphine and his friends enliven by their uninvited presence, Epicene finds her tongue and displays an obstreperous temper. Morose, in despair, agrees that if Delphine can obtain a divorce he will settle an allowance on him and make him his heir. Delphine then reveals that Epicene is a boy in disguise.

Erminia, in Tasso's *Jerusalem Delivered* (1575), a Syrian maiden in love with the courteous and chivalric Tancred, although he had conquered her father, the King of Antioch, who was slain in his last battle, and had made a prisoner of herself. During the siege of Jerusalem by the crusaders under Tancred, she donned the armor of Clorinda, sallied out into the Christian camp and after many adventures found her hero, wounded almost to death, and nursed him back to life and health. Her subsequent fate is not recorded.

Escarbagnas, Countess d', in Molière's comedy of that name (1671) is a caricature of the flatulent pretence of the rustic noblesse. Ignorant and silly, she has brought back from a two months' visit to Paris a cheap imitation of Parisian ways and words —to the great bewilderment of her peasant servants. She finds her neighbors insupportable with "their airs of impertinent equality," but to pass the time away she flirts with Monsieur the Councillor and Monsieur the Receiver of Taxes, while her heart is given to a young town gallant who makes fun of her behind her back.

Esher, Sir Ralph, hero of Leigh Hunt's historical romance, *Sir Ralph Esher, or Memoirs of a Gentleman of the Court of Charles II* (1832), cast in the form of an autobiography.

Sir Ralph tells how he happened to catch a vagrant feather from the cap of Miss Stewart, which he presented to the lady with so much grace, that King Charles was moved and invited him to Court. There he gained the confidence of Lady Castlemaine, discovered an old acquaintance in Nell Gwynne, found sometimes a friend, and sometimes an enemy in the versatile Duke of Buckingham, fraternized with many eminent literary men, fought against the Dutch under the Duke of York, won the esteem of Sir Philip Herne, was his confidant in a love affair and braved the plague of London for his sake, became enamored of a young lady believed to be the natural daughter of the Duke of Ormond, but who turns out to be the lawful offspring of Lord Waringstown, and finally closes the narrative with the double marriage of Sir Philip Herne and himself to the ladies of their affection.

Esmeralda, in Victor Hugo's *Notre Dame de Paris* (1831), a gypsy girl who, with tambourine and goat, dances in the streets of mediæval Paris. Her beauty is unadorned almost to the point of nudity, yet she remains pure and undefiled. She is in love with a captain in the gendarmerie of Louis XI, but the creature who loves her best is Quasimodo, the hunchback bell-ringer, for whom she feels only a mixture of repugnance and pity. When she is accused of witchcraft she flies to the belfry where Quasimodo conceals her for a time, but she is eventually gibbeted. Esmeralda is one of the many imitations of Goethe's Fenella (*q.v.*).

Esmond, Beatrix, in Thackeray's novel, *Henry Esmond* (1852), a brilliant, heartless, capricious beauty, the daughter of Lady Castlewood, who failing in her efforts to become the wife of a duke or the mistress of a king, marries her brother's tutor, for whom she secures by intrigue the rank of bishop. " She was imperious," we are told, " she was lightminded, she was flighty, she was false. She had no reverence for character and she was very, very beautiful." Yet she was of the earth earthy. She reappears in the *Virginians* (1857) as the aged Baroness de Bernstein, her face red with rouge and redder with punch, hobbling about on her tortoise-shell cane, and making modest youths and maidens blush for her coarseness.

Thackeray is believed to have found a prototype for her, not in real life, but in history. She is a rifacimento, so it is asserted, of the famous and infamous Elizabeth Chudleigh, who in George II's day claimed to be the Duchess of Kingston, who really was the Countess of Bristol, who set British Parliament and people by the ears in the effort to decide her pretentions, who was finally adjudged guilty of bigamy and escaped to Europe, where she filled the Imperial Court of St. Petersburg and the Papal Court at Rome with the noise of the scandals of her later life. See CROCODILE, LADY.

Esmond, Henry, the hero and the feigned autobiographer of the *History of Henry Esmond,* a historical novel by W. M. Thackeray (1852).

Reputed to be the illegitimate son of Thomas Esmond, Viscount of Castlewood, he is baptized Thomas, but in boyhood is taken to the family seat and renamed Henry. His father is killed at the battle of the Boyne. The Castlewood estate and titles pass to Francis Esmond, by whom, and by his wife Rachel, Harry is kindly treated and educated with their children, Beatrix and Frank. Francis Esmond, mortally wounded in a duel with Lord Mohun, on his deathbed confesses to Harry that he is really legitimate and the rightful heir. Harry keeps the confession to himself. He plans to bring over the Pretender in disguise. That volatile gentleman (see JAMES STUART) falls in love with Beatrix and forfeits all his chances by an amatory escapade. The two Esmonds renounce their allegiance, break their swords in James's presence, and return just in time to hear George I proclaimed king of England. Beatrix follows the prince to the continent. Harry, who had been in love with Beatrix, ends by marrying her mother and emigrates with her to America.

Ethelberta, heroine of *The Hand of Ethelberta,* a novel (1876) by Thomas Hardy. The daughter of Chickerell, a butler, she becomes a governess in the home of Sir Ralph Petherwin, elopes with and marries the son; loses husband and father-in-law soon afterward; and takes a position as companion to her mother-in-law. She shocks Lady Petherwin by publishing a volume of poetry and, being cut off in her will, becomes a public entertainer with a shrewd eye to whatever may offer in the matrimonial way. Eventually she accepts Lord Mountclerc, an aristocratic debauchee, whose wealth enables her to provide for her none too reputable brothers and sisters.

Ettrick Shepherd, one of the conversationalists at the *Noctes Ambrosianæ,* of which Christopher North was the presiding genius. He is easily recognizable as James Hogg.

Euphorion, in Goethe's *Faust* (Part II, Act iii), the result of the union between Faust and the Greek Helena, summoned up by magic arts from the shades. He is a beautiful boy, representing modern poetry, with Byron as the concrete personality in whose traits the abstract idea has been clothed. A wild, free, aspiring child, Euphorion throws himself singing from a rock, expecting to fly, and falls dead at his parents' feet. From the abode of shades his spirit calls to his mother and draws her after him.

Euphorion, the winged son of Faust and Helen, . . . is the genius of modern poetry in its most finished form, romantic passion clad in the perfection of classical beauty. With the lyre in his hand he rises singing from the earth and the parents, full of anxiety and delight, listen to the strange, full-sounding, heart-moving tones of his voice. It is well known that Goethe intended in this wilful and wanton sprite to commemorate the life of Byron, the poet whom, among moderns, he admired and valued above all others.—H. H. BOYESEN: *Goethe and Schiller*, p. 264.

Euphrasia, in Arthur Murphy's tragedy, *The Grecian Daughter* (1772), saves from starvation her aged father Evander, King of Syracuse, when he was dethroned by Dionysius the Younger and confined in a rocky dungeon, by nourishing him with milk from her own breast. In his baffled rage Dionysius would have put Evander to death but Euphrasia stabbed the tyrant to the heart. Murphy invented his history for the occasion. The tale was originally told by Valerius Maximus (*De Pietate in Parentis*, v. 4) of a young Roman matron who in this fashion nourished her imprisoned mother. Festus, a later writer, changed the mother into the father, and Murphy, accepting Festus's version, laid the scene in ancient Syracuse and altered names and circumstances to suit himself. There was, however, a Grecian daughter Xantippe, who so preserved the life of her father Cimonos when he was imprisoned in a dungeon in Rome, on the site of the church of St. Nicholas in Carcere. Byron visited the dungeon and describes it in *Childe Harold's Pilgrimage* (iv, 148):

There is a dungeon in whose dim drear light
What do I gaze on?
An old man, and a female young and fair
Fresh as a nursing mother in whose veins
The blood is nectar.
Here youth offers to old age the food
The milk of his own gift . . . It is her sire
To whom she renders back the debt of blood.

Euphrasia, heroine of Beaumont and Fletcher's drama, *Philaster* or *Love Lies Bleeding* (1608), whose love for the hero leads her to don male apparel and enter his service. She unintentionally excites his mad jealousy by attracting the love of the Princess Arethusa, but all comes right when her true sex is revealed.

Euphrasia's passion is a child's wholly imaginative worship springing from a child's preconceived ideal of the manhood she sees embodied in visible shape by the hero of her visions. Her passion asks for and wins no recompense of love, demands no response, claims nothing save the inalienable right to give, and throughout no jarring note of premature womanhood taints the freshness and freedom of the image, and no words in all the play ring truer than her own appraisement of the life she is eager to surrender:

'Tis not a life,
'Tis but a piece of childhood thrown away.

Euphues, hero of two romances by John Lyly: *Euphues, or the Anatomy of Wit* (1581), and *Euphues and his England* (1582). The name is derived from Roger Ascham, who in his *Schoolmaster* (1570) had enumerated among the essential qualities of a child that which Socrates had called Εμφυες, or personal attractiveness of mind and body. Euphues, a native of Athens, goes to Naples and there wooes Lucilla, daughter of the governor, who is already pledged to his friend Philautus. The friends quarrel and exchange long letters full of extravagant conceits, but when Lucilla jilts Euphues for a third lover they are reconciled and join in bewailing the inconstancy of woman. Euphues returns to Athens and writes long letters to his friends on education and religion. These constitute the bulk of the book, and it was for their sake that it was written. The work is far more serious and earnest than is generally supposed. Charles Kingsley calls it " as brave, righteous and pious a book as any man need desire to look into; " but it is full of the verbal affectations, quaint conceits and painful elaboration of style, which, though common enough in the court circles of Queen Elizabeth, were first given literary form in this book, and hence gained the name of " Euphuism." The book was held in high estimation by most of Lyly's contemporaries, and was extensively imitated. Euphuism became the rage. Shakespeare, however, ridiculed it in the character of Armado in *Love's Labor's Lost*, as did Ben Jonson in Fastidious in *Every Man out of His Humor*. The character of Sir Percie Shafton, in Scott's

Monastery, is a not very successful attempt to recreate a Euphuist who had modeled his conversation upon Lyly's romance.

In *Euphues and His England* Euphues and Philautus visit England, to mingle in friendly intercourse with its inhabitants, especially the female part thereof, with whom they never tire of holding long, conceited dialogues and exchanging long, conceited letters. A lady named Camilla, especially, attracts Philautus, but though she esteems him as a friend, as a conversationalist and as a correspondent, she does not love him, and he is finally led by a prudent matron, named Flavia, to the possession of a wife in the young lady Violet.

Eusebio, hero of *The Devotion to the Cross* (Spanish, *La Devocion de la Cruz*, 1634) a drama by Pedro Calderon de la Barca, the greatest of all the Spanish dramatists. Eusebio, after various disorders, takes to the mountains, becomes a robber, a murderer and a ravisher, but never amid all his crimes has renounced his devotion to the cross, nor his confidence that in the end he must be saved by this devotion. And, indeed, when the end comes, he finds his confidence has not been misplaced.

It must not be supposed that Eusebios belong merely to the region of imagination. Fowell Buxton (*Memoirs*, 1848, p. 488) visited, in the prisons of Civita Vecchia, a famous Italian bandit, Gasparoni, who having committed two hundred murders, had never yet committed one upon a Friday. —R. C. TRENCH, *The Genius of Calderon*, p. 67.

Eustace, Lady Elizabeth, heroine of Anthony Trollope's novel, *The Eustace Diamonds* (1873), an opulent and aristocratic lady of the Becky Sharp type.

The *Eustace Diamonds* achieved the success which it certainly did attain, not as a love story, but as a record of a cunning little woman of pseudo fashion, to whom in her cunning there came a series of adventures, unpleasant enough in themselves, but pleasant to the reader. As I wrote the book, the idea constantly presented itself to me that Lizzie Eustace was but a second Becky Sharp; but in planning the character I had not thought of this, and I believe that Lizzie would have been just as she is though Becky Sharp had never been described.—ANTHONY TROLLOPE: *An Autobiography*, p. 298.

Eva, Little, in Mrs. H. B. Stowe's *Uncle Tom's Cabin*, the daughter of Tom's owner, St. Clare, and the mistress and friend of Topsy, the colored girl. Her early death is probably a reminiscence of "Little Nell" Trent's in Dickens's *Old Curiosity Shop*.

Evadne, the principal character though not the titular heroine of *The Maid's Tragedy* (1619), by Beaumont and Fletcher. Sister of Melantius, general of the army of Rhodes, she has been seduced by the king. To conceal the amour the culprits agree that she must marry some one who shall be a husband only in name. Amintor is the king's choice. Though already engaged to Aspatia (*q.v.*) friendship to Melantius and loyalty to his monarch forbid his refusal. On the wedding night Evadne reveals the shameful truth. Amintor, in horror, appeals to Melantius, who overwhelms his sister with reproaches and wrings from her a promise to kill the king, which is promptly fulfilled. Meanwhile Aspatia, assuming male apparel, seeks her recreant lover, picks a quarrel with him, throws herself upon his sword and expires. Amintor then runs the sword through his own body and Evadne, recognizing herself as the cause of all these calamities, stabs herself.

The character of Evadne—her naked, unblushing impudence, the mixture of folly with vice, her utter insensibility to any motive but her own pride and inclination, her heroic superiority to any signs of shame or scruples of conscience from a recollection of what is due to herself or others, are well described.—HAZLITT.

Evadne, titular heroine of a tragedy, *Evadne, or the Statue* (1819), by Richard Lalor Shiel, who acknowledges some indebtedness to *The Traitor*.

Sister to Colonna, a Neapolitan noble, in love with and beloved by Vicentio, she is the object of dishonorable advances from the King of Naples, who desists after she has drawn his attention to the statue of her father by whom his life had once been saved. Concealed behind this same statue the king overhears the confession of another plot against his life and throne by his favorite Ludovico. The latter is killed by Colonna and Evadne is united to her lover.

Evander, in Arthur Murphy's tragedy, *The Grecian Daughter* (1772), the father of Euphrasia (*q.v.*). Murphy, in defiance of history, makes him King of Syracuse, who had dethroned Dionysius the Elder and was in his turn dethroned and imprisoned by Dionysius the Younger.

Evangeline, titular heroine of a poem (1849) by Longfellow, founded on the expulsion of the Acadians from Nova Scotia (see ACADIA). Evangeline Bellefontaine and her lover, Gabriel Lajeunesse (*q.v.*), are separated during the exodus. She traces him from Louisiana to the west and then back again to the east, always just failing to meet him. At last, after she herself has become a Sister of Mercy in Philadelphia, she finds him dying in a hospital of the plague.

Evans, Sir Hugh, in Shakespeare's comedy, *The Merry Wives of Windsor*, a Welsh parson (the title is one which in Elizabethan days was given to clergymen.)

An excellent character in all respects. He is as respectable as he is laughable. He has "very good discretions, and very odd humours." The duel scene with Caius gives him an opportunity to shew his "cholers and his tremblings of mind," his valour and his melancholy, in an irresistible manner. In the dialogue, which at his mother's request he holds with his pupil, William Page, to shew his progress in learning, it is hard to say whether the simplicity of the master or the scholar is the greatest.—HAZLITT: *Characters of Shakespeare's Plays.*

Evelina, heroine of a novel by Madame D'Arblay entitled *Evelina, or a Young Lady's Entrance into the World.* See AVELING, EVELINA.

Everdene, Bathsheba, heroine of Thomas Hardy's novel, *Far from the Madding Crowd.* She inherits a farm from her uncle and being generously equipped, both bodily and mentally, carries it on with the assistance of a bailiff. She might have married a neighboring farmer, William Boldwood, but is fascinated by the showy accomplishments of Sergeant Troy whom after marriage she turns adrift as a ne'er-do-well. He is reported drowned. Again Bathsheba would have married Boldwood but Troy reappears, as insolent and impudent as ever, and she shoots him. Condemned to death, her sentence is commuted to penal servitude for life. Gabriel Oak, who had risen on her estate from shepherd to bailiff, renews his old-time attentions and ends by marrying her.

She is a rustic beauty fond of admiration, loving her independence, without much heart but with a brave spirit, a sharp hand at a bargain, an arrant flirt overflowing with vanity, but modest withal. "As a girl, had she been put into a low dress, she would have run and thrust her head into a bush; yet she was not a shy girl by any means. It was merely her instinct to draw the line dividing the seen from the unseen higher than they do in towns." "She has her faults," says Oak to the toll-keeper, after his first meeting with her, "and the greatest of them is—well, what it is always —vanity." "I want somebody to tame me," she says herself; "I'm too independent." Oak is not the man to perform so difficult an achievement. He has too many Christian characteristics and too limited a power of utterance to succeed with Bathsheba.—*Saturday Review.*

Every Man, a sort of synopsis of human life and character, a representative of all humanity, titular hero of an anonymous " morall playe " probably of the time of Edward IV, whose sub-title runs as follows: " A Treatise, how the hye Fader of Heven sendeth Dethe to somon every creature to come and gyve a counte of theyr lyves in this Worlde."

Eyre, Jane, heroine of a novel of that name by Charlotte Brontë (1847), a stiff little Puritanical governess, homely, shy and reserved, but inwardly shaken with emotions and passions that cry for an outlet. Charlotte Brontë undoubtedly drew to some extent on herself for this portrait, and to that extent *Jane Eyre* is the outlet she needed.

George Henry Lewes (not a person of the finest fibre) said of *Jane Eyre* that the grand secret of its success, as of all great and lasting successes, was its reality: " In spite of crudities, absurdities, impossibilities, it remains most singularly and startlingly alive. In *Jane Eyre* Charlotte Brontë comes for the first time into her kingdom of the inner life. She grasps the secret, unseen springs; in her narrow range she is master of the psychology of passion and of suffering, whether she is describing the agony of the child Jane, shut up in that terrible red room, or the anguish of the woman on the morning of that wedding day that brought no wedding."

Ezzelin, Sir, in Byron's poem, *Lara* (1814), a " stern stranger " who recognizes Lara at the table of Lord Otho, but, ere he distinctly formulates his charge, accepts the proposal made by Otho that the matter shall be decided by a duel. At the appointed time Lara appears but Ezzelin is never heard of more. It is dimly hinted, however, that on the fatal eve a serf had seen a huntsman cast a dead body into the river dividing Lara's lands from Otho's and that a star of knighthood blazed upon the corpse's body. The reader is left to his own conclusions.

F

Fadden, Chimmie (*i.e.*, Jimmie), the hero of various stories and sketches by Edward M. Townsend and also of a drama. He was a direct study from life, the original being one Patrick O'Connell, better known as " Chuck Conners " (1852-1913), who, because of his familiarity with the Chinese quarter in New York and his influence over its denizens, was often called " The White Mayor of Chinatown."

It was his inimitable Bowery speech which made Chuck so popular. He became a celebrity because of his quaint philosophy delivered in the Bowery dialect. His saloon became a place for every slum visitor to see, and they would stand and wait for some of the wisdom of the east side to drop from his lips in his own vernacular. Chuck did not hesitate to take advantage of this, and capitalized it for all it was worth. It was Conner's wife who wrote his book, *Bowery Life*, which had quite an extensive sale.

All over the country Americans who have made trips through New York's Chinatown will discuss Chuck Conners to-day. Few of those who visited the place failed to see him. Many of them were in the parties he guided through the mysterious underground passages and dark ways of that quarter.—*N. Y. Globe*, May 10, 1913.

Fadladeen, in Moore's *Lalla Rhook* (1817), the chamberlain of Aurengzebe's harem, appointed to escort Lalla Rhook from Delhi to Cashmere. " A judge of everything from the pencilling of a Circassian's eyelids to the deepest questions of science and literature," he is severely critical of the tales recited by a minstrel in the

lady's train and correspondingly chagrined when the poet turns out to be her affianced bridegroom and his future master. The portrait was recognizably drawn from Francis Jeffrey, whose " sententious smartness " is cleverly imitated. Fadladeen's remorse and contrition at his mistake is thought to have been suggested by the change which came over the mood of the *Edinburgh Review* when it discovered that Byron was a Whig. Hence it is amusing to find in Jeffrey's review of *Lalla Rhook* an allusion to

the omniscient Fadladeen, the magnificent and most infallible grand chamberlain of the Haram (*sic*)—whose sayings and remarks, we cannot help observing, do not agree very well with the character which is assigned to him—being for the most part very smart, sententious and acute, and by no means solemn, stupid and pompous, as was to have been expected."—F. JEFFREY: *Essays*, p. 449.

Fag, in Sheridan's comedy of *The Rivals*, a lying servant to Captain Absolute, who " wears his master's wit as he does his lace, at secondhand."

I am quite conscious of my own immunities as a tale-teller. But even the mendacious *Mr. Fag* . . . assures us: that, though he never scruples to tell a lie at his master's command, yet it hurts his conscience to be found out.—SIR W. SCOTT.

Fagin, in Dickens's novel, *Oliver Twist*, a fawning, crafty old Jew, a receiver of stolen goods, employing a number of confederates, chiefly boys, whom he trains up as pickpockets and petty thieves. After a long life of crime he is sentenced to death for complicity in the murder of Nancy Sikes.

It was eighteen years since Ivanhoe had appeared, and what a contrast between its Jewish personage and the character in this the next work of a great English writer in which a Jew plays a prominent rôle! In the one the charm, in the other the disgrace of the work; in the one the possessor of all human virtues, in the other of all human vices; the one a plea for kindness toward a community at that time still unrecognized as worthy of the rights of men and women, the other calculated to reawaken all the old thoughts if ever they had died out, of the baseness and wickedness of the Jews.—DAVID PHILIPSON: *The Jew in English Fiction*, p. 89.

Fairchild Family, an interesting group described by Mrs. Sherwood in *The History of the Fairchild Family, or the Child's Manual* (1818), which enjoyed a vast popularity with several generations of child readers. A new edition was called for in 1889.

The family consisted of Mr. and Mrs. Fairchild, their three children, and two servants, John and Betty. They lived in the country, and it does not appear that Mr. Fairchild had any particular occupation, except being oppressively good. A sort of married Mr. Barlow, without his fund of general information, he never lost an opportunity of giving a religious turn to the conversation.

Mrs. Fairchild was as solemn and instructive as her husband, though she was a lady with a past. There had been a time, as she informed her children, when " if she could but escape punishment, she did not care what naughty things she did." In these unregenerate days, she would pinch Shock, her aunt's lap-dog, or pull his tail and she also " used the cat ill." As might be expected the children were prodigies of precocious piety.

Fairfax, Jane, in Jane Austen's novel, *Emma*, a gentle, patient girl, an anticipation of Anne Elliot in *Persuasion*.

Fairford, Alan, in Scott's *Redgauntlet* (1824), a young Scotch solicitor, son of Alexander or Saunders Fairford, and the devoted friend of the hero, Darsie Latimer, whose sister he marries. According to Lockhart, Scott drew his own portrait in this character.

Faithful, in Bunyan's prose allegory, *The Pilgrim's Progress* (1678), a companion of Christian on a part of his journey toward the Celestial City At Vanity Fair both pilgrims are seized. Faithful is condemned by Justice Hategood to be burned alive. His soul is taken to heaven in a chariot of fire.

Faithful Jacob, hero of a sea-tale by Captain Frederick Maryatt—*Jacob Faithful, or the Adventures of a Waterman* (1835). Born on a Thames lighter, Jacob, up to the age of eleven, has never set foot on shore. The craft is manned by his father, mother and himself. One of his first acts, on beginning life ashore, is to sell his mother's asses for £20. At fourteen he is bound apprentice to a waterman, when his real adventures begin.

Fakredeen, in Disraeli's *Tancred*, a young emir who is always head over heels in debt but finds a certain joy in the fact. " Fakredeen," says the author, " was fond of his debts; they were the source, indeed, of his only real excitement, and he was grateful to them for their stirring powers." In this respect he resembled young Disraeli;—nor in this respect alone:

There is in the emir's political character the most curious mixture of lofty aims and ambiguous conduct, of faith in an idea and faith in intrigue; and this is characteristic of Disraeli himself when he is about to throw himself into active political life.—GEORGE BRANDER.

Faliero, Marino, the forty-ninth Doge of Venice, elected 1354, is the hero of two great tragedies named after him, one by Byron (1819), the second by Casimir Delavigne (1829). When 75 years of age he married Angiolina, a young beauty. Soon after the union a giddy young nobleman, Michel Steno, whom he had had occasion to rebuke in public, stuck up some indecent lines on the chair of state purporting that the Doge kept a young wife for the benefit of others   The Senate condemned Steno to a month's imprisonment; whereupon the Doge, incensed at the inadequacy of the sentence, joined in a plot against the republic. Betrayed by Bertram, a fellow conspirator, the Doge was beheaded on the Giant's Staircase.

Falkland, the real hero of William Godwin's novel, *Caleb Williams* (1794). A proud aristocrat, jealous of his good name and that of his family, he is goaded by intolerable insult to murder a dangerous enemy, Tyrrel. Two innocent men suffer for the crime. Falkland, tearful of disgrace more than death, remains silent. Finding that his secret is known to his secretary, Caleb Williams, he makes him swear never to reveal it, threatening terrible penalties if the oath be broken. " I am," he warns his dependant, " as much the fool of fame as ever; I cling to it as my last breath; though I be the blackest of villains, I will leave behind me a spotless and illustrious name; there is no crime so malignant, no scene of blood so horrible, in which that object cannot engage me." Finally the truth comes out, and Falkland dies of shame and a broken heart. See WILLIAMS, CALEB.

Falstaff, Sir John, figures in I and II *Henry IV* (1588), and in *The Merry Wives of Windsor* (1596). The epilogue to *II Henry IV* promises that " our author will continue the story with Sir John in it " but Shakespeare obviously changed his mind, for the fat knight does not appear in the next play of the series, *Henry V*, though his death is announced by Dall Tearsheet in a famous passage (II, iii). He makes his appearance, outside of the Shakespearean cycle, in operas by Balfe, Verdi and Nicolai, and also in a comedy by William Kenrick (1766) entitled *Falstaff's Wedding, A Sequel to the 2nd part of Henry IV.* The latter, intended originally for publication in book form alone, was remodelled by the author for the stage and performed, April 12, 1766, for the benefit of Love, who took the titular rôle. See also

FASTOLFE, SIR JOHN, and OLD-CASTLE, SIR JOHN.

Perhaps the most substantial comic character that ever was invented. Sir John carries a most portly presence in the mind's eye and in him, not to speak it profanely, "we behold the fulness of the spirit of wit and humor bodily." We are as well acquainted with his person as his mind, and his jokes come upon us with double force and relish from the quantity of flesh through which they make their way, as he shakes his fat sides with laughter, or "lards the lean earth as he walks along." . . . Falstaff's wit is an emanation of a fine constitution; an exuberance of good-humor and good-nature; an over-flowing of his love of laughter and good fellowship; a giving vent to his heart's ease, and over-contentment with himself and others.—WILLIAM HAZLITT: *Characters of Shakespeare's Plays.*

He is a man at once young and old, enterprising and fat, a dupe and a wit, harmless and wicked, weak in principle and resolute by constitution, cowardly in appearance and brave in reality, a knave without malice, a liar without deceit, and a knight, a gentleman and a soldier without either dignity, decency, or honor.—MAURICE MORGANN: *On the Dramatic Character of Sir John Falstaff* (1777).

That Queen Bess should have desired to see Falstaff making love proves her to have been, as indeed she was, a gross-minded old baggage. Shakespeare has evaded the difficulty with great skill. He knew that Falstaff could not be in love; and has mixed but a little, a very little, *pruritis* with his fortune-hunting courtship. But the Falstaff of the *Merry Wives* is not the Falstaff of Henry IV. It is a big-bellied impostor, assuming his name and style, or, at best, it is Falstaff in dotage.—HARTLEY COLERIDGE: *Essays and Marginalia.*

Fang, a sheriff's officer in the second part of Shakespeare's *King Henry IV.*

Fang, Mr., the justice in Dickens's novel of *Oliver Twist;* intended, it is said, for a Mr. Laing, " a coarse magistrate," who " felt," we are told, " the power of the novelist, and was glad to resign."

Fanny, heroine of a poetical satire of that name (1819) by Fitz Greene Halleck. The daughter of a " codfish aristocrat," she and her father make a temporary splurge in New York City and then subside into poverty and obscurity.

There is no story in *Fanny* or none to speak of, and the most that we can say of it is that it is an imaginary sketch of the social experiences of its heroine, the daughter of a shopkeeper in Chatham Street, who, having amassed what was then considered a comfortable little fortune, proceeded to make a brilliant, brief splurge in society and concluded his career by going where the woodbine twineth. What the subject-matter of such a poem as *Fanny* could be in the hands of a true poet was shown at a later period by Thomas Hood in Miss Kil-mansegg.—R. H. STODDARD: *Lippincott's Magazine*, XLIII, p. 892.

Fantine, the chief female character in Victor Hugo's *Les Miserables* (1862), enforcing his favorite moral of the possible redemption of fallen womanhood through the reawakening of its better impulses. She is intro-duced in Book iii (named after her) in a characteristic setting of students celebrating a holiday with the gri-settes as their companions. Nemesis follows in desertion, shame, poverty, and the struggle between womanly pride and maternal love. The origi-nally pure, confiding and beautiful girl degenerates into a jealous, reck-less, abandoned woman, redeemed only by the love of little Cosette. Then, when society has consummated its monstrous wrong, M. Madeleine (see VALJEAN, JEAN) appears as a sort of *deus ex machina;* his pity pene-trates the heart which agony and despair had deadened; another victim is snatched from the moral death which (we are shown) is the penalty of misfortune rather than wickedness.

Take the pathetic story of Fantine, for instance, which forms but a fragment of the whole book; Hugo here takes the coldest reader deep into misery. He knows better than any writer of the time how to excite physical horror, and it is in general to his ability to excite sympathetical physical sen-sations that nine-tenths of his success is due. In the case before us our blood runs cold at the description of the poor girl's sufferings: she sells her hair for money, she sells her teeth, and finally herself, and it is perhaps as grim a picture as even Hugo has drawn, that is made of it all. He is as pitiless as fate or as a newspaper reporter: he spares us none of the tragedy.—T. S. PERRY.

Fardarougha, in *Fardarougha, the Miser, or the Convicts of Lisnamond,* an Irish novel by William Carleton, a miser whose generous instincts are still dormant under a layer of avarice and greed.

Farintosh, Marquis of, in Thack-eray's novel, *The Newcomes,* a young English nobleman of great wealth, good looks, distinguished ancestry, and meagre intelligence; spoiled by flattery from his cradle and launched upon society as a full-blown egotist and coxcomb. Believing that every daughter of Eve was bent upon mar-rying him, he is not merely pained, but shocked and astonished when Ethel Newcome throws him over be-cause of his past. M. B. Field in his *Memories,* p. 132, says Thackeray told him that the original of this character was the Marquis of Bath.

Farrell, Aminta, heroine of George Meredith's novel, *Lord Ormont and his Aminta* (1894). She makes a secret marriage with his lordship, a sulky Achilles of an Englishman, rebels against his treatment of her and the false position to which a mere whim condemns her, and is thrown into renewed association with a former schoolboy lover, Matthew Weyburn. Weyburn has been ap-pointed secretary to Lord Ormont, whom he greatly admires, and is revolving plans for an international school which is to produce men on the English pattern. Constant asso-ciation renews the old love and at last the two leave England together and are happy forever after. They set up the school and in the end Lord Ormont commits to their keeping his grand-nephew.

Fashion, Sir Brilliant, in Arthur Murphy's comedy, *The Way to Keep Him* (1760), a man of the world who " dresses fashionably, lives fashion-ably, wins your money fashionably, loses his own fashionably, and does everything fashionably."

Fashion, Tom, nicknamed " Young Fashion " in Vanbrugh's *The Relapse* (1697), and in Sheridan's rifacimento of that comedy, *A Trip to Scarborough* (1777), the younger brother of Lord Foppington, who personates that nobleman and wins his destined bride, Miss Hoyden Clumsy. Through his consideration and courtesy he fully reconciles the snobbish Sir Tunbelly, her father, after the fraud has been discovered and has been crowned by marriage.

Fastolfe, Sir John (who must not be confounded with Falstaff), a character in *I Henry VI* where he is portrayed as "a contemptible craven." He was a real personage (1377–1459), one of the most famous of the English knights who won their spurs in the French wars. It was at the siege of Patay (1430) that he incurred the imputation of cowardice which Shakespeare, following Holinshed, has fixed upon him. But at the most he seems to have done no more than to have withdrawn his troops from what seemed to him inevitable defeat, and the regent Talbot must have been satisfied with his explanation, for none of his honors were taken away from him and he continued in high favor with the English government until his resignation of his-commands in 1440.

> This dastard at the battle of Patay
> Like to a trusty squire did run away
> *I Henry VI*, iii, 2.

Fathom, Ferdinand, Count, hero of Smollett's novel, *The Adventures of Ferdinand, Count Fathom* (1753), an unmitigated villain, whose career is a series of fiendish knaveries. There had been a precedent for such a fiction in Fielding's *Jonathan Wild;* and Smollett did his best, by introducing characters of romantic virtue, and by leading the scoundrel himself through a succession of scenes affording scope for circumstantial description, to impart to the tale the necessary amount of interest.

Unlike Fielding, he does not bring his hero to the gallows, but crushes the vice out of him by a gradual accumulation of miseries, and then remits him to a life of further probation under a feigned name. As if to prove the wisdom of this procedure, Fathom reappears in a subsequent novel in the guise of a thoroughly reformed gentleman neatly dressed in black, with a visage of profound melancholy, and doing much good in his neighborhood.

Faulconbridge, Philip, nicknamed "the Bastard," natural son of Richard I and Lady Faulconbridge in Shakespeare's drama, *King John.* A man of wit and high spirits, he can mock with no great delicacy at his own natal misfortune. Large-hearted and large-brained, he has yet an insular contempt for all foreigners.

Faulkland, in Sheridan's comedy, *The Rivals,* lover of Julia Melville, a morbid, over-anxious, self-tormenting weakling.

Fauntleroy, Little Lord, in Mrs. Frances Hodgson Burnett's story of that name (1886), the hereditary title of the seven-year-old hero. His father had been disinherited by the grandfather, an English earl, because of his marriage with an American, but when the father dies the Earl relents toward the grandson he has never seen. The boy had been living in New York in poor and vulgar surroundings, against which his gentle and tender mother (known to him as "Dearest"), was the sole counteracting influence. He is summoned to England on condition that his mother shall not accompany him, but the boy's frank and loyal and generous nature triumphs over all prejudices against his mother as well as himself.

Faust, or **Faustus,** a name famous in legend and literature, is identified in real life with one Giorgius Sabellicus Faustus, Junior, a German student of magic first mentioned in a letter, dated August 20, 1507, from the Benedictine monk Trithimius to the astrologer Johann Windurg at Hasfurth. Trithimius denounced him as a mountebank. Melanchthon, on the contrary, believed that he was really in league with the devil. From these and other contemporary authorities we learn that he travelled around Europe performing many marvels; that he was popularly believed to have sold himself to the devil, who accompanied him in the shape of a black poodle; and that one morning he was found mysteriously dead. Hence he was thought to have been killed in the night by his master who had carried off his soul to hell. Eventually there crystallized around Faust's memory the various mediæval or earlier legends concerning a compact between a mortal and the devil, whose original heroes had been Virgil, Pope Silvester, Friar Bacon or Michael Scott, all of which could find a common origin in pre-Christian Jewish sources. The earliest collection of Faustus legends was published by John Spies at Frankfurt in 1587, and was followed by similar books and pamphlets in almost every European country. He became a favorite figure in the German puppet shows. Marlowe introduced him to the English stage in 1594 (see FAUSTUS, DR.). Following in the wake of the German legend, Marlowe made Helen of Troy his mistress. Goethe's Faust (1798) was practically the first to introduce a new love element in Gretchen, the German diminutive of Margueret. This gave rise to an extensive musical literature which utilized this episode in Goethe's play, the chief being *La Damnation de Faust* (1846) by Hector Berlioz, and *Faust and Marguerite* (1859), an opera by Gounod.

Faustus, hero of Marlowe's tragedy, *The Tragical History of Dr. Faustus* (1590), founded on an English paraphrase (1588) of Johann Spies's chapbook by Bishop Aylmer (see FAUST). As in the original legend, the main interest is supernatural; Faust's compact with Mephistophilis whereby he dooms his soul to hell after twenty-four years of earthly power and glory and unlimited sensual gratification, the magic feats and the ridiculous tricks by which the fiend amuses his master's leisure, and finally the victim's repentance, his vain attempts to escape from his bargain; his awful end, when after exhorting his disciples to take warning by his fate, Faust is carried off to hell. There is a slight love interest. Mephistophilis, at Faust's command, summons Helena of Troy from the shades. `She becomes Faust's mistress and bears him a child.

Faustus himself is a rude sketch, but it is a gigantic one. This character may be considered as a personification of the pride of will and eagerness of curiosity, sublimed beyond the reach of fear and remorse.— WILLIAM HAZLITT, *Literature of the Age of Elizabeth*, Lecture ii.

Favorita, La, title of Donizetti's opera (1842) and pet name of the heroine, Leonora de Guzman, the favorite mistress of Alfonso XI of Castile. His son Ferdinando falls in love with her. Alfonso is obliged to consent to the marriage in order to save himself from excommunication. When Ferdinando discovered the true state of affairs he indignantly spurned the lady and became a monk.

Featherstone, Mr., in George Eliot's novel of English country life, *Middlemarch*, a miser who affords a death-scene and a will-reading scene which seem to show the completed ideal of what Dickens was trying for in *Chuzzlewit*. He is as sordid and limited as Tennyson's *Northern Farmer*, with his burden of "propputy, propputy." "There's one thing I made out pretty clear when I used to go to church, and it's this: God A'mighty sticks to the land. He promises land, and he gives land, and he makes chaps rich with corn and cattle."

Fedora, titular heroine of a drama (1883) by Victorien Sardou. Her full name is Fedora Romazof; she is a princess, young, beautiful, wealthy, living in St. Petersburg in 1882. Her betrothed, Yarischkine, has been mysteriously slain. Suspicion rests upon Count Louis Ypanof, who flees to Paris. Thither Fedora follows him. With the knowledge and sanction of the police she encourages him to fall in love with her in order to obtain from him the confession of his crime, but becomes in her turn infatuated with him. Just when she has well-nigh abandoned her suspicions he confesses the crime. She gives the alarm. But in the next interview, which is to betray him into the hands of the police, he explains that he had killed Yarischkine because he had seduced his (Ypanof's) wife. To her horror Fidora finds that she had delivered him up to death for the sake of a man who was faithless to her. His arrest follows, he discovers that he has been betrayed by a woman, but does not know her name. Fedora drinks poison, confesses everything, and dies with his kiss of forgiveness upon her lips.

Fedora in Balzac's *Peau de Chagrin* the " woman without a heart " whom Raphael (*q.v.*) worships as his first love. She is the representative of that " society " which in Paris, more even than elsewhere, is the goal of a certain class of ambitious youth. Success in the contest means only disillusionment and can be attained only at the sacrifice of what is best and truest in the human heart. Fedora is to be won only by a man who is as calculating and self-centred as herself. Raphael might have been saved by Pauline, the type of real love—love self-sacrificing, self-effacing, constant, ennobling—but he meets her too late. Blinded by sordid ambition, he continued to follow the woman without a heart to his eventual ruin.

Feenix, Cousin, in Dickens's novel, *Dombey and Son*, an aristocratic personage, tireless in his allusions to his " lovely and accomplished relative," the wife of Mr. Dombey.

Feignwell, Colonel, hero of Mrs. Centlivre's comedy, *A Bold Stroke for a Wife* (1718). His name rather too blatantly proclaims his most prominent trait; he was an ingenious strategist who could flatter and cozen with a straight countenance. His bold strike was that of winning the heiress, Anne Lovely, by passing himself off as Simon Pure (*q.v.*), and insinuating himself into the confidence and good-will of her four guardians, each a man of marked peculiarities.

Felton, Septimius, hero of a novel of that name left unfinished by Nathaniel Hawthorne and published posthumously in 1872. From Indian ancestors, Septimius inherits a touch of savage passions not quite eliminated by puritanical training. On another side he is descended from an ancient English family, one of whose members had committed a murder and ever afterwards left behind him the track of a bloody footstep wherever he travelled. Septimius, under the burden of this double heritage,

grows up moody and skeptical. When the American Revolution breaks out he is more disposed to bury himself in meditation than to take part in the struggle; but by a strange accident he is involved in the fight at Lexington, and kills a young English officer in spite of himself. He withdraws all the more decidedly into his own thoughts and he devotes himself to the quest for an elixir of life which will bestow immortality upon him.

Septimius may be taken as in some sense an 'ideal representation of Hawthorne himself, and of the consequences of the revolt of a fine but ill-balanced nature against the prosaic realism of modern life.

Fenella, in Scott's *Peveril of the Peak*, is trained by the villainous Edward Christian, her real father, in the belief that she is the daughter of his brother, the murdered William Christian, and that to avenge William's death is her " first great duty on earth." As a pretended deaf-mute and a " base eavesdropper " she spends her girlhood in the Countess of Derby's household. Her hopeless love for Julian Peveril redeems her. To be near him and to save him she assumes the fresh disguise of " Zarah, the Moorish sorceress " and helps to deliver him from prison. The character, like Bulwer's Nydia, evidently owes something to Goethe's Mignon. Sir Walter is his 1831 introduction cites the parallel case of a wandering woman resident in his grandfather's house, who was believed to have feigned deafness and dumbness for some years. But the evidence of her deceit rests solely on the testimony of " a mischievous shepherd boy."

Feramors, the name assumed by the Prince when disguised as a Cashmerian minstrel in Moore's *Lalla Rookh*.

Ferdinand, in *The Tempest*, is the son of the King of Naples, and in love with Miranda, daughter of the banished Duke of Milan, Prospero.

Ferdinand, King of Navarre in Shakespeare's *Love's Labor's Lost*, a scholarly prince who sets up a " little Academe," a school of culture, for himself and three companions. He is evidently drawn from Henry IV of France. In Shakespeare's *Tempest* Ferdinand is the name of a shipwrecked prince, son of the usurping King of Naples, who wooes and wins Miranda on Prospero's enchanted island.

Fernando of Portugal, Don, uncle of Alphonso V, King of Portugal, and grandson on his mother's side of the English John of Gaunt, is the hero of *The Steadfast Prince*, a tragedy by Calderon.

Taken captive in an unfortunate African expedition, he refused liberty on the terms offered him by the Moorish king and wins his place among the noble army of martyrs by the patient endurance of protracted agonies for the sake of his faith.

It is impossible, when we compare the lowly Ferdinand with his cousin and contemporary, Henry V, to deny that the selfish glory of the victor of Agincourt looks poor in the purer light which encircles the preserver of Ceuta, nor can we help wishing that the mightier genius, who in Prince Hal bequeathed a fascinating but dangerous model to future royal scions, had known and depicted the loftier type of prince which fate reserved to the hand of Calderon.— *Saint Paul's Magazine*, October, 1873.

Ferrars, Endymion, hero of a political novel *Endymion* (1880), in which the Earl of Beaconsfield, then Prime Minister of England, has undertaken to describe certain features in the career of the Right Hon. Benjamin Disraeli.

The hero of the book, at least the young man who gives the name to it, is an almost colorless effigy of humanity who is moved on through the pages by the alternate efforts of his sister and the woman whom he admires and afterwards marries, to the position of prime minister, a position utterly remote from the logical consequences of his intellect or will. He is the creature of accident, friendliness and destiny, and as he is shoved along a step higher at each turn of the story, the reader comes to watch for his appearance higher up with curiosity but without the least apprehension.—*N. Y. Nation.*

Ferrars, Myra, in Lord Beaconsfield's novel *Endymion* (1880), twin sister to the titular hero and his great helper in his upward climb. She strikes the keynote of her brother's character and career when she says to him: "Power and power alone should be your absorbing object, and all the accidents and incidents of life should only be considered with reference to the main result." In order to assist her brother's ambitions she marries Lord Roehampton, and, when widowed, she for the same reason accepts the crowned adventurer (a caricatured portrait of Napoleon III) who had, as Prince Florestan, long admired her during his exile in England.

Ferroll, Paul, hero of two novels by Mrs. Caroline Wigley Clive: *Paul Ferroll* (1856) and *Why Paul Ferroll Killed His Wife* (1862). The wife, a woman of violent temper and unscrupulous methods, had separated Paul from Elinor, his first love, in order to secure him for herself. He murders her, marries Elinor and for a time escapes suspicion, but confesses when an innocent party is found guilty of the crime, and escapes to America. He had deposited an account of the dead, with an explanation of its motives, in the coffin of his victim; this is found and constitutes the sequel to the first novel.

Festus, hero and title of a dramatic poem (1835) by Philip James Bailey, which gives a modernized version of the Faust legend.

The hero is a human soul of the highest gifts and attainments, doomed to despair and melancholy and unwillingly ensnared by sin. The mode in which he becomes the plaything of the archspirit of evil is impressive, but hardly intelligible; nor are the relations of the tempter to his victim ever realized in a vividly dramatic or narrative way. It would be an almost impossible feat to separate the story or plot of *Festus* from its lyrical and rhetorical ornament.—E. W. GOSSE: *Portraits and Sketches.*

Festus, in Robert Browning's *Paracelsus*, the old and faithful friend who believes in Paracelsus from the first. He is the husband of Michal, and both, at various stages in his career, influence for good the mind of the hero of medicine.

Feverel, Sir Austin, in George Meredith's novel, *The Ordeal of Richard Feverel* (1859), father of the hero—a pseudo philosopher who strives to make the world square with his ideals and to fashion his son in his own mould. He cannot forget the part played by woman in the fall of man, hence he names the instinct of sex the Apple Disease. " We are pretty secure from the Serpent till Eve sides with him " is his favorite apothegm. So his system consists largely in protecting his son against the approaches of this malady; but Nature beats his system.

Feverel, Richard, titular hero of George Meredith's novel, *The Ordeal of Richard Feverel, A Tale of Father and Son* (1859). The elder Feverel (see above) is a philosopher who tries to make the world square with his philosophy and to bring up Richard, his son, to the highest limit of human perfection by shaping all the circumstances of his youth. The system breaks down—the boy is miserable, the circumstances turn out the worst in which he could have been placed. Philosophy is beaten by the attractions which the outer world, and especially the outer world of women, will ever offer to the most virtuous and most ingenuous. The boy who is kept in entire seclusion manages to meet a farmer's niece by moonlight, and marries her before he is twenty. When he is married and his father is playing off the batteries of the most philosophical anger so as to drive him to the exact stage and kind of repentance most desirable, the fascinations of the unsystematic world again triumph over the system, and the young husband is carried away by the trickery and arts of a much naughtier woman than the young wife from whom his father contrives for a time to separate him.

Fidele, in Shakespeare's *Cymbeline*, the name assumed by Imogen when she dons male attire.

Fidessa, in Spenser's *Faërie Queene*, the name assumed by Duessa when she wished to beguile the Red Cross Knight.

Fifine, subject of Browning's philosophical poem, *Fifine at the Fair* (1872), a beautiful strolling actress in whom the husband of Elvire (un-

named himself but obviously meant as a modern adumbration of Don Juan) finds his text for an apologia. With great fertility of illustration he seeks to convince the wife whom he loves that he does well in occasionally toying with the Fifines who appeal to his lusts. Browning provides the arch voluptuary with a defence of inconstancy in marriage which lies quite beyond the speculative capacity of the traditional Juan.

Figaro, hero of two comedies by Beaumarchais, *Le Barbier de Seville* (1775) and *Le Mariage de Figaro* (1784). The latter play was reproduced in English by Thomas Holcroft under the title, *The Follies of a Day* (1784). Several operas have been founded on the two plays, notably Mozart's *Nozze di Figaro* (1786), Paisiello's *Il Barbiere di Seviglia* (1810), and Rossini's *Il Barbiere di Seviglia* (1816).

In the first play Figaro is a barber, in the second a valet, and each avocation gives him ample opportunity to exhibit his consummate adroitness in evading the consequences of his own audacity in stratagem and intrigue, and in preserving his *sang froid* and alertness of mind in the most embarrassing situations.

In Figaro, Beaumarchais has personified the *tiers état*, superior in wit, industry, and activity to birth, rank, or fortune, in whose hand lies the political power; so that the idea of the piece is not only a satirical allegory upon the government and nobility of that epoch, but a living manifesto upon the inequality, just or unjust, of society.—ROSE.

Fillpot, Toby, hero of *The Brown Jug,* a favorite English drinking song by Rev. Francis Fawkes (1721-1777). It opens

Dear Tom, this brown jug which now foams with mild ale
(In which I will drink to sweet Nan of the vale)
Was once Toby Fillpot, a thirsty old soul,

and goes on to explain the process of his metamorphosis from human clay to earthenware.

Filomena, St., in the Roman Catholic calendar, a saint who tended the sick and wounded. A famous picture in Pisa by Sabatelli represents her floating down from heaven attended by two angels bearing a lily, a palm and a javelin. In the foreground are patients cured by her intercession. A curious coincidence in name and mission suggested Longfellow's poem of *Santa Filomena*, written in praise of Florence Nightingale (1820–1900), the first and most famous of war nurses. Filomena (see PHILOMEL) means " nightingale."

> Nor ever shall be wanting here
> The palm, the lily, and the spear:
> The symbols that of yore
> St. Filomena bore.
> LONGFELLOW: *Sta. Filomena.*

Finch, Miss, the heroine of Wilkie Collins' novel, *Poor Miss Finch* (1872). She is a beautiful blind girl engaged to Oscar Dubourg whose twin brother Nugent is also in love with her. Oscar takes nitrate of silver for epileptic fits, and as a result of the treatment turns·all over to a permanent blue color. Now, Miss Finch has personal prejudices on the score of complexion, together with the natural antipathy of the blind to anything dark. Were she once to detect the dyeing of his skin, her instincts would infallibly prove far too strong for her love. The consequence is, constant precautions against betrayal, and a series of dangerous mystifications. However, the secret is kept, and plays into the hands of the twin brother. Nugent fights his passion for a long time before he yields to it. Then he becomes almost unnaturally a scheming villain. But, recollecting that this pair of Dromios is identical, down to the tones of the voice, in everything except their characters and complexions, it is easy to see how ingeniously circumstances are made to complicate themselves in the hands of a planner of labyrinths so experienced as Mr. Collins.

Finn, Huckleberry, a character in Mark Twain's *Adventures of Tom Sawyer* (1876) who reappears as the hero of *Adventures of Huckleberry Finn* (1885), an autobiographical tale of boyish adventure along the Mis-sissippi River told as it appeared to Huck Finn.

> In *Tom Sawyer* we saw Huckleberry Finn from the outside; in the present volume we see him from the inside. He is almost as much a delight to any one who has been a boy as was Tom Sawyer. But only he or she who has been a boy can truly enjoy this record of his adventures, and of his sentiments and of his sayings. Old maids of either sex will wholly fail to understand him or to like him, or to see his significance and his value. Like Tom Sawyer, Huck Finn is a genuine boy; he is neither a girl in boy's clothes like many of the modern heroes of juvenile fiction, nor is he a "little man," a full-grown man cut down; he is a boy, just a boy, only a boy. The contrast between Tom Sawyer, who is the child of respectable parents, decently brought up, and Huckleberry Finn, who is the child of the town drunkard, not brought up at all, is made distinct by a hundred artistic touches, not the least natural of which is Huck's constant reference to Tom as his ideal of what a boy should be.—*Saturday Review.*

Finn, Phineas, hero of *Phineas Finn, the Irish Member* (1869), a novel by Anthony Trollope, and its sequel, *Phineas Redux.* Starting as the impecunious son of an Irish country doctor, he gets into Parliament at five and twenty, is in the Ministry a year or two afterwards, fights a duel, rides an unmanageable horse, saves a cabinet minister from the hands of garroters, and being as strong as a coalheaver and as handsome as an Apollo is besieged by several ladies of rank and wealth. At the call of duty he leaves London to settle down in contented obscurity at Cork with a poor Irish girl whose only merit is that she is more deeply in love with him than any of the rest. In the sequel she dies and he returns to London and politics.

Firmilian, hero of a burlesque tragedy of that name by W. Edmonstone Aytoun, published (1854) under the pseudonym of T. Percy Jones. A student at the University of Badajoz, Firmilian is determined to be a poet. He is writing a tragedy, *Cain*, that " shall win the world by storm." He finds himself handicapped because he has no personal experience of the agonies of remorse. To supply this deficiency he poisons the wine of three friends in a tavern. Yet this first essay proves to be a mistake. They drink and die while he is absent. He had failed to witness their dying throes. So he blows up a cathedral with gunpowder and watches the catastrophe from the pillar of St. Simeon Stylites. Even now he is not satisfied. Priest, choir and worshippers were all strangers to him. Had there been a benefactor, a relative among them he might, indeed, have felt wicked. As mere incidents he kills a rival poet and a critic and then plunges into sensuality, hoping that adultery may furnish those glorious qualms of conscience which murder fails to yield. He is hounded by the Inquisition, becomes the victim of his own haunted imagination, finally falls over a precipice and is killed.

Firmin, Dr. George Brandon, in Thackeray's *Adventures of Philip,* father of the hero, an unctuous hypocrite, handsome, polished, attractive to women. Under the name of George Brandon he had already made his appearance in *A Shabby Genteel Story* as the seducer of Catherine Gans (*q.v.*).

Firmin, Philip, hero of Thackeray's novel, *The Adventures of Philip* (1861). Rough, boisterous and uncouth, he is a self-determined contrast to the smooth villainy of his father, Dr. Brandon Firmin. Because Brandon was polished and polite, Philip looked upon those qualities as masking insincerity and treachery, and so eschews them with loud disdain. Being big and strong, red-haired and red-bearded, he can exhibit to some purpose his quarrelsome and aggressive yet not ungenerous temper, and too often alienates friend or would-be friend by a determination to indulge his headlong independence of speech and action.

Fitz Boodle, George Savage, the autobiographic hero of various tales and sketches by W. M. Thackeray, collected together under the general title, *The Fitz Boodle Papers,* and the feigned narrator of *Men's Wives.* He is represented as the indolent and rather impudent younger son of a country baronet with considerable

knowledge of fast life both in Bohemia and in Belgravia, whose passion for tobacco proves disastrous in some of his love affairs.

Fitzborn, in Disraeli's novel, *Vivian Grey,* a supposed portrait of Sir Robert Peel.

Fixlein, Quintus, hero and title of a romance by John Paul Richter.

Flamboroughs, The Miss (*sic*), in Goldsmith's *Vicar of Wakefield,* daughters of Solomon Flamborough, an over-loquacious farmer. Their simplicity and wholesomeness are favorably contrasted with the airs assumed by pseudo ladies of fashion introduced by Squire Thornhill.

Flanders, Moll, heroine of and feigned autobiographer of *The Fortunes and Misfortunes of Moll Flanders* (1722), a realistic novel by Daniel Defoe. A thief and a harlot, she went to the bad early in life, was five times married without any regard for the laws against bigamy, but ends as a penitent.

Flash, Sandy, in Bayard Taylor's novel, *The Story of Kennett,* is the notorious highwayman, Fitzpatrick, the traditions of whose deeds of daring still survive in Chester County, Pennsylvania. Long after his death in the early nineteenth century searches were made for the treasures he was reputed to have buried in the neighborhood of Castle Rocks.

Fleaunce, in Shakespeare's *Macbeth,* the son of Banquo. He fled to Wales on his father's murder, married a Welsh princess, and became the ancestor of the royal house of Stuart.

Fleming, Contarini, hero of a novel of that name (1832) by Benjamin Disraeli, in which he has obviously drawn his own portrait as he pictured himself in youth. Contarini would fain be a poet, but his worldly wise father (Isaac D'Israeli?) dissuades him and he enters politics.

Fleming, Farmer, in George Meredith's novel, *Rhoda Fleming,* father of the heroine, an excellent specimen of the sturdy British yeoman, masking a kind heart under a stern and unyielding exterior, whose ideas are very simple, but obstinate and deep-

rooted in proportion. He is over-
whelmingly grateful to Algernon
Blanco the man who had seduced
and afterwards married his daughter Dahlia, though he knows him to
be a villain, and he insists on her
joining her husband, though this
means certain and enduring misery
to both.

Fleming, John, hero of T. B.
Aldrich's short story, *Marjorie Daw*,
and of the same author's *Queen of
Sheba*.

Fleming, Paul, the hero of Longfellow's *Hyperion* (1839). A young
American poet, he starts out on a
European tour under the shadow of a
great affliction. He has lost his young
wife and his child. Plunged at first
into deep despair, his youth finally
reasserts itself and, though chastened
and subdued by the ordeal through
which he has passed, he recovers
some measure of cheerfulness and
finds that there still lies before him
a world of duties and hopes and aspirations. In this mood he meets and
falls in love with Mary Ashburton
(*q.v.*), but she repels his suit.

Fleming, Rhoda, titular heroine of
a novel by George Meredith (1865),
the younger sister of Dahlia, who has
brought shame upon herself and her
family and fled from their presence.
Rhoda goes in search of Dahlia and
never rests until she has found her
and, as she thinks, righted her wrong,
though in truth her fierce obstinacy
has only shattered her poor sister's
returning gleam of long-deferred
happiness. Convinced at last that
she had been mistaken, and that she,
too, had something to repent of, the
proud nature melts and we have a
final glimpse of her, tamed and softened, in the keeping of Robert Arm-
strong, the lover who deserved her
so well.

Flestrin, Quinbus, the name which
the Lilliputians in *Gulliver's Travels*
apply to Gulliver. Swift explains
that in the Lilliputian language this
means "man-mountain."

Fleur de Marie, in Eugene Sue's
Mysteries of Paris, a young maiden,
the lost daughter of Rudolph, Grand

Duke of Gerolstein, and his mistress
(he believes her to be dead), who is
brought up amid murderers, prostitutes and thieves in the lowest
quarters of the French metropolis;
but who has retained through all
surroundings her innate purity of
soul, delicacy of sentiment and
warmth of heart.

Florac, Comte de, in Thackeray's
novel, *The Newcomes* (1855), the
son of a saintly Catholic lady who
in her youth had loved and been beloved by Colonel Newcome. The
colonel takes a great interest in the
young man when he comes to London,
though he is strangely unlike his
mother. A mixture of good sense and
good breeding with amazing levity
and ludicrous oddities, he becomes a
general favorite by reason of his bon-
homie, his prodigality, his perennial
high spirits. His Franco-English
speech is a linguistic triumph.

Florestan, Prince, in Lord Beaconsfield's novel, *Endymion* (1880), with
"his graceful bow that always won
a heart," who sets out from England
in a yacht, and conquers his kingdom
in ten days after writing a pretty note
to Lady Roehampton (Lady Palmerston), is a sort of caricature portrait
of the Emperor Napoleon III.

The character of Louis Napoleon's counterpart is carefully and skilfully drawn. He
first appears as a boy entrusted to the care
of Mr. Sidney Wilton by his mother, Queen
Hortense, who is introduced under the ill-
omened name of Agrippina. His English
guardian renounces his acquaintance when
he breaks his parole in a second attempt to
recover his throne. His final attainment of
his object is accomplished after the fashion,
not of the third, but of the first Napoleon.
His ambiguous position in England, his real
or professed belief in destiny, and his resolute use of opportunities, are happily described.—*Saturday Review.*

Floriani, Lucretia, in George Sand's
romance of that name (1846), an
actress who—surfeited with the noisy
life of the theatres, with illicit
amours, with fame itself—retires to
a villa on Lake Como. One of her
former friends, Salvador, brings to
her retreat a stranger, Prince Karol.
He is melancholy, neurotic and con-
sumptive. His extreme refinement
and delicacy had revolted at what he

had heard of Lucretia's past; nevertheless he now falls passionately in love with her; despite a violent struggle against himself; despite all reactions of despair and remorse. As to Lucretia, she allows herself to be loved and even to love, in a caressing, maternal way, and yields herself to him but only in such measure as her solicitude for his welfare will permit. He becomes insanely jealous; he resents Salvador's tone of familiarity toward the former " friend," he tortures Lucretia with his doubts, suspicions, accusations, upbraidings, until at last she breaks away from him.

In this book George Sand has told with a few necessary changes of detail the story of her own liason with Frederick Chopin, the musician. She denied, of course, that Chopin was Prince Karol, but contemporaries were not to be deceived. Liszt in his biography of Chopin quotes many passages from the novel. Furthermore, Chopin recognized himself and was greatly annoyed.

Florimel, the Fair, in Spenser's *Faëry Queene,* books iii–iv (1590–1596), a maiden whose hand was sought by Sir Satyrane, Sir Peridure and Sir Calidore, but herself in love with the unresponsive Marinel. At last, when Marinel was reported slain by Britomart, she started out to discover what truth was in the rumor. Proteus intercepted her and shut her up in a dungeon " deep in the bottom of a huge, great rock." One day Proteus gave a banquet to the sea gods which Marinel and his mother attended and he, wandering from the table, overheard Florimel bewailing the hard fate that had befallen her " and all for Marinel." His heart was touched, and with the aid of Neptune he released the maiden and married her.

She wore a golden girdle, once the cestus of Venus, but forfeited by that goddess when she wantoned with Mars, its peculiar property being that it " loosed or tore asunder " if clasped around the waist of an unchaste woman. A witch made a counterfeit Florimel out of Riphæan, snow mixed with " fine mercury and virgin wax," and for a time this imposed upon her friends and lovers, but the enchantment was finally dissolved and she melted into nothingness, leaving no wrack behind but the golden girdle.

Her name is compounded of two Latin words meaning honey and flowers, thus betokening the sweet and delicate elements of which her nature is moulded. She seems to express the gentle delicacy and timid sensitiveness of woman; and her adventures, the perils and rude encounters to which those qualities are exposed in a world of passion and violence. She flees alike from friend and foe, and finds treachery in those upon whom she had thrown herself for protection; and yet she is introduced to us under circumstances not altogether consistent with feminine delicacy, as having left the court of the fairy queen in pursuit of a knight who did not even return her passion.—GEORGE S. HILLIARD.

Florinda, the Helen of Spain. She is the heroine of Southey's epic, *Roderick, the Last of the Goths* (see RODERICK). Landor, in his *Count Julian,* calls her Cava. She was Julian's daughter; Roderick ravished her and thus sent Julian into the enemy's camp and paved the way for the Moorish occupation of Spain. At the finale Roderick (now become a monk) receives the dying confession of Julian and is recognized by Julian's daughter:

. . . Round his neck she threw
Her arms, and cried, " My Roderick; mine in heaven!"
Groaning, he claspt her close, and in that act
And agony her happy spirit fled.
SOUTHEY: *Roderick, etc.,* xxiv.

Florisel, Don, hero of the *Exploits and Adventures of Don Florisel of Nicea* (1835), a ninth book in the *Amadis* series added by Feliciano de Silva Burgos. In the mien of a shepherd he wooes a princess, herself disguised as a shepherdess, and his was therefore an appropriate name for the prince in *The Winter's Tale* (see FLORIZEL). The story became one of the most popular romances of the *Amadis* cycle, and was speedily translated from the Spanish into French and Italian, though apparently not into English.

Florizel, in *The Winter's Tale* (1611), the son of Polixenes, King of Bohemia, full of the innocence and chivalry of unstained youth, who falls in love with Perdita (*q.v.*) and courts her, little dreaming of her lofty lineage, under the name of Doricles.

George IV assumed the name of Florizel in his correspondence with Mrs. Mary Robinson, actress and poet, whom he addressed as Perdita, the part in which he first saw her and fell in love with her.

Floyd, Aurora, heroine of a novel of that name (1863), by Miss M. E. Braddon.

> The secret of Aurora Floyd is much better managed than the secret of Lady Audley, and it required much courage in Miss Braddon to choose exactly the same substance of the secret—namely, the previous marriage of the principal character of the story, and try her hand at writing it again so as to make herself perfect in it.—*Saturday Review.*

Fluellen, in Shakespeare's historical play, *Henry V* (1599), a Welsh captain in the English army, valorous, voluble and amusingly pedantic. A famous example of his logical futility is his parallel between Henry V and Alexander the Great: "One was born in Monmouth and the other in Macedon, both which places begin with M and in both a river flowed" (Act iv, Sc. 7).

> Fluellen the Welshman is the most entertaining character in the piece. He is good-natured, brave, choleric, and pedantic. His parallel between Alexander and Harry of Monmouth, and his desire to have "some disputations" with Captain Macmorris on the discipline of the Roman wars, in the heat of the battle, are never to be forgotten. His treatment of Pistol is as good as Pistol's treatment of his French prisoner.—HAZLITT: *Characters of Shakespeare's Plays.*

Flush, the canine hero of Mrs. Browning's stanzas, *To Flush, my dog.* He was a gift to the poet from her " dear and admired " friend, Miss Mitford, and belonged to "the beautiful race she has rendered celebrated among English and American readers."

Flutter, Sir Fopling, in Sir George Etheredge's comedy of *The Man of Mode or Sir Fopling Flutter* (1676), is a coxcomb in whom the Francomania of the day is satirized. "He went to Paris," says his friend Dorimant, "a plain, bashful English blockhead, and is returned a fine, undertaking French fop." An exquisite who wears gloves up to his elbows, curls his hair with painful precision, orders every article of his wardrobe direct from Paris, and engages none but French servants, he is never more delighted than when he is taken for a Frenchman. Beau Hewit is generally held to have sat for the character, though many of Etheredge's contemporaries traced in it great resemblances to himself.

Flying Dutchman. See VANDER-DECKEN.

Fogarty, Phil, hero of Thackeray's burlesque, *Phil Fogarty, a Tale of the Onety-Oneth,* in *Punch's Prize Novelists.* A parody of Lever's military novels so true to the original that Lever humorously declared he might as well shut up shop, and actually did alter the character of his novels.

Fogg, Mr., in Dickens's *Pickwick Papers,* partner in the firm of Dodson and Fogg, solicitors—"an elderly pimply-faced, vegetable diet sort of man . . . a kind of being who seemed to be an essential part of the desk at which he was writing and to have as much thought or sentiment.

Fogg, Phileas, hero of Jules Verne's novel, *Around the World in Eighty Days.* A typical French ideal of the typical Englishman, respectable, methodical, and phlegmatic to the point of imperturbability, Mr. Fogg wagers in his London club that he can make the circuit of the world in eighty days. He starts that night. Passepartout, his French valet, goes with him. All obstacles are conquered by his iron will, invincible coolness, unfailing resource and Napoleonic readiness to sacrifice everything else to the essential—save only humanity. Twice he risks defeat by this exception. He saves the beautiful Hindoo widow Aouda from suttee; he rescues Passepartout from an infuriated Chinese mob. On the eightieth day, ten minutes before the appointed time, he reaches his club.

Foker, Harry (*i.e.*, Henry), in Thackeray's novel, *Pendennis*, a gay young man, generous, kindly, eccentric, effusive, and impartially friendly to high and low, for he is the grandson of an earl on his mother's side, and on his father's the descendant of a wealthy house of brewers, which, as we learn from *The Virginians*, was founded by one Foker or Voelker in Queen Anne's time.

Foker differs from Thackeray's other characters, for there can be little doubt it was an accurate portrait of Andrew Arcedeckne of the Garrick Club. It was probably this which was the cause of Thackeray's being blackballed at the Traveller's Club, where the ballot is by members and not by the committee, on the grounds that the members feared they might appear in some later novel. It is said that Arcedeckne was small in stature and eccentric in his mode of dressing, drove stagecoaches as an amateur, loved fighting-cocks and the prize-ring, and had a large estate in Norfolk. The Hon. Henry Coke says he was so like a seal that he was called "Phoca" by his intimates. It was Arcedeckne who criticised Thackeray's first lecture on "The Four Georges." "Bravo, Thack, my boy! Uncommon good show! But it'll never go *without a pianner!*" There was, however, no enmity between them. Thackeray declared his model to be "not half a bad fellow;" and Arcedeckne remarked, "Awfully good chap old Thack was. Lor' bless you, he didn't mind me a bit. But I *did* take it out of him now and again. Never gave him time for *repartie*."— LOUIS MELVILLE: *Some Aspects of Thackeray*.

Fondlove, Sir William, in Sheridan Knowles' comedy, *The Love-Chase*, a sprightly sexagenarian who presumes too much upon his self-imagined youthfulness when he marries a woman of forty.

Fool, in Shakespeare's *King Lear*.

The fool is no comic buffoon to make the groundlings laugh . . . He is as wonderful a creation as Caliban; his wild babblings and inspired idiocy articulate and gauge the horrors of the scene.—COLERIDGE.

Foppington, Lord, a typical English coxcomb who appears in Sir John Vanbrugh's comedy, *The Relapse* (1697), and successively in Cibber's *Careless Husband* (1704), Sheridan's *Trip to Scarborough* (1777), and Buchanan's *Miss Tomboy* (1890). He is the Sir Novelty Fashion in Cibber's *Love's Last Shift* (1696), raised to the peerage and converted from a mere puppet into a brilliant caricature. Cibber was much pleased with the compliment, and as he had acted the part of Sir Novelty in his own play so a year later he appeared as Foppington in its sequel, earning thereby, as a comedian, "a second flight of reputation" (CIBBER: *Apology*). Vanbrugh makes his hero express equal delight in his new dignity. "Strike me dumb— 'my Lord,' 'your lordship'—sure whilst I was a knight I was a very nauseous fellow." He is the true fop of the period with all his qualities exaggerated. So he finds his life a perpetual " round of delights " and believes himself agreeable to all and irresistible to women. "God's curse, Madam!" he cries in dismay when Amanda strikes him in self-defence, "I am a peer of the realm ! "

Voltaire gallicised Lord Foppington as Le Comte de Boursouffle.

Ford, Master, in Shakespeare's comedy, *The Merry Wives of Windsor*, a gentleman of fortune residing near Windsor, whose middle-aged wife is an object of desire to Sir John Falstaff. Ford assumes the name of Brook (see BROOK, MASTER) in order to pass as a stranger, wins the knight's confidence, and learns from him the entire course of the wooing which at first he takes to be serious and is correspondingly troubled. When he learns the joke he humors Falstaff to the top of his bent and helps to plan and carry out the final exposure.

Ford, Mistress, one of the Merry Wives (see above), Mistress Anne Page being the other. Both are besieged by Falstaff, who writes identically the same love letter to each. They exchange confidences and agree to lure the knight on to a catastrophe which makes him a public laughing stock.

Fore and Aft, in Rudyard Kipling's story, *The Drums of the Fore and Aft*, a nickname given derisively to a regiment of raw recruits (real title, " Fore and Fit "), in memory of a sudden calamity which befalls them in an Afghan pass when, but for the two little blackguard "drums" or drummer boys, they would have been cut to pieces, as they were routed, by a dashing troop of Ghazis. The two little heroes, Jakin and Lew, who conquer only to die, are stunted "gutter birds" who swore, smoked and drank and were the disgrace of the regiment, and had but one ambition—to wipe away the stigma of being bloomin' non-combatants.

Foresight, in Congreve's comedy, *Love for Love* (1695), a ridiculous old astronomer, father of Angelica, with whom Valentine Legend is in love.

Formal, Sir, a grandiloquent and conceited character in Shadwell's comedy, *The Virtuoso* (1676). He has been saved from oblivion only by an allusion in Dryden's *MacFlecknoe*, which insinuates that Shadwell's caricature was really a bit of self-portraiture, and that his own style was as inflated and pompous as Sir Formal's:

And when false flowers of rhetoric thou
    wouldst call,
Trust nature, do not labor to be dull,
But write thy best, and top; and in each line,
Sir Formal's oratory will be thine:
Sir Formal, though unsought, attends thy
    quill.   *MacFlecknoe*, l. 165.

Fortinbras, in Shakespeare's tragedy, *Hamlet*, the Prince of Norway, who at the head of his conquering army appears in the last scene to pronounce a eulogy over Hamlet's corpse.

Fosco, Count, in Wilkie Collins's novel, *The Woman in White* (1860), a plausible and ingenious scoundrel of Italian birth.

Shortly after the publication of *The Woman in White*, Lady Lytton had written to Wilkie Collins: "The great failure in your book is the villain; Count Fosco is a very poor one, and when next you want a character of that sort I trust you will not disdain to come to me. The man is alive and constantly under my gaze. In fact, he is my own husband." This epistle was forwarded by Collins to Lytton, and could at one time be seen among the Knebworth papers."—J. H. Escott, *Edward Bulwer, First Baron Lytton.*

Fotheringay, Miss, in Thackeray's novel, *The History of Pendennis*, the stage name of Miss Emily Costigan, a beautiful actress excellently drilled

to make a showing on the stage but languid, emotionless and unintelligent in private life. Arthur Pendennis falls in love with her, (though she is twenty-six and he only eighteen) when she makes her epochal appearance in the Chatteris theatre. Her father encourages her to accept him but breaks the engagement on learning the boy has no money. A London manager invites her to the metropolis; she makes a great hit there, marries the elderly Sir Charles Mirabel and leaves the stage to become an ornament to society. A suggested original is Miss Eliza O'Neill, an actress who eventually became Lady Becher. See especially FITZGERALD: *The Garrick Club*, pp. 57-176.

Fountain, Lucy, heroine of *Love me Little, Love me Long* (1857), a novel by Charles Reade; a pretty, freakish, emotional creature, noble at heart but given to coquettish deceits and uncertain moods until steadied by her love for David Dodd, whom she marries.

Fracasse, Captain (sometimes roughly Englished as Captain Hurly-Burly), the stage name assumed by the young Baron de Sicognac in Théophile Gautier's novel, *Le Capitaine Fracasse* (announced in 1840; not published until 1863), when he joins a troupe of strolling actors. He is partly impelled by love for Isabella but partly by want, for he is living in dire poverty on his ancestral estate, Chateau de Misere, in Gascony.

The novel presents the adventures of a company of strolling players of Louis XIII's time—their vicissitudes, collective and individual, their miseries and gayeties, their loves and squabbles, and their final apportionment of worldly comfort—very much in that symmetrical fashion in which they have so often stood forth to receive it at the fall of the curtain. It is a fairy-tale of Bohemia, a triumph of the picturesque. In artistic "bits," of course, the book abounds; it is a delightful gallery of portraits. The models, with their paint and pomatum, their broken plumes and threadbare velvet, their false finery and their real hunger, their playhouse manners and morals, are certainly not very choice company; but the author handles them with an affectionate, sympathetic jocosity of which we so speedily feel the influence that, long before we have finished, we seem to have drunk with them, one and all, out of the playhouse goblet to the confusion of respectability and life before the scenes.—HENRY JAMES.

Franceschini, Guido, in Robert Browning's narrative poem, *The Ring and the Book* (1868–1869), an impoverished nobleman of Arezzo, tempted by a large dowry into a loveless mesalliance with Pompilia. She is the putative child of Pietro and Violante, who, when the aristocrat shows them the cold shoulder, declare that Pompilia was not really their child but the offspring of a Roman wanton. Violante, who confessed that she had hatched the plot, applies to the courts for the return of the dowry. Guido's indifference to his young wife turns to hatred; his cruelty drives her to an elopement with the Canon Giuseppe Caponsacchi (*q.v.*), he pursues the fugitives and has them arrested. Caponsacchi is suspended for three years. Pompilia is sent to a convent but, when she proves to be with child, is restored to her putative parents. Guido murders all three. His trial before the Pope divides Rome into rival functions, one justifying Guido, the other insisting on the innocence of Pompilia and Caponsacchi.

Franchi, Louis, and **Fabian de,** heroes of a drama, *The Corsican Brothers,* which Boucicault translated from the French. Twin brothers whose mysterious sympathies with one another create startling complications.

François, hero of Dr. S. Weir Mitchell's historical novel, *The Adventures of François* (1898), a street arab adrift in Paris during the Terror, a light-hearted, irresponsible little rascal who tells his own story.

Frankenstein, in Mrs. Shelley's fantastic novel, *Frankenstein, or the Modern Prometheus* (1817), a student at the University of Ingoldstadt, Genevese by birth, who from childhood has been obsessed with a morbid passion for the occult. From fragments of bodies collected in churchyards and dissecting room he constructs a monster and animates it with a vital spark from heaven. The

creature turns against its creator. Huge, hideous, soulless, full of animal passions, it pursues Frankenstein and every one he loves to the bitter end. It murders his closest friend, Henry Clerval, brings his adopted sister, Elizabeth, to an untimely end, and pursues Frankenstein himself from land to land, from sea to sea. Finally, on the Arctic Ocean, the modern Prometheus breathes his last. And over his dead body hovers the horrid shape of the man-machine.

Frankenstein's Man Monster, who has no other name, the *deus ex machina* in Mrs. Shelley's *Frankenstein (supra).* The story of this creature who can find no fellowship among men, is either consciously or unconsciously an allegorical portrayal of the character of Percy Bysshe Shelley, who in *Alastor* has painted himself as an idealist isolated from human sympathy. Helen Moore in her *Life of Mrs. Shelley* has a chapter on this subject.

Frederick, in Shakespeare's *As You Like It,* the usurping brother of the exiled duke, whom even his daughter Celia calls a man of harsh and envious mind. He appears to be perpetually actuated by gloomy fancies, suspicion and mistrust. He repents and reforms in the last scene, hands back the dukedom to the rightful heir, and retires to a hermitage.

Freeport, Sir Andrew, in Addison's and Steele's *Spectator,* a member of the imaginary *Spectator* (*q.v.*) club represented as an eminent London merchant of sense and sensibility.

Fresh, F. N., hero of a comedy, *Fresh the American* (1881), by Archibald Clavering Gunter.

A member of the New York Stock Board, he is put in the midst of European surroundings and in contact and contrast with European and Oriental Characters. Having made millions he goes abroad to enjoy them. His characteristics are all anti-European. He opens the play by breaking the bank at Monte Carlo; travels through Europe in his yacht *Greenback;* thinks nothing of paying 100,000 francs for the jewels of the

Ex-Khedive; slaps Achmed Pacha on the back and calls him Arch. His virtues are courage, generosity, chivalry toward women, domesticity and humanity. Any suggestion of cruelty, particularly to the weak and defenseless, arouses him to wrath. Other forms of immorality may excite his curiosity, interest or sense of humor; inhumanity alone makes him indignant.

Fribble, in Thomas Shadwell's comedy, *Epsom Wells*, a haberdasher, surly, inflated, conceited and unduly proud of his deceitful wife, who has her own way under an outer aspect of submission. Garrick borrowed the name for a still more popular character in his comedy *Miss in her Teens* (1753). Here Fribble is a weak-minded fop and mollycoddle, complaining of weak nerves, deeply interested in all the details of female dress, and learned in pastes and cosmetics.

Friday, or **Man Friday,** in Defoe's novel, *Robinson Crusoe*, the aboriginal attendant, and for a considerable period the sole companion, of Crusoe on his uninhabited island. He was so named after the day of the week on which his master has saved him from being killed and eaten by his cannibal foemen and fellow-savages.

Friday is no real savage, but a good English servant without plush. He says muchee and speakee, but he becomes at once a civilized being and in his first conversation puzzles Crusoe terribly by that awkward theological question, why God did not kill the devil—for, characteristically enough, Crusoe's first lesson includes a little instruction upon the enemy of mankind. He found, however, that it was not so easy to imprint right notions in Friday's mind about the devil as it was about the being of a God.

Fridolin, in Schiller's ballad, *The Message to the Ford* (Ger. *Der Gangnach den Eisenhammer*), a handsome page in the service of Countess Savern. Robert, the envious huntsman, maligns him and her to the Count. The latter gives orders to the workmen at the forge that they shall cast into the furnace the first person who puts to them the question, " Have you fulfilled the master's order? " Fridolin, the destined victim, is delayed on his way and Robert,

hurrying to find if his vengeance has been gratified, is hurled into the flames.

Frietchie, Barbara, titular heroine of a war ballad by J. G. Whittier (1863), based on the reported patriotic act of a woman at Frederick, Maryland, when that city was occupied, September 6, 1862, by Confederates under " Stonewall " Jackson. Whittier received the story from Mrs. E. D. E. N. Southworth, but he subsequently acknowledged that not the aged Mrs. Frietchie, but the comparatively young Mrs. Mary A. Quantrell, raised a Union flag on her house when Jackson and his men marched by. She was not molested. Some of the officers raised their hats to her saying, " To you, madam, not to your flag." Barbara Frietchie, however, did follow Mrs. Quantrell's example when, six days later, the Federal troops under Burnside passed her house. She was then ninety-six years old. See *American Notes and Queries*, October 6, 1888.

Frollo, Archdeacon Claude, in Victor Hugo's novel, *Notre Dame*, and in all the plays, burlesques and operas based upon it, a fanatic priest so absorbed in his search for the philosopher's stone that he can think of nothing else until his eye falls upon Esmeralda when he loses all control over his carnal desires and, forfeiting all claims to sanctity, pursues her to her death and his. See QUASIMODO.

Fromme, Ethan, hero of a novel of that title (1911) by Edith Wharton, a young farmer in Connecticut. He is tied to a wife seven years older than himself, a bleak New England woman, stern, silent, unyielding, domineering. She discerns that he is in love with her orphaned niece who forms the third member of the household, and her jealous harshness compels a terrible catastrophe.

Front de Bœuf, Sir Reginald, in Scott's romance, *Ivanhoe*, a follower of Prince John, a Norman noble, " very big and very fierce," whose life " had been spent in public war or in private feuds and broils." He lent his castle of Torquilstone to

Brian de Bois-Guilbert and Maurice de Bracy for the imprisonment of Cedric and his party. Wounded when defending the castle against the Black Knight's attack, he died in the ruins, forgotten by all but Ulrica, his old time mistress.

Frontoni, Jacopo, hero of J. Fenimore Cooper's romance of Venetian life, *The Bravo*, a young man of unblemished character who in the hope of rescuing his father—falsely imprisoned by the Senate—consents to assume the character and bear the odium of a public bravo or assassin.

Froth, Lord and **Lady,** in William Congreve's comedy, *The Double-Dealer* (1693)—he all devotion to fashion and she to learning—form a well-contrasted couple.

Lady Froth, the charming young bluestocking, with her wit and her pedantry, her affectation and her merry vitality, is one of the best and most complex characters that Congreve has created.—E. W. GOSSE.

Frou-Frou (a French word denoting the rustling of silks and other stuffs), the nickname of Gilberte Brigard, heroine of *Frou-Frou*, a five-act drama in prose by Henri Meilhac and Ludovic Halévy, produced with great success at the Gymnase in Paris, October 30, 1869, and subsequently reproduced in almost every European language. Charles Yriarte had given the nickname Frou-Frou to a character described in his *Parisian Life* (*La Vie Parisienne*).

Gilberte, frivolous, light-hearted and fascinating, has earned her nickname from the perpetual rustling of her dresses as she skips and dances about. She is sought in marriage by the staid and sensible M. de Sarboris, with whom her elder sister Louise is secretly in love. Louise, ever willing to sacrifice herself for her motherless sister, counsels acceptance. Frou-Frou agrees, though indifferent to him and indeed indifferent to everything save her own pleasures. After marriage she neglects home, husband and child for a round of social frivolity. Sartoris induces Louise to come and live with them and take charge of the household. For some time this

arrangement seems to give general satisfaction. Suddenly Frou-Frou is brought to her senses by the appearance of a lover whom she vaguely likes. Appalled at her danger, she turns back to her domestic duties. But she cannot change the result of years. Louise has innocently supplanted her in the affections of her husband and her child. After a brief struggle to regain what she has lost she turns in a frenzy of jealousy upon her sister.

"You have taken from me my home, my husband, my child," she cries, "well then, take everything!"

Rushing from the house she joins her lover in Venice. The brilliant comedy now degenerates into ordinary melodrama. Sartoris follows Frou-Frou to Venice and kills the lover, and in the fifth act the repentant Frou-Frou comes home to die, to crave forgiveness, and to obtain from her husband a promise to marry Louise.

Frugal, Luke, in Massinger's comedy, *The City Madam* (1632), a ruined spendthrift supported on the charity of his brother, Sir John Frugal, and ostensibly a meek and oily-tongued dependent. Sir John, feigning retirement into a convent, puts him in possession of all his property, when he changes into a monster of selfish avarice and cruelty, consenting even to send his sister-in-law and her daughters to Virginia to be sacrificed to the devil. His brief dream of wealth and power collapses, and Lady Frugal and her daughters are effectually cured of their affectations and pretensions.

Fudge Family, in a series of satirical epistles in verse, *The Fudge Family Abroad*, by Thomas Moore, consists of Phil Fudge, Esq., a parvenu Englishman of Irish descent, hack-writer, spy and Bourbon sympathizer, his son Robert, his daughter Biddy and a poor relation, Phelim Conner, who as an ardent Bonapartist and an Irish patriot acts as a foil to the overwrought cockney enthusiasms, prejudices and misunderstandings of his kin. The quartette visit Paris just after the fall of Bonaparte and reveal their characters in the self-told stories of their adventures abroad.

Fulkerson, in W. D. Howells's *A Hazard of New Fortunes* (1889), a Western man who comes to New York to exploit a great idea—" the greatest idea that has been struck since the creation of man. I don't want to claim too much, and I draw the line at the creation of man. But if you want to ring the morning stars into the prospectus, all right! " The idea takes shape in *Every Other Saturday*, a fortnightly periodical financed by Jacob Dryfoos.

He is the flower of Western audacity, shrewdness, and optimism transplanted to New York. Daring schemes are his inspiration. There is just the touch of charlatanism about him which, in the right environment, would make him a showman. But you are not offended, because he has a fine genial way of taking you into his confidence and showing you the beauties of the joke.— *N. Y. Life.*

Fuzzy-Wuzzy, hero of one of the *Barrack Room Ballads* of Rudyard Kipling, in which Tommy Atkins voices his admiration for the " big, black, bounding beggar " in the Soudan expeditionary force who fought and broke the square.

G

Gabler, Hedda, heroine of Ibsen's drama of that name.

I am wholly in agreement with Mr. Archer when he says that he finds it impossible to extract any sort of general idea from *Hedda Gabler*, or to accept it as a satire of any condition of society. Hedda is an individual, not a type, and it was as an individual that she interested Ibsen. We have been told, since the poet's death, that he was greatly struck by the case which came under his notice at Munich of a German lady who poisoned herself because she was bored with life, and had strayed into a false position. Hedda Gabler is the realization of such an individual case.—E. W. GOSSE: *Ibsen*, p. 191.

Gabrielle, heroine and title of a five-act comedy in verse (1849) by Emile Augier. The wife of Julien Chabrière, she finds life a blank because that honest, hard-working attorney is only a good husband and a good father, not a hero. In his secretary, Stephen, she finds an ideal who is willing to fill the void in her life. The husband, warned in time, appears on the scene when the two are together, and with pathetic eloquence adjures his wife to restore him her love, to save her honor, to protect her child. His speech acts as a revelation. The wife sees her husband in a new light. She contrasts his frankness, his tenderness, his generosity, with the pusillanimity of her lover. She dismisses the latter, seizes the hand of Julien, and the curtain goes down as she utters the line which forms the keynote of the play,

Oh père de famille, oh poete, je t'aime!

This artistic rehabilitation of the household, this effort to set a halo round the bold pate of paterfamilias, came upon the Parisian playgoers with all the delighted surprise of a new sensation.

Galatea, in William S. Gilbert's comedy, *Pygmalion and Galatea* (1871), the statue carved by Pygmalion (*q.v.*), which at his earnest prayer became animated.

Galeoto, The Great, in Jose Eschegary's tragedy of that name (1881), a sort of personification of public gossip, more terrific than the English Mrs. Grundy because placed in the more emotional medium of the Spanish race. In Dante's *Inferno*, Francesca da Rimini says that Galeoto was the book which prompted her and Paolo to sin (see GALEOTO and RIMINI, FRANCESCA DI, in Volume ii). Eschegary tells how Julian's young wife, thrown into daily contact with Ernest, her husband's secretary and adopted son, becomes, though guiltless, the object of suspicion and slander. Julian turns a deaf ear at first to all gossip but finally fights a duel in vindication of his honor and is borne dying to Ernest's chamber. There he finds his wife and, despite her asseverations of innocence, he expires in the belief that she is guilty. Ernest kills his slayer, and cries as the curtain falls,

" This woman is mine. The world has so decreed and I accept the world's decision. It has driven her to my arms. You cast her forth. We obey you. But should anybody ask who was the go-between in this business you should say, ' Ourselves, all unwilling, and the stupid chatter of gossip.' "

Gallagher, hero and title of a short story (1891) by Richard Harding Davis, an impish Irish-American office boy on a daily paper. In an exciting episode he runs to earth the criminal whom all the reporters are after.

Gama, Vasco da, the great Portuguese explorer (1469–1524), is the hero of Camoen's epic, *The Lusiad,* which deals with his exploit in rounding the Cape of Good Hope and discovering the ocean passage to the Indies. Here the hero is exalted into a demigod. Indeed he is so obviously the favorite of heaven that his deeds are minimized by the very power which smiles upon and smooths his path. Not a hair of his head is ever in real danger of being singed. The elements are lashed into their angriest moods only to waft the new Ulysses in triumph to his port. The great gods, with Venus at their head, combine against the hostile might of Neptune. Spirits of wind and wave sport before his prow, and ease the shock of impinging billows. The stars in their courses fight only for the honor of guiding his bark onward. So extreme a panegyric was bound to create reaction, and the facts brought out by recent research have done much to reduce the hero of this modern Odyssey nearer to the ordinary level. Yet they prove him to have been no common man.

Game Chicken, The, in Dickens' *Dombey and Son,* a professional boxer and prize-fighter, with very short hair, a broken nose, and a considerable tract of bare and sterile country behind each ear. He is a friend of Mr. Toots, whom he knocks about the head three times a week for the small consideration of ten and six per visit.

Gammon, Oily, in Samuel Warren's novel, *Ten Thousand a Year,* a slimy, slippery, hypocritical solicitor who takes up Tittlebat Titmouse's claim to a fortune.

Gamp, Mrs. Sarah, in Dickens's novel, *Martin Chuzzlewit,* an unprofessional nurse who is ever ready to hire herself out in many capacities for which she is scantily fitted by nature and training—monthly nurse, sick nurse or layer-out of the dead. " She was a fat old woman with a husky voice and a moist eye. She wore a very rusty black gown, rather the worse for snuff, and a shawl and bonnet to correspond. The face of Mrs. Gamp—the nose in particular—was somewhat red and swollen and it was difficult to enjoy her society without becoming conscious of a smell of spirits " (Chap. xix). See HARRIS, MRS.

Gander cleugh, an imaginary town situated on the imaginary river Gander in the central part, the navel, of Scotland, the residence of Sir Walter Scott's Jedediah Cleishbotham.

Ganderetta, heroine of Somerville's burlesque poem *Hobbinol* (*q.v.*).

Bright Ganderetta tripped the jovial queen
Of Maia's joyous month profuse in flowers.

Gann, Caroline Brandenberg, the unfortunate heroine of Thackeray's novelette, *A Shabby Genteel Story,* who afterwards appears as Mrs. Brandon (" the Little Sister ") in *The Adventures of Philip.* In the novelette, Caroline, Cinderella of a vulgar household, falls victim to a mock marriage contrived by her libertine lover, " Mr. Brandon." The latter's real name was Brand Firmin, he rises to be a great doctor in the novel and is the father of Philip. Mrs. Brandon having become a nurse, known familiarly as " The Little Sister," meets him again in the course of her professional duties, but forgives him and spares him all humiliation for the sake of the great love she bears to Philip.

Garcias, Pedro, a licentiate referred to in the preface to Le Sage's *Gil Blas,* which tells how two scholars at Salamanca discovered a tombstone inscribed, " Here lies interred the soul of the licentiate Pedro Garcias," and dug up a leathern purse containing a hundred ducats.

Gardiner, Sir Christopher, hero of Longfellow's *Rhyme of Sir Christopher Gardiner* in the *Tales of a Wayside Inn* (1873), was a historical character of mysterious origin who in the early seventeenth century flashed across the monotonous stage of New England, mingling for a while with the prosaic life of the seaboard settlements with an equally mysterious female companion, and then disappeared forever.

Such melodramatic personages are not common in Massachusetts history, and accordingly Sir Christopher long since attracted the notice of the writers of fiction. Here were great possibilities. And so as early as 1827 Miss Sedgwick introduced him, under the name of Sir Philip Gardiner, into her novel of *Hope Leslie*. He is the walking villain of that now-forgotten tale. The historian Motley next tried his hand upon him in his story of *Merrymount*, published in 1849. Then, in 1856, Mr. John T. Adams, the writer of several historical romances, went over the ground once more in his *Knight of the Golden Melice*. Finally, in 1873, Longfellow put the *Rhyme of Sir Christopher Gardiner* in the mouth of the landlord as the last of the *Tales of a Wayside Inn*. Both Motley and Adams, as well as Longfellow, present the knight under his own name, and, so to speak, in his proper person. They adhere more or less to the record, which Miss Sedgwick does not. They have all, however, made somewhat droll work with the facts of history.— *Harper's Magazine.*

Gargantua, a traditional French giant whom Rabelais made the hero of Book I in a huge satirical work, *The Life of Gargantua and Pantagruel* (1832). He and the book in which he is celebrated were apparently an afterthought, for Book I was published after the appearance of Book II, and only in the completed reissue did it take its now accepted precedence.

Gargantua is the gigantic heir to a gigantic race, and his birth is celebrated by a tremendous feast, a burlesque of unlimited trencher work. His education involves a satire on the monastic and pedantic systems taught in the schools, from which his father Grangousier withdraws him to place him under Ponocrates and Panurge. The first teaches him the value of labor; the second introduces him to the world of bohemian delights. Gargantua is recalled from Paris when war breaks out between Grandgousier and Picrochole. Though Picrochole is defeated, our hero learns a useful lesson about the horrors of bloodshed. He founds the Abbey of Thelema as a protest against both war and monasticism.

Gargery, Joe, in Dickens' *Great Expectations*, a blacksmith, blundering, ungrammatical and overgrown, a kind of domestic Titan, helpless in speech and of no education, but pathetic from his affectionate fidelity, and almost sublime through the naked instinct of duty.

Joe Gargery is one of a large class of characters which Dickens delighted to create—men in whom solid integrity of heart and conduct can find no adequate expression through the brain and the tongue. His brain can only stutter when his heart swells to its utmost capacity; and his favorite expression, "which I meantersay," is more eloquent than the lucid sayings of less simple and noble natures. Dickens was so captivated by Joe Gargery that he undertook the task of devising a new language for him, governed by a novel grammar, and with rules for the construction of sentences which must naturally surprise the student of Blair, Kaimes, Campbell, or Whately.— E. P. WHIPPLE.

Gargery, Mrs. Georgiana Maria, Joe's wife; sister to Pip, and a thorough shrew.

Garland, Anne, a miller's daughter, heroine of Thomas Hardy's novel, *The Trumpet Major* (1880). Though personally lovely and attractive, though amiable, innocent, generous and tender-hearted, she makes sad havoc of the heart of a worthy man, not wilfully but by dint of her inborn, involuntary, unconscious, emotional organism. She recognizes John Loveday's goodness, his self-abnegation, his lovableness, and she can no more justify herself in not loving him than she can in loving his scamp of a brother, Bob. Despite all considerations of self-respect, gratitude and expediency, she marries Bob and sends John to die on a Spanish battlefield.

Garland, Mr., in Dickens's novel, *Old Curiosity Shop,* a fat, kindly little man who befriends Kit Nubbles and takes him into his service. His wife and his son Abel are as placid and kindly as himself.

Garth, Caleb, in George Eliot's novel, *Middlemarch,* a strong, silent, capable man, father of Mary Garth. As in the case of Adam Bede, George Eliot found the suggestion of Caleb's character in her own father.

Mary Garth and Fred Vincy, the shrewd young woman and the feeble young gentleman whom she governs, do not carry us away, and Caleb Garth, though he is partly drawn from the same original as Adam Bede, is unimpeachable but a faint duplicate of his predecessor.—SIR LESLIE STEPHEN: *George Eliot.*

Garulilies, a nonsense word invented by Samuel Foote. See PANJANDRUM.

Gas, Charlatan, in Disraeli's novel, *Vivien Grey,* an empty but noisy politician who is supposed to be drawn from Canning.

Gascoigne, Sir William, Lord Chief Justice of England under Henry IV and Henry V, appears in Shakespeare's historical play, *II Henry IV.* One of the legends concerning wild Prince Hal is that he gave the justice a cuff on the ear and was sent to prison for it by Sir William. In Act V, Sc. 2 the story is alluded to as a fact by the justice; he defends his action and is unexpectedly praised for it and retained in office by the young king.

Gastibelza, the Madman of Toledo, hero of a ballad by Victor Hugo included in *Les Rayons et les Ombres* (1840). Gastibelza, " the man with the rifle," crazed by the perfidy of Donna Sabine, shouts his despair to the winds in words " in which all the sweet and bitter madness of love, strong as death is distilled into deathless speech " (SWINBURNE). The poem was set to music by Hippolyte Monpou, and Roger's singing carried it into all the saloons and concerts of Paris. An opera called *Gastibelza* was founded on the ballad by Dennery and Corman, with music by Maillart and produced at the Opéra National in Paris, November 15, 1847.

Gaunt, Griffith, in Charles Reade's novel of that name (1867), a poor young Englishman who has married Catherine Peyton, an heiress and a devout Catholic. He develops an unreasonable jealousy for her spiritual adviser, Father Leonard, and leaving his home in high dudgeon is nursed through a dangerous illness by Mercy Vint, an innkeeper's daughter, whom he marries under the name of his illegitimate half-brother and physical double, Thomas Leicester. The latter discovers his crime and denounces him to Mrs. Gaunt. There is a terrible scene between them, Gaunt disappears, a body supposed to be his is found in the mere near his house, and Mrs. Gaunt, arrested and tried for his murder, might have been convicted, but Mercy appears and proves that Gaunt is still alive and that the body is Leicester's. The novel was dramatized by Daly in 1866 and later by the author himself under the title of *Jealousy.*

Gauthier, Marguérite, the heroine of the younger Dumas' novel and drama *La Dame aux Camelias* (known in this country as Camille) was drawn from a real personage,—Madeleine Duplessis, a well-known leader of the demi-monde in Paris, who amid all the errors of her life preserved the grace of shame and a yearning after a better life. Marguérite's youth, her beauty, the malady that preyed upon her life, the efforts of an aged nobleman to save her from her degradation on account of her startling likeness to his dead daughter, are all facts in the career of the real woman.

Gaviota, La (Sp., *The Sea-gull*) in Fernan Caballero's novel of that name (1851), is the nickname of the heroine Marisalada. A fisherman's daughter, dowered with bizarre beauty and an exquisite voice, she captures the love of a young German named Stein, who finds his way to her village, he teaches her music and develops her voice, but though she marries him she feels nothing higher than friendliness for him; indeed she has been actually repelled by his midnight wooings and talk of " the infinite." Chance carries the couple to Seville, where Maria sings in the opera with extraordinary success, and where she falls disastrously in love with Pepe Vera, a matador in the bull-ring. The story ends as such a story would naturally end in real life, and the last impression is the cry of the teasing dwarf who first gave the nickname,—" *Gaviota fuistes, Gaviota eres, Gaviota serás!*" As applied to Marisalada, the nickname points to one of those harsh, angular, unsympathetic natures which, when armed with beauty or some powerful natural gift, seem made for the torture of those most intimately concerned with them.

Gavroche, in Victor Hugo's *Les Misérables*, vol. x (1863), the representative street *gamin* of Paris, whose doughty deeds and death in the barricades of Paris in 1832 are perhaps exaggerated, but whose impish love of mischief, ready flow of " chaff," native kindliness and unselfishness are vividly presented.

Gawrey, in Robert Pultock's romance, *Peter Wilkins* (1750), the name given to the flying women among whom the hero is accidentally thrown, after being shipwrecked. See YOUWARKEE.

Gawtrey, Stephen, in Lord Lytton's *Night and Morning*, a character illustrating the force of circumstances in driving a man of strong passions, but naturally honest disposition, to commit offences against society and its laws.

Gay, Lucien, in Disraeli's *Coningsby*, is intended for Theodore Hook.

Gay, Walter, in Dickens's *Dombey and Son*, a young man in the employ of Mr. Dombey; nephew to Sol Gills. He falls in love with Florence Dombey, but is soon afterward sent to Barbadoes to fill a junior situation in the counting-house there. The ship is lost at sea, and it is long thought that he went down with her; but he finally returns and marries Florence.

Very lovable is Walter Gay, cheerful and merry, with his fair face, bright eyes, and curly hair. How he lights up the atmosphere of the old instrument maker's shop, where in ten days but two people had called —the man who came to ask for change for a sovereign, and the woman who wanted to know the way to Mile End turnpike. The good boys of fiction are too often uninteresting, but this charge cannot be urged against old Solomon Gill's nephew. The frank ingenuousness of his nature, added to a spice of romance and a love of the marvellous, forms a combination which must win all hearts, let alone that of Florence Dombey. And without "Wal'r," how forlorn a figure would be Captain Cuttle.—*Pall Mall Budget.*

Gaylord, Marcia, in Howells's novel, *A Modern Instance*, the New England country girl who is wooed and won by Bartley Hubbard, only to be forsaken when dissipation gets him into financial and domestic troubles. Beautiful but slightly vulgar, jealous, passionate and vindictive, yet preserving her innocence against temptation, she is the product of a soil where religion has run to seed and men and women are living by traditions which have faded into a copybook morality.

Gebir, in Landor's poem of that name (1797), an Iberian prince, sovereign of what is now Gibraltar. His father had imposed upon him a solemn oath to conquer Egypt, which had been wrested from their ancestors. Gebir, however, falls in love with Charoba, the youthful Queen of Egypt, marries her, and dies on the wedding day through the agency of a poisoned shirt (see NESSUS) with which he had been treacherously invested. The subject of this poem was suggested to Landor by a chapter in a story by Clara Reeve. Its moral aim is to rebuke warlike ambition and to extol the more durable victories of peace in the respective persons of Gebir and his shepherd brother, Tamar.

Geierstein, Anne of, heroine of Scott's historical novel of that name (1829), the daughter of Count Albert of Geierstein, president of the secret tribunal of Westphalia. Known popularly as "the Maiden of the Mist," she did not hesitate to disabuse the mind of Sir Arthur de Vere of the "absurd report" concerning her supposed supernatural powers.

Gellatley, Davie, in Scott's *Waverley*, an "innocent," dependent on the charity of the Baron of Bradwardine. " Simply a crack-brained knave, who could execute very well any commission which jumped with his own humour, and made his folly a plea for avoiding every other." He was avowedly drawn from a local celebrity known as Jock Gray.

Jock, or John, Gray was by no means so "daft" as the Davie Gellatley of *Waverley*. He lived at a place in the south of Scotland called Gilmanscleugh, and is said to have been known over an extent of fifty miles around by a singular kind of wit that mingled with his half wit. There seems, indeed, to have been a division of parties about him in Peebles, in Selkirk, and other regions, as to whether he was really crackbrained, or was only assuming that manner in order to conceal a deeper purpose, as Alcibiades at the banquet spoke more freely from his mask of intoxication. His power of singing was good, and this, with his mimic talent, and a tenderness for his halfwitted condition, procured for him a welcome in the farmers' cottages in the whole region around.—MONCURE D. CONWAY: *The Scott Centenary at Edinburgh (Harper's Magazine).*

General, Mrs., in Dickens's *Little Dorrit* (1857), a widow lady of fortyfive whom Mr. Dorrit, after his release from the Marshalsea, engages to " form the mind " and manners of his daughters. She is of a dignified and imposing appearance, immovable, imperturbable in her rigid propriety. She had no opinions. " Her way of forming a mind was to prevent it from forming opinions. She had a little circular set of mental grooves or rails on which she started little trains of other people's opinions which never overtook one another and never got anywhere." She teaches Little Dorrit to say Papa instead of Father: " Father is rather vulgar, my dear. The word Papa, besides, gives a pretty form to the lips. Papa, potatoes, poultry, prunes and prism are all very good words for the lips; especially prunes and prism. You will find it serviceable in the formation of a demeanor if you sometimes say to yourselves in Company— on entering a room, for instance— Papa, potatoes, poultry, prunes and prism, prunes and prism.''

Genevieve, titular heroine of a ballad by Coleridge.

I've seen your breast with pity heave,
And therefore love I you, sweet Genevieve!

Genevieve is also the heroine of his poem, *Love*:

And so I won my Genevieve,
My bright and beauteous bride.

Geraint, in the Arthurian cycle, a Knight of the Round Table and hero of *Geraint, the Son of Erbin* in the Welsh *Mabinogion*, a story which Tennyson has elaborated in *Enid*, one of his *Idylls of the King*.

Tennyson's Geraint is the impersonation of doubt and all the confusion and misery and wild uncertain ghosts it breeds. He is the first to suspect Guinevere, and in his jealous terror he carries his bride Enid away from Arthur's court. Waking one night he misunderstands her broken words of self-accusation that she was no true wife, meaning that she had lured him away from his duty to the King. Then the two go forth, at the moody man's command, on aimless adventures which end in Geraint's falling, desperately wounded, after he has put to flight the retainers of Earl Limours. Enid's wifely devotion in nursing him back to health renews his faith in her and he implores forgiveness. In the elder legends the motive is simpler. Geraint thinks it is his uxorious indolence that has forfeited Enid's regard, and he starts out to show her that his arm has not yet lost its cunning—to win back her love by some high deed.

Geraldine, a name introduced into English literature by Henry Howard, Earl of Surrey, who in a series of sonnets addressed Lady Elizabeth Fitzgerald, daughter of the ninth Earl of Kildare, as the Fair Geraldine. At the time the series was begun (1537) she was only nine years old. Scott sings in *The Lay of the Last Minstrel*:

That favoured strain was Surrey's raptured line;
That fair and lovely form, the Lady Geraldine.

The poet Nash adopted the lovestrains of Surrey as the basis of romantic fictions, in which the noble lover is represented as travelling in Italy, proclaiming the matchless charms of his beloved, and defending her beauty in tilt and tournament.

Coleridge gives the name of Geraldine to the witch in *Christabel*, and Mrs. Browning makes use of it in her ballad, *Lady Geraldine's Courtship* (1844), where a high-born lady stoops to a poet of low degree after a period of pretended disdain.

Geraldine, in Coleridge's unfinished poem, *Christabel*, a fair witch who possesses magic influence over the titular heroine.

Geraldine, so far as she goes, is perfect. She is *sui generis*. The reader feels the same terror and perplexity that Christabel in vain struggles to express, and the same spell that fascinates her eyes. Who and what is Geraldine.—Whence come, whither going, and what designing? . . . Was she really the daughter of Roland de Vaux and would the friends have met again and embraced? We are not among those who wish to have *Christabel* finished. The theme is too fine and subtle to bear much extension.—J. G. LOCKHART: *Quarterly Review*, lii, p.29.

Gerolstein, Rudolph, Grand Duke of, in Eugene Sue's *Mysteries of Paris*, a young sovereign prince, gifted with vast wealth, irresistible fascinations and prodigious strength, who goes about in various disguises; as he describes it—" playing Providence," relieving misery, righting wrongs and punishing crime. His judgments and inflictions, however, are sometimes hardly more scrupulous than the methods of the criminals whom he detects and crushes. He puts out the eyes of one hardened murderer by way of rendering his punishment appropriate and lingering. He lets loose one woman of preternatural profligacy and fascinations on a notary whose crimes he wishes to unveil, under orders to drive him into frenzy by perpetually provoking desire and never gratifying it.

Géronte, a favorite name with Molière and, after him, in French dramatic literature and popular humor, for a bourgeois and philistine paterfamilias. The Géronte of *Le Médecin Malgré Lui* (1666) wishes to force his daughter Lucinde into a distasteful marriage with Horace. In *Les Fourberies de Scapin* (1671) Géronte is the father of Léandre and Hyacinthe, who reluctantly opens his purse in response to Scapin's hoaxes.

Gerontius, in *The Dream of Gerontius*, a poem which expresses Cardinal Newman's conception of the last great change through which a faithful Catholic passes when he leaves this world for the world of spirits. Gerontius becomes aware of the presence of his guardian angel in the hollow of whose hand he is borne to judgment, and also of evil beings who are hungering after him, and seeking to renew in him the old spirit of rebellion. He hears the songs of the angels as he speeds through their hosts and the prayers of those kneeling around his death-bed which are borne into the very presence of God, and finally the eager spirit dashes from the hold of its guardian angel and precipitates itself at " the dear feet of Emmanuel."

Gertrude, in Shakespeare's *Hamlet*, Queen of Denmark and mother of the prince. In Saxo-Grammaticus her name is given as Geruth or Gerutha.

Gertrude of Wyoming, heroine of a poem of that name (1809) by Thomas Campbell, dealing with the Indian invasion and devastation of the Valley of the Wyoming in Pennsylvania in 1778. Roaming among the forests or reposing in sequestered nooks with a volume of Shakespeare, Gertrude grows up to lonely womanhood. In Albert Waldegrave, an orphan whom the Indian Outalissi had saved alive from slaughter by a British force and whom her father had adopted, she unexpectedly discovers the lover she had dreamed of; they are married and after three months of wedded bliss are both killed in the invasion of Brant and his warriors.

Gerund, or **Gerundio, Friar,** hero of a famous satirical romance by Padre Isla, known in the original Spanish as *Fray Gerundio de Campazas* (1758). The fun is directed against the itinerant preachers of the peninsula and the bad taste, false wit, bombast and bathos of their sermons.

Giafar, or, more correctly, *Jaffar, the Barmecide,* vizier to Haroun Alrashid, both in historical fact and in the fiction of the *Arabian Nights' Entertainment.* He accompanied that caliph in all his nightly rambles and hair-breadth adventures until his fall from power in 802. See BARMECIDE.

Giaour, The. The word simply means an infidel. In Byron's poem of that title, the Giaour steals from the seraglio of the Caliph Hassan the beautiful slave Leila. The caliph pursues and captures Leila, whom he casts into the sea but is himself slain. On his death-bed the Giaour confesses and requests that he be buried without a name.

Gibbie, Goose, in Scott's *Old Mortality,* the half-witted servant of Lady Bellenden.

Gigadibs, in Robert Browning's poem, *Bishop Blougram,* a young poet of thirty, immature, desultory, impulsive, who criticises Blougram and serves to draw out his ideas on religion and the proper conduct of a successful life.

Gilfil, The Rev. Maynard, titular hero of George Eliot's *Mr. Gilfil's Love-Story* in *Scenes of Clerical Life* (1858), an excellent old gentleman who smoked very long pipes and preached very short sermons. For all his odd ways and slipshod talks he never lost the respect of his parishioners nor the affection of their children. The story concerns an episode of his youth when " he had known all the deep secrets of devoted love, had struggled through its days and nights of anguish and trembled under its unspeakable joys."

Gilmour, Elizabeth, nicknamed Elly, heroine of a novel by Anne Thackeray Ritchie, *The Story of Elizabeth.* When she is 18 her mother is only 36 and is jealous of the attentions that Elly receives. Jealousy deepens to hatred when Sir John Dampier, whose boyish fancy the mother had caught in her girlhood, is now fascinated by Elly's fresh beauty and winsome ways. Having madly loved him for twenty years, Mrs. Gilmour conceived that she had

by her constancy won the sole right to his affections.

Gilpin, John, hero of a humorous ballad by William Cowper, *The Diverting History of John Gilpin, showing how he went further than he intended, and came safe home again,* printed anonymously in 1782. A linen draper and a train-band captain in London, his wife suggests that they shall take their first holiday on the twentieth anniversary of their marriage. The family proceeds by coach to Edmonton. Gilpin arranged to join them there for dinner, but he elects to go on horseback and, being a poor rider, meets with ludicrous and disconcerting misadventures, finds it impossible to rein up at Edmonton, and finally turns his horse back to London, which he reaches dinnerless and bedraggled. Lady Austin gave the hint to the poet by telling him a similar story, and a true one, concerning one Beyer of Paternoster Row, who died in 1791.

Ginevra, in Ariosto's *Orlando Furioso,* an innocent lady who during the absence of her true love, Ariodantes, is falsely accused by a wicked duke. Rinaldo champions her cause, slays the duke in single combat and restores the lady to Ariodantes, who opportunely reappears. Spenser utilizes the story in his *Tale of Irena,* and Shakespeare himself borrows a hint from it in the underplot of Hero and Don John, *Much Ado about Nothing.*

Ginevra dei Benci, a Florentine lady whose portrait by Ghirlandajo is in Santa Maria Novella, is the heroine of a popular tradition versified by Samuel Rogers in *Italy* (1822). The evening before her marriage, playing hide and seek, Ginevra hid in a trunk; the heavy lid closed upon her, the lock snapped fast. Search was in vain. Her fair fame suffered at the hands of malicious women jealous of her beauty. Years later the chest was opened. Her remains were found, with the peculiar perfume she used still lingering in her hair, one hand grasping the jewel her bridegroom had given her to fasten the front of her gown. A similar story is told in the anonymous English ballad, *The Mistletoe Bough.*

Ginx's Baby, in a satirical novel of that name (1870) by Edward Jenkins, the thirteenth child in a destitute family. His father proposed to drown him for a nuisance but was persuaded to hand him over to a Roman Catholic Sister of Mercy. The Protestant Detectoral Association rescued him from " Papistical " hands to find that they had squandered in public meetings, salaries and tracts all the funds raised for his support by benevolent zealots. The parish squabbled over him with another parish and, after ruinous litigation, turned him back to Ginx, who left him on the doorstep of a club. The club brought him up to be a page, but discharged him when he took to stealing silver spoons, whereupon Ginx's baby leaped from Vauxhall Bridge and there was an end of him.

Glaucus, the hero of Bulwer-Lytton's historical novel, *The Last Days of Pompeii* (1834), with whom Nydia is in love.

Glenarvon, hero of a novel of that name (1816) by Lady Caroline Lamb. He is a somewhat malicious obvious caricature of Lord Byron, with whom the lady had been deeply infatuated.

I suppose you have seen *Glenarvon?* Madame de Stael lent it to me to read from Coppet last summer. It seems to me that if the authoress had written the truth and nothing but the truth—the whole truth— the romance would not only have been more romantic, but more entertaining. As to the likeness, the picture can't be good. I did not sit long enough.—BYRON: *Letter to Moore,* December, 1816.

Glendinning, Edward, in Scott's romance, *The Monastery,* reappears in its sequel, *The Abbot* as Father Ambrose, last abbot of Saint Mary's. In the " days of tribulation " which " wrenched asunder the allegiance of Christians to the Church," he was " turned out of house and homestead," and deprived of " the temporalities of that noble house of God." But with undiminished zeal he devoted himself to Queen Mary's release, not scorning to " wear the garb

of a base sworder, and run the risk of dying the death of a traitor."

Glendower, Owen (1359–1415), a Welsh rebel lord of Glyndwr, who proclaimed himself Prince of Wales in 1402 and next year joined the rising under Harry Percy—the famous " Hotspur." They were defeated at Shrewsbury, June 21, 1403. Shakespeare introduces him into *I Henry IV* (Act iii, Sc. 1) as a vainglorious boaster, confident that he possesses supernatural powers and can summon spirits from the vasty deep. Hotspur laughs at him:

Why so can I and so can any man
But will they come when you do summon them?

Glenthorn, Lord, hero of Miss Edgeworth's novel, *Ennui* (1809). Brought up by a tricky but indulgent guardian as the heir to a immense estate in England and Ireland, he is blasé from his teens. He tries travelling, gambling, feasting, hunting, pugilism, coach-driving, love-making, all in vain. He even thinks seriously of suicide. The lucky discovery that he was changed at birth saves him. He magnanimously surrenders everything to the rightful owner, now a blacksmith, studies law, suceeds at the bar, and ends by marrying the ex-blacksmith's heiress. Lord Jeffrey, in a review of Alfieri's *Life (Essays,* p. 145), detects a marked resemblance between the poet and the imaginary peer, and opines that " if these *Memoirs* had been published when Miss Edgeworth's story was written, it would have been impossible not to suppose that she had derived from them everything that is striking and extravagant in her own narrative.

Gloriana, in Spenser's *Faërie Queene,* the Queen of Fairyland; a personification both of Glory and of Queen Elizabeth, as Spenser explains in his introductory letter to Sir Walter Raleigh: " In that Faërie Queene I mean *Glory* in my general intention, but in my particular I conceive the most excellent and glorious person of our soveraine the Queene." She is thus introduced in Canto I, St. iii:

Upon a great adventure he was bound,
That greatest Gloriana to him gave,
That greatest glorious Queene of Faery
  Land,
To winne him worship, and her grace to
  have.

Glorvina, Lady, heroine of *The Wild Irish Girl* (1801), a novel by Sidney Owenson, afterwards Lady Morgan. Glorvina is the daughter of the Prince of Inismore, one of the ancient Irish nobility. A gentlemanly stranger, hurt by a fall, is taken into her home and the young people fall in love. Glorvina is bound by an engagement to an elderly English nobleman, though bound only by gratitude, and when it afterwards turns out that the young man is the son of the nobleman to whom she is affianced, the latter gallantly surrenders her.

Gloucester, Earl of, father of Edgar and Edmund, in the episode which Shakespeare has taken from Sidney's story of the blind King of Paphlagonia in *The Arcadia* and woven into the texture of *King Lear.*

Shakespeare found there the father, loving, kind-hearted, but suspicious, and weak in principle and in mind; the bastard, an ungrateful villain; the legitimate son, a model of filial affection; the attempt of his suspicious and deceived father to kill him; and even the loss of Gloucester's eyes, and his contrivance to commit suicide by getting his son to lead him to the verge of a cliff, whence he might cast himself down: all is there,—the incidents, the personages, and their characters.—RICHARD GRANT WHITE.

Gloucester, Richard, Duke of. See PLANTAGENET and RICHARD III. He is first called Gloucester in *III Henry VI*, iii, 2.

Glover, Catharine, heroine of Scott's novel, *The Fair Maid of Perth,* "universally acknowledged to be the most beautiful young woman of the city or its vicinity." Daughter of Simon, the old glover, she eventually becomes the bride of Henry Gow, known also as Henry Smith, the armorer. See CONACHAR.

Glowry, Mr., the owner of Nightmare Abbey, in Peacock's novel of that name.

Glubdubrib, in Swift's *Gulliver's Travels* (1726), one of the imaginary islands visited by Gulliver. It was peopled by sorcerers who summoned up for his amusement the shades of people famous in the past.

Glumdalclitch, in Swift's *Gulliver's Travels* (1726), a little girl nine years old and forty feet high, who had charge of Gulliver while he dwelt in Brobdingnag.

Gobbo, Launcelot, in Shakespeare's comedy, *The Merchant of Venice,* a mixture of servant and buffoon who leaves Shylock's service for that of the Christian Bassanio. The scene with his father, Old Gobbo, in Act ii, 2, is a favorite bit of clownish humor greatly expanded in the usual performance by traditional " business " that has no warrant in the text.

Gobseck, Esther Van, in Balzac's *Grandeurs et Misères des Courtisanes* and in other novels, the great grandniece of Jean Esther Van Gobseck. She early became a prostitute, like her mother. When she met Lucien de Rubempré each fell in love with the other. Lucien foolishly took her to the opera, where she was unmasked and insulted. Later, Jacques Collin, the powerful and dangerous protector of Lucien, saw and fell in love with her. He converted her to Catholicism and installed her in a suite of rooms. She was only allowed to take a promenade at night. Baron de Nucingen unearthed the mysterious beauty and by the power of money won her from Collin. By 1830 she owned a fine house in Rue St. George, which eclipsed that of any other courtesan. She died by suicide, all unknowing that she was heiress to seven million francs which had been left to her by her grand uncle.

Gobseck, Jean Esther Van, a miser and usurer, is the titular hero of Balzac's *Papa Gobseck* and flits through the pages of *Father Goriot, Cæsar Birotteau,* etc. The son of a Jew and a Dutch woman, born in Antwerp in 1740, he travelled all over the world and finally settled in Paris. The accumulation of gold and the power won by gold were his only joy. In Paris he became head centre of many businesses, establishing himself on the Rue des Gres, where, arrayed in his dressing gown, he lived most sordidly despite his enormous wealth.

Godfrey of Bullogne, the cheif character of Tasso's *Jerusalem Delivered* (1575), and the title under which Edward Fairfax published (1600) his translation, in the Spenserian stanza. A version by Richard Carew had already appeared, in 1594, in the same measure, under the title of *A Boke called Godfrai of Bulloign, an heroicale poem of S. Torquato Tasso, Englished by R. C.* Godfrey of Boulogne (the modernized spelling) appears also in Walter Scott's romance, *Count Robert of Paris.* Godfrey, Duke of Lorraine, was proclaimed king of Jerusalem when the Crusaders temporarily conquered the Holy Land.

Godiva, or **Godgifu,** a historical character (about 1040–1080), wife of Leofric, first Earl of Mercia. Tennyson makes her the heroine of a poem, *Godiva, a Tale of Coventry* (1842), which is founded on a legend first printed by Roger of Wendover in his *Flores* (1237) and later (1613) versified by Drayton, *Polyoblion,* xiii. In Tennyson's version Godiva begs her husband to remit an oppressive tax under which Coventry had grown restive. He heedlessly agreed on what he thought was the impossible condition that she should ride naked through the town at midday. She took him at his word (first giving notice that all doors and windows in the town should be closed and that no one should stir abroad that noon) and Sir Leofric kept his word. See WALSH: *Curiosities of Popular Customs,* p. 471.

Goldtip, Spiffington, familiarly known as " Spiffy," a social promoter in Laurence Oliphant's satirical novel, *Picadilly* (1870), who launches rich vulgarians into Mayfair.

Golightly, in Kipling's story *The Arrest of Lieutenant Golightly* in *Plain Tales from the Hills,* a fastidious and dandified officer whose outfit is ruined by a tremendous rainfall, so that, dirty and dishevelled, he is arrested by mistake for a deserter.

Goneril, in Shakespeare's *King Lear,* one of the monarch's ungrateful daughters who, after he has been deposed, plots against her sister Regan, poisons her, and dies (v, 3).

The monsters Goneril and Regan are gorgons rather than women, such as Shakespeare has nowhere else conceived. The aspect of Goneril can almost turn to stone; in Regan's tongue there is a viperous hiss. Goneril is the more formidable because the more incapable of any hatred which is not solid and four-square. Regan acts under her sister's influence, but has an eager venomousness of her own.—DOWDEN.

Goodenough, Dr., in Thackeray's *Pendennis,* the physician who attends Arthur when dangerously ill of fever. He is mentioned in *The Newcomes* (ix, ixxx) and reappears in *The Adventures of Philip* as the friend and adviser of the Little Sister and of Philip, though he dislikes and distrusts Philip's father, Dr. Firmin. The writing of *Pendennis* was interrupted by the dangerous illness of its author. Dr. John Elliotson, who attended him, refused to accept any fee from a literary man, as Dr. Goodenough refused if from Philip. When *Pendennis* was finished Thackeray dedicated the book to him.

Goody Two-Shoes, in a nursery tale of that name (1765) attributed to Oliver Goldsmith. Little Margery has been used to only one shoe and is so tickled when presented with a pair that she shows them to everyone exclaiming " Two Shoes! " Hence her nickname. It appeared anonymously from the press of Newberry. Goldsmith did much hackwork for this publisher and the internal evidence of style points to him. The book has a spontaneous and playful humor not often found in the work of professional hackwriters. The very advertisement and title-page are characteristic:

"'We are desired to give notice that there is in the press, and speedily will be published, either by subscription or otherwise, as the public shall please to determine, the History of Little Goody Two Shoes, otherwise Mrs. Margery Two Shoes; with the means by which she acquired learning and wisdom, and, in consequence thereof, her estate; set forth at large for the benefit of those

"Who from a state of rags and care,
And having shoes but half a pair,
Their fortune and their fame should fix,
And gallop in a coach and six." ' "

The name, at least, existed before Goldsmith's time. Charles Cotton in his burlesque, *Journey to Ireland* (1670), describes a dinner with the Mayor of Chester, when this colloquy occurs:

Mistress mayoress complained that the dinner was cold,
"And all along of your fiddle faddle," quoth she.
"Why then, Goody Two-Shoes, what if it be?
Hold you, if you can, your tittle tattle," quoth he.

Gorboduc, hero and title of the first English tragedy (1561) by Thomas Norton and Thomas Sackville, Lord Buckhurst. Gorboduc was a semimythical king of Britain whose story, as told by the ancient chroniclers, is here closely followed. Succeeding to the crown shortly after Lear, he profited so little by that monarch's sorry example that during his life he divided his realm between two sons, Ferrex and Porrex. The princes soon fell into dissension; Porrex stabbed Ferrex and was himself slain by his mother, who preferred her first-born; and the people, rising in rebellion, dethroned Gorboduc and his consort and put both to death.

Gordon, Lord George (1750–1793), the instigator of the famous "No Popery" riots in England in 1779, is a prominent character in Dickens's *Barnaby Rudge* (1841), the hero of which enlists himself among the rioters.

Goriot, Father, titular hero of Balzac's novel, *Père Goriot* (1835), the story of King Lear modernized and reduced from semi-barbaric royalty to the humdrum bourgeoisie of Paris. Mesdames de Restaud and de Nucingen are the representatives of Regan and Gonerie, but the parental victim, who is a retired grocer, is allowed no solace in the shape of a Cordelia.

Gosling, Giles, in Walter Scott's *Kenilworth*, landlord of the Black Bear Inn, near Cumnor Place, where he lives with his daughter Cicely.

Gotthelf, Jeremias, hero of Albert Bitzius's story, *The Mirror of Peasants.* He is a poor Swiss villager whose trust in Providence is finally rewarded. Bitzius subsequently used his hero's name as his own pseudonym.

Gradasso, in Bojardo's *Orlando Innamorato* and Ariosto's *Orlando Furioso,* a boastful, arrogant yet valiant king of Sericana who invades France in a quest for the sword and horse of Rinaldo. His vassals who accompany him are all crowned kings but they dare not address him save on their knees.

Gradgrind, Thomas, in Dickens's *Hard Times* (1854), a retired wholesale hardware merchant. "A man of realities; a man of facts and calculations; a man who proceeds upon the principle that two and two are four, and nothing over, and who is not to be talked into allowing for anything over; Thomas Gradgrind, sir,—peremptorily Thomas, Thomas Gradgrind; with a rule and a pair of scales, and the multiplication-table always in his pocket, sir, ready to weigh and measure any parcel of human nature, and tell you exactly what it comes to. It is a mere question of figures, a case of simple arithmetic." So the author describes him and later makes him reveal himself in his advice to the teacher, Mr. M'Choakumchild:

"Now, what I want is facts. Teach these boys and girls nothing but facts. Facts alone are wanted in life. Plant nothing else, and root out everything else. You can only form the minds of reasoning animals upon facts: nothing else will ever be of any service to them. This is the principle on which I bring up my own children, and this is the principle on which I bring up these children. Stick to facts, sir!"

Graeme, Roland, in Scott's historical romance, *The Abbot* (1820), a foundling brought up as a page in the household of Sir Halbert Glendenning, Knight of Avenel. He is transferred to the service of Mary Stuart, Queen of Scots, then imprisoned in Lochleven Castle, and takes gallant part in the loyalist plot that frees her from captivity (1568). He marries his true love, Catharine Seyton, daughter of Lord Seyton and maid of honor to the queen, when it is discovered that he is the true heir to the barony of Arundel, and consequently her equal.

Granada, Archbishop of, in Le Sage's *Gil Blas* (vii, 3), the prelate to whom the hero attaches himself as private secretary. The archbishop begs " whenever thou shalt perceive my pen smack of old age, and my genius flag, do not hesitate to tell me of it, for I mistrust my own judgment, as that may be biased by self-love." After an attack of apoplexy Gil Blas ventures to hint that his grace's last discourse " had not altogether all the energy of his former ones." The archbishop demurs. " You are yet too young to make proper distinctions," he says; " know, child, that I never composed a better sermon. Go tell my treasurer to give you a hundred ducats. Adieu, Master Gil Blas; I wish you all manner of prosperity with a little more taste."

Grandcourt, Henleigh, in George Eliot's *Daniel Deronda* (1876), suitor for the hand of Gwendolen Harleth and subsequently her husband.

Grandcourt, to whom Gwendolen sacrifices herself, is compared to a crab or a boa-constrictor slowly pinching its victim to death: to appeal to him for mercy would be as idle as to appeal to "a dangerous serpent ornamentally coiled on her arm." He is a Tito in a further stage of development—with all better feelings atrophied, and enabled, by his fortune, to gratify his spite without exerting himself in intrigues. Like Tito, he suggests, to me at least, rather the cruel woman than the male autocrat. Some critic remarked, to George Eliot's annoyance, that the scenes between him and his parasite Lush showed the "imperious feminine, not the masculine character." She confronted herself by the statement that Bernal Osborne—a thorough man of the world—had commended these scenes as specially lifelike. I can, indeed, accept both views, for the distinction is rather too delicate for definite application. One feels,

I think, that Grandcourt was drawn by a woman; but a sort of voluptuous enjoyment of malignant tyranny is unfortunately not confined to either sex.—LESLIE STEPHEN: *George Eliot.*

Grandet, Eugenie, heroine of Balzac's novel of that name, was the only daughter of Felix Grandet, born 1796 at Saumar. Strictly raised by a pious and gentle mother and a miserly father, her life knew no other love than a platonic one for her cousin, Charles Grandet. He forgets her when away in the Indies, returning with a large fortune and a titled bride. Eugenie, now an orphan of thirty-one, gives her hand to the elderly Cruchot de Bonfours, who had sought it for nine years. Widowed at 36 and still a virgin she returns to the sombre paternal house at Saumar to devote the rest of her life to benevolence and charity.

Grandet, Pere Felix, in Balzac's *Eugenie Grandet,* the father of the heroine, a portentous figure of concentrated avarice.

Grandison, Mrs. Caroline, in George Meredith's novel, *The Ordeal of Richard Feverel* (1859), a character thus described by the author: " She was a colorless lady of an unequivocal character, living upon drugs, and governing her husband and the world from her sofa. Woolly Negroes blessed her name, and whiskered John Thomases deplored her weight." She had rapidly produced eight daughters, and felt the solemnity of woman's mission. A son was denied her. Her husband, " quite unobjectionable gentleman, lost heart after the arrival of the eighth, and surrendered his mind to more frivolous pursuits. After that disappointing eighth she also lost heart and ' relapsed upon religion and little dogs.' "

Grandison, Charlotte, in Richardson's novel, *Sir Charles Grandison* (1754), a sister to the titular hero, sprightly and vivacious but curiously deficient in good manners. Lady Mary Wortley Montague, commenting on Charlotte's failure to distinguish between pert folly and humor—between ill nature and spirit—says roundly that she should have been treated like a humorsome child and well whipped (see Dobson's *Samuel Richardson*, pp. 158–159). It has been suggested that Richardson borrowed certain of her traits from his friend and constant correspondent, Lady Bradshaigh. Certainly some of Charlotte's most individual expressions are to be found in that lady's letters, who, moreover, confesses to " saucy freedoms and impertinences " with which she " is too naturally inclined to treat her best friends."

Grandison, Sir Charles, hero of a novel of that name (1754) by Samuel Richardson, representing the author's ideal man. Sir Charles conquered his own generation but to-day the critic is inclined to dismiss him as a self-conscious prig— " the exponent of a courtesy which has more of buckram and punctilio than of genuine benevolence and propriety "(AUSTIN DOBSON). Taine flippantly suggested that he should be canonized and stuffed. Austin Dobson holds that there can be nothing in Johnson's suggestion, as reported in Miss Seward's *Anecdotes* (ii, 223), that Grandison was modelled on Mr. Robert Nelson of the *Festivals and Fasts*, who died in 1715.

He is an ideal but so very, very tame that it is hard to justify his existence. He is too perfect to be of the slightest moral use to anybody. He has everything he wants, so that he has no temptation to be wicked; he is incapable of immorality, so that he is easily quit of all inducements to be vicious; he has no passions, so that he is superior to every sort of spiritual contest; he is monstrously clever, so that he has made up his mind about everything knowable and unknowable; he is excessively virtuous, so that he has made it up in the right direction. He is, as Mr. Leslie Stephen remarks, a tedious commentary on the truth of Mrs. Rawdon Crawley's acute reflection upon the moral effect of five thousand a year. He is only a pattern creature, because he has neither need nor opportunity, neither longing nor capacity to be anything else.—W. E. HENLEY: *Views and Reviews*, p. 219.

Grantley, Archdeacon, in Anthony Trollope's *Barchester Towers* and other novels.

My archdeacon, who has been said to be lifelike, was the simple result of my moral consciousness. It was such as that, in my opinion, that an archdeacon should be—or, at any rate, would be with such advantages

as an archdeacon might have possessed:—and lo! an archdeacon was produced who has been declared by competent authorities to be an archdeacon to the very ground.— TROLLOPE: *Autobiography*.

Grantorto (It. *Great Wrong*), in Spenser's *Faërie Queene*, Book V, a personification of rebellion in general, but more specifically of the Irish rebellion of 1850. A huge giant who attempts to keep Irena (Ireland) out of her inheritance is finally beaten in single combat and decapitated by Sir Artegal.

Gray, Auld Robin, hero of Lady Anne Barnard's ballad, *Auld Robin Gray* (1772), and of two sequels written many years later.

Gray, Dorian, hero of Oscar Wilde's novel, *The Portrait of Dorian Gray* (1891), a debauchee who carries his love of pleasure to unmentionable extremes. The record of his downfall is kept by a portrait which grows old and hideous while the sensualist himself preserves all his youthful beauty until a sudden collapse makes himself and his portrait contemporaries.

Gray, Duncan, in Robert Burns's ballad of that name (1792), a Scotch peasant lad who, treated coldly by Maggie when he wooes her, takes her affected disdain too seriously so that she fell sick and was like to die until his eyes are opened and he wooes her back to life. The refrain is well known:

Ha, ha! the wooing o't!

Graziella, in Lamartine's story of that name, the heroine of a true episode in the author's youth when he was rusticating on the coast of Italy. Ingratiating himself with a fisherman's family, he was taken into their home and unwittingly fell in love with the daughter of the house. Her parents would betroth her to a wealthy cousin, but Graziella runs away in the night. The hero finds her under remarkable circumstances and restores her to her family, but she tears herself away and shortly after he hears of her death.

Graziella of course was published as a romance, but Lamartine never imagined or invented romances. He lived them and then wrote them out. Graziella was the girl's real name. Her family still live near Naples. One of them—a curé—was recently interviewed about her by a contributor to one of the Italian magazines. "Graziella?" he said, "Ah, yes, she was my aunt. Her mother had a lodger—a Frenchman—a M. Lam—Lam—yes I think it was as you say Lamartine." And Lamartine himself says expressly in his *Memoires* that the story, save for one or two trivial details, was true. He had gratified his vanity by describing Graziella as a coral polisher, whereas in point of vulgar fact, she was a cigarette-maker.—FRANCIS GRIBBLE: *The Passions of the French Romantics.*

Greaves, Sir Launcelot, hero of Smollett's romance, *The Adventures of Sir Launcelot Greaves* (1762), written to beguile the time during his imprisonment for debt. The story is a somewhat absurd travestie of Don Quixote. In lieu of the Spanish Knight we have a young English squire of naturally noble disposition, but half crazed by love, riding with his groom along English country roads, in quest of wrongs to be redressed, and, after sundry adventures, in which other odd characters figure, restored in the end to sound sense and his Amelia. In the course of the story, however, the author leads the hero through a series of situations, affording matter for social description and satire; and he takes care to conduct him at sufficient leisure through the King's Bench.

Grecian Daughter, The. See EU-PHRASIA.

Green, Verdant, in the novel of that name (1860) by Cuthbert Bede (Rev. Edward Bradley), an unsophisticated undergraduate at Oxford, nicknamed Gig-lamps from the large spectacles he wore. After being the favorite victim of practical jokes in his first year, he in turn victimizes the greener youths who succeed him in the lower classes. The tautological name (verdant of course is Anglicized Latin for green) seems to have been no invention of the author's. In *Notes and Queries* Series II, i, 87, John Murray writes: In reading a letter of the date 1744 I came across the name Verdant Green as a familiar allusion. Can anyone help me to discover who or what this prototype of Cuthbert Bede's famous character was? " The appeal received no response.

Gregory, Miss, heroine of a series of stories by Perceval Gibbon, bound together under the title, *The Adventures of Miss Gregory* (1912). She is an Englishwoman of wealth, birth and breeding, fifty years old, when she is introduced to us with " just the least touch of the arrogance of the high caste " but " composed, shrewd and friendly." A professional spectator, she seeks adventures all alone in the heart of Africa, in Russia, in Germany, and finally in her native England.

Gretchen, a German diminutive of Margaret (*q.v.*).

Grey, Agnes, heroine and title of a novel (1847) by Anne Brontë (" Acton Bell ") which is in part autobiographical and gives the story of a governess in a north of England family who goes through many of the humiliations that Anne herself had experienced in a like situation.

Grey, Henry, in Mrs. Humphrey Ward's novel of *Robert Elsmere* (1888), is to a certain extent drawn from Thomas Hill Green, the historian and the most persuasive master of philosophic thought in modern Oxford. Mrs. Ward acknowledges that she had him in mind, but adds that the character of Grey is in no sense a portrait.

"Reality suggested many points in the description, but I was writing a novel and not a biographical study."—*McClure's Magazine.*

Grey, Maggy, heroine of Mrs. Alexander's novel, *The Wooing O't* (1873). A familiar type of the Victorian heroine with her eyes of changing blue, pensive and sensitive, her shy mouth, indescribable nose, frank, open forehead, delicately formed neck, and pretty figure, always modest, always natural, always charming. Beloved by Lord Torchester and her cousin John Grey she cares only for Geoffrey Trafford (*q.v.*), who at first deems himself too old for her.

Grey, Vivian, hero of a novel of that name (1827) by Benjamin Disraeli.

A brilliant, impudent, audacious youth bubbling over with epigrams and paradoxes, often truer than they sound, he is the son of a noted man of letters. While still in his teens he meets at his father's table a dull but distinguished statesman, the Marquess of Carabas (*q.v.*), and inveigles him into a cabal against his own party which ends disastrously to all concerned. Vivian, having unintentionally killed an opponent in a duel, goes abroad and the rest of the book describes his adventures in Europe. Disraeli's own likeness to Vivian has been often urged, probably with as much truth and in the same sense as Thackeray's resemblance to Pendennis and Bulwer's to Pelham. See LORRAINE, MRS. FELIX.

Grieux, Chevalier des. See LESCAUT, MANON.

Grieve, David, hero of a novel, *The History of David Grieve* (1892) by Mrs. Humphrey Ward. David and his sister Louie are the children of a Scotch workingman and a French grisette. The girl inherits all her mother's nature, the boy just enough to play havoc with his dour Scotch virtue in a single episode. He rescues himself from his seducer; marries a girl who is in no way his equal, and remains faithful to her in the belief that marriage is an inviolable institution.

> I have come to think the most disappointing and hopeless marriage, nobly borne, to be better worth having than what people call ideal passion—if the ideal passion must be enjoyed at the expense of one of those fundamental rules which poor human nature has worked out, with such infinite difficulty and pain, for the protection and help of its weakness.—Book iv, Chap. 7.

Grif, hero and title of a novel by B. L. Farjeon. He is a sort of an Oliver Twist in the Australian diggings at the time of the Gold Rush, a street arab and a thief by force of circumstance, but capable of developing all the virtues.

Grimes, Peter, hero of the twenty-second tale in George Crabbe's *The Borough* (1810), a drunken and thievish prodigal who makes away with

three of his sons by neglect or abuse but escapes conviction through lack of evidence and dies raving mad in the parish poor house.

Grip, in Dickens's novel, *Barnaby Rudge,* an evil-looking and all-too-knowing parrot whom Barnaby carries in a basket at his back. The bird's favorite cries, which it uses at all inappropriately appropriate emergencies, are " Halloa! " " I'm a devil," " Never say die! " " Polly put the kettle on." During the Gordon riots its vocabulary was augmented by the war cry of the mob, " No Popery! " The raven in the story was, the author tells us, a compound of two great originals, of which he was, at different times, the possessor, and one of which, stuffed, was sold, after Dickens's death, for the sum of £120. See the preface to the " Charles Dickens " edition.

Grippy, Leddy, in Galt's novel, *The Entail,* one of the author's most humorous characters.

Griskinissa, in W. B. Rhodes' burlesque tragedy, *Bombastes Furioso,* the affianced wife of Bombastes (*q.v.*), whom the King of Atopia would fain marry.

Grogan, Tom, in F. Hopkinson Smith's novel of that title, the assumed name of the heroine. Her husband, a stevedore in New York harbor, dies; she conceals the fact in order to carry on the business in his name and is thereafter herself known as Tom. She combines a powerful physique and great strength of will with a tender, maternal love for her daughter Jenny and her crippled boy Patsy. Her success excites the jealousy of rival stevedores and of the Knights of Labor whose union she had refused to join. Though they resort to blackmail, arson and attempted murder, she proves more than a match for them in the end.

Grundy, Mrs., now accepted as a personification of that awesome prig, the British Matron, with her narrow, inflexible rules of propriety, originally appeared as a minor character in J. M. Morton's comedy, *Speed the Plough* (1798). Dame Ashfield, a farmer's wife, is jealous of her neighbor Grundy's prosperity, but is under the social sway of his wife so that she can do nothing without wondering " what will Mrs. Grundy say ?" The play opens with a scene of a farmhouse, where Farmer Ashfield is discovered at a table enjoying his pipe and ale:—

Ashfield. Well, dame, welcome whoam. What news does thee bring vrom market?
Dame. What news, husband? What I always told you—that Farmer Grundy's wheat brought five shillings a-quarter more than ours did.
Ashfield. All the better vor he.
Dame. And I assure you, Dame Grundy's butter was quite the crack of the market.
Ashfield. Be quiet, woolye? Always ding, dinging Dame Grundy into my ears. *What will Mrs. Grundy zay?* Why don't thee letten Mrs. Grundy alone? I do verily think that when thee goest to t'other world, the vurst question thee'll ax 'll be, if Mrs. Grundy's there?

Guenn, heroine of a novel of that name by Blanche Howard Teufel (1883), a fisher girl of Brittany, wild, shy, passionate and proud. Her exuberant feelings are wasted in a generous love for the artist Hamor, who secures her for a model. His picture done, he departs as lightly as he came, leaving the poor child broken-hearted but not dishonored.

Guest, Stephen, in George Eliot's novel, *The Mill on the Floss* (1860), a typical provincial coxcomb " whose diamond ring, attar of roses and air of nonchalant leisure at twelve o'clock in the day are the graceful and odoriferous result of the largest oilmill and the most extensive wharf in St. Ogg's." But he is emotional and fond of music and represents to Maggie Tulliver the æsthetic element she longs for. Though Stephen is engaged to her cousin, Lucy Deane, though Maggie herself is half pledged to Philip Wakem, he makes passionate love to her and she, after passing through a "fierce battle of emotions," presently finds herself drifting to sea with him in a boat, and is only arrested by her conscience at the last moment when she is some way toward Gretna Green. Maggie's passion for Guest has ever been a puzzle

to male critics. Swinburne calls him a " counter-jumping Adonis."

George Eliot did not herself understand what a mere hair-dresser's block she was describing in Mr. Stephen Guest. He is another instance of her incapacity for portraying the opposite sex. No man could have introduced such a character without perceiving what an impression must be made upon his readers. We cannot help regretting Maggie's fate; she is touching and attractive to the last; but I, at least, cannot help wishing that the third volume could have been suppressed.—LESLIE STEPHEN: *George Eliot.*

Guiderius and **Arvirgarus,** in Shakespeare's *Cymbeline,* sons of that monarch, who pass under the names of Polydore and Cadwal as supposed sons to Morgan, who had kidnapped them in infancy in revenge for his banishment.

Guildenstern, in Shakespeare's *Hamlet,* a courtier. See ROSENCRANTZ.

Guinevere, in Tennyson's *Idylls of the King,* the consort of Arthur, to whom she proves unfaithful with Sir Lancelot. In the idyll which bears her name her guilt has been made public; Lancelot in his own realm beyond seas has been defending himself against Arthur; and the queen, concealed in a nunnery, is oscillating between remorse and regret, when the king himself makes his appearance. He has stopped on his way to the fatal battle where a whole generation of heroes were finally to disappear. It only remained to show her what ruin she had wrought, to forgive her, and to part forever.

Gulbeyaz, in Byron's *Don Juan,* vi (1824), the sultana who ransoms Juan and smuggles him into the harem in female disguise. Finding that he and Dudu have reached an understanding that is agreeable to both, she commands that they be stitched up in a bag and thrown into the Bosphorus. Juan escapes to survive many other adventures.

Gulliver, Lemuel, hero and pretended author of a satirical romance (1726), by Jonathan Swift, *Travels in Several Remote Nations of the Earth by Lemuel Gulliver.* Originally a surgeon in London, he becomes the captain successively of several ships. Four of his voyages are made to countries so remarkable that he deems it right to publish his experiences.

I. He is wrecked off the coast of Lilliput (*q.v.*), a country inhabited by a race of pigmies only 6 inches high who name him Quinbus Flestrin or " Man Mountain."

II. A roc carries him to Brobdingnag (*q.v.*). Here the telescope is reversed. In Lilliput one of our inches represents a foot; in Brobdingnag one of our feet represents an inch.

III. He is driven to Laputa (*q.v.*), the country of quacks, pretenders, empirics and impostors.

IV. He visits the land of the Houyhnhnms (*q.v.*), a race of horses, blessed with more than human reason and cursed with no human follies or vices.

Gulnare, in Byron's *Corsair* (1814), the wife of the Sultan Seyd. She assists Conrad (*q.v.*) to escape from prison and follows him disguised as a page. She reappears in the same author's *Lara* as Kaled, Lara's page, who turns out to be a woman.

Gunga Din, in Rudyard Kipling's poem of that name (*Barrack Room Ballads*) is the regimental water carrier, a Hindoo lad whose singleminded devotion to duty leads to a heroic death on the battlefield. We are told that

'E didn't seem to know the use o' fear.

Nevertheless he was not heroic to the view:

The uniform 'e wore
Was nothin' much before
An' rather less than 'arf o' that be'ind.

Gurth, in Scott's *Ivanhoe*, the " born thrall," or serf, of Cedric of Rotherwood. A faithful and cautious drudge, he nevertheless forsook his herd of swine to attend his master's disinherited son at Ashly-de-la-Zouch. Later, with Wamba, he took a leading part in the attack on Front de Boeuf's castle.

Gurton, Gammer (*i.e.,* **Grandmother**), the leading character in the earliest of English comedies, *Gammer Gurton's Needle*, doubtfully attributed to John Still, afterwards Bishop of Bath and Wells. It was first printed in 1579. Gammer Gurton, a diligent, notable old dame, possesses the only needle in the parish and loses it in mending her man Hodges's breeches. Dicken the Bedlam, a mischief-making wag, accuses Dame Chat of stealing it and the resultant squabbles embroil the whole neighborhood.

In 1810 John Ritson edited a collection of old English nursery rhymes which he entitled *Gammer Gurton's Garland, or the Nursery Parnassus.* Gammer Gurton, whose name is here used as a typical English grandmother, was evidently put out as a rival of Mother Goose, whose *Melodies* had been collected probably under Oliver Goldsmith's supervision and published not later than 1760. It contains much of the same material with additions. Mother Gurton's reign was shortlived and she at no time succeeded in ousting Mother Goose from her preëminence.

Guyon, Sir, in Spenser's *Faërie Queene*, Book ii (this book celebrates the triumph of temperance over intemperance), the personification of temperance in its largest sense, meaning control alike over the sensual appetites and the meaner mental impulses. It is his task successively to meet and subdue Amavia, or intemperance of grief; Braggadochio, intemperance of the tongue; Furor, intemperance of anger, Pyrocles and Cymocles, dual representatives of sexual excess; Phædria, intemperance of pleasure, and Mammon, or the inordinate love of gold. But the prime object of his quest and the final crown of his achievements is the destruction of Acrasia (*q.v.*) and her Bower of Bliss.

Gwilt, Lydia, in Wilkie Collins's novel, *Armadale* (1866), a precocious criminal, who at twelve years of age forges a letter to deceive a father into allowing his daughter to throw herself away. Though hateful and hideous, Lydia draws a certain pity by reason of her lonely childhood and her strength of character. In the end she gives her life to save her lover from the fatal consequences of her own crime.

Gwynplaine, hero of Victor Hugo's historical romance, *The Man Who Laughs* (*Fr., L Homme qui Rit*, 1869). To deprive him of a heritage he had in childhood been disfigured out of recognition. An artist in what was known to the England of James II as comprachico, had cut both sides of his mouth upward to the ears, leaving on the face for life a hideous and ineffaceable grin. The wretched victim had the air of perpetually laughing. Yet it was by virtue of this very deformity that Gwynplaine caught the fancy of the Duchess Josiana who yearned either for a god or for a monster. He is saved from her wiles by his love for the blind girl Dea. Sightless, she sees with the keener, truer vision of the soul. Snatched when an infant, by the hand of the boy, from the breast of her dead mother in the fatal snowdrift, Dea has grown to feel a woman's love blend with her sense of grateful trust in the man's strong arm and ardent will. The outcast and butt of the mob is to her the ideal of manly form. His voice, his step, his presence, are those of a god. To him she is the guardian angel who keeps his animal nature in subjection. The thought of her breaks the spell which Josiana had cast over him. But Dea dies and Gwynplaine commits suicide.

Gynt, Peer. A kind of Norse Faust, celebrated in the folk legends of Norway, whose superabundant imagination threatens him with destruction unless he is saved by a woman. Ibsen took him as the titular hero of a dramatic poem (1867) usually reckoned his masterpiece. Gynt is here introduced as a peasant lad living in poverty with his widowed mother Åse. Full of great ideas and glorious plans for the future, his youthful arrogance knows no bounds. He attends a wedding and carries off Solvejg, the bride, to a mountain, where he soon deserts her. After many adventures he finds himself in the hall of the King of the Dovre Mountains, whose daughter he wooes. Banished by the king, he returns home to find Åse dying. After her death he sails for foreign climes, eventually landing, rich and powerful, on the coast of Morocco where he realizes some of his early dreams but without any of the expected happiness. Finally, old, gray and disenchanted, he returns to the faithful Solvejg, who receives him with open arms.

H

Hafed, leader of the Ghebers in *The Fire-Worshippers*, the third tale in Moore's *Lalla Rookh* (1817). He falls in love with Hinda, daughter of Al Hassan, an Arabian emir come to extirpate the remnants of his tribe in their rocky fastnesses. After a desperate defence in which all his tribe are slain, Hafed immolates himself upon a funeral pyre. Hinda, a witness to his fate from a nearby galley, leaps into the water and is drowned.

Haidee, in Byron's *Don Juan*, Cantos ii, iii and iv, " the beauty of the Cyclades," motherless daughter of a Greek pirate named Lambro. Don Juan, shipwrecked on her island, was nursed by her in a cave and they fell mutually in love. On a report that Lambro was dead Juan issued from his concealment and gave a grand banquet which was interrupted by the reappearance of the pirate. Don Juan was seized and sold as a slave, Haidee broke a blood-vessel and died.

Hajji Baba, hero of an oriental romance by James Morier, *The Adventures of Hajji Baba of Ispahan* (1824), a sort of Persian Gil Blas, a volatile, unprincipled adventurer who, beginning life in his father's barber shop at Ispahan, becomes successively one of a band of Tar-comans, a menial servant, a pupil of the physician-royal of Persia, an attendant on the chief executioner, a religious devotee, and a dealer in tobacco pipes in Constantinople. Stratagem enables him to win the hand of a rich Turkish widow; he rises to be an official to the Shah, is appointed Secretary to the mission of Mirza Firouz, and accompanies the Russian ambassador to London. A sequel, *Hajji Baba in England* (1828), was less successful.

The Persian Picaroon, with his morals sitting easy about him, a rogue indeed, but not a malicious one, with as much wit and cunning as enable him to dupe others, and as much vanity as to afford them perpetual means of retaliation; a sparrow-hawk, who, while he floats through the air in quest of the smaller game, is himself perpetually exposed to be pounced upon by some stronger bird of prey, interests and amuses us, while neither deserving nor expecting serious regard or esteem; and like Will Vizard of the hill, "the knave is our very good friend."—SIR W. SCOTT.

Hal, Bluff King, a popular nick-name for King Henry VIII of Eng-land, which has given a title to a dozen pantomimes in which he is the hero. Alternate nicknames are Bluff Harry and Burly King Harry.

Ere yet in scorn of Peter's pence,
  And numbered bead and shift,
Bluff Harry broke into the spence
  And turned the cowls adrift.
              —TENNYSON.

Hal, Prince, the familiar abbrevia-tion for Henry, Prince of Wales, son of Henry IV, who succeeded him as Henry V. He appears in Shake-speare's *I* and *II Henry IV*. See also HENRY V.

The Prince whom Shakespeare admires and loves more than any other person in English history, afterwards to become Shakespeare's ideal King of England, cares little for mere reputation. He does not think much of himself and of his own honor; and while there is nothing to do and his great father holds all power in his own right hand, Prince Hal escapes from the cold proprieties of the court to the boisterous life and mirth of the tavern. He is, however, only waiting for a call to action, and Shake-speare declares that from the first he was conscious of his great destiny, and, while seeming to scatter his force in frivolity, was holding his true self, well guarded, in

reserve. May there not have been a young fellow remembered by Shakespeare, who went by night on deer-stealing frolics near Stratford, who yet kept from waste and ruin a true self, with which his comrades had small acquaintance and who now helped Shakespeare to understand the nature of the wild Prince and his scapegrace acquaint-ances?—E. DOWDEN: *Shakespeare Primer.*

Hales, the Ever Memorable John, a title applied to John Hales (1584–1656), a famous English divine.

Halevy, Jehuda ben, a Jewish poet of the fifteenth century whom Heine has taken as the titular hero of one of his most beautiful poems. Like the Crusaders he made his pilgrimage to Jerusalem; and there, amid the ruins, sang a song of Zion which has become famous among his people. A " bold Saracen," riding by, lolled over his saddle and plunged a spear into the singer's breast: " Quietly flowed the Rabbi's life-blood, quietly he sang his song to an end and his last dying sigh was Jerusalem! "

Halifax, John, hero of a novel, *John Halifax, Gentleman* (1856), by Mrs. Dinah Mulock Craik. An orphan brought up in poverty and obscurity, he finds among his dead father's effects a book autographed " John Halifax, Gentleman," and he takes this designation as an ideal to be lived up to. By faithfulness, integ-rity and grit he rises to wealth and marries a girl of gentle birth. The character is said to have been studied from Handel Cossham, the son of a Gloucestershire carpenter who be-came a wealthy colliery owner. Some of the British critics were disposed to question whether it were possible for a man of such antecedents to justify the term " gentleman " so insistently thrust upon him on the title-page. The question could never have arisen in America.

A boy who begins by being a farm-servant until he is fourteen, and then is employed in a tan-yard to fetch the skins from market, might possess all the fine characteristics bestowed on John Halifax,—his self-reliance, his energy, his integrity, his passion for self-improvement; but he would not—he could not attain the bearing and manners of a gentleman; he could not by mere effort of self-culture attain the tone of good society. —*Saturday Review.*

Hallam, Arthur, the intimate friend of Arthur Tennyson (engaged to Tennyson's sister), whose early death occasioned the series of poems bound together as *In Memoriam* (1850). Arthur Hallam (1811–1833) was the son of Henry Hallam, the literary historian of the Middle Ages.

I know not how to express what I have felt . . . I do not speak as another would to praise and admire the poems; few of them indeed I have as yet been capable of reading, the grief they express is too much akin to that they revive. It is better than any monument which could be raised to the memory of my beloved son; it is a more lively and enduring testament to his great virtues and talents that the world should know the friendship which existed between you, that posterity should associate his name with that of Alfred Tennyson.— HENRY HALLAM, letter to Tennyson in *A Memoir of Tennyson*, vol. i, p. 327.

Haller, Mrs., in Benjamin Thompson's drama *The Stranger* (1797), adapted from Kolzebue, is the name assumed by Adelaide, Countess of Waldbourg, when she eloped from her husband. The latter also dropped his identity, and, known only as "the stranger," led a roving and purposeless life. Mrs. Haller lives for three years in the service of the Countess of Wintersen and is there sought in marriage by Baron Steinfort. She confesses the truth to him, and he succeeds in finding and reconciling her husband.

Hamlet, hero of Shakespeare's tragedy, *Hamlet, Prince of Denmark*. This is the title as it appears in the Folio of 1623, the text of which differs from the five preceding quartos (1603, 1604, 1605, 1611, the last undated) as they differ more or less materially from one another.

Hamlet in his final evolution is the most interesting character in all imaginative literature. A prince of a studious and philosophic temperament, his natural melancholy is aggravated by the mysterious death of his father and the hurried wedding that followed between his widowed mother and his uncle Claudius, who had usurped the throne. The Ghost of his father appears; reveals that Claudius had murdered him, and swears him to revenge. Thereafter

Hamlet's mind is torn by doubt and indecision. He assumes an "antic disposition" partly to baffle his enemies, partly to create a veil behind which to hide his true self, partly because his whole moral nature is indeed deeply disordered (DOWDEN) —his wild and excitable state lending itself with dangerous ease to the feigning of actual derangement. He puts the Ghost's credibility to the test by hiring players to reproduce on a mimic stage a similar murder and so betrays the king into a virtual confession. Even now he delays action by every thinnest pretext. He will not kill the king when he comes upon him at prayer lest his soul be saved thereby. Yet a few minutes later, surprised by a sudden impulse of suspicion, he kills Polonius, who is concealed behind an arras, and therefore invisible. Treacherously stabbed at last by Laertes' poisoned foil, Hamlet exchanges weapons in the scuffle, wounds Laertes and then, learning of the poison and of his own imminent death, seeing ruin and destruction all around him, he plunges the weapon into the heart of Claudius.

No one of mortal mould (save Him "whose blessed feet were nailed for our advantage to the bitter cross") ever trod this earth, commanding such absorbing interest as this Hamlet, this mere creation of a poet's brain. No syllable that he whispers, no word let fall by any one near him but is caught and pondered as no words ever have been except of Holy Writ. Upon no throne built by mortal hands has ever "beat so fierce a light" as upon that airy fabric reared at Elsinore.—H. H. FURNESS.

To me it is clear that Shakespeare sought to depict a great deed laid upon a soul unequal to the performance of it. In this view I find the piece composed throughout. Here is an oak tree planted in a costly vase, which should have received into its bosom only lovely flowers; the roots spread out, the vase is shivered to pieces.—GOETHE: *Wilhelm Meister*.

It is an inherent peculiarity of a mind like Hamlet's that it should be conscious of its own defect. Men of his type are forever analyzing their own emotions and motives. They cannot do anything, because they are always as it were standing at the cross-roads, and see too well the disadvantages of every one of them. It is not that they are incapable of resolve, but somehow the band between the motive power and the operative faculties is relaxed and loose. The engine works, but the machinery it should drive stands still. . . . (Hamlet) is the victim not so much of feebleness of will as of an intellectual indifference that hinders the will from working long in any one direction. He wishes to will, but never wills. His continual iteration of resolve shows that he has no resolution. He is capable of passionate energy where the occasion presents itself suddenly from without, because nothing is so irritating as conscious irresolution with a duty to perform. But of deliberate energy he is not capable, for there the impulse must come from within and the blade of his analysis is so subtle that it can divide the finest hair of motive twixt north and northwest side, leaving him desperate to chose between them.—J. R. Lowell: *Shakespeare Once More.*

Hamlet, Young, in George Eliot's satirical poem, *A College Breakfast Party,* the chief guest at Horatio's table:

Blond metaphysical and sensuous
Questioning all things, and yet half convinced
Credulity were better; held inert
Twixt fascinations of all opposites
And half suspecting that the mightiest soul
(Perhaps his own?) was union of extremes.

There is reason to believe that the portrait was drawn from William Hurrell Mallock.

Hamlin, Jack, *i.e.,* **John,** in Bret Harte's *Gabriel Conroy* and in several of his short tales, a professional gambler of amiable disposition and gentlemanly manners who, despite his exterior air of gayety, is deeply dissatisfied with his lawless and predatory manner of existence. In *Bohemian Days in San Francisco* Bret Harte gives some account of a real person who doubtless was Jack Hamlin's prototype as well as John Oakhurst's (*q.v.*). Harte describes his handsome face, his pale southern look, his slight figure, the scrupulous elegance and neatness of his dress, his genial manner and the nonchalance with which he set out for the duel that ended in his death.

The type was a new one and it completely revolutionized the ideal of the gambler which had long obtained both in fiction and on the stage. As a London critic very neatly said, with this dainty and delicate California desperado Bret Harte banished forever the turgid villains of Ainsworth and Lytton.— H. C. Merwin: *Life of Bret Harte.*

Han, hero of a romance, *Han of Iceland* (Fr. *Han d'Islande,* 1823), by Victor Hugo. Claiming descent from Ingulph the Exterminator, a monster of hoary antiquity famous for his hatred of mankind except as articles of uncooked food, he carries out the family traditions under modern dietary restrictions, especially after the loss of his son, and finally, sated with carnage, arson, and pillage, he surrenders himself to justice. Addressing his judges he says, " I have committed more murders and set more fires than you have pronounced unjust judments in all your lives. . . . I would gladly drink the blood in your veins. It is my nature to hate men, my mission to harm them. Colonel, it is I who crushed a battallion of your regiment with fragments of rock. I was avenging my son. . . . Now, judges, my son is dead; I come here to seek death. . . . I am tired of life, since it cannot be a lesson and an example to a successor. I have drunk enough blood, I am no longer thirsty; now, here I am, you can drink mine."

He is accordingly condemned to death. Finding the ordinary processes of justice too tardy, however, and being, as we have seen, of an impetuous disposition, he sets fire to his prison and perishes in the flames with his few surviving enemies.

Handy Andy, the nickname of Andy Rooney, the *deus ex machina* in Samuel Lover's novel of Irish life, *Handy Andy* (1842). It was given to him in pure irony because, in the author's own words, Andy " had the most singularly ingenious knack of doing everything the wrong way." By his inveterate blundering he furnishes matter alike for mirth and wrath to all who are in any way connected with him. Yet in the end his very blundering saves the situation and turns the tables against villainy in favor of virtue and honesty, so that all his world rejoices with him when Andy proves to be the lawful heir to the title and estates of Lord Scatterbrain and weds his pretty cousin

Oonah despite all matrimonial complications brought about by his own recklessness.

Happy Valley, in Dr. Johnson's oriental romance, *Rasselas*, an abode of continual but monotonous felicity, which Rasselas abandons in the search for more strenuous joys. He returns to it thoroughly disillusioned with the outside world.

Harapha of Gath, a character, original with Milton, in his dramatic poem of *Samson Agonistes*. Harapha scoffs at Samson in his chains, but is afraid of his strength and keeps at a safe distance.

Hardcastle, Squire, in Goldsmith's comedy, *She Stoops to Conquer*, a jovial, generous, but prosy country gentleman, old-fashioned himself and fond, as he says, of " everything that's old—old friends, old manners, old times, old books, old wine " (Act i, Sc. 1). His wife, Lady Hardcastle, on the other hand is fond of the latest fashions and the genteelest society, but never having been in London has scant opportunity for enjoying either. By her first marriage she is the mother of Tony Lumpkin; her second has yielded her a daughter, Kate Hardcastle, who " stoops " to conquer Young Marlow (*q.v.*).

Hardy, Letitia, the eponymic " belle " in *The Belle's Stratagem* (1780) by Mrs. Cowley. Daughter to the fond and foolish but well-meaning Mr. Hardy, Lydia is affianced to Doricourt, a fashionable man about town, elegant and volatile, but essentially honorable, who irks at the bondage of an enforced betrothal. To win his love she appears in disguise at a masquerade, and Doricourt falls an easy victim to " the beautiful stranger." Old Hardy now feigns sickness and from his pretended deathbed urges Doricourt to an immediate marriage. He unwillingly consents. His chagrin is changed to joy when Letitia appears in her masquerade dress and reveals the " stratagem."

Harleth, Gwendolen, the principal female character in George Eliot's novel, *Daniel Deronda* (1876). A beautiful young lady, hard, cold, brilliant, misled by worldly considerations into a loveless marriage with the middle-aged Mallinger Grandcourt, who is harder and colder than herself. He reduces her to such chaotic despair that when he is accidentally drowning she withholds the hand that might have rescued him. She is ultimately saved, " as though by fire" through her unreturned love for Daniel Deronda. Gwendolen is akin to Rosamond Vincy in *Middlemarch*—as selfish, as dead to duty and tenderness, as confident and unscrupulous.

Rosamond is perhaps more consistently selfish, after the common idea; but there is an intense, enduring strength of egotism in Gwendolen which is surely not less repulsive. Gwendolen, however, has this superiority conferred upon her, that she is not one of the narrow-brained women who through life regard all their own selfish demands as rights. She has a root of conscience in her. But the reader cannot forget that this conscience was never aroused, and to all appearance never would have been aroused, till Deronda's eye rested on her; and he is not willing to see the great moral difference between one outside conscience and another, between being guided by the opinion of society and being guided by the judgment of one extremely attractive person. Rosamond dreads being despised by the world. Gwendolen is always saying to Deronda, "You despise me," and is represented as learning to despise herself through his eyes. But interesting young men are not always impersonations of the Law and the Gospel, and the world would be no gainer were Gwendolen's way of deferring to a single conscience invested with such attractive externals, rather than to the aggregate conscience of society, to become the generally accepted rule.—*London Saturday Review*, September 23, 1876.

Harley, or **Young Harley,** hero of Henry McKenzie's novel, *A Man of Feeling* (1771), a youth of the most exquisite sensitiveness, a mere bundle of nerves forever quivering on the verge of collapse. Loving his neighbor's daughter, Miss Walton, he is too shy to avow his passion until he is bedfast, and when his lady accepts him he dies of the shock.

Harlowe, Clarissa, heroine and title of a novel by Samuel Richardson (1751). Having drawn in *Pamela* the portrait of a poor girl subjected to temptation, Richardson here submits a young lady to similar experi- ences. Clarissa belongs to a good country family in eighteenth century England. She is wooed by the notorious profligate Lovelace, whose suit is frowned upon by the Harlowes, including at first even Clarissa herself. But she is secretly taken by his dashing ways. He succeeds in abducting her and so seriously compromising her that she dies of shame. Lovelace (*q.v.*) is killed in a duel by her cousin, Colonel Morden.

All incomplete as she is, she remains the Eve of fiction, the prototype of the modern heroine, the common mother of all the self-contained, self-suffering, self-satisfied young persons whose delicacies and repugnances, whose independence of mind and body, whose airs and ideas and imaginings are the stuff of the modern novel. With her begins a new ideal of womanhood; from her proceeds a type unknown in fact and fiction until she came. When after outrage she declines to marry her destroyer and prefers death to the condonation of her dishonor, she strikes a note and assumes a position till then not merely unrecognized but absolutely undiscovered.—W. E. HENLEY: *Views and Reviews*, p. 221.

Harold, Childe, the titular hero of *Childe Harold's Pilgrimage*, a narrative and descriptive poem by Lord Byron. Cantos 1 and 2 appeared in 1812. Childe Harold (evidently Byron's own ideal of himself) is a gloomy, haughty, imperious youth, the freshness of whose feelings has been exhausted in a round of unholy pleasure. Satiated and heart-sick, he leaves behind him his lemans and his fellow bacchanals, bids farewell to England, and wanders over the continent of Europe, viewing its fairest scenes with the abstracted gaze of one who is in them but not of them, whose thoughts are not the thoughts of other men, who has risen superior to either hope or fear. Yet through all this affection of scowling cynicism Byron shows that his heart can still beat high with generous enthusiasm for what is great, beautiful and heroic, his nerves still tingle with contempt for what is base and ignoble.

Harpagon, the titular " Miser " in Molière's comedy, *L'Avare* (1667), an impersonation of grasping and rascally parsimony painted from the comic rather than the tragic side. The cunning folly of his economics, the bewildered stupidity that results from his absorption in one idea; the violent despair into which he is thrown by the supposed loss of his treasure-box—all are suffused with so broad a light of humor that they leave no sting behind them; you feel only kindness for a character that has furnished so much fun. His own man-of-all-work, under pressure from the miser himself, thus reports some current tales:

"One neighbour says that you have private almanacks printed, in which you double the ember-days and vigils in order to oblige your household to observe more fasts than others; another, that you have always a quarrel ready to pick with your servants at "boxing" time, or when they are leaving you, so as to have a pretext for giving them nothing. Another says that you once had a warrant out against the cat of one of your neighbours for having eaten up the remains of a leg of mutton; another, that you were caught one night coming to steal your own horse's oats, and that your coachman—my predecessor—gave you, in the dark, I don't know how many blows with a stick, about which you never said anything."

The *Avare* of Molière, though taken from the *Aulalaria* of Plautus, differs widely from the Latin piece. Plautus's Miser is a man who loves gold for its own sake, for the sake of amassing it, hoarding it up, and reserving it for solitary enjoyment, whereas Harpagon, to the pure love of gold adds also the love of lucre, and to bring in more money will part with, and put in circulation, that which he already possesses. He is a usurer, and there lies the essential difference between the miser of Plautus and the *Avare* of Molière. It is the difference between avarice and avidity.—*Edinburgh Review.*

Harper, in Cooper's novel, *The Spy;* the name under which George Washington hides his personality.

Cooper cannot be congratulated upon his success in the few attempts he has made to represent historical personages. Washington, as shown to us in *The Spy*, is a formal piece of mechanism, as destitute of vital character as Maelzel's automaton trumpeter. This, we admit, was a very difficult subject, alike from the peculiar traits of Washington, and from the reverence in which his name and memory are held by his countrymen. Harper under which name Washington is introduced, appears in only two or three scenes; but, during these, we hear so much of the solemnity and impressiveness of his manner, the gravity of his brow, the steadiness of his gaze, that we get the notion of a rather oppressive personage, and sympathize with the satisfaction of the Whartons, when he retires to his own room, and relieves them of his tremendous presence.

Harrington, hero and title of a novel by Maria Edgeworth, whose object is to raise the Jewish race in the estimation of English readers. The theme was suggested by an American correspondent, a Miss Mordecai, who gently reproached Miss Edgeworth for having so often made Jews ridiculous and begged that she would write a story about an estimable Jew. The theme lay outside of her own experience and she had to evolve a Jew out of her own moral consciousness who was unsatisfactory even to the Jews. So says Miss Zimmern, herself a Jewess:

Her zeal outran her judgment; her elaborate apology is feeble; and if the Jews needed vindication they could hardly be flattered by one of this nature, for she does not introduce us to a true Jew at all. Her views were based upon that rare and beautiful character, Moses Mendelssohn, a character as little typical of the Jewish as of any other race or religious creed, but common to all men who think and feel philosophically and have raised themselves above the petty prejudices of mankind. This was as much as to say that only a Jew who was no Jew was admirable and estimable.—HELEN ZIMMERN: *Maria Edgeworth*, p. 168.

Harrington, Evan, hero and title of a novel (1861) by George Meredith. Like Meredith himself Evan is the son of a tailor, most mirth-provoking of trades; but he has the fortune or misfortune to have been bred as a gentleman and to have the instincts and manners that go with gentle birth. Half against his will he is taken for a member of a well-known family bearing the same name, is welcomed to the house of a baronet and the heart of a baronet's daughter. The tailor wins the lady in the character of a gentleman. Rose's maid kindly informs him how her mistress shuddered when she repeated to herself the awful word " snip " which some malignant who suspected the truth had suggested in regard to her lover. But whenever honesty distinctly bids him to own he is a tailor he does so, and after he has been led by love to avow his passion he summons up

his courage and tells Rose he is the snip she detests. She is all frankness, loyalty and generosity, vows she will never desert him, and goes straight to her parents to inform them that a tailor is to be their son-in-law.

Harris, George, in Mrs. H. B. Stowe's *Uncle Tom's Cabin*, a mulatto slave on a Kentucky estate. His wife Eliza is sold to an alien and distant owner. Both he and she run away—to meet at last on the free soil of Canada. He is " possessed of a handsome person and pleasing manners " and such " adroitness and ingenuity " that he has " invented a machine for the cleaning of hemp, which displays quite as much mechanical genius as Whitney's cotton gin." Naturally he finds disguise easy. Here is how he looks when on the second day of his flight he alights at a Kentucky hotel:

"He was very tall, with a very dark Spanish complexion, fine expressive black eyes, and close curling hair, also of a glossy blackness. His well-formed aquiline nose, straight thin lips, and the admirable contour of his finely formed limbs, impressed the whole company instantly with the idea of something uncommon."

Harris, Mrs., in Dickens's *Martin Chuzzlewit*, an alleged friend of Mrs. Gamp, whom she was continually citing in approval of her own acts or in illustration of some point at issue, but whom no one in her circle of acquaintance had ever seen and who was finally disposed of by Mrs. Prig in the famous phrase, " I don't believe there's no sich a person."

"Bother Mrs. Harris!" said Betsey Prig. Mrs. Gamp looked at her with amazement, incredulity, and indignation; when Mrs. Prig, shutting her eye still closer, and folding her arms still tighter, uttered these memorable and tremendous words:—
"I don't believe there's no sich a person!"
After the utterance of which expressions, she leaned forward, and snapped her fingers once, twice, thrice, each time nearer to the face of Mrs. Gamp; and then rose to put on her bonnet, as one who felt that there was now a gulf between them which nothing could ever bridge across.—*Martin Chuzzlewit.*

Harrison, Rev. Dr., in Fielding's novel, *Amelia*, a model parson, " well worthy," says the author, " of the cloth he wore, and that is I think, the

highest character a man can attain."
Half his fortune he has given away
or been defrauded of by the plausible
tales of insidious friends. Yet he can
be just and even stern when he knows
he is right. He takes in execution the
goods and person of his friend Booth
because Booth, while pleading poverty, was buying expensive jewelry.

Harum, David, the principal character in a novel of that name (1898)
by Edward Noyes Westcott, a banker
and dealer in horses in a village in
Central New York who possesses a
shrewdness, humor and homely
philosophy that temper his utter
lack of principle in horse-selling and
horse-trading, and who can and does
rise to occasional heights of charity
and self-abnegation of which he is
bashfully reticent.

Harvey, Belinda, titular heroine of
Belinda (1803), a novel by Maria
Edgeworth. While spending a winter
in London with Lady Delacour, a
brilliant and fashionable woman, she
meets Clarence Harvey. Mutual
love attracts, mutual distrust sets
them apart. Not till the resultant
comedy of cross purposes has involved the entire Delacour household
is the tangle straightened out, and a
reconciliation effected.

Hatchway, Lieutenant Jack, a
retired naval officer, on half-pay, in
Smollett's novel, *The Adventures of
Peregrine Pickle.* He is represented
as living with Commodore Trunnion
as a companion.

> He who can read the calamities of Trun-
> nion and Hatchway, when run away with
> by their mettled steeds, . . . without
> a good hearty burst of honest laughter, must
> be well qualified to look sad and gentleman-
> like with Lord Chesterfield or Master
> Stephen.—Sir W. Scott.

Havisham, Miss, in Dickens's *Great
Expectations* (1860), the foster mother
of the heroine Estella. She lived a
hermit life in her magnificent but
neglected home, Satis House, left to
her by her father, a wealthy brewer.
A great tragedy had ruined her life.
She had been engaged to be married
to a man she passionately loved,
Compeyson, a showy and shallow
gallant, who jilted her on the appointed wedding day. She received
the fatal letter when she was dressing
for church. Her life was despaired
of. When she recovered from a long
illness, she laid waste her heritage,
stopped all the clocks at twenty
minutes to nine—the time of her
receiving the letter—and never afterwards looked upon the light of day.

Hawk, Sir Mulberry, in Dickens's
Nicholas Nickleby (1838), a gambler
and a roué "especially remarkable
for his tact in ruining young gentlemen of fortune. . . . He made
them his butts in a double sense for
he emptied them with good address,
and made them the laughing stocks
of society." (Chap. xix.) He fails
in his efforts to seduce Kate Nickleby
and is soundly thrashed by Nicholas.
Later he fights a duel with his head
pupil and chief dupe, Lord Frederick
Verisopht, in which the latter is killed.

Hawthorn, Jerry, one of the heroes
of Pierce Egan, Jr's. *Life in London,
or the Day and Night Scenes of Jerry
Hawthorn and Corinthian Tom* (1824)
—a collection of sketches describing
the sports and amusements of London
in the days of the Regency. Illustrated by George Cruikshank, it had
enormous contemporary vogue. A
drink called Tom and Jerry is still
compounded in American bar-rooms.

Hayes, Catherine, notorious in
English criminal annals, who was
burned alive in 1726 for the murder
of her husband, is the heroine of
Thackeray's novel *Catherine.*

Hazard, Myrtle, heroine of Dr.
Oliver Wendell Holmes's novel, *The
Guardian Angel.* The descendant
from ancestors of divergent races and
characteristics, herself born in the
tropical climate of oriental India, she
is brought up from the age of fifteen
in the New England village of Oxbow
by an austere and provincial aunt,
who utterly fails to understand her
or to curb her. Fortunately she falls
by accident under the care of Professor Gridley, whom she rightly calls
her Guardian Angel, and her final
reformation is wrought by her experiences as a hospital nurse during

the Civil War. " In the offices of mercy which she performed . . . the dross of her nature seemed to be burned away. The conflict of mingled lives in her blood had ceased.'' Myrtle is especially interesting as the first character of fiction in which the dual influences of heredity are discussed by a scientist of literary ability.

Headlong, Squire, the hero of *Headlong Hall* (1815), a novel by Thomas Love Peacock, which is more a series of discussions on life and letters than a connected narrative. The principal interlocutors are a perfectibilian, a deteriorationist, a statu-quo-ite and a reverend doctor who has won the squire's fancy by a learned dissertation on the art of stuffing a turkey. The squire himself is an amiable eccentric whose special fad is the collection and exploitation of human curios.

Headrigg, Cuddie (*i.e.*, Cuthbert), in Walter Scott's novel, *Old Mortality*, a ploughman in Lady Bellenden's service; a mixture of "apparent dulness with occasional sparkles which indicated the craft so often found in the clouted shoe.''

Heath, Sir Massingbird, in James Payn's novel *Lost Sir Massingbird* (1864), a Georgian roué who had hobnobbed with royalty itself as represented by the Prince Regent and returned financially ruined to Fairburn Hall, an entailed estate of which he could not dispose save by the death of the heir-presumptive, his nephew Marmaduke Heath, who is carefully shielded from his evil designs by the lad's friends. In his hot youth Sir Massingbird had secretly married a gipsy whom he drove mad with his cruelty. She laid on him the curse, " May he perish inch by inch within reach of aid that shall not come.'' The curse was fulfilled in his old age. He disappeared mysteriously and months later his bones were found in an old oak tree. It was supposed that he had climbed the tree to look around for poachers, and that a misstep had precipitated him into the hollow trunk.

Heathcliff, hero of Emily Brontë's novel, *Wuthering Heights* (1847), a man of stormy, untrained nature, brought as a child to Wuthering Heights, the owner of which, Mr. Earnshaw, had picked him up as a stray in the streets of Liverpool. His affection is as terrifying as is his hatred; despairing but unconquered he starves himself at last, dying with a sneer on his lips, and is buried beside the woman he had loved and tortured —a side of whose coffin he had torn away years before.

" How did you contrive to preserve the common sympathies of human nature when you resided here? '' writes Heathcliff's young bride to the old servant. " I cannot recognize any sentiment which those around share with me. . . . Is Mr. Heathcliff a man? '' And at the end the servant herself, who tells the story, asks: " Is he a ghoul or a vampire? . . . Where did he come from, the dark little thing, harbored by a good man to his bane? '' Cruelty, and not love, cruelty of the living and of the dead, is the master passion of the book. If one were looking for a parallel to the sufferings of those who are the sport of this inhuman passion, it would be found in the diabolism that surrounds Webster's Duchess of Malfi:

I'll tell thee a miracle;
I am not mad yet, to my cause of sorrow.

Hebron, in the first part of *Absalom and Achitophel*, by Dryden, stands for Holland, but in the second part, by Tate, it stands for Scotland.

Heep, Uriah, in Dickens's *David Copperfield* (1894), a repugnant hypocrite and sneak, clerk to Mr. Wickfield. Under a cloak of abject humility he hides a jealous, malignant, meddlesome disposition. His evil designs are frustrated by Mr. Micawber.

"I am well aware that I am the umblest person going, let the other be who he may. My mother is likewise a very umble person. We live in a numble abode, Master Copperfield, but have much to be thankful for. My father's former calling was umble; for he was a sexton.''—*David Copperfield*, Chap. xvi.

Heep, articled clerk, articled out of charity whom to describe description fails; he is a sinister, crouching, fawning imp of humility; viperous in soul and body; long-fingered and splay-footed and red-eyed with damp exudations of the cuticle, a frog-like hand; altogether a "moist, unwholesome body."—*London Times.*

Helbeck of Bannisdale, hero and title of a novel by Mrs. Humphry Ward (1898). He is an English Catholic of ancient lineage, great wealth and corresponding responsibilities. The novel portrays with insight and skill the spiritual battle that an austere and devout Catholic must fight before he can yield so far to passion as to contemplate marriage with a girl who not only has no knowledge of and no sympathy with any religion, but has inherited a positive scorn for the Catholic faith and an impertinent contempt for the rules and ceremonies of the Church. Poor little Laura Fountain, equally troubled, cuts the knot by committing suicide.

Heldar, Dick (*i.e.*, Richard), hero of Rudyard Kipling's novel *The Light that Failed* (1896). An English artist, an orphan who had been brought up with another waif called Maisie by the hard-hearted Mrs. Jennett. In early manhood he goes to the front as a war-artist, and receives a sabre cut which threatens his eyesight. He determines to produce one great masterpiece before he goes blind. The light fails just as he has finished his picture, and that is destroyed by a model who owes him a grudge. Maisie refuses to marry him. Darkness of mind and body settled down upon him, and he sacrifices his life in the Soudan.

Helen, heroine of a ballad, *Sister Helen* (1870), by Dante Gabriel Rossetti. The tale is supposed to be told by her little sister.

A girl forsaken by her highborn lover turns to sorcery for help in her revenge on him; and with the end of the third day come three suppliants, the father and the brothers of the betrayer, to whom he has shown the secret of his wasting agony, if haply they may bring him back, not life, but forgiveness at her hands. Dying herself of anguish with him and with the molten figure of her making, she will remit nothing of her great revenge; body and soul of both shall perish

in one four-fold death: and her answers pass, ever more and more bitter and ardent through the harmless mouthpiece of a child. —SWINBURNE.

Helen, subject and title of two poems by Edgar Allan Poe, addressed to different individuals. The first, a lyric of two five-lined stanzas, was written at the age of fourteen, and first published in 1831. It was addressed to Mrs. Jane Stanard, the friend and confidante of his boyhood, who inspired him, in his own words, with " The one idolatrous and purely ideal love of my passionate boyhood." It contains the well known lines

To the glory that was Greece,
And the grandeur that was Rome.

In spite of technical defects this is one of his most exquisite lyrics. " Its confusion of imagery," says Stedman, " is wholly forgotten in the delight afforded by melody, lyrical perfection, sweet and classic grace." The other and later poem is in blank verse, and commemorates the first time he saw the poetess Sarah Helen Whitman, a lady who was subsequently one of his greatest friends. This was when he was on his way to Boston to lecture. Restless, at midnight, he wandered from his hotel at a place near where she lived, and saw her walking in a garden.

Helena, in the second part of Goethe's *Faust*, an avatar of Helen of Troy, summoned from the shades by Mephistopheles.

The Helena of the Second Part of *Faust* is a pure abstraction, but it should never be forgotten that the character was not originally intended to be made such. A long series of years had intervened since the period when the youthful Goethe first conceived the idea of his *Faust* upon the basis of the popular tradition embodied in the ancient puppet-play, where Faust forces Mephistopheles to procure for him Greek Helen, the fairest of women. As late as the year 1800, when already engaged upon the re-modelling of the entire First Part, he expressed his regret to Schiller that he must turn Helena into a mere "mask and face" (*Fratze*). The Helena of the Second Part is a mere allegory, representing Classicism as opposed to Romanticism (symbolized in the person of Faust), and giving birth, after her union with him, to Euphorion, who, as Goethe allowed to be known, was to typify the brief union of both literary tendencies in Lord Byron.—*Saturday Review.*

Helena, in Shakespeare's comedy, *All's Well That Ends Well* (1598), the only daughter of a doctor, Gerard de Narbon, herself so skilled in medicine that she cured the King of France of an apparently fatal disorder. In return he promised her the hand of any one among his courtiers. She chose Bertram, Count of Rousillon, who married her under duress and then immediately forsook her. She won him back by stratagem; he had pursued a maiden named Diana with wanton love; Helena substitutes herself for Diana at the assignation and plays her part so well that later, when she convinces Bertram that it was herself and not Diana with whom he had spent the night, he gladly takes her back. This stratagem is imitated by Amanda in Colley Cibber's *Love's Last Shift.*

Helena is a young woman seeking a man in marriage. The ordinary laws of courtship are reversed, the habitual feelings are violated: yet with such exquisite address this dangerous subject is handled, that Helena's forwardness loses her no honor. Delicacy dispenses with her laws in her favor.—LAMB.

Helmer, Nora, heroine of Henrik Ibsen's drama, *The Doll's House* (1879), is a sort of Scandinavian Frou-Frou portrayed with a greater depth of earnestness, sympathy and insight than her French predecessor. She is in fact a type of nineteenth century womanhood, brought up in the innocent ignorance which was the contemporary ideal and quite unable to comprehend and contend with the sterner realities of life. Through pure ignorance she commits forgery and contemplates suicide. She is saved by her husband, who takes upon himself the burden of guilt. By a clumsy expedient he also is saved.

Heloise, or **Eloise,** the real heroine of one of the most famous of love romances, the mediæval episode of Heloise and Abelard. Peter Abelard (1079–1142) was the profoundest scholar, the most skilful dialectician, the greatest orator of his day. He fell in love with Heloise, his pupil, daughter of Canon Fulbert, she reciprocated and they fell, but she

refused the reparation he offered her by marriage. Pope, in his *Epistle from Eloisa to Abélard,* makes this refusal arise from an abstract predilection for the name of mistress above that of wife; it was really due to disinterested affection which would not stand in the way of the high ecclesiastical preferment which seemed naturally due to his talents and services.

Heloise, The New, a name which Jean Jacques Rousseau gives to Julie, the heroine of his romance, *La Nouvelle Heloise* (1760), who was drawn from an actual flame of his own, the Countess d'Houdetot. See JULIE.

Helstone, Caroline, in Charlotte Brontë's novel, *Shirley,* an orphan brought up by her uncle, the rector. In her loyalty, devotion and generosity she is faithfully copied from Miss Brontë's schoolfellow and warm and steadfast friend through life, Ellen Nussey. It was to Miss Nussey that Charlotte wrote, "If we had but a cottage and a competency of our own, I do think we might live on till death, without being dependent on any third person for happiness."

Helstone, Mr., in Charlotte Brontë's novel, *Shirley.*

In the seldom recurring holidays Charlotte made sometimes short visits with those of her companions whose homes were within reach of school. Here she made acquaintance with the scenes and prominent characters of the Luddite period; her father materially helped to fix her impressions, for he had held more than one curacy in the very neighborhood which she describes in *Shirley.* He was present in some of the scenes, an active participator as far as his position permitted. Sometimes on the defensive, sometimes aiding the sufferers, uniting his strength and influence with the Mr. Helstone of *Shirley.* Between these two men there seems to have been in some respects a striking affinity of character which Charlotte was not slow to perceive, and she blended the two into one, though she never personally beheld the original of Mr. Helstone, except once when she was ten years old. He was a man of remarkable vigor and energy, both of mind and will. An absolute disciplinarian, he was sometimes called "Duke Ecclesiastic," a very Wellington in the Church.

Mr. Brontë used to delight in recalling the days he spent in the vicinity of this man. Many a breakfast hour he enlivened by his animated relations of his friend's unflinching courage and dauntless self-reliance,—and how the ignorant and prejudice population around misunderstood and misrepresented his worthiest deeds.—*Reminiscences of Charlotte Brontë.*

Henriette, in Molière's comedy, *Les Femmes Savantes* (1672), a bright and winning girl who acts as an agreeable foil to the absurdities of the titular " Learned Ladies "— especially her mother Philaminte and her sister Armande. She shares with her father the opinion that household duties and not science and philosophy constitute woman's true field of action, and might therefore be accepted as the pioneer anti-suffragette in modern drama.

Henriette is nature itself and straightforward simplicity; she is essentially womanly; she has a wholesome charm and a feminine grace. Perhaps it is not too much to say that Henriette embodies Molière's ideal of the French girl, just as Rosalind may represent Shakespeare's ideal of the English girl. . . . As the type of maidenly ignorance Molière gives us Agnès, where Shakespeare presents us with Miranda; and as the representative of all that is most attractively feminine, he depicts Henriette where Shakespeare has imagined Rosalind.—BRANDER MATTHEWS: *Molière*, p. 297.

Henry IV (1366–1413), the first of the Lancastrian kings, appears in the two Shakespearean plays that bear his name and also in *Richard II*, where he is called Bolingbroke from the town in which he was born. He was Duke of Hereford during Richard's reign.

Henry IV is the same Bolingbroke who had been so greatly conceived in King Richard II; only he is no longer in the full force of his manhood. He is worn by care and toil, harassed by the troubles of the unquiet times, yet still resolved to hold firmly what he has forcibly attained. There is a pathetic power in the figure of this weary, ambitious man, who can take no rest until the rest of death comes to him.—EDWARD DOWDEN: *Shakespeare Primer.*

Henry VIII, last of the Tudor kings of England, is the hero of a historical play doubtfully attributed to Shakespeare.

Henry, if we judge him sternly, is cruel and self-indulgent; but Shakespeare will hardly allow us to judge Henry sternly. He is a lordly figure, with a full abounding strength of nature, a self-confidence, an ease and mastery of life, a power of effortless sway, and seems born to pass on in triumph over those who have fallen and are afflicted. —E. DOWDEN: *Shakespeare Primer.*

The character of Henry VIII is drawn with great truth and spirit. It is like a very disagreeable portrait, sketched by the hand of a master. His gross appearance, his blustering demeanor, his vulgarity, his arrogance, his sensuality, his cruelty, his hypocrisy, his want of common decency and common humanity are marked in strong lines. His traditional peculiarities of expression complete the reality of the picture. His authoritative expletive "Ha!" with which he intimates his indignation or surprise, has an effect like the first startling sound that breaks from a thundercloud. He is of all the monarchs in our history the most disgusting, for he unites in himself all the vices of barbarism and refinement without their virtues.—HAZLITT.

In foreign literature the most striking portrait of Henry VIII appears in Calderon's drama *La Cisma de Inglaterra* (*The English Schism*), which narrates the monarch's quarrel with the church (for which Wolsey and not himself is made responsible), and more especially his amour with Anne Boleyn, an astute, alert, and very politic lady.

Hereward, in Walter Scott's romance, *Count Robert of Paris* (1831), a Saxon Crusader, one of the Varangian guard of Alexius Comnenus, Emperor of Greece. He is vanquished by the titular hero in single combat with battleaxes, after which he enlists under Count Robert's banner, and in the countess's maid, now called Agatha, discovers his Saxon love Bertha.

Hereward, whom Charles Kingsley took as the hero of his novel, *Hereward the Wake* (1866), was the son of Leofric, Earl of Chester, and Lady Godiva (*q.v.*). From early boyhood he showed such insubordination that his father obtained his banishment from the country. After many strange adventures he married a noble maiden named Torfrida and returned with her on hearing of the invasion of England by the Normans. Finding most of his family slain and the ancestral hall in possession of the invaders, he collected a band of Saxons, easily rescued his patrimony and then took refuge on the Island of Ely. This he held until in 1072, he was betrayed by some of his adherents, but even then he cut his way through the Norman forces. Finally he made peace with William the Conqueror through the influence of the Lady Elfrida, a widow, for whose sake he repudiated Torfrida. But he never prospered after this faithlessness and was finally slain by Norman besiegers of his home.

Heriot, Blanche, heroine of a short story in Albert Smith's *Pictures of Life* (1841), afterwards turned into a melodrama by the same author under the title, *Blanche Heriot, or the Chertsey Curfew* (1842). The plot is founded upon the legend connected with the Old Chertsey Church. Blanche was a heroic girl during the Wars of the Roses who in order to gain time for her lover's pardon to arrive, and so save his head from " rolling on the Abbey mead," clung to the clapper of the great bell in the belfrey tower and so prevented it from announcing the hour set for the execution. The theme has been borrowed by Rosa Harthwicke Thorpe in her ballad *Curfew Shall not Ring To-night,* who changes the heroine's name to Bessie and the time of action to Cromwell's day. David Belasco, in *The Heart of Maryland,* uses the same expedient.

Hermann, farmer hero of Goethe's pastoral poem, *Hermann and Dorothea.* See DOROTHEA.

Hermia, an Athenian maiden, heroine of Shakespeare's comedy, *A Midsummer Night's Dream* (1592). Egeus, her father, had promised her in marriage to Demetrius. But she, loving Lysander, eloped with him and was pursued by Demetrius. He in his turn was followed by Helena, who was devotedly in love with him. All four fell asleep in a forest and dreamed the dream that forms the basis of the comedy. Through the help of a magic herb in the hands of Puck, Demetrius awakes in love with Helena and resigns Hermia to Lysander.

Hermione, heroine of the first part of Shakespeare's *A Winter's Tale,* daughter of the Emperor of Russia and consort of Leontes. The victim of her husband's jealousy, she is believed to be dead for fifteen years and is restored to him in the last act, her character fully vindicated.

Hermione is, I suppose, the most magnanimous and noble of Shakespeare's women; without a fault she suffers, and for sixteen years, as if for the greatest fault.—F. J. FURNIVALL.

The character of Hermione is as much distinguished by its saint-like resignation and patient forbearance, as that of Paulina is by her zealous and spirited remonstrances against the injustice done to the queen, and by her devoted attachment to her misfortunes. Hermione's restoration to her husband and her child, after her long separation from them, is as affecting in itself as it is striking in the representation.

Hermit, The, the otherwise unnamed hero of Thomas Parnell's poem so entitled. The story he found in Howell's *Familiar Letters* (Book iv, Section ix, 2), who in his turn avowed obligation to " Sir P. Herbert in his late *Conceptions.*" The hermit, anxious to renew for a period his relations with the world, starts out from his cell and is joined by a young stranger. That night they are hospitably entertained by a nobleman. The youth steals his golden goblet. Next night they are reluctantly entertained by a miser to whom the youth presents the goblet. On the third day the youth strangles the infant child of another entertainer; on the fourth he drowns the guide who had led the wanderers to safety. When the hermit started to curse the youth he turned into a radiant angel who explained that he had stolen the goblet to teach the rich lord not to trust to worldly wealth; he had given it to the miser to show that kindness always meets a reward; he had strangled the infant because the father loved it better than he loved God; he had drowned the guide to prevent him from committing a contemplated murder.

Hernani, hero of a tragedy by Victor Hugo entitled *Hernani or Castilian Honor* (1830). A mysterious bandit and revolutionary leader, he is in love with Dona Sol, the betrothed of Ruy Gomez, her guardian, in whose house she lives. She reciprocates Hernani's passion. To complicate matters she is beloved by the king, Charles V. Hernani is discovered at night in Ruy Gomez's house planning an elopement. King Charles, who had smuggled himself into the house on his own account, saves the bandit by claiming him as a member of his suite. Later Hernani returns the compliment by saving the king when in his power. Still later Charles pursues the outlaw to the gates of Ruy Gomez's castle. The sacred rites of hospitality force Gomez to grant sanctuary to the fugitive. "His head or yours!" shouts Charles. "Take mine!" calmly returns the Duke. Overcome by such generosity Hernani presents Ruy Gomez with a horn. He swears to forfeit his own life whenever Gomez demands it by blowing the horn. The occasion comes in the last act, at his own wedding with Dona Sol, which is presided over by the magnanimous Charles, now an emperor. The fatal horn is heard in the midst of the festivities; Ruy is implacable; Hernani is true to his vow. One dose of poison suffices for bridegroom and bride. Ruy Gomez stabs himself over their corpses.

Hero, in Shakespeare's *Much Ado About Nothing* (1600), daughter of Leonato, governor of Messina, whose quiet decorum forms an excellent contrast to the brilliant insousciance of her cousin Beatrice. A cruel plot devised by the malignant Don John separates her at the very altar from her betrothed, Don Claudio, but Beatrice, with Benedict's help, succeeds in establishing the truth.

"When they are both on the scene together," says Mrs. Jameson, "Hero has little to say for herself; Beatrice asserts the rule of a master spirit, eclipses her by her mental superiority, abashes her by her raillery, dictates to her, answers for her. But Hero, added to her grace and softness, and all the interest which attaches to her as the sentimental heroine of the play, possesses an intellectual beauty all her own."

The supposed death and subsequent marriage of Hero were suggested by the 22nd novella of Biondello's collection, whose scene is laid, as in the comedy, at Messina. Hero's father is called Leonato, and her lover's friend Don Piero, or Pedro.
The mode in which the innocent Hero before the altar at the moment of the wed-

ding, and in the presence of her family and many witnesses, is put to shame by a most degrading charge—false indeed, yet clothed with every appearance of truth—is a grand piece of theatrical effect in the true and justifiable sense. The impression would have been too tragical had not Shakespeare carefully softened it, in order to prepare for a fortunate catastrophe.—SCHLEGEL.

Herrick, Robert, in R. L. Stevenson's romance, *Ebbtide* (1894), a man who has failed in life not through vice, but weakness—a fatal incapacity for fixed aim and deliberate action. In his beginnings a gentleman and a scholar, a graduate of Oxford, he degenerates into a beachcomber and becomes the companion of outcasts who man a stolen ship. He tries suicide and fails even in that. "I am broken crockery," he cries; "I am a burst drum; the whole of my life has gone to water; I have nothing left that I believe in, except my living horror of myself." It is barely possible that the author drew some hints for this character from his cousin, Robert A. M. Stevenson, who shared Herrick's brilliant incapacity but not his guilt. Will H. Low, in *A Chronicle of Friendship*, quotes a letter from Stevenson which contains this sentence: "A little while ago Henley and I remarked about Bob 'how strange it was that the cleverest man we knew was starving.'"

Hester, subject of Charles Lamb's poem of that name, written on the death of Hester Savory (1777–1803), "a young Quaker you may have heard me speak of as being in love with for some years while I lived at Pentonville, though I had never spoken to her in my life."—LAMB: *Letter to Manning*, March, 1803. Some attempts have been made to identify her with the Alice W—— of *Dream Children*, but Alice was fair and Hester Savory dark as a gipsy, as may be seen from the miniature reproduced in Lucas's *Life of Charles Lamb*, vol. I, p. 328.

Hiawatha, titular hero of Longfellow's epic (1855), who according to Indian traditions was the son of Mudjekeewis (the west wind) and Wenonah. He wrestled with and conquered Mondamin (maize) and gave it to be the food of man. He subdued Mishea Nahma the sturgeon and taught man how to extract its oil for lighting and cooking purposes. He introduced the arts of navigation, medicine, and picture writing. By his marriage to Minnehaha he set the example of monogamy. After her death and the advent of the white man he departed for the kingdom of Ponemah, the land of the hereafter.

High-Heels, in Swift's *Gulliver's Travels,* a faction or party in Lilliput opposed to the **Low-Heels,** each of whom has its own idea as to whether high or low heels should be the everyday fashion for shoes. High-heels, so they averred, were most loyal to the spirit of the constitution, nevertheless the Emperor of Lilliput appointed only Low-Heels to office. The satire is directed against the High-church and Low-church factions in English religion and the Whigs and Tories in British politics.

Hilda, in Nathaniel Hawthorne's romance, *The Marble Faun,* a New England maiden, unspotted of the world, studying art in Rome. Her first knowledge of sin and its consequent suffering comes to her through the guilt of others. Accident makes her a witness to Donabello's murder of the monk Antonio. She is overwhelmed by a sense of the wickedness thus thrust upon her. Her understanding of the old painters and her skill in copying them, dependent as they are upon the whiteness of her own soul, are temporarily suspended by this merely vicarious smirch. She can neither keep nor betray her terrible secret, and in this dilemma seeks the secrecy of the Catholic confessional.

Hilda's Tower, formerly known as the Torre della Scimia, is still pointed out in Rome. Here she kept a legendary lamp burning before the shrine and fed her doves until another's crime drove her from her maiden refuge.

In the biography of his father Julian Hawthorne says that in Hilda there was something of his mother. He denies an imputed likeness between Hilda and a certain Miss Shepard who was with the Hawthornes in Italy. As to the name, the same authority in *Hawthorne and his Circle* tells us that it was suggested by the Abbey of St. Hilda at Whitby, on the Yorkshire coast, England.

Hildegarde, in *The Initials,* by Baroness Von Tautphoeus. See ROSENBERG, HILDEGARDE.

Hoax, Stanislaus, in Disraeli's novel, *Vivian Grey,* a practical jester presumably drawn from Theodore Hook. See GAY, LUCIEN.

Hobbididance, the "prince of dumbness," a friend referred to by Edgar in *King Lear,* Act iv, Sc. 1. Shakespeare evidently found the name in Harsnet's *Declaration of Egregious Popish Impostures.* See MODU.

Hobbinol, in William Somerville's burlesque pastoral, *Hobbinol, or the Rural Games* (1740), is the great man of his village in the Vale of Eversham, who presides over the games wherein his son, Young Hobbinol, and Ganderetta, a near relation, are respectively King and Queen of the May. See HOBINOL.

Hobinol or **Hobbinol,** in the *Shepherd's Calendar* (1572), a pastoral poem by Edmund Spenser, a fellow-swain of Colin Clout, who sympathizes with him in his love for Rosalind (Eclogue iv) and later (Eclogue ix) holds a dialogue with Diggon Davie on Popish abuses. As Colin Clout is meant for Spenser, so Hobinol represents his classmate and life-long friend Gabriel Harvey (1545-1630), a physician and an LL.D., a respectable poet and one of the most learned men of his day.

Hogsflesh, Mr., the hero of a farce, *Mr. H.,* by Charles Lamb, which was emphatically damned on the one night of its performance, December 10, 1806.

"The story," as the author wrote to Manning, "is a coxcomb appearing at Bath, vastly rich—all the ladies dying for him—all bursting to know who he is; but he goes by no other name than Mr. H." At length, "after much vehement admiration, when his true name comes out—Hogs-flesh—all the women shun him, avoid him, and not one can be found to change their name for him," until he obtains permission from the king " to take and use the surname and arms of Bacon," and is happily united to his Melesinda.

Curiously enough the little play was frequently brought out success-fully in the United States.

The first pope who changed his name on assuming the pontificate—thereby setting a precedent that has been followed by all his successors—was named Pietro Osporca or Peter Hogsmouth. Some authorities attribute the change to the apparent arro-gance of assuming to call himself Peter II. But the general impression is that he was glad to rid himself forever from all associa-tion with his family name by assuming the title of Sergius II.

Hohensteil-Schwangau, Prince, in Robert Browning's poetical soliloquy, *Prince Hohensteil Schwangau, the Savior of Society* (1872), is evidently painted from Napoleon III.

With plausible and ingenious cas-uistry the Prince passes in review the leading events of his own life. He acknowledges that they conform to no ideal standard and justify no plaudits which hero-worshipping his-torians might bestow upon them, yet he claims that in this world any Utopian scheme of government would be worse than useless, that it is the duty of a ruler to adjust himself to existing conditions, and assist his subjects to live the life into which they were born; and that his own policy, vacillating as it might seem to the ingenuous, was dictated throughout by the higher law of public expediency.

Holdfast, Aminadab, in Mrs. Cent-livre's comedy, *A Bold Stroke for a Wife* (1710), a friend of Simon Pure.

Holgrave, Mr., in Hawthorne's romance, *The House of the Seven Gables*, assumed name of a daguerro-typist who persuades Hepzibah Pyn-cheon to rent him a room in one of the " seven " gables. His real name is Maule, his family being hereditary enemies of the Pyncheons.

Hollingsworth, in Hawthorne's *The Blithedale Romance* (1852), the leading spirit in the Blithedale community, a strong man physically and mentally but narrowed down to a single idea: " He had taught his benevolence to pour its warm tide exclusively through one channel, so that there was nothing to spare for other great manifestations of love to man, nor scarcely for the nutriment of individ-ual attachments unless they could minister, in some way, to the terrible egotism which he mistook for an angel of God." Both the gentle Pris-cilla and the passionate Zenobra are in love with him.

Holmes, Sherlock, the amateur detective in novels and stories by Sir Arthur Conan Doyle, avowedly imi-tated from the M. Dupin (*q.v.*) of Edgar Allan Poe. He first appears in *A Study in Scarlet* (1887), is a lead-ing character in *The Sign of the Four* (1889), *The Adventures of Sherlock Holmes* (1891), and *The Hound of the Baskervilles* (1902), is apparently killed off at the close of *The Memoirs of Sherlock Holmes* (1904), but is somewhat awkwardly and uncon-vincingly resuscitated (for commer-cial reasons, it is suspected, quite as much as for literary) in *The Return of Sherlock Holmes* (1904).

A slave to cocaine, eccentric and brusque in manner, Holmes never-theless displays rare detective skill and unravels the most intricate crimi-nal snarls. His forte is *à posteriori* reasoning which enables him so to group apparently unimportant effects as to discover the most remote and apparently disconnected causes.

The death of the original of Sherlock Holmes early this month at his home near Edinburgh leads the *Dial* to remind its readers that it is not far from a score of years since Dr. Joseph Bell, an instructor of Sir Arthur Conan Doyle, unwittingly gave him more than the formal lessons bargained for, by supplying him with the germinal idea from which grew the detec-tive stories that made his reputation. Dr. Bell, who was born in 1837, early showed such skill in the application of inductive methods to the practice of his profession that, long before the creation of Sherlock Holmes, he was chosen assistant to Dr. Littlewood, official adviser to the crown in cases of medical jurisprudence. It was his application of the same methods in a half-playful vein to the affairs of everyday life that caught the attention and stimulated the imagination of the youthful Doyle, although Dr. Bell himself is said to have deprecated the notoriety thus thrust upon him as the alleged model of Holmes, and to have maintained that his use of the faculty of observation was nothing more than could be learned from any good manual of general medical practice.—*N. Y. Nation.*

Holofernes, in Shakespeare's comedy, *Love's Labor's Lost* (1594), a pedantic schoolmaster in whom are ridiculed the affectations and pomposity of contemporary pedagogues, and especially those who adopted the preciosity of Lyly's *Euphues.* Shakespeare probably took the name, directly or indirectly, from Rabelais *Gargantua,* the hero of which was instructed in Paris by a pedant named Holoferne.   Much ingenuity has been wasted in identifying the character with John Florio (d. 1625), an Italian philologist and lexicographer settled in London, who might have provoked Shakespeare's spleen by attacking all English dramas as " neither right comedies nor right tragedies, but perverted histories without decorum."   It has been pointed out that Holofernes is an imperfect anagram of Johannes Florio, or rather a perfect anagram of Hnes Florio, but the imperfection is a little too glaring.

Holt, Felix, hero of George Eliot's novel, *Felix Holt the Radical,* an ardent but level-headed champion of the workingman believed to be drawn from Gerald Massey.

No doubt, Felix is an honourable man, for he refuses to live upon a quack medicine or to look leniently at bribery when it is on his own side.   But there is a painful excess of sound judgment about him.   He gets into prison, not for leading a mob, but for trying to divert them from plunder by actions which are misunderstood.   He is very inferior to Alton Locke, who gets into prison for a similar performance.   The impetuosity and vehemence only comes out in his rudeness to Esther and plain speaking to her adopted father; and in trying to make him an ideal of wisdom, George Eliot only succeeds in making him unfit for his part.—LESLIE STEPHEN: *George Eliot.*

Holy Bottle (Fr. *Dive Bouteille*), in Rabelais's satiric romance *Pantagruel* (1545), an oracle whose quest occupies much of the time of Pantagruel and his friend Panurge. After

seeking it vainly in many lands, in order to question it as to the advisability of Panurge's marriage, they finally locate it in the island of Lanterns.   Here the Bottle is kept in an alabaster fount in a great temple. The attendant priestess throws something into the waters which begins to bubble, and from out the mouth of the oracular bottle proceeds the single word Trinc! (Drink!)   The advice is taken and the story ends in an orgy.   An order of the *Dive Bouteille* was instituted in France in the sixteenth century avowedly to carry out the philosophy of Pantagruelism.

Homburg, Prince of, hero and title of a romantic drama by Heinrich von Kleist.

In a battle fought by Frederick William, Elector of Brandenburg, against the Swedes the Prince, disobeying orders at a critical moment, rushes in and turns defeat into victory.   Nevertheless he is arrested for disobedience and condemned to death. Nathalie, the Elector's niece and adopted daughter, who is secretly betrothed to the Prince pleads for pardon which Frederick agrees to grant if the culprit will sign a statement that his sentence is unjust.   The Prince recognizes that he cannot do this.   Even his own officers clamoring for his release cannot sway his purpose.   The Elector, however, has only been trying him, the Prince is 'pardoned and formally betrothed to Nathalie.   A similar theme is treated by Schiller in his *Fight with the Dragon.*

Homespun, Cecily, in George Colman, Jr.'s comedy, *The Heir at Law* (1797), an innocent little country girl betrothed to Dick Dowlas.   Like her brother Zekiel she was the prototype of a whole line of beings long popular upon the British stage—the original of the simple rustic maiden whose wardrobe was contained within a cotton pocket handkerchief, who trusted and believed in everybody and wept with everybody and was as innocent of London ways as one of her own lambs.

Homespun, Zekiel, in George Colman, Jr.'s comedy, *The Heir at Law* (1797), an honest, warm-hearted, simple-minded rustic, the prototype of a long line of similar characters upon the English stage. Colman was one of the first who awoke sympathy for the woes of the lowly born. He may be said to have created the ebulient and kindly peasant, ever lugging out his small stock of money, ever eager to bestow his last shilling on any teller of a pitiful tale, ever spouting sentiment and morality, as ready with his fists as with his tongue, and invariably expressing joy by stamping his hob-nailed boots and singing " Ri ti tol di iddity, tol de iddity, tol de iddity." This noble creature, after being the idol of pit and gallery for over half a century, was finally slain in the burlesques of H. J. Byron.

Homunculus, in Goethe's *Faust*, Part II, is a small human being whom Wagner, the Famulus of Faust, discarding all natural methods of generation, has succeeded in fashioning by artificial means.

The meaning of Homunculus may be better grasped if we remember that Wagner stands for the letter as Faust for the spirit. The letter without the spirit killeth; the spirit without the letter could make no revelation of itself. Letter and spirit are alike necessary, but only in harmonious union. Faust has recourse to the Mothers—to the Infinite, the Absolute the realm of the Idea. Wagner works in the world of natural forces, concerns himself with methods of expression. Grammar, rhetoric, history—all these human arts are typified by Homunculus. As the Earth-Spirit prepares the garment of Life which the Deity wears, so Wagner prepares the garment of expression with which the idea must clothe itself.

Honeyman, Miss, in Thackeray's novel, *The Newcomes*, aunt to Clive Newcome and sister of Rev. Charles Honeyman, a little, brisk old lady, cheerful, frugal, honest, laborious, charitable, who lets out lodgings in Steyne Gardens and whose superior manners and prosperity win her from the neighboring tradespeople the title of Duchess.

Honeythunder, Mr. Luke, in Dickens's *Edwin Drood*, chairman of the Convened Composite Committee of Central and District Philanthropists, a large man, with a tremendous voice, and an appearance of being constantly engaged in crowding everybody to the wall.

Honeywood, hero of Goldsmith's comedy, *The Good-natured Man* (1767), a young man of good family and ample fortune, whose aim in life is to be generally beloved, and whose motto is " universal benevolence." He can neither refuse nor contradict; he gives away with lavish liberality to worthy and unworthy alike; he suffers his servants to plunder him; he tries to fall in with the humor of every one and to agree with every one. Goldsmith himself is the undoubted original of this character. At last Honeywood is reformed through the influence of his uncle, Sir William, and of Miss Richland, whom he married, and in the last act he confesses that his system of universal benevolence had been a fatal mistake. " Though inclined to the right, I had not courage to condemn the wrong; my charity was but injustice, my benevolence but weakness, and my friendship but credulity."

Honeywood, Sir William, in the same comedy, the uncle of the above, a generous and high-minded gentleman, whose benevolence, however, is limited by the demands of good sense, and who strives to bring his nephew within the same judicious bounds.

Honoria, subject of Dryden's poem, *Theodore and Honoria*, imitated from a story in Boccaccio's *Decameron*, 8th day. The mounted spectre of a knight pursues with dogs the ghostly form of the woman who in life had scornfully repelled his love. In Boccaccio's story the names are given as Guido Cavalcante and Nostalgia degli Onesti.

Hope, Evelyn, heroine of a poem by Browning in *Men and Women* (1855). Evelyn, a maid of sixteen, is dead. He who had loved her, a man " thrice as old," contemplating her as she lies in the beauty of death and asking himself whether his love was all in vain, replies that love is eternal, that there never will be one lost good, and that he will claim her in the life to come or in worlds not yet created, and be more worthy of her then than now.

Horatio, in Shakespeare's *Hamlet*, the faithful friend and counsellor of the titular hero.

Horatio is the only complete man in the play—solid, well-knit and true; a noble, quiet nature with that highest of all qualities, judgment, always sane and prompt, who never drags his anchors for any wind of opinion or fortune, but grips all the closer to the reality of things. He seems one of those calm, undemonstrative men whom we love and admire without asking to know why, crediting them with the capacity for great things, without any test of actual achievement, because we feel that their manhood is a constant quality, and no mere accident of circumstance and opportunity. —J. R. LOWELL: *Literary Essays, Shakespeare Once More.*

Horner, Gilpin, a goblin page of somewhat baffling characteristics, introduced by Sir Walter Scott in his *Lay of the Last Minstrel* (1805).

Lord Cranstoun's page is somewhat unearthly. It is a little misshapen dwarf whom he found one day when he was hunting in a solitary glen and took home with him. It never speaks except now and then to cry "Lost! lost! lost!" and is on the whole a hateful, malicious little urchin with no one good quality but his unaccountable fidelity and attachment to his master.— FRANCIS JEFFREY: *Essays from the Edinburgh Review—Walter Scott.*

Hortense, in Dickens's *Bleak House*, the French maid to Lady Dedlock. She looks "like a very neat she-wolf imperfectly tamed." She imperfectly guesses Lady Dedlock's secret, shoots Mr. Tulkinghorn, and disappears, still defiant, in the custody of Mr. Inspector Bucket.

Hosier, Admiral, the subject of Richard Glover's ballad, *Admiral Hosier's Ghost* (1739), was a British officer who in command of 20 ships and 3000 men was sent to the Spanish West Indies with orders to blockade but not to attack. His men were decimated by disease; he himself died of a broken heart at this enforced inaction. The poem tells how, after Vernon's victory, the ghosts of Hosier and his men arose "all in dreary hammocks shrouded, which for winding sheets they wore" and lamented their lost opportunities.

Hotspur, a popular nickname given to Harry Percy (1364–1403), the son of the Earl of Northumberland, on account of his fiery temper. Shakespeare adopts the pseudonym in the two parts of *Henry IV*.

Hotspur, who to bring him into contrast with the Prince is made much younger than the Harry Percy of history, is as ardent in the pursuit of glory as the Prince seems to be indifferent to it. To his hot temper and quick sense of personal honor, small matters are great; he does not see things in their true proportions; he lacks self-control, he has no easiness of nature. Yet he is gallant, chivalrous, not devoid of generosity nor of quick affections, though never in a high sense disinterested.—DOWDEN: *Shakespeare Primer.*

Houyhnhnms, in Swift's *Gulliver's Travels*, a race of horses endowed with reason and bearing rule over the degraded yahoos—the latter being caricatures of humanity as the former are sublimations of the animal creation. The name is obviously onomatopoetic and is meant to suggest the neighing of a horse.

Nay, would kind Jove my organs so dispose
To hymn harmonious *Houyhnhnms* through
    the nose,
I'd call thee *Houyhnhnm*, that high-sounding
    name;
Thy children's noses all should twang the
    same.
                        POPE.

Howe, Miss, in Richardson's *Clarissa Harlowe* (1751), the friend and correspondent of the heroine.

Miss Howe is an admirably sketched character, drawn in strong contrast to that of Clarissa, yet worthy of being her friend— with more of worldly perspicacity, though less of abstracted principle; and who, when they argue upon points of doubt and delicacy, is often able, by going directly to the question at issue, to start the game, while her more gifted correspondent does but beat the bush. Her high spirit and disinterested devotion for her friend, acknowledging, as she does on all occasions, her own inferiority, show her in a noble point of view; and though we are afraid she must have given honest Hickman (notwithstanding her resolution to the contrary) rather an uneasy time of it after marriage, yet it is impossible not to think that she was a prize worth suffering for.—SIR WALTER SCOTT.

Miss Howe, who is called a young lady of sense and honor, is not only extremely silly, but a more vicious character than Sally Martin, whose crimes are owing at first to seduction and afterwards to necessity; while this virtuous damsel without any reason insults her mother at home and ridicules her abroad; abuses the man she marries and is impertinent and impudent with great applause.—LADY M. W. MONTAGU: *Letter to the Countess of Bute*, March 1, 1752.

Hubbard, Bartley, the chief character in Howells' novel, *A Modern Instance* (1882).

A rascal of the most frequent American pattern. He is neither cruel nor a slave of his passions, nor has he any desire to sacrifice others to himself. On the contrary, he is very good-natured and amiable, and likes to see everybody happy about him. But of honor or principle he has no idea whatever. In fact, for the old-fashioned notion of principle he has substituted a new idea—that of the primary importance of "smartness"—*i.e.*, of that quality which enables a man to get ahead of his fellow by short cuts, dodges, tricks, devices of all kinds which just fall short of crime.—*N. Y. Nation.*

Huddibras, Sir, in Spenser's *Faërie Queene* (II, ii), the suitor of Perissa (who typifies extravagance), and himself described as a man " more huge in strength than wise in works."

Hudibras, Sir, titular hero of a burlesque epic in octosyllabic verse by Samuel Butler, published in three parts (1663, 1664, 1678). The name is derived from the Sir Huddibras (*q.v.*) of Spenser; the setting is imitated from *Don Quixote*, though the spirit is quite different. Cervantes smiled Spain's chivalry away because he deemed it obsolete; Butler would dismiss Puritanism with a kick because he deemed it a still dangerous innovation, scotched but not killed. Hudibras is a true-blue Presbyterian, ignorant and conceited, but a pedantic pretender to learning, who starts out on a crusade against the follies and amusements of the time, bent on reforming them by " apostolic blows and knocks." His attendant squire is Ralpho, an Independent and an evident recrudescence of Sancho Panza. Hudibras is variously said to be drawn from Sir Samuel Luke or Sir Henry Rosewell. He is represented as humpbacked and pot-bellied. His orange-tawny beard is long and unkempt because he had vowed not to trim it until the monarchy was overthrown. His horse,

blind on one side and wall-eyed on the other, is reminiscent of Don Quixote's Rosinante and Gargantua's mare.

Hudson, Sir Geoffrey, a famous dwarf (1678–1698), court jester to Henrietta Maria, the Queen of Charles II of England, is introduced into Scott's novel, *Peveril of the Peak.* He tells Julian Peveril the true story of how the late queen had caused him to be enclosed in a pie which was served up at a royal banquet.

Humorous Lieutenant, The, chief comic character (otherwise unnamed) in a tragi-comedy of that title by Beaumont and Fletcher (1616). A sort of privileged jester at the Court of Antigonus, King of Macedon, he accidentally drinks up a love-potion prepared by the royal order for a recalcitrant maiden named Celia. Thereupon the Lieutenant becomes violently enamored of the king and exhibits his passion in various absurd ways.

Humphrey, Master, in Dickens's *Old Curiosity Shop,* a deformed, misshapen old clockmaker who according to the original scheme was to have been the narrator of the story, as may be gathered from the earlier chapters which appeared (1840) as part of a serial, *Master Humphrey's Clock.* Sam Weller and his father were resuscitated from the *Pickwick Papers* to assist the sale, but only two tales were included in the publication, (completed in 1841) and these (*Barnaby Rudge* and *The Old Curiosity Shop*) were afterwards republished separately. From that time, says Dickens, *Master Humphrey's Clock,* "as originally constructed, became one of the lost books of the earth, which, we all know, are far more precious than any that can be read for love or money." The original " clock " is said to be in existence.

The town of Barnard Castle is most picturesque, with a ruined castle of the Baliols. Dickens in early life used frequently to come down and stay there with some young artist friends of his. The idea of Humphrey's Clock first sprang from Humphrey, the watchmaker in the town, and the picture in the beginning of the book is of the clock over the door of his shop.—AUGUSTUS J. C. HARE, *The Story of My Life*, vol. ii, p. 275.

Hunter, Mr. and **Mrs. Leo,** in Dickens's *Pickwick Papers*, a couple who, as their name implies, are indefatigable hunters of society lions so as to exhibit them in their own parlors.

Hur, Judah Ben, hero of a historical romance, *Ben Hur, a Tale of the Christ,* by Gen. Lew Wallace. The head of a wealthy and noble family in Jerusalem, he is wrongly accused by his false friend Messala of attempted murder on the Roman governor, is stripped of all his possessions and condemned to the galleys. His galley is attacked and sunk by robbers; his bravery in its defence leads to his being adopted by the tribune Arrius; he defeats Messala in a famous chariot race; after many vicissitudes he, his mother and sister are healed of leprosy by the Messiah. He witnesses the baptism, miracles, trial and crucifixion of Christ and turns Christian himself.

Hurlothrumbo, hero of a dramatic extravaganza (1730) by the English actor-dramatist, Samuel Johnson, which had a great contemporary vogue.

Consider, then, before, like Hurlo-Thrumbo,
  You aim your club at any creed on earth,
  That, by the simple accident of birth,
You might have been high-priest to Mumbo-
      Jumbo. THOMAS HOOD.

Hyde, Mr. See DR. JEKYLL.

I

Iachimo, in Shakespeare's *Cymbeline* (1605), a friend of Posthumus, who accepts the latter's wager that he cannot seduce Imogen from her wifely fidelity to Posthumus. When he finds her incorruptible, Iachimo manages to get smuggled into her chamber and as she sleeps he takes a mental inventory of its contents, notes certain marks on her body, and possesses himself of her bracelet. The evidence convinces Posthumus; he repudiates his wife and hands Iachimo the stakes, his own diamond ring. Later, Imogen disguised as a boy page, is brought before King Cymbeline and, being bid to demand a favor, asks that Iachimo shall reveal how he obtained the diamond ring upon his finger, whereupon the whole truth comes out.

Iago, in Shakespeare's *Othello*, the " ancient," or ensign, to the Moor, his secret enemy and his pretended friend. He hates Cassio for having been promoted to an office over his own head; he hates Othello for having promoted him; he believes or pretends to believe that the latter has been intimate with his wife, Emilia; he despises Desdemona's simplicity, and he sets to work at the plot that ruins Cassio, kills Desdemona, and makes a murderer and suicide of Othello.

Simple minded critics have been of opinion that Shakespeare constructed Iago on the lines of the historic Richard III— that is to say found him in literature, in the pages of a chronicler. Believe me, Shakespeare met Iago in his own life, saw portions and aspects of him on every hand throughout his manhood, encountered him piecemeal as it were on his daily path, till one fine day when he thoroughly felt and understood what malignant cleverness and baseness can effect, he melted down all these fragments, and out of them cast this figure. —COLERIDGE.

There is no character in Shakespeare's plays so full of serpentine power and serpentine poison as Iago. The Iachimo of *Cymbeline* is a faint sketch in water colors of the absolute villain Iago. He is envious of Cassio, and suspects that the Moor may have wronged his honor; but his malignancy is out of all proportion to even its alleged motives.—E. DOWDEN: *The Shakespeare Primer.*

Ianthe, in classical mythology the maiden for whose sake Iphis was changed from female to male. Sir William Davenant, in *The Siege of Rhodes* (1656), took the name for his leading female character. Pepys's *Diary* often refers to Mrs. Betterton as Ianthe, because that was the part in which he most admired her. Shelley and Byron have made the name familiar to modern readers. Shelley's Ianthe in *Queen Mab* (1810) is the maiden to whom the queen appears in a dream. Byron's Ianthe, to whom he dedicated his *Childe Harold* in the introductory stanzas written in 1813, was Lady Charlotte Stanley, daughter of the Earl of Oxford, who at that time was only fifteen years old. Before either Byron or Shelley, Landor had applied the name to Miss Sophia Jane Smith—afterwards Countess Molande—in some early amatory verses. In Byron's case Landor resented the appropriation, as appears from some verses preserved by Colvin in his monograph on Landor:

Ianthe, who came later, smiled and said,
I have two names and will be praised in
      both;
Sophia is not quite enough for me,
And you have simply named it, and but
      once.
Now call the other up . . .
I went and planted in a fresh parterre
Ianthe; it was blooming, when a youth
Leaped o'er the hedge, and snapping at the
      stem
Broke off the label from my favorite flower,
And stuck it on a sorrier of his own.

Ibbetson, Peter, hero of a novel of that name by George du Maurier (1891).

Even the "esoteric" part of Peter Ibbetson—the fantastic theory that the soul may relive, in dreams, its own and the entire life of its race in time, and anticipate both in eternity—appealed to the imagination by the simple fervor with which it was set forth, and melted the heart by a sweet if deceitful glimpse of consoling and compensating possibilities. Peter Ibbetson was the sort of book which one reads and decides to keep, and does not lend to everybody.—*Atlantic Monthly.*

Ichabod. When the ark of the Covenant was captured from the Israelites by the Philistines at Ebenezer, Hophni and Phinehas, sons of Eli, were slain. Eli perished on hearing the news, and Phinehas's wife gave premature birth to a child: "And she named the child Ichabod, saying, the glory is departed from Israel for the ark of God is taken" (I Samuel, Chap. iv). Ichabod is a compound of the Hebrew word for glory and a negative. J. G. Whittier applied the term to Daniel Webster in a poem intended to rebuke his change of attitude toward the question of slavery, as shown in his "Seventh of March Speech" (1850) in defence of the Fugitive Slave Law. Thirty years later, in *The Lost Occasion*, Whittier made such amends as he deemed proper for whatever injustice he might have done to Webster's memory.

The poem of Ichabod has been compared to Browning's *Lost Leader* (*q.v.*). Stedman couples with these a third poem, strangely overlooked, as he deems, by anthologists—the *Lines on a Great Man Fallen*, written by William W. Lord after the final defeat of Clay, but here the scorn is visited on the popular judgment that to be defeated is to fall.

Ida, Princess, heroine of Tennyson's poem, *The Princess; a Medley* (1847). Daughter of King Gama, Ida has been betrothed in childhood to a prince she has never seen. In womanhood she repudiates an engagement not of her own making, and having ideas on the reformation and regeneration of women she retires from the world with a number of attendants and founds a university for women only,

With prudes for proctors, dowagers for
   deans.

The poem shows how the prince, after many rebuffs, finally comes into his own. It has been suggested that the germ of the poem is found in the last chapter of Johnson's *Rasselas,* "The Princess thought that of all sublunary things knowledge was the best. She desired first to learn all sciences, and then proposed to found a college of learned women in which she would preside; that, by conversing with the old and educating the young, she might divide her time between the acquisition and communication of wisdom, and raise up for the next age models of prudence and patterns of piety." But in fact the idea dates back still earlier—to the play, *A Female Academy*, by Margaret, Duchess of Newcastle, and just a hint of it may be found in Aristophanes's *Lysistrata*.

If, Castle of (Fr. *Chateau d'If*), the scene of the imprisonment of Edmund Dantes in Dumas's *Monte Christo*, is a real castle, built by Francis I in 1530, which occupies an island in the Gulf of Lyons and was once the centre of defence of the roadstead, the chief of the twenty-two forts or batteries distributed along the coast from Cape Croisette to Cape Couronne. The spot on the battlements from which Dumas feigns that Dantes was thrown is pointed out by the custodian. Off in the distance appears the island to which he swam. A more orthodox identification is that of the cell in which the Man of the Iron Mask was actually confined during the greater part of his imprisonment. Equally historic is the cell of the Abbé Faria who was a real character actually confined here at the date given by Dumas. It is a fact likewise that the Abbé died in prison. But even the *gardien* smiles when he shows the remains of the tunnel constructed between Faria's cell and that of Edmund Dantes.

Ignaro, in Spenser's *Faërie Queene*, (1590), foster-father of Orgoglio, an old dotard who walked one way and looked another and had one answer to all questions, " I don't know." It will be remembered that the members of a secret organization in America, known as the Native American Party, were familiarly known as Know-Nothings because they answered, " I know nothing about it," to all interrogatories concerning their society. Similarly during the trial of Queen Charlotte in England (1820) the Italian witnesses answered " Non mi ricordo " (" I don't remember ") to most of the questions asked them. In Mrs. Inchbald's comedy, *Such Things Are* (1786), Lord Flint, minister of state to an Indian sultan, parries every embarrassing question with the stock phrase, " My people know, no doubt, but I cannot recollect."

Ilchester, Janet, in George Meredith's *Adventures of Harry Richmond*, a spoilt child who develops into a noble woman. When Squire Beltham disinherits his grandson, the hero of the novel, she becomes the heiress to all his property but she saves the situation by marrying Harry.

Illyria, King and **Queen of.** In Daudet's *Kings in Exile* these are portraits of the Neapolitan Francis II and his wife, a sister of the Empress of Austria. See CHRISTIAN II.

Ilyitch, Ivan, the principal and practically the only character in Tolstoy's gruesome novelette, *The Death of Ivan Ilyitch*.

There are many deaths in literature, but there is none, I think, in which the gradual processes of dissolution are analyzed and presented with such knowledge, such force, such terrible directness, as here. The result is appalling, but the final impression is one of encouragement and consolation.
W. D. HOWELLS.

Imlac, in Dr. Johnson's oriental romance, *Rasselas* (1759), son of a rich merchant of Goima, Egypt, a poet philosopher and traveller who accompanies Rasselas on his search for happiness and moralizes on all they see and experience.

Imogen, heroine of Shakespeare's *Cymbeline* (1605) and daughter of the titular hero. Her husband, Posthumus Leonatus (*q.v.*), makes vicarious trial of her virtue much after fashion of Cervantes's *Curious Impertinent* (see LOTHARIO), accepts as true the lies told him by the baffled and revengeful Iachimo (*q.v.*), and orders his servant Pisanio to assassinate her. Pisanio instead informs the lady of his instructions, and on his advice she assumes the disguise of a page and enters the service of Lucius, the Roman general in Britain.

Of all Shakespeare's women she is perhaps the most tender and the most artless. Her incredulity in the opening scene with Iachimo, as to her husband's infidelity, is much the same as Desdemona's backwardness to believe Othello's jealousy. Her answer to the most distressing part of the picture is only "My lord, I fear, has forgot Britain." Her readiness to pardon Iachimo's false imputations and his designs against herself is a good lesson to prudes; and may show that where there is a real attachment to virtue it has no need to bolster itself up with an outrageous or affected antipathy to vice.—HAZLITT: *Characters of Shakespeare's Plays* (1817).

Imogine, the Fair. See ALONZO THE BRAVE.

Imogine, the Lady, in Maturin's romance, *Bertram* (1816), the wife of

St. Aldobrande, who renews her love for an old flame, the titular hero, with disastrous results. See BERTRAM.

Imoinda, in Mrs. Aphra Bell's *Oronooko* (1696), the daughter of a white man, commander of the forces of Angola, a negro king, and the wife of Prince Oronooko (*q.v.*).

Indiana, heroine and title of the first novel (1832) written entirely by George Sand and published under the famous pseudonym. It embodies her first attack upon the marriage system. Indiana is a creole united in loveless bondage to Colonel Delmare, a hot-tempered rheumatic old soldier, brutal to his inferiors, peevishly censorious toward his wife. She falls in love with Raymon de Ramière and through the help of her English cousin, Sir Ralph Brown, escapes from the island of Bourbon in the hope of joining Raymon, but finds that, unknown to her, he has married in Paris. Sir Ralph thereupon proposes that they return to the island of Bourbon and commit suicide by leaping into a favorite waterfall. They do leap but by some unexplained circumstance — Sir Ralph thinks a blue-eyed angel interfered— they survive, and, the husband having died in the interval, live happy ever after.

It is from this model that we have one of the favorite types of woman in literature for the next twenty years—the misunderstood woman (*la femme incomprise*). The misunderstood woman is pale, fragile and subject to fainting. This fainting was not due to bad health. It was the fashion to faint. The days of nerves and languid airs had come back. The women whose grandmothers had walked so firmly to the scaffold and whose mothers had listened bravely to the firing of cannon under the Empire were now depressed and tearful like so many plaintive elegies. It was just a matter of fashion.—RENÉ DOUMIC, *George Sand*, p. 81.

Inez, Donna, in Byron's *Don Juan* Canto i, 10–30 (1819), the mother of the titular hero, supposedly drawn from Byron's wife. A prude and a bluestocking, she worried Don Jose, her husband, into his grave and made her son recalcitrantly improper through an educational overdose of the proprieties.

Infant Phenomenon, in Dickens's *Nicholas Nickleby* (1838), the name which her fond father Nicholas Crummles gives to his eight-year-old daughter Ivinetta, and under which he bills her in his programmes.

The *American Notes and Queries*, February 23, 1889, preserves a communication from an old English actor who identifies the Infant Phenomenon with the daughter of a strolling player named Davenport.

She borrowed my wig and played Peter Teazle well at the age of twelve. Those little English villages are often merely one long street, and Davenport would pick out a lodging which all the churchgoers would have to pass Sunday morning. He would dress up the infant phenomenon and make her sit dancing a big doll where she could be seen in the window, and the people would stand in groups open-mouthed in wonder at the baby who played with her doll in the morning and trod the boards at night as Macbeth. Then the family formed in procession with prayer-books in their hands and the vanity of earthly joys in their faces, and went to church. Davenport went first, his wife behind, and the phenomenon in the rear, and always managed to reach the church just after everybody else was seated, and marched up the aisle to the communion-table in a style of pure melodrama, thus attracting the attention of all to the phenomenon.

Ingenu, The, in Voltaire's story of that name (Fr. *L'Ingenu*, 1767), a young Canadian half-breed, sprung from European forefathers and a Huron mother who comes by chance to live with his surviving relatives in France. He is described as a being of impossible virtue, summing up all the best qualities of man in his natural and unsophisticated state—the satire of the story lying in the contrast between his simple and noble nature, and the meanness, hypocrisy and falsehood of the civilized beings whom he looks up to as his superiors.

Inglesant, John, hero and title of a historical romance by John Henry Shorthouse. The scene is laid in the time of Charles I. Inglesant is a sensitive, imaginative, dreamy young man with a Protestant head and a Catholic heart who has developed consummate tact through the Jesuit training intended to fit him for the task of mediator between the Catholics and Protestants in England.

The author's power as a story-teller is shown in his tacitly saying to the reader "My hero is weak, but I defy you to despise him!" The hero is, indeed, the tool of a Jesuit, but so noble a tool that we forgive him for being one; he loves a woman not by any means above the average, but because he is true to her we respect his marriage; and he is willing to die with a lie that disgraces him on his lips, that the lie may save the honor of a king whom he does not greatly love, and serve the purpose of a religious party to which he does not openly belong.—*Saturday Review.*

Ingoldsby, Thomas, the feigned editor of the *Ingoldsby Legends*, which are supposed to have been disinterred from the family chest of the Ingoldsbys.

These legends are a medley of prose and verse, the latter remarkable for their exuberant spirits and their grotesque felicities of rhyme and rhythm. The real author was Rev. Richard Harris Barham.

Inkle, Thomas, hero of the story, *Inkle and Yarico*, in Addison and Steele's *Spectator.* See YARICO.

Innes, Evelyn, heroine of a novel of that name (1898) by George Moore and of its sequel, *Sister Teresa* (1901). An impassioned young woman of odd antecedents and of great musical genius, she falls under the influences, successively, of an agnostic man of the world, of an artist and a mystic, and of a Catholic priest. Conscience drives her to give up an immoral life, enter a Catholic sisterhood, as the " Sister Teresa " of the sequel, and devote the rest of her life to penance.

Insarof, Demetri, in Tourgenief's *On the Eve,* a young Bulgarian patriot who devotes his life to freeing his country from the Turkish yoke. Elena Strashof, a brilliant, imaginative girl, an artist's model, of noble but impoverished lineage, falls in love with him. Insarof would fain break away from her lest she interfere with his self-imposed mission but she shows that she is willing to abandon home and country for his sake. The struggle between passion and patriotism, intensified by his dread of involving her in peril, ends in a dangerous illness from which he recovers long enough to marry her and then falls back into a fatal relapse. She joins the sisters of Mercy in the Bulgarian army.

Interpreter, Mr., in Bunyan's *Pilgrim's Progress,* Part I (1678), lord of a house, a little beyond the Wicket Gate, where Christian is relieved of his doubts. He may be taken as a symbol of the Holy Ghost in its action upon hearts that are well disposed.

Ionè, to whom some of Landor's early verses were addressed, was a Miss Jones. The process by which the name was hellenized is thus poetically explained in some verses of Landor's which Professor Colvin has preserved in his Life of the poet:

Ionè was the first. Her name is heard
Among the hills of Cambria, north and south,
But there of shorter stature, like herself:
I placed a comely vowel at its close,
And drove an ugly sibilant away.

Ippolito, Don, in Howells's *A Foregone Conclusion* (1875). A Venetian priest whom circumstances and not belief or inclination have forced to take orders. Not only does he chafe under a lack of faith that he acknowledges to himself and to his intimates, but he finds the priesthood an obstacle to his normal development as an inventor. Falling in love with the American, Florida Vervain, she pities him but is horrified when he declares himself, and her refusal of him is the remote cause of his death.

Irena, in Spenser's *Faërie Queene,* v (1596), a personification of Ireland. Deprived of her inheritance by Grantorto (the rebellion of 1580), Sir Artegal was dispatched to her aid and succeeded in restoring her to her own.

Irene, subject of a poem by Edgar Allan Poe, which originally appeared under that name in a juvenile volume (1831) but was later republished as *The Sleeper*—an apostrophe to the lady Irene, who lies dead upstairs, from her distracted lover, who has risen from his bed at night to pace under her casement.

Irene, heroine of *Smoke,* a novel by Ivan Tourgeneif. An unprincipled, selfish and pitiless coquette, she had jilted Litvinof for a more brilliant match, but accidentally meeting him when he is engaged to another she does all in her power to revive the old flame still smouldering in his heart. He only partly trusts her, respects her less and really does not love her. Nevertheless for her sake he breaks his betrothal vows, abandons all the purposes and hopes of his life, and but for her capricious and cowardly retreat at the last moment would have plunged with her into utter disgrace and ruin.

Irene, Countess, in Berthold Auerbach's novel, *On the Heights* (*Auf der Hohe*) (1865), a young beauty whom her father, Count Eberhard von Wildenort, a recluse, has placed in a German court. Her vivacity, intelligence and unconventional ways capture the fancy of the king, wearied as he is of the dull monotony of state and the pious sentimentality of his queen. He betrays his passion by kissing a statue of Victory for which she had sat as model. We are given to understand that she falls with him, but whether in an actual sin of sense or merely of the imagination is left to the reader to determine. At all events she is the chief sufferer. She writes her guilt to the queen and plans to drown herself but is saved by Walpurga, wet-nurse to the king's son, who takes her to her own mountain home. Here Irma for a year lives " on the heights," literally and metaphorically, occupying her time with a journal of philosophical and religious rhapsody. Finally she dies in the presence of the reconciled king and queen.

Ireson, Flood, hero of Whittier's ballad, *Skipper Ireson's Ride,* was in real life Captain Benjamin Floyd Ireson. The poem tells how the skipper for his hardheartedness in sailing away from a leaking ship in Chaleur Bay was

Tarred and feathered and carried in a cart
By the women of Marblehead.

In his *History and Traditions of Marblehead,* Samuel Roads has shown that Ireson was a much maligned man. A terrific gale was blowing when his ship *The Betty* sighted the wreck, and the crew decided not to risk their own lives for others. In vain Skipper Ireson proposed to stay by the wreck all night, or until the storm should abate, and then go to the rescue. " To this they also demurred and insisted on proceeding homeward without delay. On their arrival in Marblehead, fearing the just indignation of the people they laid the entire blame upon the skipper." Acknowledging a presentation copy of Roads' book Whittier wrote: " I have no doubt that thy version of Skipper Ireson is the correct one. My verse was solely founded on a fragment of rhyme which I heard from one of my early schoolmates, a native of Marblehead. I supposed the story to which it referred dated back at least a century. I knew nothing of the particulars and the narrative of the ballad was pure fancy. I am glad for the sake of truth and justice that the real facts are given in thy book. I certainly would not, knowingly, do injustice to any one, dead or living."

Ironsides, Old, a popular nickname for the American frigate *Constitution* launched at Boston September 20, 1797, which had won no small fame by the capture of the British *Guerriere* and other exploits in the war of 1812. In 1825 a proposal was made to break it up. Much indignation was aroused in Boston near which town, in the Charleston Navy Yard, the vessel was lying. To this public feeling Oliver Wendell Holmes, then a stripling of sixteen, gave voice in a spirited little poem, *Old Ironsides* first published in a Boston newspaper, and then circulated about the country. The verses are characteristic. The ship

No more shall feel the victor's tread
    Or know the conquered knee;
The harpies of the shore shall pluck
    The eagle of the sea.

The effect was so great that the proposal was abandoned.

Isaac of York, in Scott's historical romance, *Ivanhoe,* the father of Rebecca. Befriended by Ivanhoe he and his daughter show their gratitude by tending him when he is wounded. " Detested by the credulous and prejudiced vulgar, and persecuted by the greedy and rapacious nobility," he found that in wealth lay " the only road to power and influence." But while following this road he was " trampled down like the shorn grass, and mixed with the mire of the ways." Ultimately he and Rebecca leave England and go to live abroad.

Isaacs, Mr., in Marion Crawford's novel of that name, a study of the development of a man's higher nature through a woman. A professed Mussulman married to three wives whom he regards with kindly but contemptuous tolerance, he meets a noble and beautiful Englishwoman, Miss Westonhaugh, and falls hopelessly in love with her and she with him.

Isabella, heroine of Thomas Southerne's tragedy, *The Fatal Marriage or the Innocent Adultery* (1694), the supposed widow of Biron. Disinherited for marrying he has gone to the wars and is reported dead. After seven years, she is driven by poverty to marry Villeroy. Next day Biron returns; he is slain by the minions of his younger brother Charles, who accuses Villeroy. Isabella goes mad and dies. In 1770 a revised version of the play was brought out by Garrick as *Isabella*, and under that title it was ever afterwards acted.

The character of Isabella is well conceived and worked out with great sympathy. Her gradual yielding to the importunate advances of Villeroy, her second husband, and her grief and horror at the discovery that Biron, her first husband, is alive and has returned to her, are depicted with considerable power. The introduction of Isabella's and Biron's child is a stroke of dramatic genius and must have materially strengthened the play, as the same device has strengthened many a popular drama since. —CHARLES WHIBLEY: *The Cambridge History of English Literature,* viii, 217.

Isabella, in Shakespeare's comedy, *Measure for Measure* (1603), the sister of Claudio. She is pursued by Angelo, but even to save her brother from death, she will not yield her purity. The disguised duke, however, persuades her to a stratagem. She " assents in words " and substitutes Mariana in her stead (see MARIANA).

The plot of *Measure for Measure* is similar to that of Whetstone's drama *Promos and Cassandra* (1578), which he turned into a prose story in his *Heptameron of Civil Discourses* (1582). Before him the theme had been treated by Giraldi Cinthio in a tragedy, *Epithia*, and a novella (*Hecatommithi,* viii, 5). As Shakespeare has called his heroine Isabella and not Cassandra he is generally assumed to have borrowed from Whetstone rather than directly from Cinthio. He was less obviously indebted to Robert Greene's *Never too Late* (1590), whose heroine, Isabel, has a very similar adventure. Deserted by her husband, she is tempted and threatened by Bernardo, one of the burgomasters of the city of Caerbranck, but successfully resists him. He then has her brought before the council, of which he is executive head, and accused of adultery by a false witness whom he has suborned. Isabel is condemned and sentenced, but the witness suddenly repents of his perjury and confesses, whereupon Signor Bernardo is heavily fined and deposed from office.

Isadore, title and subject of a poem by Albert Pike, beginning

Thou art lost to me forever! I have lost thee, Isadore!

Pike claimed that Poe had plagiarized from him the metre and the motive of the poem *Lenore.*

Isbosheth, in Dryden's satirical poem, *Absalom and Achitophel* (1681), is meant for Richard Cromwell, son of Oliver, the great Protector, who is called Saul in the poem. The analogy is very close. Ishbosheth, like Richard, was the only surviving son of his father. He was accepted as king on the death of his father by all except the tribe of Judah, just as Richard was acknowledged " protector " by all except the royalists. Both ruled but a few months.

Ithuriel, in Milton's *Paradise Lost,* Book iv, the angel of truth whose spear, by the lightest touch, exposes deceit. Gabriel sends him and Zephon to find Satan who had eluded the vigilance of the angelic guards and won his way into Paradise. They found him " squat like a toad, close at the ear of Eve " whispering to her as she slept

Vain hopes, vain aims, inordinate desires
Blown up with high conceits engendering pride.
Him thus intent Ithuriel with his spear
Touched lightly for no falsehood can endure
Touch of celestial temper but returns
Of force to its own likeness; up he starts
Discovered and surprised.

The name and the character seem to have been invented by Milton. Klopstock in *The Messiah* (iii, iv) borrows both and makes Ithuriel the guardian angel of Judas, who retires when Satan enters the traitor's heart.

Ivanhoe, Sir Wilfrid, Knight of, hero of Scott's historical novel, *Ivanhoe* (1819). His father, Cedric of Rotherwood, disinherits him because of his love for Rowena, whom Cedric, as her guardian, had betrothed to Athelstane. He follows Richard I to the Crusades, returns to England disguised as a palmer and appears at a tournament at Ashby under the name of the Disinherited Knight, overthrows Bois-Guilbert and four other knights; reveals himself after he has named Rowena queen of the tournament; is still rejected by his father; finds shelter with the Jew, Isaac of York, and his beautiful daughter Rebecca, champions the latter's cause when she is accused of sorcery; accidentally overcomes Bois-Guilbert; is finally reconciled to his father and marries Rowena.

Ivanhoe, like an honorable gentleman, curbs his passion for Rebecca and is true to Rowena, though we see that the memory of Rebecca never leaves his heart. Ivanhoe

behaves as in his circumstances Scott would have behaved instead of giving way to passion. It would have been more to the taste of to-day if the hero had eloped with the fair Hebrew, but then Ivanhoe and Rebecca are persons of honor and self-control. I found in Scott's papers a letter from an enthusiastic schoolboy, a stranger— "Oh, Sir Walter, how could you kill the gallant cavalier and give the lady to the crop-eared Whig?" This was the remark of the natural man. Scott kept the natural man in subjection.—ANDREW LANG.

Ivanovitch, Ivan (literally " John Johnson "), an imaginary personage embodying the peculiarities of the Russian people in the same way that John Bull represents the English. Browning in a poem under this title (1879) makes Ivan the name of a Russian carpenter who hears a mother tell the ghastly tale of how she threw her little children to the wolves to save herself. The story is an old one but Browning adds a new end. Ivan, when the poor frightened woman had confessed, lifted up his axe and cut off her head. The mother's sin was out of Nature: the punishment should be outside of ordinary law. So thinks Ivan, so think his neighbors; so the village judge decides.

Ixe, Mademoiselle, heroine of a novel of that name (1891), by Lanoe Falconer. A Russian governess in an English family, the Merringtons, she excites suspicion by her reticence and reserve. At a ball given by the Merringtons she shoots a Russian count, a visitor in the neighborhood, with the aid of Evelyn, a daughter of the house. The count survives his wounds, Evelyn escapes, and three years later, on the occasion of her marriage, she receives a letter of congratulation from a Russian prison signed simply X.

J

Jack, Colonel, titular hero of Defoe's novel, *The History of the Most Remarkable Life and Extraordinary Adventures of the Truly Hon. Colonel Jacque, Vulgarly called Colonel Jack* (1722).

Colonel Jack is a young Arab of the streets—as it is fashionable to call them nowadays—sleeping in the ashes of a glasshouse by night, and consorting with thieves by day. Still the exemplary nature of his sentiments would go far to establish Lord Palmerston's rather heterodox theory of the innate goodness of man. He talks like a book from his earliest infancy. He once forgets himself so far as to rob a couple of poor women on the highway instead of picking rich men's pockets; but his conscience pricks him so much that he cannot rest till he has returned the money.—LESLIE STEPHENS: *Hours in a Library.*

Jacques, from Latin *Jacobus,* the French for James, which, being the most common of all Christian names in France, is used slightingly or contemptuously like the English Jack, to which it is etymologically akin.

Jacques, titular hero of a novel by George Sand.

Jacques discovers that Octave and his wife are in love with each other. There are various alternatives. He can dismiss his rival, kill him, or merely pardon him. Each alternative is a very ordinary way out of the difficulty. Jacques cannot resign himself to anything ordinary. He therefore asks his wife's lover whether he really cares for his wife, whether he is in earnest and whether the attachment will last. Satisfied with the results of this examination he leaves Fernande to Octave. He then disappears and kills himself, but he takes all necessary precautions to avert the suspicion of suicide, in order not to sadden Octave and Fernande in their happiness . . . Jacques is "a stoic." George Sand has a great admiration for such characters. Personally I look upon him as a mere simpleton.—RENÉ DOUMIC: *George Sand,* p. 88.

Jacques, Pauvre, hero of a song of that name by the Marchioness de Travanet which was highly popular for some years before the French Revolution. Marie Antoinette, when she conducted her imitation Swiss village in the Little Trianon, sent for a real Swiss girl to heighten the illusion. The stranger grew melancholy and was often overheard sighing for *Pauvre Jacques,* whereupon the queen sent for Jacques, made him marry the girl and settled a handsome dowry on the pair.

Jaffier, in Thomas Otway's tragedy, *Venice Preserved,* a protégé of the Senator Priuli, who rescues his daughter Belvidera from shipwreck and after a brief courtship marries her clandestinely. Priuli wrathfully discards them both whereupon Jaffier is induced by Pierre to join a conspiracy against the lives of the Venetian senators. Belvidera induces him to confess all to Priuli, under promise of pardon to the conspirators but Priuli condemns all to death save Jaffier. The latter slays his friend Pierre to save him from death on the wheel and then kills himself. Belvidera dies raving mad.

In Jaffier we have a vivid portrait of the man who is entirely governed by the affections, and who sways from the ardent resolution to a weakness hardly distinguishable from treachery, as friendship and love alternatively incline him. The little that we know of Otway warrants the impression that he was such a man and assuredly he could not have excited such warm interest in a character so feeble in his offence, so abject in his repentance, and in general so perilously verging on the despicable, without a keen sympathy with the subject of his portrait *Tout comprendre e'est tout pardonner.* RICHARD GARNETT: *The Age of Dryden.*

Jaggers, in Dickens's novel, *Great Expectations* (1860), a lawyer of Little Britain, Pip's guardian and Miss Havisham's man of business. A hard, logical man, suspicious of others but personally above suspicion.

There is hardly in literature a more finished specimen of the legal bully, perfect in the art of hectoring witnesses, terrifying judges, and bamboozling juries. Even when there is no case to be tried he cannot get rid of the contentiousness of mind and manner he has acquired in the criminal courts. In private conversation, where no point is to be gained, he refuses to admit anything, and cross-examines everything and everybody.— E. P. WHIPPLE.

James I of England and **VI** of Scotland (1566-1625), called by his flatterers "the English Solomon" and by Sully "the Wisest Fool in Christendom," is admirably drawn in Scott's historical novel, *The Fortunes of Nigel:*

"He was deeply learned, without possessing useful knowledge; sagacious in many individual cases, without having real wisdom; fond of his power, and desirous to maintain and augment it, yet willing to resign the direction of that, and of himself, to the most unworthy favourites; a big and bold assertor of his rights in words, yet one who tamely saw them trampled on in deeds; a lover of negotiations, in which he was always outwitted; and one who feared war, where conquest might have been easy."

In gentle King Jamie he had a model of which the grotesque absurdity needed pruning rather than exaggerating, and of all Scott's many portraits of kings the slobbering, trotting figure of James is the most truthful and the most comic.—ANDREW LANG.

James, Truthful, the supposed narrator of several of Bret Harte's poems, including *The Society on the Stanislaw* and *The Heathen Chinee.* The latter was originally published as *Further Language from Truthful James.*

Janos, the principal character in *Janos the Hero,* narrative poem (1844) by Alexander Petofi, a strange medley of epic and extravaganza based on popular traditions. A German translation by Kertbeny appeared in 1851, and an English one by Sir John Bowring.

Janos, a herdsman, dismissed in disgrace because in his love for Duska he has neglected his sheep, joins a band of Magyar Hussars, under Mathias Corvin, who are marching to aid France against Turkish invaders. They traverse Tartary, the land of the Saracens, Italy, Poland and India—the geographical confusion being in purposed imitation of the chivalrous romances—and at last reach France. In a pitched battle with the Turks, Janos slays their pasha and rescues the King's daughter from the clutches of the infidel, refuses to marry her but is richly rewarded and returns on a dragon's back to his native village to find Duska dead. Once more the Hero wanders forth, this time in heartbroken search for death, but after numerous weird adventures in Giant Land, in the Land of the Witches, etc., he reaches Fairyland, where Duska is magically restored to life and to her lover, and they are King and Queen of Fairyland to this day.

Jansoulet, hero of Alphonse Daudet's novel, *The Nabob.* He emigrates from Paris to Tunis with only half a louis in his pocket. He returns with more than twenty five millions and becomes the prey of a horde of penniless adventurers whose greed even his prodigality cannot satisfy. His dining-room in the Place Vendome is the rendezvous of projectors and schemers from all parts of the world. Finally he fails.

Jaquenetta, in Shakespeare's *Love's Labor's Lost,* a country girl who excites the jealous rivalry of Don Adriano de Armado and Costard.

Jaques, in Shakespeare's comedy, *As You Like It* (1598), one of the lords attendant on the banished duke in the forest of Arden. His soliloquy, known as the Seven Ages, occurs in Act ii, Sc. 1. Lamb in a sonnet speaks of the fair domain of Arden:

Where Jaques fed his solitary vein.

The Folio of 1623 spells the name Jaques, or rather Iaques, but other editions sanction the intercalary *c* that recognized its Latin origin in Jacobus, through the French Jacques. Shakespeare makes it a dissyllable.

Jaques is the only purely contemplative character in Shakespeare. He thinks, and does,—nothing. His whole occupation is to amuse his mind, and he is totally regardless of his body and his fortunes. He is the prince of philosophical idlers; his only passion is thought; he sets no value upon anything but as it serves as food for reflection. He can "suck melancholy out of a song, as a weasel sucks eggs;" the motley fool, "who morals on the time," is the greatest prize he meets with in the forest. He resents Orlando's passion for Rosalind as some disparagement of his own passion for abstract truth; and leaves the Duke, as soon as he is restored to his sovereignty, to seek his brother out who has quitted it, and turned hermit.—HAZLITT: *Characters of Shakespeare's Plays.*

Jaques, Maitre, in Molière s comedy, *L'Avare* (1668), a factotum playing the combined rôle of cook and coachman in Harpagon's niggardly household. Whenever he is addressed in a capacity unsuited to his costume he solemnly changes smock for livery, or vice versa—a bit of by-play that never fails to find the audience.

Jarley, Mrs., in Dickens's *Old Curiosity Shop* (1840), the merry and kind-hearted proprietor of a travelling wax-work show, " the only stupendous collection of real wax-work in the world " containing one hundred figures the size of life—" the delight of the nobility and gentry, and the peculiar pet of the royal family and the crowned heads of Europe." She befriends Little Nell and engages her to display the wax-works to visitors.

Jarndyce, John, in Dickens's novel, *Bleak House,* a kindly optimist of sixty, guardian of Richard Carstone, Ada Clare and Esther Summerson, one of the parties in the suit of Jarn-

dyce *v.* Jarndyce which has occupied
the Court of Chancery for nearly half
a century. When things went wrong
he was sure that the wind was " in
the East," but when they righted
themselves the wind was "due west."

Jarvie, Bailie Nicol, in Scott's
novel, *Rob Roy,* a kinsman of Rob's.
He is a Glasgow magistrate, and a
pawky, petulant purseproud Lowland tradesman, full of his own and
his father's local dignity, full also
of mercantile and Presbyterian for-
malities, but kindly, good-natured,
and ever humorous. " The idea of
carrying him to the wild, rugged
mountains among outlaws and desper-
adoes—at the same time that he
retained a keen relish of the comforts
of the Saltmarket at Glasgow and a
due sense of his dignity as a magistrate—completes the ludicrous effect
of the picture " (CHAMBERS: *English
Literature*). There is no known
original, but Charles Mackay of the
Edinburgh Theatre Royal fulfilled
Scott's ideal to the life. " I am not
sure," writes Scott to Joanna Baillie,
" that I ever saw anything possessing
so much truth and comic effect. At
the same time he is completely the
personage of the drama, humane and
irritable in the same moment, and
the true Scotsman in every turn of
thought and action; his variety of
feelings towards Rob Roy whom he
likes and fears and despises and admires and pities all at once is exceedingly well expressed."

Jarvis, in Edward Moore's domestic tragedy, *The Gamester,* a devoted
servant who strives to wean Beverley
from his passion for the gaming table.

Jeames, the original English form
of James, retaining that pronunciation, even after the change in spelling,
among the London flunkies and the
classes in which they moved and from
which they sprang. Hence the significance of the name in Thackeray's
burlesque, *Jeames's Diary,* the original of which is a footman who comes
into a large fortune and assumes the
name of Jeames de La Pluche.

Jeddler, Dr. Anthony, in Dickens's
Christmas story, *The Battle of Life*

(1846), a self-imagined " great philosopher," kindly at heart but reneging
his own kindliness to pose as a cynic
who looks on the world as a gigantic
joke. His daughters, Grace and
Marion, are both in love with Alfred
Heathfield, who loves Marion but is
by Marion induced to marry Grace.

Jekyll, Dr., in R. L. Stevenson's
allegorical tale of the dual personality
in man, *Dr. Jekyll and Mr. Hyde*
(1886), is an eminent and most reputable physician. Mr. Hyde is the
worser self that dwells within his
members. The doctor is genial,
handsome, loving and beloved by
society. Hyde is loathsome, skulking,
dwarfish, as evil in looks as he is in
morals. Dr. Jekyll accidentally discovers how to separate these two
personalities. When he is wearied of
the virtues of Jekyll he can become
Mr. Hyde and revel in vice until, surfeited, he welcomes a return to virtue.
All the time he is conscious that the
ape-like thing within him grows
stronger for each fresh liberation. At
last he can no more be transferred
back into Dr. Jekyll. There is no
longer a Dr. Jekyll left, only a Mr.
Hyde, waiting for the hangman, and
yet it is the soul of Jekyll that cries
frantically from the lips of Hyde.

As long as man remains a dual being, as
long as he is in danger of being conquered
by his worst self, and, with every defeat,
finds it the more difficult to make a stand,
so long Dr. Jekyll will have a personal and
most vital meaning to every poor struggling
human being. *Mutaio nomine de te fabula
narratur,* so craftily is the parable worked
out that it never obtrudes itself upon the
reader or clogs the action of the splendid
story. It is only on looking back, after he
has closed the book, that he sees how close
is the analogy and how direct the application.—CONAN DOYLE, *National Review,* vol.
14, p. 647.

Jellyby, Mrs., in Dickens's *Bleak
House* (1852). A sham philanthropist
who is not all a sham, for she succeeds
in deceiving herself as to the sincerity
of her interest in public matters and
especially in the scheme of unloading
Britain's superfluous population into
Borrioboola-Gha on the left bank of
the Niger in Africa. So entirely is
she immersed in this project that she
neglects herself and her household,

her children grow up ignorant and unkempt, and her husband becomes a bankrupt. Her eldest daughter "Caddy" (Caroline) gets so disgusted copying unending letters to uncountable correspondents that she gladly marries "Prince" Turveydrop, exchanging a life of drudgery for domestic happiness.

Jellicot, Old Goody, in Scott's *Woodstock*, servant at the underkeeper's hut at Woodstock.

Jenkins, Peter, in Mrs. Gaskell's *Cranford*, brother to the Misses Deborah and Mattie Jenkins. He runs away from home as a boy and returns to restore the family fortunes. Miss Deborah is a prim old maid, a great stickler for form and ceremony and a profound admirer of Dr. Johnson. Miss Mattie is gentle, sweet-tempered and a general favorite.

Jenkins, Winifred, in Smollett's novel, *Humphrey Clinker*, maid to Miss Tabitha Bramble.

Not even the Malapropism of Sheridan or Dickens is quite as riotously diverting, as rich in the unexpected turns, as that of Tabitha Bramble and Winifred Jenkins, especially Winifred, who remains delightful even when deduction is made of the poor and very mechanical fun extracted from the parody of her pietistic phraseology. That it could ever have been considered witty to spell "grace" "grease," and Bible "byebill," can only be explained by the indiscriminate hostility of the earlier assailants of Enthusiasm.—AUSTIN DOBSON, *Eighteenth Century Vignettes*, ii, 140.

Jenkinson, Dr., in W. H. Mallock's satire, *The New Republic* (1877), is meant as a caricature of Dr. Benjamin Jowett (1817–1893), Master of Baliol College, Oxford, and translator of Plato. Dr. Jenkinson preaches a latitudinarian sermon barely distinguishable, if at all, from out-and-out infidelity, which it is said annoyed Dr. Jowett very much.

Jenkinson, Ephraim, in Goldsmith's *Vicar of Wakefield*, a swindler who imposes upon Dr. Primrose by his venerable appearance, his piety, his fluent talk about "cosmogony," and his approval of the vicar's pet theory concerning monogamy.

Jenkinson, Mrs. Mountstuart, in George Meredith's *The Egoist*, a widow, wealthy, clever and domineering, who rules society in the county where Sir Willoughby Patterne lives.

Jennico, Basil, in *The Pride of Jennico* (1898), a novel by Agnes and Egerton Castle, a young Englishman who inherits the castle of Tollenddhal in Bohemia on condition that he shall marry none but a woman of noble blood. Accident throws in his way the Princess Marie Ottilie and her waiting maid who have exchanged characters in a mad prank, and the novel shows how he married the disguised princess through that lady's stratagem although he had wooed and won the substitute.

Jenny, subject of a short poem by D. G. Rossetti, an analysis of the life and feelings of a courtesan. The poem is uttered in the person of one who has half accidentally dropped again into a momentary companionship, such as had once been too familiar with him, and soliloquizes over the poor mercenary beauty who has fallen into the unexpected slumber of pure weariness.

Jermyn, Matthew, in George Eliot's *Felix Holt*, a lawyer, the father of Harold Transome, and himself secretly married to Mrs. Transome.

Jerome, Edwards, hero of Mary Wilkins Freeman's novel, *Jerome*. A poor young man with no apparent prospects. he promises that he will give away to the town poor all his wealth if he ever makes it. Two incredulous rich men, taunted by the jibes of the company, declare that if within ten years he receives and gives away as much as $10,000 they on their side will give away to the poor one-fourth of their property. Jerome comes into a fortune, keeps his promise, and the rich men fulfil their agreements.

Jeronimo or **Hieronymo,** hero of a play of that name by Thomas Kyd, and its sequel, *The Spanish Tragedy* (1597). His verbal peculiarity is to address himself—"Go by, Jeronimo"—when things happen awry. This expression caught the fancy of Elizabethan playgoers and was multitudinously caricatured by Elizabethan playwrights.

Hostess: You will not pay for the glasses you have burst?
Sly: No, not a denier. Go by, Jeronimy, go to thy cold bed and warm thee.
SHAKESPEARE: *Taming of the Shrew, Induction.*

Jess, heroine of a novel of that name by H. Rider Haggard (1887). The scene is laid mainly on an ostrich farm in the Transvaal during the first Boer insurrection in 1880. The main incident of the story is the hackneyed one of two lovers who sacrifice their own happiness for the sake of a third who has the conventional right of prior engagement. Jess and Captain Niel are doubtless actuated by heroic motives in renouncing each other because Niel is affianced to Bessie, the baby-faced sister of Jess, but a more reasonable solution of the same problem has been presented by Howells in *The Rise of Silas Lapham.*

Jessica, in Shakespeare's *Merchant of Venice,* the daughter of Shylock, who elopes with Lorenzo and carries off with her a casket full of money. Thus she prompts the agonized cry " My daughter and my ducats! " which may have suggested to Molière a remote analogy in Harpagon's lament for *les beaux yeux de ma casette.*

Jim, Lord, the title of a novel (1900) by Joseph Conrad and the sobriquet of its hero.

A young officer in the mercantile marine whose courage is tempered by too much imagination, he momentarily loses his head in a dire emergency, is cashiered, and seeks to redeem himself and recapture his ideals by a career of self-devotion among the savages of Malaysia.

Jingle, Alfred, in Dickens's *Pickwick Papers* (1836) a swindler of easy manners, affable address, and abounding impudence who for a time imposes upon the members of the Pickwick Club. His conversation is a hurried jumble of staccato phrases. Henry Irving made a great success of the part of Jingle in a dramatization of the *Pickwick Papers.*

Jiniwin, Mrs., in Dickens's *Old Curiosity Shop,* the mother of Mrs. Quilp.

Jip, in Dickens's *David Copperfield,* the pet dog of Dora Spenlow.

Joan (see DARBY). Joan is sometimes the name of Punch's wife though she is usually called Judy. Discredited legend tells of a mythical Pope Joan, a disguised female who is said to have reigned as Pope John VIII (855–858) and to have died in childbirth during a public procession.

Joan of Arc (Fr. *Jeanne Darc*), known to history as the Maid of Orleans from her chief exploit in relieving the city of Orleans of its English besiegers May, 1429. She crowned Charles VII at Rheims, July 17, 1429, and then, her mission accomplished, would fain have returned to her mother. Charles prevailed on her to remain. But now the militant girl prophetess, hitherto so strangely successful, failed in almost everything. Only sixteen months after her first appearance at Vaucouleurs to announce her mission to Robert de Baudricourt she was taken prisoner by the English at Compiègne. On May 30, 1431, she was burned at the stake as a witch. Her extraordinary career and the peculiar combination in her of simplicity and shrewdness, of fire and gentleness, of the peasant girl with the mystic and the saint, have made her a favorite study of dramatists, poets and romancers. Early English slander portrayed her as a termagant sorceress, even Shakespeare—if Shakespeare did write the First Part of *Henry VI* in which she appears—reviled her as " a railing Hecate." Worse than all her own countryman, Voltaire, vilely slandered her in *La Pucelle* (written 1738, published 1755), the most disgraceful poem ever written by a man of European influence. Posterity has done her justice. History has cleared her name. Her personality, so strong, pure and simple, emerges from the fiercest light of criticism without a serious blot. Poetry and fiction have supplemented history. The German Schiller led the way in his tragedy, *The Maid of Orleans* (*Jungfrau von Orleans*), and a great transatlantic humorist, Mark Twain, has brought up the rear in a historical romance, *Personal Recollections of Joan of Arc* (1896). The American feigned that this was an authentic memoir written by " the Sieur Louis de Conte, her Page and Secretary."

Joblilies. A nonsense word invented by Samuel Foote. See PANJANDRUM.

Jocelyn, in Alphonse Lamartine's poem of that name, a young student of divinity cast out of Paris by the Revolution, who takes up his abode in a cave. Here he harbors two other refugees, one of whom, Laurence, turns out to be a girl. He flees from temptation, becomes curate of a small Alpine village, whither in his old age Laurence, now a great lady but weary of the penalties of greatness, comes to make her last dying confession.

Jocelyn, Rose, in George Meredith's novel, *Evan Harrington*, a high-spirited girl, daughter of the kindly and sensible Lady Jocelyn. She meets Evan in Portugal and eventually marries him.

Joe, the Fat Boy, in Charles Dickens's *Pickwick Papers*, Mr. Wardle's page, who could be waked up to duty but invariably went to sleep again. " Damn that boy, he's asleep again! " is a favorite expression with Mr. Wardle and his friends. Mr. F. G. Kitton tells us that the original of this character was probably one James Budden, whilom landlord of the Red Lion Inn in Military Road, Chatham.

John, Don, in Shakespeare's *Much Ado About Nothing* the bastard brother of Don Pedro, Duke of Arragon—

He is composed and framed of treachery.

He trumps up a false accusation against Hero on the eve of her marriage.

John, Dr., the nickname of Graham Bretton, in Charlotte Brontë's novel, *Villette*, the brilliant physician for whom Lucy Snowe cherishes a " one-sided friendship " which she describes as " half marble, half life,"—indignantly repelling any accusation of " warmer feelings." According to the autobiographic heroine this paragon was " handsome, bright-spirited and sweet-tempered, a curled darling of Nature and of Fortune "—possessing in short all the graces which had been denied herself—" born a conqueror as some are born conquered."

In *Villette* my mother was the original of Mrs. Bretton; several of her expressions are given verbatim. I myself, as I discovered, stood for Dr. John. Charlotte Brontë admitted this to Mrs. Gaskell, to whom she wrote: "I was kept waiting longer than usual for Mr. Smith's opinion of the book and I was rather uneasy, for I was afraid he had found me out and was offended.— SIR GEORGE MURRAY SMITH: *In the Early Forties, N. Y. Critic,* vol. 38, p. 59.

John, Friar, in Rabelais's romance, *Pantagruel,* an unclerical cleric whose gluttony, debauchery and unquenchable high spirits furnish much of the fun of the book. When an army from Lerne pillaged his convent vineyard Friar John seized a cross and pummelled the rogues without mercy, beating out their brains, smashing their limbs, cracking their ribs, gashing their faces, breaking their jaws and dislocating their joints (*Gargantua* i, 27). He is an inseparable companion of Panurge in the search for the oracle of the Holy Bottle.

Throughout the book, he dashes on, regardless of every thing in this world or the next. If there is a shipwreck or a skirmish, Friar John is foremost in the bustle; fear is unknown to him; if a joke more than usually profane is to be uttered, Friar John is the spokesman. The swearing, bullying phrases are all put in the mouth of Friar John. Rabelais loved this lusty friar, this mass of lewdness, debauchery, profanity, and valor. He is the "fine fellow" of the book; and the author always seems in a good humor when he makes him talk.— *For. Qu. Rev.*

John, King, hero of a play (1595) of that name by Shakespeare, the first of his historical dramas. An earlier drama on the same subject, *The Pageant of King John,* by Bishop Bale (supposed to be written in the reign of Edward VI), was bitterly and even brutally polemic in its anti-popery bias. Shakespeare's play is founded upon *The Troublesome Reign of King John* (1591), which is some-sometimes attributed to him, but in the later version he has toned down or rejected all that could be offensive to Catholics.

So long as John is the impersonator of England, of defiance to the foreigner, and opposition to the Pope, so long is he a hero. But he is bold outside only, only, politically; inside, morally, he is a coward, sneak and skunk. See how his nature comes out in the hints for the murder of Arthur, his turning on Hubert when he thinks the murder will bring evil to himself, and his imploring Faulconbridge to deny it.—F. J. FURNIVALL, editor, *The Leopold Shakespeare.*

Johnstone, Christie, in Charles Reade's novel of that name (1855), a female vender of fish in Newcastle, England, whose native refinement, brightness and generous impulses end in her capture of an artist, Charles Gatty, after having captivated a peer—Viscount Ibsden.

Jones, Tom, hero of a novel by Henry Fielding, *The History of Tom Jones, a Foundling* (1749), whose character is meant to be representative of the typical young Englishman of the period, a generous, good-natured, free-living youth, prodigal and profligate, hating only lies and hypocrisy, honest and truthful in his ordinary habit but with no sensitive scruples of conscience in accepting anything that was offered him in the way of pleasure or profit, however tainted in origin or degraded by association.

I cannot say that I think Mr. Jones a virtuous character; I cannot say but that I think Fielding's evident liking and admiration for Mr. Jones show that the great humorist's moral sense was blunted by his life, and that here in art and ethics there is a great error. . . . A hero with a flawed reputation, a hero sponging for a guinea, a hero who cannot pay his landlady, and is obliged to let his honor out to hire, is absurd, and his claim to heroic rank untenable."—THACKERAY.

José, Don, in Byron's *Don Juan,* the husband of Dona Inez and father of Juan.

Josiana, Lady, heroine of Victor Hugo's historical romance, *The Man Who Laughs* (Fr. *L'Homme qui Rit,*

1869). A natural child of James II of England whom the King had made a duchess in her cradle and betrothed (with the additional stimulus of a magnificent dowry) to Lord David Dirry Moir. At the age of 23 she still spurned the matrimonial yoke, not from coldness of temperament but from mingled pride and love of freedom.

Bold yet inaccessible, "a possible Astarte in a real Diana," Josiana had sounded every depth but fallen into none. Everything about her was two-fold. She had one eye blue, the other black. Light and darkness, good and evil, love and hate, mingled in her very looks. Lovers she had none in the flesh, yet she was not chaste of spirit. She possessed every virtue without any innocence. Men she disdained; she yearned for a god or a monster. Failing the god, accident threw in her way the alternative of her dreams. This modern Titania fell in love with Gwynplaine (*q.v.*).

Josselyn, hero of George Du Maurier's novel, *The Martian,* a brilliant youth who comes under the influence of the invisible Egeria, a visitor from Mars, and dwindles into a vague abstraction. .

Jouarre, Abbess of, the name of a drama by Ernest Renan (1888), and the semi-official title of its heroine, Julie de Saint Florent. She is in love with the Marquis d'Arcy, who loves her. In the dark hours of the French Revolution both are condemned to the guillotine. Left alone in their last moments, natural impulses over-master conventional canons. Julie succumbs to the arguments of the marquis that the laws of chastity which they have hitherto respected are no longer binding. Those laws were invented merely for the sake of future generations. As no future, no marriage, no family, no children exist for these lovers there is nothing to stand in the way of the closest union. "Assigned to a most imminent death we are free; the laws established in view of the necessities of a durable society exist no longer for us. Very soon we shall be in the absolute of truth, which knows neither time nor place. Let us anticipate the hours, dear Julie." The lovers pass to the death cart radiant with a perfect happiness which seems to them a foretaste of heaven. But, at the very last, he alone is sent to death while she is spared. In an agony of despair she attempts her life but fails. She lives to become a mother, and in after years the wife of the young nobleman who had snatched her from death.

Jourdain, Monsieur, the principal character in Molière's comedy, *Le Bourgeois Gentilhomme* (1670). An elderly tradesman, ill-educated and ill-bred, who has suddenly acquired great wealth, he is filled with the desire to educate himself in accordance with his new station in life. So he hires an entire corps of professors. Dancing master, fencing master, professor of music, etc., all play upon his vanity and help to expose his follies and his weaknesses to the audience. M. Jourdain is particularly astonished to learn from his professor of philosophy that for forty years he has been speaking prose without knowing it.

Joyce, in Mrs. Oliphant's novel of that name (1888), is a gracious figure, gentle-born and peasant-bred, cultured through her natural attraction for whatever is noble, and sympathetic as she would not have been by a more artificial training.

Juan, Don, the arch libertine of European literature, whose popularity is second only to that of Faust, the arch sceptic. His legend has a remote basis in fact. Don Juan Tenorio, member of an illustrious Seville family in the fourteenth century, killed Commander Ulloa after seducing his daughter Giralda. A statue of Ulloa placed above his tomb in the convent of St. Francis was destroyed by an incendiary. The monks, suspecting the Don, are said to have lured him into the convent and killed him. They encouraged or connived at the wild stories which crystallized around the memory of

the prodigal. These first took literary shape in a drama by Tirso de Molino (Gabriel Tellez, 1626) entitled *Ee Burlador de Seville y el Convidado de piedra (The Blasphemer of Seville or the Stone Guest).* We are here shown how the sensual excesses of Don Juan so undermined his faith in God or devil that he brazenly visited the commander's tomb and invited his statue to sup with him. The statue accepts, keeps the appointment and in return bids Don Juan sup with him on the morrow. When the Don appears at the rendezvous, the statue seizes him by the hand, and amidst thunderings and flashes of lightning, the earth opens and swallows him up.

The story passed into Italy, was dramatized at Naples by Onofreo Giliberti (1652), appeared in France (1658) in a translation of Giliberti's drama, and definitely assumed its place among the great masterpieces of literature when Molière produced his *Festin de Pierre* (1665). In Molière's hands Don Juan becomes the type of the hardened and irreclaimable yet brilliant and fascinating libertine, the literary ancestor of all the modern race of seducers from Lothario to Lovelace. His own servant Sganarelle describes him as " the wickedest man that ever trod this earth—a madman, a dog, a devil, a Turk—a heretic fearing neither heaven, nor saint, nor God, nor hobgoblin, spending his life like a mere brute-beast, a hog of Epicurus, a regular Sardanapalus." Nevertheless Juan's high courage, his gallant bearing, his light-hearted grace make one almost forget the wickedness which is so constantly and steadily pursued that it excites a bastard admiration.

From the dramatic stage the character passed to the operatic in Mozart's *Don Giovanni* (1787). Byron took the name but not the legend for his own *Don Juan (q.v.)* a very different character. Very different also is the hero of Browning's *Fifine at the Fair (q.v.).*

Juan, Don, titular hero of a satirical and narrative poem by Lord Byron, in sixteen cantos. Cantos 1 and 2 were published in 1819, Cantos 3, 4 and 5 in 1821, Cantos 6, 7, 8 and 9, 10, 11 and 12, 13, 14 at different dates in 1823, and Cantos 15 and 16 in 1824.

Byron's Don Juan has little in common with the Don Juan of legend except the name. He is a young Spanish grandee, who having been seduced into an amour with a married woman older than himself, is obliged to flee from her husband. His ship founders at sea and he is cast upon a little island in the Ægean. Here he is succored by Haidee, a Greek girl with whom he falls in love. Their union is celebrated by splendid festivities, in the midst of which Lambro, the pirate-father of Haidee, who had been given up for dead, suddenly reappears. Juan is disarmed, carried to Constantinople and sold for a slave. His purchaser is the Sultana, Gulbayez, who introduces him, disguised, into the seraglio (see DUDU). Afterwards he escapes, arrives before the city of Ismail, then besieged by the Russians, distinguishes himself in the storming of that place and is sent as special messenger to convey the news to the Empress Catherine. He rises so far in the favor of the Court of St. Petersburg that he is appointed ambassador to England. The poem abruptly ends with a number of satirical pictures of life and society in the latter country.

Jubal, titular hero of a poem by George Eliot (1874) founded on the Old Testament story of the son of Lamech and Adah who invented the " harp and organ."

Jubal invents the lyre, teaches his tribe how to use it, and then wanders away in quest of new musical inspiration. Returning, an old man, he finds the people celebrating his anniversary and glorifying his name, but when he declares himself they treat him as a lunatic and cast him out into the desert.

The immortal name of Jubal filled the sky
While Jubal, lonely, laid him down to die.

Jude the Obscure, the familiar nickname of the hero of Thomas

Hardy's novel, *Jude the Obscure.* An orphan brought up by his great aunt Miss Fawley, he assists her in her bakery and then becomes apprentice to a stonemason, dreaming dreams, meanwhile, of college and a great career. His life is wrecked by an entanglement with Arabella Donn who traps him into mismated matrimony. The girl he loves, Sue Bridehead, marries the village schoolmaster but leaves him for Jude. When both get a divorce Sue objects to a legal tie. The couple have two children of their own and with them bring up the morbid sensitive son of Jude's first marriage who ends by hanging himself after murdering the other offspring. Sue remorsefully returns to her schoolmaster and Jude to Arabella. Jude dies in an effort to reach Sue again.

Julia, in Shakespeare's *Two Gentlemen of Verona* (1594), a young woman who disguises herself as a page, accompanies Proteus on a journey, and so wins back that recreant lover.

Here first Shakespeare records the tender and passionate history of a woman's heart, and the adventures to which love may prompt her. Julia (who is like a crayon sketch of Juliet, conceived in a way suitable to comedy instead of tragedy) is the first of that charming group of children of Shakespeare's imagination which includes Viola, Portia, Rosalind and Imogen—women who assume, under some constraint of fortune, the disguise of male attire, and who while submitting to their transformation forfeit none of the grace, the modesty, the sensitive delicacy, or the pretty wilfulness of their sex.—E. DOWDEN: *Shakespeare Primer.*

Julia, a more or less imaginary sweetheart whom the Rev. Robert Herrick (1591–1674) addressed or alluded to in amatory poems so decidedly unclerical in tone that Cromwell in 1648 ejected him from his church living, thus reducing him to the grade of Robert Herrick, Esq.

Mr. Gosse assures us that Julia really walked the earth and even gives us some details of her mundane pilgrimage; other critics smile and shake their heads and doubt. It matters not, she lives and will continue to live when we who dispute the matter lie voiceless in our graves. The essence of her personality lingers on every page where Herrick sings of her. His verse is heavy with her spicy perfumes, glittering with her many colored jewels, lustrous with the shimmer of her silken petticoats.— AGNES REPPLIER: *Points of View: English Love Songs* (1891).

Julia, heroine of *The Hunchback* (1832), a drama by Sheridan Knowles. The scene is laid in the time of Charles I. Julia, brought up as the ward of a hunchback named Master Walter, in unsophisticated ignorance of her own origin and of the world at large, falls in love with and engages herself to Sir Thomas Clifford. A season of fashionable frivolity in London turns her head, she breaks with Sir Thomas and is affianced to a young man who poses as the Earl of Rochdale. Sir Thomas loses his fortune and becomes the humble dependent of the Earl. He appears on the appointed marriage day to announce the coming of his master. Julia breaks down and announces that it is he whom she had always loved. Then the hunchback appears and discloses that he is the true Earl of Rochdale, the father of Julia, and the secret mover of an elaborate plot to recall her to the right path.

Julian, one of the two interlocutors in Shelley's poem, *Julian and Maddalo.* He stands for Shelley himself —as Maddalo stands for Byron.

Julian, Count, semi-mythical hero of a legend which has been versified in Scott's *Vision of Don Roderick,* Southey's *Don Roderick,* and Walter Savage Landor's *Count Julian.* He was one of the principal lieutenants of Roderick the Goth (*q.v.*), but when that prince violated his daughter Florinda or Cava, Julian allied himself with Musca, the Caliph's lieutenant in Africa, and countenanced the invasion of Spain by a body of Saracens and Africans, commanded by Tarik, from whom Jebel Tarik, Tarik's Rock—that is, Gibraltar—is said to have been named. The issue was the defeat and death of Roderick and the Moorish occupation of Spain. A Spaniard, according to Cervantes, may call his dog, but not his daughter, Florinda.

Juliana, heroine of John Tobin's comedy, *The Honeymoon.* See ARANZA, DUKE OF.

Julie, heroine of Jean Jacques Rousseau's sentimental romance, *Julie ou la Nouvelle Héloise* (1760), who was drawn from an actual flame of his own, the Countess d'Houdetot. Rousseau himself, under the name of Saint Preux, figures as the modern Abelard, in love with his pupil, but too honorable to play the part of Abelard. His highborn pupil loves him in return, but they are parted and she marries M. de Wolmar, who is better suited to her in rank and wealth. Later the lover is invited to return and he lives with the married couple in Arcadian simplicity and innocence. See SAINT PREUX.

Juliette, in George Sand's romance, *Leone Leoni* (1835), an infatuated young girl who follows over Europe the most faithless, unscrupulous and ignoble, but also the most irresistible of charmers.

It is *Manon Lescant,* with the incurable fickleness of Nanon attributed to a man; and as in the Abbé Prévost's story the touching element is the devotion and constancy of the injured Desgrieux, so in *Leone Leoni* we are invited to feel for the too closely clinging Juliette who is dragged through the mire of a passion which she curses and which survives unnamable outrage.—HENRY JAMES.

K

Kaled, in Byron's poem, *Lara* (1814), a boy page in attendance on the hero. When the latter is slain by an arrow it turns out that the page was a girl in male disguise:

He saw the head his breast would still sustain,
Roll down like earth to earth upon the plain;
He did not dash himself thereby, nor tear

The glossy tendrils of his raven hair,
But strove to stand and gaze, but reeled and fell,
Scarce breathing more than that he loved so well.
Than that *he* loved! Oh! never yet beneath
The breast of *man* such trusty love may breathe!
That trying moment hath at once revealed
The secret long and yet but half concealed;
In baring to revive that lifeless breast,

Its grief seemed ended, but the sex con-
fessed;
And life returned,—and Kaled felt no
shame—
What now to her was Womanhood or Fame?
Lara, Canto ii, l., 1151.

Karénina, Alexis, in Tolstoy's
novel, *Anna Karénina* (1869), the
unloved husband of the heroine.

A bureaucrat, a formalist, a poor creature,
he has conscience; there is a root of goodness
in him, but on the surface and until deeply
stirred he is tiresome, pedantic, vain, ex-
asperating . . . Alas! even if he were
not all these, perhaps even his pince-nez
and his rising eyebrows, and his cracking
finger joints would have been provocation
enough!—MATTHEW ARNOLD: *Essays in
Criticism.*

Karénina, Anna, heroine and title
of a novel by Count Lyof Tolstoy
(1869, English translation 1886).
A Russian noblewoman, young and
beautiful and emotional, she is married to a man much older than herself.
Count Vronsky, a young officer of
superficial brilliancy, falls in love with
her and she with him, and the story
deals with her struggles against temptation, her eventual yielding, her
raptures, her terrors, her despair and
final suicide.

Karol, Prince, in George Sand's
novel, *Lucretia Floriani* (See FLORI-
ANI), was evidently drawn from François Chopin, with whom the authoress
lived for eight years.

It may have been to the glory of Prince
Karol to resemble Chopin, but it was also
quite creditable to Chopin to have been the
model from which this distinguished neuras-
thenic individual was taken . . . What
concerns us is that George Sand gives with
great nicety the exact causes of the rupture.
In the first place, Karol was jealous of
Lucretia's stormy past; then, his refined
nature shrank from certain of her comrades
of a rougher kind. The invalid was irritated
by her robust health, and by the presence,
and we might almost say the rivalry of the
children. Prince Karol finds them nearly
always in his way, and he finally takes a
dislike to them. There comes a time when
Lucretia finds herself obliged to choose between the two kinds of maternity, the
natural kind and the maternity according
to the convention of lovers.—RENÉ DOUMIC:
George Sand.

Karshish, in Robert Browning's
poem, *An Epistle, containing the
Strange Medical Experience of Karshish* (*Men and Women*, vol. i, 1855),
an Arab physician who meets the
risen Lazarus and reports his version

of the miracle to his teacher Ahib.
He strives to display no more than a
scientific interest in the story as a
mere case of mistaken trance, yet his
imagination is haunted by the mental
transfiguration of the man who in
his own belief has brought back into
time eyes that have looked upon
eternity, and he cannot repress a
mysterious awe at the bare possibility
of the truth of the story.

Keeldar, Shirley, the heroine of
Charlotte Brontë's novel, *Shirley*
(1849), a young woman of free and
independent spirit, loving nature,
hating shams and conventions, joining feminine wilfulness to a will-
power more than masculine.

The heroine is Emily Brontë as she might
have been if the great god Wunsch who
inspires day dreams had given her wealth
and health. One might as readily fancy the
fortunes of a stormy sea petrel in a parrot's
gilded cage. Shirley cannot live with Jane
Eyre.—ANDREW LANG: *Good Words*, vol.
xxx, p. 239.

Kehama, hero of an oriental legend
which Southey has versified in his
epic poem, *The Curse of Kehama*
(1809). Mighty lord of earth and
heaven, he claimed dominion also
over hell but was punished for his
presumption by being condemned to
" the immortality of death," and in
this state to become the fourth supporter of the throne of Yamen the
Mahommedan Pluto. See LADURLAD.

Kenneth of Scotland, in Scott's
romance of the Crusades, *The Talisman,* the name assumed by David,
Earl of Huntington, when as an obscure adventurer he enters the service
of Richard Cœur de Lion in Palestine.
He is also known as the Knight of the
Sleeping Leopard from the device on
his shield. Though in the opening
chapter he fights bravely against
Saladin (disguised as Sheerkohf) and
later signalizes himself in a secret
mission to the hermit Theodorick, he
falls a victim to a practical jest played
by Queen Berengaria, is surrendered
to Saladin by Richard, returns disguised as the mute Nubian slave
Zohauk, a present from Saladin, saves
Richard's life from the dagger of an
assassin, successfully champions his

master's cause in a trial by combat with the traitor Conrade of Montserrat, and being acclaimed under his true name becomes the avowed suitor of Edith of Plantagenet whom he had ever loved.

Kent, Earl of, in Shakespeare's tragedy, *King Lear,* is banished by Lear for remonstrating against his treatment of Cordelia, but under the guise of Caius, a servant, follows the King in his misfortunes and brings about the meeting with Cordelia in the final scene.

Kent is perhaps the nearest to perfect goodness in Shakespeare's characters, and yet the most individualized. There is an extraordinary charm in his bluntness, which is that only of a nobleman arising from a contempt of overstrained courtesy and combined with easy placability where goodness of heart is apparent.—COLERIDGE.

Kenwigs, Mr. and **Mrs.,** in Dickens's *Nicholas Nickleby,* an ivory turner and his wife who for various reasons looked upon themselves as highly genteel and were generally looked up to as desirable acquaintances. Their daughters were pupils of Nicholas Nickleby.

Kenyon, in Hawthorne's *Marble Faun,* a New England sculptor resident in Rome where he falls in love with Hilda.

Mrs. Elizabeth Akers Allen, whose first husband was Paul Akers, furnished this note to the correspondents' column of the New York *Sun* in November, 1891: "While it is true that W. W. Story's statue of Cleopatra is mentioned in the *Marble Faun,* it is also true that the Pearl Diver and the grand calm head of Milton commented on at some length in the dialogue between Miriam and Kenyon in his studio were not works of Story but of the late Paul Akers, a personal friend of Hawthorne in Rome, a native of the same state and an artist in whose studio Hawthorne often passed a social hour. In his preface to the *Marble Faun* Hawthorne expressly speaks of Mr. Akers and credits these marbles to him. In the text of the romance the personal description of Kenyon is a portrait of Mr. Akers.

Kerouec, Alain de, Marquis de Rochebriante. The principal character in Bulwer-Lytton's novel, *The Parisians,* a young aristocrat bred in the great traditions of his house who cannot fraternize with the flippant *jeunesse dorée* of the metropolis. Although impoverished by his father's extravagance he never dreams of selling his chateau or going to work for a living. What he does do is to marry the daughter of a great financier.

Keyber, Conny, a nickname which Henry Fielding applied to Colley Cibber in *The Author's Farce* (1731). A burlesque of *Pamela* entitled *An Apology for the Life of Mrs. Shamela Andrews* (1741), whose pretended author is "Mr. Conny Keyber," is attributed to Fielding, and the attribution is all the more plausible because at that date it would seem that Fielding believed Cibber to be the author of *Pamela* (see Dobson's *Samuel Richardson,* pp. 43–45).

Killingworth, originally Kenilworth, a town in Connecticut founded 1663 which is probably the scene of Longfellow's poem, *The Birds of Killingworth.*

I found among his papers a newspaper cutting—a report of a debate in the Connecticut legislature upon a bill offering a bounty upon the heads of birds believed to be injurious to the farmers, in which debate a member from Killingworth took part. The name may have taken his fancy and upon this slight hint he may have built up his story.—SAMUEL LONGFELLOW: *American Notes and Queries,* v, 198.

Kilmansegg, Miss, heroine of Thomas Hood's satirical poem, *Miss Kilmansegg and her Golden Leg,* an heiress with great expectations and with an artificial leg of solid gold.

Who can forget her auspicious pedigree, her birth, christening and childhood, her accident, her precious leg, her fancy ball, her marriage *a la mode,* followed in swift succession by the Hogarthian pictures of her misery and death.—E. C. STEDMAN: *Victorian Poets,* p. 80.

Kim, the nickname of Kimball O'Hara, hero of Kipling's novel *Kim* (1901), a precocious little vagabond of Irish parentage, orphaned when a baby and left to shift for himself in the depths of the native quarter of Lahore. He meets a Thibetan priest, Tesleo Lama, who is seeking the All-healing River of the Arrows or Stream of Immortality, becomes his disciple, and roams through India in his company. Eventually Kim is recognized, reclaimed and adopted by the Irish regiment to which his father belonged.

His apprenticeship to the secret service gives him unique insight into the shady walks of Anglo-Indian life.

King of the Mountains, hero of a novel by Edmond About (1856) exposing the brigandage and maladministration of modern Greece. The narrative is placed in the hands of a young German, who with two ladies, the wife and daughter of a London banker, are represented as falling into the hands of the king of the mountains —a brigand named Hadji Stauros.

Kirkwood, Maurice, in O. W. Holmes's novel, *A Mortal Antipathy* (1885), a young man of good presence and good family, suffering from a singular malady. As a child he had been dropped from the arms of a girl cousin. Ever after, the presence of a beautiful woman caused a violent derangement of the heart's action and endangers life. He cherishes the hope that as like cures like some lovely woman may lift the curse from his life. His hope is justified.

Kite, Sergeant, in Farquhar's comedy, *The Recruiting Officer* (1706). By sheer audacity and vulgar aplomb he coaxes, wheedles or bullies recruits into the army. Thoroughly frank in self-understanding and self-description he says of his own characteristics— "the whole sum is: canting, lying, impudence, pimping, bullying, swearing, drinking, and a halberd."

Kitty, the name under which Matthew Prior celebrated Catherine Hyde (1700–1777), who in 1720 married the third Duke of Queensbury and is also famous as the patron of Gay and Swift. She was high-spirited and whimsical—a spoiled child, a beauty and a wit at odds with the tyrannous conventions of her time—but her character was unblemished. Bolingbroke called her *La Singularité.* Walpole spoke of her frankly as " an out-pensioner of Bedlam." Yet four years before her death her still triumphant charms extorted from this most persistent of her detractors the following *amende*:

> To many a Kitty, Love his car
> Will for a day engage,
> But Prior's Kitty, ever fair
> Obtained it for an age!

Klesmer, Herr, in George Eliot's *Daniel Deronda* (1876), a German musician, poor and proud and of high ideals, who teaches Gwendoleth Harleth and incidentally seeks to convert her to the doctrine of hard work and self-sacrifice.

Knight, Henry, the second lover of Elfrida in Hardy's novel, *A Pair of Blue Eyes* (1873). He is an author, inclined to Quixotry and even priggishness, a little stilted and something of a purist in his notions about women.

Knight is a genuine man, and it is not his fault if he is uninteresting in proportion as he is literary. Since Pendennis and Warrington, many personages of our calling have figured in fiction, and they have nearly all been bores; and some blight of tiresomeness seems in novels to fall upon a class who in life are so delightful. It is to be said of Knight, that he is something more than the conventional literary man of fiction; but he at no time gives us the sense of entire projection from the author's mind that Stephen Smith does, and that, in a vastly more triumphant way, Elfrida does. He remains more or less dependent, more evidently a creature of the plot; but he very imaginably serves as the object of Elfrida's adoring love, after her heart has helplessly wandered from its first ignorant choice.—W. D. HOWELLS in *Atlantic Monthly*, October, 1873.

Knight of the Burning Pestle, a title assumed by the hero of a burlesque of that name (1611) by Beaumont and Fletcher. Like Don Quixote, which was translated in 1612, the satire is aimed at the exaggerations and affectations of the tales of chivalry. In a play within a play Ralph, a grocer's boy, sallies out in quest of adventures. "Hence my blue apron!" he cries. "Yet in remembrance of my former trade, upon my shield shall be portrayed a burning pestle, and I will be called the Knight of the Burning Pestle."

Krook, Mr., in Dickens's *Bleak House,* the drunken proprietor of a rag and bone shop, who died under circumstances that suggested spontaneous combustion.

Kunigunde, in German legend the Lady of the Kynast, and in French annals the heroine of the story of *The Glove,* which Schiller has versified. See LORGE, DE.

L

Lacy, Sir Hugo de, in Scott's novel, *The Betrothed,* Constable of Chester and Lord of the Marches, a crusader and " one of the most redoubted warriors of the time." He left his betrothed, Lady Eveline Berenger, under the protection of his nephew, Sir Damian de Lacy, and returned after three years to find she had married the nephew.

Randal de Lacy in the same novel is a remote kinsman of Sir Hugo, " a decayed reveller," who turns up at intervals in various disguises, a merchant, a hawkseller, a robber captain.

Ladislaw, Will, in George Eliot's novel, *Middlemarch* (1872), a clever, good-natured and easy-going Bohemian who flirts with Rosamund Vincy though in love with Dorothea, and who marries the latter after she has been widowed by the death of Casaubon.

Ladislaw is almost obtrusively a favourite with his creator. He is called "Will" for the sake of endearment; and we are to understand him as so charming that Dorothea's ability to keep him at a distance gives the most striking proof of her strong sense of wifely duty. Yet Ladislaw is scarcely more attractive to most masculine readers that the dandified Stephen Guest. He is a dabbler in art and literature; a small journalist, ready to accept employment from silly Mr. Brooke, and apparently liking to lie on a rug in the houses of his friends and flirt with their pretty wives. He certainly shows indifference to money, and behaves himself correctly to Dorothea, though he has fallen in love with her on her honeymoon. He is no doubt an amiable Bohemian, for some of whose peculiarities it would be easy to suggest a living original, and we can believe that Dorothea was quite content with her lot. But that seems to imply that a Theresa of our days has to be content with suckling fools and chronicling small beer.—SIR LESLIE STEPHEN: *George Eliot.*

Ladurlad, in Southey's epic, *The Curse of Kehama* (1809), incurred that curse by killing Kehama's son Arvalan for attempting to dishonor his daughter Kailyal. The curse had manifold clauses, among them that water should not wet him nor fire consume him nor sleep bless him nor death release him. In the end the curses turned to blessings for by them he was enabled to release his daughter from a burning pagoda, to deliver her lover Lorrimite from his captivity

under the ocean, and to wreak vengeance against Kehama in hell. When Kehama drank the cup of " immortal death," Ladurlad was taken up to paradise.

Lady of the Lake, in Arthurian romance, a name sometimes given to Vivien, mistress of the enchanter Merlin. Her palace was situated in the midst of a delusive lake, a mirage whose mere semblance protected it from approach. Scott has given the same name to Ellen Douglas, heroine of his poem, *The Lady of the Lake,* a former favorite of King James IV of Scotland, then living in banishment in a secret retreat in Loch Katrine.

Ladylift, Elinor, in Mrs. Archer Clive's novel, *Why Paul Ferrol Killed his Wife,* the girl with whom Ferrol (*q.v.*) was in love, though he was inveigled into marrying Laura Chanson in her stead.

Laertes, in Shakespeare's tragedy, *Hamlet,* brother to Ophelia and son of Polonius, a young courtier, gallant and courteous enough when things go well with him, but easily jarred by adversity so that his naturally choleric temper bursts out into noisy rhodomontade and he can even be persuaded into treachery. The king induces him to fight Hamlet in a sham duel with a poisoned foil. After he has inflicted a deadly wound the foils are accidentally exchanged; thus Laertes and Hamlet both perish.

La Fayette, Louise de (1616–1665) was for two and a half years the closest friend and confidante of Louis XIII, but retired to a convent when he proposed to make her his mistress. On this episode Madame de Gentis founded a historical romance *Mlle. de La Fayette* (1813), which gives only the platonic side of the story, paints Louise in glowing colors, hides as far as possible the weakness and imbecility of Louis, and presents Richelieu as the hypocritical knave and Boisenval as the traitor of melodrama.

Lagado, in *Gulliver's Travels* (1726), by Dean Swift, the capital city of Balnibari, a continent subject to the

King of Laputa. Here stands the great academy of inventors and projectors, engaged in all sorts of fanciful schemes, ridiculing the speculative philosophers and pretenders of Swift's own day. Some seek to extract sunshine from cucumbers, to calcine ice into gunpowder, to build houses from the roof down, etc. But Swift's greatest scorn is ironically reserved for a set of political projectors who were proposing schemes for persuading monarchs to choose favorites on the score of wisdom, capacity and virtue, for teaching ministers to consult the public good and for ensuring the rewards of life to eminent services and great abilities.

La Garaye, Countess of, heroine of a poem by Hon. Mrs. Norton, *The Lady of La Gayare* (1862). A newly-wedded and most devoted wife, she insists on accompanying the count to the hunting field and there meets with an accident which cripples her for life. Her only fear is that she will be unable to hold the affections of her husband, but he removes her doubts by word and deed.

Laird's Jock, The. See ARM-STRONG, JOHN.

Lajeunesse Gabriel, in Longfellow's poem, *Evangeline*, the lover of the titular hero. See EVANGELINE.

Lalla Rookh, titular heroine of Moore's poem of that name (1817). Daughter of the great Aurengzebe, she is betrothed to Aliris, the young King of Buchuria, and sets out to meet him in the Valley of Cashmere. Her journey is beguiled by four tales recited to her by Feramorz, a young Persian poet with whom she falls in love. Great is her delight on arriving at her journey's end to find that the poet is in reality her affianced prince.

Lambro, in Byron's *Don Juan* (Canto iii), the father of Haidee and a Greek pirate who has built himself a home on "one of the wild and smaller Cyclades." Coleridge praises this as one of the finest of all Byron's characters. There was a real Major Lambro, captain in 1791 of a Russian piratical squadron which plundered the islands of the Greek archipelago

and was attacked by seven Algerine corsairs. Major Lambro was wounded but escaped with his life.

"Upon the whole, I think the part in *Don Juan* in which Lambro's return to his home, and Lambro himself, are described, is the best—that is, the most individual—thing in all I know of Lord B.'s works. The festal abandonment puts one in mind of Nicholas Poussin's pictures."—COLERIDGE.

Lamia, in Keats's narrative poem of that name (1820), a serpent who assumes the form of a fair lady and wooes to his own destruction a young man of Corinth. Keats found the story in Burton's *Anatomy of Melancholy* who gives it on the authority of Philostratus (*De Vita Apollonii*, Bk. iv). According to Philostratus Menippus Lycius, a young man of twenty-five was met on his way between Cenchreas and Corinth by a phantasm of this sort who carried him home to her house in the suburbs of Corinth.

The young man, a philosopher, otherwise staid and discreet, able to moderate his passions, though not this of love, tarried with her a while to his great content, and at last married her, to whose wedding, amongst other guests, came Apollonius; who, by some probable conjectures, found her out to be a serpent, a lamia; and that all her furniture was, like Tantalus's gold, described by Homer, no substance but mere illusions. When she saw herself described, she wept, and desired Apollonius to be silent, but he would not be moved, and thereupon she, plate, house, and all that was in it, vanished in an instant: many thousands took notice of this fact, for it was done in the midst of Greece.—BURTON: *Anatomy of Melancholy*, part 3, sect. 2, memb. 1, subs. 1.

Lammle, Alfred, in Dickens's novel, *Our Mutual Friend* (1864), a "mature young gentleman with too much nose on his face, too much ginger in his whiskers, too much torso in his waistcoat, too much sparkle in his studs, his eyes, his buttons, his teeth." He married Miss Sophronia Akersheim, "a mature young lady with raven locks and complexion that lit up well when well powdered." Each imagined that the other was wealthy and both were bitterly disillusioned after marriage.

Lancelot or **Launcelot of the Lake,** the most famous of the Knights of the Round Table. Son of King Ban of Brittany, he received his surname from having been stolen in infancy by Vivian, the Lady of the Lake, who brought him up in her own palace until he was about eighteen, and then took him to the court of King Arthur to be knighted. He won for himself the reputation of being the greatest warrior and the most accomplished Knight of the Round Table. The one blot upon his name was his adulterous passion for Queen Guinevere, which not only brought misery into his own life, but according to Tennyson was eventually the cause of the death of King Arthur and the breaking up of the Round Table.

Tennyson has taken the traditions in regard to Lancelot and infused into them a depth of meaning quite out of the reach of the old romancers. He has given us no grander conception than that of the erring knight in the *Idylls of the King.*

The moment this strong, sad, tender, heroic figure comes upon the scene the whole atmosphere is changed. He is the embodiment of truth itself warped into falsehood, honor itself turned into dishonor. We have no glimpse of Lancelot in the first triumph and feverish exultation of his sin. He has found it all out, its enormity of evil, its bitterness, its growing and gathering mesh of falsehoods, its kindred with everything that is most opposed to all the impulses of his nature, before he becomes known to us. It is a bondage which he cannot break. Were he even strong enough to break it, his loyalty to Guinevere could not brook that he should be the first to suggest such a severance. He is her slave to do her will, in that great wondering shame and pity which amid all his love he has for the woman who has yielded to him. Never from him can the word of parting come. His honor is rooted in dishonor, his faith unfaithful is beyond the touch of change. He moves about that court where every man suspects him but Arthur, his face marred and his spirit veiled by the shadow of his sin, in everything but this spotless as Arthur's self, the soul of knightly nobleness and grace. —*Blackwood's Magazine.*

Langeais, The Duchess of, heroine of Honoré de Balzac's novel of that name. Montriveau, a man mature in all save knowledge of the world and of women, is suddenly thrown into dangerous intimacy with the Duchesse de Langeais, whose luxurious leisure tempts her to practise all her arts of seduction, but whose native coldness protects her against the moral dangers of such a pastime. Gradually they change places, the Duchess against her will is drawn into a real love, but Montriveau had learned her true character and contrives a terrible revenge. The original of the character is said to have been Balzac's quondam friend, The Duchess de Castries.

Langham, Edward, in Mrs. Humphry Ward's novel, *Robert Elsmere,* an Oxford tutor whose excellent qualities of head and heart are neutralized and rendered almost abortive by morbid shyness, introspection and indecision. Mark Pattison (see CASAUBON) has been suggested as the original of this character, but Mrs. Ward explained in a subsequent introduction that it was drawn from her conception of Amiel, whose *Journal* she had recently translated.

Langham owes his being entirely to the fact that in 1885 I had published a translation of Amiel's "Journal Intime." Some of the phrases in the description of Langham are taken or paraphrased from the "Journal Intime." And yet, of course, Langham is no more Amiel than Grey is T. H. Green as soon as he enters the little world of the novel.—MRS. HUMPHRY WARD in *McClure's Magazine.*

Languish, Lydia, in *The Rivals,* a comedy (1775) by Richard Brinsley Sheridan, a beautiful heiress, the object of the titular rivalry between Bob Acres and "Ensign Beverley." She is a gushing and romantic young lady, full of high-flown fancies borrowed from the current heroines of fiction, and with an unhealthy imagination that despises the robust commonplace of life and seeks to be wooed and won in some novel and startling fashion. Knowing this, Captain Absolute assumes the name of Ensign Beverley in order to court her in the manner she desires. With his revelation of himself in his true character everything ends happily.

Laon, hero of Shelley's juvenile poem, *The Revolt of Islam* (1817). An enthusiast for civil and religious liberty, he inculcates with his own principles the beautiful and high-spirited Cythna, who unconventionally surrenders herself to him. Othman the tyrant seizes Cythna for his harem, she escapes, finds Laon bound to the stake and perishes with him by her own wish. The poem was originally published under the title *Laon and Cythna,* and in this first edition Shelley made hero and heroine brother and sister, " not," says Symonds, " because he believed in the desirability of incest, but because he wished to throw a glove down to society and to attack the intolerance of custom in its stronghold."

Lapham, Irene, in *The Rise of Silas Lapham* (see below), daughter of Silas. Beautiful and intelligent, she is sensitive about the plebeian ways of her parents, but bears her troubles in silence and is equally undemonstrative and self-sacrificing when Tom Corey whom she loves, declares his passion for her sister.

Lapham, Silas, the principal character in W. D. Howells' novel, *The Rise of Silas Lapham* (1885).

His big hairy fist, his ease in his shirtsleeve, his boastful belief in himself, his greed, his coarseness, his mixture of ignorance and shrewdness, his queer glimmerings of sensitiveness not only to the call of conscience but to the finer issues of honor, make him a typical self-made American sprung from obscurity—as Balzac's Cæsar Birotteau is a typical Frenchman of like origin. Each also is a business man whom success floats to the crest of the wave only to let him be overwhelmed by disaster, and each—broken, beaten, bankrupt—develops in his feebleness a moral strength he had not known in his days of power.

Silas Lapham is one of the great triumphs of modern fiction. He is a type, and yet he is intensively individual. John T. Raymond, who personated Colonel Sellers all over the United States for several seasons, once told me that there was scarcely a town in which some man did not introduce himself to the comedian as the original of Sellers, saying, "Didn't Mark ever tell you? Well, he took Sellers from me!" And there is scarcely a town in New England or in that part of the Middle West which was settled from New England in which there is not more than one man who might claim to be the original of Silas Lapham. Strong, gentle, pushing, pertinacious, bragging un-

consciously, scrupulous with the scrupulousness of the New England conscience, provincial, limited in his ideas, and yet not hostile to the light in so far as he can perceive it, Silas Lapham is an American type which has never before been so boldly presented.—BRANDER MATTHEWS: *London Saturday Review.*

Laputa, in *Gulliver's Travels* (1726), a flying island inhabited by scientific quacks so immersed in their own thoughts that attendants called Flappers were appointed to strike them with blown bladders on the mouth and ears to bring them back to a realization of the world around them.

Lara, hero and title of a narrative poem by Lord Byron (1814). A chief, long absent from his own domain, he returns unheralded, accompanied by a single page. The mystery that surrounds him is increased by his proud isolation, his weariness of the world, his scowling contempt for his fellow-men, his aloofness from the very people with whom he associates.

Born of high lineage, linked in high command,
He mingled with the Magnates of his land;
Joined the carousals of the great and gay,
And saw them smile or sigh their hours away;
But still he only saw, and did not share,
The common pleasure or the general care.

At a banquet given by his neighbor, Lord Otho, a stern stranger, Sir Ezzelin, accuses him of being—what or whom? The words Ezzelin would have spoken are stopped in mid flow. A duel is arranged for—but Ezzelin is never seen again. Lara is subsequently slain in heading a rebellion. His page Kaled turns out to be a girl in boy's clothes, and dies of a broken heart. It is hinted that on the eve of the appointed duel with Ezzelin a peasant had witnessed the concealment of a body. The reader is left to his own inferences. Was Lara none other than Conrad the Corsair? Was Kaled, Gulnare? Was it Lara or Kaled who had gotten rid of Ezzelin? Any of these surmises will fit the given facts.

Lariat, The, in Mark Twain's jocose book of travels, *Innocents Abroad,* one of his fellow pilgrims who, having a

15

fondness for writing doggrel, instals himself as Lariat (Laureate) of the journey. The portrait was drawn from a real personage, Bloodgood H. Cutter (1817–1900), a Long Island farmer who published some very poor verses. Having inherited a fortune sufficient to gratify his passion for travel he could pack up and start at a moment's notice. His house at Littleneck, Long Island, came under the hammer after his death and revealed an eccentric collection of curios gathered by himself from all parts of the world.

Larpent, Lady Louisa, in Miss Burney's novel *Evelina*, an excellent specimen of the die-away lackadaisical ladies of quality that frequented the old watering places of England.

Lars, hero of a narrative poem, *Lars, A Pastoral of Norway*, by Bayard Taylor; a Norwegian peasant. Yielding to the custom of his people he fights a duel, seriously wounds his adversary and, thinking he has killed him, flees to Pennsylvania, where he adopts the Quaker faith. Years after he returns to Norway to destroy the tyrannous custom of the duello.

Lasca, hero and title of a poem of the great American west, by Frank Desprez.

Last, Dr., a character in Foote's satirical play, *The Devil on Two Sticks*, originally acted with great success by Weston. Long after the play itself, as a complete work, had vanished from the stage the scenes in which Dr. Last appears lingered as a farcical interlude. The name and the character were borrowed by Isaac Bickerstaffe in *Dr. Last in his Chariot* (1769), an adaptation of Molière's *Le Malade Imaginaire*.

Latimer, Darsie, hero of Scott's novel, *Redgauntlet* (1824), supposed to be the son of Ralph Latimer, but eventually discovered to be Sir Arthur Darsie Redgauntlet, heir to the family estates.

Launce, in *The Two Gentlemen of Verona* (1592), a clownish servant to Proteus, much addicted to puns and conceits.

Launce, accompanied by his immortal dog, leads the train of Shakespeare's humorous clowns: his rich, grotesque humanity is worth all the bright fantastic interludes of Boyet and Adriano, Costard and Holofernes, worth all the dancing doggrel or broad-witted prose of either Dromio.— E. DOWDEN: *Shakespeare Primer.*

Laura, heroine of Byron's poem, *Beppo.*

Laurence, Friar, in Shakespeare's *Romeo and Juliet*, a Franciscan friar who marries the lovers (ii, 6) and gives Juliet a sleeping potion (iv, 1.)

The reverend character of the friar, like all Shakespeare's representations of the great professions, is very delightful and tranquillizing, yet it is no digression but immediately necessary to the carrying out of the plot.—COLERIDGE.

Laurie, Annie, heroine of the famous Scotch song by William Douglas (written about 1705), was a real character, the eldest daughter of Sir Robert Laurie. The poet wrote the words of this song during the progress of his courtship which was unsuccessful, for Annie married James Fergusson of Craigdarrock in 1709 and became the mother of Alexander Fergusson, the hero of Burns' poem, *The Whistle.* Douglas himself was the hero of a popular song, *Willie was a Wanton Wag.*

The air that now accompanies the words of *Annie Laurie* is of comparatively recent origin. It was composed by Lady John Scott. A touching incident in connection with the song is told in Bayard Taylor's, *An Incident in the Camp.*

Lavengro, hero of George Borrow's semi-fictitious autobiography, *Lavengro the Scholar, the Gipsy, the Priest* (1851), and its sequel *The Romany Rye* (1857). The two books describe Borrow's wanderings over Great Britain and Ireland, his strange adventures, literary struggles in London, vagrancy with gypsies, etc., all with a veil of mystery purposely thrown over them so as to blend romance and realism in an enchanting fashion.

Lavinia, heroine of an episode in Thomson's *Seasons, Autumn* (1730). She is the daughter of Acasto, to whom Palemon, a young squire, owes his fortune. Acasto, dying, leaves Lavinia and her mother destitute; she comes among the gleaners in Acasto's fields, he sees her and falls in love with her, but fights against the prospect of a mesalliance, until he discovers that she is the daughter of his old friend and patron, when he proposes and is accepted. The story is evidently inspired by the old Testament story of Ruth.

Lavinia, in Shakespeare's *Titus Andronicus,* daughter of Titus, becomes the wife of Bassanius, is dishonored and mutilated by the Goths (ii, 3, 5) and is killed by her father (v, 3).

Lawrence, Lazy, hero of one of Miss Edgeworth's stories in *Parent's Assistant* who is adequately described by this nickname. Probably the author had in mind a popular chapbook entitled *The Infamous History of Sir Lawrence Lazie,* the hero of which was arraigned under the laws of Lubberland for having served the Schoolmaster, his Wife, the Squire's Cook and the Farmer. Sir Lawrence successfully explained away the treasons laid to his charge.

Lawson, Sam, a shrewd, illiterate, shiftless, humorous Yankee villager, the supposed narrator of the stories collected in *Old Town Folks* (1869) by Mrs. Harriet Beecher Stowe. With all his worthlessness he has amusing streaks of God-fearing piety and law-abiding reverence for magistrates and dignities.

Leandre. Three of Molière's characters bear this name—the rival of Lélie in *L'Etourdi,* the son of Geronte in *Les Fourberies de Scapin,* and the lover of Lucinde in *Le Médecin Malgré Lui.*

Lear, Lir, or **Lier,** a mythical king of Britain, especially notable in literature as the hero of Shakespeare's tragedy, *King Lear* (written 1605, printed 1608). The success of Shakespeare's play prompted the publication of the older play on which it was founded, doubtless with the hope that it might be passed off for Shakespeare's. The title page ran: *The True Chronicle History of King Leir and his three Daughters, etc., as it has been divers and sundry times lately acted.* Its last appearance on the stage had been in 1594. This play is not a tragedy; it ends happily in accordance with the original legend wherein Cornel'a defeats her sisters and reinstates her father on the throne. The germ of the story appears in the *Gesta Romanorum,* the hero being a Roman emperor. It was first transferred to the mythical British king by Geoffrey of Monmouth in his *Chronicle.* Thence it passed into various lamentable ballads describing the death of King Leyr and his Three Daughters of which the catastrophe probably suggested to Shakespeare his own tragic conclusion.

Learoyd, a Yorkshire private in an Indian regiment, the companion of Mulvaney and Ortheris, in *Soldiers Three* and other tales and sketches by Rudyard Kipling.

Of these three strongly contrasted types the first and the third live in Mr. Kipling's pages with absolute reality. I must confess that Learoyd is to me a little shadowy. . . . It seems as though Mr. Kipling required, for the artistic balance of his cycle of stories, a third figure, and had evolved Learoyd while he observed and created Mulvaney and Ortheris, nor am I sure that places could not be pointed out where Learoyd, save for the dialect, melts undistinguishably into an incarnation of Mulvaney.—EDMUND GOSSE: *The Century.*

Leatherstocking, the nickname under which Natty Bumppo (*q.v.*) appears in Cooper's novels, *The Pioneers* and *The Prairie.* He has other nicknames in other books of the series, but as this represents him in his maturity and age it has become most closely identified with him. Hence the five novels are known to the public and to the book trade as the Leatherstocking Series.

Leatherstocking is indeed a most memorable and heroic yet pathetic figure, as living and impressive almost as any we know, and we should be sorry to believe that the world will ever willingly let die the delightful books which tell of his battles, his friendships, his unhappy love, his integrity and grand simplicity of character, his ungrudging sacrifices for others, his touching isolation and his death on the lonely prairie. American fiction has no other such character.—*London Spectator.*

Lecks, Mrs., one of the heroines of Frank R. Stockton's mock serious extravaganza, *The Casting Away of Mrs. Lecks and Mrs. Aleshine* (1886). Two elderly New England ladies, in a wreck which they had discounted in advance, are thrown into the sea and floated there for some days on life-preservers. Their housewifely pre-science had provided them with all the necessaries and some of the lux-uries suitable for the emergency. From their pockets they produced Westphalian sausages, carefully canned and bread hermetically sealed and ship biscuit and a bottle of whiskey, without which Mrs. Lecks declared that she never travelled—not to mention the fact that both ladies had put on black stockings having heard that sharks never snapped at colored people.

Lecoq, Monsieur, a detective who figures brilliantly in Gaboriau's novel of that name and its sequel, *The Honor of the Name.*

Sherlock Holmes might have taught Lecoq many little dodges, but Lecoq was by far the greater intellect—an intellect that moved in larger curves on a higher plane, for in the sequel especially he had to unravel the threads of a vast and compli-cated politico-social intrigue rooted in the national life of France.—*Saturday Review.*

Lecouvreur, Adrienne, a famous French actress (1690–1760), whose house in Paris became the resort of the best society including the ladies of the court. She not only succeeded in raising her profession, hitherto scorned, to something like esteem, but she revolutionized the mannerism and artificiality of the contemporane-ous stage and introduced the natural and unaffected delivery ever since cultivated by her successors. Eugene Scribe and Legouvé made her the heroine of a tragedy, *Adrienne Le-couvrier* (1849), which was adapted by Fanny Davenport in *Adrienne the Actress* (1853). The story turns upon the love of Maurice de Saxe for Adrienne, who at first knows him only as an officer without fame or rank, whom she loves for himself alone. She has a terrible rival in the Prin-cesse de Bouillon, a woman who stops at nothing to gain her own ends, and who finally poisons Adrienne by means of a bouquet, which is made to appear a present from Maurice de Saxe. The dramatists make her a passionate, loving, worthy woman, on whom the artificial life of the stage has exercised no perceptible influence, capable under the influence of jeal-ousy of forgetting for a while most self-imposed restraints, but incapable of any action that is not defensible from the code of feminine morality which is accepted by the majority of women, or that springs from any degrading motive.

Lee, Annabel, subject of a lyric of that name by E. A. Poe, in which he celebrates his love for his childwife Virginia Clemm and his despair over her early death. The poem originally appeared in the *New York Tribune* on October 9, 1849, two days after Poe's death. In 1851 Poe's friend, Thomas H. Chivers of Georgia (1807–1858), published a collection of poems, *Eonchs of Ruby,* in which appears a poem called *Rosalie Lee,* that has a far-off resemblance to Poe's lyric. It is impossible to say which was written first.

Lee, Simon, hero and title of a poem by Wordsworth. The poet sees old Simon Lee at work on the root of an old tree, and helps him to get over a difficulty. The old man thanks him. The incident suggests nearly a hundred lines, the whole history of Simon being sketched, and the sorrow of bleak age shown stealing over the brightness of youth and the power of manhood.

Le Fevre, a poor lieutenant whose death is related in *The Story of Le Fevre,* an episode in Sterne's novel, *The Life and Opinions of Tristram Shandy.*

Legeia, heroine and title of a short story by E. A. Poe.

Legeia, the devoted wife of the narrator of the story, holds the theory which was a favorite with Bulwer, that will ought to be able to conquer death. She, however, dies of con-sumption but apparently haunts her successor, the second wife, till the latter dies of the mere oppression on her spirits. Then by a vast spiritual effort, the tentatives of which are attended with ghastly physical effects, Legeia enters the dead body of her rival and for one brief moment brings back the exhausted organism to life in her own person. Legeia was a favorite name with Poe. He had already used it in his juvenile poem, *Al Aaraf*:

> Legeia, Legeia,
> My beautiful one,
> Whose lightest idea
> Will to melody run.

See LIGEA.

Legend, Benjamin, known familiarly as Ben without prefix or affix, in Congreve's *Love for Love* (1695), the prodigal son of Sir Sampson Legend, who runs away to sea and becomes a common sailor, kindly at heart but rough in exterior, full of picturesque sea-slang and harmless oaths like " Mess! " This was Bannister's favorite character.

What is Ben—the pleasant sailor which Bannister gives us—but a piece of satire . . . a dreamy combination of all the accidents of a sailor's character, his contempt of money, his credulity to women, with that necessary estrangement from home? . . . We never think the worse of Ben for it, or feel it as a stain upon his character.—C. LAMB.

Legend, Valentine, hero of Congreve's comedy *Love for Love* (1695), a young Cambridge man, a lover of the classics and eke of pleasure, who, partly out of pique because Angelica, the beautiful heiress, will not marry him, has wasted all his fortune and is reduced to the husks of the prodigal son.

Legree, Simon, in Mrs. Stowe's novel, *Uncle Tom's Cabin* (1853), a slave dealer and slave-driver brutalized to callousness by the exigencies of his trade. Though he dies a harrowing death in this novel, Thomas Dixon resuscitates him in *The Leopard's Spots* and " reconstructs " him as a Republican leader under the carpet-bag régime.

Leicester, Robert Dudley, Earl of, a historical character (1532–1588), who forfeited the love of Queen

Elizabeth by his marriage to Amy Robsart (*q.v.*). He is the hero of Scott's romance, *Kenilworth*.

Leigh, Sir Amyas, hero of Charles Kingsley's historical romance, *Westward Ho! or the Voyages and Adventures of Sir Amyas Leigh in the Reign of Queen Elizabeth* (1855). He is a trifle over-muscular but he is also a man endowed with strong poetic feelings, a keen sensibility to all beauty of art and nature and an amiability that is only disturbed when he meets or when he merely thinks of the Spaniards whom it is his object in life to drive off the face of the earth—and the sea.

The gigantic Amyas Leigh was the legitimate parent of a lusty progeny, which has become a considerable nuisance in these latter days. He was, for example, the undoubted ancestor of Guy Livingstone and a host of huge blundering male animals of the heavy dragoon species, with a "most plentiful lack of discretion," and a terrible superfluity of muscular development. . . . And thus Mr. Kingsley's dislike for the excesses of asceticism or sentimentalism, and generally for a stunted and one-sided development of human nature, was easily pressed into the service of people who were anxious to develop the inferior instincts at the expense of the superior. Moreover, there is no more annoying form of affectation than the affectation of simplicity; and Mr. Kingsley's frequent denunciations of morbid self-consciousness made some of his disciples too obtrusively and demonstratively unconscious of themselves. It is hard to be fair to him when we are suffering from the excess of the qualities which he admired. And yet we must admit that, when the balance is rightly struck, there is really something to be said for the genuine Amyas Leighs. Manliness and simplicity are after all good qualities, thought the factitious imitations of them are detestable. And in Mr. Kingsley's pages they were certainly not intended to imply any predominance of merely physical excellence.—*Saturday Review*, January 30, 1875.

Leigh, Aurora, heroine of a narrative poem of that name (1856) by Mrs. E. B. Browning. The brilliant daughter of an Englishman by an Italian mother, she is orphaned at an early age, is disinherited by her father's will and after many vicissitudes marries Romney Leigh, the high-minded cousin who had involuntarily supplanted her in the possession of the family estate.

Leila, in Byron's narrative poem, *The Giaour* (1813), the beautiful slave of the Caliph Hassan, who falls in love with the titular hero, escapes from the seraglio, is overtaken and cast into the sea. Another Leila appears in Byron's *Don Juan* (Canto viii). A Turkish child, Juan rescues her at the siege of Ismail and takes her first to St. Petersburg and then to London, where the adventures of both come to an abrupt close.

Lelia, heroine of a romance, *Lelia* (1833), by George Sand, a beautiful woman who having been once deceived has foresworn love and laughs at men. She plays a cruel joke upon Stenio (*q.v.*) by substituting for herself in a pretended assignation her own sister Pulcherie (*q.v.*), a courtesan who is her physical double. She turns a deaf ear to all the advances of Magnus, a priest whose faith cannot cure him of his passion for her. Stenio ends by committing suicide. Magnus, driven mad by the austerities he has imposed upon himself, slays Lelia.

Lelie, the titular " blunderer " in Molière's comedy *L'Etourdi*, which is imitated from Nicolo Barbieri's *L'Inavvertito* and has in turn been imitated by Dryden in *Sir Martin Marall*, by Mrs. Centlivre in *Marplot*, and others. Lelie is a conceited and scatterbrained youngster whose capacity for blundering confounds all the schemes devised by his ingenious and unscrupulous valet to secure the person of the slave girl Clélie. Mascarille (*q.v.*) cajoles, lies, and thieves with indefatigable perseverance and marvellous adroitness; but each new plan is foiled, almost in its inception, by the stupidity of the marplot in whose behalf he labors.

Lenore, heroine of a lyric poem of that name by Edgar A. Poe, and, in the same poet's *Raven*, the name of the " rare and radiant maiden " whose death has plunged the hero into gloom.

Lenore, heroine of a German ballad of that name by Gottfried August Burger, which has been translated by Sir Walter Scott, D. G. Rosetti and many others of less note. Her lover dies and she blasphemously cries for him to come to her, he appears at night in ghostly form, places her behind him on his spectral steed and rides madly to the graveyard where their marriage is celebrated by a crew of howling goblins. In one form or other the story is common to most European nations. Burger confesses his obligations to an old Dutch ballad. See also ALONZO THE BRAVE.

Leonato, in Shakespeare's *Much Ado about Nothing* (1600), governor of Messina and father of Hero. Merry, light-hearted and indulgent, he is weakly credulous when scandal assails his daughter.

Leoni, Leone, the titular hero of a romance by George Sand (1835), an infamous young seigneur, a swindler and a libertine, with a special penchant for the women of the pavement. He yet succeeds in inspiring Juliette, who tells the story, with a passion that sweeps away all scruples and triumphs over all revolts of conscience.

The subject of the story is the sufferings of an infatuated young girl who follows over Europe the most faithless, unscrupulous and ignoble, but also the most irresistible of charmers. It is *Manon Lescaut* with the inconceivable fickleness of Manon attributed to a man, and as in the Abbé Prévost's story the touching element is the devotion and constancy of the injured and deluded Desgrieux, so in Leone Leoni we are invited to feel for the too closely-clinging Juliette who is dragged through the mire of a passion which she curses and yet which survives unnamable outrage.—H. JAMES.

Leontes, King of Sicilia in Shakespeare's *A Winter's Tale*, the husband of Hermione, whom he unjustly suspects of infidelity and casts away from him.

Besides the ripe comedy, characteristic of Shakespeare at his latest . . . there is also a harsh exhibition in Leontes of the meanest of the passions, an insane jealousy, petty and violent as the man who nurses it. For sheer realism, for absolute insight into the most cobwebbed corners of our nature, Shakespeare has rarely surpassed this brief study which in its total effect does but throw out in brighter relief the noble qualities of the other actors beside him, the pleasant qualities of the play they make by their acting.— ARTHUR SYMONS: *Henry Irving Shakespeare*, vol. II, p. 320.

Leporello, in Mozart's opera of *Don Giovanni* (1787), usurps the place of Sganarelle as valet to Don Juan. The name is first heard of on the mimic stage in Shadwell's drama of *The Libertine* (1676).

Lerouge, Claudine, the *corpus delicti* in Émile Gaboriau's detective novel *L'Affaire Lerouge*. A woman of worthless character, she has been the nurse of an illegitimate son of the Count of Commarin by a mistress whom he adored. The Count bribes her to substitute the infant for his legitimate heir by a wife he dislikes. She was baffled by her husband, an honest suitor, but the Count thinks the substitution has been effected. The bastard, when he grows up, plots to assert his pretended rights and first finds it necessary to rid himself of the former nurse. Hence the murder of Claudine Lerouge, which needs all the detective skill of Lecoq to unravel.

Lescaut, Manon, titular heroine of a novel by the Abbé Antoine Prévost, a female profligate of winning grace and beauty and perennial gayety and good humor. Des Grieux, a youngster at college, sacrifices brilliant prospects to elope with her. Although strongly attached to him she is vain, reckless, luxurious. To provide for her wants she descends to the most disgraceful expedients, while he becomes a gamester and a cheat and assists Manon in extorting money from her base admirers. Finally an ill-concerted fraud throws Manon into the clutches of the law. She is convicted and transported to New Orleans. Her lover follows her despite all the efforts of his family and friends. In the new world they reform and give a striking example of constancy and devotion until Manon's death. See DES GRIEUX, CHEVALIER.

The amiable chevalier Des Grieux and the seductive Manon meet by accident, fall mutually in love and abandon their families to elope together, never thinking there is ought else but love. Falling soon into poverty, one makes a commerce of her charms, the other learns to cheat at cards. How do these two characters inspire such lively interest, carried at last to the highest degree? It is because there is, here, passion and truth; because this woman, always faithful to Des Grieux even in betraying him, who loves nothing better than him, who mingles so great a charm with her infidelities, whose

voluptuous imagination, whose graces, whose gaiety have taken so strong a hold upon her lover—because such a woman is as seductive in fiction as in fact. The enchantment that surrounds her by the author's art never leaves her even in the cart that carries her to the hospital.—LA ROUSSE: *Grand Dictionaire Universelle.*

Lesley, Bonnie, in Robert Burns's song of that name, was in real life Miss Leslie Baillie, one of the two daughters of an Ayrshire gentleman. Father and daughters called upon the poet at Dumfries when on their way to England. Burns mounted his horse, rode with the travellers for fifteen miles and composed the song on his return home. William Black, in his novel *Kilmeny*, makes Bonnie Leslie the pet name of his heroine.

Lestrange, Nelly, the autobiographical heroine of Rhoda Broughton's novel, *Cometh up as a Flower* (1868).

She smells neither of bread and butter nor of the stables, two almost equally odorous extremes between which the heroines of most English novels vibrate, and is at the widest removed from the metaphysical and strong-minded nondescripts affected by our writers. She is merely a very genuine little girl, innocent, passionate and with a genius for loving, the story of whose love and troubles is told with a simplicity and truth to nature which we think quite exceptional. —*N. Y. Nation.*

Lesurques, Joseph, the hero of a drama, *Le Courrier de Lyon*, 1850 (*The Lyons Mail* incorrectly translated by Charles Reade, 1854, as *The Courier of Lyons*) founded on fact by Eugene Moreau, in collaboration with Sirandan and Delacour. Even the real names of the leading characters are retained. On April 27, 1796, the Lyons mail coach was attacked between Melun and Lieussant by robbers who shot postilion and courier. Five years later, Dubosc, the leader of the gang, was guillotined. In the interim the innocent Lesurques had been convicted and executed on circumstantial evidence, which included an extraordinary resemblance to the murderer. The French drama inexorably follows every tragic detail. The English version alters the catastrophe; Lesurques is saved at the last moment and Dubosc is sent to the gallows. The play has always been a favorite on the French stage because it affords excellent opportunity to a versatile and melodramatic actor who assumes the double part of the criminal Dubosc and the upright, courageous Lesurques.

Levi, Isaac, in Charles Reade's novel, *It is Never too Late to Mend* (1856), a representative of the better class of Jews who had hitherto been scurvily treated in English fiction. From the Jew that Shakespeare drew to those of Thackeray and Dickens none wins our cordial sympathy. Disraeli sought to make a change, but his gorgeous Sidonia is too idealistic for everyday wear. Levi himself is somewhat theatrical, but he is wise, charitable, kindly—the instrument by which wrong-doers are punished and the good vindicated. Love for home and for his dead wife exalts him, and there is something even nobler when he turns to his reviler, and, disclaiming all intention to threaten, says solemnly: "Be advised then. Do not trample upon one of my people. Nations and men that oppress us do not thrive." See HARRINGTON.

Levine, Constantine Dmitrich, in Lyof Tolstoy's novel of *Anna Karenina*, a character in which many traits are drawn from the author's own character and history.

By birth and wealth Levine belongs to the world of great people, but he is not a man of the world. He has read much and thought more; he would fain better the condition of his retainers; he is interested in schools and agriculture. But he is shy, suspicious, touchy, impracticable and quite out of his element in the gay world of Moscow. In Levine's religious experiences Tolstoi was relating his own.—MATTHEW ARNOLD: *Essays in Criticism*, 2nd Series.

Lewis, in Charles Kingsley's dramatic poem of *The Saint's Tragedy*. Landgrave of Thuringia, and husband of Elizabeth. He is intended as a type of the husbands of the Middle Ages, and of the woman-worship of chivalry.

Liberty Hall, a place where every one may do as he chooses. The term first occurs in Goldsmith's comedy,

She Stoops to Conquer Act i, Sc. 2 (1773). Young Marlow and Hastings mistake Squire Hardcastle's house for an inn and disport themselves accordingly. The squire, though taken aback, determines to enter into the spirit of his guests and assures them: "This is Liberty Hall, gentlemen; you may do just as you please here."

Licentiate of Glass, hero and title of a tale by Cervantes, a scholar and a gentleman who never succeeds in life until he goes mad and attracts the attention of the great by his disorderly wit. Unfortunately he gets cured and is compelled to leave the court.

Lieschen, in Carlyle's *Sartor Resartus*, bed-maker and stove-lighter, washer and wringer, cook, errandmaid, and general provider to Professor Teufelsdröckh.

Life-in-Death, in Coleridge's eerie poem, *The Ancient Mariner*, a spectre who throws with Death for the shipwrecked crew. Death, it would appear, wins the first throw or throws and has seized upon all the comrades of the hero, but Life-in-Death wins the final cast for the Mariner himself. He is reserved, in other words, for a living death. The spectre is thus described:

> Her lips were red, her looks were free,
>   Her locks were yellow as gold:
> Her skin was as white as leprosy,
> The Night-mare Life-in-Death was she
>   Who thicks man's blood with cold.
>
>   Part III, l. 190.

It is difficult to reconcile the description of Life-in-Death with the subsequent adventures of the Mariner. She is apparently a personification of lawless pleasure, and has a bold and evil beauty. Apart from the sequence it would seem as though the text, "She that liveth in pleasure is dead while she liveth" (I Timothy v, 6), had been in the poet's mind. Perhaps Coleridge wished to bring her before us as a general embodiment of one dead in sin, without regard to her particular part in the poem.—HENRY S. PANCOAST: *Standard English Poems* (1899), Notes, p. 687.

Ligea, a water nymph inhabiting the river Severn; celebrated by Milton in the song *Sabrina Fair* in *Comus*:

> And fair Ligea's golden comb
> Wherewith she sits on diamond rocks
> Sleeking her soft alluring locks.

There seems to be here a curious anticipation of Heine's Lorélei (*q.v.*).

Lilian, Airy, Fairy. First line of *Lilian*, a short poem by Alfred Tennyson.

Lilliput, in Swift's *Gulliver's Travels*, an imaginary country peopled by a diminutive race who describe Gulliver as the Man-Mountain. Their sovereign, whose dominions extend within a dominion of no less than twelve miles, is taller by the breadth of Gulliver's nail than any of his subjects, which alone is sufficient to strike all with awe. He describes himself as " the delight and terror of the universe, whose dominions extend to the extremities of the globe, monarch of all monarchs, whose feet press down to the centre and whose head strikes against the sun; at whose nod the princes of the earth shake their knees."

Lillyvick, Mr., in Dickens's *Nicholas Nickleby*, a collector of water rates, uncle to Mrs. Kenwigs. The entire Kenwigs family, his expectant heirs, are alarmed and disgusted when he marries Henrietta Petowker, an actress, newly engaged for the Crummles company at Portsmouth. They are correspondingly elated when she runs away with a half-pay captain, and Lillyvick returns to his own family.

Limmason, Lieut. Austin, the titular hero of Kipling's short story, *The Man who Was*, in *Life's Handicap* (1890). He is brought in—" a limp heap of rags "—while the mess of the White Hussars are entertaining Dirkovitch, a Cossack officer. He is white, he speaks English, he answers to a number and discloses a disconcerting knowledge of mess matters. At sight of the Cossack he grovels with abject fear and in reply to a question tells of a long period in Siberia. The rolls of the regiment are searched. Under date, " Sebastopol, 1854," Lieutenant Austin Limmason is recorded as missing. The man remembers his name but dies before many days. A dramatization by F. Kingsley Peile was produced in London by Beerbohm Tree who played Austin Limmason.

Lindabrides, heroine of a romance, *The Mirror of Knighthood*, one of the books in Don Quixote's library (*Don Quixote*, Part I, i, 6) whose name has survived as a cant term for a courtesan, a woman of ill fame.

Linden, in W. D. Howells's novel, *A Hazard of New Fortunes*. A German socialist, a hater of the capitalistic class, who is employed on *Every Other Week* but who resigns when he discovers that it is financed by the millionaire Dryfoos. Colonel Higginson tells us that among all Howells's characters in fiction, the one who most caught Whittier's fancy was " that indomitable old German, Linden," whom he characterized, in writing to Mrs. Fields, as " that saint of the rather godless sect of dynamiters and atheists—a grand figure."

Lindores, The Ladies, in the novel of that name by Mrs. M. O. W. Oliphant (1883), are the daughters of a gentleman who has been leading a needy life abroad but succeeds to a Scotch peerage just as his girls grow up, and is straightway transformed from a useless dilettante into a stern, scheming man of the world. To the lasting sorrow of the elder daughter, " poor Lady Car," and to the scorn and dismay of the younger one, Edith, they are made pawns in the game their father is playing. In a sequel—*Lady Car* (1889)—the further fortunes of the elder are continued through the blankness of widowhood to the disillusion of a second marriage with the lover of her youth.

Lindsay, Margaret, heroine of a rather lachrymose novel, *The Trials of Margaret Lindsay* (1823), by John Wilson.

Linkinwater, Tim, in Dickens's *Nicholas Nickleby*, the cheerful, kindly, business-like old clerk, ultimately the business partner, of the Cheeryble Brothers (*q.v.*), said to have been drawn from an actual employee of the Grant Brothers.

Punctual as the counting-house dial . . . he performed the minutest actions, and arranged the minutest articles in his little room in a precise and regular order.

paper, pens, ink, ruler, sealing-wax, wafers, . . . Tim's hat, Tim's scrupulously folded gloves, Tim's other coat, . . . all had their accustomed inches of space. . . . There was not a more accurate instrument in existence than Tim Linkinwater.—DICKENS: *Nicholas Nickleby*, xxxvii (1838).

Lionel, The Late (Fr. *Feu Lionel*), hero of a comedy by E. Scribe produced in 1858 at the Théatre Français, Paris.

Lionel is a young man who is saved from committing suicide, and who thenceforth drops his real name—hence the title "*feu* Lionel." Considerable embarrassment is afterwards caused by his difficulty in establishing his identity.

Lirriper, Mrs., a lodging-house keeper in two Christmas stories by Dickens, *Mrs. Lirriper's Lodgings* (1863) and *Mrs. Lirriper's Legacy* (1864).

She is quite the lodging-house keeper, fills her home as well as she can, hates Miss Wozenham, her rival, with a true professional hatred, and yet she has a goodness, an overflow of humor and sense, and a benevolence quite her own. The abundance of bye-remarks that proceed from her is inexhaustible, and although by the characteristic oddity of expression they are tolerably well connected with her they are often instances of the drollest and happiest fancies that have come from Mr. Dickens. —*Saturday Review*, December 12, 1863.

Lisa, heroine of George Eliot's poem, *How Lisa Loved the King* (1869), which versifies a tale from Boccaccio (*Decameron*). A lovely Italian maid of wealthy but plebian parents, she looks coldly on her suitors, for she is pining away with a hopeless passion for the king. A poet puts her story into a song that is sung to beguile the royal leisure. The king, interested beyond his wont, is yet more caught up by learning that the love thus recited is a real and not an imaginary thing, and resolves, in perfect purity of purpose, to have an interview with the lovelorn damsel. He visits her, promises to wear her colors in the tourney, and to be her faithful knight, and having brought back the rosy health to her cheeks, advises her to marry one who has long loved her. Lisa takes the good counsel, and the King, in his

nobility of soul, settles a principality upon the husband.

Lisa, Monna, mother of Tessa, in George Eliot's *Romola*.

Lishmahago, Captain, in Smollett's novel, *Humphrey Clinker* (1771), a superannuated officer on half-pay, the favored suitor of Miss Tabitha Bramble. He is a hard-headed and hard-featured Scotchman, vain, pedantic, disputatious, dogmatic; eccentric in manner and in dress, but with a jealous sense of honor and a bigoted pride of country. Scott acknowledges that he was in some sense a forerunner of Dugald Dalgetty. Hazlitt sees in him a faint imitation of Don Quixote. Thackeray recognizes a family likeness in all three:

What man who has made his estimable acquaintance—what novel reader who loves Don Quixote and Major Dalgetty—will refuse his most cordial acknowledgments to the admirable Lieutenant Lishmahago?— THACKERAY, *English Humorists*.

Lismahago is the flower of the flock. His tenaciousness in argument is not so delightful as the relaxation of his logical severity when he finds his fortune mellowing in the wintry smiles of Mrs. Tabitha Bramble. This is the best-preserved and most severe of all Smollett's characters. The resemblance to "Don Quixote" is only just enough to make it interesting to the critical reader without giving offence to anybody else.—HAZLITT.

Littimer, in Dickens's *David Copperfield*, the confidential servant of Steerforth; an embodiment of aggressive and awesome respectibility. "He surrounded himself with an atmosphere of respectibility, and walked secure in it. It would have been next to impossible to suspect him of anything wrong, he was so thoroughly respectable. Nobody could have thought of putting him in a livery, he was so highly respectable. To have imposed any derogatory work upon him would have been to inflict a wanton insult on the feelings of a most respectable man."

Livingstone, Guy, hero of G. A. Lawrence's novel (1857), *Guy Livingstone, or Thorough*, a young aristocrat of considerable wealth, of enormous bodily strength and of an implacable temper—a Berseker out of his element in an age of peace and civilization—who finds vent for his pent-up energies in libertine amours and physical sports. Despite his cruelty and egotism he is immensely popular, especially with women. He is a direct descendant of Rochester and an ancestor of St. Elmo.

Liza, heroine of Tourgenief's novel, *A Nest of Nobles,* and the name under which the book itself has been translated into English by W. R. S. Ralston. Fedor Lavretsky, when a boy in heart though a man in years, had fallen in love with and married a frivolous woman of society who proved false to him. Shocked and outraged, he left her to return to his home. Here he meets Liza, whose serious, frank, and loyal nature restores his faith in womanhood, and just as he becomes interested in her he receives news of his wife's death. He declares his love; Liza confesses her own. After a moment of happiness their dream is rudely broken by the return of the wife, the report of her death having been false. Liza, with lofty resignation, counsels Fedor to receive and forgive his erring wife; he bows to what he recognizes as his duty, and Liza goes into a convent.

Lobaba, in Southey's oriental epic, *Thalaba the Destroyer* (1801), one of the sorcerers connected with Dom-Daniel, who had vowed himself to kill Thalaba. He approached him (Book III) in the garb of a merchant, and under pretence of guiding him to Babylon led him astray into the wilderness and there raised up a whirlwind to destroy him. The whirlwind, however, proved a boomerang that destroyed Lobaba and let his intended victim escape.

Lochiel, Donald Cameron of (1695–1748), generally known as Gentle Lochiel, is the titular hero of Thomas Campbell's poem, *Lochiel's Warning.* The Highland seer who is the speaker vainly warns him to beware of the day—

When the Lowlands shall meet thee in battle array.
For a field of the dead rushes red on my sight,
And the clans of Culloden are scattered in flight

This is a prophetic glimpse of the battle of Culloden, April 16, 1746, where Lochiel, fighting for the Pretender, was wounded and the clans defeated by the Duke of Cumberland.

Lochinvar, Young, titular hero of a ballad by Sir Walter Scott, a young Highlander who, being invited to the enforced wedding of the maiden he himself loves, induces her only too easily to become his partner in a dance; then, watching his opportunity, swings her over the saddle of his horse and gallops away to the dismay of her family, the bridegroom and the wedding guests.

Locke, Alton, hero of Charles Kingsley's novel, *Alton Locke, Tailor and Poet* (1849). A man of infinite yearnings, brought up in sordid surroundings and among narrow-minded dissenters, he is thrown upon the world by his mother at the instigation of a clerical bigot. He works as a tailor, sees much of the distressful trade carried on in the sweater's den, educates himself, writes poems that are published by subscription, supports himself for a while with his pen, but drifts back among his Chartist friends; is innocently mixed up with the burning of a farm, is sentenced to three years' imprisonment, and dies shortly after his release.

Lockit, in Gay's *Beggar's Opera* (1728), the harsh and cruel jailer of Newgate who refuses Captain Macheath's request for candles in his cell. The quarrel between the two was contemporaneously recognized as a topical hit at Walpole and Lord Townshend, who had come into personal collision.

Lockit, Lucy, daughter of the above. She falls in love with Macheath and helps him to escape from Newgate in return for his promise to marry her. He is recaptured and then confesses that he already has a wife in Polly Peachum.

Locksley, or " Diccon Bend-the-Bow," in Walter Scott's romance, *Ivanhoe,* the names under which a mysterious stranger is introduced. He eclipses all the other archers in the passage-of-arms at Ashby-de-la-

Zouch, and afterwards he and his men, under the leadership of the Black Knight, relieve the prisoners in Front-de-Bœuf's castle. Finally he reveals himself to Richard I: "Call me no longer Locksley, my Liege," he says, "but know me under the name which, I fear, fame hath blown too widely not to have reached even your royal ears—I am Robin Hood of Sherwood Forest."

Locksley Hall, a feigned country seat, obviously in Lincolnshire, which Tennyson makes the scene of two poems *Locksley Hall* (1842) and *Locksley Hall; Twenty Years After* (1886). Here the unnamed hero has spent his orphaned youth under the guardianship of an uncle; here has met, loved and been jilted by his cousin Amy. In the first poem he pours out his scorn for Amy, her wealthy boor of a husband, her mother and the entire social order. He wildly protests that he will abandon civilization and take to wife some savage woman who shall rear him a dusky brood. Finally he schools himself to self-conquest by dwelling on the insignificance of the individual; the mighty meaning of the race and the glorious possibilities of the future. In the second *Locksley Hall* the image of old age is as clear and true as the image of youth in its predecessor.

The old lover of Locksley Hall is exactly what the young man must have become, without any change of character by force of time and experience, if he had grown with the growth of his age. For that reason alone the poem in its entirety has a peculiar historical importance as the impersonation of the emotional life of a whole generation. Its psychological portraiture is perfect, its workmanship exquisite, and its force and freshness of poetic fervor wonderful.— LORD ROBERT BULWER LYTTON, letter to Mary Anderson quoted in Hallam Tennyson's *Life* of his father, vol. II, p. 330.

Lodore, hero of a novel of that name (1835) by Mrs. Shelley, a morbid sentimentalist who has a liaison with a married woman of title, marries a girl of the lower classes, is horrified to find his illegitimate son attempting a flirtation with his wife, leaves her and dies in a duel in New York. Luckily she is rescued from the dangers that surround her by her love for a noble being named Horatio Saville, an evident portrait of Shelley.

Lodowick, Friar, in Shakespeare's *Measure for Measure*, the name assumed by Duke Vincentio (*q.v.*).

Loftus, Father Tom, in Lever's *Confessions of Harry Lorrequer*, a kind-hearted, good-tempered, rollicking Irish priest, fond of telling a good story and of assisting at the emptying of a bowl of punch. The character has been borrowed by Boucicault in the Father Tom of his *Colleen Bawn*. Lever drew him from a Father Comyns of Kilkee, in Clare, whose hospitality had been extended to the author for three months while the latter was in hiding from his Dublin duns. Father Comyns recognized the portrait at once, and in a letter to the mutual friend who had introduced him to Lever, protested against this breach of hospitality. In spite of all Lever's attempts at extenuation, the priest never gave his absolution to the author of the *Confessions*.

Lofty Jack, in Goldsmith's comedy of *The Goodnatured Man*, a gentleman who makes his way among his creditors by the magnificent audacity of his lies. He claims to have the ear of parliament and of the King, to be the bosom friend of the ministers and the intimate acquaintance of all persons of rank and fashion, with more offices in his gift than any other man in England. The character is almost identical with that of Beau Tibbs in the *Citizen of the World*, only he is placed in better circumstances.

Longaville, in Shakespeare's comedy, *Love's Labor's Lost* (1594), a young lord attending on Ferdinand, King of Navarre (*q.v.*). No sooner has he signed the compact of solitary study for three years than he falls in love with Maria. "A man of sovereign parts" and glorious in arms, his only fault

Is a sharp wit matched with too blunt a will;
Whose edge none spares that come within
his power.   Act ii, Sc. 2.

Lorenzaccio, in Alfred de Musset's tragedy of that name (1833), dramatizing an episode in mediæval Florentine history.

The Lorenzaccio of De Musset, the filthy wretch who is a demon and an angel, with his fierce, serpent-tongued repartees, his subtle blasphemies, his cynical levity playing over a passion of horror at the wickedness and cowardice of the world that tolerates him.—G. B. SHAW: *Dramatic Opinions*, ii, 294.

Lorenzo, in Shakespeare's *Merchant of Venice*, a high-spirited, care-free, romantic boy who elopes with Jessica. We should like Jessica better if she had not deceived and robbed her father, and Lorenzo, if he had not married a Jewess, though he thinks he has a right to wrong a Jew. The dialogue between this newly-married couple by moonlight, beginning " On such a night," etc., is a collection of classical elegancies.

Lorenzo, an atheist and evil liver in Young's *Night Thoughts*, held up as a warning and example to others. It has been thought to be a portrait of the poet's son, who was something of a prodigal. Dr. Johnson points out, however, that in 1741, when the poem was written, " this Lorenzo, this finished infidel, this father to whose education vice had for some years put the last hand, was only eight years old." He is inclined to believe that Lorenzo was entirely a fictitious person.

Lorge, De, hero of a ballad, *Der Handschuh (The Glove)*, versifying a legend which Schiller found in Froissart's *Chronicles*. De Lorge, one of the courtiers of Francis I of France, one day sat making love to his lady in the gallery of the amphitheatre above the wild beasts. From sheer levity and hardness of heart she threw her glove into the arena and challenged her lover to bring it back as a test of his boasted love. He descended and recovered it, then flung it into her face, all his love changed to contempt by this revelation of her character. Bulwer's translation is very good. Leigh Hunt and Robert Browning have a poem on the same subject, Leigh Hunt closing as Schiller does by leaving the lady silent and ashamed in the midst of the assembly. Browning, who tells the story in the person of Ronsard, a pretended wit-

ness to the event, goes on to vindicate the lady by a curious analysis of the motives that prompted her to this test of her lover's truthfulness and makes De Lorge end by marrying a mistress of the king, who takes particular pleasure in sending her spouse after her gloves.

Lorraine, Mrs. Felix, in Disraeli's *Vivian Grey*, a clever, designing, vicious and unscrupulous woman, who sometimes aids and sometimes thwarts the plans of Vivian and finally, becoming his implacable enemy, tries to poison him. Says Vivian to himself: " A horrible thought sometimes comes over my spirit. I fancy that in this woman I have met a kind of double of myself—the same wonderful knowledge of the human mind, the same directness of voice, the same miraculous management which has brought us both together under the same roof, yet do I find in her the most abandoned of all beings, a creature guilty of that which even in this guilty age I thought was obsolete." The character was undoubtedly drawn from Lady Caroline Lamb.

Lorrequer, Harry, hero of Charles Lever's novel, *The Confessions of Harry Lorrequer* (1837), a young Irishman of good family who, after campaigning with Wellington on the Continent, comes home to Ireland and, shifting from Cork to Dublin and then back again to Germany, gets himself tangled up in tragi-comic perplexities from which he is invariably extricated by dint of his own high spirits, or the good-nature and cleverness of others.

We are not interested in Harry's love affairs, but in his scrapes, adventures, duels at home and abroad. He fights people by mistake whom he does not know by sight, he appears on parade with his face blackened he wins large piles at trente et-quarante; he disposes of coopers of claret and bowls of punch, and the sheep on one thousand hills provide him with devilled kidneys. The critics and the authors thought little of the medley but the public enjoyed it and defied the reviewers.—ANDREW LANG: *Essays in Little*, p. 164.

Lost Leader, The, is the title of one of Browning's most famous poems

.—a passionate invective upbraiding some person unnamed for having been tempted by a few paltry rewards, to desert his cause. There has been some question as to the person aimed at—Wordsworth, Goethe and Southey—all of whom changed in mature life from the radicalism of their youth to extreme conservatism —being suggested by rival disputants. But the controversy was settled by a letter inserted in Grosart's edition of the *Prose Works of William Wordsworth*:

19, WARWICK-CRESCENT, W.
DEAR MR. GROSART: Feb. 24, '75.

I have been asked the question you now address me with, and as duly answered it, I can't remember how many times; there is no sort of objection to one more assurance, or rather confession, on my part, that I did in my hasty youth presume to use the great and venerated personality of Wordsworth as a sort of painter's model; one from which this or the other particular feature may be selected and turned to account: had I intended more, above all, such a boldness as portraying the entire man, I should not have talked about "handfuls of silver and bits of ribbon." These never influenced the change of politics in the great poet; whose defection, nevertheless, accompanied as it was by a regular face-about of his special party, was to my juvenile apprehension, and even mature consideration, an event to deplore. But just as in the tapestry on my wall I can recognize figures which have *struck out* a fancy, on occasion, that though truly enough thus derived, yet would be preposterous as a copy, so, though I dare not deny the original of my little poem, I altogether refuse to have it considered as the "very effigies" of such a moral and intellectual superiority.

Faithfully yours,
ROBERT BROWNING.

Lothair, titular hero of a novel (1871) by Benjamin Disraeli, a young English nobleman who succeeds to an immense fortune after a long minority. The Catholic Church and the Revolutionary societies run a race against each other for his money and influence. The latter win chiefly through his platonic love for Theodora, the wife of an American general who is the inspiring element of the Italian patriots. After adventures with both parties he finally escapes to England, where he recovers his senses, saves the remainder of his fortune, and marries the Lady Corisande.

The immediate provocation for the novel was the conversion of John, second Marquis of Bute, a young and enormously wealthy peer, to the Church of Rome. He had been received on Christmas Eve, 1868. Lothair's coming of age is copied faithfully from the picturesque ceremonials with which Lord Bute's majority had been celebrated in September, 1868, and the intrigues concocted in order to make Lothair a Roman Catholic bear a close resemblance to those which were said to have entrapped Lord Bute. But there the similarity ended. In appearance, character, and tastes Lothair has no resemblance to Lord Bute, and whereas Lord Bute succumbed, Lothair emerged triumphant from his encounter with the proselytizers.

Lothario, in Cervantes's story, *The Curious Impertinent* (*Don Quixote*, i, iv, 6), a Florentine cavalier, the friend of Anselmo. The latter, proud of his wife Camilla and convinced of her virtue, challenges Lothario to put it to the test. Lothario's attack, begun reluctantly enough in a spirit of bravado, ends in a serious passion; the lady succumbs and the pair elope. Anselmo dies of grief, Lothario is slain in battle and Camilla retires to a convent where she, too, shortly dies. Rowe undoubtedly took the name of Lothario from the hero of this story.

Lothario, in Rowe's tragedy, *The Fair Penitent* (1703), a young Genoese nobleman, a brilliant, handsome and perfidious libertine, who seduces Calista and is killed in a duel by Altamont, her husband. He undoubtedly suggested the Lovelace of Richardson and thus became the prototype of a long line of splendid but treacherous villains in fiction and drama. In Act v, Sc. 1, occurs the line which has always been accepted as succinctly descriptive.

Is this that haughty, gallant, gay Lothario?

The character of Lothario seems to have been expanded by Richardson into that of Lovelace; but he has excelled his original in the moral effect of the fiction. Lothario, with gaiety which cannot be hated, and bravery which cannot be despised, retains too much of the spectator's kindness. It was in the power of Richardson alone, to teach us at once esteem and detestation; to make virtuous resentment overpower all the benevolence which wit, and elegance, and courage, naturally excite; and to lose at last the hero in the villain.—DR. JOHNSON.

Lothario, in Goethe's *Wilhelm Meister's Lehrjahre,* a magnificent German aristocrat, the friend and patron of Wilhelm. The portrait is evidently drawn after Karl August of Weimar, who stood in the same relation to Goethe.

Loti, Pierre, the pseudonym of Louis Marie Julien Viaud, a French naval officer who has distinguished himself in literature. Though energetic in action, young Louis was so bashful and self-effacing that his comrades nicknamed him Loti after a modest little Indian flower which shuns the light. His early novel, *Rarahu* (1880), was republished in 1882 under the title of *The Marriage of Loti.* It is largely autobiographical. So are its successors, *Le Roman d'un Spahi* and *Madame Chrysantheme,* whose hero is still named Loti, and remains a naval officer voyaging from port to port, who enters into a series of morganatic marriages with the native women of the countries he visits. See RARAHU.

Lotte, in Goethe's novel, *The Sorrows of Werther,* the diminutive by which Charlotte, the wife of Albert, is known in her own family circle. She was drawn from Charlotte (Lotte) Buff whom Goethe met at a ball in Wetzlar in May, 1772. She was the betrothed of his friend Kestner, a dry, formal and upright man, too short-sighted to understand that Lotte and his brilliant friend were fast falling in love with each other. Indeed Goethe himself did not realize that he was playing with fire until one moonlight night Lotte unintentionally revealed the secret. Then he incontinently fled from Wetzlar, partly from altruistic loyalty to Kestner and partly from egoistic regard for his own comfort. Love that might lead either to scandal or to matrimony was not a desirable contingency. See WERTHER.

Louis XI of France is the hero of a drama by Casimir de la Vigue, and is introduced as a prominent character in two of Scott's novels, *Quentin Durward* and *Anne of Gierstein.*

Lovegold, in Fielding's *The Miser,* a paraphrase of Molière's *L'Avare,* is an old man of sixty engaged to marry a designing young miss of nineteen, Marianna, who so alarms him by her pretended extravagance in ordering jewelry and dresses that he gladly pays £2000 to be let off the bargain, and she marries Lovegold's son.

Lovel, Lord, hero of *The Mistletoe Bough* (1839), a song by Thomas Haynes Bayley. On the night of his wedding to a baron's daughter the bride plays a game of hide and seek and shuts herself up in an old oak chest whose lid closes in upon her by its spring lock. In vain the bridegroom seeks her far and wide; no clue is discovered until years afterwards when the old chest is sold and the purchaser discovers a skeleton in bridal array. The same story is told by Rogers in *Italy.* See GINEVRA.

Lovel, Peregrine, in Rev. J. Townley's farce *High Life below Stairs* (1759), a wealthy commoner who, suspecting his servants of extravagance and dishonesty, pretends to withdraw into the country, disguises himself as an Essex bumpkin, applies for service in his own town house and is hired by the unsuspecting butler Philip. He discovers that Philip has invited to supper a large company of gentlemen's gentlemen and their sweethearts, that they assemble under the names and titles of their respective masters and mistresses, drink his rarest wines and feed at his expense on the best that the markets afford. At the height of the fun he breaks up the revels by announcing himself.

Lovelace, Robert, the hero-villain of Richardson's novel, *Clarissa Harlowe,* who lays siege to the heroine's virtue and finally accomplishes her ruin by means of a drug. See LOTHARIO.

Is there anything better than Lovelace in the whole range of fiction? Take Lovelace in all or any of his moods, suppliant, intriguing, repentant, triumphant—above all triumphant—and find his parallel if you can. Where, you ask, did the little printer of Salisbury Court—who suggests to Mr. Leslie Stephen "a plump white mouse in a wig"—where did Richardson discover so much gallantry and humanity, so much romance and so much fact, such an abundance of the heroic qualities and the baser veracities of mortal nature? Lovelace is, if you except Don Quixote, the completest hero in fiction. He has wit, humor, grace, brilliance, charm; he is a scoundrel and a ruffian, and he is a gentleman and a man; of his kind and in his degree he has the right Shakespearean quality.—W. E. HENLEY: *Views and Reviews*, p. 220.

Loveless, Edward, with his wife Amanda, the leading characters in Colley Cibber's comedy, *Love's Last Shift or the Fool in Fashion* (1695); in its sequel *The Relapse, or Virtue in Danger* (1696) by Sir John Vanbrugh; and in an adaptation of the latter comedy by Sheridan rechristened *The Trip to Scarborough.*

In the first play Loveless, a young rake, recently married to Amanda, wearies of her monotonous virtues and abandons her to pursue a dissipated career in the European capitals. After ten years he returns and is told that she is dead. This is only a ruse. Amanda is alive and still in love with him. She has him introduced into her house by candlelight and passes herself off as a lady fond of gallantry. Charmed with her feigned looseness of behavior, he falls in love with a supposed mistress who had wearied him as a wife. When she has him securely in her toils, she reveals the truth.

In *The Relapse* Vanbrugh paints Loveless' second fall from marital integrity;—his pursuit of the, apparently, only too willing Berinthia who, however, only toys with him to arouse the jealousy of her real object, Colonel Townly. Amanda is almost tempted to retaliation, but at the critical moment recovers herself and dismisses first Mr. Worthy, for whom she has some esteem, and next the profligate and foolish Sir Foppington whom she holds in contempt. Her recreant husband overhears the scene with the latter and is once more restored to fealty and repentance.

Lovell, Archie, in the novel of that title (1866) by Mrs. Annie Edwardes, a pretty young hoyden, innocently audacious, who scandalizes the " shady English " by her tomboy manners and defiance of convention. She escapes by only the narrowest margin from the disastrous consequences of a wild adventure with a young man undertaken in perfect ignorance of the ways of the world.

Lovely, Anne, heroine of Mrs. Centlivre's comedy, *A Bold Stroke for a Wife* (1718), an orphan whose father has left her £30,000 which she will forfeit if she marries without the consent of four guardians,—each so full of idiosyncrasies that " they never agreed on any one thing." Colonel Feignwell, whom she favors, succeeds in ingratiating himself with each and all by sheer audacity.

Love-o'-women, the nickname of Larry Tighe and the title of a story in Rudyard Kipling's *Many Inventions.* A handsome man, " wicked as all hell," his favorite amusement was the seduction of innocent women. Mulvaney meets him in later life a victim of torturing remorse.

It is worth a hundred addresses on Social Purity platforms and yet is written with an artistic reliance which is beyond all praise.—*London Athenæum.*

Lowrie, Joan, heroine of *That Lass o' Lowrie's* (1877), by Mrs. Frances Hodgson Burnett. She works at the mouth of a Lancashire coal pit. Her father, a savage miner, is accustomed to beat her when he is drunk. Touched by the kindness of a pleasant young engineer when she is suffering from one of the paternal castigations, she in return saves him from her father's hatred, helps rescue him, half dead, from the mine after a terrible accident, and consents to marry him on finding that he had long been in love with her.

Lucasta, the name under which Richard Lovelace (1618-1658) celebrated his ladylove, Lucy Sacheverell, in a series of lyrics. *Casta* is Latin for chaste and the name has been alternatively interpreted as " Chaste Lucy " or " Chaste Light " (*Lux* *casta*). Amarantha and Althea appear to have been other names for the same sweetheart. Tradition asserts that Lovelace was betrothed to her; but on his being taken prisoner in one of the wars of the time and reported to be dead, she hastily married another. He soon returned to his native land, imprecated anathemas upon the sex, declined into a vagabond and died miserably in a cellar. It must be added that the posthumous poems of Lovelace contain no reference to Lucasta's broken troth. His place in literature is maintained to-day by two among his many lyrics: *To Lucasta, on going to the Wars*, and *To Althea from Prison*.

Lucetta, in Shakespeare's comedy, *The Two Gentlemen of Verona*, maid to Julia. She is sharp enough to discover the true character of Proteus.

Lucile, titular heroine of a novel in verse (1860) by Robert, Lord Lytton ("Owen Meredith"). A correspondent of the London *Literary World* first pointed out that Book i is a mere reproduction in English anapæsts of George Sand's prose tale, *Lavinia*, with the situations and motif so modified as to make them acceptable to the conventional standards of Anglo-Saxon morality.

Lucile, beautiful, impassioned and accomplished, had been betrothed in extreme youth to Lord Alfred Hargrave. Circumstances had parted them. For ten years she had borne a smiling face and an aching heart in brilliant French society. He meanwhile, a blasé man of the world, had been seeking peace of mind and conscience in travel. Learning of his engagement to Matilda Darcy, a cousin, Lucile writes the letter which opens the book asking that he return her letters in person. The old passion revives. There is now a rival in the field, a fiery French legitimist, the Duke of Luvois. Lucile refuses him. With diabolical ingenuity he suggests base suspicions to Alfred, thus frustrating a union which could alone have filled up the void in two desolate natures. The Englishman marries his cousin; the Frenchman takes to

family pride and military glory. Again and again these two men are brought into collision and protected from each other by the lonely Lucile. Alfred's son falls in love with the Duke's niece. They are forbidden to think of each other. The boy takes service in the Crimea and, wounded, is tended by Sœur Seraphine, a nursing nun who proves to be Lucile. She learns his secret. The might of the persuasion of one so suffering and so religious ends in the reconciliation of the old enemies and the union of the young people.

Luck, Thomas (so named at a rough christening by a miner), the child-hero of Bret Harte's story of life (and birth and death) in a California mining camp, entitled *The Luck of Roaring Camp*. The story deals with the unexpected appearance of the baby amid these rough surroundings, the death of its mother, the only woman in camp, and later of the child itself after it has performed its mission of civilizing the camp up to the point that it was actually proposed to build a hotel and invite a few decent families to reside there for the sake of "the Luck"—who it was hoped would profit by female companionship.

Lucretia, heroine of *Lucretia, or Children of the Night* (1847), a romance by Bulwer-Lytton. Discovering the weakness and perfidy of Mainwaring (*q.v.*), who engages himself to her while really loving her cousin Susan Mivers, Lucretia, an orphan of great talents and fierce passions, elopes to France with her tutor, Dalibard, a French emigré, clever, unscrupulous and atheistical. Presently he seeks to deliver himself from his shrewish wife. She finds herself under the influence of slow poison. If Dalibard lives she must die. She betrays him to an assassin. Having once tasted blood she develops into a fiend. Returning to England she ruins the domestic happiness of Mainwaring, marries a Methodist minister and poisons him, attempts other crimes, and, inadvertently poisoning her own son, ends her life in a madhouse. Mainwaring's original was Thomas Griffith Waignewright.

Lucullus, in Shakespeare's *Timon of Athens,* a false and fawning friend. Timon's servant calls him "thou disease of a friend."

Lucy, heroine of a ballad, *Lucy and Colin,* by Thomas Tickell. Lucy is betrothed to Colin but he forsakes her for a bride "thrice as rich as he." At his wedding he catches sight of her, standing silent and apart and, all his heart going out to her with pity and love, "the damps of death bedewed his brow." She also dies and is buried with him. Vincent Bourne has translated the poem into Latin verse. Goldsmith calls it the best ballad in our language.

Ludington, Miss, heroine of Edward Bellamy's fantastic novelette, *Miss Ludington's Sister.* A beautiful girl changed by misfortune and sickness into a sad and faded woman, she preserves an early portrait of herself and conceives the idea that what she was once must still exist somewhere. The delusion is furthered by impostors who undertake to materialize the wraith and introduce their tool to Miss Ludington as her soul-sister, but the go-between breaks down and confesses.

Ludlow, Johnny, the pretended author of a series of stories and sketches (1874 and 1880) by Mrs. Henry Wood. Johnny is the ward of a Worcestershire squire, whose healthy country life enables him to exercise his faculties of observation upon a number of oddities in different walks of life, and his descriptive powers upon not a few domestic tragedies and romances. Johnny acts as a sort of chorus; sometimes he plays a minor part.

The admirable way in which Mrs. Wood preserves throughout the genuinely boyish tone is not the least of the merits of her book.—*Spectator.*

Luggnagg, in *Gulliver's Travels,* an imaginary island, about a hundred leagues southeast of Japan, the inhabitants of which have received the gift of eternal life, without the corresponding accompaniments of health and intellect.

Luke, hero of Massinger's *City Madam,* who, from a state of poverty, suddenly comes into the possession of unbounded wealth, a type of vindictive hypocrisy.

Lumpkin, Tony, in Goldsmith's comedy, *She Stoops to Conquer* (1773), a coarse, good-natured, fun-loving country booby, whose love of practical joking leads him to point out his own home, the house of his stepfather, Squire Hardcastle, as an inn. Hence Young Marlow and Hastings arrive there under a misapprehension and the consequent comedy of errors is not fully cleared up until Tony confesses his complicity. See MARLOW, YOUNG.

Tony is one of the especial favorites of the theatre-loving public, and no wonder. With all the young cub's jibes and jeers, his impudence and grimaces, one has a sneaking love for the scapegrace; we laugh with him rather than at him; nor can we fail to enjoy those malevolent tricks of his when he so obviously enjoys them himself.

Luria, in Robert Browning's tragedy of that name (1846), a Moor, captain of the army of France in the war against Pisa. He loves Florence; Florence mistrusts him. The Pisan general Tiburzio warns him that the day of his expected victory will also be that of his condemnation, offering him the Pisan command if he will leave the ungrateful Florentines. True to the end Luria leads his troops out to victory and then swallows poison. Tiburzio meanwhile is taken captive and has told his story. Luria dies surrounded by the repentant captain and others who had mistrusted him—the true human soul in each breaking its artificial barriers, reaching toward and doing fealty to the enthusiasm of the greater spirit which attracts and absorbs their own.

Lycidas, a shepherd in Virgil's *Third Eclogue.* Hence Milton in his poetical monody, *Lycidas* (November, 1637), adopts the name for his friend and former college companion, Edward King, son of Sir John King, Secretary for Ireland, who was drowned on the passage from Chester to Ireland, August 10, 1637.

Lydgate, Dr., in George Eliot's *Middlemarch*, an enthusiast ruined by an unfortunate marriage. At twenty-seven he comes to Middlemarch with high aims. He marries Rosamond Vincy, pretty, petty, obstinate, self-willed. The paradise of sweet laughs and blue eyes over which he has dreamed since he first met her proves a disastrous disillusion. At the age of forty Dr. Lydgate, of magnificent possibilities, is thoroughly disenchanted. Instead of completing the unfinished work of his ideal, one Doctor Bichat, he has become a fashionable physician at bathing places, and distinguished himself by writing a treatise on the gout. In the prime of life, his hair still brown, now and then conscious of visitations from his earlier self, he closes his career.

The skill with which Lydgate's gradual abandonment of his lofty aims is worked out without making him simply contemptible forces us to recognize the truthfulness of the conception. It is an inimitable study of such a fascination as the snake is supposed to exert upon the bird; the slow, reluctant surrender, step by step, of the higher nature to the lower, in consequence of weakness which is at least perfectly intelligible.—SIR LESLIE STEPHEN: *George Eliot.*

Lygia, in H. Sienkiewicz's historical romance, *Quo Vadis* (1897), a beautiful Christian maiden living in the household of Aulus Plautius, a Roman noble during the reign of Nero. Vinicius, one of the emperor's guards, lays siege to her virtue and, being repeatedly foiled, denounces her as a Christian. She is exposed to the wild beasts in the amphitheatre, is saved therefrom by her attendant Ursus, a gigantic savage, and ends by marrying Vinicius, who has been converted to Christianity by the preaching of St. Peter and St. Paul.

Lyndon, Barry, the autobiographic hero of *The Memoirs of Barry Lyndon* (1844), a satirical romance of the picaresque order by W. M. Thackeray. His real name is Redmond Barry; the name Lyndon he assumes on his marriage. Telling his own story, he frankly reveals himself as an unmitigated blackguard, a profligate, a gambler and a sharper, who, after a riotous youth, a manhood of infamy and an old age of merited ruin and beggary, looks upon himself, gravely and in good faith, as a wronged and virtuous gentleman—" the victim," as he is made to say on his own title-page, " of many cruel persecutions, conspiracies and slanders."

As Thackeray paints the portrait it is worthy to hang in any rogue's gallery—as the original was worthy to be hanged on any scaffold. The villain double-dyed is very rare in modern fiction, and Barry Lyndon is an almost incomparable scoundrel, who believes in himself, tells us his own misdeeds, and ever proclaims himself a very fine fellow —and honestly expects us to take him at his own valuation, while all our knowledge of his evil doings is derived from his own self-laudatory statements!—BRANDER MATTHEWS: *The Historical Novel and other Essays,* p. 157.

Lys, Diane de, titular heroine of a novel by Alexander Dumas fils (1851), and its dramatization (1853) by the author. Married for her money by a titled libertine and busy man of affairs who neglects her, she meets Paul Aubrey, a young sculptor who has amused himself with facile loves but has never experienced a *grande passion.* Both have ardent, imaginative natures, both are in search of some one on whom to lavish the wealth of their affections. The inevitable happens with tragic consequences.

Lysander, in Shakespeare's *A Midsummer Night's Dream*, a young man of Athens who flees from that city with Hermione, closely pursued by Demetrius, to whom Egeus, the lady's father, has betrothed her. Following Demetrius is another lady, Helena, who is madly in love with him. The four ill-assorted lovers fall asleep and dream a dream about the fairy court of Oberon and Titania, in the course of which Puck, by means of a magic herb known as "Love-in-idleness," rearranges matters in a thoroughly satisfactory manner. Demetrius wakes to find himself in love with Helena and out of love with Hermione. Egeus, arriving in quest of the fugitives, accepts the situation.

Lysimachus, in Shakespeare's comedy, *Pericles, Prince of Tyre* (1608), the governor of Mitylene who marries Marina.

M

Macaire, Robert, at one time a generic name for any French *chevalier d'industrie* whose characteristics ran the gamut from petty vice and political chicanery to the gravest crimes against law and order. The term doubtless originated with the chevalier Richard (not Robert) de Macaire, who in 1371 murdered Aubrey de Montdidier in the Forest of Bondi, Paris. The assassin was apprehended on suspicions aroused by the conduct of Montdidier's faithful dog, Dragon, which had witnessed the attack. In 1814 the story was put into a play by Pixericourt, *The Dog of Montargis* (*q.v.*), which was later rehabilitated with the dog feature omitted, in *L'Auberge des Adrets* (see below). Here Macaire was recreated as a bold, humorous and reckless thief and murderer. Just about this time Daumier, the famous caricaturist of the Paris *Charivari*, borrowed the name for a series of sketches in which Robert Macaire was successively depicted as a banker, an advocate, a journalist, etc., in whom were personified perverseness, impudence, and charlatanism. They were remarkable as portraitures of abstract qualities, and it is largely owing to their favorable reception on the part of a good-natured public that Daumier has come to be known in later times as the "Aristophanes of French caricature." And in this way Robert Macaire came to be the sportive designation of a certain class of Frenchmen.

Macaire, Robert, the leading character in a French melodrama, *L'Auberge des Adrets*, by Benjamin Antier and Saint Amand. The plot turns on a murder committed at a wayside inn by the adventurer, Robert Macaire, the blame of which is thrown on a poor woman passing the night there who is eventually found to be the murderer's neglected wife. Frederick Lemaitre, the greatest French actor of his day, saw that the leading characters in the story would admit of being treated from a humorous standpoint. Associating himself with the original authors he turned the melodrama into an extravaganza entitled simply *Robert Macaire*, whose satirical strictures upon political and commercial chicanery were entirely foreign to the original conception, and so had a success of a different character as an exposure of passing vices and follies. Although Lemaitre's treatment of Macaire was purely farcical he found opportunities for emitting real flashes of tragical genius, so striking, so terrifying indeed that his capacity for throwing himself with overwhelming force into a situation was completely established.

McAndrews, who exploits himself in *McAndrews Hymn*, by Rudyard Kipling, a Scottish engineer who loved his engine with something of the same irreverent reverence that he bestowed upon his God.

Macbeth, King of Scotland in Shakespeare's tragedy of that name, is introduced in Sc. i, 3, where he meets the witches; murders Duncan, II, 1, and succeeds him as king; causes the murder of Bangno, III, 1, and of Macduff's family, iv, 1, 2; meets the English army at Dusinane, Act V, and is slain by Macduff, v, 8. According to authentic history he was not killed at Dusinane, but at Lumphanan two years later (1057). Furthermore, he appears to have been a benign and beneficent ruler. In the play Lady Macbeth complains of him (I, 5) that he is "too full of the milk of human kindness," and indeed it is only his wife's influence that decides his first murder and later that of Banquo. Struggling with remorse of conscience he confuses it, as Coleridge says, with the feeling of insecurity and plunges into more crimes in order to safeguard himself against the results of the first.

Macbeth himself appears driven along by the violence of his fate, like a vessel drifting before the storm. He is not equal to the struggle between fate and conscience. In thought he is absent and perplexed, sudden and desperate in act, from a distrust of his own resolution. His energy springs from the anxiety and agitation of his mind. His blindly rushing forward on the objects of his ambition or revenge, and his recoiling from them equally betray the harassed state of his feelings. This part of his character is admirably set off by being brought in connection with that of Lady Macbeth, whose obdurate strength of will and masculine firmness give her the ascendancy over her husband's faltering virtue. She at once seizes the opportunity that offers for the accomplishment of their wished-for greatness, and never flinches from her object till all is over.—HAZLITT: *Characters of Shakespeare's Plays.*

Macbeth, Lady, in Shakespeare's *Macbeth*, the hero's consort who impels him to crime the moment she hears of the witch's prophecy that he shall succeed Duncan as King of Scotland.

The magnitude of her resolution almost covers the magnitude of her guilt. She is a great bad woman, whom we hate, but whom we fear more than we hate. She does not excite our loathing or abhorrence, like Regan and Goneril. She is only wicked to gain a great end; and is, perhaps, more distinguished by her commanding presence of mind and inexorable self-will, which do not suffer her to be diverted from a bad purpose, when once formed, by weak and womanly regrets, than by the hardness of her heart, or want of natural affections.— HAZLITT: *Characters of Shakespeare's Plays.*

Macbride, Miss (*née* McBride), heroine of a satirical poem, *The Proud Miss Macbride,* by John G. Saxe. She was "terribly proud" of everything concerning herself; though her boasted "high-birth" was under a skylight, and though her Phœnix-like rise had been from the ashes of a chandlery. She scorned a fractional tailor, was "up to snuff" with a tobacconist and "nonsuited" an attorney, but accepted the plausible and worthless fortune hunter "dapper Jim." Her pride had its fall; instead of "reversion" came "reverses;" lover and friends fled; the vulgar mocked; and Miss Macbride was left alone in her sorrow.

Macduff, thane of Fife in the time of Edward the Confessor, figures anachronistically in Shakespeare's *Macbeth.* One of the witches had warned Macbeth to beware of the thane of Fife, another had added that "none of woman born should have power to harm him." In England Macduff raised an army to dethrone Macbeth, who having attacked his castle and slain his wife and all his children, meets him at last face to face on the fatal field at Dusinane.

Macbeth tauntingly repeats the witch's prophecy. Macduff retorts that he was not born of woman, but "was from his mother's womb, untimely ripped." Seeing all hope lost, Macbeth boldly cries:

> Lay on Macduff
> And damned be he who first cries Hold! Enough!

They fight and Macbeth is slain.

MacFarlaine, Ailie, in Mrs. Oliphant's novel, *The Minister's Wife* (1869), a Scotch lassie, with golden hair and mystical blue eyes and a delicate, half hectic color, who is converted at a revival and whom a brother enthusiast, a newly reformed sinner, claims in the name of the Lord, urging her to become his bride and help him to convert the world.

It is not easy to depict the visions which sweep across the mental eye of one whose brain religious enthusiasm has almost crazed, without rendering them ludicrous, but there is unmixed pathos in the picture which Mrs. Oliphant has drawn of this poor Lowland maiden as she knelt before the open Bible on her bed, and remained there lost "in one long trance of prayer and reverie, while the short autumn day came to an end, and the twilight closed around her,"collecting her energies in order that she might submit to the marriage which she dreaded far more than she would have feared the scaffold or the stake.—*Saturday Review,* July 3, 1869.

McFingal, hero of John Trumbull's *McFingal,* a political satire in Hudibrastic verse (1774–1782), which deals with the events of the American Revolution and finds matter for humor in both Whig and Tory,—but especially the latter. McFingal, a New England Scotchman, represents the British and the Tories, Honorius the Whigs and the patriots. After undergoing many ludicrous adventures, and getting the worst of every argument, McFingal is hoisted to the top of a flagpole and let down again to receive a coat of tar and feathers. The most famous lines in the poem are frequently quoted as coming from *Hudibras,*

> No thief e'er felt the halter draw
> With good opinion of the law.

MacFlecknoe (*i.e.,* son of Flecknoe), the name under which Dryden caricatured his rival Thomas Shadwell (1640–1692) in a satirical poem, *Mac-*

Flecknoe, or a Satire on the True Blue Protestant Poet T. S. (1682). Richard Flecknoe was an Irishman who had died in 1678. Though he had done some good work in prose and verse, he had been the butt of Andrew Marvell and was accepted by his English contemporaries as a typical dullard. His character was estimated perhaps from his repeated failures as a dramatist. This man is depicted by Dryden as the king of " the realm of nonsense," conscious of his approaching end and anxious for the election of his successor. In a strain of ludicrous panegyric, he discusses the grounds of his son Shadwell's claims to the vacant throne. He reflects with pride on the exact similarity, as well in genius as in tastes and features, which exists between himself and his hopeful boy. Shadwell's coronation is then described with more humor than is common with Dryden, though the conclusion of the poem evinces a sudden change from banter to ferocity, and betrays the bitterness of the feelings which had prompted it. This admirable satire—to which Pope is indebted for the plot of the *Dunciad*—is certainly to be numbered among Dryden's most successful efforts.

M'Flimsey, Miss Flora, heroine of *Nothing to Wear*, a satirical poem by William Allen Butler. A dweller in Madison Square, then the fashionable headquarters of New York City, she is the discontented and indeed desolate possessor of extravagant gowns and jewelry and native and foreign finery, but still insists that she has nothing to wear.

Macheath, Captain, in *The Beggar's Opera* (1728), by John Gay, a handsome, reckless ruffian adored by the ladies and feared by all men save the accomplices who share his booty. He is married to Polly Peacham whom he really loves and who loves him in return, but this does not prevent his paying attentions to Lucy Lockit and other beauties. It is Macheath who sings the famous song,

How happy could I be with either
Were t'other dear charmer away.

Betrayed by Polly's father he is lodged in Newgate gaol. His escape, recapture, trial, condemnation to death and reprieve make up other episodes in his career which ends with his making Polly a promise that he will be true to her for the rest of his life.

MacIan, Gilchrist, in Scott's historical novel, *The Fair Maid of Perth*, the chief of Clan Quhele. Just before the birth of Eachin MacIan (see below) he had lost seven sons in battle with Clan Chattan, ominous prophecies had induced him to apprentice the eighth son to Simon Glover. Eighteen years later he suffered himself to be persuaded that Eachin's presence was necessary to ensure the defeat of Clan Chattan by Clan Quhele. Luckily he died before witnessing his son's disgrace.

MacIan, Ian Eachin (*i.e.*, Hector), in Scott's historical romance of the fourteenth century, *The Fair Maid of Perth* (1828). Son of Gilchrist MacIan (*supra*) he was " born under a bush of holly and suckled by a white doe," and under the name of Conachar was brought up in obscurity as Simon Glover's apprentice. He is the rival of Henry Gow for the hand of Catharine Glover, but is afflicted with " a quick fancy that overestimates danger " and is acutely conscious of his own faint-heartedness. Nevertheless he bears himself gallantly in the struggle with Clan Chattan until he is left alone face to face with his deadly enemy, Henry Gow. Then " his heart sickened, his eyes darkened, his ears tingled, his brain turned giddy " and he ignominiously fled from the field. In his tenderness towards this involuntary coward, Scott expiated the harshness he had visited on a ne'er-do-well brother Thomas, who had shown the white feather in the West Indies. This harshness he subsequently repented.

McIvor, Fergus (called also Vich Ian Vohr), in Scott's novel, *Waverley* (1814), the chief of Glennaquoich, a gallant Highland Jacobite of fiery temper and uncompromising loyalty.

He is the brother of Flora McIvor, with whom Edward Waverley is in love.

Fergus MacIvor has a much more possible prototype in Colonel Alexander Ranaldson Macdonnell of Glengarry, one of the most typical Celts of his race. His pride and heat of temper were quite equal to those of the hero of fiction. He was the last Highland chief who really kept up the state and customs of ancient gaeldom to their full extent. When he travelled he did so as a Gaelic prince, with a full retinue of kilted attendants, not a single articulus lacking of a Highland chieftain's tail. He was a great friend of Scott's, who writes of him in glowing terms (see Lockhart). On 14 January, 1828, he was killed in the attempt to get ashore from the wrecked steamer *Stirling Castle*. His grand ideas about the state of a Macdonald chief helped to embarrass the estates, the whole of which were sold partly in his son's and partly in his grandson's time.—S. R. CROCKETT: *The Scott Originals*.

McIvor, Flora, in *Waverley*, the sister of Fergus, and like him devotedly attached to the house of Stuart and the Catholic religion. In her unswerving loyalty to an unpopular faith and a losing cause, a loyalty which though " wildly enthusiastic " " burnt pure and unmixed with any selfish feeling," in her passionate attachment to principle and her final renunciation of woman's tenderest prerogatives she anticipates Rebecca of York. After a touching farewell scene with Waverley she retires to the convent of the Scotch Benedictine nuns in Paris. One incident embodied in the novel really happened to a fair Jacobite friend of the author, a Miss Nairne. As the Highland army rushed into Edinburgh Miss Nairne, like other Tory ladies, stood waving her handkerchief from a balcony. A ball, accidentally discharged, grazed her forehead. " Thank God," she said, on recovering her senses, " that the accident happened to me whose principles are known. Had it befallen a Whig they would have said it was done on purpose."

Mackaye, Saunders, a leading character in Charles Kingsley's novel, *Alton Locke* (1850), obviously drawn from his intimate friend, Thomas Carlyle.

He has some real humor, a quality in which Kingsley was for the most part curiously deficient; but one must suspect that in this case he was drawing from an original. It is interesting to read Mr. Carlyle's criticism of this part of the book. "Saunders Mackaye," he says (*Life*, vol. i, p. 244), "my invaluable countryman in this book, is nearly perfect; indeed, I greatly wonder how you did contrive to manage him. His very dialect is as if a native had done it, and the whole existence of the rugged old hero is a wonderfully splendid and coherent piece of Scotch bravura." Perhaps an explanation of the wonder might be suggested to other people more easily than to Mr. Carlyle; but at any rate Mackaye is a very felicitous centre for the various groups who play their parts in the story.—LESLIE STEPHEN: *Hours in a Library.*

Mackenzie, Sheila, heroine of *The Princess of Thule,* by William Black (1874), who receives that nickname because her father rules unquestioned over the fisher peasants of " Borva," the remotest of the Hebrides isles. " The girl," we are told, " was somehow the product of all the beautiful aspects of nature around her. It was the sea that was in her eyes, it was the fair sunlight that shone in her face, the breath of her life was the breath of the Moorland winds." Lavender, an artist, clever and attractive, but something of a snob, transplants this delicate northern flower to the hot-house air of London, where she pines and withers until his neglect drives her to escape back to the freedom of her natural life,—only to find that its brightness and contentment have flown. Her loss startles Lavender into recognition of his better self and she succeeds in making him a true man.

Macleod, Colin or **Cawdie,** in Richard Cumberland's comedy, *The Fashionable Lover* (1780), a Scotch servant in the employ of Lord Abberville, who supervises the household finances with such strict economy and integrity that he earns the hatred of his fellow domestics and eventually checks his young master on the road to ruin. Cumberland's avowed object in drawing this portrait was " to weed out the unmanly prejudice of Englishmen against the Scotch."

Macleod of Dare, Sir Keith, hero of *MacLeod of Dare,* a novel by William Black (1878), a Highland chief, intense, untamed and passionate, yet fine-strung and chivalrous, spending most of his time in Scotland with a chorus of wild retainers, yet occasionally lured to London. Here he wrecks his happiness by a misplaced passion for Gertrude White, a fine and fickle lady, an actress spoiled by adulation. His dethroned and distempered reason prepares for both betrayer and victim a shocking catastrophe.

Macquart, Gervaise, heroine of Zola's novel, *L'Assomoir* (1877), who reappears in others of the Rougon Macquart series. At fourteen, and already a mother, she was driven from her home and accompanies her lover to Paris. He deserts her and two children. She marries Coupeau, a tinsmith. At first they are happy, but poverty and vice disintegrate what might have been a family into mere units of misery, wretchedness and corruption. Zola pitilessly traces their downfall.

MacSarcasm, Sir Archy, in C. Macklin's comedy, *Love à la Mode* (1779), a Scotch knight especially proud of his descent. He tells Charlotte Goodchild whom he is wooing that " in the house of MacSarcasm are twa barons, three viscounts, six earls, one marquisate, and twa dukes, besides baronets and lairds oot o' a' reckoning." Believing that Charlotte has lost her fortune he repents of his wooing and informs her that he has just received letters " frae the dukes, the marquis, and a' the dignitaries of the family expressly prohibiting my contaminating the blood of Macsarcasm wi' onything sprung from a hogshead or a coonting house."

MacSycophant, Sir Pertinax, in Macklin's comedy, *The Man of the World* (1764), a hard, practical, shrewd and worldly old Scotchman, ambitious for his son's sake rather than for his own and careless of how sordid or disgraceful the means whereby his ambitions may be realized.

Madeline, heroine of Keats's narrative poem, *The Eve of St. Agnes*

(1820). The poem is based on the old superstition that if a maiden goes to bed supperless on the vigil of St. Agnes' feast she will see her destined husband on awaking. Madeline, in love with Porphyro, tries this spell and Porphyro, obtaining surreptitious access to her virgin bower, watches her reverently till she sinks in slumber, arranges a dainty dessert by her couch, and gently arousing her with a favorite air, persuades her to steal from the castle under his protection.

Maimuna, in Southey's epic, *Thalaba* (Books vii–ix), an old woman whom Thalaba finds spinning in her house in Kaf. Expressing surprise at the extreme fineness of her thread he was invited to break it if he could. Incredulously Thalaba wound it around his wrists, but found it impossible to disentangle it again and became utterly powerless. Maimuna with the help of her sister Khwala conveyed him helpless to the island of Mohareb. Later she repented, turned to Allah and liberated Thalaba.

Maison Rouge, Chevalier de (literally the Knight of the Red House), hero and title of a romance by Alexander Dumas. A young French nobleman, the chevalier is incited by chivalric love for Marie Antoinette to a heroic plan for liberating her from the Tower. By an unfortunate combination of circumstances he arrives just in time to frustrate a better plot conceived by cooler heads, and willingly allows himself to be slain by the baffled conspirators. G. LeNotre, in *The Real Maison Rouge* (1894), shows that this hotheaded youth was in actual life known as A. D. J. Gonze de Rougeville. He did take a bold part in the attempts to free Marie Antoinette, but he was a less chivalric person than his double in fiction. In fact he was an impostor of plebeian birth who usurped the name of de Rougeville. Nor was he a victim of the Revolution. He survived until 1814.

Maitland, Dean, hero of *The Silence of Dean Maitland* (1886), a novel by " Maxwell Grey " (Miss

M. G. Tuttiell). As a young curate the future dignitary of the Church of England had seduced a girl, committed manslaughter to avoid the consequences, and allowed an innocent friend to be condemned to penal servitude on circumstantial evidence. Despite severe twinges of conscience Maitland had led a good and useful life until the friend is released from prison and unconditionally forgives him, when he makes public confession and dies.

Malagigi (the Italian form of the French *Maugis*), in Ariosto's *Orlando Furioso* (1516), one of Charlemagne's paladins, brother of Aldiger and Vivian and cousin to Rinaldo. He was brought up by the fairy Oriana, and in his turn became a famous magician.

Malagrowther, Sir Malachi, the feigned author of a series of letters contributed by Sir Walter Scott to the *Edinburgh Weekly Journal* in 1826. Their object was to antagonize a proposal by the British government that the circulation of bank notes in Scotland should be restricted to those of £5 or more. Lockhart assures us that "these diatribes produced in Scotland a sensation not inferior to that of the Drapier letters in Ireland." What is more to the point they defeated the proposed measure.

Malagrowther, Sir Mungo, in Scott's historical romance, *The Fortunes of Nigel*, a crabbed old courtier whose natural peevishness is increased by his misfortunes. He takes delight in making everybody as unhappy as himself.

Malbecco, in Spenser's *Faëry Queen* (Book III, ix, 10), designed to represent the self-inflicted torments of jealousy.

> The sight could jealous pangs beguile,
> And charm *Malbecco's* cares awhile.
>   SIR W. SCOTT.

Malcolm, in Shakespeare's *Macbeth*. A son of Duncan.

Malefort, in Massinger's *Unnatural Combat*, an incestuous ruffian who pays the penalty of his crimes by direct interposition from heaven. The character is probably modelled on that of the Italian villain Francesco Cenci (*q.v.*).

Malfi, Duchess of, heroine of a tragedy of that name by John Webster (*circa* 1618). Her marriage to her steward Antonio Bologna maddens her brothers when they discover the secret. One, a cardinal, hires Bosola to slay Antonio. A more terrible end for the Duchess is planned by her twin brother Ferdinand, Duke of Calabria. He calls upon her in a darkened room, pretends to be reconciled, then suddenly uncovers three waxen figures smeared with blood whom she takes for her slaughtered children and husband. After having sufficiently feasted on her mental tortures, Ferdinand sends a troop of madmen into her room who leap and howl around her. Then follow the executioners, with a gravedigger and a coffin, who sing a mournful dirge before they strangle her. The two children are likewise strangled.

Mall, Mistress, alluded to in Shakespeare's *Twelfth Night*, i, 3, a famous thief and murderess who dressed in man's clothing and infested Hounslow Heath. Her chief exploit was the robbery of General Fairfax, for which she was sent to Newgate. Her real name was Mary Frith. Under the nickname of Moll Cutpurse she is the heroine of *The Roaring Girl* (1611) by Middleton and Decker.

Mallinger, Sir Hugo, in *Daniel Deronda*, represents the aristocracy in the form most indulgently viewed by George Eliot—that of a wealthy, easy country gentleman of ancient descent and large means; but, as a comfortable, easy aristocrat must be either stupid or malignant, he is characterized by "that dulness towards what may be going on in other minds, especially the minds of children, which is among the commonest deficiencies even in good-natured men like him, when life has been generally easy to themselves, and their energies have been quietly spent in feeling gratified."

Maltravers, Ernest, hero of a novel of that name (1837) by Bulwer-

Lytton, and its sequel, *Alice, or the Mysteries.* He is put forward as the type of genius. At eighteen a marvel of precocious wisdom and learning, he comes home from a brilliant university career in Germany, meets a burglar's daughter, the beautiful and unsophisticated Alice, and lives with her until the burglar reclaims her. He falls in love with other ladies, married and unmarried; enlarges his mind by foreign travel; becomes famous in London as a poet, and is affianced to Lady Florence Lascelles, a kindred genius, a beauty and an heiress. She dies; he transfers his affections to a mysterious young woman, Evelyn Cameron; she turns out to be the daughter of the long lost Alice—presumably by himself. He is in despair. Eventually everything is cleared up. Alice's daughter had died, and Evelyn had been substituted in her place by Lord Vargrave, who had married Alice and died. Evelyn is happily disposed of to a colonel in the army; Maltravers is free to return to Alice.

Malvolio, in Shakespeare's comedy, *Twelfth Night*, steward to Olivia, solemn, pompous and puritanical, an easy butt for practical jokes.

The analogy between Malvolio and Don Quixote occurs inevitably. For both were men of lofty bearing, cursed with an exaggerated sense of their missions, and in both of them this sense was used by irreverent creatures to entice them into ludicrous plights. But the analogy does not go further than that. I cannot subscribe to Charles Lamb's ingenious paradox that Malvolio was in himself a fine fellow, whose dignified bearing had solid basis in a dignified nature. Malvolio does not, indeed, at the beginning of the play, say anything which would contradict this theory. But that is due to Shakespeare's slap-dash technique. Shakespeare's real opinion of Malvolio is shown in the words which he puts into the mouth of Olivia: "O, you are sick of self-love," etc. Malvolio is meant to be an egomaniac—a state quite inconsistent with true dignity. He is intrinsically absurd.—MAX BEERBOHM in *Saturday Review.*

And what a wonderful touch is that which opens all the sadder side of life in the very heart of the jest, by showing, within the pedantic gravity of Malvolio, a folly more intense than all the other folly combined, the half-tragic absurdity of self-importance and mad vanity, latent, and wanting only the stimulus of the simplest practical joke to call it forth!—MRS. OLIPHANT, *Molière.*

Mambrino, in Ariosto's *Orlando Furioso*, a pagan king of Bithynia who was specially famous for a golden helmet that made its wearer invisible. Mambrino is killed by Rinaldo, but the helmet is stolen from him by Scaripante and passes through many hands. In *Don Quixote* the mad knight sees a barber who has clapped upon his head a brazen basin to protect his hat from a sudden shower of rain. The Don insists that this is Mambrino's helmet. Taking possession of it he wears it as such. In Part I, iii, 8, the galley slaves snatch the basin from Quixote's head and break it to pieces. Cervantes, evidently forgetful of this episode, makes it turn up again in book IV, ch. xv, where the gentlemen at the inn sit in judgment on it, humor the Don's whim and gravely decide that it is not a basin but an undoubted helmet.

Mamillius, in Shakespeare's *A Winter's Tale*, a precocious and loving boy, son of Hermione, who dies in consequence of his mother's disgrace (III, 2).

The beautiful suggestion that Shakespeare as he wrote had in mind his own dead little son still fresh and living at his heart, can hardly add more than a touch of additional tenderness to our perfect and piteous delight in him.—SWINBURNE.

Mammon, Sir Epicure, in Ben Jonson's comedy, *The Alchemist* (1610), a conceited and purse-proud dupe who is easily cozened into supplying Subtle, the alchemist, with the funds necessary for carrying on his researches.

Epicure Mammon is the most determined offspring of its author. It has the "whole matter and copy of the father—eye, nose, lip, the trick of his frown." It is just such a swaggerer as contemporaries have described Old Ben to be. Meercraft, Bobadil, the Host of the New Inn, have all his image and superscription. But Mammon is arrogant pretension personified. Sir Samson Legend in *Love for Love* is such another lying, overbearing character, but he does not come up to Epicure Mammon. What a "towering bravery" there is in his sensuality. He affects no pleasure under a sultan.—CHARLES LAMB.

Man, The Last, lyric by Thomas Campbell turning on the gruesome fancy of a man who is left in utter loneliness after all the race has perished. The same idea occurs in Byron's *Darkness*, and a useless discussion was started between the two poets and their followers as to who was the plagiarist. Byron's poem was published first, but Campbell insisted that his own lyric was written first and had been shown in MS. to Byron.

Man in Black, an eccentric philanthropist in Goldsmith's *Citizen of the World* (1759), an evident combination of some of those Goldsmith family traits which were afterwards so successfully recalled in Dr. Primrose, Mr. Hardcastle, and the clergyman of the *Deserted Village*.

The contrast between his credulous charity and his expressed distrust of human nature, between his simulated harshness and his real amiability, constitutes a type which has since been often used successfully in English literature.—AUSTIN DOBSON, *Eighteenth Century Vignettes*, i, 121.

Man Who Laughs, hero and title of a novel by Victor Hugo. See GWYNPLAINE.

Manders, Pastor, in Ibsen's *Ghosts*, the clerical adviser to Mrs. Alving, a kindly and childish man with a good deal of moral cowardice and futility posing as virtue.

Mandeville, hero and title of a romance by William Godwin (1817), a furious misanthropist suffering from what modern psychopaths would call the mania of persecution. All mankind, he thinks, have conspired against him, and he commits strange deeds nor hesitates at crimes to protect himself against this visionary combination.

Manette, Dr. Alexander, in Dickens's *Tale of Two Cities*, a physician of Paris, for eighteen years a prisoner in the Bastille because of his professional acquaintance with the misdeeds of a noble family. Released just before the outbreak of the Revolution, his daughter Lucie devotes herself to him during his remaining years. See CARTON, SYDNEY, and DARNAY, CHARLES.

Manfred, in Horace Walpole's romance, *The Castle of Otranto* (1764), a mediæval baron who tyrannizes over his wife and beautiful daughter, but is finally overawed by a gigantic apparition.

Manfred, Count, hero of Byron's dramatic poem, *Manfred* (1811), a moody person of high intellect and indomitable will who has been guilty of some monstrous crime (apparently an unholy love for his own sister) and wanders in agony over the earth seeking oblivion. When introduced he has made his final abode in an Alpine solitude. He calls upon the spirits of the unbounded universe (all but the great Supreme) and vainly pleads with them for the gift of forgetfulness. In his last agony demons assail him, but he defies their power. See ASTARTE.

It is a grand and terrific vision of a being invested with superhuman attributes in order that he may be capable of more than human sufferings, and be sustained under them by more than human force and pride. —JEFFREY: *Essays from the Edinburgh Review.*

Manisty, Edward, in Mrs. Humphry Ward's novel of *Eleanor* (1900), is believed to be drawn from William H. Mallock. It is no flattering portrait. Self-centred and egotistical, moody and taciturn, Manisty adds to these qualities the ungraciousness of peculiarly bad manners. He falls in love first with his cousin, the titular heroine, and then with a pretty American. Eleanor, though she is in love with him, sacrifices herself to bring about the match.

Manly, Captain, in Wycherley's comedy, *The Plain-dealer* (1674), is evidently based to some extent on the Alceste of Molière's *Le Misanthrope* (1666). In externals there certainly seems small likeness between Wycherley's surly and uncouth sea captain and the polished but impatient cynic painted by Molière. Both alike, however, have been soured by the wickedness and hypocrisy of the age. Manly's infatuation for straightforward conduct and "plain-dealing" blinds him to the real qualities of men and women, and while he sees through superficial pretence and affectation he is like a child in the hands of those who humor his whims.

Wycherley borrowed Alceste and turned him—we quote the words of so lenient a critic as Mr. Leigh Hunt—into "a ferocious sensualist, who believed himself as great a rascal as he thought everybody else." The surliness of Molière's hero is copied and caricatured. But the most nauseous libertinism and the most dastardly fraud are substituted for the purity and integrity of of the original. And to make the whole complete, Wycherley does not seem to be aware that he was not drawing the portrait of an eminently honest man. So depraved was his moral taste that while he firmly believed that he was producing a picture of virtue too exalted for the commerce of this world he was really delineating the greatest rascal that is to be found even in his own writings.—MACAULAY: *Essays Comic Dramatists.*

Mannering, Colonel Guy, in Sir Walter Scott's *Guy Mannering* (1815), a retired English officer, wealthy, a widower of aristocratic tastes and prejudices, with a turn for astrological studies. Despite his caustic speech and reserved manner he has a fund of affection which his daughter Julia learns eventually to value. In chapter xvii, however, we find her writing, " It is impossible to say whether I love, admire or fear him the most. His success in life and in war—his habit of making every object yield before the energy of his exertions, even when they seemed insurmountable—all these have given a hasty and peremptory cast to his character, which can neither endure contradiction nor make allowances for deficiencies."

Mannering, Julia, heroine of Scott's *Guy Mannering,* the lively, dark beauty who is wooed and married by Vanbeest Brown. Andrew Lang holds that she is " a portrait from the life " of Miss Charpentier, who became Scott's wife: " In personal appearance the two ladies are unmistakably identical and Miss Charpentier in a letter of November 27, 1797, chaffs her lover exactly as Julia Mannering chaffs her austere father."

Mar, Helen, heroine of Jane Porter's historical romance, *The Scottish Chiefs* (1809). Though she is in love with Sir William Wallace she respects his devotion to his dead wife and does not aspire to be more than his sister. Wallace and Bruce rescue her when she is abducted to France. She is based on a real character of that name, the daughter of Lord Mar.

Marall, Sir Martin, the principal character in Dryden's comedy, *Sir Martin Marall, or the Feigned Innocent* (1667). See MARPLOT.

> The most entire piece of mirth . . . that certainly ever was writ . . . very good wit therein, no fooling.—PEPYS *Diary.*

March, Basil, in W. D. Howells's novels appears first with his newly married wife Isabella as the hero of *Their Wedding Journey.* He is a Boston journalist, amiable, unselfish, unpretentious, with a dry humor that tends towards self mockery, especially when he affects to be playing the favorite American matrimonial rôle of the Man-afraid-of-his-wife. Like Arthur Pendennis he and Isabella March reappear in many of Howells's novels as a sort of chorus on the main action, but he assumes an especially important part in *A Hazard of New Fortunes* as the editor of *Every Other Week.*

March, Jo (*i.e.,* Josephine), one of the titular *Little Women* (1867) in Louisa M. Alcott's juvenile story of that name. Like her own author she develops literary tastes and begins her career by contributing " blood-and-thunder stories " to the sensational weeklies, but desists for conscience sake at the very period when they begin to pay well.

Marcia, heroine of Addison's tragedy, *Cato* (1713), beloved by both Sempronius and Juba.

Marck, William de la (the " Wild Boar of Ardennes "), in Scott's historical romance, *Quentin Durward,* a notorious robber and murderer on the frontiers, excommunicated by the pope for a thousand crimes, whose head is the price by which may be won the hand of the Countess de Croye.

Margaret (diminutive *Gretchen, i.e.,* Maggie; in French Marguerite), the heroine of the first part of Goethe's *Faust* and of Gounod's opera based upon Goethe's drama. Name and character are Goethe's own inventions. In the original Faust chap-books a love-episode is passingly alluded to. Helen of Troy, sum-moned from the shades for Faust's gratification, bears him a son named Justus. Marlowe amplified this episode. He gave Helen an important share in the action. Not until 1728 do we come across any hint of Mar-garet. In a little chapbook Faust falls in love with " a beautiful but pure girl who would permit him nothing out of matrimony." Faust declares he will marry her. The fiend points out that marriage had been interdicted in the compact and cows him into submission. It was but a step from this idea to that of seduc-tion through the connivance of Mephistopheles. Gradually the per-sonage who at the creative touch of Goethe was to become the most charming figure in the story grew in importance. There is reason to be-lieve that even in advance of Goethe the story of Faust and his sweetheart was acted in the German puppet shows somewhat as we know it now. But it was Goethe who gave the maiden her name and her distinctive personality. The name was evidently suggested by Goethe's first love, the maid-servant Gretchen (Maggie), who returned his passionate ardor with sisterly affection. Some traits may have been borrowed from her. But Frederike Brion, the girl whose heart he almost broke, was more nearly in his thoughts.

Margaret is one of Goethe's most exquisite creations. A daughter of the people, simple, joyous, artless, full of innocent vanity, of naïve pert-ness, of sweet girlish love and faith, her very lack of the heroic qualities makes the pathos of her story com-plete.

Faust's feeling for her speedily changes from mere desire to some-thing more spiritual, from lust to love, or, rather, to a mixture of love and lust. The better nature struggles for the mastery, but in the end the coun-sels of Mephistopheles prevail. Lust triumphs; the maiden is seduced. Her shame becomes known. She

kills the infant to whom she has given birth and is thrown into prison. Here Faust finds her, crazed with suffering, singing wild snatches of song. He strives to make her fly with him, but flight is impossible. Morning dawns and finds her dying. Mephistopheles appears and forces Faust to leave her to her fate.

Margaret, the titular heroine of a romance of New England life (1845), by Rev. Sylvester Judd.

Judd had a delicate purity of mind which made him extremely felicitous in reproducing the simplicity of child-life and moral innocence. Margaret's pathway, amid hideous shapes of depravity in her family associations, is as redolent of inno-cence as the pathway of Una and her lion. The graceful fancies that play about her in her walk to and from church, her spiritual experiences in the evening on the hills, the sweetness that radiates like moonlight from her pure soul, are singularly child-like. She walks in a tainted atmosphere, but the miasma has failed to strike in.—*Century.*

Margaret of Anjou, daughter of King René, consort of Henry VI of England, appears in all three parts of Shakespeare's *Henry VI* as succes-sively maid, wife and widow, and reappears in the latter character in *Richard III.* Under her reverses her character develops from a high-spir-ited princess to a " bloody minded Queen."

Margaret in her widowhood is also a leading character in Scott's romance *Anne of Geierstein,* where she strives to secure the aid of Charles the Bold against the " usurper " Edward IV. Shakespeare violates history through-out. He makes her fall in love with Suffolk (*I Henry VI,* v, 5), a sheer in-vention. There is no evidence that she stabbed York (*III Henry VI,* i, 3, or had a hand in Gloucester's death. She died in 1482 and Richard III did not commence his reign until 1483. Nevertheless her presence in the play of *Richard III* is dramatically effect-ive, as she appears only to pour out curses and watch greedily for their fulfilment.

Marguerite, in Gounod's opera, *Faust.* See MARGARET.

Mariana, in Shakespeare's comedy, *Measure for Measure* (1603), a young lady betrothed but not actually married to Angelo whom he ha, abandoned to a solitary life. " There at the moated grange resides the dejected Mariana," says the duke to Isabella (Act iii, Sc. 1). Acting on this hint Tennyson in two of his shorter poems, *Mariana* (1830) and *Mariana in the South* (1832), has pictured the distress and desolation of Shakespeare's heroine when Angelo left her to wear out her life in solitary tears at the moated grange.

Marianne, titular heroine of a novel (1731) by Pierre Carlet de Marivaux.

A simple country girl who tells her own story,—she comes up to Paris and falls under the guardianship of a middle-aged roué with great pretences to sanctity. She indignantly repels all his advances, flies for refuge to a convent and eventually falls in love with a worthy young man who proves to be her persecutor's nephew.

Marianne has been said to be the origin of *Pamela*, which is not exactly the fact. But it is certain that it is a remarkable novel and that it gave rise to the singular phrase Marivaudage with which the author, not at all voluntarily, has enriched literature. The real importance of *Marianne* in the history of fiction is that it is the first example of the novel of analysis rather than of incident.—GEORGE SAINTSBURY.

Marigold, Dr., narrator of the story *Dr. Marigold's Prescriptions* (1865), by Charles Dickens. A " Cheap Jack" or itinerant auctioneer, he loses both his daughter and his wife and adopts a little deaf-mute.

Marina, heroine of Shakespeare's *Pericles, Prince of Tyre* (1608), and daughter of the titular hero, so called because she was born at sea. She was perfidiously sold as a slave at Mytilene, where Pericles eventually discovered her. She herself discovered her mother Thasia (supposed to have died in childbirth) in the priestess officiating at the oracle of Diana at Ephesus.

Marinel, in Spenser's *Faërie Queene* (Books iii–iv), is the recalcitrant lover of Florimel. Living in a rocky cave he allows nobody to pass without challenge. Britomart proved more than a match for him, however, for when he forbade her progress she simply knocked him " grovelling on the ground " with her spear. His love story is told under Florimel.

Marius, titular hero of Walter Pater's *Marius the Epicurean* (1853), a young Roman noble at the time when Marcus Aurelius, by precept and example, encouraged people to take their old religion seriously. Like the Emperor, Marius is an exponent of the finer tendencies of his day, a reminiscence at once of Roman greatness in the past and a prophecy of the Christian future. His philosophy, based on Cyrenaicism or Epicureanism, altered more or less, ebbed and flowed, touched very closely on Stoicism, as true Epicureanism naturally does, and nearly welled over into Christianity. So great was the æsthetic impression made on the hero by early Christian services, and so strong his apprehension of the tranquil happiness and corporate existence in the Church of Christian men, that he was " almost persuaded to be a Christian." He died, too, while still young, in such circumstances that the generosity of the Church regarded him as a martyr.

Marjoribanks, Lucilla, heroine of Mrs. Oliphant's novel *Miss Marjoribanks* (1865). Daughter of the hard-headed, unromantic doctor of Carlingford, who early in the story is left a not inconsolable widower, she resolves to devote her energies to the task of being " a comfort to dear papa," and incidentally of reforming and reshaping the unsatisfactory condition of Carlingford society. The doctor, possessing a keen sense of humor, is greatly tickled by the grand air with which his daughter occupies her new position and still more delighted at her success.

Markheim, hero and title of a short story by R. L. Stevenson in *The Merry Men* (1887). A man who has failed through weakness, eventually falls into crime, and deliberately murders a man for gain. He is confronted by his own soul, which drives him to repentance and confession.

Here is the germ that eventually developed into *The Strange Case of Dr. Jekyll and Mr. Hyde* (1886).

In *Markheim* the devil is akin to the German *Doppelgänger*. He is Markheim's worst self, or represents in the flesh his worst possibilities, coming at a crucial moment to tempt the man who has slipped away from good to commit himself irrevocably to evil. Here, in half-a-dozen pages, is compressed the whole history of a weak mortal's gradual descent from innocent youth, highly aspiring, to most iniquitous manhood. Markheim is going, as thousands of Markheims infirm of purpose have gone, morally straight to hell. He is stayed at the last moment by a flash of defiance, of revolt against the malignant shape that would bind him fast for ever. Only George Eliot's Tito Melema is comparable in drawing to Markheim, and Mr. Stevenson does not lose in force by brevity.—*N. Y. Nation*, May 19, 1887.

Marko, Prince, in George Meredith's novel, *The Tragic Comedians*, a rival of Dr. Alvan (*q.v.*) for the hand of Clotilde von Rudiger. He kills the other in a duel. The novel is based upon the tragic story of Ferdinand Lassalle's death. Alvan is Lassalle, Prince Marko in real life was Yanko von Racowitza.

Marlow, Young, in Goldsmith's *She Stoops to Conquer* (1773), son of Sir Charles Marlow, who sends him on a visit to his old friend Squire Hardcastle and describes him to that gentleman as a miracle of shyness and modesty. Marlow's shyness afflicts him only in the unaccustomed society of ladies; with women of other classes he is quite at his ease. He mistakes Hardcastle's house for an inn and his daughter for the barmaid. She, knowing who he is, humors the mistake and wins him first to an outburst of passion and then to a confession of honest love.

Marner, Silas, the leading character in George Eliot's novel, *Silas Marner, the Weaver of Raveloe* (1861). A handloom weaver afflicted with catalepsy, he had known strange spiritual experiences in youth, but his nearest friend had robbed him at once of his sweetheart and his good name, falsely accusing him of theft; and Silas, bewildered, distrusting God and man, had retired to a lonely hut. Here he found his only solace in gloat-ing over a little heap of gold scraped together by miserly means. One day he is robbed. He is saved from his own despair by the chance finding of a little child. On this baby girl he lavishes all the latent love of his thwarted nature, and her filial affection redeems him and fits him once more for human companionship when, after sixteen years, the real thief is discovered and Silas's good name is restored.

Marphurius, in Molière's comedy, *Le Marriage Forcé* (1664), a pyrrhic philosopher, unable to make up his mind upon any subject. Sganarelle consults him about his marriage: "Perhaps, it may be so; everything is uncertain," replies the sceptic. Sganarelle repays him in his own coin. He thrashes him and, when Marphurius threatens an action for damages, he retorts, "Perhaps, it may be so; everything is uncertain." (Sc. 11.)

Marplot, the hero of Mrs. Susanna Centlivre's comedy, *The Busybody* (1709), and its sequel, *Marplot in Lisbon* (1711). An inquisitive and impertinent booby, continually intruding, to his own discomfiture and that of others, into the affairs of his neighbor. He owes his being in part to Molière's *L'Etourdi* and its English imitations (Dryden's *Sir Martin Marall* and the Duke of Newcastle's *Sir Martin Marplot*), but is in essentials an original character of genuine humor, differing from his predecessors "by committing a succession of exploits in action as well as in speech. He is the parent of that long-lived favorite of our own days, Paul Pry, and some of his unexpected apparitions, especially one down the chimney, are irresistibly ludicrous." (A. W. WARD: *English Dramatic Literature*, p. 491.)

Marplot, Sir Martin, hero of a comedy of that name translated or adapted, with little more than a change of venue, from Molière's *L'Etourdi*, by William Cavendish, Duke of Newcastle, who was assisted in the staging by Dryden. Mrs. Centlivre borrowed the name Marplot, shorn of its knightly title, for the hero of her comedy *The Busybody*, who differs materially from his predecessor. See LELIE.

Marrall, Jack, in Massinger's comedy, *A New Way to Pay Old Debts* (1625), a Term-Driver, a vile tool of Sir Giles Overreach, whom the usurer utilizes in his dirty work. Marrall, convinced that Sir Giles's nephew and chief victim, Frank Wellborn, is engaged to an heiress, seeks to curry favor with him by betraying his employer, and is finally involved in the old man's ruin and kicked off the stage, to the applause of everybody.

Marsac, Gaston de Bonne, Sieur de, hero of Stanley Weyman's *A Gentleman of France* (1893), a historical romance dealing with France just before the accession of Henry IV. An impoverished nobleman, chivalrous, adventurous and thoroughly loyal to the cause of Henry of Navarre, he involves himself in a plot for the abduction of Turenne's niece, Mademoiselle de Vire, and wins that high-spirited lady from sworn enmity to love and marriage.

Marse Chan (the name by which he is known to his negro servant, who tells the story), a gallant Southerner, hero and title of a short story by Thomas Nelson Page, published in volume, *In Old Virginia* (1887). He loves a lady who loves him in return, but treats him in true Lady Disdain fashion until she learns of his death on the battlefield, when she mourns for him as for a husband all the rest of her life.

Marshmont, Allegra, in I. Zangwill's novel, *The Mantle of Elijah* (1900), the daughter of an English prime minister, full of high ideals, under whose influence she makes a deplorable marriage with Robert, a plausible but vulgar demagogue. Through the influence of Raphael Dominick she is disillusioned and returns to her own family.

Martano, in Ariosto's *Orlando Furioso*, Books viii–ix, (1516), a braggart and a coward, who presented himself before King Norandino of Damascus in the armor he had stolen from Gryphon, the victor in a great tournament, and so robbed him not only of his prizes but also of his faithless lady-love, Origilla. The villainy was unmasked by Aguilant, who seized the precious pair and returned with them to Damascus. Martano was hanged and Origilla imprisoned. Spenser imitated the character of Martano in his Sir Bragadocchio, *Faërie Queene*, iii, 8, 10.

Martext, Sir Oliver, in Shakespeare's *As You Like It*, a vicar determined that " ne'er a fantastical knave of them all shall flout me out of my calling."

Martha, in Goethe's *Faust*, a garrulous and foolish matron, a friend of Margaret, who allows Mephistopheles to make pretended love to her while Faust is carrying out his plans for the seduction of the younger woman.

Martin, Mabel, heroine of a narrative poem by J. G. Whittier, originally published (1860) under the title of *The Witch's Daughter*, afterwards (1875) revised and enlarged and republished as *Mabel Martin*. The daughter of a reputed witch who had been legally murdered, she sits at a husking frolic alone and despised, and is finally driven away with taunts and insults. Esken Harden, the host of the occasion, touched by her beauty and her sorrow, follows and brings her back to introduce her as his bride to the company assembled.

Martine, in Molière's *Le Médecin Malgré Lui* (1666), the wife of Sganarelle. When the latter beats her she screams for help, but when Robert, a neighbor, would champion her, she resents his interference. " It is my wish to be beaten!" she cries, and Sganarelle transfers the stick to Robert's shoulders for meddling with matters that do not concern him.

Marwood, Alice, in Dickens's novel, *Dombey and Son* (1846), a precocious criminal who had been transported in girlhood for participation in a burglary. Returning to England she was seduced by Carker. She was assisted in securing revenge by her mother, " Mrs. Brown," a former mistress of Mrs. Skewton's brother-in-law. Through this illegitimate connection Alice rightly came by a striking family resemblance to Edith Skewton, Mr. Dombey's second wife. with whom Carker eloped. See DOMBEY, EDITH.

Mascarille (Italian *maschera*, a mask, under which disguise Molière himself played the part), one of Molière's best known characters, who appears in *l'Etourdi* (1653), in *Le Depit Amoureux* (1654), and *Les Précieuses Ridicules* (1659). He is imitated from the Davus and Tranio of classic comedy, and in his turn gave way to Sganarelle and Scapin, the fruits of Molière's maturer imagination. An ever-faithful yet ever-lying valet, he cheats, steals and perjures himself for his master, but is always true to his interests and develops an amazing fertility of trickery in seeking to advance them.

Maskwell, in William Congreve's comedy, *The Double-Dealer* (1700), a suave and cunning hypocrite whose conscious villainy is more fiend-like than human. Lady Touchwood, herself a woman of low morals, cherishing a lawless passion for her husband's nephew, Mellefont, describes him as "a sedate, a thinking villain whose black blood runs temperately bad." Knowing her secret, Maskwell attempts to use it for Mellefont's discomfiture and his own conquest of Cynthia Pliant, to whom Mellefont is affianced, all the while pretending to be the latter's best friend.

The heartless treachery of Maskwell is overdone. He is a devil, pure and simple, and not a man at all.—E. W. GOSSE.

Maslova, heroine of Tolstoi's novel, *Resurrection* (1900). As a young girl out at service she had been seduced by Prince Dimitri Ivanovitch Nekludoff, a profligate Russian aristocrat. Plunging into a life of shame, she is finally brought to trial for the murder and robbery of one of her lovers. Nekludoff is on the jury that finds her guilty. So great is his remorse for the past that he forswears all the privileges of rank and wealth, follows her to Siberia and succeeds in reforming her, but fails in his effort to marry her. She loves him, indeed, but she will not accept so great a sacrifice at his hands. He devotes the rest of his life to good works and especially the weeding out of social abuses.

Mason, Lady, heroine of Anthony Trollope's *Orley Farm,* 1862.

Her mixture of guilt and innocence, her strength and weakness and her power of making herself loved whatever she does, constitute altogether one of the best conceived types of mixed character neither good nor bad that modern English fiction has to show.—*Saturday Review,* October 11, 1862.

Massingbird, Lost Sir. See HEATH, SIR MASSINGBIRD.

Master, The Old, a leading figure in Dr. O. W. Holmes's *Poet at the Breakfast Table,* who divides conversational honors with the Poet. "I think," says the Poet, "he suspects himself of a three-story intellect, and I don't feel sure that he isn't right."

Matchin, Maud, the central figure and the best drawn character in John Hay's *The Breadwinners* (1884). A beautiful, hard, sordid and commonplace girl whose mind is warped by wild desires for social advancement; she is the exponent as well as the victim of a badly regulated education in the public schools.

Mathilde, in Rossini's opera, *Guglielmo Tell* (1829), sister of Gessler the tyrannical Austrian governor of Switzerland. She is in love with Arroldo, a Swiss, and marries him after her brother's death.

Matilda, heroine of Sir Walter Scott's narrative poem, *Rokeby* (1812). Daughter of the Knight of Rokeby and niece of Mortham, she was beloved by Wilfred, but herself loved her father's page. After the course of true love had run roughly for a period it was made smooth by the discovery that the humble page was the son and heir of Mortham.

Matsys, Quentin (1466–1530), a noted Flemish painter, is the hero and title of a novel by Caroline Pichler founded on fact. Originally a blacksmith in Antwerp, Quentin fell in love with Liza, whose father, Johann Mandyn, a famous painter, declared that only a painter might win his daughter. Thereupon the blacksmith gave up the anvil for the secret study of art. One day he visited Mandyn's studio surreptitiously and on the leg of a pictured angel he painted a bee. So life-like was the insect that Mandyn, returning, tried to shoo it away with his handkerchief. One revelation leading to another, the old painter gladly welcomed the young one as his son-in-law.

Matthias, in J. R. Ware's drama, *The Polish Jew* (1874), a German miller haunted by the memory of a terrible crime. One Christmas Eve a Jew pedlar had stopped at his house for refreshment and driven off in his sleigh. Matthias had followed and murdered him for the money he had carelessly exhibited, then flung the body to be consumed in a limekiln. Every Christmas eve after that, the imagined sound of sleighbells drives Matthias almost mad with horror. Finally he dreams that he has been put into a mesmeric sleep, forced into confession, and executed. The shock kills him. Ware's drama was founded on a short story, *Le Juif Polonais*, by Erckmann-Chatrian. Henry Irving won his first great success in the part of Matthias and he repeatedly brought out the play under the title of *The Bells.*

Maud, heroine of a narrative poem by Alfred Tennyson, of whom we are told little more than that at sixteen she was tall and stately and had a classical profile. Her lover, uꞋnamed, who tells the story, draws himself at full length as a sort of modernized Ravenswood, though even more peevish and hysterical.

Tennyson held a volume of *Maud* in his hand and was talking about it, as he loved to do: "I want to read this to you because I want you to feel what the poem means. It is dramatic; it is the story of a man who has a morbid nature, with a touch of hereditary insanity, and very selfish. The poem is to show what love does for him. The war is only an episode. You must remember that it is not I myself speaking. It is this man with the strain of madness in his blood

and the memory of a great trouble and wrong that has put him out with the world."
—HENRY VAN DYKE, *Century Magazine,* vol. 45, p. 539.

Maugis, one of Charlemagne's paladins, a magician as well as a warrior, and the Nestor of French romance. He is the Malagigi of Pulci and Ariosto.

Maul, in Bunyan's *Pilgrim's Progress,* Part II (1684), a giant fond of sophistical reasonings, whereby he deluded and deceived the young. He attacked Mr. Greatheart with a club, but Greatheart pierced him under the fifth rib, and then cut off his head.

Mauley, Sir Edward, in Scott's romance of *The Black Dwarf* (1816), is known as the Black Dwarf from his physical deformities. A misshapen monster with only " a distorted resemblance to humanity," he is morbidly sensitive to his defects and is moreover the prey to an acute conscience. Born to great wealth which his parents designed should become greater by his union with a kinswoman, Letitia, he was tricked out of his promised bride by Richard Vere, a bosom friend, while he lay in jail for defending that friend from a would-be assassin whom he had slain. Losing faith in humanity he goes into retirement and is suspected to be a magician in league with the devil, but gradually wins popular confidence by acting as physician to mind and body of any who sought his aid. Though professing that his only object is the misanthropic one of " perpetuating the mass of human misery," he acts always with wisdom, generosity and exuberant liberality. He reveals himself at last as Sir Edward Mauley in order to baulk Richard Vere in his plans for marrying Isabel Vere, his daughter, to the unworthy Langley.

Mauprat, Adrien de, the lover and husband of Julie in Bulwer Lytton's drama, *Richelieu.* A colonel in the army of Louis XIII, he is described as " the wildest gallant and bravest knight of France." The king shut him up in the Bastille for braving his displeasure by the surreptitious marriage, but Richelieu after a due period of suspense procured his release and pardon.

George Sand has taken the name *Mauprat* as the title and hero of a romance embodying the character and career of the last of a fierce race of robber barons in France.

Mause, Old, in Scott's romance, *Old Mortality,* a covenanter, the mother of Cuddie Headdrigg.

Mauves, Madame de, titular heroine of a short story by Henry James in *A Passionate Pilgrim and other Tales.*

A very subtle study of the contrast between a pure American girl's idealistic view of the old French *noblesse*, and her actual experience of a selfish and worthless French husband of long descent whom she has married out of the depths of her girlish enthusiasm—the contrast being pointed, of course, by the appearance of the right man on the scene when it is too late to have any effect on the development of the story, except by eliciting a deeper shade of depravity in the husband and a finer shade of moral idealism in the wife.—*Spectator.*

Mavering, Dan, hero of W. D. Howells's novel, *April Hopes* (1887), a Harvard graduate of good family who marries Alice Pasmer. She is a high bred New England girl with a Puritan conscience and an ironclad code which makes no allowance for human nature.

Mawworm, in Isaac Bickerstaff's comedy, *The Hypocrite* (1768), a vulgar and ignorant imitator of his patron Dr. Cantwell and a co-conspirator against the comfort and dignity of Sir John Lambert's family. He shares in Cantwell's downfall when their plans miscarry. Cantwell is modelled on Molière's *Tartuffe*, but Mawworm is an original conception of Bickerstaff's, introduced to enforce the satire against the later puritan dissenters. In his attitude of pretended humility he anticipates Uriah Heep: " Do despise me," he pleads; " I'm the prouder for it. I like to be despised " (Act ii, Sc. 1). He is the best drama character in the play, and in the hands of successive exponents, from Weston and Quick to the elder Matthews and Liston, enjoyed almost unexampled prosperity.

Bickerstaff's comedy, *The Hypocrite,* is a fairly brisk and entertaining piece founded upon *Tartuffe.* Instead of coming directly through the French, it reaches us through Cibber's adaptation *The Nonjuror* (1717), which substituted for Tartuffe an English Catholic priest seducing an English gentleman into treasonable practices. Colley Cibber provoked the wrath of the Jacobite faction and was responsible for the endless series of attacks to which he was thenceforward subject. With the expiration of Jacobite hopes the political aspects of the play lost their significance. Bickerstaff returned to the original motive, and by the introduction of Mawworm directed the satire against the late development of puritanical dissent.—*London Athenæum.*

Maxime, in Chaucer's *Second Nun's Tale* in *The Canterbury Tales* (1388), an officer of the prefect Almachius, who during the Diocletian persecution was ordered to slay Valerian and Tiburce, contumacious Christians who refused to worship the image of Jupiter. Instead he compassionately took them home with him, was converted and baptized by them and when they were martyred declared that he saw angels conveying them to heaven. Thereupon Almachius had him flogged to death.

Maylie, Rose, in Dickens's *Oliver Twist,* adopted daughter of Mrs. Maylie. She eventually marries Harry Maylie and turns out to be the aunt of Oliver whom the family had befriended in his need.

May Queen, in the poem of that name by Tennyson, is the bright-eyed merry Alice who in Part 1 begs her mother to call her early next morning:

For I'm to be queen o' the May, mother,
  I'm to be queen o' the May.

In Part 11 Alice is lying bedridden on New Year's eve, and again she begs to be called early, for another reason:

But I would see the sun rise upon the glad
  New Year,
So if you 're waking, call me, call me early
  mother dear.

In Part 111 March has come. Alice has lingered until now, but breathes her last farewell with a kind word for Robin, the village lad who had loved her in her proud and wilful youth:

If I had lived—I cannot tell—I might have
been his wife;
But all these things have ceased to be with
my desire of life.

Mazeppa, Ivan Stefanovitch (1640–
1709), the hero of Byron's poem, *Mazeppa* (1819), was an historical character. By birth a Cossack, he entered
the service of John Casimir, King of
Poland. A Polish nobleman surprised him in an intrigue with his
wife, bound him naked on his own
horse, and lashed the animal out
into the steppes. The animal bore
him off to its native woods in the
Ukraine, where Cossacks released
him. He became a leader among
them and was ennobled by Peter the
Great, but deserted to Charles XII
when that Swedish monarch invaded
Russia. After the defeat at Pultowa,
he killed himself by poison.

Byron, basing his poem on Voltaire's *Charles XII*, makes Mazeppa
tell his story to Charles XII after
Pultowa. Pushkin has made Mazeppa the hero of a drama, *Pultowa*.
Hugo has a poem on the subject in
Les Orientales. Boulanger in 1827
exhibited a picture of Mazeppa bound
to his horse. Its fame, however, was
eclipsed later in the same year by two
pictures exhibited by Horace Vernet.
A portrait of Mazeppa painted from
life was discovered in 1886, at Kief,
in Southern Russia.

A melodrama, *Mazeppa*, was produced in Philadelphia in 1825 by a
handsome Englishman named Hunter,
and had a great run. In 1840 Adah
Isaacs Menken originated the idea
of substituting a woman (herself) in
the part, and her overwhelming success
in America, London and Paris made
it a favorite play with other actresses
who had a shapely form to display.

Meadows, Mr., in Madame
D'Arblay's novel of *Cecilia* (*q.v.*), is
an *ennuyé*, described by one of the
characters as "the sweetest dresser
in the world. I assure you it's a great
thing to be spoke to by him; we are
all of us quite angry when he won't
take any notice of us." He himself
complains, on one occasion, of being
"worn to a thread," because he has

been "talking to a young lady to
entertain her."

Mears, Charlie, in *The Finest
Story in the World* in Kipling's *Many
Inventions*, a bank clerk who imagines
himself a poet and a story teller. In
his own self he is absolutely without
literary gift. But we are allowed to
believe that in some former life he
had been a Greek galley-slave. Every
now and then he drags up from the
dim recesses of his brain wondrous
recollections which he looks upon as
inventions. Just as the finest story
in the world is being put together bit
by bit, the chain is snapped. Charlie
has "tasted the love of woman that
kills remembrance."

Medamothi, in Rabelais's *Pantagruel*, iv, 3 (1545), an island where
Pantagruel and his fleet landed on
the fourth day of their voyage.
Many curiosities were to be seen here,
as "an echo drawn from life," "a
picture of a man's voice," some of the
"atoms" of Epicurus, and a sample
of Philomela's needlework. Medamothi is compounded of two Greek
words and means "Never in any
place." Etymology and definition
kin it to the word Utopia.

Medora, in Byron's poem, *The
Corsair*, the wife of Conrad (*q.v.*),
who pined away and died while he
was imprisoned by the pacha Seyd.
In describing her Byron had in mind
Lady Frances Wedderburn Spencer,
his favorite of the hour. The lines,
Remember him, when Passion's Power,
and the sonnets, *To Genevra*, were
written under her spell. *The Bride
of Abydos*, which was "thrown off"
in four nights, was written to divert
his mind from his passion for this
lady, and it was in her honour that
Medora, the Corsair's bride, was
first named "Francesca."

Medoro, in Ariosto's *Orlando Furioso* (1516), a beautiful Moorish youth
of humble origin. Agramante took
him captive at the siege of Jerusalem,
brought him to Paris and made him
his page. When the lad was wounded
Angelica, his fellow countrywoman,
tended him, fell in love with him,
married him and eloped with him to

Cathay. Hence the madness of Orlando, who was in love with Angelica.

Megone, Mogg, an Indian sachem who at the bidding of a white girl brings her the scalp of her seducer, but the bloody trophy diverts her hatred from the seducer to his slayer and she murders Megone in his sleep. This Indian legend has been versified by Whittier.

Meister, Wilhelm, hero of Goethe's philosophical romance, *Wilhelm Meister's Apprenticeship* (1795–1796), and its sequel, *Wilhelm Meister's Wanderings* (Wanderjahre), the latter not published until 1821–1829. As with the drama of *Faust*, these two parts of one great whole may be taken as a sort of allegorical representation of the life of Goethe or less specifically the life of the typical Man. This interpretation seems to be implied in Goethe's own statement to Eckermann. "The critics," he complained, " seek a central point which in truth is hard to find. I should think a rich manifold life brought close to our eyes might suffice, without any determined moral tendency which could be reasoned upon. But, if this is insisted upon, it may perhaps be found in what Frederick, at the end, says to the hero, " Thou seemest to me like Saul, the son of Kish, who went out to seek his father's asses, and found a kingdom! For what does the whole say, but that man, despite all his follies and errors, led by a higher hand, reaches some higher aim at last?"

A number of brilliant episodes serve to present the different stages in Meister's spiritual evolution. The son of a German merchant, he falls in with and joins a troupe of strolling players. At first the glitter of his new life attracts him, but the tinsel eventually reveals itself. He loves Marianne and has a son, Felix, by her, but abandons both in a fit of unfounded jealousy. He meets and befriends Mignon (*q.v.*), who dies of unrequited passion for him. He abandons the bohemian life for that of solid respectability and is initiated into the ways of the great world. His development is expedited by reclaiming his son. What women and society have failed to teach him he learns from little Felix. He marries a lady of wealth and station and turns landowner.

Melaine, titular heroine of a narrative poem by N. P. Willis, an impassioned and fine-strung girl who discovers at the altar that her lover is her brother and dies.

Melbury, Grace, in Thomas Hardy's novel, *The Woodlanders* (1887).

She is an Anna Karénina called to a lower state of life. She wants the earth, and takes all she can get of it, by fair means or foul. She had a worse man for a husband than was Anna Karénina's, and a better man for a lover; thus she was saved from actual infidelity, though by no virtue in herself. Tolstoi barely condones Anna's fault, and sweeps her by the judgment of conscience to a fearful end. Mr. Hardy exalts the spirituality of Grace Melbury, and doesn't seem to think that she commits an error worth the attention of conscience. He doesn't mean, either, that her husband shall appear rather less offensive than she, yet he does; for, having been off a year or so with another woman, Fitzpiers experiences a slight diffidence in inviting his wife to live with him again.—*N. Y. Nation,* May 19, 1887.

Melema, Tito, in George Eliot's *Romola* (1863), a beautiful young Greek, winning all hearts by the sweetness of his temper and the charm of his manner, loving most things, hating nothing but pain, bodily or mental; never deliberately proposing to do anything cruel or base, but descending step by step into cruelty and baseness, simply because he tries to step away from everything unpleasant, and betraying every trust in him, simply because he cares solely for his own safety and pleasure. Among his victims are Romola and Tessa, both of whom he married, and Baldassare, who eventually strangles him to death.

Mr. Moncure D. Conway says that the brilliant woman dearly loved the characters she created even when they were wicked. Her friend Sara Hennell told him that once when at her house in London looking at some sketches of the characters in *Romola,* hanging on the wall, they stood before "Tito." After a moment's silence

George Eliot said softly, as if to herself, "The dear fellow." Sara Hennell exclaimed, "He's not a dear fellow at all, but a very bad fellow." "Ah," said "Tito's" creator, with a smile, "I was seeing him with the eyes of 'Romola.'"—*N. Y. Tribune.*

Mélisande, heroine of Maurice Maeterlinck's romantic tragedy, *Pelléas and Mélisande* (1892), a princess from a strange land, married offhand to Goland, a king's son in Allemonde, who discovers her sitting disconsolate in a forest. This Teutonic Francesca falls in love with her husband's younger brother Pelléas and he with her. Goland suspects—his jealousy strangely mingled with love for his brother and his child wife— and when suspicion ripens for him into certainty he kills Pelléas and wounds Mélisande so that she dies after premature delivery of a child.

Mélisande is one of the poet's most successful full-length portraits. She is exquisitely girlish, is charming with her strange undine airs, and is touched by a singular atmosphere of the remote. Hauptmann has realized the same ethereal type in Rautendelein. Mélisande is very romantic. At times she is on the point of melting into the green tapestry of the forest. She is a woodland creature. More melancholy than Miranda, she is not without traces of her high-bred temperament; less real than Juliet, she seems quite as passion-smitten.— JAMES HUNEKER: *Iconoclasts,* p. 402.

Mell, Mr., in Dickens's *David Copperfield* (1849), a kindly weakling, second master at Mr. Creakle's school, Salem House, who finds a solace in his flute for all worldly ills, even for the fact that his mother is in an almshouse and for Steerforth's sneers at this " degradation."

Melmoth, hero of C. R. Maturin's romance, *Melmoth, the Wanderer.*

Melmoth has bartered his soul with the devil for something like immortality and other privileges, including the unusual one of escaping his doom if he can get some one to take the bargain off his hands. This leads to numerous episodes in which Melmoth attempts to obtain substitutes, and in one of these the love-interest of the book —the, of course fatal, love of Melmoth himself for a Spanish Indian girl, Immalee, or Isidora—is related with some real pathos and passion, though with a good deal of mere sentiment and twaddle.—GEORGE SAINTSBURY: *The English Novel,* p. 186.

Melnotte, Claude, hero of Bulwer Lytton's comedy, *The Lady of Lyons* (1838). He is in love with Pauline Deschapelles, the proudest beauty in Lyons. Being only a poor gardener's son, he finds that he has no chance to win her. Two other rejected suitors, Beauseant and Glavis, conspire with him to conquer her by strategy. Claude, assuming to be the Prince of Como, dupes the lady into marriage, but is scornfully repudiated when Pauline discovers the trick. He joins the revolutionary army under the name of Morier, rises to be colonel, acquires wealth and returns to Lyons just in the nick of time. Pauline's father is on the eve of bankruptcy; she herself is on the verge of matrimony with the false Beauseant. Claude saves the situation and wins the love and admiration of his own wife.

Melun, in Shakespeare's *King John,* a French lord. Shakespeare accepts from Matthew Paris the story that before his death, which took place in London, Melun revealed to certain English barons that Louis and 16 of his earls and barons were bound by oath, in case England were conquered, to kill, banish or imprison all the English nobility as traitors or rebels.

Melville, Julia, in Sheridan's comedy, *The Rivals* (1775), a noble-hearted girl in love with the jealous Faulkland, and retaining a single-minded devotion to him despite all his unjust suspicions and galling innuendos.

Mencia of Mosquera, in *Gil Blas,* i, 11–14, a novel by Le Sage. Her husband, Don Alvo de Mells, was forced to flee after slaying a friend in a quarrel. He was reported dead and Mencia married the Marquis of Guardia, who took her to his castle near Burgos. Here among the under gardeners she recognized Don Alvo. Eloping with him, he was slain by a gang of robbers who, after immuring her in their cave, sent her back to the Marquis of Guardia. But she found him dying of grief and after closing his eyes retired to a convent.

Mendoza, Isaac, in Sheridan's comedy, *The Duenna* (1775), a Portuguese Jew, wise in his own conceit, whose fancied wit is ever outwitted by those he would make his dupes. "I'm cunning, I fancy," he chuckles to himself," a very cunning dog aint I? a sly little villain, eh? a bit roguish; he must be very wide awake who can take Isaac in!" He meets Louisa, whom he had intended to make his wife; she dupes him into the belief that she is Clara Guzman; he sends his rival Antonio to the supposed Clara and she marries him; he mistakes Louisa's duenna for Louisa and elopes with her.

Mephistopheles (a name variously spelled in German myth and English drama until the popularity of Goethe's *Faust* crystallized this form), one of the seven chief devils in the demonology of the Middle Ages, the second of the fallen angels and the most powerful, after Satan, of all the infernal host. Moncure D. Conway (*Pedigree of the Devil*) traces his lineage back to Asmodeus (*q.v.*). Under his present name, however, he was unknown to the public until the thirteenth century, and in his modern quality as the familiar demon of Faust he made his first literary appearance in an anonymous German book published (1587) by Johann Spies. Next year, under the form Mephistophilis (*q.v.*), Marlowe introduced him to an English audience in his tragedy, *Dr. Faustus*. An etymology endorsed by Conway makes the name a hybrid compound (Latin, *mephitis*, and Greek, *philos*) meaning a lover of bad smells. Dunzer suggests three Greek rootwords: *me*, not; *photos*, light, and *philos*, love = not loving light.

Be his origin what it may, he is best known to us as the cold, cynical, relentless fiend of Goethe's *Faust*,—the composite sixteenth century devil fused into a new and more coherent individuality by the typical genius of the early nineteenth. In the old Faust legends Mephistopheles's character is simple. He is a fiend, malicious, malignant and supernaturally powerful, who executes Faust's behests in order to secure his soul. Marlowe invested him with a melan-

choly dignity that may have suggested to Milton some of the traits of his Satan. Goethe's conception marked a new departure. In the first fragment of his *Faust* (published 1790, but written earlier), Mephistopheles has a marked individuality. Cynical and materialistic, but finding a man's delight in action and adventure, he seems supernatural only by virtue of his magical feats. Succinctly summed up, he is the spirit of unrest, denial and contradiction of mockery and self-mockery, in the dual nature of man, whose higher self is typified by Faust. His mission is to destroy in order that Faust may rebuild. Because he rejoices in destruction for its own sake, he is the better fitted to perform his God-appointed task. In the history of humanity he appears and reappears at all crises which call for a renewal of the old in a higher form. This conception lies immanent in the words put by Goethe into his mouth: "I am the spirit which denies! Which always wills the bad and does the good." It is artistically worked out to its end in the overthrow of Mephistopheles and the triumph of Faust, as shown in the last scene of the second part published in 1825.

Goethe was too sure an artist not to see the danger of dealing with mere abstractions and, though Mephistopheles is the embodiment of an idea, his external traits are modelled from concrete personalities. Perhaps Voltaire was to some extent in Goethe's mind,—Voltaire whom in his childhood he could have strangled for his irreverent treatment of the Bible. Grimm suggests Herder as the prototype, but he makes a little too much of this idea. Goethe himself has indicated Merck, a man who, unproductive himself and of a strongly marked negative tendency, took a malicious delight in mocking at the efforts and aspirations of others.— WALSH: *Faust, the Legend and the Poem.*

Mephistophilis, in Marlowe's drama, *Tragical History of Dr. Faustus* (1588), marks the first appearance of that fiend (see MEPHISTOPHELES) on the English stage.

The melancholy figure of Mephistophilis has a certain grandeur, but he is not the Tempter, according to the common conception, creeping to his purpose with the cunning of the serpent; nor is he the cold ironical "spirit that denies;" he is more like the Satan of Byron, with a touch of piety and much repentance. The language he addresses to Faustus is such as would rather frighten than seduce him.—G. H. LEWES: *Life of Goethe* (1855).

Mercedes, heroine and title of a drama (1883), by T. B. Aldrich. The French soldiery have invaded her native town in Spain. Poisoned wine has been prepared for them. To disarm their suspicions she drinks of it and gives her baby to drink. When twenty of the Frenchmen have followed suit the baby grows livid and dies before their eyes.

Mercutio, in Shakespeare's tragedy of *Romeo and Juliet* (1598), a kinsman to Prince Escalus and friend to Romeo. He is an elegant trifler, a light-hearted mocker who has not earnestness enough for strong passion or deep conviction, a product, by reaction, of Italian life where excess of sentiment evokes the scoffer at sentiment. His chief attribute is humor, coupled with a light, airy fancy and a tendency to puns and conceits. He always sees the ridiculous side of things and greets it with a laugh, light, airy and mercurial—like his name. See TYBALT.

Oh! how shall I describe that exquisite ebullience and overflow of youthful life, wafted on over the laughing waves of pleasure and prosperity, as a wanton beauty, that distorts the face on which she knows her lover is gazing enraptured, and wrinkles her forehead in the triumph of its smoothness! Wit ever wakeful; fancy busy, and procreative as an insect; courage; an easy mind, that, without cares of its own, is at once disposed to laugh away those of others, and yet to be interested in them—these and all congenial qualities, melting into the common copula of them all—the man of rank and the gentleman, with all its excellences and all its weaknesses—constitute the character of Mercutio!"—COLERIDGE.

Mercy, in the second part of Bunyan's *Pilgrim's Progress* (1684), a young woman who accompanied Christiana on her pilgrimage. At the Wicket Gate she swooned for fear she might be denied admission, but her fears were unnecessary. Mr. Brisk would fain have married her, but desisted when he learned that she was poor, and she became the wife of Christiana's eldest son, Matthew.

Merdle, Mr., in Dickens's novel, *Little Dorrit* (1857), a banker who was hailed as the " Master Mind of the Age," but developed into " the greatest forger and greatest thief that ever cheated the gallows " by suicide. Evidently there is some reminiscence here of the character and career of Hudson " The Railway King."

Meredith, Janice, heroine and title of a romance (1900) of the American Revolution by Paul Leicester Ford. The daughter of an uncompromising Tory, she falls in love with Charles Fownes, a man of gentle birth but fallen fortunes, who has been indentured to her father as one of a shipload of convicts brought over from England to New Brunswick, N. J. Her fidelity to her lover and to the American cause land her as a captive first in one camp and then in the other, until her status is officially recognized by General Washington. Her lover, whose real name turns out to be Brereton, enlists under Washington and has risen to the rank of general when they are formally affianced.

Merle, Madame, in Henry James's novel, *The Portrait of a Lady,* a plausible lady posing as a model of propriety, yet in reality the mistress of a married man and the mother of an illegitimate daughter who, in all the innocence of ignorance, is being brought up by her unsuspecting stepmother.

Merman, Forsaken, The, in Matthew Arnold's poem of that name, a Sea King married to a mortal maiden named Margaret. She forsook him and her children under the Christian conviction that she must return from his kingdom beneath the sea to the upper world to pray for her soul.

Merrilies, Meg, in *Guy Mannering,* one of Scott's weirdest and most effective creations. An aged gipsy, half sibyl, half lunatic, she had been young Mannering's nurse in infancy, and she is the first to recognize him when, all ignorant of his origin, he returns as Henry Bertram to the home of his unsuspecting kindred—

the place whence he had been kidnapped.

> She is most akin to the witches of Macbeth, with some traits of the ancient Sibyl ingrafted on the coarser stock of a gipsy of the last century. Though not absolutely in nature, however, she must be allowed to be a very imposing and emphatic personage, and to be mingled both with the business and the scenery of the piece with the greatest possible skill and effect.—FRANCIS JEFFREY: *Essays.*

> Old Meg she was a Gipsy,
>   And liv'd upon the Moors:
> Her bed it was the brown heath turf,
>   And her house was out of doors.
>
> Old Meg was brave as Margaret Queen
>   And tall as Amazon:
> An old red blanket cloak she wore;
>   A chip hat had she on.
> God rest her aged bones somewhere—
>   She died full long agone!
>   KEATS: *Meg Merrilies* (1844).

Mertoun, Mordaunt, in Scott's novel, *The Pirate,* son of Basil Mertourn, an ex-pirate, who loves and eventually marries Brenda Troil.

Messala, in Gen. Lew Wallace's *Ben Hur, a Tale of the Christ* (1880), a young Roman patrician, treacherous and supercilious, despising Ben Hur because he is a Jew, but feigning friendship until the time comes when he can betray him to the galleys and seize upon his property. Ben Hur achieves a long-nurtured vengeance in the famous chariot race, where he defeats Messala and maims him with his chariot wheel.

Meyrick, Hans, in George Eliot's *Daniel Deronda,* a friend of the hero, a volatile artist of German blood who owns himself a dilettante in virtue and whose improvised words even in sorrowful moments have inevitably some drollery. He introduces Daniel to his household:—the mother keen and sensible; the sisters all openhearted and unselfish, and each with a separate little oddity.

Micawber, Wilkins, in Dickens's *David Copperfield* (1849), an eccentric individual, law-writer to Uriah Heep, whose villainy he eventually exposes, who, with his adoring wife, Emma, furnishes the broadest fun to the novel. Unpractical, visionary, ever buoyant and self-satisfied under the most distressing and humiliating circumstances, he reproduces Dickens's own father not only in character, but in the principal incidents of his amusing career. Forster's *Life of Dickens* (1871) first revealed this fact to the public. The continual struggle with bad luck, the shabby devices for eking out a genteel existence; the repeated compromises with creditors, the final crash, and the sojourn in the debtors' prison, and then the court of bankruptcy—not only were these facts common to the career of Wilkins Micawber and John Dickens, but also such minor matters as the petition of the debtors to the throne,—"not for the abolition of imprisonment for debt, as David Copperfield relates, but for the less dignified but more accessible boon of a bounty to drink his Majesty's health on his Majesty's forthcoming birthday,"—and that well-known financial statement by Mr. Micawber, that the difference between misery and happiness lay in the odd pence of an income overspent or underspent.

> The Micawbers live better on nothing than most people do on a little; they fluctuate between tears and smiles; they pass from despair to hot punch, and from the immediate prospect of starvation to a sanguine gaiety. Mr. Micawber survives a thousand contingencies when his flower had been cankered. A hundred times has the die been cast and the flower been cankered, yet a hundred times he emerges buoyant and cheery. Alnaschar is nothing to him, in a forlorn tenement, beyond the City Road: he calculated the expense of putting out a bow window from his aircastle in Picadilly. As to exterior, Mr. Micawber is stout and bold; he wears shabby clothes, an enormous shirt-collar and an eyeglass dangling for ornament, not use.—E. P. WHIPPLE.

Michael, in the narrative poem of that name by William Wordsworth, a herdsman near Grasmere whose toil and vigilance had cleared away from debt his heritage of a few acres, but who lost half his little all by the failure of a nephew for whom he was surety. He received his death blow by the subsequent defalcation of his only son, the child of his middle period, the pride and hope of his age, who had gone to London with high hopes and noble aims, but had fallen a victim to metropolitan temptations.

Midas, Sir Gorgius, a favorite figure in the society caricatures which George DuMaurier contributed to the London *Punch.* The artist confided to a friend that he was drawn from life. It is to be hoped he never recognized himself. Sir Gorgius is a vulgar, purse-proud parvenu of hesitant h's, but of unlimited self-confidence and self-assertion until brought face to face with a real aristocrat, when he sinks into the ordinary British toady.

Middleton, Clara, in George Meredith's novel, *The Egoist,* a high-spirited, clever girl, daughter of the learned and sententious Dr. Middleton. She fancies herself in love with Sir Willoughby Patterne, but breaks off the engagement when longer acquaintance reveals his self-centred pride. While Laetitia Dale's story exposes the cruel side of egotism Clara's brings to light the absurdity of it. With her sense of fun and healthy instincts of liberty and enjoyment, the distress Sir Willoughby occasions her is nothing to the agonies she makes him undergo.

Middleton, Ellen, titular heroine of a novel (1844), by Lady Georgiana Fullerton. In a momentary fit of anger, when a girl, she had accidentally killed a child. Two persons know the secret. Throughout her married life she is pursued by the malice of one and the mischievous advocacy of the other, a man who loves her. The novel presents a vivid picture of Ellen's fear and penitence, flight and peaceful death.

Middleton, Sir John, in Jane Austen's novel, *Sense and Sensibility,* the squire of the neighborhood where Mrs. Dashwood settles with her daughters.

Sir John and Lady Middleton have also their several claims to consideration, though there is amiability about Sir John, with his passion for what he calls "little hops," and "for collecting parties of young people to eat ham and chicken out of doors," even in late October. Lady Middleton was "reserved, cold, and had nothing to say for herself beyond the most commonplace inquiry or remark." But she had a greedy eagerness for flattery, and even the elder Miss Steele, with her terrible talk of conquests and "smart beaux," knows how to get invited to stay with her two months.

Miggles, heroine of a story of that name by F. Bret Harte in volume, *Luck of Roaring Camp.*

"Miggles," who retires into the wilds with the paralyzed wreck of the man who had been good to her in her prosperous but naughty days, and who will not throw a sop to Mrs. Grundy by marrying him, because then she would be *bound* to do what she did of her own accord—is another instance of good in bad; a diamond picked out of the gutter. There is no talk with her about regret for the past—only practice. When the coach (storm-bound) has left her dwelling, and the passengers arrive at the next halt, and the judge, "solemnly taking off his white hat," and making sure that all the glasses are full, says: "Here's to Miggles. God bless her!" it would have been a hard heart indeed that would not add, Amen!— *Atlantic Monthly.*

Miggs, Miss, in Dickens's novel *Barnaby Rudge* (1841), the handmaiden and comforter of Mrs. Varden. Tall and gaunt and shrewish, she holds all mankind in contempt, making a secret exception, however, of Simon Tappertit, who scorns her. She upholds her mistress as a suffering martyr, " the mildest, amiablist, forgivingest-sperited, longest-sufferingest female in existence," and denounces poor Gabriel Varden as an inhuman Nero. Baffled in all her matrimonial schemes, she ended her life as female turnkey to a county Bridewell.

Mignon, in Goethe's *Wilhelm Meister's Apprenticeship,* a mysterious Italian maiden of peculiar and elfish charm, daughter of a wandering harpist. Wilhelm rescues her in her girlhood out of the hands of rope dancers whose manager had cruelly mistreated her, and from the day of her rescue the slender, black-haired, star-eyed maid clings to him with ardent but unconfessed and unrequited love which finally kills her. Walter Scott in Fenella and Victor Hugo in Esmeralda have imitated this weirdly attractive character.

In Mignon and the Harpist Goethe has introduced into his novel those mysterious forces, beyond the reach of human knowledge and control, which play a significant part in our lives. The one rises up out of ourselves, it lies in the invisible depths in our own souls; this force is personified in Mignon. The other lies outside us, in the influence of divinely favored spirits, whose

highest and most genuine representative
is the poet; it appears as the Harpist.
BIELSCHOWSKY: *Life of Goethe*, ii, 230.—
Atlantic Monthly.

Mikado, The, hero of a comic opera
of that name by William S. Gilbert,
music by Arthur Sullivan. The plot
turns upon the complications which
follow upon the crusade this mythical
monarch of Japan had instituted
against flirting:

So he decreed in words succinct,
That all who flirted, leered or winked,
Unless connubially linked,
Should forthwith be beheaded.

Milan, Duke of, in Massinger's
tragedy of that name, is a high-
minded gentleman inordinately fond
of his wife, Marcelia.

He is represented as excessively uxorious,
and his passion takes this very disagreeable
turn of posthumous jealousy. He has instructed Francisco to murder the wife whom
he adores, in case of his own death during
the war, and thus to make sure that she
could not marry anybody else. On his
return the wife, who has been informed by
the treachery of Francisco of this pleasant
arrangement, is naturally rather cool to
him; whereupon he flies into a rage . . .
His affection returns in another scene, but
only in order to increase his jealousy, and
on hearing Francisco's slander he proceeds
to stab his wife out of hand. It is the action
of a weak man in a passion, not of a noble
nature tortured to madness.—LESLIE
STEPHEN: *Hours in a Library.*

Mildmay, Frank, the autobiographic hero of Captain Marryat's
novel, *Frank Mildmay, or the Naval
Officer* (1829). He is autobiographic
in two senses, for not only is Mildmay
made to write his own story, but the
story itself is in many respects that
of Marryat's own early life, including
his entrance into the navy as a midshipman under Lord Cochrane, afterwards Earl of Dundonald, and his
service in the Mediterranean, at
Walcheren and in the Burmese War
of 1824. Lord Cochrane appears in
the novel under the transparent
mask of an initial.

Millamant, in Congreve's comedy,
The Way of the World, a fashionable
belle, in love with Mirabell and capturing him by the witchery of her
very faults.

Millamant is the perfect model of
the accomplished fine lady: the ideal

heroine of the comedy of high life,
who arrives at the height of indifference to everything from the height
of satisfaction; to whom pleasure is
as familiar as the air she draws; elegance worn as a part of her dress; wit
the habitual language which she hears
and speaks; love, a matter of course;
and who has nothing to hope or to
fear, her own caprice being the only
law to herself, and rule to those about
her. Her words seem composed of
amorous sighs—her looks are glanced
at prostrate admirers or envious
rivals. She refines on her pleasures
to satiety; and is almost stifled in the
incense that is offered to her person,
her wit, her beauty and her fortune.

Miller, Daisy. "Daisy" is the
family nickname for Anna Miller,
heroine of Henry James's short story,
Daisy Miller (1878). A young girl
from Schenectady, "strikingly, admirably pretty," who travels about
Europe with her placid mother and
her terrible little brother, Randolph,
and meets premature death at Rome.

A girl of the later eighteen-seventies, sent
with such a mother as hers to Europe by a
father who remains making money in
Schenectady, after no more experience of
the world than she had got in her native
town, and at a number of New York dinners
among people of like tradition; uncultivated
but not rude, reckless but not bold, inex-
pugnably ignorant of the conventional right,
and spiritedly resentful of control by cri-
terions that offend her own sense of things,
she goes about Europe doing exactly what
she would do at home, from an innocence
as guileless as that which shaped her conscience in her native town. She knows no
harm, and she means none; she loves life,
and singing and talking and dancing and
"attentions," but she is no flirt, and she is
essentially and infinitely far from worse.—
W. D. HOWELLS: *Heroines of Fiction.*

Millerin, Luise, heroine of Schiller's drama, *Love and Intrigue*. A poor
musician's daughter, she is loved by
Ferdinand von Walther, son of the
prince in one of the petty German
principalities of the eighteenth century. His father makes no demur so
long as he believes Ferdinand contemplates a mere liaison, but is horrified (like Major Pendennis in the
case of Arthur) when he finds his
intentions are honorable. He arrests
father Millerin and persuades the

daughter that she can save him only
by writing a compromising letter to
a court libertine. She consents and
swears never to reveal the truth.
Ferdinand refuses to believe that the
letter is genuine, but Luise remains
faithful to her oath.

Mills, Miss, in Dickens's *David
Copperfield* (1849), the bosom friend
of Dora Spenlow. She is fond of
posing as a victim of blighted love,
an outcast in " the desert of Sa-
hara."

Millwood, Sarah, in George Lillo's
tragedy, *George Barnwell* (1732), the
courtesan who seduces George into
robbery and murder and then informs against him. See BARNWELL.

Milly, in a narrative poem by
Adelaide Anne Procter, *Milly's Expiation* (1862), is a noble-minded Irish
girl whose lover is accused of murder.
She saves him by a falsehood on the
witness stand and subsequent events
prove him to be innocent. But to the
surprise of all she refuses to marry
him. Only her lover and the parish
priest who tells the story know that
this is her self-imposed expiation for
the perjury she had committed.

Milo, in *Troilus and Cressida*, ii, 3,
an athlete of Crotona, a Greek city
of Southern Italy, one of whose feats
was the carrying of a living bull on
his shoulders through the race course
at Olympia, anachronistically introduced. See MILO in vol. II.

Milton, John, is the hero of a dramatic poem, *Milton*, by Bulwer-
Lytton, based upon the legend of an
Italian lady who chanced to find the
young poet asleep on some primrose
bank of his native country. Struck
with admiration, she left by his side
an epigram appreciative of his singular beauty which she borrowed from
Guarini, a poet of her own land. The
story is a myth belonging to the lives
of other poets besides Milton. Bulwer makes Milton meet the lady in
his subsequent journey to Italy. In
old age she again crosses the seas to
look her last upon the love of her
youth. Francois Coppee tells the
story in a different fashion in *Le
Passant (The Passerby)*.

Minna, in Scott's novel, *The Pirate*,
is, with her sister Brenda, one of the
heroines.

Minnehaha (Indian, *Laughing
Water*), in Longfellow's poem, *Hiawatha*, the wife of the titular hero and
daughter of the arrow-maker of the
Dacotahs. She was named after a
waterfall between St. Anthony and
Fort Snelling.

Mirabel, in Beaumont and
Fletcher's comedy, *The Wild Goose
Chase* (1652), a travelled Italianate,
gentleman, a cynical philanderer who
loves women but abhors marriage.
He is pursued matrimonially by
Oriana, the " witty follower of the
chase," who employs artifices crude
and coarse in the effort to entrap him.
When the ingenuity of the dramatists
is exhausted Mirabel succumbs to
Oriana's wiles. Farquhar, in *The
Inconstant* (1702), borrowed the
names and modernized the theme.
His Oriana is assisted in her matrimonial desires by the strategy of Old
Mirabel, and the combined force of
concupiscence and chicanery finally
drives young Mirabel into the net
from which he shies.

Mirabell, Edward, in Congreve's
comedy, *The Way of the World* (1700).

Mirabella, in Spenser's *Faërie
Queene*, vi, 6–8 (1596), a fairmaid who,
because of scorn and pride and the
cruelties she had inflicted upon her
lovers, was condemned in Cupid's
judgment hall to ride through the
world clad in mourning weeds,
mounted on a mangy jade and accompanied by a lewd fool called
Disdain until " she had saved as
many lovers as she had slain." It is
conjectured that in this character
Spenser paid a back-handed compliment to the lady who had jilted
him in real life and whom he addressed poetically as Rosalind (*q.v.*).

Miranda, in J. R. Lowell's *Fable for
Critics* (1848), a Boston bas-bleu in
classic apparel.

She is an evident satire upon Margaret Fuller, afterwards Countess
Ossoli (1810–1850), who also furnished some hints for Hawthorne's
Zenobia (*q.v.*). Before and shortly

after her early and tragical death Margaret Fuller had a reputation as great and peculiar, if not as extensive, as susceptible ambition and feminine vanity could desire. Her personal qualities endeared her to a circle of intimate friends, by whose worship she was no doubt spoilt. How impatiently her pretensions were endured, and how deeply her somewhat offensive assumption of superiority and her naïve but intense egotism were resented, by outsiders, may be seen in the severity of Lowell's merciless satire, " Miranda " being almost the only writer of whom he speaks with anything like aversion or bitterness.

Miranda, in Shakespeare's comedy, *The Tempest* (1609), daughter of Prospero, who brings her up on an enchanted island where her only companions are such monsters as Caliban and such ethereal sprites as Ariel. Consequently her maiden innocence and ignorance are only too likely to be captivated by the first man she sees. Luckily it is the gentle and noble Prince Ferdinand, son of her uncle Antonio, the usurping duke, who first falls across her path through shipwreck and fulfils her destiny.

Mirèio, titular heroine of a Provençal poem by Frédéric Mistral. Because of her love for Vincen, the poor weaver's son, she rejects more eligible suitors. Her father, learning the reason, furiously swears she shall never see her lover again. Then in the night she remembers that Vincen once said if ever she was in trouble she must go to the three Saint Maries of Baux; and so she rises and flies, and crossing the wide sea-meadows to their chapel on the seashore, is sunstruck and dies there, just as father, mother, and lover arrive in search of her. The best English translation is by Harriet W. Preston (Boston, 1872). An opera entitled *Mireille* was set to music by Gounod in 1864. The original version was in five acts and followed the poem to its tragic termination. This was found objectionable in a work so distinctively lyrical, and it was afterwards compressed into

three acts and the sufferings of true love were crowned by a joyous union.

Miriam, in Whittier's poem of that name (1870), a Christian girl whose example wins from her Moslem lord for those who have offended him that mercy which he sees to be in all creeds and finds so little practised in life.

Miriam, in N. Hawthorne's romance, *The Marble Faun* (called *Transformation* in England), a beautiful art-student in Rome. Her nationality and her origin are purposely involved in mystery, as well as her relations with Brother Antonio, a model, who continually dogs her footsteps and whose evil influence she evidently dreads. At last, during a moonlight excursion on the Capitoline Hill, her friend, Count Donatello, enraged beyond endurance, and encouraged by a glance from Miriam, flings him over the Tarpeian rock to his death. From that moment Miriam and Donatello become linked together by their guilty secret, and the happy, heedless, faunlike Italian is changed into the conscience-stricken sinner. In the end he surrenders himself to justice and Miriam disappears.

G. P. Lathrop in his *Study of Hawthorne* finds the inspiration for the character of Miriam in the profound impression made upon the author by Guido Reni's (alleged) portrait of Beatrice Cenci. This necessarily implies that the mysterious model was Miriam's father and that her justification for conniving at murder was the same as Beatrice's. Julian Hawthorne (*Life of Hawthorne*, vol. ii, p. 236) mentions a theory which originated with Dean Stanley and was partly sanctioned by Hawthorne himself, viz., that Miriam was suggested by Mademoiselle Deluzy, whose suspected complicity in the murder of the Duchesse de Praslyn had stirred up French society in 1847. "Well, I dare say she was," quoth Hawthorne, when the subject was brought up by Henry Bright, "I knew I had some dim recollection of some crime, but I didn't know what, but," he added, "the story isn't meant to be explained; it's cloudland."

Mirvan, Captain, in Fanny Burney's novel, *Evelina*, a rough seadog, " excellently conceived," says Austin Dobson, " but only partially exhibited." Indeed, Evelina acknowledges that she cannot report his conversation verbatim because " almost every other word he utters is accompanied by an oath which I am sure would be as unpleasant for you to read as for me to write. And besides he makes use of a thousand sea terms which are to me quite unintelligible."

In a letter (1780) from Bath to "Daddy" Crisp, Miss Burney says that certain naval officers she met there would not accept Captain Mirvan as a type. But she declares her impenitence: "The more I see of sea-captains the less reason I have to be ashamed of Captain M., for they have all so irresistible a propensity to wanton mischief, to roasting beaux and detesting old women, that I quite rejoice I showed the book to no one ere printed, lest I should have been prevailed upon to soften his character."

Mirza, in Addison's allegory, *The Vision of Mirza* (No. 159 of the *Spectator*), a pious Moslem who, falling asleep on the fifth day of the moon, has unfolded to him a panorama of human life. Time is symbolized as a prodigious tide of water rolling through a valley with an impenetrable mist at each end. Over it stretched innumerable bridges of life over which men were passing. Some fell prematurely and were engulfed; others reached the island abodes of the blest.

Mite, Sir Matthew, in Foote's comedy, *The Nabob,* a returned East India merchant, purse-proud, vulgar, dissolute, hating the aristocracy yet eager to be numbered among them, turning a cold shoulder to the humble friends of his youth, ostentatiously rewarding his panderers and flatterers, and amazing the ignorant by his braggadocio talk of lacs and rupees.

Moby Dick, in Herman Melville's novel of that name (1850), a huge and ferocious whale, so styled by the whalers of New Bedford and Nantucket in the mid-eighteenth century. Captain Ahab of the whaler *Pequod* loses a leg in his first unsuccessful encounter with the monster. He swears revenge. He attains it in a three days' battle with Moby Dick, admirably described, which ends in the death of the whale, but not until he has demolished the boats and sunk the *Pequod.*

Mock Doctor, hero of a farce (1733) by Henry Fielding, paraphrased from *Le Médecin Malgré Lui* (1666), of Molière. Sganarelle, the faggot-maker, is here called Gregory.

Modish, Lady Betty, in Colley Cibber's comedy, *The Careless Husband* (1704), a fashionable young woman who coquets with Lord Foppington merely to arouse the jealousy of Lord Morelove, whom she really cares for, though she will not admit it until brought to terms by his retaliatory flirtation with Lady Graveairs.

Mogli the Frog, in Kipling's *Jungle Books* (1894–1895), the name given by Mother Wolf to a native baby, named Nathoo, found by her in a forest. The man-cub is suckled along with her litter of four cubs and brought up in the jungle. He learns jungle law and jungle lore from Baloo the Bear and Baghiera the Black Panther, and in due course is accepted as one of the Free People at a Pack Meeting, despite threats and protests from Shere Kan, a lame tiger who had claimed the baby as its victim. Shere Kan remains his sworn enemy. When Mogli has grown to boyhood the tiger's plot against his life is foiled through the lad's boldness and fertility of resource, but he is forced to leave the Pack and seek a dwelling among men. While acting as village herd he killed his old enemy Shere Kan. He married the daughter of Abdul Gafur, who gives birth to a child that is seen playing with a wolf.

Mokanna, the "Veiled Prophet of Korassan" in the first story of Moore's *Lalla Rookh* (1817), a Moslem impostor, Hakem ben Haschem, so nicknamed from a silver-gauze veil worn to hide his face. He seduces Zelica by magic arts; her lover Azim in revenge joins the invading army of the Caliph, and Mokanna, despite all his valor and energy, finding his followers reduced to a mere remnant, poisons them and himself plunges into a bath of corrosive chemicals which dissolve all the elements of his body. Zelica assumes the fatal veil, and being mistaken for Mokanna rushes upon the spear of Azim and receives his forgiveness in death. Moore found the historical original of his prophet in D'Herbelot's *Bibliothe que Orientale* (1697).

Monaco, King of, in Sardou's political drama, *Rabagas* (1872), a monarch who could never please his people nor their mouthpiece, Rabagas. If he went out he was " given to pleasure;" if he remained in he was given to idleness; if he declared war he was " wasteful of the public money;" if he preserved peace he was " pusillanimous;" if he ate he was "self-indulgent;" if he abstained he was " priest-ridden."

Moncada, Matthias de, in Scott's novel, *The Surgeon's Daughter*, a merchant stern and revengeful who arrests his daughter Zilia the day after her confinement of an illegitimate son.

Monflathers, Miss, in Dickens's novel, *The Old Curiosity Shop*, xxxi (1840), the mistress of a boarding and day school who is greatly shocked when Little Nell on Mrs. Jarley's behalf asks her to patronize the waxwork show. " Don't you know," she asks, " it is very naughty to be a wax child when you might have the proud consciousness of assisting, to the extent of your infant powers, the noble manufacturers of your country? "

Monimia, titular heroine of *The Orphan* (1610), a tragedy by Thomas Otway. The ward of Lord Acasto, she is in love with Acasto's son, Castallo, who marries her secretly. Another son, Polydore, gains admission to her chamber on the bridal night by passing himself off as his brother. Monimia commits suicide when dawn reveals the deception and Polydore, now for the first time aware of her marriage, provokes a quarrel with Castallo and immolates himself on the latter's sword.

The nature of its central incident has kept it from the stage for the last eighty years, but from the time that Mrs. Barry first played Monimia the character has been a favorite with many of our best actresses, down to Miss O'Neill . . . A victim of love ill fated, worthy for sadness to rank with Penthea in *The Broken Heart*, although she is altogether more lovable and life-like than that somewhat shadowy personage.

Indeed Otway might be called a belated Ford, with tempered horrors and mitigated gloom, yet with fully as intense a sympathy for ill-starred love and the sickness of a heart broken with griefs.—*Temple Bar*, vol. 118, p. 378.

Monoplies, Richard, in Scott's historical romance, *The Fortunes of Nigel*, the honest, obstinate and faithful Scotch servant of Lord Nigel Olifaunt.

Monmouth, Marquis of, in Disraeli's novel, *Coningsby, or the New Generation* (1844), father of the titular hero, a nobleman of vast wealth, great political influence, rare sagacity, unbending will, intense selfishness and licentious habits, intended as a portrait of that famous voluptuary, the third Marquis of Hertford whom Thackeray also utilized in his Lord Steyne.

Lord Monmouth is finely conceived and admirably drawn, and is a far more interesting and attractive figure than either his original or Thackeray's Lord Steyne. Heartless, self-indulgent and devoid of scruple as he is, he has a certain grandeur of his own as the type of a Sulla-like patrician, arrogant but dignified, sublimely selfish, but also self-sufficient, and alike in good and evil fortune undaunted in his bearing.—MONEYPENNY: *Life of Benjamin Disraeli*.

Monsoon, Major, in Charles Lever's novel *Charles O'Malley* (1841), a good-natured, blustering, military braggadocio of distinctly Irish characteristics—said to be drawn after the O'Gorman Mahone (see MULLIGAN, THE). Lever used to feast this gentleman daily at his table while the novel was in course of construction. As it appeared serially in the *Dublin University Magazine*, the Major soon recognized the uses to which he was put, but Lever's wine was so good that he contented himself with an occasional growl at his host when the touches in the portrait seemed a little too free.

Modern English literature has not produced a more Shakespearean—I might say a more original—comic character . . . But Major Monsoon is well known to be a minutely accurate portrait of the character,—a faithful chronicle of the sayings and doings of a real living personage.—G. P. MARSH: *English Language and Literature*, p. 567.

Montargis, Dog of. The animal hero of a melodrama by Guilbert de Pixérécourt, *La Foret de Bondi on le Chien de Montargis* (1814), which dramatized a historical fact. During the reign of the French Charles V, Aubrey de Montdidier was murdered in the forest of Bondi near Paris. Vainly did his faithful hound seek to protect him. The dog was successful, however, in revealing the murderer. He flew at the Chevalier Richard de Macaire whenever he saw him in the streets of Paris. Suspicion was aroused. Macaire was known to have been an enemy of Montdidier. Charles V ordered chevalier and dog into his presence. He decided the matter could be settled only by the ordeal of battle. The chevalier was to be armed with a club, the dog was to have an empty cask to retire to. The singular combat, fought on October 8, 1371, lasted so long that the man fainted from fatigue. On coming to he confessed the crime. A bas relief picturing this event was sculptured in the great hall of the now ruined castle of Montargis. Hence the name given to the dog. It had no other connection with the Montargis family.

Monte Christo, Count of. See DANTES, EDMOND.

Montesinos, in the Charlemagne cycle of legends, a paladin who for some fancied slight retired from the French court to La Mancha and took up his abode in a cavern some 60 feet deep which is still known as the Cave of Montesinos. Cervantes makes Don Quixote (II, ii, 5) penetrate half-way into this aperture, when he falls asleep and is visited by strange visions wherein his own Dulcinea is enchanted into the appearance of a country wench and members of the court of Charlemagne are befooled by Merlin.

Montgomery, Ellen, heroine of a novel, *The Wide Wide World* (1851), by Susan Warner (" Elizabeth Wetherill "), which once enjoyed extraordinary popularity. Ellen's parents going to Europe place the child under the tutelage of a narrow-minded,

sharp-tempered relative of her father's, Miss Fortune Emerson; she is rescued from the blight of Puritanism by a kind friend, Alice Humphrey.

Moor, Karl, hero of Schiller's first play *The Robbers* (1781), a high-spirited and naturally noble youth, of good family, who turns bandit and, with a gang of kindred spirits, wages war against society, because it tolerates and even sanctions the polished villainy of a brother who has cruelly wronged him. Incidentally the play was a protest against all outworn conventions and artificial restraints of mind and soul. In Germany it created a sensation only second to that of its less violent precursor, Goethe's *Werther*, and its influence extended all over Europe.

Moray, Captain Robert, in Gilbert Parker's historical romance, *The Seats of the Mighty* (1896), an officer in Lord Amherst's regiment held on parole as a hostage in Quebec, at the critical period of the war between the French and English. Imprisoned on a false charge of being a spy he is saved from execution by Doltaire (*q.v.*), who attempts to secure certain papers from him and who being his rival in love wishes Moray to survive and witness his own triumph. He escapes, however, brings valuable information to the besiegers under Wolfe and after the capture of Quebec recovers the lady (Alixe Duvarney) whom he had secretly married on the eve of his escape. Moray is avowedly drawn from a little known historical personage, author of an autobiographical work, *Memoirs of Major Robert Stobo.*

The narrative was written in a very ornate and grandiloquent style, but the hero of the memoirs was so evidently a man of remarkable character, enterprise and adventure that I saw in the few scattered bones of the story which he unfolded the skeleton of an ample historical romance. There was necessary to offset this buoyant and courageous Scotsman, adventurous and experienced, a character of the race which captured him and held him in leash till just before the taking of Quebec. I therefore found in the character of Doltaire—which was the character of Voltaire spelled with a big D—purely a creature of the imagination, one who, as the son of a peasant woman and Louis XV, should be an effective offset to Major Stobo. There was no hint of Doltaire in the "Memoirs." There could not be, nor of the plot on which the story was based, because it was all imagination. Likewise, there was no mention of Alixe Duvarney in the "Memoirs," nor of Bigot and Mme. Cournal and all the others. They too, when not characters of the imagination, were lifted out of the history of the time.— SIR GILBERT PARKER: *Introduction to Novels.*

More, Sir Thomas, the famous Lord Chancellor of England (1478–1535), figures in Shakespeare's historical drama *Henry VIII* (iv, i; v, 3), but only under his official title as Lord Chancellor. In v, 3, he sentences Thomas Cromwell to the Tower. A full length sketch of More is presented by Anne Manning in her historical romance *The Household of Sir Thomas More* (1869). This purports to be a diary kept by his daughter Margaret who married Roper. The story begins with More as a private gentleman, a great lawyer and a friend of Erasmus, then shows him as first favorite in the court of Henry VIII and ends with his downfall and death on the scaffold.

Morella, in Edgar Allan Poe's story of that name, a wife who had pried deeply into mystical writings on personal identity until the subject held a kind of unholy fascination for both herself and her husband. Dying, she bears a daughter into whom it soon becomes evident that the personal soul of the mother had entered.

Morgan, James, in Thackeray's novel, *Pendennis*, the valet of Major Pendennis, anticipating all his wants, supplying him with backstairs gossip about fashionable folk and generally a model of discreetness until his head is turned by continued prosperity and he seeks to blackmail his employer through his knowledge of Colonel Altamont's secret. The Major neatly checkmates him in an interview which Morgan begins as a lion and ends as a lamb.

Morland, Harry, hero of Henry Brookes's novel, *The Fool of Quality* (1760), is the second son of the Earl of Morland and is nicknamed " fool " by his parents because he appears to

sad disadvantage beside his brilliant elder brother. Eventually he proves that he was only an ugly duckling who in his swanhood eclipses all his family. Charles Kingsley, perhaps because the hero foreshadowed the Muscular Christianity of which Kingsley was a prophet, brought out a new edition of the novel in 1873, with an eulogistic introduction.

Morose, in Ben Jonson's *Epicene*, a lover of quiet, exquisitely impatient of rude sounds and loquacity, who lived in a retired street, and barricaded his doors with mattresses to prevent disturbance to his ears.

Morris, Dinah, the real heroine of George Eliot's *Adam Bede* (1859), a publicly recognized Wesleyan field-preacher "acting under directions." In private life she works in a cotton-mill. With the enthusiasm of a fair, gentle and unselfish spirit, and an in-born delicacy that saves her from any errors of tact or taste, she becomes a ministering angel in her simple way to the rude and ignorant among whom her lot is cast. Dinah was copied from Mrs. Elizabeth Evans, the author's aunt, who had been a female preacher at Wirksworth in Derbyshire.

One Sunday afternoon Mrs. Evans happened casually to mention that in her youth she had, with another pious woman, visited an unhappy girl in prison, stayed with her all night, and gone with her to execution. "This incident," adds George Eliot, "lay on my mind for years on years, as a dead germ apparently, till time had made my mind a nidus in which it could fructify. It then turned out to be the germ of *Adam Bede.*"

Mosby, the villain of the anonymous drama, *Arden of Feversham* (1592), which has sometimes been attributed to Shakespeare. Having seduced Arden's wife he is baffled in repeated attempts to murder him but finally hires two ruffians to do the deed. They rush in at a given signal when Mosby and Arden are seated playing a game of draughts. The whole gang are apprehended and executed in strict accordance with the facts of the case; the story being

18

true. In 1739 the old play was re-vised and rewritten by George Lillo.

Moth, in Shakespeare's *Love's Labor's Lost,* page to Don Adriano, a saucy and playful youngster.

Mou-Mou, hero of a story of that name by Tourgenief, a deaf mute, a serf, who has led an unhappy, lonely life, whose only friend is a little dog. His mistress, who has absolute power over her slaves, a nervous, fretful woman, fancies herself kept awake by the dog's barking, and gives orders that it be put to death. The serf is himself its executioner; he washes the dog, gives it a good meal, takes it out with him upon the river, throws it overboard, and rows hastily away.

Mowcher, Miss, in Dickens's *David Copperfield,* hair dresser and masseuse, —" a fussy dwarf of about forty or forty-five, with a very large head and face, a pair of roguish grey eyes, and such extremely little arms that to enable her to lay a finger archly against her snub nose, as she ogled Steerforth, she was obliged to meet the finger half-way and lay her nose against it." Kindly cheery and well intentioned despite her vulgarity—her favorite expression is " ain't I volatile? "

Mudjekeewis, in Longfellow's *Hiawatha,* the father of the titular hero.

Muller, Maud, heroine and title of a ballad by J. G. Whittier. Maud, a shy and pretty maiden, stops in her haymaking to help the judge to a cup of water. He drives away and never sees her again. But each has been strangely moved. A little more for-wardness on the part of either might have changed the destiny of both. Such is the evident moral of the closing couplet:

Of all sad words of tongue or pen
The saddest are these "It might have been."

Bret Harte's clever parody, *Mrs. Judge Jenkins,* assumes that the judge did marry the maid and sums up the result of the mesalliance as follows:

There are no sadder words of tongue or pen
Than "It is, but it hadn't orter been."

Mulligan, of Ballymulligan, The, in Thackeray's Christmas book, *Mrs. Perkins's Ball,* a fire-eating Irishman, self-described as a descendant from the Irish kings, who forces Titmarsh to take him to the ball where he frightens his partner by making her dance a double shuffle jig, and ex-changes high words with Mr. Perkins over the wine. He is a composite of William John O'Connell, brother of the Liberator, facetiously called Lord Kilmallock from his native town, and Charles James Patrick Mahone, who chose to style himself the O'Gorman Mahone.

Mulvaney, Terence, hero of many of Rudyard Kipling's best stories. With his friends and fellow soldiers, the cockney Stanley Ortheris and the Yorkshire John Learoyd, he made his first appearance in *The Three Muske-teers,* a tale bound up in *Tales of the Hills,* first published in Calcutta in 1888. Here is the opening sentence: " Mulvaney, Ortheris and Learoyd are privates in B Company of a Line Regiment and personal friends of mine. Collectively, I think, but am not certain, they are the worst men in the regiment so far as genial blackguardism goes."

Mulvaney, the Irish giant, who has been the "grizzled, tender, and very wise Ulys-ses" to successive generations of young and foolish recruits, is a great creation. He is the father of the craft of arms to his asso-ciates; he has served with various regiments from Bermuda to Halifax; he is "old in war, scarred, reckless, resourceful, and in his pious hours an unequaled soldier." Learoyd, the second of these friends, is "six and a half feet of slow-moving, heavy-footed Yorkshireman, born on the wolds, bred in the dales, and educated chiefly among the carriers' carts at the back of York railway-station." The third is Ortheris, a little man as sharp as a needle, "a fox-terrier of a cockney," an inveterate poacher and dog-stealer.—E. W. GOSSE: *The Century.*

Münchausen, Baron, titular hero of a burlesque book of travels, the first edition of which, a pamphlet of 48 pages, was published in London and in the English language under the title *Baron Munchausen's Narra-tive of his Marvellous Travels and Campaigns in Russia.* Rewritten and finally enlarged to its present proportions the book ran through five editions before 1787, when it was introduced to the German public in a preface by G. A. Burger, the poet, who not unnaturally passed in Germany for its author. Not until 1824 was the authorship definitely fixed upon Rudolf Eric Raspe (1737–1794) by a communication from Karl von Reinhard.

Raspe, however, was more compiler than author. From Bebel's *Facetiæ*, Lange's *Mendacia Ridicula*, Castiglione's *Cortegiano* and other sources he borrowed the stories he attributed to Baron Munchausen. In the preface to the first edition he thus identified his hero: " Baron Munchausen, of Bodenwerder, near Hameln, on the Weser, belongs to the noble family of that name, which gave to the King's German dominions the late Prime Minister and several other public characters equally illustrious. He is a man of great original humor."

Murdstone, Edward, in Dickens's *David Copperfield*, the hero's cruel stepfather who broke the heart of the widow Copperfield in the attempt to be " firm " with her. His sister Jane is as gloomy and obstinate as himself.

Musketeers, The Three (Fr. *Les Trois Mousquetaires*), in Dumas's romance of that name (1844), a military trinity, made up of Arthos, Aramis and Porthos (see these separate names) which the advent of D'Artagnan changes into a quartette.

Musketeer may be translated into less literal but more idiomatic English as Guardsman. Hence, in *Trilby*, Du Maurier borrows and amplifies the name into " The Three Guardsmen of the Pen," applying it to an amiable trio of bohemian artists in Paris: Little Billee, a Londoner (William Bagot); "The Laird," a Scotchman, and " Taffy," a Yorkshireman.

A reminiscence of Dumas's trio may also have suggested to Kipling his Soldiers Three (see MULVANEY). In French a Mousquetaire might be any soldier armed with a musket, but the word was applied specifically to a company of gentlemen who formed a mounted guard to the King of

France from 1661 to 1791, when they were suppressed. They were clad in scarlet, hence their quarters were known as the Maison Rouge. In peace they followed the king as protectors in the chase; in war they fought either afoot or on horseback.

Mylrea, Daniel, in Hall Caine's novel, *The Deemster* (1887), son of the bishop of the Isle of Man and nephew of the Deemster Thorkell Mylrea. A richly endowed nature suddenly arrested in a prodigal and unworthy career by a great tragedy. He kills his own cousin in a duel forced upon him and is sentenced to be cut off forever from his own people. None may look upon him or speak to him or give him aid. A pestilence breaks out; Daniel wins a new place in public esteem by his courage and devotion.

Myriel, Monseigneur Bienvenu, Bishop of D., in Victor Hugo's *Les Miserables*, Part I (1862), an ideal of exalted charity, united to a chastened sprightliness and absolute mental serenity. When raised to the episcopate his first act was to turn his palace into a hospital and take the hospital for his episcopal residence. He reserves for himself only one fifteenth of his salary, the rest goes to the poor. He visits his diocese on foot or riding a horse or a donkey. His mission is to assuage human suffering. He passes his days in study, prayer and the consolation of the afflicted—a short interval only being snatched for the frugal meal, a veritable dish of herbs. See VALJEAN, JEAN.

Myrrha, in Byron's historical tragedy, *Sardanapalus* (1819), an Ionian slave, the best-loved of the monarch's concubines—beautiful, heroic, loving and devoted—ashamed of her enforced degradation, half ashamed even of loving a barbarian but using all her influence over him to ennoble as well as to lighten his existence. She rouses him to action against the conspiracy of Arbaces, and when all is lost, induces him to mount a funeral pyre which she fires with her own hand, then leaps into the flames to share his death.

N

Nadgett, in Dickens's *Martin Chuzzlewit* (1844), a sort of non-professional private detective employed by Montague Tigg as manager of the fraudulent Anglo-Bengalee Company.

Nana, heroine and title of a novel by Emile Zola which takes up the fortunes of the daughter of Gervaise Macquart, heroine of *L'Assommoir*. In this first novel she is a little girl precociously familiar with evil courses, now she is full fledged and a fair representative of the Parisian courtesan of the Second Empire. The volume opens with an account of her appearance on the stage, in one of the burlesques that were common at that time, when Offenbach was looked upon as a great musical composer. She cannot sing a note; she knows nothing of acting, but her beauty wins the day, and she is at once successful. Men of fashion go crazy over her, and so launch her upon a career of squalid splendor that ends in disaster.

Nancanou, Mrs. Aurora, and her daughter **Clothilde,** the two heroines, equal in charm and not greatly disparate in age, of George W. Cable's novel of creole life in New Orleans, *The Grandissimes.*

No dearer or delightfuller figures have been presented by the observer of an alien race and religion . . . In this mother and daughter the parental and filial relations are inverted with courageous fidelity to life, where we as often see a judicious daughter holding an impulsive mother in check as the reverse. Clothilde is always shocked and troubled by her mother's wilful rashness, and Aurora, who is not so very much her senior, is always breaking bonds with a girlish impetuosity, which is only aggravated by the attempt to restrain it.—W. D. HOWELLS: *Heroines of Fiction,* vol. II, p. 236.

Narcissa, in Pope's *Moral Essays* (1731), the subject of the famous lines:

"Odious! In woollen? 'Twould a saint
    provoke!"
Were the last words that poor Narcissa
    spoke.
"No, let a charming chintz and Brussels
    lace
Wrap my cold limbs and shade my lifeless
    face;
One would not, sure, be frightful when one's
    dead!
And, Betty, give this cheek a little red!"
                    Essay, i, l. 246.

Pope here alludes to the current story that Nance Oldfield, the famous actress (1683–1730), was buried by her own orders in a " very fine Brussels lace headdress, a new pair of kid gloves, and a robe with lace ruffles and a lace collar." The place of interment was Westminster Abbey; for two days previous the body lay in state in the Jerusalem Chamber, watched over by two noblemen.

Narcisse, in G. W. Cable's novel, *Dr. Sevier* (1883), an amiable light-minded creole with infinite confidence in himself and in the future. He asks to be called Papillon or Butterfly " 'Cause," says he, "thass my natu'e. I gatheth honey eve'y day fum eve'y opening floweh, as the baod of Avon wemawked."

Nathan, hero of G. E. Lessing's drama, *Nathan the Wise* (1779), a Jew trader in Jerusalem at the time of the Crusades, a broad-minded philosopher who, though a Jew by race and nominally by religion, has risen above the trammels of that most exclusive sect and has learned to look upon all religions as different forms of the one great central Truth which no human intellect can grasp in its entirety. In the crucial scene of the book he explains his position to Saladin by the apologue of the three indistinguishable rings given to his three sons by an impartial father who could not bear to set one above the other. In the end it turns out that Nathan's adopted daughter Recha and a young Templar who loves her are brother and sister and the children of Saladin's brother by a Christian wife. Jew, Christian and Mussulman, therefore, are united into one family, knit together by ties of blood and mutual good offices.

Nathaniel, Sir, in Shakespeare's *Love's Labor's Lost*, the curate of Holofernes, described as " a foolish mild man, an honest man look you and soon dashed."

Nauhaught, subject of a poem, *Nauhaught the Deacon*, by J. G. Whittier. A baptized Indian, poor and on the verge of starvation, he dreams one night that an angel presents him with a gold piece. Next morning he finds a purse of gold. After a hard battle with his savage instincts, he restores it to the owner, who hands him a gold piece from its contents. Thus the dream is fulfilled.

Naulahka, in the novel of that name (1892) by Rudyard Kipling and Walter Balestier, is a priceless necklace that Nicholas Tarvin, a hustling American from the Western states, secures after many terrific adventures in India—thereby winning the hand of Kate Sheriff. Naulahka means the nine-lakher, "the thing worth nine lahks of rupees"= £90,000, or $450,000.

Nell, Little, in Dickens's *Old Curiosity Shop*. See TRENT, NELLY.

Nerissa, in Shakespeare's *The Merchant of Venice*, a bright, pert, waiting maid to Portia whom she imitates. She is close kin to Lucetta in *The Two Gentlemen of Verona*.

Nestor, in Greek myth the oldest and most experienced of all the chiefs gathered before Troy. Homer credits him with great powers of persuasion, Shakespeare introduces him into *Troilus and Cressida*. In Act i, Sc. 3, Ulysses describes how Patroclus mimics Nestor and his infirmities in order to make sport for Achilles.

Neuha, heroine of Byron's narrative poem *The Island*. A native of Toobonai, one of the Society Islands whereon the mutineers from the *Bounty* had landed, she gave her hand in marriage to a mutineer named Torquil. When a British vessel was sent out to capture the outlaws, Neuha withdrew with her husband into a cave of which she knew the secret and they remained there until all danger was past.

Neville, Miss, in Goldsmith's comedy, *She Stoops to Conquer* (1773), a friend and confidante of Miss Hardcastle, lively, coquettish and handsome. Mrs. Hardcastle has destined her for her son Tony Lumpkin, but neither cares for the match and when Miss Neville falls in love with Hastings Tony eagerly helps the latter to outwit Mrs. Hardcastle.

Newcome, Barnes, in Thackeray's *The Newcomes*, eldest son of Sir Brian and Lady Ann, a cold-blooded, cowardly, mean-spirited, selfish man of the world, a roué in secret, a moralist by public profession, clever in speech, in politics and business, ruling all his family except his sister Ethel, who recognizes that he is a sham, and tyrannizing over his wife (Lady Clara Pulleyn) until she elopes with Jack Belsize (Lord Highgate).

Newcome, Clive, in Thackeray's novel, *The Newcomes*, Colonel Newcome's only son, an artist, frank, generous, open-hearted, in love with his cousin Ethel Newcome, whom he marries after the death of his first wife, Rosa Mackenzie, has freed him from a disastrous mesalliance.

Newcome, Ethel, in Thackeray's *Newcomes*, eldest daughter of Sir Brian and Lady Ann, a brilliant, beautiful, high-spirited girl. Loving truth and scorning sham, she is a little too quick in detecting affectation or insincerity in others, too impatient of dulness or pomposity. "Truth looks out of her bright eyes and rises up armed and flashes scorn or denial, perhaps too readily when she encounters flattery or meanness or imposture. After her first appearance in the world, if the truth must be told, this young woman was popular neither with many men nor with most women " (Chap. xxiv). But none could fail to pay tribute to her beauty. Even the famous Diana in the Louvre to which Clive compared her was not more perfect in form or face.

Thackeray wrote *The Newcomes* after his visit to the United States in 1852. Mrs. Julia Ward Howe in her *Reminiscences* opines that two young women whom he met in New York gave him hints for his very un-English Ethel. Mrs. Hampton, sister-in-law of General Wade Hampton, was one: "She told me that she recognized bits of her own conversation in some of the sayings of Ethel Newcome." The other is mentioned later in the same book: "I have little doubt that in depicting the beautiful and noble though wayward girl Thackeray had in mind something of the aspect and character of the lovely Sally Baxter." General James Grant Wilson quotes from a letter he received from Sally's surviving sister in 1900. Thackeray, she says, used to call her mother Lady Castlewood and her sister Miss Beatrix. "It is not true," she adds, "as has been often said, that the character of Ethel Newcome was drawn from my sister, although some of the scenes in *The Newcomes* were no doubt suggested by seeing my sister holding her court in New York ball-rooms."

Newcome, Colonel Thomas, the chief character in Thackeray's novel *The Newcomes* and one of the greatest figures in fiction, claiming kinship with Thackeray's own favorites Don Quixote, Sir Roger de Coverley, Uncle Toby and Natty Bumppo, all of whom he half laughingly acknowledged were in his mind as he wrote. The Colonel is simple, unworldly, pure minded, humble, God-fearing, a gentleman in externals and in all his instincts, generous up to the limit of his means, and obsessed by a punctilious sense of honor that proves his own undoing. The "Adsum!" which he utters on his death bed in the Greyfriars (chap. lxxx), singularly is reminiscent of the "Here!" of another famous death scene, that of Natty Bumppo in Cooper's *The Prairie*. Lady Anna Thackeray Ritchie in raising a monument to Thackeray's stepfather, Major Carmichael Smith, has placed the ejaculation "Adsum!" over the epitaph, thus showing that the family realizes the Major was in some respects the prototype of Colonel Newcome.

Newman, Christopher, in Henry James's novel of *The American* (1877), is a self-made American. He has gathered a great fortune before the age of 35, has gone to Paris to spend it, and naïvely resolves to take him a wife out of the Faubourg St. Germain. He gains the entree to that difficult stronghold and very nearly succeeds in his project. But alas! "The Old World crushes the representative of the New. It erects before him a cruel incomprehensible barrier and sucks the soul out of him and remorselessly cuts off all his hopes. He is no match for it, though he thinks at first that he is far more than a match. This is the way in which aristocratic France deals with the American. It baffles him, confounds him, cuts off his ambition and his ideal, and makes an end of what was to have been so good—his future, the reward of his exertions, the fine dream upon which he had concentrated all his hopes."—*Blackwood's Magazine.*

Nick of the Woods, hero and title of a novel by Robert Montgomery Bird. In early boyhood Nick had seen his home destroyed and his family and friends butchered by Indians. He devotes his life to revenge, and eventually succeeds in killing not only every member of the band of devastators but hundreds of other red fiends. The body of every victim is marked by a rude cross cut upon the breast. Astounded at this wholesale slaughter by an unseen and undetected foe the Indians identify him with their devil Jibbenainosay.

Nickleby, Mrs. Mary, in Dickens's *Nicholas Nickleby*, mother of the hero and his sister Kate. She is weak and vain and foolish, rambling in her mind and delightfully irrelevant and inconsequent in her talk. While Mrs. Malaprop only messes up her words, Mrs. Nickleby creates inextricable confusion in ideas. "The name began with 'B' and ended with 'g' I am sure. Perhaps it was Waters"—this is the sort of thing wherein she weltered. In a letter to Leigh Hunt, Dickens expressly stated that Mrs. Nickleby was drawn from his mother, as Micawber was drawn from his father. He never forgave either of his parents for placing him as a boy in a blacking bottle establishment. See FORSTER, *Life of Dickens,* iii, 8.

Nickleby, Nicholas, hero and title of a novel (1838), by Dickens. Son of a poor country gentleman who left him fatherless at an early age, Nicholas had to make his own way in the world. He was successively an usher at the infamous Dotheboys Hall, a Yorkshire school run by Wackford Squeers; the first walking gentleman in Mr. Crummles's theatrical company; a clerk in the office of the

Cheeryble Brothers; and finally a London merchant on his own account. He marries Madeline Bray.

Nicholas Nickleby is Dickens's first romantic novel because it is his first novel with a proper and romantic hero, which means, of course, a somewhat chivalrous young donkey . . . Mr. Vincent Crummles had a colossal intellect; and I always have a fancy that under all his pomposity he saw things more keenly than he allowed others to see. The moment he saw Nicholas Nickleby, almost in rags and limping along the high road, he engaged him (you will remember) as first walking gentleman. He was right. Nobody could be more of a first walking gentleman than Nicholas Nickleby was before he went on to the boards of Mr. Vincent Crummles's theatre and he remained the first walking gentleman after he had come off.—G. K. CHESTERTON.

Noggs, Newman, in Dickens's novel, *Nicholas Nickleby*, a man of gentle breeding who has been ruined by Ralph Nickleby and enters his service to ruin him in turn. At last he has the satisfaction of telling him what he has done, " face to face, man to man and like a man." He is described as a tall man with two goggle eyes, of which one is a fixture, a rubicund nose, a cadaverous face and ill-fitting clothes, much the worse for wear and very much too small. He rarely spoke unless spoken to, and had a trick of rubbing his hands slowly over each other, cracking the joints of his fingers and squeezing them into all possible distortions.

Nolan, Philip, hero of E. E. Hale's story, *The Man Without a Country* (1863). An officer of the United States Navy, he is implicated in the treason of Aaron Burr and has doubly damned himself by expressing a hope that never again would he hear the name of the United States. He is taken at his word; passed from one man-of-war to another, never allowed to talk on national affairs, nor to see an American paper, nor to read a history of the United States, nor to hear the name of his country until at last, homesick and heartsick after an exile of fifty-five years, he dies praying for the fatherland which he had disowned and which had disowned him in return. Subsequently Mr. Hale

made him the hero of a novel, *Philip Nolan and his Friends,* which was never popular.

Norna of the Fitful Head, the sobriquet of Ulla Troil in Scott's *The Pirate,* a mysterious personage who imagines herself gifted with supernatural powers. Scott explains that she is meant to be " an instance of that singular kind of insanity " which imposes upon itself as well as upon others. Deeming that her father's death had taken her from humanity to be " something pre-eminently powerful, pre-eminently wretched " she claimed to be the Sovereign of the Seas and Winds, and her claims were generally allowed by the superstitious.

Norna is a new incarnation of Meg Merrilies, and palpably the same in the spirit. Less degraded in her habits and associates and less lofty and pathetic in her denunciations, she reconciles fewer contradictions and is on the whole inferior perhaps to her prototype but is far above the rank of a mere imitated or borrowed character.— FRANCIS JEFFREY: *Essays.*

Norris, Aunt, in Jane Austen's novel, *Mansfield Park* (1814), a bustling, self-important, miserly, irritable old woman who worries her niece Fanny Price by continual harrying and nagging.

A mean, stingy busybody, Aunt Norris is the most amusing widow in fiction. She talks Sir Thomas into adopting Fanny Price, and talks him out of expecting her to take any share in the concurrent expenses with equal facility. She sponges on Mrs. Rushworth's housekeeper till she goes home laden with plants, cream cheeses and golden pheasants' eggs, which are to be hatched in Lady Bertram's coops. She bullies poor Fanny mercilessly. She schemes for the marriage of the dull Rushworth with the handsome Maria, and so enjoys planning the green baize curtain for the theatricals that she actually winks at the indecorum of "Lovers' Vows," and is so busy saving the absent Sir Thomas "at least two shillings in curtain rings" as to be quite blind to Maria's flirtations.—ROWLAND GREY.

North, Christopher or **Kit,** the pseudonym under which Prof. John Wilson contributed to *Blackwood's Magazine.* It first arose in connection with the famous series of dialogues, *Noctes Ambrosianæ,* which were supposed to take place in the " blue parlor " of a tavern kept by one

Ambrose in Prince's Street, Edinburgh. The protagonist of the occasion and the ruler of the roast was ever Christopher North;—his principal interlocutors were Timothy Tickler, an idealized portrait of Robert Sym (1750–1844), an Edinburgh attorney; and the Ettrick Shepherd, a good-natured caricature of the poet Hogg. Wilson collected his miscelleanous essays into book form under the title *Recreations of Christopher North* (1842), but his poems and novels appeared under his own name.

Northumberland, Henry Percy, Earl of, in Shakespeare's *Richard II* and in the two parts of *Henry IV*, a powerful nobleman who joins Bolingbroke's rebellion against Richard and having helped to make him Henry IV joins in a rebellion against him. At Shrewsbury he is "crafty sick" and fails to go to the aid of his son (see HOTSPUR) and allies. In *II Henry IV* he again fails the allies and Henry triumphs. Warwick truthfully says of him:

King Richard might create a perfect guess
That great Northumberland then false to him
Would, of that seed, grow to a greater falseness.
II Henry IV, iii, 1.

Norval, Old, in John Home's tragedy, *Douglas* (1757), a Scotch shepherd who finds the infant heir of the Douglases exposed in a basket and brings him up as his own son.

Young Norval, the lad, at the age of eighteen, saves the life of Lord Randolph and is rewarded by a commission in the army. Now Lord Randolph is the second husband of Lady Douglas. Glenarvon, his heir, seeks to stir up strife by exciting Lord Randolph's jealousy. Young Norval kills Glenarvon. Lord Randolph kills Norval and then finds too late that he has slain his wife's son by her first marriage; the wife in despair throws herself over a precipice.

Nourmahal (*Persian*, the Light of the Harem), heroine of the fourth and last tale in Moore's *Lalla Rookh* (1817), called after her *The Light of the Haram* (sic). The favorite Sultana of the Emperor Selim, she quarrels with her consort during the Feast of Roses in the Vale of Cashmere. Repenting after the sullen fit has passed she applies to an enchantress, who invokes a spirit to teach her an irresistible song. She sings it masked to the offended monarch and when his heart is softened by its sweetness throws off her disguise and springs with fonder welcome than ever into his outstretched arms.

Nurse to Juliet, in Shakespeare's *Romeo and Juliet.*

The Nurse is a coarse, kindly, garrulous, consequential old body, with vulgar feelings and a vulgarized air of rank; she is on terms of long standing familiarity with her master, her mistress, and Juliet, and takes all manner of liberties with them; but love has made Juliet a woman and independent of her old foster mother.—E. DOWDEN: *Shakespeare Primer.*

Nydia, in Bulwer's *Last Days of Pompeii*, a blind girl who weaves garlands of flowers and sells them in the public places of the doomed city. A Greek of noble birth and gentle nurture, she had been stolen in infancy from her parents, sold into slavery and rescued from a brutal taskmaster by the hero, Glaucus. She repays him with the love of an intense and passionate heart, but the love,— unrequited, even unsuspected by its object, embittered by despondency and jealousy,—finally drives her to crime, despair and death. Not only in her history, but in her beauty, her simplicity, her purity, her wayward and capricious childishness, Nydia is obviously borrowed from Goethe's Mignon, with, perhaps, a few hints from Fenella and Esmeralda, the characters in which Walter Scott and Victor Hugo followed the same great original.

Nym, in Shakespeare's *Merry Wives of Windsor*, a corporal under Falstaff. He does not appear in *Henry IV*, but in *Henry V* he emerges again as an ensign. An arrant rogue and a coward, he and Bardolph are hanged. To nym is a cant word still extant among English thieves, meaning to pilfer, to steal.

O

Oakhurst, John, a professional gambler in the California mining camps of 1849, a favorite creation of Bret Harte who brings him into many of his short stories. He is incidentally sketched in *The Luck of Roaring Camp*,—" Oakhurst, a gambler, had the melancholy air and intellectual abstraction of a Hamlet "—and he commits suicide from the noblest motives in the next sketch in the same volume, *The Outcasts of Poker Flat.* He was resuscitated whenever Mr. Harte needed him for the purpose of his plot. See HAMLIN, JACK.

We think it probable that none but a man would care for the portrait of such a gambler as Mr. John Oakhurst, or would discern the cunning touches with which it is done, in its blended shades of good and evil . . . Perhaps Oakhurst would not, in actual life, have shot himself to save provisions for a starving boy and girl; and perhaps that poor ruined Mother Shipton was not really equal to the act ascribed to her: but Mr. Harte contrives to have it touch one like the truth, and that is all we can ask of him.—W. D. HOWELLS.—*Atlantic Monthly*, May, 1870.

Obermann. Hero and title of a famous book (1804)—a psychological study rather than a novel—in which the author, Etienne de Senancour, reveals the workings of his own morbid yet noble mind. Through the medium of a series of letters written from day to day without any recorded answers, Obermann voices his disappointments, his disillusions, his empty hopes, his vague and restless aspirations. Looking back at the weariness and satiety which eclipsed the pagan world he recognizes the new life that came in with Christianity; laments the gradual waning of the lifegiving faith and confesses himself unable to join in the hopes held out by the newer faith now supplanting it. What shall be in the future is not for him to share because he is hopelessly wedded to a past that is no more.

I turn thy leaves! I feel their breath
  Once more upon me roll;
That air of languor, cold, and death,
  Which brooded o'er thy soul.

* * * * * * * *

A fever in these pages burns
  Beneath the calm they feign;
A wounded human spirit turns,
  Here, on its bed of pain.
    MATTHEW ARNOLD, *Stanzas in Memory of the Author of Obermann*, 1849.

Oberon, in Shakespeare's *Midsummer Night's Dream*, the king of the fairies, consort of Queen Titania. He was the dwarf Alberich in the *Nibulengen Lied* who guarded the treasure of the Nibelungs but was overcome by Siegfried. He was the Auberon of the legendary history of the Merovingian dynasty, where he figures as a magician and the brother of Merovee. He was Alberich, king of the dwarfs, who aids Ortnit in his wooing. He makes his first appearance as Oberon, king of the fairies, in *Huon of Bordeaux* where Shakespeare undoubtedly found him and made him his own. See OBERON in vol. II.

Oblonsky, Prince Stépane Arcadievitch, best known to his own circle as Stiva, a character in Tolstoy's novel *Anna Karenina*.

To think of him as anything except Stiva is difficult. His air souriant, his good looks, his satisfaction; his "ray" which made the Tartar waiter at the club joyful in contemplating it; his pleasure in oysters and champagne, his pleasure in making people happy and in rendering services; his need of money, his attachment to the French governess, his distress at his wife's distress, his affection for her and the children; his emotion and suffused eyes, while he quite dismisses the care of providing funds for household expenses and education; and the French attachment, contritely given up to-day only to be succeeded by some other attachment to-morrow—no never, certainly, shall we forget Stiva.

Ochiltree, Edie, in Scott's novel *The Antiquary*, one of the "King's bedesmen;" a travelling beggar licensed by the crown who was on familiar terms with gentle and simple alike. He was drawn from Andrew Gemmels, an Ayrshire man, a native not of Ochiltree but of Old Cumnock the adjacent parish. Like Edie he fought at Fontenoy. When his soldiering days were over, he assumed the Blue Gown of the bedesman and drifted into the vagrant life which characterized his remaining years. He died in 1793, according to his tombstone, aged 106.

[Andrew] was the best known gaberlunzie on both sides of the border. His stories of his campaigns and adventures in foreign countries, his flow of wit and drollery, his skill at the dambrods (draughts) and other agreeable qualities rendered him a general favorite, and secured him a cordial reception and free quarters in every shepherd's cottage and farm kitchen within the sphere of his peregrinations. Scott's description of him is that of a remarkably fine old figure, very tall, and maintaining a soldier-like manner and address . . . Unlike the Edie of fiction Andrew was somewhat fond of the "siller" and was supposed to carry considerable sums about his person.—W. S. CROCKETT: *The Scott Originals*, p. 137.

O'Ferrall, Trilby, heroine of George du Maurier's novel *Trilby* (1895), an artist's model seventeen years old and in love with "Little Billee" Bagot when the story begins. She was an orphan, the daughter of an Irish gentleman in English orders who had lost his living through drink and married a Paris barmaid, illegitimate but of aristocratic connections. Trilby's love opens her eyes to the fact that her antecedents are shady, that posing, especially "in the altogether" (nudity) is not respectable and that otherwise she has so erred against the social code as to be unfit to enter the Bagot family. So though she had agreed to an engagement with Little Billee she breaks it for his sake and disappears out of his life to reappear as a famous singer hypnotized into melodic utterance by a villain named Svengali (*q.v.*).

Oldbuck, Jonathan, in Scott's novel *The Antiquary*, the Laird of Monkbarns, whose antiquarian tastes make him the sponsor for the novel. An old bachelor, full of learning, wit and drollery, he knows how to express sound thought in quaint and pregnant sentences. Scott owns that the character was drawn from an old friend of his father's, George Constable (1719–1803), a retired lawyer whose tastes and whimsies kinned him to Oldbuck.

Constable spent many of his Edinburgh Sundays with the Scotts—ever a welcome break in the austerity of the day to the younger generation, who coaxed Constable to turn the conversation from its severely Calvinistic tone to subjects of history and auld lang syne. He remembered the Jacobite uprising of '45 and told excellent stories, with a strong dash of peculiar caustic humor. See S. R. CROCKETT: *The Scott Originals*, p. 123.

Oldcastle, Sir John, Shakespeare's original name for Falstaff in both parts of *Henry IV* (1588). A drama called *Sir John Oldcastle*, now known to be by Arthur Munday, and printed in 1600, was ascribed to Shakespeare on the title page. A knight of the same name also figures in an old play of uncertain date and authorship, *The Famous Victories of Henry V*, as one of Prince Hal's boon companions. Shakespeare took some of his material from this play, including the name of Oldcastle, which was speedily changed to the immortal one of Falstaff. This is evident from 3 oversights in the printed texts. In the quarto of 1600 the syllable *Old* remains prefixed to a speech of Falstaff's. Not only in this quarto but also in both Folios and consequently in all subsequent printings a now meaningless pun is retained in an allusion to Falstaff as "My Old Lad of the Castle" (*I Henry IV*, I, ii, 48), together with another allusion to Falstaff as "page to Thomas Mowbray, Duke of Norfolk" (*II Henry IV*, III, ii, 28), which is true of the historical Oldcastle. This historical Oldcastle is better known as Lord Cobham, the Lollard martyr. Lastly, in the Epilogue to *II Henry IV*, Shakespeare wrote: "Falstaff shall die of a sweat unless he be killed with your hard opinions, for Oldcastle died a martyr and this is not the man." Rowe says that Elizabeth acting on behalf of the Cobhams of that day ordered the change of name. The disclaimer in the epilogue, therefore, was probably no more than an ingenious artifice to ward off the resentment of a powerful family as well as to make that appear a gratuitous recognition of propriety which was in reality obedience to a royal command.

Did you never see
The play where the fat knight, hight Oldcastle,
Did tell you truly what this honor was.
            FIELD: *Amends for Ladies* (1618).

Old Mortality, in Scott's novel of that name (1816), the nickname of

Robert Paterson (1715–1801) a religious enthusiast who left his home about 1758 to wander about until his death, repairing and erecting gravestones to the memory of the persecuted Covenanters. The story—which describes the conflict of the Covenanters in 1670–1671 with the royal forces under Claverhouse—purports to have been told by Paterson to the author as Jedediah Cleishbotham and licked into proper narrative shape by Cleishbotham's assistant Pattieson. It was Scott's friend Joseph Train who suggested to him that a story about Claverhouse might be put into the mouth of Old Mortality,—" Would he not do as well as the Minstrel did in the *Lay."* " Old Mortality?" asked Scott; " who is he?" "Never shall I forget," says Train, " the eager interest with which he listened while I related to him what I knew of old Robert Paterson, the wandering inscription cutter." On departing, Train promised that on his return to Galloway he would collect all available particulars. Scott himself had met the famous original in 1793.

Oliver, in Shakespeare's *As You Like It,* elder brother to Orlando who plunders his brother of his poor inheritance through sheer jealousy. He is suddenly converted when Orlando saves his life, proposes to give up all his possessions to Orlando and marries Celia under her feigned name of Aliena, imagining that she is a poor and lowly shepherdess.

Olivia, in Shakespeare's *Twelfth Night,* a beautiful woman beloved by the duke Orsino. She falls in love with Cesario, his messenger, unaware that the lad is simply Viola in male disguise. She readily transfers her affections to Sebastian, Viola's twin brother. She anticipates Priscilla Mullens by telling the ambassador:

But would you undertake another suit ?
I had rather hear you to solicit that
Than music from the spheres.

Omnium, Palliser Plantagenet, Duke of, one of Anthony Trollope's most successful characters who first appears as Plantagenet Palliser, with his wife Glencora, in *Can You Forgive Her* (1864), and gathers in importance as he passes through *Phineas Finn* (1866) and *Phineas Redux* (1874) until at last he reaches the height of his ambition as English premier in *The Prime Minister* (1876). The series was concluded in 1880 with *The Duke's Children.* He is a typical English gentleman, cold, shy, sensitive, proud, scrupulously honest and honorable, devoted to his country's service, cherishing high ideals but absolutely without charm or magnetism. Lady Glencora, like himself, is universally respected but nowhere popular.

I think that Plantagenet Palliser, Duke of Omnium, is a perfect gentleman. If he be not, then I am unable to describe a gentleman. She is by no means a perfect lady; but if she be not all over a woman, then am I not able to describe a woman. I do not think it probable that my name will remain among those who in the next century will be known as the writers of English prose fiction; but if it does, that permanence of success will probably rest on the character of Plantagenet Palliser, Lady Glencora, and the Rev. Mr. Crawley.—ANTHONY TROLLOPE: *An Autobiography,* p. 313.

Oneiza, in Southey's *Thalaba the Destroyer,* books vi and vii, daughter of Moath, a well-to-do Bedouin who is carried off by violence to the paradise of pleasure, and there meets Thalaba, who rescues her and himself before either had been contaminated by its temptations. They are married but she dies on the bridal night.

Ophelia, in Shakespeare's *Hamlet,* daughter of Polonius and intended wife of Hamlet. He is high-handed and tyrannic over her in carrying out his assumed madness. The death of her father drives her insane (Act iv, Sc. 5) and she ends by drowning herself, unintentionally, in a brook (iv, 7).

Ophelia is a character almost too exquisitely touching to be dwelt upon. Oh rose of May, oh flower too soon faded! Her love, her madness, her death, are described with the truest touches of tenderness and pathos. It is a character which nobody but Shakespeare could have drawn in the way that he has done, and to the conception of which there is not even the smallest approach, except in some of the old romantic ballads. —HAZLITT: *Characters of Shakespeare's Plays.*

Opimian, Dr., in Thomas L. Peacock's prose satire *Gryll Grange* (1860), a lover of Greek and Madeira, evidently drawn from the author himself and serving as a vehicle for his reactionary views on education, modern inventions, reforms and reformers. Dr. Opimian sums up the material side of his own character in the phrase " Whatever happens in the world never let it spoil your dinner."

Orgon, in Molière's comedy *Tartuffe,* brother-in-law of the titular character, whose faith in that religious hypocrite transcends even that of his mother so that he virtually abdicates all authority in favor of the usurper. The rest of the family, including his beautiful young wife, his son and daughter, his brother and the servant are all banded together in opposition. The self-deception of Orgon is indeed almost too complete throughout the early part of the play. One may endure that a woman should be thus hoodwinked, but a man is expected to know the world better.

Oriana, in the mediæval romance *Amadis of Gaul,* a daughter of the mythical Lisuarte, King of England, and the lady love of Amadis (*q.v.*). Being represented as the gentlest, loveliest and most faithful of women, hers was a favorite name of compliment. The literary courtiers of Queen Elizabeth styled her the " fair " or " matchless " Oriana. A series of madrigals addressed to her as Oriana was published in 1601. They celebrate her beauty and chastity at sixty-eight. Ben Jonson borrowed the term for Anne the queen of James I.

Origilla, in Ariosto's *Orlando Furioso* (Books viii–ix), the faithless love of Gryphon who forsook him for Martano.

Orion, hero and title of an epic poem (1843), by Robert Hengist Horne, meant, as the author subsequently explained, " to present a type of the struggle of man with himself— that is to say, the contest between the intellect and the senses, when powerful energies are equally balanced." He is a truly practical believer in his gods and his own conscience; a man with the strength of a giant, innocently wise; with a heart expanding towards the largeness and warmth of nature and a spirit unconsciously aspiring to the stars.

Orlando, hero of Shakespeare's *As You Like It* (1598) and lover of Rosalind. The younger son of Sir Rowland de Boys, his elder brother Oliver through jealousy neglects his education, persecutes him and even seeks to kill him. In a wrestling bout at the court of the usurping duke, Orlando wins the love of Rosalind, but when he flees to the forest of Arden he fails to recognize his fellow exile in the masculine garb of Ganymede until she reveals the truth.

In choosing the names Orlando and Oliver, Shakespeare was influenced by the Italian romances (see next entry) and the same influence is curiously evident in other parallelisms, even to the selection of the Forest of Arden as the scene of the comedy. Ariosto's Orlando hangs up poems to Angelica in the Forest of Arden.

Orlando, hero of a famous triad of Italian poems, Pulci's *Morgante Maggiore* (1488); Bojardo's *Orlando Innamorato* (1495) or *Orlando in Love* and Ariosto's *Orlando Furioso* (1516) or *Orlando Mad.* Orlando is Italian for Roland and the hero is the Carlovingian Paladin placed among newly invented circumstances (which ignore or modify the elder French legends) and treated mockheroically with a good deal of license and levity. Pulci's poem is an independent narrative of Orlando's adventures as the companion of giants and the foe of enchanters, Morgante Maggiore being a huge creature he had converted to Christianity. Bojardo accepts the general theme of a war between Charlemagne and the Saracens, but places the scene under the walls of Paris, which is simultaneously besieged by Agramante, Emperor of Africa, and Garcilasso, King of Sericana. The immaculate Roland becomes in his hands the gallant Orlando, the recreant husband of Aldabella, the sport of a light o' love named Angelica, who has come from farthest Asia to sow dissensions among the Christians. Here Bojardo left her. Ariosto took up the thread of the narrative. Angelica succeeds in seducing Rinaldo, who at first had scorned her and abandons him for Medoro, a captive Moor in Paris. She marries the latter and elopes with him to her native Cathay, planning to make him king. Orlando follows and, growing mad with jealousy and baffled love, wanders far and wide performing prodigious deeds of strength on men, cattle and trees. Finally he is cured by Astolfo, who has made a visit to the moon and there in the Paradise of Fools has recovered the lost wits of his friend.

Orleans, Bastard of, in Shakespeare's *I Henry VI*, is the Count of Dunois, famous as one of the greatest soldiers of his time and the devoted admirer of Jeanne Darc.

Ormont, Lord, hero of a novel, *Lord Ormont and his Aminta* (1894), by George Meredith; a sulky and whimsical nobleman who refuses to make public his marriage to Aminta Farrell. Chafing under her anomalous position, she is thrown much in the society of Ormont's secretary, Matthew Weyburn, between whom and herself there had been a boy and girl love in their schooldays. Finally with the approval of the author Matthew and she elope to set up a school where true honor is to be taught and in the end Lord Ormont commits to their keeping his grandnephew.

Oronooko, hero and title of a novel by Mrs. Aphra Behn and of a tragedy (1696) by Thomas Southern, founded thereon. The novel belongs to the same class of humanitarian literature as Mrs. Stowe's *Uncle Tom's Cabin* and Tourgenief's *Notes of a Sportsman,* but differs from them in being only an embellishment of actual facts that had come under the author's notice. Oronooko, and his grandfather, an African king, both fell in love with Imoinda, a girl of their own tribe, whom the monarch ordered to his harem. Oronooko, in despair, forced his way to her chamber at night; was discovered, but made good his escape. The girl was sold into slavery, and Oronooko, lured on board an English slave ship, was shortly afterwards sold to a planter in Surinam (the colony where Mrs. Behn was then living), who, by a strange coincidence, had become the owner of Imoinda. Oronooko plotted a revolt among his fellow-slaves; the plan was discovered, and he was brutally flogged. Enraged at the indignity, he escaped into the woods with Imoinda, who was then pregnant. But fearing she might fall into the hands of their pursuers, and determined never to be the father of a slave, he slew her, and some days afterwards was captured near her dead body, half insensible from grief and hunger. He was tied to a post, hacked to pieces and burned. Southern's chief deviations from the novel are in the introduction of a comic underplot, rightly censured for its indecency, and in the catastrophe where Oronooko kills first the Governor of Surinam and then himself.

Orsino, Duke of Illyria, in Shakespeare's *Twelfth Night,* " a fresh and stainless youth," in love with Olympia. In the end he transfers his affections to Viola who, disguised in male attire, had served him as a page.

Osborne, Mr., in Thackeray's novel, *Vanity Fair,* an ignorant, vulgar, hard, purseproud English merchant, who has risen from poverty to wealth and with a continually inflated sense of his own importance.

Osborne, George, in Thackeray's *Vanity Fair,* a captain in the British army, son of old Osborne, whom he despises for his ill breeding and social lapses, but on whose continued favor he complacently counts. He goes too far, however, in the one good deed of his selfish, vainglorious life, his loyalty to Amelia Sedley whom he had been engaged to since childhood, but whom his father would have him forswear when the Sedleys are overwhelmed in financial difficulties. Irritated by his father's obstinacy; softened also by Dobbin's story of her sufferings, he marries her offhand, thereby incurring his father's lasting wrath. Six weeks later he would have been ready to elope with Becky Sharp. He is killed at Waterloo.

O'Shanter, Tam, hero and title of a poem (1790) by Robert Burns. According to his wife Tam was:

A blethering, blustering, drunken blellum.

Nevertheless in his historian's words:

Kings may be blest but Tam was glorious
O'er a' the ills o' life victorious!

Late one night, unusually "glorious," he was riding home, when he noticed that the kirk of Alloway was illuminated and peeping inside discovered "warlocks and witches in a dance" while old Nick blew the bagpipes. Tam's involuntary shout of "Well done Cutty Sark!" applausive of a witch in a short sark or petticoat, brought the whole pack after him as he fled. He spurred for the River Doon, knowing that no witch would cross running water, and had safely passed mid-stream when she whom he had called Cutty Sark reached over and snatched off his mare's tail.

Osric, in *Hamlet*, a courtier who has no business in the play except to carry Laertes' challenge to Hamlet in Act v, 2.

He exists it cannot be doubted merely as a foil for Hamlet's wit and melancholy. When the mind is wholly taken up with tragic issues, when it is brooding on a great sorrow, or foreboding a hopeless event, the little daily affairs of life continue unaltered; tables are served, courtesies interchanged, and the wheels of society revolve at their accustomed pace. Osric is the representative of society; his talk is of gentility, skill in fencing, and the elegance of the proffered wager.—WALTER RALEGH: *Shakespeare,* in *English Men of Letters* series, p. 146.

Othello, hero of Shakespeare's tragedy, *Othello the Moor of Venice* (1604), a Moorish general in the service of Venice who marries Desdemona, daughter of a senator, against her father's will, is exonerated by the senate of having used any unlawful means in gaining the maiden (Act i, Sc. 3), is aroused to jealousy by the malignant insinuations of Iago (iii, 3) and kills Desdemona and himself in v, 2. "The noblest man of man's

making," Swinburne calls him. He is not prone to jealousy, but on the contrary is naturally trustful, "with a kind of grand innocence," says Dowden, "retaining some of his barbaric simpleness of soul in midst of the subtle and astute politicians of Venice." Great in simple heroic action, he is unversed in the complex affairs of life and "a stranger to the malignant deceits of the debased Italian character." The germ of the story is contained in *Un Capitano Moro, A Moorish (or Arab) Captain,* in Cinthio's *Hecatommithi,* published in Venice in 1565. Shakespeare borrowed the outlines of the story but none of the names except that of Desdemona. There is historical evidence that a certain Moro was governor of Cyprus in the fifteenth century and that his wife died under mysterious circumstances. This may have been the basis of Cynthio's tale.

Coleridge has justly said that the agonized doubt which lays hold of the Moor is not the jealousy of a man of naturally jealous temper, and he contrasts Othello with Leontes in *The Winter's Tale* and Leonatus in *Cymbeline.* A mean watchfulness or prying suspiciousness is the last thing that Othello could be guilty of. He is of a free and noble nature, naturally trustful, with a kind of grand innocence, retaining some of his barbaric simpleness of soul in midst of the subtle and astute politicians of Venice. He is great in simple heroic action, but unversed in the complex affairs of life and a stranger to the malignant deceits of the debased Italian character.— E. DOWDEN: *Shakespeare Primer.*

Otranto, Manfred, Prince of, hero of Horace Walpole's romance, *The Castle of Otranto* (1764). The father of Conrad,—betrothed to Isabella, daughter of the Marquis of Vicenza, —Manfred decides to marry that lady himself when Conrad is found in the castle court dashed to pieces under an enormous helmet. Numerous portents ensue to prevent his carrying out his purpose, and in the meantime Isabella escapes to Friar Jerome, through the instrumentality of a peasant named Theodore. Drops of blood flow from the nose of the statue of Alphonso, the prince from whose heirs the dukedom had been wrested, and in the end the walls of the castle are overthrown by an earthquake and the statue of Alphonso cries out from the ruins, "Behold in Theodore the true heir of Alphonso." Manfred then resigns Isabella to Theodore.

O'Trigger, Sir Lucius, in Sheridan's comedy, *The Rivals*, a fire-eating, fortune-hunting Irish gentleman, always as ready to forgive as to fight. The rôle was a failure on the first appearance of the play partly from the incompetence of the actor, but partly also because it was looked upon as a reflection on the Irish. "If any gentlemen," wrote Sheridan, "opposed the piece from that idea, I thank them sincerely for their opposition; and if the condemnation of this comedy (however misconceived the provocation) could have added one spark to the decaying flame of national attachment to the country supposed to be reflected on, I should have been happy in its fate, and might with truth have boasted that it had done more real service in its failure than the successful morality of a thousand stage novels will ever effect." In its original form *The Rivals* was played twice, and then withdrawn for alterations. After an interval of ten days it was reproduced, and forthwith obtained the popularity it has never forfeited since. The part of Sir Lucius was taken from Lee and entrusted to Clinch,—a clever actor who so distinguished himself by the impersonation that Sheridan gave him the farce of *St. Patrick's Day* to produce upon the occasion of his benefit at the close of the season.

Ottilia, Princess, in *The Adventures of Harry Richmond*, a novel by George Meredith.

Ottilia was one of those women whom men love passionately and know very little about. Once in a life a man may see such a face—in lonely glimpses; hear such a voice—a music broken by long pauses of absence. She creates a tropical storm in his imagination; he gives her his dreams, thinks he must die for want of her, and lives to take a Janet Ilchester to wife. Janet is of the type most Englishmen desire to have their wives, although human weakness may lead their erring fancy towards Ottilia. *Daily News*, November 6, 1871, reported in *George Meredith, Some Early Appreciations*, 1909, by Maurice Buxton Forman.

Overreach, Sir Giles, the principal character in Philip Massinger's comedy, *A New Way to Pay Old Debts* (1625). A usurer and an extortioner, he is no miser, because he finds that an outer appearance of splendor and luxury furnishes his best snare for the weak and the gullible. He lives luxuriously, keeps many servants, is profuse in his expenditures. He encourages the extravagances of the prodigal, especially of Frank Wellborns his own nephew, whom he reduces to pecuniary straits, from which he reaps his own profit, and then seeks to drive into crime, so that the gallows may rid him of a dangerous victim. He goads his neighbors into lawsuits in order that he may ruin them and absorb their lands. His final purpose is to marry his daughter (through a preliminary seduction planned by himself) to a nobleman and so enjoy a triumph over the lords and ladies whom he has beggared, but who still snub him. Finally the nephew enters with other victims into a plot which beats him at his own game and Overreach goes mad when he discovers how the tables have been turned. Edmund Kean in England and E. L. Davenport in America were especially famous in this part.

The original of Overreach has been traced to Sir Giles Mompesson (1584-1651), a notorious usurer who was finally banished from England for his misdeeds. He shared with Sir Francis Michell in the profits of a patent for the exclusive manufacture of gold and silver lace which Macaulay denounced as "the most disgraceful of all patents in our history."

P

P. P., Clerk of this Parish, the hero of a burlesque, *Memoirs*, written in ridicule of Burnet's garrulous *History of My Own Times* and usually published among Pope's works, but largely, if not entirely, the composition of John Arbuthnot. P. P.'s pomposity, pedantry and egotism have earned him a high place among the braggarts of fiction.

Packlemerton, Jasper, in Dickens's novel, *The Old Curiosity Shop*, xxviii (1840), one of the principal wax-figures in Mrs. Jarley's collection. In Mrs. Jarley's words: "Jasper courted and married fourteen wives and destroyed them all by tickling the soles of their feet when they were asleep."

Paddington, Harry, in Gay's *The Beggar's Opera* (1727), one of Macheath's gang of thieves, but a recognized failure among them, "a poor, petty-larceny rascal," says Peacham, "without the least genius. That fellow," continues this severe critic, "though he were to live for six months, would never come to the gallows with credit" (Act i, 1).

Paeana, in Spenser's *Faërie Queene*, book iv, 9 (1596), the daughter of Corflambo, lovely to the eye, but "too loose of life and eke too light." She fell in love with Amias, a captive in her father's dungeon, but his affections were otherwise engaged. Now Amias had a friend, Placidas, who was exactly like him in face and figure. Placidas, coming to release him, was mistaken for Amias and brought before Paeana; she was delighted to find her love reciprocated and married the stranger even though he had undeceived her. Thenceforth she reformed her ways.

Page, Master, in Shakespeare's comedy, *The Merry Wives of Windsor* (1596), a gentleman living in Windsor whose wife is coveted by Sir John Falstaff and laid siege to simultaneously with the wife of his friend Ford (*q.v.*).

Page, Mistress, wife of Page, as above, who being courted by Falstaff, plans with Mrs. Ford to outwit him and make him ridiculous.

Page, Mistress Anne, daughter of the above. A young woman, bright and clever and pretty, who loves and is loved by young Fenton. But inasmuch as she has inherited a legacy of £700 she attracts two other suitors: Dr. Caius, favored by her mother, and Slender, whom her father prefers. Fenton wins her by a stratagem.

Page, William, a schoolboy, a brother to Anne.

Palemon, the lover of Lavinia in Thomson's poetical paraphrase of the story of Ruth, included in *The Seasons* —*Autumn* (1730). Falconer took the same name for the hero of his narrative poem, *The Shipwreck* (1756), who is the son of a rich merchant and the lover of Anna. The purseproud merchant is wroth at the threatened mesalliance, for Anna's father, Albert, is master of one of his ships; so he sends Palemon on a voyage with Albert. The ship is wrecked near Cape Colonna in Attica, and Palemon, though rescued from the waves, dies of the wounds he has suffered in the struggle.

Palfrey, Prudence, heroine of a novel of that name (1874), by T. B. Aldrich.

Miss Prudence has traits of a veritable girlhood; it is but too sadly natural that her heart should waver in its true allegiance, when she finds Dillingham at first indifferent and then devoted, and, above all, wanted by all the other girls! She gives you the sense of a pretty, sufficiently wilful, sufficiently obedient, natural, good-hearted girl, and that is as much as one ought to ask of any heroine.—W. D. HOWELLS.

Pallet, in Smollett's novel, *The Adventures of Peregrine Pickle* (1751), a boorish painter, "a man without any reverence for ancient customs and modern etiquette."

Dr. John Moore, best known as the author of *Zeluco*, was when nineteen years of age the companion and cicerone of Smollett in Paris, helping him with his superior knowledge of French. Smollett made no secret that he was picking up characters to be introduced into his novel. Moore remembered particularly one English artist whom they encountered perpetually in the picture galleries and other places of resort, and who disgusted Smollett by his incessant talk about *vertù*. Smollett had evidently marked this man for his purpose; and, accordingly, in his *Peregrine Pickle*, published shortly after his return to England, Moore had no difficulty in recognizing the unfortunate painter in the character of Pallet.

Palliser, Plantagenet, an English aristocrat, who appears in many of Trollope's novels. See OMNIUM, DUKE OF.

Mr. Plantagenet Palliser had appeared in *The Small House at Allington*, but his birth had not been accompanied by many hopes.

In the last pages of that novel he is made to seek a remedy for a foolish false step in life by marrying the grand heiress of the day; but the personage of the great heiress does not appear till she comes on the scene as a married woman in *Can You Forgive Her?* He is the nephew and heir to a Duke—the Duke of Omnium—who was first introduced in *Doctor Thorne* and afterwards in *Framley Parsonage.*—TROLLOPE: *Autobiography.*

Pambo, poem by Browning in volume, *Jocoseria* (1883). Pambo asking of a learned man how he was to acquire wisdom was referred to the 39th Psalm, 1st verse, " I said, I will take heed to my ways, that I sin not with my tongue." He was struck dumb by the greatness as well as the simplicity of the lesson and went his way to practise it. When last heard from he was still grappling with the initiatory lesson of wisdom.

Pamela, titular heroine and title of a novel by Samuel Richardson (1741). The full title is *Pamela; or Virtue Rewarded. In a Series of Letters from a Beautiful Young Damsel to her Parents. Published in order to cultivate the principles of Virtue and Religion in the minds of the youth of both sexes.* Richardson was indebted for the incidents of the story to some circumstances in real life which were related to him while visiting in the country.

Pamela, the daughter of a small farmer and a pretty and ladylike girl of seventeen or eighteen, is waiting-maid and half companion to a dowager lady of great fortune in Bedfordshire, and, as a matter of course, inspires her son, who is only named as Mr. B., with a dishonorable passion. The gentleman does little or nothing towards the accomplishment of his purpose till his mother's death, and even then is held back for some time by a grave doubt whether Pamela's station in society is good enough to qualify her for his mistress. This painful scruple being at length overcome, he proceeds to pay court to her in the usual way, as one accustomed to conquest, and not dreaming of resistance. To his surprise he is rebuffed and he then tries the effect of regular proposals, a handsome allowance for herself, and all manner of good things for her

parents. These likewise being rejected, he is driven to have recourse to abduction, but is once more baffled and as a last resort offers her his hand and fortune, which are joyously accepted.

Panchine, in Ivan Tourgenief's novel, *Liza, or a Nest of Nobles,* the typical representative of that class of Russians whom scratching is supposed to metamorphose into Tartars. Panchine is all lacquer and gilding. He possesses many accomplishments, occupies himself with literature and art, and can express on occasion the most liberal and philanthropic sentiments. But his real nature is dull, cunning, and selfish. He has provided himself with a stock of Western ideas, just as a Turkish pasha orders steam-engines and power-looms, and to equal purpose. The ideas and accomplishments are laid one by one on the shelf, and Panchine becomes an ordinary Russian official.

Pancrace, Doctor, in Molière's *Forced Marriage,* a pedantic philosopher who applies the logical method of Aristotle to the most trivial acts and occurrences and convinces himself of the truth of absurdities.

Pandarus, in Shakespeare's tragedy of *Troilus and Cressida* (1609) and in Chaucer's poem (1380) similarly entitled,—a go-between or procurer, the uncle of the lascivious Cressida. There is a hero of this name in the *Iliad* and another in the *Æneid,* but neither has any connection with the more modern figure, which seems to have been invented by Boccaccio and inserted by him into the story of Cressida's loves.

His name, shortened to Pandar, has passed into the English language as the synonym for a procurer. According to Shakespeare he invoked this future curse upon his own head. In *Troilus and Cressida,* III, ii, 200, he says to the eponymic hero and heroine, " If ever you prove false one to another, since I have taken such pains to bring you together, let all pitiful goers-between be called to the world's end after my name, call them all Pandars; let all constant men be

Troiluses; all false women Cressidas and all brokers-between Pandars! Say Amen."

Pandosto, hero of a prose pastoral, *Pandosto the Triumph of Time* (1588), which Robert Greene based upon a Polish tale. The subtitle, *The History of Dorastus and Fawnia,* superseded the original title in later editions. Its chief interest to-day lies in the fact that Shakespeare drew from it the materials of *A Winter's Tale* (1611). Pandosto is Leontes, Dorastus is Florizel and Fawnia Perdita. In Greene's story Pandosto falls in love with his own daughter, not knowing her to be such, and is finally seized by a fit of melancholy madness in which he slays himself.

Pangloss, Dr., in Voltaire's satirical novel, *Candide* (1759), a professional optimist, tutor to the hero.

Dr. Pangloss proved admirably that there is no effect without a cause, and that in this best of possible worlds, the castle of the baron was the most beautiful of castles, and the baroness the best of possible baronesses. It is demonstrated, he would say, that things cannot be other than they are; for as everything was made for one end, everything is necessarily for the best end. Remark well that the nose is formed to wear spectacles; so we have spectacles. The legs were obviously instituted to be breeched and we have breeches. Pigs were made to be eaten; we eat pork all the year. Hence, those who have asserted that all is well uttered folly; we must maintain that all is best.—JAMES PARTON: *Life of Voltaire,* vol. ii, p. 212.

Pangloss, Dr. Peter, in *The Heir-at-Law* (1797), a comedy by Colman the Younger, a poor, but mercenary pedant, who pompously describes himself as " an LL.D. and an A.S.S.," and is delighted to be raised from the condition of a muffin-maker in Milk Alley to that of tutor to Dick Dowlas at £300 a year. He is fond of big words and of quotations; to the latter he always appends full credit, as " Lend me your ears—Shakespeare, hem! "

To the character of Dr. Pangloss *The Heir-at-Law* no doubt owes the chief portion of the vitality it still enjoys; so lively and vigorous a caricature in the hands of a competent interpreter could scarcely fail to afford very hearty amusement. Whether the character ever possessed any

distinct foundation in nature cannot now be discovered. The Doctor's appellation is derived, of course, from Voltaire's *Candide* and the character has been plausibly traced to *Fortune in her Wits,* an unacted comedy by Charles Johnson, published in 1705, and translated from Cowley's Latin play of *Naufragium Joculare.* In this work appears a pedantic tutor, called Sententious Gerund, who travels to Dunkirk with his pupils, Grim and Shallow, and indulges in quotations from classic authors and the poets, very much after the manner of Colman's Pangloss. Although well known to be a student of old plays, it is still quite possible that Colman was unacquainted with Johnson's comedy or its original, and that Pangloss is to be accounted as a wholly independent creation.

Panjandrum, The Great. A name sometimes used, like the American " Great Muck-a-Muck," to characterize a boaster, a poseur, a person inflated with his own imaginary importance. The term seems to have been invented by Samuel Foote, dramatist and comedian, in a farrago of nonsense written down to test the memory of old Mackein who claimed that he could learn anything by heart on hearing it once: " So she went into a garden to cut a cabbage-leaf to make an apple-pie; and at the same time, a great she-bear coming up the street pops his head into the shop—What! no soap? So he died and she very imprudently married the barber; and there were present the Picninnies and the Joblilies and the Garalilies and the Great Panjandrum himself. And they all fell to playing the game of catch-as-catch-can, till the gunpowder ran out at the heels of their boots."

Pantagruel, hero of Parts ii–v of Rabelais's *Chronicles of Gargantua.* He is the worthy son of the famous giant, though of lesser stature,—an epicurean philosopher, fond of guzzling, gorging and gormandizing, a jolly host, a responsive guest, an exhilarating companion, rising buoyantly above all the ills of life. Some commentators have seen in him a personification of Henry II, and his inappeasable appetite, devouring the substance of the masses, suggests an allegory of royalty. With his inseparable companion Panurge, he starts in search of the Oracle of the Dive-Bouteille (see HOLY BOTTLE) and meets extraordinary adventures on the way.

Panurge, the inseparable companion of Pantagruel in Rabelais's *Chronicles of Gargantua*, Parts II–V. A jovial, hard-drinking, bottle-nosed, pimply-faced, fatsided glutton, laughing at everything save fear, for he is an arrant coward, a man of great wit and intelligence, but well-nigh bereft of morality,—a drunkard, a profligate, a spendthrift and a trickster—he is the most puzzling character in all Rabelais. In Book iii he determines to marry, a determination which leads him to consult a vast number of authorities, each giving occasion for satire of a more or less complicated sort. Finally it is decided that with Pantagruel and Friar John he shall sail to consult the oracle of the Dive-Bouteille. See HOLY BOTTLE.

Panza, Sancho of Adzpetia, in Cervantes's *Don Quixote* (1605), squire to the titular hero, whose shrewdness, homely common sense and coarse and vulgar wit form an excellent foil to the other's crack-brained idealism. "A little squat fellow with a tun belly and spindle shanks" (Part I, ii, 1), he rides an ass called Dapple, is fond of the gross pleasures of the table, and is always pat and pertinent in his use of racy proverbs.

At first he is introduced as the opposite of Don Quixote, and used merely to bring out his master's peculiarities in a more striking relief. It is not until we have gone through nearly half of the First Part that he utters one of those proverbs which form afterwards the staple of his conversation and humor, and it is not till the opening of the Second Part, and indeed, not till he comes forth in all his mingled shrewdness and credulity as the governor of Barataria, that his character is quite developed and completed to the full measure of its grotesque, yet congruous, proportions.—TICKNOR: *Spanish Literature*, ii, 146.

Paracelsus, Philippus Aureolus, who was originally Theophrastus Bombastus von Hohenheim, a famous German-Swiss physician and alchemist (1493-1541). A strange mixture of charlatanism and really advanced views in science, he was popularly believed to keep a familiar or small demon in the hilt of his sword. Browning has made him the hero of a philosophic and narrative poem entitled *Paracelsus* (1835). At the age of twenty he thinks that knowledge is the *summum bonum* or greatest good of human life. His friends Festus and Michal advise him to retire to a seat of learning, but he emerges at the expiration of eight years entirely disillusionized. Falling in with Aprile, a young and enthusiastic poet, he alters his creed and determines to seek the *summum bonum* in love. Again he is disappointed and he finally decides to drop his ideals and make the material world yield up to him such enjoyment as it possesses.

Paris, in Shakespeare's tragedy, *Romeo and Juliet*, a suitor for Juliet who is commanded by her parents to accept him. Romeo (Act V, 3) kills him at Juliet's grave.

Parisina, in Byron's poem of that name (1816), the wife of Azo, chief of Ferrara. Betrothed to Hugo, an illegitimate son of Azo before her marriage and still loving him afterwards, the lovers now found freer scope for indulging their passion. One night Azo woke to overhear his wife confess her guilt while asleep. He had his son beheaded and, though he spared Parisina's life for the nonce, no one ever knew her subsequent fate. Byron founded his poem on an incident recorded in Gibbon's *Antiquities of the House of Brunswick*.

Trizzi, in his *History of Ferrara*, gives a different and more authentic story: Niccolo III of Ferrara (the historic name) married for the second time Parisina Malatesta. Because she detested his bastard, Niccolo sent Ugo to escort Parisina on a journey. Love succeeded to aversion, the secret of the guilty pair was betrayed by a servant and both were beheaded.

Parolles, in *All's Well that Ends Well* (1598), a follower of Bertram, a braggart and a coward:

I know him a notorious liar,
Think him a great way fool, solely a coward.
I, i, III.

Parolles, the vilest and basest character, although not the most wickedly malicious, that Shakespeare wrought.—R. G. WHITE.

The comic part of the play turns on the folly, boasting, and cowardice of Parolles, a parasite and hanger-on of Bertram's, the detection of whose false pretensions to bravery and honour forms a very amusing episode. He is first found out by the old lord Lafeu, who says, "The soul of this man is in his clothes"; and it is proved afterwards that his heart is in his tongue, and that both are false and hollow. The adventure of "the bringing off of his drum" has become proverbial as a satire on all ridiculous and blustering undertakings which the person never means to perform.—HAZLITT: *Characters of Shakespeare's Plays.*

Partington, Mrs., a famous character invented by Sydney Smith in a speech made at Taunton in 1831, ridiculing the rejection of the Reform Bill by the House of Lords: "I do not mean to be disrespectful, but the attempt of the lords to stop the progress of reform reminds me very forcibly of the great storm of Sidmouth, and the conduct of the excellent Mrs. Partington on that occasion. In the winter of 1824, there set in a great flood upon that town; the tide rose to an incredible height, the waves rushed in upon the houses, and everything was threatened with destruction. In the midst of this sublime storm, Dame Partington, who lived upon the beach, was seen at the door of her house with mop and patterns, trundling her mop, and squeezing out the sea-water, and vigorously pushing away the Atlantic Ocean. The Atlantic was roused, Mrs. Partington's spirit was up; but I need not tell you that the contest was unequal. The Atlantic Ocean beat Mrs. Partington. She was excellent at a slop or a puddle, but she should not have meddled with a tempest."

Attempts have been made to prove that there was really a Mrs. Partington, living as stated on the beach at Sidmouth, Devonshire, England, who engaged in vigorous contest with the incoming flood during the storm of November, 1824.

In truth, Sydney never had the weakness of looking too closely to see what the enemy's advocate is going to say. Take even the famous, the immortal apologue of

Mrs. Partington. It covered, we are usually told, the Upper House with ridicule, and did as much as anything else to carry the Reform bill. And yet, though it is a watery apologue, it will not hold water for a moment. The implied conclusion is, that the Atlantic beat Mrs. Partington. Did it? It made, no doubt, a great mess in her house, it put her to flight, it put her to shame. But when I was last at Sidmouth the line of high-water mark was, I believe, much what it was before the great storm of 1824, and though the particular Mrs. Partington had, no doubt, been gathered to her fathers, the Mrs. Partington of the day was, equally without doubt, living very comfortably in the house which the Atlantic had threatened to swallow up.—GEORGE SAINTSBURY.

Partington, Mrs. Ruth, an eccentric creation of the American humorist B. P. Shillaber. Her name was evidently a reminiscence of Sydney Smith's invention, but in her mistaken use of big words and her nice derangement of epitaphs, she establishes a clear line of descent from Sheridan's Mrs. Malaprop, Hook's Winifred Jenkins and Smollett's Tabitha Bramble.

Partridge, in Fielding's *Tom Jones,* the devoted companion of the hero in all his wanderings after leaving Squire Alworthy's house. Timid, simple-minded, blundering and eccentric, he manages to involve himself and his master in all sorts of misadventures. But he has a good heart and a semi-cultivated brain, stored as it is with odds and ends of classical literature. Before throwing in his lot with Jones he had been the village schoolmaster and later a barber under the alias of Mr. Benjamin. It may be presumed, therefore, that the latter was his Christian name.

Passepartout, in Jules Verne's romance, *Round the World in Eighty Days,* the French valet of Phileas Fogg, who had saved him from murder by a Chinese mob.

Pastorius, Daniel, hero of J. G. Whittier's poem, *The Pennsylvania Pilgrim* (1872), was a real character, a young German scholar of the seventeenth century who, turning Quaker, came to the new land of Penn and helped to found Germantown, a suburb of Philadelphia. Here he married and lived a long, calm, useful life, tilling the soil, reading good books, corresponding with savants and sought alike by the neighboring Indians and by such gentle enthusiasts as wandered into that haven of peace.

Patelin, hero of an ancient French farce by P. Blanchet, *L'Avocat Patelin, Lawyer Patelin.* Full of flattery and insinuating ways, he contrives to obtain on credit, from William Josseaume, six ells of cloth, by artfully praising the tradesman's father. To him is credited the proverbial expression, *Revenons a nos moutons,* "let us return to our sheep," or "to our muttons," as English humor will sometimes insist on translating it.

Patterne, Sir Willoughby (the name may have some punning allusion to the willow pattern, once famous in chinaware), the titular hero of George Meredith's novel, *The Egoist.*

Living entirely in and for himself, the views he takes of that self and of the duties of his position in society are all based on pride and conceit. As Providence has made him the greatest magnate in the county, it is not for him to frustrate the divine intentions, by cultivating the acquaintance of those who are his equals or possibly, his superiors. Being only a baronet, he mistrusts the peerage. London he feels to be the destruction of all individuality. Patterne Hall alone gives him room and verge enough for the proper display of his talents. There he is in his element, worshipped by the countryside in general and by Laetitia Dale (*q.v.*) in particular.

The Egoist is a satire, so much must be allowed, but it is a satire of a singular quality, which tells you nothing of that obvious mote which is engaged from first to last with that invisible beam. It is yourself that is hunted down, these are your faults that are dragged into the day and numbered, with lingering relish, with cruel cunning and precision. A young friend of Mr. Meredith's (as I have the story) came to him in agony. "This is too bad of you," he cried. "Willoughby is me!" [sic!] "No, my dear fellow," said the author, "it is all of us." I have read *The Egoist* five or six times and I mean to read it again; for I am like the young friend of the anecdote—I think Willoughby an unmanly but a very serviceable exposure of myself.—R. L. STEVENSON.

Pattieson, Mr. Peter, in the introduction to Scott's *Heart of Midlothian*

and again in the introduction to *The Bride of Lammermoor,* is feigned to be an assistant teacher at Glandercleugh, where he wrote *The Tales of My Landlord,* published after his death by Jedediah Cleishbotham.

Paul, hero of a romantic idyl, *Paul and Virginia* (1788), by Bernardin de St. Pierre, the illegitimate son of one Margaret, who has retired to hide her shame in Port Louis, in the Mauritius. In childhood he is the playmate, in early manhood he becomes the ardent and respectful lover, of Virginia (*q.v.*), his nearest neighbor, the daughter of an aristocratic French widow, Madame de la Tour.

Paulina, in Shakespeare's comedy, *A Winter's Tale,* a loud and voluble champion of Queen Hermione against the jealous king.

Paulina, *née* Home, who becomes the Countess de Bassompierre and eventually marries "Dr. John" (Graham Bretton), is a dainty, ideal creature, "an airy fairy thing," in Charlotte Brontë's novel, *Villette.* She is sketched from infancy to womanhood.

"I felt that this character lacked substance," said Miss Brontë, herself; "I fear the reader will feel the same."

Pauline, in Bulwer-Lytton's comedy, *The Lady of Lyons* (1838), the daughter of a wealthy merchant, M. Deschappelles, who marries Claude Melnotte. See MELNOTTE.

Pauline, heroine of a narrative poem by Robert Browning.

It is the half-delirious self-revealing of a soul maddened by continued introspection, by the irrepressible craving to extend its sphere of consciousness, and by the monstrosities of subjective experience in which this self-magnifying and self-distorting action has involved it. The sufferer tells his story to a woman who loves him, and to whom he has been always more or less worthily attached; and ends by gently raving himself into a rest which is represented as premonitory of death, and in which the image of a perfect human love rises amidst the tumult of the disordered brain, transfusing its chaotic emotions into one soft harmony of life and hope.—*Contemporary Review.*

Peachum, in *The Beggar's Opera* (1728), by John Gay, the ostensibly respectable patron of Captain Macheath and his gang of highwaymen, who is really a pimp and a fence. Though eloquently indignant when his honor is impeached he betrays his confederates when it suits his purposes and his pocket. In all his crookedness he enjoys the moral support of his wife, but the pair shock and alienate their daughter Polly.

Peachum, Polly, the daughter of Peachum and bride of Captain Macheath. She is represented as preserving her purity unsullied among evil surroundings, refusing even the compromise suggested by her Machiavellian mother to be " somewhat nice in her deviations from virtue." Polly's constancy to Macheath, despite his multitudinous divagations after other " charmers," wins his tardy recognition in the last act. The part of Polly was a favorite with pretty actresses of good voices, no less than three of whom sang their way direct from the stage to the peerage.

It was Polly as impersonated by the fascinating Lavinia Fenton (in 1728) that made the success of *The Beggar's Opera.* She dressed the part in the most simple manner, and the pathetic naïveté with which she delivered the lines—

" For on the rope that hangs my dear
    Depends poor Polly's life "—

had such an effect that applause burst forth from every part of the house. The work had up to this moment gone but poorly. Its triumph was now assured, and the enthusiasm of the public went on increasing till the fall of the curtain.—HENRY SUTHERLAND EDWARDS: *The Prima Donna* (1888).

Pearl, Little, in Hawthorne's *The Scarlet Letter,* the elfish result of Arthur Dimmesdale's liaison with Hester Prynne. She is the torment and the only treasure of her mother.

Peckham, Silas, in Oliver Wendell Holmes's romance, *Elsie Venner* (1861), is a hustling Yankee pedagogue, who " keeps a young lady's school exactly as he would have kept a hundred head of cattle—for the simple unadorned purpose of making just as much money in just as few years as can be safely done." He finds a notable assistant in Mrs. Peckham, an honest, ignorant woman, " who could not have passed an examination in the youngest class," but who without a qualm looks after " the feathering, cackling, roosting, rising and general behaviour of these hundred chicks."

Pecksniff, Seth, in Dickens's novel, *Martin Chuzzlewit,* a consummate humbug and hypocrite, ostensibly an architect and land-surveyor, " though he never designed or built anything and his surveying was limited to the extensive prospect from the windows of his house." In conversation and correspondence he exudes morality. He is fuller of virtuous precept than a copybook. " Some people likened him to a direction post which is always telling the way to a place and never goes there; but these were his enemies, the shadows cast by his brightness, that was all." His person is sleek, his manner soft and oily. Ultimately he is exposed and degenerates into " a drunken, begging, squalid, letter-writing man." He has two daughters, **Mercy** and **Charity,** known respectively as Merry and Cherry,—the first marries Jonas Chuzzlewit and becomes deeply penitent, the second cherishes for life the feeling that she is a victim of misplaced confidence in having been deserted at the altar by Mr. Augustus Moddle. Samuel Carter Hall was generally looked upon as the original of Pecksniff.

With him was often seen the egregious Mr. Pecksniff (as Samuel Carter Hall was commonly known to his acquaintances since the publication of *Martin Chuzzlewit* ten years before). Hall was a genuine comedy figure. Such oily and voluble sanctimoniousness needed no modification to be fitted to appear before the footlights in satirical drama. He might be called an ingenuous hypocrite, an artless humbug, a veracious liar, so obviously were the traits indicated innate and organic in him rather than acquired Dickens, after all, missed some of the finer shades of the character; there can be little doubt that Hall was in his own private contemplation as shining an object of moral perfection as he portrayed himself before others. His perversity was of the spirit, not of the letter, and thus escaped his own recognition. His indecency and falsehood were in his soul, but not in his consciousness; so that he paraded them at the very moment that he was claiming for himself all that was their opposite. No one who knew him took him seriously, but admired the ability of his performance, and so well was he understood that he did little or no harm beyond the venting of a spite here and there and the boring of his auditors after the absurdity of him became tedious.—JULIAN HAW-THORNE in *Hawthorne and his Circle.*

Pedlington, Little, an imaginary English village, in John Poole's *Little Pedlington and the Pedlingtonians* (1839). Small as it is, quackery, humbug, cant, selfishness and other social vices flourish within its bounds.

Pedro, Don. Prince of Arragon, in *Much Ado About Nothing;* the "villain" of the play, who slanders the fair heroine.

Pedro, Dr., in Cervantes's *Don Quixote,* the more familiar name for Dr. Pedro Rezio de Aguero, court physician in the island of Barataria. With a whalebone rod in his hand he posts himself at the dinner table to limit the diet of Sancho Panza, newly elected governor of the island, within proper hygienic limits. Partridges are "forbidden by Hippocrates," olla podridas are "most pernicious," rabbits are "a sharp-haired diet." These are accordingly whisked off the table. "A few wafers and a thin slice or two of quince" are recommended by the doctor and sniffed at by Sancho. Finally the latter is suffered to fall to upon a dish of beef hashed with onions. He is quite content: "Look you, signor doctor," he says, "I want no dainties, for I have always been used to beef, bacon, pork, turnips and onions" (II, iii, 10).

Peebles, Peter, in Scott's novel, *Redgauntlet,* a vain, litigious, arrogant, hard-headed and hard-hearted Scotchman, the plaintiff in the famous case of Peebles against Plainstanes, which for fifteen years had dragged its slow length from court to court until it had reached the British parliament. Peter meanwhile had made shipwreck of fortune, character and understanding and become "the old scarecrow of Parliament House," a liar, a drunkard and a pauper, but still glorying in his fancied eminence as a suitor in the law courts.

Peeping Tom, a comparatively recent interpolation into the legend of Lady Godiva (*q.v.*). When that lady announced that she would ride naked through the town of Coventry at noon on a certain day she requested that all citizens should remain at home with their doors and windows shut.

Then she rode back clothed on with chastity,
And one low churl, compact of thankless
      earth,
The fatal byword of all years to come,
Boring a little auger-hole in fear,
Peeped—but his eyes before they had their
      will,
Were shrivelled into darkness in his head
And dropt before him.
                  TENNYSON: *Lady Godiva.*

Peerybingle, John, and his wife, **Mary,** known as "Dot," an humble, but kindly and devoted couple in Dickens's *Cricket on the Hearth* (1845). See SLOWBOY, TILLIE.

Peg, in Arbuthnot's satirical *History of John Bull,* is intended to personify the Church and State of Scotland. "Peg had, indeed, some odd humours and comical, for which John would jeer her. 'What think you of my sister Peg,' says he, 'that faints at the sound of an organ, and yet will dance and frisk at the noise of a bagpipe?' Lord Peter [the Pope] she detested; nor did Martin Luther stand much better in her good graces; but Jack [Calvin] had found the way to her heart."

Peg of Limavaddy, title and heroine of a ballad by William Makepeace Thackeray.

Peggotty, Clara, in Dickens's *David Copperfield,* the homely but kindly nurse of David in childhood and his friend through life. She is generally believed to have been founded on Dickens's own nurse, Mary Weller. She marries Barkis after a peculiar courtship.

Peggotty, Daniel, brother to Clara (*q.v.*), fisherman and dealer in shellfish, a hearty whole-souled bachelor of a primitive simplicity, living at Yarmouth in a house constructed out of a turned-up boat, with his nephew Ham, his niece Emily, and Mrs. Gummidge. Ham turns out as sturdy, staunch and simple as himself. Emily grows up into a beautiful girl, is engaged to her cousin Ham, but

runs away with James Steerforth.
Daniel sets forth to find her and bring
her home, travels, mostly afoot, over
a great part of the continent and at
last comes upon her traces in London.
Meanwhile Steerforth is wrecked at
Yarmouth. Ham endeavors to rescue
him and both are drowned. Daniel
Peggotty with Mrs. Gummidge and
Emily emigrates to Australia where
he prospers as he deserves.

Pelham, the hero of Bulwer-
Lytton's novel, *Pelham, or The Adventures of a Gentleman* (1828). In
accordance with the subtitle, Pelham
attempts to realize Etherege's ideal
of a complete gentleman as exemplified in the code of Sir Fopling Flutter,
that a gentleman ought to dress well,
fence well, have a genius for love-
letters and an agreeable voice for a
chamber. Pelham, however, alter-
nates his round of empty pleasure by
taking an active interest in the political events of his time.

Pell, Solomon, in Dickens's *Pickwick Papers* (1826), an attorney in
the Insolvent Debtors' Court, by
whose aid Tony Weller contrives to
get his son Sam imprisoned in the
Fleet for debt, so that he may be
near Mr. Pickwick to wait upon him
and protect him.

Pelleas, in Arthurian legend—as it
found final shape in Mallory's *Morte
D'Arthur* and Tennyson's *Idylls of
the King: Pelleas and Ettare* (1870)
—the sinless youth, who cherishing a
maiden passion for a maid and finding
her false, goes mad at the discovery
of sin. Tennyson introduces him as
the happiest in the happy throng at
the jousts at Carleon. For the lady
Ettare has accepted his love and she
is beautiful and as pure as Guinevere
and Guinevere as pure as heaven and
every lady spotless and every knight
true and, under God, the god-like
Arthur ruled the world. Soon Ettare
changes. She wearies of his very
innocence. "I cannot bide Sir Baby!"
she cries. Pelleas, hard to be undeceived, trusts Sir Gawain when that
gay knight offers to win back Ettare's
love for him. Gawain proves unfaithful and Pelleas discovers his

unfaithfulness and the unworthiness
of Ettare.

Pendennis, Arthur (called Pen for
short), the hero of Thackeray's novel,
The History of Pendennis (1848–50).
A sentimentalist by nature whose
milk of human kindness has been
curdled into a mild cynicism by
contact with bohemian and fashionable life, he cultivates "a belief
qualified with scorn in all things
extant." Emerson rather neatly sums
up the same Thackerayan philosophy in the epigrammatic phrase
" We must renounce ideals and accept
London." Doubtless Pendennis represented one phase of Thackeray's
mind and was consequently a favorite
with him. " Being entirely occupied
with my two new friends Mrs.
Pendennis and her son, Arthur," he
wrote to the Brookfields, " I got up
very early again this morning, and
was with them for more than two hours
before breakfast. He is a very good-
natured, generous young fellow, and I
begin to like him considerably. I wonder if he is interesting to me from
selfish reasons, and because I fancy we
resemble each other in many parts."
Pendennis's career was in many respects reminiscent of his creator's.

Pendennis, Major Arthur, in
Thackeray's novel, *Pendennis* (1848–
1850), the uncle of the hero, a major
retired on half pay with ample leisure
to cultivate the aristocratic classes,
whom he worships with a sort of sub-
limated snobbery. He is the typical
old beau, a model of neatness and
external decorum. " Pendennis's
coat, his white gloves, his whiskers,
his very cane were perfect of their
kind as specimens of a military man
en retraite." He knows everybody
and is rejoiced when his doings are
recorded in the fashionable news.
" He was a very useful and pleasant
person in a country house. He entertained the young men with queer
little anecdotes and *grivoises* stories
on their shooting parties or in their
smoking room, where they laughed at
him and with him. He was obsequious with the ladies of a morning
in the rooms dedicated to them."

He has real affection for his nephew, shows tact and diplomacy in rescuing him from the Costigans and demonstrates his courage and fertility of resource in getting the better of his recalcitrant valet, Morgan.

Pendennis, Helen, in Thackeray's *Pendennis,* the widow of a surgeon, John Pendennis, and mother of Arthur, affectionate and over-indulgent to him, and in all other relations of life kindly self-sacrificing, patient and charitable except when her maternal jealousy is awakened.

Penfeather, Lady Penelope, in Scott's novel, *St. Ronan's Well,* an eccentric lady of fashion who, being cured of some imaginary complaint by the waters of St. Ronan's Spring, brings celebrity to the place, poses as its tutelary divinity, and attracts thither "painters and poets and philosophers and men of science, and lecturers and foreign adventurers," and is not herself discovered " to be a fool unless when she set up for being remarkably clever."

Penruddocke, Nigel, in Disraeli's *Endymion* (1835), student friend of the hero at Oxford, a type of the Tractarian religious movement, compounded of Cardinal Manning and Cardinal Newman. Like his prototypes Nigel goes over to Rome and eventually becomes a Cardinal.

Percy, Rosamond, in Maria Edgeworth's *Patronage,* warm-hearted, generously impulsive, sprightly, who according to Maria's own testimony resembles her creator.

Perdita, in *A Winter's Tale* (1611), daughter of King Leontes and Queen Hermione, of Sicily, who because the father suspected the mother's virtue, was abandoned on the coast of Bohemia, was rescued by a shepherd, who called her Perdita and brought her up in his own ignorance as to her origin,—and was wooed and won by Prince Florizel (*q.v.*), disguised for the nonce as the shepherd Doricles. Because of the opposition of Florizel's father, King of Bohemia, the lovers fled to Sicily where the mystery of her birth was cleared up and the repentant Leontes accepted her as his daughter.

George IV when Prince of Wales called himself Florizel and Mrs. Robinson, Perdita, in his lover's correspondence with that actress.

Shakespeare shows us more of Perdita than of Miranda, and heavenly as the innocence of Miranda was, we yet feel that Perdita comes to us with a sweeter, more earthlike charm, though not less endowed with all that is pure and holy, than her sister of the imaginary Mediterranean isle. —F. J. FURNIVALL.

Peri (pl. **Peris**), in Oriental mythology, certain gentle spirits,—offspring of the fallen angels and themselves constituting a link between man and angel,—who dwell in air and live on perfumes and, though themselves banished for a time from Paradise, go about this lower world doing good, especially in pointing out to the pure the way to heaven. In *Paradise and the Peri,* the second tale in Moore's *Lalla Rookh* (1817), one of these spirits standing disconsolate by the entrance to Eden, is told by the Angel of the Gate that she may obtain admission if she will bring thither " the gift that is most dear to Heaven." She scours the earth and brings back with her successively a drop of patriot blood shed by a dying warrior, then the last sigh of a maiden who had died nursing her plague-stricken lover, and lastly a tear dropped by an aged sinner who had been converted by a child's innocent prayer.

Perrichon, M., hero of a comedy *The Journey of M. Perrichon,* by Eugene Labiche. A Paris shopkeeper, wealthy, vain, simple-minded, touring Switzerland with his daughter.

Petruchio, in Shakespeare's *The Taming of the Shrew* (1594), often known as *Katherine and Petruchio,* from its leading characters, a gentleman of Verona who deliberately undertakes to marry Katherine Molina, locally famous as " the Shrew," in order to tame her into a model wife. He accomplishes this seemingly impossible feat, not by chastisement, but by mental and moral suasion. Vigorous in mind and body, high-spirited, but with perfect control over his temper, with an unfailing sense of humor and with an iron will he scares, persecutes and laughs her into submission.

Philaminte, in Molière's comedy, *Les Femmes Savantes* (1672), the *maitresse femme* or strong-minded woman of Molière's time, a self-imagined *bel esprit*, imperious and dominating, whose henpecked husband, the honest bourgeois Chrysale, makes only a feeble protest against her extravagances. With her daughter Armande and her sister-in-law Bélise, she seeks to found a learned circle over which she shall be queen, her prime minister or right-hand man being a poet-taster named Trissotin (*q.v.*).

Philammon, the leading male character in Charles Kingsley's historical romance, *Hypatia* (1838), a young Christian monk, self-immured in one of the rock monasteries on the upper Nile, but burning with a desire to rescue his fellow-men from sin and destruction. He removes to Alexandria, where his intellect is dazzled and confused and his faith shaken by the spectacle of the ancient classic culture, serene in its splendid certainties, making a final stand against the clashing hosts of Christian disputants, all seemingly destined to perish in internecine strife about doctrinal trifles. The best of the old philosophy seems to him embodied in the person of the historical Hypatia, a lecturer on Neo-Platonism, who has aroused the antagonism of priests and monks and is finally torn to pieces by a Christian mob.

Philander, in Ariosto's *Orlando Furioso* (1516), a gentleman of Holland, who being entertained by Argeo, baron of Servia, had the misfortune to provoke the love of Argeo's wife Gabrina. Imitating Joseph's conduct in the Potiphar affair, Philander had exactly Joseph's luck. Falsely accused he was cast into a dungeon. Thither Gabrina followed him, begging that he would defend her against a wicked knight. When he consented she tricked him into killing her own husband, then forced

him to marry her under threat of betrayal, and, tiring of him soon afterwards, poisoned him.

Philaster, hero of Beaumont and Fletcher's comedy, *Philaster, or Love Lies Bleeding.* Ludwig Tieck with small reason suggests that in this character the authors designed to give Shakespeare a hint as to how a prince deprived, like Hamlet, of his rights, ought to behave, just as in *The Two Noble Kinsmen*, they indirectly attacked Ophelia by showing how ladies disappointed in love should demean themselves.

Pickle, Peregrine, titular hero of Smollett's novel, *The Adventures of Peregrine Pickle* (1751), a young scapegrace overfond of practical jokes.

The savage and ferocious Pickle, besides his gross and base brutality, besides his ingratitude to his uncle, and the savage propensity which he shows in the pleasure he takes to torment others by practical jokes, resembling those of a fiend in glee, exhibits a low and ungentlemanlike tone of thinking, only one degree higher than that of Roderick Random. . . . We certainly sympathize very little in the distress of Pickle, brought on by his own profligate profusion and enhanced by his insolent misanthropy. We are only surprised that his predominating arrogance does not weary out the benevolence of Hatchway and Pipes, and scarce think the ruined spendthrift deserves their persevering and faithful attachment."—SIR W. SCOTT.

Pickwick, Samuel, hero of *The Posthumous Papers of the Pickwick Club* (1837-39) by Charles Dickens, an eccentric and benevolent Londoner, middle-aged and of the middle classes, unsophisticated, hot-headed, but essentially amiable, easily angered, easily pacified and easily led. He is pictured with a bald head, a smooth round face, a bland and childlike expression, spectacled nose, a rotund paunch, and short stubby legs thrust into black gaiters that reach up to his knee. His faithful attendant is Sam Weller (*q.v.*). See also BARDELL, MRS.

Many comic writers have drawn a clever rascal and his ridiculous dupe; here, in a fresh and very human atmosphere we have a clever servant who was not a rascal, and a dupe who was not ridiculous. Sam Weller stands in some ways for a cheerful knowledge of the world; Mr. Pickwick stands for a still more cheerful ignorance of the world. —G. K. CHESTERTON, *Studies in Dickens.*

Picninnies. A nonsense word invented by Samuel Foote. See PANJANDRUM.

Pinchwife, Mr., one of the principal male characters in Wycherley's comedy, *The Country Wife* (1672), a London citizen who has married an unsophisticated girl from the country and is only too conscious of the dangers to which rustic innocence is exposed in the town. As usual in Restoration plays his jealous care and caution overreach themselves and precipitate the very calamity he wishes to guard against.

Pinchwife, Mrs. Margery, the heroine of Wycherley's comedy, *The Country Wife,* an ignorant and innocent rustic beauty who has her eyes opened only too widely when she is transferred from country to city. The plot of the play is largely borrowed from Molière's *L'Ecole des Femmes* and Margery is a brutalized British version of Agnes (*q.v.*). In David Garrick's adaptation from Wycherley, *The Country Girl* (1766), Margery Pinchwife becomes Peggy Thrift (*q.v.*).

Compare the *Ecole des Femmes* with *The Country Wife.* Agnes is a simple and amiable girl, whose heart is indeed full of love, but of love sanctioned by honor, morality and religion. Her natural talents are great. They have been hidden, and as it might appear destroyed by an education elaborately bad. But they are called forth into full energy by a virtuous passon. Her lover, while he adores her beauty, is too honest a man to abuse the confiding tenderness of a creature so charming and inexperienced. Wycherley takes this plot into his hands and straightway it becomes a licentious intrigue of the lowest and least sentimental kind, between an impudent London rake and the idiot wife of a country squire.—MACAULAY ESSAYS: *Leigh Hunt.*

Pinkerton, The Misses, in Thackeray's *Vanity Fair,* a couple of dignified and self-important ladies who kept an educational establishment for young ladies on Chiswick Mall. Here Amelia Sedley went to school and Rebecca Sharp was a pupil teacher.

I cannot help thinking that, although *Vanity Fair* was written in 1845 and the following years, it was really begun in 1817, when the little boy so lately come from India found himself shut in behind those filagree iron gates at Chiswick, of which he writes when he describes Miss Pinkerton's establishment. Whether Miss Pinkerton was or was not own sister to the great Doctor at the head of the boarding school for young gentlemen on Chiswick Mall, to which "Billy boy" (as the author of *Vanity Fair* used to be called in those early days) was sent, remains to be proved. There is certainly a very strong likeness between those two majestic beings—the awe-inspiring Doctor and the great Miss Pinkerton—whose dignity and whose Johnsonian language marked an epoch in education.—ANNE THACKERAY RITCHIE. Introduction to *Vanity Fair.*

Pip, familiar nickname of Philip Pirrip, hero of Dickens's *Great Expectations* (1860). An orphan, he is brought up by Joe Gargery (*q.v.*) and his shrewish wife. Abel Magwitch, an escaped convict whom he unwittingly helps, takes a fancy to the boy, and when he becomes a wealthy sheep farmer in Australia deposits £500 a year with lawyer Jaggers to educate Pip and make a gentleman of him. In the end Pip marries Estella, who has been adopted in infancy by Miss Havisham and who turns out to be Magwitch's daughter.

Pipchin, Mrs., in Dickens's novel, *Dombey and Son* (1846), an ill-favored old woman with mottled cheeks and gray eyes, who has devoted all the energies of her mind to the study and treatment of infancy. " She was generally spoken of as a ' great manager ' of children and the secret of her management was, to give them everything that they didn't like and nothing that they did." While she lived on buttered toast and sweetbreads her charges were starved. Paul Dombey is sent to board with her and she eventually becomes Mr. Dombey's housekeeper.

Pippa, in Robert Browning's drama *Pippa Passes* (1841), an innocent, sprightly Italian peasant maid in Asolo, who spends her New Year holiday by wandering through the old town and its environs, singing simple and tender little songs. When she returns home at nightfall she little thinks how vitally she has affected a number of hearers, the guilty lovers Sebald and Ottima, the artist Jules and his wife, Luigi and his mother and Monsignor the Bishop. All these people have their lives changed by suggestions from her songs floating in upon them at a critical moment.

Pisanio, in Shakespeare's *Cymbeline*, servant to Posthumus, who being commissioned to murder his master's wife Imogen, persuades her to escape in boy's clothes to Milford Haven, and sends to Posthumus a bloody handkerchief as evidence that the murder has been done.

Pizarro, Francisco (1471-1541), a Spanish soldier, conqueror of Peru, is the hero of a drama by Kotzebue entitled, *Spaniards in Peru,* which in 1799 was paraphrased in English as *Pizarro,* nominally by R. B. Sheridan, but really by one of his hacks. The play deals with a war between Pizarro and Ataliba (Atahualpa), inca of Peru. In the Sheridan version Pizarro is slain in combat by Alonzo, one of Ataliba's officers. This is a departure from Kotzebue and a violation of historical truth. Pizarro survived to become the conqueror of Peru and was assassinated in his palace at Lima by the adherents of his one-time friend Amalgro whom he had executed in 1538.

Placidas, in Spenser's *Faërie Queene,* Book iv (1596), the physical double of his friend Amias. See PACANA.

Plagiary, Sir Fretful, in Sheridan's comedy, *The Critic,* an affected, supercilious and oversensitive dramatist, obviously drawn from Sheridan's pet antipathy, Richard Cumberland. One charge, which Sneer flings at Sir Fretful might, with almost equal reason, have been applied to Sheridan himself, that he kept stray jokes and pilfered witticisms in his commonplace book with as much method as the ledger of the Lost and Stolen Office.

Pleydell, Paulus, in Scott's novel, *Guy Mannering,* an Edinburgh advocate described by the author as " a lively, sharp-looking gentleman, with a professional shrewdness in his eye, and, generally speaking, a professional formality in his manners. But this,

like his three-tailed wig and black coat, he could slip off on a Saturday evening when surrounded by a party of jolly companions, and disposed for what he called his altitudes." In his diary, under date June, 1830, Scott alludes to " the painting by Raeburn of my old friend Adam Rolland, who was in the external circumstances, but not in frolic or fancy, my prototype for Paul Pleydell." Rolland died at an advanced age in 1819. The " High Jinks " side of Counsellor Pleydell was probably furnished by Andrew Crosbie, who died thirty years before Guy Mannering was published, but left a jocund memory about the Parliament House. " His portrait still adorns its walls, and in Scott's young advocate days, Crosbie's meteor-like career was one of the chief traditions of Bench and Bar. (S. R. CROCKETT: *The Scott Originals,* p. 97).

Pliable, in Bunyan's *Pilgrim's Progress,* Part I (1678), a neighbor of Christian's, who accompanied him as far as the Slough of Despond and then turned back discouraged.

Plornish, Thomas, in Dickens's *Little Dorrit,* a plasterer, a long-legged, loose-jointed, smooth-cheeked, fresh-colored, sandy-whiskered man of thirty. He generally chimed in conversation by repeating the words of the speaker. Thus when Mrs. Plornish tells a visitor " Miss Dorrit darsn't let him know," Plornish echoes " Dursn't let him know." Mrs. Plornish's name is Sally. Her peculiarity is to preface all her remarks with " Well, not to deceive you." Thus: " Is Mr. Plornish at home? " " Well, sir, not to deceive you, he's gone to look for a job."

Plume, Sir, in Pope's *Rape of the Lock,* an empty-headed fop, who talks sententious nonsense freely interlarded with fashionable oaths:

Sir Plume, of amber snuff box justly vain,
And the nice conduct of a clouded cane,
With earnest eyes and round, unthinking face,
He first the snuff box opened, then the case.

Pope admitted that the portrait was drawn from Sir George Brown.

Speaking of the effect produced by the poem he said: "Nobody but Sir George Brown was angry and he was a good deal so and for a long time. He could not bear that Sir Plume should talk nothing but nonsense (SPENCE: *Anecdotes*). Yet the biography of Coke of Norfolk claims that Thomas Coke, great grandfather of Lord Melbourne, and Vice-Chamberlain to Queen Anne, was the real Sir Plume.

Plummer, Caleb, in Dickens's *Cricket on the Hearth* (1845), a poor toymaker, devoted to his blind daughter, Bertha, whom he deludes into the idea that they are living in comfort and that everything and everybody around them are delightful.

Plyant, Sir Paul, in William Congreve's comedy, *The Double-dealer* (1694), a henpecked husband of choleric temper in general, but so thoroughly dominated by his second wife that he dare not touch a letter addressed to himself until my lady has read it, and so infatuated that he would not believe his own eyes and ears if they bore testimony to her faithlessness. Yet under his very nose she carries on a transparent intrigue with Ned Careless.

Sir Paul Plyant with his night-cap made out of a piece of a scarlet petticoat, tied up in bed out of harm's way, and looking, with his great beard, like a Russian bear upon a great drift of snow, is wholly delightful.— E. W. GOSSE: *Life of Congreve*, p. 55.

Plymley, Peter, the feigned author of *Peter Plymley's Letters*, a series of epistles written by Rev. Sydney Smith, and advocating the removal of the secular disabilities of Roman Catholics in England. Peter is a Londoner writing to his brother Abraham, the parson of a rural district, who is evidently a kind-hearted, honest and conscientious man; but dull and ignorant and dreadfully scared at a bogy of his own imagining —a Popish conspiracy against crown, church and commonwealth. Abraham communicates his alarms to his brother Peter in London and Peter's letters are replies to these outpourings.

Podsnap, Mr. John, in Dickens's *Our Mutual Friend*, a pompous, self-satisfied person, who imagines himself a shining member of society, patronizes his acquaintances and takes Providence under his protection. The author sums up the articles of his faith as Podsnappery. "They were confined within close bounds, as Mr. Podsnap's own head was confined by his shirt-collar; and they were enunciated with a sounding pomp that smacked of the creaking of Mr. Podsnap's own shoes."

His wife is a "fine woman for Professor Owen, quantity of bone, neck and nostrils like a rocking horse, hard features" and a majestic presence.

Podsnap, Miss Georgiana, their daughter, is an undersized damsel, with high shoulders, low spirits, chilled elbow, and a rasped surface of nose. She is the personified "Young Person," to Podsnap's mind,—an "institution" which required everything in the universe to be filed down and fitted to it. The question about everything was, Would it bring a blush to the cheek of the young person? "And the inconvenience of the young person was that, according to Mr. Podsnap, she seemed always liable to burst into blushes when there was no need at all. There appeared to be no line of demarcation between the young person's excessive innocence and another person's guiltiest knowledge."

Pogram, The Honorable Elijah, in Dickens's *Martin Chuzzlewit*, a member of the American Congress and "one of the master minds of our country," whose acquaintance Martin Chuzzlewit makes on his return from Eden to New York. He is especially noted as the author of the "Pogram Defiance," "which rose so much con-test and preju-dice in Europe."

Poins, in both parts of Shakespeare's *Henry IV*, a madcap companion of Sir John Falstaff, witty, dissolute and reckless.

Poirier, M., a Parisian shopkeeper in *Le Gendre de M. Poirier*, 1855 (*The Son-in-law of Mr. Poirier*), by Emile

Augier and Jules Sandeau. Having made a fortune, he aspires to political and social honors and gladly accepts as his daughter's husband a penniless young nobleman, the Marquis de Presles (*q.v.*). Through reckless folly the patrician husband involves himself in serious troubles from which he is twice rescued by his plebeian wife.

Polixenes, in Shakespeare's comedy, *A Winter's Tale* (1594), the King of Bohemia. While a guest in Sicilia the jealousy of Leontes is aroused against him. He would have been murdered but for Camillo, who warns him and flees with him to Bohemia. He opposes the marriage of his son Florizel to Perdita, until the truth about the shepherdess is revealed.

Pollexfen, Sir Hargrave, the villain in *Sir Charles Grandison*, who is foiled in his attempted abduction of Miss Harriet Byron, by the titular hero of the novel.

Polonius, the lord chamberlain in Shakespeare's *Hamlet*, father of Laertes and Ophelia. He is kindly, but vain, pompous and self-satisfied; at times insufferably tedious and prolix; yet his advice to his son and to his daughter (both in Act i, Sc. 3), is full of worldly wisdom pointedly put. Hamlet slays him in Act iii, Sc. 4.

Polonius is a perfect character in its kind; nor is there any foundation for the objections which have been made to the consistency of this part. It is said that he acts very foolishly and talks very sensibly, There is no inconsistency in that. Again, that he talks wisely at one time and foolishly at another; that his advice to Laertes is very excellent, and his advice to the King and Queen on the subject of Hamlet's madness very ridiculous. But he gives the one as a father, and is sincere in it; he gives the other as a mere courtier, a busy-body, and is accordingly officious, garrulous, and impertinent. In short, Shakespeare has been accused of inconsistency in this and other characters, only because he has kept up the distinction which there is in nature, between the understandings and the moral habits of men, between the absurdity of their ideas and the absurdity of their motives.—HAZLITT: *Characters of Shakespeare's Plays.*

Pomfret, Barbara, heroine of Amelie Rives's novelette, *The Quick or the Dead* (1888), a morbid, introspective, hysterical young woman, torn by the conflict between loyalty to her dead husband, Valentine Dering, and her passion for a living man, John Dering, his cousin who so closely resembles him in manner, face and figure, that she finds it difficult to keep the two identities distinct. In the end the Dead triumphs over the Quick and " Jock " is dismissed.

Pomona, the servant girl in Frank R. Stockton's *Rudder Grange* (1880). With her taste for violent reading, her ingenuity in devices and her experiences as a newly married bride she furnishes much of the humor of the story. In a sequel, *Pomona's Travels*, she has developed into the presentable wife of Jone, writing letters descriptive of England, where she is enjoying her honeymoon, with just enough departure from the correct usage of the English tongue to make them in keeping with her character and not so much as to cheapen them.

Pompilia, heroine of Robert Browning's poem, *The Ring and the Book*. See FRANCESCHINI, GUIDO.

Pons, Sylvain, a simple-hearted old musician, hero of Balzac's novel, *Cousin Pons* (1847), the story of whose gradual breaking down under insults and humiliations from his purse-proud relatives, the Marvilles, makes the staple of the novel. It belongs to the series *Scenes from Parisian Life.*

Poquelin, Jean-ah, hero and title of a short story by George W. Cable in *Old Creole Days* (1879), a wealthy Creole who lives in seclusion in an old house with but a single attendant, a deaf-mute negro. His secretiveness excites suspicion, he is mobbed by a crowd of idlers and dies of his injuries. As the solitary mourner at his funeral there appears Jean's brother, a leper, long supposed dead, but now ready to give himself up to lifelong exile in the abhorrent *Terre aux Lepreux*, from which the dead man had so long shielded him.

Porter, Sir Joseph, K.C.B., in Gilbert and Sullivan's comic opera, *H.M.S. Pinafore*, the admiral who " stuck close to his desk and never went to sea " and hence rose to be "ruler of the Queen's navee." The character is a supposed skit on William H. Smith, head of a gigantic newspaper combine, who was actually First Lord of the Admiralty at the time.

Porthos, in Dumas's romance, *The Three Guardsmen* (Mousquetaires), one of the immortal trio, a good-natured giant, vain and stupid as is the nature of giants, yet with sense enough to place his superabundance of strength at the command of his more keen witted companions. In real life he was Isaac de Portau, from Pau, in the Pyrenees, and his birth was so humble that the " de " was of no distinction whatever.

Portia, in Shakespeare's *Julius Cæsar* (1607), the wife of Brutus. Unwilling to be excluded from her husband's counsels she secretly inflicted a severe wound upon herself to show that she was worthy of his confidence. This is Plutarch's story. In the method of her suicide on hearing of the death of Brutus, Shakespeare follows Valerius Maximus: " She being determined to kill herself took hot burning coals into her mouth, and kept her lips closed till she was suffocated by the smoke."

> With this she fell distract
> And, her attendants absent, swallowed fire.
> *Julius Cæsar,* Act iv, Sc. 3.

Portia, heroine of Shakespeare's *Merchant of Venice,* a rich heiress in love with Bassanio, for whose sake she undertakes to rescue his friend Antonio. Borrowing a lawyer's robe she appears in court and unrecognized by any one conducts the trial in such brilliant fashion that Antonio triumphs against his Jewish enemy. See SHYLOCK.

> Shakespeare's Portia, my ideal of a perfect woman,—the wise, witty woman, loving with all her soul and submitting with all her heart to a man whom everybody but herself (who was the best judge) would have judged her inferior; the laughter-loving, light-hearted, true-hearted, deep-hearted woman, full of keen perception, of active efficiency, of wisdom prompted by love, of tenderest unselfishness, of generous magnanimity; noble, simple, humble, pure, true; dutiful, religious and full of fun; delightful above all others, the woman of women.— FRANCIS ANNE KEMBLE: *An Old Woman's Gossip.*

Posa, Marquis of, in Schiller's *Don Carlos,* a Spanish nobleman in whom the author has embodied his own ideals.

> Schiller wrote for the great ideas of the Revolution; he destroyed the intellectual Bastiles; he built at the Temple of Liberty, and indeed at that great temple which should enclose all races like a brotherly community, for he was cosmopolite. He began with that hatred of the past which we see in his "Robbers," where he is like a little Titan who has played truant from school, and drunk schnapps, and smashed in Jupiter's windows, and ended with that love for the future which we already see blooming in "Don Carlos" like a forest of flowers, he himself being the Marquis of Posa, who is at once prophet and soldier, and who under a Spanish cloak bears the noblest heart which ever loved and suffered in all Germany.—H. HEINE.

Posthumus, Leonatus, in Shakespeare's *Cymbeline,* the husband of Imogen.

> His jealousy is not heroic like Othello's, it shows something of grossness unworthy of his truer self. In due time penitential sorrow does its work; his nobler nature reasserts itself.—DOWDEN.

Pother, Doctor, in Dibdin's farce, *The Farmer's Wife* (1780), an apothecary, " city register and walking story book," who furnished George Colman, the younger, with a hint for his Doctor Ollapod (1802).

Potion, Mr., the apothecary in Smollett's novel, *Roderick Random,* a caricature of Mr. John Gordon, an eminent surgeon, to whom the novelist was bound apprentice in the earlier years of his life, and to whom he does greater justice by the mouth of Matthew Bramble in *Humphrey Clinker.*

Potiphar, Mr. and Mrs., in George William Curtis's satirical sketches of New York Society, *The Potiphar Papers* (1853), a parvenu couple, ignorant, ill bred and affected, who strive to make a great splurge on their suddenly acquired wealth. Mr. Potiphar's knowledge of art may be gathered from the interest he displays in " Giddo's Shay Doover."

Pourceaugnac, M. de, hero and title of a comedy (1660), by Molière, —a man from the provinces who comes to Paris to wed a young woman and who returns baffled, after having been tormented and turned into ridicule by valets and other underlings, whom a more fortunate rival has commissioned to persecute him.

Powell, Mary, the first wife of John Milton, the poet, is the heroine of a novel (1850), by Anne Manning, *The Maiden and Married Life of Mary Powell.* Mary herself is the feigned autobiographer. She describes her meeting with the poet, their courtship and marriage, their London life, the estrangement that led to his tract on divorce and their eventual reconciliation.

Power, Paula, the heroine of Thomas Hardy's novel, *A Laodicean, or the Castle of the De Stancys* (1881). The daughter of a wealthy but plebeian railroad builder, she succeeds to the possession of Castle Stancy, the estate of an old and ruined family, and is consequently distracted between her natural bent in loving a person more nearly of her own class and an attempted reconstruction of the old family through marriage with one of its poor and disreputable offshoots.

Poyser, Mrs., in George Eliot's novel *Adam Bede,* a farmer's wife, shrewd, sharp, epigrammatic, whose rustic wit and wisdom form a sort of chorus to the story. The character is said to have been inspired by the author's mother.

Adam Bede for most of us means preeminently Mrs. Poyser. Her dairy is really the centre of the whole microcosm. She represents the very spirit of the place; and her influence is the secret of the harmony of the little world of squire and parson and parish clerk and schoolmaster and blacksmith and carpenter and shepherd and carter. Each of these types is admirably sketched in turn, but the pivot of the whole is the farm in which Mrs. Poyser displays her conversational powers . . . It is, indeed, needless to insist upon her excellence; for Mrs. Poyser became at once one of the immortals. She was quoted by Charles Buxton—as George Eliot was pleased to hear—in the House of Commons before she had been for three months before the public: "It wants to be hatched over again, and hatched different." One is glad to know that Mrs. Poyser's wit was quite original. "I have no stock of proverbs in my memory," said George Eliot; "and there is not one thing put into Mrs. Poyser's mouth that is not fresh from my own mint."—SIR LESLIE STEPHEN: *George Eliot.*

Prasildo, in Bojardo's *Orlando Innamorato* (1495), a Babylonish nobleman, who falls in love with Tisbina, wife of his friend Iroldo. Tisbina promises to return his love if he will perform certain feats that she deems impossible. He succeeds, however, and husband and wife seek to poison themselves to avoid the alternative. Prasildo resolves to join them, but learns from their apothecary that they have swallowed only a harmless drink. Prasildo informs his friend, he leaves the country and Prasildo marries Tisbina. Later Prasildo hears that his friend's life is in danger, whereupon he starts out to rescue him at the hazard of his own.

Pratt, Miss, in Susan Ferrier's novel, *The Inheritance,* an old maid of irrepressible and buoyant inquisitiveness, a feminine Paul Pry, who appears and reappears wherever she is least expected and least wanted.

Miss Pratt humiliates the proud and outrages the dignified. She interrupts lovers' confidences, and listens to political news not meant for her and finally precipitates the end of Lord Rossville by alighting at his door from a hearse—the omnibus of death being the only vehicle he could find to speed her on the way through a heavy snow-storm. Miss Pratt is never in greater form than when she talks about her invisible nephew, Anthony Whyte,—a stroke of genius, and the anticipation of a stroke of genius in an author with whom Miss Ferrier has much in common.—C. T. COPELAND: June, 1893, *Atlantic Monthly.*

The reference, of course, is to Charles Dickens and his Mrs. Harris (*q.v.*) in *Martin Chuzzlewit.*

Precieux (fem. **Précieuses**), a French term given to belated successors of the English Euphuists, who originated towards the end of the reign of Louis XIII in a praiseworthy effort made by leaders of society to correct the prevalent coarseness in speech and literature, but had degenerated under Louis XIV into absurdity and affectation. Like the Euphuists, the Precieux cultivated a taste for rare and obsolete words, for verbal conceits, for delicate sentiments, for romance, for ultra refinement in manners and speech. Molière came back to Paris at a time when the fad was at its height; and gave it a death-blow in his comedy *Les Précieuses Ridicules* (1659). Madelon, the daughter, and Cathos, the niece of Gorgibus, the two Précieuses of the comedy, decline with rudeness the suitors whom Gorgibus has chosen for them, because they are not ideal *Precieux*. The rejected ones in ferocious revenge send their respective valets, Mascarille and Jodelet, disguised the one as a marquis, the other as a viscount—to visit the ladies. The shams are received with open arms and a ridiculous interview follows which is ended by the appearance of the two masters and the exposure of the plot.

Presles, Marquis Gaston de, in *The Son-in-Law of M. Poirier*, comedy by Eugene Augier and Jules Sandeau, a ruined and profligate nobleman, whom Poirier (*q.v.*) has purchased for his daughter Antoinette. To Gaston's own astonishment her nobility of character effects his reformation and makes him fall in love with his plebeian wife, whom he began by slighting and neglecting.

Prettyman, Prince, in *The Rehearsal* (1671), a burlesque by the Duke of Buckingham, is alternately a prince and a fisherman. He is a caricature on the Leonidas of Dryden's *Marriage à la Mode*.

Prig, Betsey, in Dickens's *Martin Chuzzlewit*, a bosom friend of Mrs. Gamp—of the same build, " but not so fat; and her voice was deeper and more like a man's. She had also a beard." These two ladies " often nuss together, turn and turn about, one off, one on."

Primrose, Rev. Dr. Charles, the titular hero of *The Vicar of Wakefield* (1766), a novel by Oliver Goldsmith. Devout, charitable, unworldly, he unconsciously reveals his own character in his feigned autobiography and allows us to smile at his amiable weaknesses.

Dr. Primrose cherished no idea of superiority over his neighbors and parishioners. His relations with

them were of the friendliest and won him their heartiest love. He went to the fair to sell his own colt and thought nothing of having a friendly glass over the transaction at the inn. When troubles came and the poor vicar was taken to a debtor's prison, his flock came gallantly to the rescue and would have beaten the sheriff's officers if the vicar had not prevented them.

In Lupton's *Wakefield Worthies,* p. 182, it is pointed out that the character of Dr. Primrose may have been drawn from the Rev. Benjamin Wilson, Vicar of Wakefield from 1750 to 1764 and that Goldsmith probably had paid a visit to Wakefield before writing his novel. There is a "Thornhill" near Wakefield and a "Primrose Hill" in the city.—*Notes and Queries*, II, iv, 216.

Primrose, George, elder son of the Vicar, who goes to Amsterdam to teach the Dutchmen English, but quite forgets that an antecedent knowledge of Dutch would be requisite. He eventually joins the army, becomes Captain Primrose and marries Miss Wilmot, an heiress. Moses, the younger son, achieves a blunder equally famous at a fair where he is induced to trade a good horse for a gross of green spectacles rimmed with copper.

Primrose, Olivia, elder daughter of the Vicar of Wakefield; enthusiastic, imaginative and easily duped, she falls an apparent victim to the wiles of the libertine Squire Thornhill, but the marriage he had imagined to be a mock marriage turns out to be legal.

Sophia, the younger sister, is sought and secured in honorable marriage by the profligate's respectable uncle, Sir William Thornhill, who masquerades as Mr. Burchell until the psychological moment has arrived.

Princes in the Tower, the name popularly given to the two young sons of Edward IV,—Edward (who for a short period bore the title of Edward V) and Richard, Duke of York. Imprisoned by their uncle, who usurped the title of Richard III, they were put to death in the Tower by hired assassins. Their fate forms a pitiful episode in Shakespeare's

20

historical play *Richard III*, iii and iv, 2, 3. Their ghosts appear to Richard in v, 3.

Priscilla, in Hawthorne's *Blithedale Romance* (1852), a fragile, pretty, simple girl, a sempstress, whose very helplessness appeals to John Hollingsworth and Miles Coverdale, as the more splendid and full-bodied charms of Zenobia fail to do. Both are in love with her, but she is absolutely dominated by Hollingsworth.

Prospero, in Shakespeare's comedy *The Tempest*, the banished Duke of Milan, father of Miranda. His absorption in the pursuit of magic had cost him his throne; for his wicked brother Antonio had easily usurped it and then sent him and his little daughter to perish at sea. But " the rotten carcass of a boat " survived and landed the pair upon an island wilderness, inhabited only by monsters and sprites whom he readily mastered. (See ARIEL, CALIBAN, SYCORAX.) After fourteen years spent in this comparative solitude Prospero raises a tempest by magic arts which casts upon the shores of his island all the occupants of a shipwrecked vessel, among them his nephew, Ferdinand, son of the usurping duke.

Prospero, the great enchanter, is altogether the opposite of the vulgar magician. With command over the elemental powers, which study has brought to him, he possesses moral grandeur, and a command over himself; in spite of occasional fits of involuntary abstraction and of intellectual impatience he looks down on life and sees through it, yet will not refuse to take his part in it . . . It has been suggested that Prospero is Shakespeare himself and that when he breaks his staff, drowns his book and dismisses his airy spirits, going back to the duties of his dukedom, Shakespeare was thinking of his own resigning of his powers of imaginative enchantment.

I should describe Prospero as the man of genius, the great artist, lacking at first in practical gifts which lead to material success, and set adrift on the perilous sea of life, in which he finds his enchanted island, where he may achieve his works of wonder. He bears with him Art in its infancy—the marvellous child, Miranda. The grosser passions and appetites—Caliban—he subdues. Prospero's departure from the island is the abandoning by Shakespeare of the theatre, the scene of his marvellous works.—EDWARD DOWDEN.

Protocol, Peter, in Scott's *Guy Mannering*, an Edinburgh attorney employed by Mrs. Margaret Bertram, of Singleside.

Proudie, Dr., in Anthony Trollope's *Framley Parsonage, Barchester Towers* and other novels, a devoted and zealous clergyman, a martinet in his official capacity, but a serf in his home, who rises to be Bishop of Barchester. He is henpecked by his wife, a strong-willed, strong-voiced lady, voluble of advice that is meant for and meekly accepted as command. She has positive opinions on every phase of social, moral, and ecclesiastical law and has no hesitation in expressing them. Trollope carried her triumphantly from novel to novel and finally killed her off on overhearing a conversation between two clergymen at the Athenæum Club. Discussing Trollope's novels and especially this character, they agreed that they would not write novels at all unless they could invent new figures. Trollope went home and straightway killed the bishop's wife, but regretted her to the end of his days.

Mrs. Proudie is not merely a shrew and a scold, though she is a shrew and does scold the bishop dreadfully, and put him to shame before those who should believe him master in his house and office. It is less her ambition than her nature to govern, and she cannot help extending her domain from the bishop to the diocese and meddling in things which it is mischievous as well as indecorous for her to concern herself with. But in all this she is mainly of a conscientious zeal; she has done so much to forward the fortunes of her husband and to promote his rise from among the inferior clergy to a spiritual lordship that she cannot help arrogating power and attributing merit to herself in the management of his affairs.—W. D. HOWELLS: *Heroines of Fiction*, vol. ii, p. 124.

Pry, Paul, in Poole's comedy of that name (1825), a bustling, inquisitive but amiable busybody who makes it his daily task to inquire into everybody's affairs except his own and keep *au fait* with the latest scandal and the last bit of gossip in London town. With smiling face and conciliating air he breaks into the most private *tête-à-tête* and disturbs the most intimate domestic scene—always deprecating his intrusion by a favorite phrase—" I hope I don't intrude." Poole is said to have drawn the character from Thomas Hill who was also the original of Thackeray's Archer in *Pendennis* and is remembered as a friend of Lamb and Hazlitt. No one knew the date or place of his birth. Lamb declared that the record had perished in the Great Fire in London.

A writer in *T. P.'s Weekly*, March 18, 1910, who knew Hill well, thus describes him:

I never knew anyone who managed to make "eleven buckram men out of two," in such an insidious mode. He could swell a herring to a whale and put a Jonas within it before anyone was aware what he was about. It was a species of monomania with him to argue himself into a belief that the unfounded thing with which he began should terminate in a solemn averment of its reality; in other words, to metamorphose the pure fiction with which he commenced into an honest fact in winding up. Never was there such a busybody. He had the virtue amidst all of being a harmless, undesigning man against his neighbour. No one ever heard of his doing another an injury.

Prynne, Hester, heroine of Hawthorne's romance *The Scarlet Letter*, the wife of Master Prynne, an English physician living in Amsterdam. The latter, deformed in body and overstudious in mind, has never succeeded in capturing her love. She is shipped to Boston to await his coming and when, two years later, he arrives there, the first sight that meets his eye is his wife standing in the public pillory with a babe in her arms and the letter A, a badge of shame, embroidered in scarlet on her breast. Despite earnest appeals from Rev. Arthur Dimmesdale, a young clergyman, she refuses to divulge the name of her seducer. Prynne now assumes the name of Roger Chillingworth and attaches himself to the Rev. Arthur. His suspicions are confirmed. Arthur is the culprit, and in token thereof (it is hinted), a cancerous growth has imprinted upon his flesh the scarlet badge that Hester must flaunt before the world. She pities his sufferings, tries to bolster up his failing spirits, and lighten the melancholy that is killing him, and finally takes her

place beside him in the pillory where he has climbed to make public confession of his guilt.

Puck, in Shakespeare's *A Midsummer Night's Dream*, court jester to Oberon, King of the Fairies, ever ready to play a prank or perform a service.

Puck, or Robin Goodfellow, is the leader of the fairy band. He is the Ariel of the *Midsummer Night's Dream;* and yet as unlike as can be to the Ariel in *The Tempest.* No other poet could have made two such different characters out of the same fanciful materials and situations. HAZLITT: *Characters of Shakespeare's Plays.*

Puck, in Rudyard Kipling's *Puck of Pook's Hill* (1906), self-described as " the Oldest Old Thing in England," who introduces to the children, Dan and Una, a procession of men who have lived or thriven on a spring from the soil of Old England. He is variously spoken of as the Faun, Robin Goodfellow, Lob-lie-by-the-fire and Nick o' Lincoln. He occurs in all the stories of *Puck of Pook's Hill* and in most of the second series, entitled *Rewards and Fairies*, 1910.

Puff, Mr., in Sheridan's burlesque, *The Critic* (1779), a Grubstreet hack, who having failed in every other attempt at earning a living takes to criticism as a last resort. "I am a practitioner in panegyric," he says of himself, " or to speak more plainly, a professor of the art of puffing." Foote had already used the name for a publisher in his farce, *The Patron* (1764). This Mr. Puff has no belief in the saleable qualities of " panegyric and praise." Nobody he thinks will give money to be told that Mr. Such-a-one is a wiser and better man than himself. "No, no; 'tis quite and clean out of nature. A good sousing satire, now, well powdered with personal pepper, and seasoned with the spirit of party, that demolishes a conspicuous character and sinks him below our own level—there, there we are pleased; there we chuckle and grin, and toss the half-crowns on the counter."

Puff, Orator, in the poem of that name by Thomas Moore, in *M. P. or the Blue-Stocking,* an operetta (1811), a public speaker who cultivates two voices for use in his orations. Falling down a coalhole one night a disgusted would-be rescuer leaves him to his fate. As there are two of you, he says, you can help each other out. The moral is conveyed in the final lines of each stanza:

Oh ho! Orator Puff,
One voice for an orator's surely enough!

Pumblechook, in Dickens's *Great Expectations*, a well-to-do corn-chandler, uncle to Joe Gargery, who makes himself peculiarly offensive to Pip by his pompous patronage and his habit of springing mathematical problems on him for instant solutions. When Pip realizes his expectations Uncle Pumblechook abases himself but he recovers his self-poise when Pip is once more in reduced circumstances, piously explaining the lad's reverses as the vengeance of Providence on his ingratitude to Pumblechook.

Punch, nickname of the boy hero of *Baa Baa Black Sheep*, in Rudyard Kipling's volume of short stories, *Wee Willie Winkie*. The child of Anglo-Indian parents, Punch with his sister is committed to the care of an aunt in England and undergoes a series of petty torments, professedly designed for the good of his soul, which reduce him to a condition of sullen suspicion and stubbornness that is only lifted by the arrival of his mother. " Punch lives with an intense vitality," says Edmund Gosse, " and here without any indiscretion we may be sure that Mr. Kipling has looked inside his own heart and drawn from life."

Pure, Simon, in Mrs. Centlivre's comedy, *A Bold Stroke for a Wife* (1718), a young Quaker from Pennsylvania who comes to London to attend the quarterly meeting of his sect. He is armed with a letter of introduction from Aminadab Holdfast to Obadiah Prim, a strict and rigid Quaker, who is one of the four guardians of an heiress, Anne Lovely. Colonel Feignwell, a suitor for Anne's hand, gets possession of this letter by strategy, passes himself off as Simon Pure and ingratiates himself not only

with Friend Prim, but with the three other guardians. When the real Simon Pure turns up he is treated as an impostor and it is not until Feignwell has won the heiress that he succeeds in obtaining credentials and witnesses to his identity.

Purple Island, the name which Phineas Fletcher applies to the human frame in his poem, *The Purple Island or the Isle of Man* (1633). It is divided into 12 cantos each of which is sung by a shepherd to his companions. The first five deal with the body, whose muscles, bones, arteries and veins are minutely pictured as hills, dales, streams and rivers. The remaining cantos deal with the mind. The King of the Isle of Man is Intellect, whose eight counsellors are Common Sense, Fancy, Memory and the Five Senses. The Vices attack the human fortress, and a fierce contest is waged for the possession of the human soul. Finally an angel (King James I) appears on the scene and promises victory to the Virtues. Fletcher may have profited by a hint from Spenser's *Body Castle;* he may have suggested one for Poe's *Haunted Palace.*

Pyncheon, Hepzibah, sister to Clifford and to the Judge (see below), in *The House of the Seven Gables.*

Hepzibah Pyncheon, struggling in an agony of shame and impotence to submit to the rude contact of the world, is the true parent of all those stiffened lonely women that haunt the scenes of Mrs. [Mary E. Wilkins] Freeman's little stage. Only there is this signal difference: poor blighted Hepzibah is part of a great drama of the conscience which in its brooding over the curse of ancestral sin can only be compared with the Atè of the Æschylean theatre.—PAUL MORE, *Shelburne Essays, Second Series, Hawthorne.*

Pyncheon, Judge, in Hawthorne's novel of New England life, *The House of the Seven Gables,* a hypocrite and a Pharisee, who masks under a suave and specious exterior a grasping, greedy and relentless spirit. The chapter in which stricken suddenly by heart disease he sits dead in his chair all night while the author moralizes over him is a terrible and searching bit of analysis. Hawthorne was half annoyed and half amused by an indignant protest from the descendant of a real Judge Pyncheon, a Tory and refugee resident in Salem at the time of the Revolution, and " a most exemplary old gentleman," who thought it monstrous that the virtuous dead could not be suffered to rest peacefully in their graves.

"The joke of the matter is," says Hawthorne in a letter to his publisher (FIELD: *Yesterdays with Authors*), "that I never heard of his grandfather, nor knew that any Pyncheons had ever lived in Salem, but took the name because it suited the tone of my book and was as much my property for fictitious purposes as that of Smith. I have pacified him by a very polite and gentlemanly letter, and if you ever publish any more of the *Seven Gables* I should like to write a brief preface expressive of my anguish for this unintentional wrong and making the best reparation possible, else these wretched old Pyncheons will have no peace in the other word nor in this."

Pyrocles and **Musidorus**, in Sir Philip Sidney's *Arcadia* (1590), two princes who are shipwrecked in that land of fable and make love to King Basilius's daughters, Philoclea and Pamela. Pyrocles dons Amazon's attire and under the name of Zelmane is admitted to the King's lodge. He inspires love in both Basilius and his Queen, the one deeming him a woman, the other detecting a man under his disguise. He appoints a meeting with each in a certain cave at midnight trusting that they will not recognize each other in the darkness. Thus he unwittingly fulfils a mysterious oracle delivered to Basilius:

Thou with thy wife adultery shalt commit.

The situation of Pyrocles in female attire anticipates many Elizabethan dramas that turn upon confusion of sex; the innocent adultery may also have given a hint to Shakespeare in the case of Bertram and Helena.

Q

Quarll, Philip, hero of an anonymous romance, *The Hermit* (1727), which was one of the numerous imitations following in the wake of *Robinson Crusoe*. Like Robinson, Philip is wrecked upon a desert island. A rather startling innovation is that of making an ape, instead of another Man Friday, his sole companion and sharer of his home.

Quasimodo, in Victor's romance, *Notre Dame de Paris* (1831), the hunchback bell ringer, bow-legged, deaf and one-eyed who lives sequestered in the furthest recesses of the Cathedral and has grown to manhood almost unvisited by the light of day. He loves Esmeralda the gypsy girl. She has only a shuddering pity for him, but seeks his aid when the mob proclaims her a witch. He hides her till she is enticed away by the archdeacon, Claude Frollo, who cherishes a base passion for her that she does not return. Enraged, Frollo surrendered her to the mob and she was hanged. Quasimodo throws Frollo over the battlements of Notre Dame and disappears. Two years later his skeleton was found in the cave of Montfaucon clasping that of Esmeralda. He had crept into the cave where her body had been cast and died by her side.

Quayle, Glory, heroine of Hall Caine's novel, *The Christian* (1897). The beautiful granddaughter of a parson in the Isle of Man, she is beloved by John Storm, son of the local magnate Lord Storm. But she will not marry him. Both find their way to London. Storm, who has taken orders, devotes his life to work among the poor in the slums, while she becomes first a hospital nurse and later a musical artist. Storm's earnest, but unpractical attempts at social reform antagonize not only his ecclesiastical superiors but the adversaries of the church, and he dies of wounds received in a street brawl. Glory marries him on his death bed.

Quickly, Mistress, in Shakespeare's *The Merry Wives of Windsor* (1601), a servant of all work for Dr. Caius, the French physician, cheerfully acting as the go-between for three suitors of Anne Page, distributing among them her disinterested wishes for the success of each.

Quickly, Mistress Nell, in both parts of *Henry IV* and in *Henry V*, hostess of a tavern in Eastcheap frequented by Prince Hal and his boon companions, Falstaff, Poins and their friends. In *II Henry IV*, Mistress Quickly arrests Falstaff for debt, but dismisses the bailiffs on hearing of his commission as captain and expresses increased and indeed unlimited affection for and trust in " the honey sweet " old knight. Her description of Falstaff's death occurs in *Henry V*, Act ii, Sc. 3. She herself dies before the end of this play, after marrying Pistol, " the lieutenant of Captain Sir John's army."

Quilp, Daniel, in Dickens's *Old Curiosity Shop* (1840), a dwarf hunchback, hideous alike in mind and body, cunning, malicious, malignant, rejoicing in cruelty for its own sake, and especially delighting to torture his meek little wife Betsey. He makes a living in devious ways and is drowned in attempting to escape from arrest.

Quince, Peter, in Shakespeare's *Midsummer Night's Dream*, a carpenter who takes the part of stage-manager in the interlude of *Pyramus and Thisbe.*

Quirk, Thady, the supposed narrator of the memoirs of the Rackrent family of Ireland as they appear in the pages of Maria Edgeworth's novel *Castle Rackrent* (1782).

Quixote, Don (in England usually pronounced as it is spelled; in the United States, conforming to Spanish usage, as Ke-ho-tay), hero of one of the most famous mock-heroic ro-

mances in all literature, Cervantes' *History of the Renowned Don Quixote de la Mancha* (1605-1615). He is represented as a gentle and generous enthusiast, who has brooded over the romances of chivalry until they have disordered his brain, so that he imagines they are true, and himself a knight-errant predestined to sally out into the world, rescue damsels in distress, slay dragons and giants and generally to right wrongs, defend the oppressed, and avenge the injured. Accordingly he makes for himself an amateur suit of armor, mounts a battered steed whom he calls Rosinante, selects a peasant girl (see DULCINEA DEL TOBOSO) for his lady love, and chooses for his squire a middle-aged clown (see SANCHO PANZA) who is as grossly materialistic as he himself is idealist.

These two sally forth from their native village in search of adventures, of which the excited imagination of the knight, turning windmills into giants, solitary inns into castles, and galley-slaves into oppressed gentlemen, finds abundance wherever he goes; while the esquire translates them all into the plain prose of truth with an admirable simplicity, quite unconscious of its own humor, and rendered the more striking by its contrast with the lofty and courteous dignity and magnificent illusions of the superior personage. There could, of course, be but one consistent termination of adventures like these. The knight and his esquire suffer a series of ridiculous discomfitures, and are at last brought home, like madmen, to their native village, where Cervantes leaves them, with an intimation that the story of their adventures is by no means ended. In a continuation, or Second Part, published in 1615, the Don is exhibited in another series of adventures, equally amusing with those in the First Part, and is finally restored, "through a severe illness, to his right mind, made to renounce all the follies of knight-errantry, and die, like a peaceful Christian, in his own bed."—GEORGE TICKNOR: *History of Spanish Literature.*

R

Rab, the dog hero of Dr. John Brown's tale, *Rab and his Friends* (1858), a mastiff belonging to a poor Scotch carrier. The carrier's wife, Ailie, dies after an operation in the Edinburgh Hospital, and her husband soon follows her to the grave. Rab was present at both burials, and after

the second slinks home to the stable. He could not be driven from this and ultimately had to be killed. The story embodies a reminiscence of the author's student days.

Rabagas, hero of a satirical comedy of that name (1872), by Victorien Sardou. He is a compound of Gambetta and Emile Ollivier, a demagogue who flatters the passions of the mob, but aims at power only to gratify his snobbish love of rank. The scene is laid in Monaco. By cheap bribes and flattery Rabagas is won over to the side of the Duke, becomes prime minister, and, when the insurrection breaks out which he himself had planned, gives orders to shoot and imprison his old associates. Then comes a change in his fortunes. The Duke needs him no longer; the people hiss him. He is ousted from office and leaves the stage with these words: " Farewell; I go to the only country where talents like mine are appreciated—to France."

Rabbit, Br'er, the favorite hero in the plantation stories told by Uncle Remus (*q.v.*), wherein Brer Fox, his superior in strength, is usually victimized by craft and mental agility.

Raby, Aurora, in Byron's *Don Juan* (1824), introduced in canto xv as a guest in the house of Lord and Lady Amundeville. A Roman Catholic, she is young, rich, beautiful, and good —" a rose with all its sweetest leaves yet folded." Don Juan is evidently interested in her, but the poem breaks off abruptly, and the reader is left to conjecture what part the poet had designed that she should play in his hero's life.

Rackrent, Sir Patrick, in Maria Edgeworth's novel of Irish life, *Castle Rackrent* (1801), is the original Rackrent, the founder of the house and " a monument of old Irish hospitality." So says Thady Quirk, the historiographer of the Rackrent family. He is succeeded by *Sir Murtagh Rackrent*, famous for his knowledge of law and his ignorance of finance. Then comes Sir Kit, equally reckless of money, who imprisoned his Jewish wife for seven years because she refused to surrender her diamonds; and finally *Sir Condy Rackrent*, who squanders what is left of the family fortunes and dies from quaffing on a wager a great horn of punch.

Radigond or **Radigone,** in Spenser's *Faërie Queene*, the haughty Queen of the Amazons. Having been re-

jected by Bellodant the Bold, she revenges herself on all men who fall into her power by making them don woman's apparel and perform the womanly tasks of spinning and sewing. One of these victims was Sir Artegal, with whom she fell in love; but Britomart slew her and liberated the knight.

Ralph or **Ralpho, Squire,** in Butler's *Hudibras*, the attendant and companion of the hero, an Independent with a touch of the Anabaptist, who despising book lore, claims to be " learned for salvation," in the jargon of those sects, by means of " gifts " or " new light." Being a tailor by trade, he is punningly said to resemble Æneas and Dante in that he has seen " hell," a cant name in the sartorial world for a receptacle for shreds and scraps.

Raminagrobis, in Rabelais's romance *Pantagruel*, book iii, a starveling French poet, intended as a caricature of Guillaume Cretin, a now-forgotten author, highly esteemed by some of his contemporaries.

Ramona, heroine of a novel of that title (1885), by Helen Hunt Jackson. An orphan, she is bred as a foster-sister to Francis Ortegna, whose mother is passionately devoted to him, but only coldly just to the alien. The boy grows to love her; she has only sisterly affection for him. A mission Indian, Alessandro, shows her what love means, a love which Mrs. Ortegna holds to be an insult. The couple elope to be married, and to undergo frightful experiences, which kill Alessandro and throw Romona, a wreck, back into the arms of the loyal and devoted Francis. He finally marries her, or that part of her which has not died with her husband.

Ramsay, Adam, usually alluded to as Uncle Adam, because he stands in that relationship to the heroine, an eccentric character in Miss Susan Ferrier's novel, *The Inheritance.* Sir Walter Scott, in his *Journal*, under date January 20, 1829, notes: " Honest old Mr. Ferrier is dead, at extreme old age. He was a man with strong passions and strong prejudices, but with generous and manly sentiments at the same time. We used to call him Uncle Adam, after that character in his gifted daughter's novel." In the gifted daughter's novel we learn that Uncle Adam was " cross as two sticks," but his character as a whole is not unattractive and in intentions is never unamiable.

Ramsbottom, Mrs. Julia, the feigned author of a series of letters, beginning in 1820, which ran through a London newspaper, *John Bull*, and were collected in book form in 1829. Theodore Hook, the real author, here followed the traditions set by Winifred Jenkins in Smollett's *Humphrey Clinker*, and made bad spelling and ludicrous inversions of words and sentences do duty for any high form of wit or humor.

Random, Roderick, hero of Smollett's novel of that name (1748), in the main represents Smollett himself. Born in Scotland and educated in a Scotch university, Random is apprenticed to an apothecary; goes to sea in a King's ship as a surgeon's mate; makes acquaintance with all sorts of odd characters; experiences all kinds of hardship, and is present at the attack on Carthagena. Returning, he sees English town life in all its varieties and something also of English country life; forms a passion for " the belles lettres," and cultivates the society of wits and starveling poets. Finally, after two volumes of accidents and reverses, he is rewarded beyond his meagre deserts by the possession of Narcissa. Though endowed with some measure of good nature and generosity, Roderick is chiefly distinguished by reckless libertinism and love of mischief. His treatment of his devoted friend and slavish adherent, Hugh Strap (*q.v.*), is a characteristic example of heartless ingratitude.

Raphael, hero of Balzac's novel, *La Peau de Chagrin*, an untranslatable title, because *Chagrin* involves a pun, meaning, as it does, both *chagreen* and *sorrow*. Hence in English the book is usually known as *The Wild Ass's Skin*. Raphael comes into possession of a bit of parchment, which symbolizes the potential energy allotted to every human being. Temperate use may make it last through a long and useful career. Reckless egoism may exhaust it in a few years of feverish acquisitiveness or prodigal self-indulgence. Every expenditure of will and desire produces a shrinkage in the magic skin, which registers a corresponding curtailment of the owner's life. Raphael, starting with the headlong desire to squander his manhood in Sardanapalian debauch as a defiance to the powers that had tortured his youth, no sooner comprehends the relation of his existence to the talisman than he courts retrenchment. But it is too late.

Rappacini, Beatrice, heroine of N. Hawthorne's short story, *Rappacini's Daughter*, in *Mosses from an Old Manse*, has been fed upon poisons by her father, a cold-blooded scientist in Padua. She grows up, immune herself, but infectious to all animal life that comes in contact with her. Hawthorne's *American Notebook*, p. 209, contains the following quotation from Sir Thomas Browne's *Vulgar Errors*, which shows where he got his hint: " A story there passeth of an Indian King that sent unto Alexander a faire woman fed with aconytes and other poisons, with this intent complexionally to destroy him." The story has been traced back through the *Gesta Romanorum*, tale xi, to Aristotle's *Secretum Secretorum*, chap. xxviii, where a queen of India is said to have treacherously sent to Alexander, among other costly presents, pretended testimonies of her friendship, a girl of exquisite beauty, who, having been fed with serpents from her infancy, partook of their nature.

Rarahu, heroine of a romantic idyl, *The Marriage of Loti* (1880), by L. M. J. Viaud, who subsequently took as his pseudonym the name he had invented for his hero,—Pierre Loti. A French naval officer, he marries Rarahu, a South Sea maiden of 14, beautiful, imaginative, profoundly enamoured, and intelligent enough to be saddened by the intellectual gulf between them. He loves her in his own selfish way, but is not willing to observe the moral rules he lays down for her. After his departure she ceases not indeed to pine for him, but to be true to his memory and precepts. She dies of consumption at eighteen.

Rasselas, in Samuel Johnson's philosophical romance, *Rasselas, Prince of Abyssinia* (1759), has been brought up in the Happy Valley of Amhara. He and a sister Nekayah, wearying of these monotonous joys, escape from the valley, and under the guidance of the philosopher Imlac seek for happiness in the great world. Disenchantment meets them everywhere—in the hollow revelry of youth; among philosophers, whose practices ill accord with their theories; among shepherds, whose real lives belie the ideals of poetry; through crowds, whose smiling faces mask aching hearts; in the cell of the hermit, who counts the days when he shall once more mix with the world. The final disenchantment occurs when they return to the Happy Valley and find that even its happiness was an illusion of youth.

Rassendyll, Rudolf, hero of Anthony Hope's romance, *The Prisoner of Zenda* (1894), a young Englishman, who inherits some of the royal blood of the rulers of Ruritania, and comes legitimately by a striking resemblance to King Rudolf, his namesake and kinsman. The king has been seized by conspirators and imprisoned in the Castle of Zenda. The Englishman consents to personate him, and rules in his stead until the downfall of the conspirators.

Rastignac, Eugène de, a law student, journalist, and man about town, who appears in several of Balzac's novels. The eldest son of the Baron de Rastignac, he was born in 1797, and in 1819 went to Paris to study law. In *Père Goriot* he is the lover of Mme. de Nucingen, one of Goriot's daughters; in *Cousine Betty* (1838), he marries Augusta de Nucingen, daughter of his former mistress, whom he had left five years previous. In 1845 he was raised to the French

peerage, with an income of 300,000 francs. He is clever and cynical, a rake and a dandy. His favorite motto, "There is no absolute virtue; it is all a matter of circumstances," sums up his moral code.

The man whose career is most distinctly traced is perhaps Eugène de Rastignac, whose first steps in life we witness in *Le Père Goriot*. The picture is to some extent injured by Balzac's incurable fatuity and snobbishness, but the situation of the young man, well born, clever, and proud, who comes up to Paris, equipped by his family's savings, to seek his fortune and find it at any cost, and who moves from the edge of one social abyss to the edge of another (finding abysses in every shaded place he looks into), until at last his nerves are steeled, his head steadied, his conscience cased in cynicism, and his pockets filled—all this bears a deep imaginative stamp.—*Atlantic Monthly.*

Ratcliffe, Senator (from Peoria, Illinois), the principal character in an anonymous novel, *Democracy* (1880), now attributed to Henry Adams. He combines the least admirable traits of several well-known public men of the day (noticeably James G. Blaine), all easily recognizable.

No amount of cleverness in making such a character, consistent in itself and with its surroundings, can make it a truthful type of the strong party man of American politics. Ratcliffe confesses to ballot-box stuffing and to having been bribed, and glories therein, because his action was for the good of the party. No one needs to be told that, however great the shamelessness of some of our public men, to represent such a man as the probable Republican candidate for president is a perversion which must detract from the force of any picture of American politics.—*N. Y. Nation,* April 22, 1880.

In the succeeding July, Blaine was nominated for the presidency on the Republican ticket.

Rattlin, Jack, in Smollett's *Roderick Random,* a typical British tar, as Tom Bowling in the same novel is a typical naval officer. **Rattlin the Reefer,** hero of a novel of that name by Edward Howard, has often been attributed wrongly to Captain Marryat.

Rat-wife, The, in Ibsen's *Little Eyolf,* a weird, witch-like hag, lures the child-hero to his death. William Archer sees in her a symbol of death. G. B. Shaw recognizes her as "the divine messenger," who carries retribution into the household.

There cannot be the least doubt, I think, that in the poet's mind the Rat-wife is the symbol of death, the still, soft darkness that is at once so fearful and so fascinating to humanity.—WILLIAM ARCHER, Preface to English translation of *Little Eyolf*.

Enter then our old friend, Ibsen's divine messenger. The Rat-wife, alias the Strange Passenger, alias the Button Moulder, alias Ulrik Brendel, comes in to ask whether there are any little gnawing things there of which she can rid the house. They do not understand—the divine messenger in Ibsen never is understood, especially by the critics. So the little gnawing thing in the house—the child—follows the Rat-wife and is drowned, leaving the pair awakened by the blow to a frightful consciousness of themselves.— G. B. SHAW: *Views and Opinions*.

Ravenshoe, Charles, hero of Henry Kingsley's novel, *Ravenshoe*, a generous, high-spirited youth who comes into his own after many vicissitudes.

Ravenswood, Edgar, Master of, hero of Scott's novel, *The Bride of Lammermoor*, a melancholy youth, to whom his father, Allan, had bequeathed a legacy of vengeance against the Ashton family. His love for Lucy Ashton and her father's plausible pretences calm his hatred, which bursts out again with redoubled fury when his engagement to her is broken by Lucy's parents. Unable to realize the difficulties of her position during his absence, he himself dealt the last blow to her tottering reason and she dies in convulsions. On his way to a duel with Colonel Sholto Ashton, her brother, he is swallowed up by the quicksands of Kelpies Flow.

Ready-Money Jack, in Washington Irving's *Bracebridge Hall*, the nickname of Jack Tibbetts, a sturdy British yeoman. " He saw to everything himself; put his own hand to the plow; worked hard; ate heartily; slept soundly; paid for everything in cash down; and never danced except he could do it to the music of his own money in both pockets. He has never been without a hundred or two pounds in gold about him, and never allows a debt to stand unpaid. This has gained him his current name."

Ready Money Mortiboy, in the novel of that name (1872), by Walter Besant and James Rice, the nickname given to the chief character,—a skin-

flint country banker, heir to a race of misers, with all the stock attributes of the miser. His prodigal son, known locally as Roaring Dick, whom he had discarded years ago, comes back, apparently prosperous, but really with a determination to rob his father by inducing him to invest in a non-extant Mexican mine. One night the old man awakes, to find his son rifling his hoard. He is stricken by a paralytic stroke, from which he never recovers. Dick reforms, casts away his accomplice La Fleur, becomes a model of all the virtues, domestic and civic, and is eventually shot by his old-time partner.

There has recently died, at Northampton, Mr. Charles Cecil Becke, the borough coroner. In the obituary notice in *The Northampton Mercury*, it is stated that his mother " was a sister of the late Mr. Henry Billingworth of Whitworth, who amassed a large fortune, and figures in Besant and Rice's famous novel,—he was the original of Ready Money Mortiboy." It will be recalled that Mr. James Rice was a Northampton man.— *Notes and Queries*, II S., iv, 205.

Rebecca, in Scott's romance *Ivanhoe*, the daughter of the Jew, Isaac of York. She is as generous and self-sacrificing as her father is avaricious and self-seeking. She loves Ivanhoe, but knows her love is hopeless. Knowing also that Rowena is her successful rival, she yet offers Bois-Guilbert any sum he may demand for effecting the release of the Saxon maiden from imprisonment among her enemies. A famous scene is that in which she defies the passion-inflamed Templar and threatens to throw herself from the turret of the Tower of Torquilstone into the courtyard. Bois-Guilbert carries her to the preceptory of Templestone, where as a Jewess skilled in medicine she is convicted of sorcery and condemned to the stake. Allowed a trial by combat she chooses Ivanhoe for her champion. See BOIS-GUILBERT.

Rebecca was suggested in part by a Philadelphia Jewess, Rebecca Gratz, whose character was described to Scott by Washington Irving.

Scott owed his knowledge of Rebecca Gratz to Irving. On Irving's first visit to Abbottsford (1817) the two became intimate friends. Irving, habitually reticent as he was about the great grief of his life, presently told Scott of his youthful love for Mathilda Hoffman. She died at 18, but he never ceased to mourn her, and she never found even a temporary successor in his heart. Miss Hoffman's most devoted friend was Rebecca Gratz, of Philadelphia (1781–1869). She tended Irving's betrothed through her last illness, and Irving naturally mentioned her to Scott and told her own story. She loved a Christian, but would not marry him out of loyalty to the ancient faith, and for the rest of her life devoted her wealth and all her powers to philanthropy. When Scott finished *Ivanhoe*, two years after Irving's visit, he wrote: "How do you like your Rebecca? Does the Rebecca I have pictured compare well with the pattern given?"—See *Century*, September, 1882.

Redcliffe, Heir of, hero and title of a novel by Charlotte Yonge, which once had an immense vogue, especially among young ladies in their teens.

The hero, a young baronet of ancient family and immense estate, was in point of character such as no young man, whether gentle or simple, ever has been or will be. But it was an undeniably pretty and pathetic story, and aroused feminine sensibility to the highest degree. "Lor, ma'am!" an Abigail was reported to have said when arranging her lady's "things" in the morning, "whatever have you been a-doing of to your flounces?" (those were flounce days). "They're wringing wet." She had simply sat up to finish *The Heir of Redcliffe*, and drenched her dress with her tears at his death.—*Lippincott's Magazine.*

Red-cross Knight, hero of the first book of Spenser's *Faërie Queene* (1590), is meant for St. George, patron of England. His adventures typify the triumph of holiness over sin, of truth over error, of Protestantism over " Popery." With Una, who represents Evangelical purity or unity of faith, he starts out to slay the dragon, but is misled by Duessa, a double-faced minx, who passes herself off as Fidessa, or True Faith, and lures him to the palace of Lucifera. He is attacked and cast into a dungeon by Orgoglio, but Una sends Arthur (England) to his rescue. Arthur slays Orgoglio and liberates the Red-cross Knight, who now redeems himself by slaying the dragon, and then finds his way to Una whom he marries.

Redgauntlet, Sir Edward Hugh, hero of Scott's novel *Redgauntlet*

(1824). A Jacobite, unyielding, unbending, loving fiercely as he hated fiercely, his love depended on submission to his will. Even when he retired to a convent as Father Hugo, he never forgot and never repented the past, and died with his silver box about his neck bearing the legend *Haud obliviscendum.* He had a strange physical peculiarity—the mark of his family. He possessed the power of contracting his forehead into a frown, in the lines of which the shape of a horse-shoe might be traced. Sir Hugh was modelled from Scott's intimate friend the fifth Sir Robert Grierson, who died in 1839, aged 102.

Redlaw, the *Haunted Man,* in Dickens's story so entitled. Seeking to forget his own sorrows, he loses for a time his sympathy with the sorrows of others.

Regan, in Shakespeare's *King Lear*, one of the monarch's ungrateful daughters. See GONERIL.

Reignier, duke of Lorraine and Anjou and titular king of Naples, in Shakespeare's *Henry VI*, three parts. This is Shakespeare's spelling of René (*q.v.*). Suffolk describes his titles and influence in Act v, 5.

Remus, Uncle, an old plantation negro, shrewd and humorous, whose mind is stored with beast fables that always find a moral application among his hearers. He is the feigned narrator of the plantation and folklore tales collected by Joel Chandler Harris and published in *Uncle Remus* (1881), *Nights with Uncle Remus* (1883), *Uncle Remus and his Friends* (1892).

René (called Reignier by Shakespeare), duke of Anjou and titular king of Naples, appears in all three parts of *Henry VI*, and also in Scott's historical romance, *Anne of Geierstein.*

René, the autobiographic hero of a romance of that name, forming an episode in the prose epic *Les Natchez,* by François René Chateaubriand. It was published separately in 1807. René is a sort of French Werther and the precursor of the " grand, gloomy, and peculiar " heroes with whom Byron identified himself. Chauteaubriand specifically accused Byron of unacknowledged plagiarism. René, in the haughty pride, isolation, and contempt for civilization which has driven him to consort with savages (see also LOCKSLEY HALL), is evidently Chauteaubriand's reminiscence of his own stormy and moody youth. The central episode, an unholy passion felt for him by his sister, probably suggested *Manfred* to Byron.

René might surely claim some part in the creation of that one single person who had appeared in the various characters of Childe Harold, Conrad, Lara, Manfred, and the Giaour. The question which troubled Chateaubriand can perhaps be answered by those who have studied the Byron mystery, and are acquainted with René, with the chapter in the *Génie du Christianisme* entitled *Du Vague des passions*, and with the *Défense du Génie du Christianisme*—those passages of it especially which tell how Chateaubriand had fought against the humour that possessed the young men of his time to be guilty and gloomy after the fashion of Rousseau and Werther, and those other passages which sum up the character of René, and mark the different doom assigned to him and to his repentant victim. Byron persistently abstained from acknowledging any obligation to René. A reason will suggest itself to those who consult the books, and we will not unnecessarily dilate upon the hateful theme.—*Saturday Review.*

Rennepont, Count, in Sue's *Wandering Jew,* a descendant of Herodias, sister of the Wandering Jew. A century and a half before the story opens he had professed Catholicism in order to save his property from confiscation. The ruse was discovered and the whole estate was given to the Jesuits. He succeeded in saving 150,000 francs, which he put out at interest for 150 years, and it is the fate of this fund and of its claimants that makes up the story.

Revere, Paul, a famous loyalist in the American Revolution, hero of a ballad by Longfellow, *The Midnight Ride of Paul Revere* (1863). Revere rode from Boston to Concord by night (April 18, 1775), to notify the colonists of an intended British raid on the morrow. The details of the ride as presented by Longfellow are subjects of dispute among historians, but the main fact remains unshaken.

Riccabocca, Dr., in Bulwer-Lytton's *My Novel,* an intimate friend of the Caxton family, an Italian philosopher —a soft-hearted cynic, whose attributes are a large pipe, a red umbrella, and an inexhaustible stock of Macchiavellian proverbs.

Richard Cœur de Lion, son of Henry II and afterward the crusader king of England, appears in three of Scott's novels, *The Betrothed* (1825), *The Talisman* (1825), and *Ivanhoe* (1820). In the first he accompanies his father to the siege of the Castle of Garde Douloureuse and takes it by storm. In *The Talisman* he is chief of the allied princes arrayed against Saladin in Palestine, but his arrogance, recklessness, and impatience breed discord in the Christian camps, which ends in the abandonment of the enterprise. " Alas," says one of the characters, " that a creature so noble as thou art, so accomplished in princely thoughts and princely daring, so fitted to honor Christendom by thy actions and in thy calmer mood to rule it by thy wisdom, should yet have the brute and wild fury of the lion mingled with the dignity and courage of that king of the forest! "

In *Ivanhoe* Richard, disguised as the Black Knight of the Fetterlock, successfully intervenes to help Ivanhoe at a critical moment in the passage-of-arms at Ashby de la Zouch, and afterwards directed the attack of Locksley and his men on Front-de-Boeuf's castle.

Richard II (born 1367, king of England 1377–99), the eighth king of the house of Plantagenet, is the hero of the play by Shakespeare named after him. He is introduced in the first scene, where two nobles submit their differences to him for decision. The germs of all after events lie compact in his insincerity, partiality, and arbitrary self-will, and in the proud, tempestuous barons, who momentarily succumb. In Act iv, Sc. 1, he resigns the crown and is sent to the Tower; in v, 5, he is killed by Exton.

Richard, although possessed of a certain regal charm and power of attaching tender natures to himself, is deficient in all that is sterling and real in manhood. He is self-indulgent, has much superficial sensitiveness, loves to contemplate in a romantic way whatever is romantic or passionate in life, possesses a kind of rhetorical imagination, and has abundant command of delicate and gleaming words. His will is nerveless, he is incapable of consistency of feeling, incapable of strenuous action.—HAZLITT.

Richard III, in Shakespeare's historical tragedy of that name (1597), is first introduced to us as Richard Plantagenet, duke of Gloucester, in the two parts of *Henry VI*, becoming king in Part II, Act iv.

Shakespeare's plot is founded upon the chronicles of Hollingshed and Hall, with little indebtedness to two older plays, *The True Tragedie of Richard the Third* and *Richardius Tertius*, the latter written in Latin by Thomas Legge. Shakespeare's play takes up English history where *III Henry VI* had left it, after the battle of Tewkesbury in 1471, and ends with the fall of Richard at Bosworth in 1485.

There is something sublime and terrible in so great and fierce a human energy as that of Richard, concentrated within one withered and distorted body. This is the evil offspring and flower of the long and cruel civil wars—this distorted creature, a hater and scorner of men, an absolute cynic, loveless and alone, disregarding all human bonds and human affections, yet full of intellect, of fire, of power.—E. DOWDEN: *Shakespeare Primer.*

In no other play of Shakespeare's, we may surely say, is the leading character so predominant as here. He absorbs almost the whole of the interest, and it is a triumph of Shakespeare's art that he makes us, in spite of everything, follow him with sympathy. This is partly because several of his victims are so worthless that their fate seems well deserved. Anne's weakness deprives her of our sympathy, and Richard's crime loses something of its horror when we see how lightly it is forgiven by the one who ought to take it most to heart. In spite of all his iniquities he has wit and courage on his side—a wit which sometimes rises to Mephistophelean humor, a courage which does not fail him even in the moment of disaster, but sheds a glory over his fall which is lacking to the coldly correct opponent. However false and hypocritical he may be towards others, he is no hypocrite to himself. He is chemically free from self-delusion.—GEORGE BRANDES: *William Shakespeare, A Critical Study* (1898).

Richard, Poor, the pseudonym under which Benjamin Franklin issued a series of almanacs (1732–1757). They were distinguished for the "wise saws and modern instances" with which they abounded. Richard Saunders was the full name of the supposed author of the almanacs.

Richelieu, Armand Jean de Plessis, Duke of (1585–1642), made a cardinal in 1622, a famous French statesman, who was minister to Louis XIII from 1624 until his death. His policy strengthened the power of the crown and weakened that of the nobles. He figures in De Vigny's romance, *Cinq Mars* (1826); in Bulwer-Lytton's drama, *Richelieu, or the Conspiracy* (1839); in many of Dumas's romances, notably in the *Vicomte de Bragelonne;* in G. P. R. James's romance, *Richelieu* (1829), and in Stanley Weyman's romance, *Under the Red Robe* (1894) and its dramatization. De Vigny, who has been more or less followed by the others, paints Richelieu as he appeared to the contemporary French nobles—the organizer, with Father Joseph and Laubardemont, of espionage and assassination—and also in his better self as the masterful uncrowned king of France, sending his crowned manikin to the front to fight like any obscure captain, while he himself planned the victories that set France at the head of Europe.

Richmond, Harry, in Meredith's novel, *The Adventures of Harry Richmond,* is a sort of shuttlecock for his father and his maternal grandfather, each determined to set him on the right path. The father, Roy Richmond, believes himself the legitimate son of a royal personage; his friends believe him to be the son, but illegitimate. No intimation is given as to the truth of either theory, nor whether, if untrue, Roy Richmond is a conscious swindler or a monomaniac. The author rather suggests the former, the reader may incline to the latter and more charitable view. In fine contrast to the visionary father is the solid, earthly grandfather, Squire Beltham,—a rich, positive, passionate, swearing old English squire, " acred up to his lips, consoled up to his chin," but distinguished above his class by the real lucidity of his business mind, and therefore possessed with a double intensity of loathing for the hollow scheming and visionary pretensions of the son-in-law he had never welcomed.

Ridd, John, hero of R. D. Blackmore's novel, *Lorna Doone* (1871), who falls in love with and marries the titular heroine. He is a man of the moors and fields, with all the yeoman's cares in his mind; but, if slow to think, he is quick to act; if plain and unlettered, he is courageous and chivalric, and Lorna welcomes his placid strength.

Riderhood, Roger or **Rogue,** in Dickens's novel, *Our Mutual Friend* (1864), a river thief and longshoreman, who accuses Gaffer Hexam. His daughter, **Pleasant,** keeps an unlicensed pawnshop.

That unfragrant and unsanitary waif of its [The Thames's] rottenest refuse, the incomparable Rogue Riderhood, must always hold a chosen place among the choicest villains of our selectest acquaintance. When the genius of his immortal creator said, "Let there be Riderhood" and there was Riderhood, a figure of coequal immortality rose. reeking and skulking into sight.—SWINBURNE: *Charles Dickens,* p. 60.

Ridley, John James, called **J.J.** in Thackeray's novel, *The Newcomes,* a sickly, deformed youth, sensitive and imaginative, a fellow-student and a great friend of Clive Newcome. He reappears in *Philip,* and shows similar affection and devotion for that gentleman and his wife.

Riel, Herve, titular hero of a ballad (1871) by Robert Browning, which is based on historic fact. Riel, a Breton sailor, was in Louis XIV's navy, when the French fleet of 44 sail, on May 31, 1692, attacked the combined English and Dutch fleet of 99 sail, off Cape La Hogue in the English Channel. The French held their own until nightfall, when they headed for France. Twenty-two ships arrived off St. Malo, with the English in hot pursuit, the others having been run ashore and annihilated. No pilot could guide them into the security of the roadstead until Riel offered his assistance and gallantly achieved the feat. So little did he value his services

that, when told to name his reward, he asked for a day's leave of absence to visit his wife in his native village of La Croisic, South Brittany. On Easter Monday, 1912, a statue to the memory of Riel was unveiled in La Croisic.

Rienzi, Cola di, an historical personage who temporarily restored the old Roman system of government and constituted himself the tribune of the people. His project failed; in 1354 he was assassinated. Bulwer-Lytton has made him the hero of an historical romance, *Rienzi, the Last of the Tribunes* (1835).

Rigby, The Right Hon. Nicholas, in Disraeli's novel, *Coningsby,* a fawning, plotting, insolent man-of-all-dirty-work. He was immediately recognized as a portrait of John Wilson Croker. See WENHAM.

Rigdum Funnidos, in Carey's burlesque, *Chrononhotonthologos,* a courtier in the palace of the titular monarch, also a nickname bestowed by Sir Walter Scott on his friend John Ballantyne.

Rigoletto, hero and title of an Italian opera, libretto by Piave and music by Giovanni Verdi, first produced at Venice March 11, 1851. The plot is from Hugo's *Le Roi S'amuse.* The scene is transported from Paris to Mantua, and the names of the dramatis personæ are changed, so that Francis I becomes the Duke of Mantua, Triboulet becomes Rigoletto, Saint Vallier becomes the count of Monterone, etc. But the change of names entails no change of characters, and the situations, though toned down in parts, remain substantially the same. The name Rigoletto is taken, with the alteration of a single letter, from the vaudeville of *Rigoletti, or the Last of the Fools,* by Jaime and Alboize, one of the many dramatic variations of Hugo's work.

Rikki-Tikki-Tavi, in Rudyard Kipling's *Jungle Books* (1894 and 1895), a mongoose, the pet of a small English boy in India, who twice saves the lad's life and once the lives of his father and mother and so " fights his way gallantly enough into the list of Mr. Kipling's immortals" (*London Athenæum*).

Rinaldo, a famous character in mediæval romance, one of the four sons of Aymon and one of the greatest of Charlemagne's paladins. He appears as *Renaud* or *Regnault de Montaubau* in the French romances, but the Italian form Rinaldo came into general acceptance through the influence of Pulci, Ariosto, and Tasso.

In *Orlando Furioso* (1516) Ariosto makes him the rival of his cousin Orlando for the love of Angelica, who will have nothing to do with him. Tasso chose him as the hero of a juvenile epic, *Rinaldo* (1562), now practically forgotten but once of great vogue. This gathers together and synthetizes his various exploits against giants, enchanters, and Saracen kings, his dallyings with Queen Floriana, whom he forsook as Æneas forsook Calypso, and his more enduring love for Clarice, daughter of the infidel king Mambrino, whom he finally wins and weds.

Rizpah, poem by Tennyson. The modern Rizpah, dying, tells a lady who is visiting her how her son Willy, being dared to the feat by his wild mates, robbed the mail, took one purse, with the contents of which he refused to meddle, and was hanged for the deed. There are great pathos and power in the description of her last meeting with him, and in her tale of her subsequent insanity, and of her secretly burying his bones in holy ground. See RIZPAH in vol. II.

Never since the very beginning of all poetry were the twin passions of terror and pity more divinely done into deathless words or set to more perfect and profound magnificence of music; never more inseparably fused and harmonized into more absolute and sublime identity. The poet never lived on earth—such at least is my humble and hearty conviction—whose glory would not be heightened by the attribution of this poem to his hands. Thousands of readers for centuries to come, will be moved by it to trembling and to tears.—SWINBURNE.

Robarts, Lucy, in Anthony Trollope's novel, *Framley Parsonage*

(1861). Sister of the vicar, she loves and marries Lord Lufton.

I think myself that Lucy Robarts is perhaps the most natural English girl that I ever drew,—the most natural, at any rate, of those who have been good girls. She was not as dear to me as Kate Woodward in *The Three Clerks,* but I think she is more like real human life.—ANTHONY TROLLOPE: *An Autobiography*, p. 125.

Robarts, the Rev. Mr., vicar of Framley, in Anthony Trollope's novel, *Framley Parsonage*, a weak man, naturally honest, who runs unnecessarily into debt and is involved in difficulties that affect his honor.

Robert of Paris, Count, hero of Scott's romance of that name (1831), a French nobleman who, with his wife Brenhilda, has joined the first Crusade (1096-1099), is present in the camp of the emperor Alexius Commenus at Scutari, and takes part in the siege and capture of Constantinople. See HEREWARD.

Robin, Fanny, in Thomas Hardy's novel, *Far from the Madding Crowd* (1875), a country girl seduced by Sergeant Troy.

She appears only three times,—once when she meets Oak on the night of the fire when she is running away from home; a second time, wandering all alone by the riverside in the dark winter night, and attempting to attract Troy's attention by feebly throwing little fragments of snow at his barrack-room window "till the wall must have become pimpled with the adhering lumps of snow;" and a third time struggling faintly and with faltering steps to the workhouse, when her exhausted nature could scarce support the weight of the wretched burden it had to bear. The author has put out his whole force in the description of these last two incidents. The first is original. The second may have been suggested by the well-known chapter in *Adam Bede* entitled "The Journey in Despair." But, whether so suggested or not, it stands comparison not unfairly even with that most painful narrative of the shipwreck of a girl's life.—*Saturday Review.*

Robin of Bagshot, in *The Beggar's Opera* (1728), by John Gay, one of Macheath's gang of robbers. He was evidently designed to represent Sir Robert Walpole's unrefined manners, convivial temper and alleged robbery of the public. Robin was provided with both a wife and a mistress, to indicate to the public that Lady Walpole had a rival in Miss Skerrell.

Robinson, Hyacinth, in Henry James's *Princess Casamassima* (1886) the illegitimate son of the profligate Lord Frederick and an ignorant Frenchwoman, who is reared by a poor dressmaker among forlorn east-side people in London. Though his instincts are aristocratic, his sympathies are with the down-trodden. Falling an easy prey for workingmen of socialistic views, he promises, if called upon, to perform an act that may cost him his life. It is in this mood that he meets Princess Casamassima.

Robinson, Sergeant, hero of John Pendleton Kennedy's historical romance of the Revolutionary war, *Horshoe Robinson* (1836), so-called after the hero's nickname, given him from his trade as a farrier and from the returning sweep of a river near his own farm. He is a stalwart, long-headed, large-hearted man, with a quiet, dry humor and a preternatural acuteness, which, joined to his training as a backwoodsman, a hunter, and a soldier, enable him to outwit the villains. These are an English captain, St. Jermyn, who assumes the name of Tyrrel, and Sergeant Curry, a kind of darker Bothwell, whom St. Jermyn instigates to various plots and stratagems against the heroine's father, a Tory planter named Lindsay.

Robinson, What Mr., thinks, the third of the *Biglow Papers* by J. R. Lowell. The circumstances which gave rise to it were as follows: In 1855 the anti-slavery party intended to start Governor Briggs, of Massachusetts, for the presidency, in opposition to General Cass, the candidate of the Democrats, and General Taylor, the (ultimately successful) candidate of the Whigs. Mr. John P. Robinson, a country lawyer, then commenced a political tour of the State, for the purpose of discrediting Briggs and seconding Cass. The recruiting sergeants and the place-hunting politicians, who used always to accompany them, were denominated by Mr. Robinson " the apostles of American destiny."

Roche, La, hero of *The Story of La Roche,* by Henry Mackenzie, a tale founded on fact. La Roche was a Swiss pastor who, with his daughter Margaret, was befriended in sickness and poverty by David Hume. Three years later Hume was invited to Berne to attend Margaret's wedding to a young Swiss officer. He arrived to find both bride and bridegroom dead. The officer had been shot in a duel; the maiden had succumbed to grief. Hume, the arch-infidel, is represented as greatly touched by the Christian faith that sustained the old pastor in his bereavement.

Rochester, Edward Fairfax, in Miss Brontë's *Jane Eyre* (1847), ferocious and brutal in manner and bearing, but with an inner core of kindliness. The author's intent was to paint a strong nature, soured into cynicism by experience, who addresses the wondering and horrified yet admiring little governess from the height—or depth—of his worldly wisdom.

Mr. Rochester has imposed upon a good many people; and he is probably responsible in part for some of the muscular heroes who have appeared since his time in the world of fiction. I must, however, admit that, in spite of some opposing authority, he does not appear to me to be a real character at all, except as a reflection of a certain side of his creator. He is in reality the personification of a true woman's longing (may one say it now?) for a strong master. But the knowledge is wanting. He is a very bold but necessarily unsuccessful attempt at an impossibility. The parson's daughter did not really know anything about the class of which he is supposed to be a type, and he remains vague and inconsistent in spite of all his vigor.—LESLIE STEPHEN: *Hours in a Library.*

Rockminster, Lady, in Thackeray's *Pendennis,* a rigorous old woman of the great world, with as much kindness as character, with whom Laura Bell goes to live after the death of Mrs. Pendennis.

Roderick, thirty-fourth and last of the Gothic kings of Spain, the centre of a cycle of legends that have been utilized by Robert Southey in an epic poem, *Roderick, the Last of the Goths* (1824), which begins with history and ends in pure fable. In a moment of frenzy Roderick has violated Florinda, the daughter of Count Julian. Julian renounces Christianity, heads the Moors in an invasion of Spain, and drives Roderick from his throne. Humiliated, repentant, he accepts his defeat as a punishment for his crime and flees in peasant costume to the seaside. After a year of solitary penance, a vision rouses him to action, not to regain his throne, but to save his country. He is so changed by suffering that he fights unrecognized until the crisis of the battle of Covadango, when he rushes furiously on the enemy with his old war-cry, " Roderick the Goth! Roderick and victory!" to the inspiration of his followers, who cut the Moors to pieces. Then Roderick disappears forever.

Sir Walter Scott, in *The Vision of Don Roderick* (1811), modernizes the legend of Roderick's dream. He makes this occur in an ancient vault in Toledo, presided over by an oracle, where there is unveiled to him a prophetic panorama of Spanish history from his own times to those of Bonaparte and Wellesley.

Roderigo, in Shakespeare's *Othello,* a Venetian youth, surreptitiously in love with Desdemona and hating Othello as a successful rival, whose weaknesses are taken advantage of by Iago.

Roderigo's suspicious credulity, and impatient submission to the cheats which he sees practised upon him, and which by persuasion he suffers to be repeated, exhibit a strong picture of a weak mind betrayed by unlawful desires to a false friend.—SAMUEL JOHNSON: *General Observations on Shakespeare's Plays* (1768).

Roehampton, Lord, in Lord Beaconsfield's political novel *Endymion* (1880), is evidently intended for Lord Palmerston. He marries Endymion's sister Myra.

Scarcely any attempt is made to distinguish Lord Roehampton from Lord Palmerston except in the details of private life. In the ministry of Lord Melbourne Lord Roehampton is foreign secretary, and in that capacity he projects and executes the Syrian expedition of 1840. Lord Beaconsfield regards with admiration, and almost with tenderness, the statesman whom he long opposed with untiring energy, but always

with chivalrous courtesy. In accordance with his uniform practice, he disregards political differences which were, in fact, purely conventional. It pleases him to imagine the influence of such a character over a wife much younger than himself, who had originally accepted his hand for reasons of convenience, and especially in the hope of serving her twin brother Endymion.— *Saturday Review.*

Rolla, Jacques, hero of Alfred de Musset's poem *Rolla.* He is the only legitimate child of a foolish father, who has brought him up without occupation and left him an orphan at nineteen, without means enough to support existence on the only terms he considers endurable. Jacques accordingly divides his patrimony into three portions, determined that each should serve for a year of debauchery and that, all being ended, he would kill himself. His last night on earth he spends with a girl still innocent who has been trained for a life of shame. He discovers that she is an illegitimate sister and kills her and himself.

Rolleston, Helen, heroine of *Foul Play* (1868), a novel by Charles Reade and Dion Boucicault.

Being a character of Mr. Reade's creation, it is not necessary to say that Helen Rolleston is a very natural and lovable woman, admirably illogical, cruel, sagacious, and generous. Through all her terrible disasters and thrilling adventures she is always a young lady, and no more abandoned on that far-away island, by her exquisite breeding and the pretty conventions of her English girlhood, than she would be on her native croquet-ground. A delicious charm is gained to the romance by the retention of these society instincts and graces, which are made to harmonize rather than conflict with the exhibitions of a woman's greatness and self-devotion, when occasion calls forth those qualities.—*Atlantic Monthly,* August, 1868.

Romeo, hero of Shakespeare's tragedy *Romeo and Juliet* (1598), more or less founded on fact (see JULIET). The first mention of the romance was made by Masuccio of Palermo, who in 1476 wrote a novel about two lovers called Mariotto and Gianozza, of Siena, in Italy, whose story is like that of Romeo and Juliet. The theme was next handled by Luigi da Porto, who wrote a similar story of two lovers called Romeo and Giulietta and laid the scene in Verona.

In Verona the legend survives to-day
and has left tangible evidence of
itself. Tradition has long associated
with Verona the two contending
families of Montague and Capulet,
from whom Romeo and Juliet sprang.
They are known to-day as the
"Capuleti" and the "Montecchi,"
and Verona has many things to show
the traveller which claim association
with them and their feuds.

Romeo is Hamlet in love. There is the
same rich exuberance of passion and sentiment in the one that there is of thought and
sentiment in the other. Both are absent
and self-involved; both live out of themselves in a world of imagination. Hamlet
is abstracted from everything; Romeo is
abstracted from everything but his love,
and lost in it. His "frail thoughts dally
with faint surmise," and are fashioned out
of the suggestions of hope, "the flatteries
of sleep." He is himself only in his Juliet;
she is his only reality, his heart's true home
and idol. The rest of the world is to him a
passing dream.—HAZLITT: *Characters of
Shakespeare's Plays.*

Romola, heroine of George Eliot's
novel of that name (1863), daughter
of a wealthy Florentine merchant,
to whom she is entirely devoted even
when she loses her heart to Tito
Melemma (*q.v.*).

Readers in general cannot feel quite so
warmly to Romola as to the childish Maggie;
she is a little too hard and statuesque, and
drops her husband rather too coolly and
decisively as soon as she finds out that he is
capable of disregarding her sentiments. Still
she is one of the few figures who occupy a
permanent and peculiar niche in the great
gallery of fiction; and, if she is a trifle chilly
and over-dignified, one must admit that she
is not the less lifelike. She is, moreover,
the only one—to my feeling—of George
Eliot's women whose marriage has not
something annoying. She marries a thorough scoundrel, it is true, but the misconception to which she falls a victim is one
which we feel to be thoroughly natural under
the circumstances.—SIR LESLIE STEPHEN:
George Eliot.

Rondelet, Paul, in *The Monks of
Thelema,* by Besant and Rice, is drawn
from Walter Pater. (See THELEMA.)

Roper, Margaret, daughter of Sir
Thomas More (*q.v.*), who married
William Roper, is the heroine and
the feigned author of *The Household
of Sir Thomas More,* by Anne Manning. Tennyson alludes to her in *A
Dream of Fair Women.*

Morn broadened on the borders of the dark,
  Ere I saw her who clasped in her last
    trance
Her murdered father's head, or Joan of Arc,
  A light of ancient France.
      TENNYSON: *A Dream of Fair Women.*

Rosa, Aunty, in Rudyard Kipling's
short story, *Baa, Baa, Black Sheep,*
the narrow-minded, pharisaical, and
sour-tempered relative, who comes
near crushing all kindly feelings out
of little Punch (*q.v.*). The character
is very similar to that of the aunt
who brings up Dick and Maisie in
The Light that Failed.

Rosalind, heroine of Shakespeare's
As You Like It, daughter of the
banished duke, loving and beloved
by Orlando. She assumes male attire
and the name of Ganymede, and,
with her cousin Celia, sets out to find
her father in the forest of Arden.
Here she re-encounters Orlando, who
does not recognize her, and she sets
him the task of making love to Ganymede as though "he" were the Rosalind whom Orlando is perpetually
sighing for.

To every actress of distinction the
character of Rosalind has offered
irresistible attractions. It has been
played by Peg Woffington and Mrs.
Siddons, by Charlotte Cushman and
Helen Faucit, by Adelaide Neilson
and Mary Anderson, by Madame
Modjeska and Ellen Terry. The
interpreters alike of comedy and
tragedy have included it in their
repertory, viewing the part as a sort
of neutral ground, independent of
professional classification. In truth,
Rosalind is not to be described as
tragic at all; yet the romance, the
sentiment, the tenderness of the character commend it to the actresses of
tragedy, while its sportiveness, its
wit, its archness, always subject it
to the claim of those comedy actresses
who are not content merely to provoke laughter.

Rosalind . . . has vivacity and wit
enough to captivate those who like a woman
of spirit; and yet with this there is inter-
woven so much womanly tenderness and
delicacy, she is, in her gayest moods, so
truly, sometimes so touchingly, feminine,
that she wins more admirers than she
dazzles.—R. G. WHITE.

Rosalind is not a complete human being: she is simply an extension into five acts of the most affectionate, fortunate, delightful five minutes in the life of a charming woman. And all the other figures in the play are cognate impostures.—GEORGE BERNARD SHAW.

Rosalinde, the name under which Edmund Spenser celebrates his first love. Immediately on leaving college, he retired to the north of England, where he first became enamoured of the fair being to whom, according to the fashion of the day, he gave the fanciful appellation of Rosalind. She has been satisfactorily identified with Rose Daniel, sister of the poet Samuel Daniel. See *Atlantic Monthly,* vol. ii, 677.

Rosaline, in *Romeo and Juliet,* a lady for whom Romeo is represented as having cherished a hopeless passion before he saw Juliet.

No one, I believe, ever experiences any shock at Romeo's forgetting his Rosaline, who has been a mere name for the yearning of his youthful imagination and rushing into his passion for Juliet. Rosaline was a mere creation of his fancy.—COLERIDGE.

Rosalynde, heroine of Thomas Lodge's prose fiction *Rosalynde Euphues Golden Legacie* (1590), which in its turn was partly based upon *The Cook's Tale of Gamelyn,* wrongly ascribed to Chaucer. Rosalynde is the obvious original of Shakespeare's Rosalind in *As You Like It,* but he has turned a faint sketch into a brilliant picture. The Forest of Arden appears both in play and novel. When Lodge's Rosalynde and Alinda are banished by Torismond and decide to find their way thither, Rosalynde assumes male attire, because, as she explains to her cousin, " I am of tall stature and would very well become the person and apparel of a page; thou shalt be my mistress, and I will play the man so properly, that, trust me, in what company soever I come, I will not be discovered. I will buy me a suit and have my rapier very handsomely by my side, and, if any knave offer wrong, your page will show him the point of his own weapon."

Rose Mary, heroine of a ballad by D. G. Rossetti, in volume, *Ballads and other Poems* (1882). Rose Mary has in her possession a beryl stone which reveals anything to a pure maiden. But she has fallen into sin with Sir James Heronhaye, and, when she would direct her lover how to avoid an ambush prepared for him by his mortal foe the Warden of Holycleugh, she reads the stone amiss: the knight takes the wrong road, and is slain. His body is borne back to the lady's castle, but under his mail are found love tokens showing that he had plighted his troth to the warden's sister. Rose Mary cleaves the stone in twain, and so expels the evil spirits who had deceived her and restores the good angel who had been driven out by her sin. As she dies, the angel receives her and assures her of heavenly forgiveness.

Rosenberg, Hildegarde, heroine of the *Initials* (1850), an international novel by Baroness Tautphoeus. A young Englishman, Hamilton, who comes to board with the Rosenberg family in Munich, falls in love with her, while Hildegarde's sister Crescenz complicates matters by falling in love with him.

The well-born Englishman could not help feeling and showing himself superior to the bourgeois family which had received him, and such a girl as Hildegarde could not help promptly hating him for it. They met almost as enemies, and their wooing throughout had often the alarming effect of warring; at the very end, her capture is something like a hostile triumph. The affair is not the less intoxicating to the spectator; the country fought over, though difficult, is picturesque, and the manners and customs of the neutrals, as well as the belligerents, are realized as vital elements of the exciting spectacle.—W. D. HOWELLS: *Heroines of Fiction,* vol. ii, p. 140.

Rosencrantz, in Shakespeare's *Hamlet,* a courtier who, with Guildenstern, had been a school-fellow of Hamlet's at Wittenberg. They always appear together, and Hamlet realizing that they had been sent for by the king to spy upon him, grows to hate them. He calls them " adders fanged," and puts them to the blush when they own that they cannot play upon his pipe. They carry the orders concerning Hamlet to England and are themselves sacrificed.

Ross, Man of, the name by which John Kyrle (1664–1754), a citizen of the town of Ross, in Herfordshire, has been celebrated by Pope and Coleridge. It was originally given him during his lifetime, by a country friend, and the title is said to have pleased him greatly. Kyrle was a gentleman of remarkable benevolence and public spirit, who with an income of only £500 a year actually performed all the worthy deeds chronicled in Pope's tribute. This appears in *Moral Essays*, Epistle iii, and consists of but 16 lines, the concluding ones running as follows:

Whose causeway parts the vale with shady rows?
Whose seats the weary traveller repose?
Who taught that heaven-directed spire to rise?
"The Man of Ross," each lisping babe replies.

Roumestan, Numa, hero of a novel of that name by Alphonse Daudet (1881), a typical Provençal bonhomme of unusual intelligence and boundless ambition, a liar and a braggart, who gets himself elected as a deputy and rises to eminence in the French capital and international politics.

Roxana, heroine of a novel by Daniel Defoe, *The Fortunate Mistress Lady Roxana* (1724). A courtesan who preys upon the upper classes, she was originally the innocent and beautiful daughter of a French refugee. An unfortunate marriage with a fool, who levants, sends her to the bad. She accumulates much wealth in sordid and squalid ways, but is overreached in the end and dies in jail.

Roy, Rob,—*i.e.*, Robert the Red,—a real character, the Robin Hood of Scotland, who plays an important part in Scott's novel named after him.

Judged by Scott's novel, the biggest, bravest heart that ever beat beneath the MacGregor tartan was that of Rob Roy, so named from the color of his hair and his fresh, ruddy complexion. Scott did not create the Rob Roy of romance. He ideal-

izes, no doubt, but his interpretation of the character of Rob rests mainly on the popular tradition of the man. A descendant of the blood-thirsty Dugald Ciahr Mohr, Rob had all his ancestor's love of the sword and capacity for leadership, without his cruelty. His lot was cast in the most restless epoch of Scottish history. It was an age of semi-barbarism, when the passion for power was the main thing, when a pillaging of the industrious Saxon was considered the proof of manliness and bravery.—S. R. CROCKETT: *The Scott Originals*, p. 195.

Rubempré, Lucien de, journalist, author, and dandy, who appears in several of Balzac's novels, notably *Lost Illusions* (1843), *A Distinguished Provençal at Paris* (1843), and *Splendors and Miseries of Courtesans*.

After scandalizing the people of Angouleme by what is actually a platonic passion for a great lady, he repairs to Paris in her train, dreaming great dreams of the figure he will cut there as a poet. Taken up by the Cénacle, a coterie of literary men, they soon drop him. He enters journalism, finds it abominably corrupt, and, after a meteoric career, returns to his native city, ruined in health, morals, and money.

Rudge, Barnaby, in Dickens's novel of that name (1841), the half-witted son of a murderer, who levies blackmail on Barnaby's mother, Mary Barnaby. At the age of twenty-three years Barnaby is a red-haired, glassy-eyed, grotesque object, clad in a green dress with tawdry ruffles, a fantastically trimmed hat upon his head, and carrying in a basket at his back a raven known as Grip. During the Gordon riots he eagerly joins the mob in their work of destruction, his strength and agility making him a valuable auxiliary. Arrested and condemned to death, he is eventually pardoned and retires with his mother to peaceful obscurity.

Rudiger, Clotilde von, in George Meredith's *The Tragic Comedians*, the young girl for whose sake the middle-aged Dr. Alvan is killed in a duel by Prince Marko. The novel is founded solidly on fact. Alvan is Ferdinand Lassalle, Marko is Yanco von Racowitza, and Clotilde is Helene von Donniges, who subsequently to the duel married Yanco, and, as Frau von Racowitza, published in 1879 *Meine Beziehungen zu Ferdinand Lassalle*, a rather lame apologia for the part played by her in the tragedy of fifteen years previous. Every important incident in Meredith's novel is taken from Helene's book. Later she became Countess Schewitsch.

Rudin, Dimitri, hero and title of a novel (1860) by Ivan Tourgenief. He is a vainglorious charlatan, who honestly believes in himself as a great literary genius, and forces a temporary acquiescence upon others, especially female others. He imposes first upon Daria Mikhailovna, who is ambitious to figure as the head of a salon, but she is soon disillusionized. His next victim is an old lady, also a bluestocking, who dismisses him when she finds him making successful love to her daughter. Forced to leave Russia, he ends his life defending a barricade in Paris.

Rugg, Peter, hero of a fantastic little story, *Peter Rugg, the Missing Man* (1824), by William Austin, which achieved a wide but ephemeral reputation in the United States. Peter, a citizen of pre-revolutionary Boston, was caught in a storm while out driving, and, refusing all invitations to tarry with a friend, swore a fearful oath: "I will see home to-night in spite of the tempest, or may I never see home!" Hence he was compelled to wander perpetually

between Hartford and Boston in a spectral chaise drawn by a spectral horse, with a spectral child beside him, and a thunder-storm in the rear. The tale is included in Drake's *Legends of New England.*

Peter Rugg is a creation after Hawthorne's own heart; the earth hath bubbles as the water hath, and he is of them; and the place given him in *The Virtuoso's Collection* gives proof that he had met Hawthorne's eye.— T. W. HIGGINSON, in *New York Independent,* May, 1888.

Rutherford, Mark, hero of two novels by William Hale White ("Reuben Shapcott"), *The Autobiography of Mark Rutherford* (1881), and its sequel, *Mark Rutherford's Deliverance* (1885). A doubter who wishes to believe, but is too scrupulously honest to accept any compromises, Mark leaves the independent ministry for a Unitarian chapel, and then drifts into agnosticism, gives up the problem of teaching his fellowman for that of helping him in his poverty and depression, and finally returns to a greatly modified form of Calvinism and, in his softened state, marries the true and loyal woman whom he had formerly despised for her intellectual limitations.

Ryecroft, Henry, hero of *The Private Papers of Henry Ryecroft* (1903), a work wherein George Gissing puts into the form of autobiographic fiction the aspirations, struggles, and disillusionments of his own career as an author.

S

Sacharissa (Gr. *sakehar*, "sugar"), the name under which Edmund Waller wooed, but failed to win, Dorothea Sidney, eldest daughter of the Earl of Sunderland. The poems on Sacharissa and her beautiful home at Penhurst, where Waller sang his passion to the deer among the beeches or watched Vandyke painting her in the "Shop of Beauty" have immortalized lady and poet alike. He sings to Sacharissa's picture, to her painter, her friends, her servant, her coming

and going, her sleeping or not sleeping, but in vain. The Lady Dorothy chose a wooer of higher degree, Lord Spencer, afterwards created Earl of Sunderland, who was killed at the battle of Newbury. In later days we hear of another meeting between Mr. Waller and Sacharissa. "When, Mr. Waller," said the Dowager Countess of Sunderland, "will you write such beautiful verses to me again?" "When, madam," replied the poet, "your ladyship is as handsome and young again." This must surely be calumny,—so accomplished a courtier would have turned his answer more skilfully. His *Love's Farewell* is a more fitting close to the romance.

St. Clair, Eva, in Mrs. H. B. Stowe's novel, *Uncle Tom's Cabin* (1851), the daughter of Uncle Tom's master.

St. Leon, hero of a novel by William Godwin, *St. Leon, a Tale of the Sixteenth Century* (1799), a gentleman in respectable circumstances, living comfortably with his wife and children, who is morally and mentally ruined by coming into possession of the elixir of life and the philosopher's stone.

Saint Preux, hero of Rousseau's novel, *Julie, ou la Nouvelle Heloise,* evidently meant as a portrait of the author. Separated from his Julie after being her tutor and her impassioned but determinedly platonic lover, Saint Preux goes for a voyage round the world and returns. Julie is now Madame de Wolmar. M. de Wolmar, knowing all about the past, welcomes Saint Preux as an old friend, whose whilom affection was a proof of sensibility and discernment. He invites him to sit at his table, to stay in his house, and to teach his children. As a supreme proof of confidence he makes a point of leaving him alone with his wife. These incidents weave together the tangled facts of real life. The original of Julie (*q.v.*) was married to Count d'Houdetot, a complaisant husband, who made up a *menage à trois* with Saint Lambert, his wife's (most unplatonic) lover. Rousseau came near resolving the trinity into a quartette, but his own hesitancy and the lady's self-conquest at the psychological moment saved the situation. See GRIBBLE: *Rousseau and the Women he Loved.*

Saladin (1137–1193), a famous sultan of Egypt and Syria, founder of the Ayubite dynasty therein, appears in Scott's romance of the Crusades, *The Talisman,* as the chief adversary of Richard Cœur de Lion. Each loved and admired the other, " as noble adversaries ever love each other." Fond of incognito adventure,

like Haroun al Rashid, Saladin appeared in disguise as Sheerkohf of Kurdistan, fought with Kenneth of Scotland; subsequently guided him to the hermit of Engaddi, and, returning with him to the Christian camp as Adonbec the physician, cured Richard and others by the aid of his sacred talisman. He suggested to Kenneth the stratagem by which he regained his honor, and in his proper person presided over the trial by combat in which Kenneth overcame the traitor Conrade of Montserrat.

Of all Sir Walter's characters the most dashing and spirited is the Sultan Saladin. But he is not meant for a hero, nor fated to be a lover. He is a collateral and incidental performer in the scene. His movements therefore remain free, and he is master of his own resplendent energies, which produce so much the more daring and felicitous an effect.—HAZLITT: Essays, *Why Heroes of Romance are Insipid.*

Salammbo, B. C., daughter of Hamilcar Barca, general of the Carthaginians during the First Punic War, is the titular heroine of an historical romance by Gustav Flaubert. She is beloved by Matho, leader of the mercenaries who have revolted against Carthage and stolen the sacred Zaimph or mantle of the goddess Tanit. Salammbo is urged to recapture the talisman, penetrates to the tent of Matho at night, and succeeds by her blandishments in carrying it off. Carthage triumphs over her rebellious soldiery and cuts them to pieces. Matho, reserved for the sport of the capital, runs the gauntlet of hideous torture through the streets and expires at the feet of Salammbo. She herself dies while pledging the genius of Carthage, "for that she had touched the mantle of Tanit."

Salathiel ben Sadi, a mysterious Jew, who appeared and disappeared in Venice towards the close of the sixteenth century in such sudden fashion that men came to identify him with the Wandering Jew (see vol. II) and consider him as one of many avatars of the cobbler or porter who insulted Christ. Finally his name entirely supplanted that of

Ahasuerus or Cartophilos given in the earlier legends. The Rev. George Croly (1829) published a romance entitled *Salathiel*, which was revived in 1900 and renamed *Tarry Thou Till I Come*.

Sally in our Alley, song by Henry Carey (1734), which has attained a wide popularity. Of its composition the author gives this account:

A shoemaker's apprentice, making a holiday with his sweetheart, treated her with a sight of Bedlam, the puppet shows, the flying chairs, and all the elegancies of Moorfield, from whence, proceeding to the farthing pie-house, he gave her a collation of buns, cheese, cakes, gammon of bacon, stuffed beef, and bottled ale; through all which scenes the author dodged them (charmed with the simplicity of their courtship). from whence he drew this little sketch of nature; but, being then young and obscure, he was very much ridiculed by some of his acquaintance for this performance, which nevertheless made its way into the polite world, and amply recompensed him by the applause of the divine Addison, who was pleased (more than once) to mention it with approbation.

The original air to the song was also composed by Carey, but it was subsequently dropped and the words were adapted to an old ballad air, *The Country Lass*.

Sampson, Dominie Abel, in Scott's novel *Guy Mannering*, a Scotch tutor in the Mannering family,—" a poor, modest, humble scholar, who had won his way through the classics, but fallen to the leeward in the voyage of life." His favorite ejaculation, " Pro-di-gi-ous! " is constantly extorted from him by any emotion of surprise, wonder, or admiration.

Sampson, Dr., in Charles Reade's *Hard Cash* (1863), a sturdy Scotch physician, one of the author's strongest and most original characters, who despises all regular practitioners and at the crisis of the story comes to the rescue of Alfred Hardie, confined in an asylum.

Samson, hero of Milton's dramatic poem *Samson Agonistes* (1671), is the Samson of Judges xvi, blinded and bound and a sport for his Philistine enemies in Dagon's temple, but wreaking a terrible revenge by pulling down the pillars of the edifice and perishing with the spectators in the

ruins. Milton must have taken the biblical story as an allegory of his own later life. He too was after the Restoration a champion at bay, a prophet without honor in his own country, which had been delivered into the hands of the enemy, poor, blind, derided, but still militant (agonistes) and ready for vengeance in the name of the Lord.

He also was blind, as Samson had been,— groping about among the malignant conditions that had befallen him, helplessly dependent on the finding of others, and bereft of the external consolations and means of resistance to his scorners that might have come to him through sight. He also had to live mainly in the imagery of the past. In that past, too, there were similarities in his case to that of Samson. Like Samson, substantially, he had been a Nazarite,—no drinker of wine or strong drink, but one who had always been an ascetic in his dedicated service to great designs. And the chief blunder in his life, that which had gone nearest to wreck it, and had left the most marring consequences and the most painful reflections, was the very blunder of which, twice-repeated, Samson had to accuse himself. Like Samson, he had married a Philistine woman, one not of his own tribe, and having no thoughts or interests in common with his own; and like Samson, he had suffered indignities from this wife and her relations, till he had learned to rue the match.— PROF. MASSON.

Sandford, Harry, in Thomas Day's juvenile story *Sandford and Merton* (1780), the son of a poor farmer, full of all boyish virtues. He is placed, with Thomas Merton, the six-year-old son of a wealthy gentleman, under the tuition of the wise and learned Mr. Barlow, an ex-clergyman, who continually holds him up as a model and exemplar for the more or less reprehensible Tommy.

Sangrado, Doctor, in Le Sage's novel, *Gil Blas*, a famous physician in Valladolid, to whom Gil Blas attaches himself as pupil and servant. He is imitated from the Dr. Sagredo of Espinel's romance, *Marcos de Obregon*. A tall, thin, pale man of very solemn appearance, who weighed his discourse and used " great pomp of words," his system was simple enough. It consisted of profuse blood-letting, and equally profuse administration of hot water into the system. Gil Blas was reduced to a sparse diet of beans, peas, and stewed apples, but allowed to drink all the water he could.

Sans-Gene, Madame, the nickname of Marie Therese Figueur (1774–1861), who, born in Burgundy, was enrolled at the age of 19 in a cavalry regiment commanded by one of her uncles, went to Germany with the French and Batavian armies, charged at Hohenlinden, took part in the siege of Toulon, was in the Italian, Spanish, and Austrian campaigns, and fought at Austerlitz and in Russia. During the Hundred Days the Emperor conferred the Legion of Honor upon her, and she charged at Waterloo for the last time. With the Restoration she left the army to marry Marshal Lefebvre, Duke of Dantzic (1755–1820). She was then 39. Victorien Sardou, in his drama *Madame Sans-Gene*, has taken this martial character and made her a vulgarian whose comic familiarity is tolerated by Napoleon.

Saracinesca, Prince, a character in a novel by Marion Crawford, *Saracinesca* (1887), which forms the first in a series dealing with the social and domestic life of nineteenth century Roman aristocracy. The love affairs of his son Sant Ilario and of the high-souled Corona d'Astrardente, who, though haplessly married to a superannuated dandy, remains true to her husband, occupy the first volume; the solution of that entanglement is given in the second, *Sant Ilario* (1889). In *Don Orsino* (1892) the titular hero is Sant Ilario's son, who occupies himself with building speculations. The concluding volume, *Corleone* (1898), is a Sicilian episode in the history of the Saracinescas, bringing them in contact with the Corleones,—"the worst blood in Italy."

Sardanapalus, hero of Lord Byron's tragedy (1821), based on the Greek fable of the last Assyrian king who fell B.C. 823. He is here represented as generous and amiable, but so fond of pleasure, so vain and indolent, that his enemies despise him for his apparent weakness and

effeminacy. Arbaces, a Mede, and Beleses, a Chaldean soothsayer, conspire against him. With their adherents they attack the palace, and force their way into the grand hall. Sardanapalus, roused at last, fights with great bravery, astonishing his friends and appalling his enemies. But the rebels are finally victorious. Sardanapalus, at the instigation of his favorite slave Myrrha, has a funeral pile raised and immolates himself upon it. Myrrha applies the torch and then throws herself into the flames to be consumed with the king, her master. The only deviation from history in the above is in the introduction of the slave Myrrha. The soothsayer's name, however, should have been spelled Belesis, not Beleses, and the second syllable should be short.

Savage, Captain, a naval commander in Frederick Marryat's novel, *Peter Simple* (1833), daring, brilliant and successful, but a severe martinet. The character is drawn from Thomas Cochrane, tenth Earl of Dundonald, with whom the author shipped as midshipman at the beginning of his naval career. In one or other of his traits the same original may be traced in other portraits from the same hand,—the Captain C. of *Frank Mildmay* (1829), Captain M. of *The King's Own*, and Captain Maclean of *Joseph Faithful* (1834).

Savonarola, a famous Florentine preacher, religious enthusiast, and would-be reformer, figures as an important character in George Eliot's novel *Romola* (1863), and also to a lesser extent in Mrs. Harriet Beecher Stowe's *Agnes of Sorrento* (1862). George Eliot's portrait is a powerful study of ardent ideals ending in failure. Savonarola's personal aims and longings for the glory that he thought his due are made to become his ruin and to furnish the road to his defeat and death.

Savoyard Vicar, in Rousseau's novel *Emile*, a mild and gentle priest who believes more in good works than in any sectarian creed, and whose "Confessions" form an important episode in the book. The character combines the traits of two of Rousseau's early instructors, M. Gatier, his gentle, melancholy studious tutor in the Seminary of Annecy, in Savoy; and the Abbé Gaimé, whom, in his boyhood, he had met in Turin, an ecclesiastic more remarkable for the breadth and liberality than for the orthodoxy of his religious opinions. Rousseau's Vicar is a deist at heart who cannot bring himself either to accept absolutely or to reject the Gospel, but who deems that until we know more fully what the truth is it is best to respect the public order, and to refrain from disturbing the established worship, and who remains a priest in full communion with the Church for much the same reasons that actuate Browning's Bishop Blougram. The portraiture did not prove agreeable to either the advocates or the antagonists of revealed religion; the first saw in it a dangerous attack upon orthodoxy, and the latter felt it was a powerful blow against crude atheism and materialism. *Le Vicaire Savoyard*, Voltaire wrote to a friend, " deserves all possible chastisement. The Judas abandons us just as our philosophy was about to triumph."

Sawin, Birdofreedom, a character introduced into Lowell's *Biglow Papers.* A fellow-townsman of Hosea Biglow's, he enlists in the Mexican armies a volunteer, and writes home a melancholy account of the horrors into which he has been inveigled. His letters, three in number, are versified by Hosea.

Sawyer, Bob, in Dickens's *Pickwick Papers* (1836), friend and roommate of Benjamin Allen (*q.v.*), both medical students of dishevelled appearance and rollicking bohemian habits, revelling in beer and oysters, and devoting as little attention as possible to their profession. Eventually Sawyer sets up medical practice in Bristol, with small success. Sam Weller delights to call him Mr. Sawbones.

Sawyer, Tom, hero of Mark Twain's novel of that name (1876), a story of boyish adventure in a village

in Missouri on the Mississippi River. He reappears less prominently in its sequel *Huckleberry Finn* (1885). The character is undoubtedly reminiscent of the author's own youth.

Both boys have their full share of boyish imagination; and Tom Sawyer, being given to books, lets his imagination run on robbers and pirates and genies, with a perfect understanding with himself that, if you want to get fun out of this life, you must never hesitate to make believe very hard; and, with Tom's youth and health, he never finds it hard to make believe and to be a pirate at will, or to summon an attendant spirit, or to rescue a prisoner from the deepest dungeon 'neath the castle moat. But in Huck this imagination has turned to superstition; he is a walking repository of the juvenile folklore of the Mississippi Valley—a folklore partly traditional among the white settlers, but largely influenced by intimate association with the negroes.—*Saturday Review,* January 31, 1885.

Scapin (It. *Scapino*, either from *scappino*, a sock, or *scappare*, to run away), one of the famous traditionary characters of the Italian stage whom the French have borrowed, and whom Molière has immortalized in *Fourberies de Scapin.* He is the only one of Molière's valets who is entirely free from cowardice; ever ready to risk his shoulders in any adventure. Thus he may be considered the founder of a race which did not take possession of the theatre till many years after Molière's death—the race of Intrigants, Aventuriers, and Chevaliers d'Industrie, who revel in intrigue for its own sake, who hunger and thirst for the unknown and the forbidden, for excitement, change, adventure at all hazards and at any price. The Italian Scapino is one of the many descendants of the Davus and Tranio of classic comedy, and is represented as a valet of infinite wit and knavery, a trickster, a babbler, and a coward, who ingratiates himself with the prodigal son of a family by espousing his cause as against the miserly father, and by assisting him in all his intrigues, but is ruled throughout quite as much by interest as by inclination. Scapino originated in Milan.

His traditional dress, on the Italian stage, included a mask, a large plumed hat, a heavy cloak, and a wooden sword. In France he dropped his mask, and was arrayed in garments striped green and white.

Schedoni, in Mrs. Ann Radcliffe's romance *The Italian,* a wicked, able, and hypocritical monk, profligate, unrelenting, and implacable.

Schlemihl, Peter, hero and title of a tale (1813), by Adalbert von Chamisso. A poor tailor, he tells his own story. In exchange for an inexhaustible purse he had parted with his shadow to a mysterious little man in grey. At first he exults in his new opulence. But wherever he goes questions concerning his lost shadow assail him. Suspicions of all sorts are awakened. He is shunned and avoided; his very servants refuse to live with him; his betrothed jilts him; and poor Schlemihl finds refuge in a desert where there are none to mock him. One day the little man reappears and offers to return the shadow at the price of Peter's soul. Peter, in his wretchedness, is on the point of yielding, but luckily asks after a man whom he suspects of having entered into a similar compact. The devil is forced to show him the corpse of this other victim. Peter in horror flings the magic purse into a chasm, and is finally relieved of his tormentor.

Many attempts have been made to read an allegorical meaning into Schlemihl's story. Chamisso himself expressly denied any didactic purpose.

"I have seldom," he says, "any ulterior aim in my poetry; if an anecdote or a word strikes me in a particular manner, I suppose it must have the same effect on others, and I set to work, wrestling laboriously with the language, till the thing comes out distinctly. 'Schlemihl,' too, came forth in this way. I had lost on a journey my hat, portmanteau, gloves, pocket-handkerchief, and all my movable estate. Fouqué asked me whether I had not also lost my shadow, and we pictured to ourselves the effects of such a disaster." Nevertheless, consciously or unconsciously, he was influenced by a world-wide tradition.

The tale of Peter Schlemihl belongs to a family of legends which show that a man's shadow has been generally regarded as a sort of spiritual attendant of the body, which under certain circumstances it may permanently forsake. In strict accordance with this idea, not only in classic languages, but in various barbaric tongues, the word meaning "shadow" expresses also the *soul* or other self.—JOHN FISKE: *Myths and Myth-makers.*

Scholar Gipsy, in Matthew Arnold's poem of that name (1853), the hero of an Oxford tradition, that a lad in the University many years ago wandered away with the gypsies in search of their strange lore and still haunts the fields and watersides. The poet and his poet friend Arthur H. Clough, in their wanderings around Oxford, realize that the life of the vagrant scholar was finer than their own.

Schönberg-Cotta, Friedrich and **Elsè,** the feigned authors of *The Chronicles of the Schönberg-Cotta Family* (1865), by Mrs. Elizabeth Charles. Their father is an improvident printer with eight children to provide for; their aunt, Ursula Cotta, adopts Martin Luther, who is the school-fellow of Friedrich at the university of Erfurt; and a fellow monk in an Augustinian monastery. Finally the two friends go to Rome together, and their experiences in that city lead to the revolt against the Papacy, in which Friedrich becomes the faithful henchman of Luther.

Schweidler, Mary, heroine of a romance *The Amber Witch* (Ger. *Die Bernstein Hexe,* 1843), by Johann Wilhelm Meinhold. Purporting to be a contemporaneous chronicle by Herr Schweidler, pastor of Coserow in Pomerania, of certain events that took place in his parish in the early seventeenth century, the hoax for a period completely deceived the antiquarian world.

During the distress occasioned by the Thirty Years' War, Schweidler's daughter Mary has discovered a vein of amber in the Streckelburg Mountain. She tells her father. They dare not disclose their good fortune, but secretly sell the treasure, and, after supplying their own wants, devote the remaining money to the relief of the starving villagers. Mary has incurred the ill-will of Elsie, the real witch of the village, who takes advantage of her mysterious nightly visits to the mountain and her stores of unexplained wealth to accuse the maiden of a compact with Satan. She is tried and condemned to the stake. Her lover, Count Rudiger of Ravenstein, appears as her deliverer and the story comes to a triumphant close with her happy marriage.

Scriblerus Club, a short-lived association, founded in 1714, which included among its members many of the foremost wits of the Queen Anne period,—Pope, Swift, Arbuthnot, Congreve, Atterburg, Harley, and Gray. Directly or indirectly it inspired Arbuthnot's *Memoirs of Martinus Scriblerus,* Swift's *Travels of Gulliver,* and Pope's *Treatise of Bathos.*

Scriblerus, Cornelius, the father of Martinus (see below). A learned gentleman, an antiquary by profession, he has eccentric ideas on education. The boy is brought up in such manner that everything contributes to the improvement of his mind, even to his dress. Cornelius invented for him " a geographical suit of clothes, which might give him some hints of that science and likewise some knowledge of the commerce of different nations. He had a French hat with an African feather, Holland shirt and Flanders lace, English cloth lined with Indian silk; his gloves were Italian, and his shoes were Spanish. He was made to observe this and daily catechised thereupon, which his father was wont to call travelling at home." The Scriblerus family may have given hints to Sterne for his account of Tristam Shandy and his father.

Scriblerus, Martinus, hero of a curious burlesque, *Memoirs of the Extraordinary Life, Works, and Discoveries of Martinus Scriblerus,* usually published among Pope's works, but known to have been mainly written by John Arbuthnot, with occasional assistance from Pope and Swift. " To talk of Martin in any hands but yours," says Swift in a letter to Arbuthnot, " is folly. For you every day gave us better hints than all of us together could do in a twelve-month." Pope explains that the design was to ridicule all the false taste in learning, under the character of a man of capacity that had dipped into every art and science, but injudiciously in each. Under the tutelage of his father (see SCRIBLERUS, CORNELIUS), Martin was brought up a prig from childhood. He had the Greek alphabet stamped on his gingerbread, played games after the manner of the ancients, and wore a geographical suit of clothes. He became a critic, practised medicine, studied diseases of the mind, and endeavored to discover the seat of the soul. Then he started on his travels in the countries visited by Gulliver. Here the work comes to an abrupt end.

Scrooge, Ebenezer, hero of Dickens's *Christmas Carol* (1843), surviving partner of the firm of Scrooge and Marley, stockholders. " Oh! but he was a tight-fisted hand at the grindstone, Scrooge!—a squeezing, wrenching, grasping, scraping, clutching, covetous old sinner! Hard and sharp as flint, from which no steel had ever struck out generous fire; secret and self-contained and solitary as an oyster. . . . He carried his own low temperature always about with him: he iced his office in the dog-days, and didn't thaw it one degree at Christmas." The story tells how, through the agency of three midnight visitants—the Ghosts of Christmas Past, of Christmas Present, and of Christmas to-Come—he was converted into a genial and benevolent worshipper of the Christmas season.

Scudamore, Blythe, hero of Richard D. Blackmore's novel of the Napoleonic period in England, *Springhaven* (1887). Familiarly known as " Scuddy," his behavior on land and sea, in war and in love, is always brave yet considerate and chivalric. " The gentle Scuddy," his creator calls him, and proceeds to describe him as " brave and modest, wholesome and natural, facing the cannon's mouth without flinching, and recklessly flinging down his heart for a pretty, foolish girl to trample on." His sweetheart is Dolly Darling.

Scudamore, Sir, in Spenser's *Faërie Queene*, Book iv. His name is corrupted from the words *escu d'amour*, the shield of love. He was so called because, against twenty rival combatants, he had secured for himself a shield, hanging in the temple of Venus over this inscription: WHOSOEVER BE THIS SHIELD, FAIRE AMORET BE HIS.

Scythrop, in Peacock's satiric novel, *Nightmare Abbey*, a caricature of the poet Shelley. Specially pointed is the passage wherein Scythrop, loving two ladies at once, tells his distracted father that he will free himself from his dilemma by suicide. Shelley himself admitted the likeness and was amused by the caricature. After all, the portrait of the man Shelley as depicted by Peacock, directly in his *Memorials* and indirectly in this novel, is more attractive than the " divine," characterless humanitarian whom hero-worshippers love to paint.

Sebastian, in *Twelfth Night*, a young gentleman, brother to Viola; full of the rashness and impetuosity of youth. Another Sebastian, a drunken sailor, figures in *The Tempest*.

Séchard, David, in Balzac's *Lost Illusions*, a tender, melancholy, meditative young man, the friend of the hero, Lucien de Rubempré. He is born and bred in the country, and so preserves his soul unspotted from the contaminations of the city, which prove the ruin of his friend.

Sedley, Amelia, in Thackeray's *Vanity Fair*, a sweet-tempered, gentle, generous, and deeply affectionate young woman, who marries George Osborne, and cherishes his memory after death, despite Major Dobbin's persistent courtship of her and her growing fondness for him, until Becky Sharp disillusionizes her. " Couldn't forget him? " cries Rebecca, " that selfish humbug, that low-bred cockney, that padded booby, who had neither wit, manners, nor heart, and was no more to be compared to your friend of the bamboo cane than you to Queen Elizabeth."

The character is obviously akin to the Amelia Booth of Fielding, but the name Amelia was that of Thackeray's grandmother, and the character was modelled after three women of his own circle. " You know you are only a piece of Amelia," Thackeray wrote to Mrs. Brookfield. " My mother is another half; my poor little wife—*y est pour beaucoup*."

We hear that Emmy Sedley was partly suggested by Mrs. Brookfield, partly by Thackeray's mother, much by his own wife. There scarcely seems room for so many elements in Emmy's personality. For some reason ladies do not love her, nor do men adore her . . . She is not clever, she is not very beautiful, she is unhappy, and she can be jealous. One pities her, and that is akin to a more tender sentiment; one pities her while she sits in the corner, and Becky's green eyes flatter her oaf of a husband; one pities her in the poverty of her father's house, in the famous battle over Daffy's Elixir, in the separation from the younger George . . . Yes, Emmy is more complex than she seems, and perhaps it needed three ladies to contribute the various elements of her person and her character.—ANDREW LANG: *Essays in Little*.

Sedley, Joseph, commonly called " Jos," the brother of Amelia, a fat and foolish beau and *bon vivant*, lazy, peevish, timid, boastful, and self-indulgent. " He was as vain as a girl; and perhaps his extreme shyness was one of the results of his extreme vanity " (chap. iii). Timorous before ladies, yet with an ardent desire to stand well with them, he eagerly welcomes the overtures of his sister's friend Becky Sharp, but is frightened off just as he had decided to propose to her. Fond of the military, he wears moustachios and a frogged coat and accompanies the army to Brussels, but flees terror-stricken while the battle of Waterloo is raging. On his return to India, he brags so much of what he had seen and heard and done on the fateful day, that he acquired quite a reputation for courage among the ignorant and was dubbed Waterloo Sedley. He is not ungenerous or unkindly, he befriends Amelia in her poverty, and in the end falls a victim to the middle-aged wiles of his former flame, Becky Sharp.

Selika, heroine of a five-act opera, *L'Africaine* (1865), words by Eugene Scribe, music by Meyerbeer. She is the queen of an island off the African coast, who falls in love with Vasco da Gama, the Portuguese explorer, and immolates herself for his sake.

Selim, name of the hero of Byron's poem, *The Bride of Abydos* (see ZULEIKA), and also of Moore's *The Light of the Harem* in Lalla Rookh (see NOURMAHAL). Edward Moore, in a poem called *Selim the Persian* (1748), makes an ironical defence of Lord Lyttleton under this name.

Selkirk, Alexander (1676–1723), a Scotch sailor, whose story gave Daniel Defoe the suggestion for *Robinson Crusoe.* His captain, one Straddling, took offence at him, and left him on the uninhabited island of Juan Fernandez in the Pacific Ocean, where he remained for four years and four months (1704–1708), until rescued by Captain Woods Rogers. Hence Juan Fernandez has often, but wrongfully, been called Crusoe's Island (see CRUSOE). Alexander Selkirk is the subject of a famous lyric by William Cowper, beginning:

I am monarch of all I survey,
My right there is none to dispute.

Sellers, Col. Mulberry, chief character in *The Gilded Age*, a novel by Mark Twain and Charles Dudley Warner, which was dramatized in 1876, with John T. Raymond in this part. There is a suggestion of Micawber in Sellers, and it is curious to find, from Paine's *Life of Mark Twain*, that Twain's father, like Dickens's, was of the Micawber ilk. But Mr. Clemens, Sr., had only the gloomy side of Micawber. The gay and buoyant side was quite alien to that unhappy man. Mark Twain's invincible optimist, Col. Sellers, was not his father, but his mother's favorite cousin, James Lampton.

Many persons regarded "Colonel Sellers" as a fiction, an invention, an extravagant impossibility, and did me the honor to call him a "creation"; but they were mistaken. I merely put him on paper as he was; he was not a person who could be exaggerated. The incidents which looked most extravagant, both in the book and on the stage, were not inventions of mine but were facts of his life; and I was present when they were developed. John T. Raymond's audiences used to come near to dying with laughter over the turnip-eating scene; but, extravagant as the scene was, it was faithful to the facts, in all its absurd details. The thing happened in Lampton's own house, and I was present. In fact I was myself the guest who ate the turnips. In the hands of a great actor that piteous scene would have dimmed any manly spectator's eyes with tears, and racked his ribs apart with laughter at the same time. But Raymond was great in humorous portrayal only. In that he was superb; he was wonderful—in a word, great; in all things else he was a pigmy of the pigmies.

The real Colonel Sellers, as I knew him in James Lampton, was a pathetic and beautiful spirit, a manly man, a straight and honorable man, a man with a big, foolish, unselfish heart in his bosom, a man born to be loved; and he was loved by all his friends, and by his family worshipped. It is the right word. To them he was but little less than a god. The real Colonel Sellers was never on the stage. Only half of him was there. Raymond could not play the other half of him; it was above his level. That half was made up of qualities of which Raymond was wholly destitute.—MARK TWAIN: *Chapters from My Autobiography, North American Review.*

Senta, in the opera of *The Flying Dutchman*, is an interpolation by Wagner himself in order to add a love element to the mediæval legend. According to this version of the story, the Dutchman is allowed once in every seven years to come on shore, with the chance of ridding himself from his curse if he can find a woman willing to devote herself to him with her whole heart. The experiment is fraught with considerable danger to the woman, for, if she breaks faith, her punishment is nothing less than eternal perdition. Herr Wagner has made Senta quite ready to fall in love with the doomed Van der Decken, having long been in love with a portrait of him which hangs in her father's house. But she has been betrothed to Erik until the moment of the Dutchman's appearance, when she cheerfully throws over her former lover; and it is only a misunderstanding which prevents the Dutchman marrying her and living happily ever afterward. The rapidity with which Senta transfers her love from Erik to the Dutchman tends to injure a character of much beauty; and the eagerness with which Daland, her father, accepts as his son-in-law a mysterious stranger who carries about with him a chest full of treasure, gives a somewhat disagreeable aspect to the character of the proverbially bold and open-hearted seaman.

Sentry, Captain, a member of the fictitious Spectator Club, which was supposed to look after the fortunes of that paper. The character was sketched by Sir Richard Steele in the opening number and subsequently filled out by both Addison and Steele. The original of this character was Colonel Kempenfelt, of Sweden, father of an admiral in the British navy who was lost with all his crew, on board the *Royal George.*

Sevier, Dr., hero of a novel of that name (1883) by George W. Cable, a benevolent, upright, and severely strict physician of New Orleans. " His inner heart was all of flesh," we are told, " but his demands for the rectitude of mankind pointed out like the muzzles of cannon through the embrasure of his virtues."

Sewell, Rev. Mr., in W. D. Howells's novel, *The Minister's Charge* (1887), the titular " minister," whose amiable habit of telling pleasant fibs brings Lemuel down to Boston with impossible expectations and illusions.

He ministers to a very respectable Boston flock; he is sincere, in spite of his amiable fibs; he wishes to do right and to be father confessor to his people, without the faintest knowledge of moral theology or any training for the work except a good heart and some experiences of the human race in general and the Bostonian in particular.—*Catholic World.*

Seyton, Catherine, heroine of Scott's historical romance, *The Abbot,* a " waiting damsel " to Mary, Queen of Scots, who inspired Roland Græme with an enthusiasm for " the good cause " as loyal and lofty as her own.

Sganarelle, one of Molière's most famous characters, who made his first appearance in a farce called *Sganarelle, or the Imaginary Cuckold,* and was afterward introduced into other plays, with somewhat varying characteristics according to the needs of the story,—*i.e., Le Festin de Pierre,* where he is valet to Don Juan; *L'Amour Médecin* (1664), where he is father to Lucinde; *Le Médecin Malgré Lui,* where he is the husband of Martine and a wood-chopper forced to assume the character of a physician; *L'École des Maris,* where, with his brother Ariste, he brings up two orphan sisters so as to train them into model wives for themselves and both are wofully deceived; and *Le Mariage Forcé,* which, though later in production than the *Cocu Imaginaire,* is logically earlier, since the latter now forms the sequel.

Like Harlequin or Punch, Sganarelle in fact is rather an abstraction or type of character than an individual, and his various avatars are irreconcilable the one with the other.

Molière's Sganarelle, under all his various aspects of valet, of husband, of father to Lucinde, of brother to Ariste, of teacher, of wood-chopper, of doctor, is a character who belongs wholly to the poet, as Panurge belongs to Rabelais, Falstaff to Shakespeare, Sancho to Cervantes; he is the ugly side of humanity personified; the odd, surly, morose, selfish, low, cowardly side; alternately cringing and charlatanic, peevish and absurd,—the nasty side which excites derision. In certain joyous moments, as when Sganarelle touches the nurse's bosom, he resembles the portly Gorgibus, who, in his turn, reminds one of Chrysale, that other jolly round-bellied humorist. Sganarelle, paltry and pitiful as Panurge, has nevertheless managed to leave behind him a posterity worthy of both, among whom we must remember Pangloss and not forget Gringoire. —ST. BEUVE.

Shafton, Sir Piercie, in Scott's historical romance, *The Monastery,* a relative of the Duke of Northumberland on one side, on the other a grandson of old Overstich the tailor. He affects the " euphuistic " style of conversation in fashion at the Elizabethan courts, but rather overdoes it and degenerates into too obvious burlesque. In spite of his affectations he is capable of genuine energy of mind, and his chivalrous companionship with Mysie of the Mill proved him worthy of her simple devotion.

Shakespeare, William, the poet-dramatist, is the hero of W. S. Landor's dramatic colloquy, *The Examination of Shakespeare for Deer-stealing* (1834).

No play of character more sparkling occurs in any of Landor's writings than is struck out by the conjunction of such opposite types as are here presented,—the boy-poet, overflowing with genius, emotion, and animal spirits, witty, wise, joyous, and serious by turns; Sir Thomas Lucy, the justice, stupid, vain, devout, and kind-hearted; Master Silas, the chaplain, hard-headed, vulgar, malicious, and sensual; Joseph Carnaby, the chief witness, super-stitious and hypocritical, conscious of his tattered reputation while speaking truth for the nonce. Inimitable, too, is the de-scription of Shakespeare's tactics with the justice, whom he handles after the manner of an angler, baiting his hook with tempting morsels of flattery, and spinning out a line of interminable digression, which he adroitly manœuvres until his prey is caught.

Shallow, Justice Robert, sketched at full length in *Merry Wives of Windsor* (1598), appeared earlier in *II Henry IV* (1598) and later in *Henry V* (1599). He is a foo, a braggart, and a liar, boasting of sins in his youth which he never com-mitted. It has been plausibly sur-mised that the justice is a reminiscent caricature of Shakespeare's boyhood enemy, Sir Thomas Lucy of Charl-cote, near Stratford, who prosecuted him for deer-stealing and incidentally drove him from Stratford to London.

Shandy, Captain Tobias, better known as **Uncle Toby,** the real hero of Sterne's *Tristram Shandy*, a cap-tain in the British army, retired in consequence of wounds received at the siege of Namur, but still keeping up his military tastes, interests, and habits. Gallantry, simplicity, mod-esty, and benevolence are his leading traits. He is supposed to have been drawn from the author's father, who was an army lieutenant.

What shall I say to thee, thou quintes-sence of the milk of human kindness, thou reconciler of war (as far as it was once neces-sary to reconcile it), thou returner to child-hood during peace, thou lover of widows, thou master of the best of corporals, thou whistler at excommunications, thou high and only final Christian gentleman, thou pitier of the Devil himself, divine Uncle Toby! Why, this I will say, made bold by thy example, and caring nothing for what anybody may think of it who does not, in some measure, partake of thy nature, that he who created thee was the wisest man since

the days of Shakespeare; and that Shake-speare himself, mighty reflector of things as they were, but no anticipator, never arrived at a character like thine.—LEIGH HUNT.

My Uncle Toby is one of the finest com-pliments ever paid to human nature. He is the most unoffending of God's creatures; or, as the French express it, *un tel petit bonhomme!* Of his bowling-green, his sieges, and his amours, who would say or think anything amiss?—HAZLITT.

Shandy, Tristram, the nominal hero of the novel of that name by Laurence Sterne.

Shandy, Walter, in Sterne's novel, *Tristram Shandy*, the father of the titular hero.

The author supposed in him a man of an active and metaphysical, but, at the same time, a whimsical cast of mind, whom too much and too miscellaneous reading had brought within a step or two of madness, and who acted, in the ordinary affairs of life, upon the absurd theories adopted by the pedants of past ages. He is most ad-mirable contrasted with his wife, well de-scribed as a good lady of the *poco-curante* school, who neither obstructed the course of her husband's hobby-horse—to use a phrase which Sterne has rendered classical —nor could be prevailed upon to spare him the least admiration for the grace and dex-terity with which he managed it.—SIR WALTER SCOTT.

There has been a great deal said and writ-ten about the plagiarisms of Sterne; but the only real plagiarism he has been guilty of (if such theft were a crime) is in taking Tristram Shandy's father from Martin's, the elder Scriblerus. The original idea of the character, that is, of the opinionated, captious old gentleman who is pedantic, not from profession, but choice, belongs to Arbuthnot.—HAZLITT.

Sharp, Rebecca, more familiarly known as Becky, the chief female character in Thackeray's *Vanity Fair*. A friendless girl, with " the dismal precocity of poverty," she early determines to marry well and make her way in the world. Her first mark is Joseph Sedley, brother of her school friend Amelia; but he is frightened away. She next sets her cap for Rawdon Crawley, whom she wins, and learns too late that she might have had his wealthy father and that he himself is disinherited on account of his marriage. Neverthe-less, she sets up an establishment, and shows him how by cleverness and tact and cajoling her admirers she can maintain a social position, and by wheedling and ruining her tradesman she can live on nothing a year. Rawdon detects her in an intrigue with Lord Steyne. Though she stoutly maintains her innocence, he obtains a separation from her. She sinks to a tawdry bohemian existence on the Continent until Joseph Sedley once more falls in her way. She strips him of all he has and comes into his insurance money after his suspicious death.

A friend congratulated him once on that touch in *Vanity Fair* in which Becky admires her husband when he is giving Steyne the punishment that is ruining her for life. "Well," he said, "when I wrote the sentence, I slapped my fist on the table and said, '*That* is a touch of genius!'"—JAMES T. FIELDS: *Yesterdays with Authors*, p. 27.

She, abbreviated from "She-who must-be-obeyed," the official title of Ayesha, heroine of Rider Haggard's romance *She* (1887). Ayesha is a beautiful sorceress, dwelling somewhere in the darkest deeps of darkest Africa, who is reputed to be immortal and is surrounded by retainers as weird as herself. Two thousand years ago, it appears, she had treacherously compassed the death of a priest of Isis, whose descendant, a young Englishman named Leo Vincey, penetrates her fastnesses and fascinates her by his hereditary likeness. He too falls in love with her, but, the cycle having been rounded, she is consumed in the mystic flames she herself had evoked to renew her youth.

Sheppard, John, familiarly known as Jack, a famous English highway robber (1702-1724), hero of numerous ballads and imaginative works; notably *Harlequin Sheppard* (1725), a pantomime by John Thurmond, a pretended autobiography attributed to Defoe (1724), and a novel, *Jack Sheppard* (1839), by William Harrison Ainsworth. A carpenter by trade, Sheppard sprang from a long line of honest carpenters in Stepney. In, early youth he fell in with a loose woman, Elizabeth Lyon, known as "Edgeworth Bess," who with another girl, "Poll Maggott," incited most

of his crimes. His recklessness, his courage, and his generous disposition made him a sort of popular hero. He made two remarkable escapes from Newgate, excellently described in Ainsworth's romance, though the most famous of these two chapters is said to have been written by William Maginn. Two hundred thousand people attended his execution at Tyburn, November 16, 1724.

Sheva, hero of R. Cumberland's comedy *The Jew* (1776), written to justify the Hebrew race from current Christian calumnies. He is rescued by Don Carlos from an *auto-da-fé* at Cadiz and brought to London, where the don's son, Charles Ratcliffe, rescues him in turn from a howling London mob. In return Sheva makes Charles his heir and gives his sister £10,000 as her marriage portion when she weds Frederick Bertram. Modest, benevolent, and philanthropic, Sheva is "the widow's friend, the orphans' father, the poor man's protector, and the universal dispenser of charity; but he ever shrank to let his left hand know what his right hand did." The Jews of England made up a handsome purse for Cumberland to reward him for this championship of their race.

In the Old Testament Sheva was one of David's scribes (2 Sam. xx, 25). Dryden and Tate, in *Absalom and Achitophel*, Part II (1682), bestow the name upon Sir Roger Lestrange, censor of the press under Charles II and editor of the *Observator*, an unswerving royalist sheet. Dryden says:

Than Sheva, none more loyal zeal have shown,
Wakeful as Judah's lion for the throne.

Shipton, Mother, the name of a famous prophetess in the reign of Henry VIII, who is said to have successfully predicted the death of many famous men. Bret Harte gives the nickname to one of the characters in his *Outcasts of Poker Flat*, a woman of ill fame who starves herself to save a younger outcast. (See SHIPTON, MOTHER, in vol. II.)

Shore, Jane, an historical character (*circa* 1450–1527), who in 1470 forsook her husband, William Shore, to become the mistress of Edward IV. She had great influence over that king through her wit, tact, and merry disposition. After Edward's death she was accused of harlotry and witchcraft by Richard III and forced to do penance in the public streets, " going before the crosse in procession upon a Sonday with a taper in her hand." She is the heroine of a ballad preserved in Percy's *Reliques*, of an anonymous drama, *History of the Life and Death of Master Shore and Jane Shore his Wife*, and of a more famous tragedy, *Jane Shore* (1714), by Nicholas Rowe. Rowe makes her husband come to Jane's rescue in her downfall, but he is seized by the minions of Richard and Jane dies.

Shylock, in Shakespeare's comedy *The Merchant of Venice*, a Jew usurer. He hates Antonio, partly for reviling his religion, but more especially for that he spoils his business by lowering the rates of interest in Venice. Therefore, when Antonio comes to borrow money from him, he half jestingly ensnares him into a compact whereby the borrower shall lose a pound of flesh if the debt be not promptly returned at a given time. Shylock's impassioned appeal in Act iii, 1, is almost the only scene where Shakespeare shows any sympathy for him.

The diverse interpretations given by notable actors to the part of Shylock have their origin in a certain incongruity between the story that Shakespeare accepted and the character of the Jew as it came to life in his hands. Some actors, careful of the story, have laid stress on revenge, cunning, and the thirst for innocent blood. Others, convinced by Shakespeare's sympathy, have presented so sad and human a figure that the verdict of the court is accepted without enthusiasm . . . The difficulty is in the play. The Jew of the story is the monster of the mediæval imagination, and the story almost requires such a monster, if it is to go with ringing effect on the stage. Shylock is a man, and a man more sinned against than sinning. Antonio and Bassanio are pale shadows of men compared with this gaunt, tragic figure, whose love of his race is as deep as life; who pleads the cause of a common humanity against the cruelties of prejudice; whose very hatred has in it something of the nobility of patriotic passion;

whose heart is stirred with tender memories even in the midst of his lament over the stolen ducats; who in the end, is dismissed, unprotesting, to insult and oblivion.— WALTER RALEIGH: *Shakespeare.*

Sidonia, in Disraeli's novel of *Coningsby, or The New Generation* (1844) a character in whom the author paints his ideal Jew. It is drawn partly from the actual traits and deeds of Baron Alfred de Rothschild and partly from the undeveloped possibilities which the author discovered in himself at his then age of thirty-nine. Sidonia's function in the novel is to educate Harry Coningsby, as Harry in his turn is to educate the New Generation.

Sidonia is a Hebrew of immense fortune in the prime of youthful manhood and with an athletic frame which sickness has never tried; affable and gracious but, though unreserved in manner, impenetrable beneath the surface; and yet with a rare gift of expression and an intellect that, matured by long meditation, and assisted by that absolute freedom from prejudice which is the compensatory possession of a man without a country, enables him to fathom, as it were by intuition, the depth of every question.—MONYPENNY: *Life of Benjamin Disraeli.*

Sieglière, Mademoiselle de la, heroine and title of a novel by Jules Sandeau.

Very good again is *Mademoiselle de la Sieglière*, with its curious theme of an enriched peasant driven by aristocratic wiles to restore to his old seigneur the estate which the latter has forfeited by emigration.— GEORGE SAINTSBURY.

Sigismunda or **Sigismonda,** heroine of Dryden's poem *Sigismunda and Guiscardo.* (See vol. II.)

Sikes, Bill, in Dickens's *Oliver Twist*, a brutal thief and housebreaker, who murders his mistress, Nancy.

A thoroughly hardened ruffian of the sturdy English type, with a sullen ferocity which penetrates his whole nature and allies him to his true brethren, the beasts of prey; there is no room in his breast for conscience, or pity, or physical fear; his attendant and moral shadow, the dog, has a character seemingly caught from that of his master; or perhaps we should say that Sikes the dog appears to have been arrested in that process of evolution which, when allowed free course, resulted in the production of Sikes the man. The account of the murder of Nancy is one

22

of the most harrowing scenes in romance; and there is great power displayed in the description of Sikes's flight afterwards, with the phantom of his victim pursuing him, the "widely-staring eyes, so lustreless and glassy," meeting his at every turn. Dickens, when writing these scenes, realized them so intensely that they may be said to have taken possession of him. When he read the account of the murder of Nancy to his wife, she became so affected that he describes her as being "in an unspeakable state."—E. P. WHIPPLE.

Silva, Don, in George Eliot's dramatic poem, *The Spanish Gypsy* (1868), a nobleman in love with Fedalma. A beautiful and elaborate portrait, in which the author has aimed to depict a young nobleman as splendid in person and in soul as the dawning splendor of his native country. In spite of the poem being called in honor of his mistress, Don Silva is really the central figure in the work.

Silver, John, the principal character in R. L. Stevenson's romance, *Treasure Island* (1883). The *Saturday Review* declared that the book ought to have been entitled *John Silver, Pirate*, and in fact Stevenson had originally called it the *Sea-Cook.* For John Silver, pirate by profession, sailed as sea-cook aboard the *Hispaniola* when she started out on a search for Flint's buried hoard in Treasure Island.

He is a big fellow, "very tall and strong, with a face as big as a ham; plain and pale, but intelligent and smiling;" his left leg is cut off at the hip, and he carries a crutch, which he manages "with wonderful dexterity, hopping about on it like a bird." He has travelled all the world over; he has a black wife; he is master of a parrot named Captain Flint; he is so helpful and clever, so smooth-spoken and powerful and charming, that everybody is deceived in him. Of course he makes himself the most useful of men while the ship is fitting out, and of course a considerable proportion of the crew are of his discovery and recommendation. The consequences are plain to the meanest capacity. There is a mutiny, and they hoist the black flag, the noble Jolly Roger; there are fights and murders and adventures; only a few of the expedition escape with their lives; and it is all John Silver's doing.—*Saturday Review*, December 8, 1883.

Simple, David, hero of a novel by Sarah Fielding, *The Adventures of David Simple* (1744), who travels through London and Westminster "in search of a faithful friend."

A sequel, *The Familiar Letters between the Principal Characters* in David Simple (1747), was the occasion for a famous contrast which Samuel Richardson, in a letter dated December, 1756, drew between Susan and her brother, Henry Fielding. "What a knowledge of the human heart! Well might a critical judge of writing say, as he did to me, that your late brother's knowledge of it was not (fine writer as he was) comparable to yours. His was but as the knowledge of the outside of a clock-work machine, while yours was that of all the finer springs and movements of the inside." Curiously enough, this is very much the praise which, a dozen years later, Johnson, no doubt the critical judge referred to, gave to Richardson himself. "There was as great a difference between them [Richardson and Fielding]," he said, "as between a man who knew how a watch was made, and a man who could tell the hour by looking on the dial-plate."

Simplicissimus, in an historical romance of that name by J. C. von Grimmelshausen (1669), is the son of a poor Spessart farmer during the Thirty Years' War. At ten years of age his father is murdered by a band of plundering soldiers. He is educated by a hermit, he serves as page to an officer, he turns hermit himself and earns a reputation for sanctity while really supporting himself by swindling. Next he finds a congenial sphere of activity in the German army. The wild license of the soldiery and the consequent sufferings of the peasantry are vividly painted. After numerous ups and downs and two unfortunate marital experiences, he retires from the world, and goes to a desert island where he anticipates some of the experiences of Robinson Crusoe.

Skeggs, Miss Caroline Wilhelmina Amelia, in Goldsmith's *Vicar of Wakefield* (1766), the companion of "Lady Blarney," both being London courtesans whom Squire Thornhill introduces to the Primrose family to aid him in beguiling the daughters of the house.

Skewton, Mrs., in Dickens's novel of *Dombey and Son*, is the mother of Edith, afterwards Mrs. Dombey.

Skimpole, Harold, in Dickens's *Bleak House* (1852), an artist, buoyant, gay, brilliant, and ingenuously unscrupulous in money matters. Dickens rather lamely sought to defend himself from the charge of having caricatured Leigh Hunt in this character.

"Exactly those graces and charms of manner which are remembered," says Dickens, "in the words we have quoted, were remembered by the author of the work of fiction in question when he drew the character in question. He no more thought, God forgive him! that the admired original would ever be charged" [as he frequently was charged] "with the imaginary vices of the fictitious creature than he has himself ever thought of charging the blood of Desdemona and Othello on the innocent Academy model who sat for Iago's leg in the picture."

Slawken-Bergius, an imaginary author of a work on Noses, himself distinguished by a nose of phenomenal length, who was invented by Sterne in order that he might pretend to quote from his works a curious tale about a man with an enormous nose.

Slaygood, Giant, in Bunyan's *Pilgrim's Progress*, Part I, the master of a gang of thieves infesting the public highway. He fell upon Feeblemind and might have killed him, but that Mr. Greatheart came to the rescue of Feeblemind and slew Giant Slaygood.

Sleary, in Dickens's *Hard Times* (1854), the proprietor of a circus at Coketown, who was never sober and never drunk, but always kindhearted. His daughter Josephine is a notable performer in his circus.

Slender, in Shakespeare's *Merry Wives of Windsor* (1596), one of the suitors of "sweet Anne Page," a country lout uneasily conscious of his lack of ease and city polish.

He is a very potent piece of imbecility. In him the pretensions of the worthy Gloucestershire family are well kept up, and immoralized. He and his friend Sackerson, and his book of songs, and his love of Anne Page and his having nothing to say to her, can never be forgotten. It is the only first-rate character in the play; but it is in that class. Shakespeare is the only writer who was as great in describing weakness as strength.—HAZLITT, *Characters of Shakespeare's Plays.*

Slick, Sam, hero of *The Clockmaker: Sayings and Doings of Samuel*

Slick of Slickville, by Judge Thomas Chandler Haliburton, which first appeared in a series of letters in the *Nova Scotian* (1835) and were gathered together two years later in a volume. Sam reappeared in other volumes from the same pen, and finally disappeared in *The Attaché, or Sam Slick in England* (1843–1844), an inglorious ending to a rather showy beginning. For, despite some exaggerations of detail, Sam Slick, at his first appearance, was an excellent caricature of the typical New England pedlar of the period, especially as he set himself,—keen-witted, resourceful, cool, calculating, and imperturbable, —in contrast to the cautious and sluggish yet gullible Nova Scotians. With his knowledge of human nature, his mother wit, and his plentiful use of "soft sawder," Sam is more than a match for the natives among whom he has come to peddle clocks. Transferred to England he loses his individuality and his humor degenerates.

Slop, Dr., a coarse, choleric, and self-conceited physician in Sterne's novel, *The Life and Opinions of Tristram Shandy, Gent* (1759), said to have been drawn from one Dr. Burton, a man midwife of York. He is the inventor of a pair of obstetrical forceps, by whose aid he succeeds in crushing Tristram's nose *in utero* and smashing Uncle Toby's fingers to a jelly. Under this name Cruikshank and Hone caricatured Dr. (afterward Sir John) Stoddart (1773–1856), a violent anti-Bonapartist who was editor of the London *Times* from 1812 to 1816.

Slote, Hon. Bardwell, in B. E. Wolf's comedy, *The Mighty Dollar,* a caricature of the American politician. A member of Congress from the Cohosh district, he is ignorant, vain, venal, self-seeking, and unscrupulous, but not without a fund of shrewd wit and humor. A whimsical peculiarity is his passion for indicating a term or a familiar expression by initials, as H. O. G. (honorable old gentleman), P. D. Q. (pretty damn quick), K. K. (cruel cuss), and G. F. for jugful.

He is likewise an adept at malapropisms: " My ancestors," he says, " came over in the *Cauliflower* and landed at Plymouth Church."

Slowboy, Tilly, in Dickens's *Cricket on the Hearth* (1845), the simple-minded, dull-witted, but devoted maid of all work in the Peerybingle household. As dry-nurse to baby no one could have been more affectionate, but she had a surprising talent for getting it into difficulties by holding it topsy-turvy and bringing its head into contact with doors and dressers, bedposts and stair-rails.

Sludge, Dickie, nicknamed Flibbertigibbit in Scott's romance, *Kenilworth*, the dwarf grandson of Gammer Sludge, " a queer, shambling, ill-made urchin," of acute but knavish intelligence, who led Edmund Tressilian to Wayland Smith's forge. In the great pageant at Kenilworth Castle, Dickie assumed the part of the imp Flibbertigibbit, in whose memory he had been nicknamed.

Sludge, Mr., hero of a monologue in verse, *Mr. Sludge the Medium*, in Robert Browning's *Dramatis Personæ*. Mr. Sludge, a shrewd, plausible Yankee spiritualist (evidently drawn after David D. Home), is at some pains to vindicate his character and career. He grants that he is an impostor, but he claims that he is merely catering to a harmless popular appetite for deception. Clamorous for any news from the invisible world, the eager " circle " betrays the imaginative medium into reporting what it appears most to desire. Their superstition feeds his own. He is obliged to cheat in self-defence. And when a man tasks his wits successfully, if it be only to mislead the witless, he takes an artist's pride in the effort.

Slum, Mr., in Dickens's *The Old Curiosity Shop* (1840), a writer of poetical advertisements. " Ask the performers," says he, " ask the blacking-makers, ask the hatters, ask the old lottery-office keepers, ask any man among 'em what poetry has done for him, and, mark my words, he blesses the name of Slum."

Slumkey, Samuel, in Dickens's *Pickwick Papers*, the " blue " candidate for Eatanswill in parliament, as Horatio Fitzkin is the buff.

Sly, Christopher, a tinker and bear-leader, who, in the induction to *The Taming of the Shrew*, is found drunk by a nobleman and taken to his house. When he awakes he is made to believe that he himself is the lord of the manor, for whose entertainment the comedy is then performed. See ABOU HASSAN.

Smectymnuus, feigned author of a tract against Episcopacy and in answer to Bishop Hall, which was published in 1641. The name is a sort of acrostic made up from the initials of the real writers, five Presbyterian divines,—Stephen Marshall, Edmund Calamy, Thomas Young, Matthew Newcomen, and William Spurstow. In 1642 Milton published *An Apology for Smectymnuus*.

Smelfungus, in Sterne's *Sentimental Journey* (1768), is evidently a caricature of Tobias Smollett, whose *Travels through France and Italy* is one prolonged snarl, and therefore the exact antithesis to Sterne's book. " The learned Smelfungus," he says, " travelled from Boulogne to Paris, from Paris to Rome, and so on; but he set out with the spleen and the jaundice, and every object he passed by was decoloured and distorted. He thought he wrote an account of them, but it was nothing but an account of his miserable feelings." Sterne tells of meeting Smelfungus at Rome and at Turin, and finding him full of complaints and prejudices. As his visit to Italy was made in 1764, when Smollett was also there, these may be records of actual meetings.

Smike, in Dickens's *Nicholas Nickleby*, a half-witted, half-starved boy, on whom the hero takes compassion when he is assistant tutor at Dotheboy's Hall. Smike runs away to join him when he leaves the Hall, and Nicholas takes care of him until his death. Smike turns out to be the son of Ralph Nickleby by an unacknowledged marriage.

There is no real life in Smike. His misery, his idiocy, his devotion to Nicholas, his love for Kate, are all overdone and incompatible with each other. But still the reader sheds a tear. Every reader can find a tear for Smike.—ANTHONY TROLLOPE.

Snagsby, Mr., in Dickens's *Bleak House*, the law stationer in Cook's Court, a mild, bald, timid, unassuming man, living in awe of a termagant wife, whom with unconscious satire he calls "his little woman." He usually prefaces his remarks with "Not to put too fine a point upon it."

Snake, Mr., in Sheridan's *School for Scandal*, a treacherous ally of Lady Sneerwell, who brazenly confesses to her, "you paid me extremely liberally for propagating the lie, but unfortunately I have been offered double to speak the truth."

Sneak, Jerry, in Foote's comedy, *The Mayor of Garratt* (1763), a paltry, mean-spirited pin-maker, who becomes the eponymic mayor. His wife is a domestic tartar, who keeps Jerry so thoroughly crushed under her thumb that he has become the type of the henpecked husband in stage-land. Garratt is a village between Wandsworth and Tooling in England. In 1750 the inhabitants made common cause against any further encroachment on their common. The chairman of the meeting was facetiously dubbed the Mayor. It happened to be general election day, so thereafter every election day a new Mayor was appointed. The London wits seized on the idea, and poured out political squibs which feigned to be "addresses" by "the Mayor of Garratt."

Sneerwell, Lady, in Sheridan's *School for Scandal*, a widow, brilliant and beautiful, but overfond of scandalmongering. "Wounded myself," she says, "in the early part of my life by the envenomed tongue of slander, I confess I have since known no pleasure equal to the reducing of others to the level of my own reputation." (Act i, 1.) Mr. Snake says of her, "Every one allows that Lady Sneerwell can do more with a word or a look than many can with the most labored detail, even when they happen to have a little truth on their side to support it."

Snodgrass, Mr. Augustus, a member of the famous Pickwick Club, a poetically-minded young man.

Snout, Tom, in Shakespeare's *Midsummer Night's Dream*, a tinker who is cast for the part of Pyramus's father in the interpolated play, but instead plays the wall.

Snowe, Lucy, the autobiographic heroine of Charlotte Brontë's novel *Villette* (1852), who in certain respects adumbrates some phases of the career and character of the author, her catastrophic experiences as a teacher in a Belgian boarding-school; her sensitiveness, her shyness, her proud humility, her spasmodic fits of impulse, her passionate emotions concealed under an icy exterior. The very name "Snowe"—decided on after "Frost" had been discarded and originally spelled "Snow"—was admittedly chosen by Miss Brontë as "a cold name, on the *lucus a non lucendo* principle, for she has about her an external coldness."

In an interesting (unpublished) letter to her friend Ellen Nussey, which was sold at auction in New York in 1912, Charlotte Brontë reveals her consciousness of those traits which are adumbrated in personal fashion in the character of Lucy Snowe. "I will preserve unbroken," she says, "that reserve which alone enables me to maintain a decent character for judgment; but for that I should long ago have been set down by all who know me as a Frenchified fool. You have been very kind to me of late and you . . . have spared me those little sallies of ridicule which, owing to my miserable and wretched touchiness of character, used formerly to make me wince as if I had been touched with a hot iron; things that nobody else cares for enter into my mind and rankle there like venom . . . I'm an idiot" (September 26, 1836.)

This figure, as Mr. Wemyss Reid has observed with indisputable accuracy of insight, was doubtless, if never meant to win liking or made to find favor in the general reader's eyes, yet none the less evidently on that account the faithful likeness of Charlotte Brontë, studied from the life and painted by her own hand with the sharp, austere precision of a photograph rather than a portrait. But it is herself with the consolation and support of her genius withdrawn, with the strength of the spiritual arm immeasurably shortened, the cunning of the right hand comparatively cancelled, and this it is that makes the main undertone and ultimate result of the book somewhat mournfuller even than the literal record of her mournful and glorious life.— A. C. SWINBURNE: *A Note on Charlotte Brontë*, p. 81.

Snug, in Shakespeare's *Midsummer Night's Dream*, a joiner who is cast for the part of a lion in the interpolated play of *Pyramus and Thisbe*. He asks manager Quince if he had the lion's part writ out, " for," says he, " I am slow of memory." On being told that he could do it extempore, " for it is nothing but roaring," he consents to undertake it.

Sofronia, a Christian maiden residing in Jerusalem at the time of its siege by Godfrey de Boulogne; heroine of a much-admired episode in Tasso's *Jerusalem Delivered*, Canto ii. Here is how she and her lover Olindo are described:

Sofronia she, Olindo hight the youth,
  Both of one town, both in one faith were taught.
She fair, he full of bashfulness and truth,
  Loved much, hoped little, and desired naught;
He durst not speak, by suit to purchase ruth,
  She saw not, marked not, wist not what he sought;
Thus loved, thus served he long but not regarded,
Unseen, unmarked, unpitied, unrewarded.
             Fairfax's translation.

In this picture of the hopeless love of Olindo, Tasso is thought to have had in mind his own passion for the beautiful Leonora d'Este, daughter of his patron. But see TASSO. In the poem, Aladin, the Mahommedan king of Jerusalem, has deprived a Christian church of an image of the Virgin, to set it up in a mosque as a palladium against the Crusaders. It disappears during the night. Aladin, confident that a Christian has stolen it, orders a general massacre of his Christian subjects. The catastrophe is averted by Sofronia, who surrenders herself as the culprit. Olindo, finding her sentenced to the stake, disputes with her the right of martyrdom. He is condemned to suffer with her, and the pair are only saved from being burnt alive by the arrival of the famous Amazon Clorinda, come to offer her service to the Saracen king, her admirer. Sofronio, never before conscious of Olindo's love, now returns it in full, and goes with him from the stake to the marriage altar.

Soggarth Aroon, poem by John Banim in which the attachment of the Irish peasant to his priest is portrayed with touching simplicity. Soggarth Aroon means *Priest dear.*

Solness, Halvard, in Ibsen's drama, *The Master Builder* (1893), an irregularly educated architect, who has become a very successful builder, though, partly out of shrewdness, partly out of an arrogant humility, he will not call himself by the loftier title. See WRANGEL, HILDA.

Building-Master Solness is Ibsen himself. It is the old fighter looking back, surveying his long working-day, measuring what has been gained, and counting the cost. . . . Solness now finds himself "on top," but filled with a secret uneasiness and fear for his own greatness. He feels he must summon all his Titanic power and will to "overdo himself," that he may keep the proud position he has attained, and not lose ground to the younger generation.—*The Copenhagen Tilskueren.*

Sorrel, Hetty, in George Eliot's novel, *Adam Bede,* the pretty village girl, vain, empty-headed, weak, engaged to Adam Bede, but seduced by Arthur Donnithorne, who reaches her with a reprieve as she is on the point of paying the penalty for child murder.

Of all George Eliot's female figures she is the least ambitious, and, on the whole, I think, the most successful. The part of the story which concerns her is much the most forcible; and there is something infinitely tragic in the reader's sense of the contrast between the sternly prosaic life of the good people about her, their wholesome decency, and their noon-day probity, and the dusky sylvan path along which poor Hetty is tripping, light-footed, to her ruin. Hetty's conduct throughout seems to me to be eminently consistent. The author has escaped the easy error of representing her as in any degree made serious by suffering. She is vain and superficial by nature, and she remains so to the end.—HENRY JAMES: *Views and Reviews.*

Spanker, Lady Gay, in Dion Boucicault's comedy, *London Assurance* (1841), a gay and brilliant woman, devoted to horses and hunting, who keeps a whip hand over her meek little husband, Dolly Spanker.

Sparabella, in Gay's *Pastorals*, iii (1714), a shepherdess in love with D'Arfey, who prefers the ungainly Clumsilis, whereupon Sparabella resolves on suicide. But how? She discards one plan after another. A penknife is too suggestive of a squeaking pig; hanging, of a dog; drowning, of a scolding quean. So the sun goes down upon her wrath and

The prudent maiden deemed it then too late,
And till to-morrow came deferred her fate.

Sparkish, in Wycherley's *Country Wife* (1675), and Garrick's adaptation of the same, *The Country Girl* (1766), a self-imagined prince of coxcombs and a pretender to wit and letters, without common sense or common understanding. Congreve took him as the model for his Tattle in *Love for Love* (1695).

Sparrowgrass, Samson, pretended author of the *Sparrowgrass Papers* (1856), by Frederick S. Cozzens, who autobiographically describes the haps and mishaps of a young city-bred couple who set up housekeeping in Yonkers, N. Y., at that time a mere suburban village.

Spatterdash, Simon, in Samuel Beazley's farce, *The Boarding-House* (1811), a local militiaman, who indulges freely in whimsical comparisons that may have suggested one of Sam Weller's many accomplishments,—*e.g.*, " ' Come on,' as the man said to his tight boot," " ' I know the world,' as the monkey said when he cut off his tail," " ' I'm turned soger,' as the lobster said when he popped his head out of the boiler," " ' I'm down upon you,' as the extinguisher said to the rushlight." See WELLER, SAMUEL.

Spenlow, Dora, in Dickens's *David Copperfield*, the " child-wife " of the hero, who rather providentially dies when her childishness palls upon him. As a girl she had acquired in Paris some graces, but she has neither intellect nor education. Her confidante is Julia Mills, a sentimental maiden. Jip, a spaniel, is her closest companion. Mr. Spenlow poohpoohs the whole business of her marriage, but he opportunely dies, a victim, apparently, of comfortable living and uncomfortable neckcloths. Dora falls into the hands of two spinster aunts, who enjoy the engagement very much, and make a pet of it, until David has attained a sufficiency by reporting and other various labor. Romance now turns into domestic farce. There is some baby house-keeping,—the silliness of the child-wife being relieved by touches of real humor and pathos,—and in a year or two Dora dies and clears the way for Agnes Wickfield.

Copperfield's first meeting with Dora is Dickens's meeting (when little more than a boy) with a lady by no means so young as Dora is there represented. The courtship is derived from his youthful love for the original of Flora. The married life with Dora, so far as her household ways are concerned, presents Dickens's own experience, so that Dora there represents a third person, and that person his wife. And, lastly, the death of Dora and Copperfield's sorrow during the following years are drawn from the death of his wife's younger sister Mary, and the sorrow Dickens felt for years thereafter.—RICHARD A. PROCTOR: *Knowledge*, vol. vii, p. 537.

Spenlow, Francis, in *David Copperfield* (1849), a proctor to whom David was articled and father of Dora, whom David subsequently married. When he is accidentally killed in a carriage accident, Dora goes to live with his maiden sisters, Misses Lavinia and Clarissa Spenlow.

They were not unlike birds altogether, having a sharp, brisk, sudden manner, and a little, short, spruce way of adjusting themselves, like canaries.—Chap. xi.

Sprague, Scientific, hero of a series of short stories by Francis Lynde, bound together under that general title. He owes the nickname to the fact that he utilizes in business the habit of acute observation and of imaginative deduction therefrom which he has acquired in the study of natural science. All the stories are incidents in a long struggle for the retention of a single railroad in the hands of its rightful owners, and

Scientific Sprague is enabled to confound all the knavish tricks of the financial pirates who set out to plunder it.

Squeers, Wackford, in Dickens's *Nicholas Nickleby* (1838), owner of Dotheboys Hall, in Yorkshire, a rapacious, ignorant, and brutal schoolmaster. Nicholas engages himself as a scholastic assistant to this gentleman, but disapproves of his methods, vigorously interferes when he attempts to thrash Smike, and leaves, followed by Smike, the worst-treated of all the pupils. Squeers had only one eye. The blank side of his face was much puckered up, which gave him a sinister appearance, especially when he smiled, at which times his expression bordered on the villainous. He wore a white neckerchief with long ends, and a scholastic suit of black; but, his coat-sleeves being a great deal too long, and his trousers a great deal too short, he appeared ill at ease in his clothes, and as if he were in a perpetual state of astonishment at finding himself so respectable. His daughter Fanny Squeers is a grotesquely peevish and repulsive young woman.

Squintum, Dr., in Foote's farce, *The Minor,* a character introduced to burlesque George Whitfield, the Methodist preacher, who had a cast in his eye. Theodore Hook applied the nickname to the Rev. Edward Irving, who was similarly afflicted.

Squire of Dames, in Spenser's *Faërie Queene,* a young knight in love with Columbell, who sets him a difficult task ere she will yield her hand. He must travel for a twelvemonth, rescuing distressed damsels, and return to her with pledges of his exploits. At the appointed time he hands her 300 pledges, but she now tells him to take a second journey and not return to her until he could bring her pledges from 300 virgins that they would dwell in chastity all their lives. Alas! in three years' travel he finds only three virgins willing to take the pledge. One was a nun, one a satiated courtesan, the last a rustic cottager who alone was influenced by any "principle of virtue." The story is imitated from *The Host's Tale* in *Orlando Furioso,* xxviii.

Stackpole, Henrietta, in Henry James's novel, *The Portrait of a Lady* (1882), the friend of Isabel Archer and European correspondent for an American paper. She is sincere, democratic, and loyal to her national traditions.

Stalky, Your Uncle, in Rudyard Kipling's *Stalky and Co.,* nickname for Arthur L. Corkran, who with two other boys affects an aloofness from the rest of the school, playing tricks upon masters and pupils alike. He is a clever boy, mathematically inclined, resourceful, self-reliant, with a good conceit of himself. McTurk, heir to an Irish estate, is the gentleman of the company. Beetle, who occasionally sacrifices his own comfort to assist Stalky in his plots, is accepted as a self portrait of Kipling in boyhood. The likeness is emphasized by the fact that, his choice of career being limited by his spectacles, he goes out to India as a journalist.

Standish, Miles, the bluff Puritan captain (1584–1656), who plays a leading part in Longfellow's narrative poem *The Courtship of Miles Standish* (1858). Not knowing that John Alden, his clerk and nearest friend, is like himself in love with Priscilla Mullen, he bids the lad woo the maiden as his proxy in such manner as youth only knows how to assume. John, with much misgiving, accepts the mission, but the maiden guesses his secret, and archly asks him, "Why don't you speak for yourself, John?" Standish flies into a rage when he hears the story. Soon after, he disappears and is reported to have been slain by the Indians. John then deems he is justified in speaking for himself. Standish turns up at the wedding, for he had been wounded, not slain, and good-humoredly accepts the situation.

Stareleigh, Justice, in Dickens's *Pickwick Papers,* a fat, stodgy little judge, deaf and irascible, who in the absence of the Chief Justice sat in judgment at the trial of Bardell *v.* Pickwick.

Starr, David, hero of Bayard Taylor's tragedy of *The Prophet* (1874), is to some extent a poetical reminiscence of Joseph Smith, the founder of Mormonism. Starr is the only son of a hard-headed farmer, who scoffs at his pretensions, and of a wife, long barren, who when David came looked upon him as peculiarly from the Lord, yet never, despite all her pride and tenderness, gave him implicit belief. This comes only from the girl he marries. It is her loving faith, joined to the inspiring credulity of his neighbors, that works upon David till he feels himself a prophet indeed.

The Prophet begins by painfully doubting the inspiration which he is passionately eager to claim. The craft of a man of the world who sees how the prophetic authority may be made to serve his selfish purposes persuades him that his doubts have been resolved by miracle; he goes on from purely intellectual to moral delusions, becomes an instrument in the hands of his undoer, and realizes his own imposture just as death deprives him of the power to retract his pretensions.

Staunton, George, in Scott's novel *The Heart of Midlothian*, the prodigal son of the rector of Willingham and the seducer of Effie Deans. He appears under various aliases, first as Geordie Robertson, a felon, then in female disguise as the Madge Wildfire of the Porteous riots; lastly he comes into a baronetage and marries Effie. Sir George and Lady Staunton reach a prominent station in London society. He is killed by a gipsy boy known as "The Whistler," who proves to be his own and Effie's son, the illegitimate issue of the seduction.

The lover of Effie Deans is far too melodramatic, too "Satanic." For once, in his failure of a character, Scott was imitating Byron's heroes, whether he knew it or not, as Byron imitated figures like the Schedoni of Mrs. Radcliffe.—ANDREW LANG: *Sir Walter Scott.*

Steerforth, James, in Dickens's *David Copperfield*, an intimate friend of the hero, who worships him with the enthusiasm of trustful and unspoiled youth. Despite his engaging manners, his captivating ways, his personal magnetism, Steerforth is thoroughly bad,—hard, cruel, selfish, domineering. Introduced to the Peggotty household, he deliberately seduces Ham's cousin and betrothed wife, Little Emily. On the eve of her intended marriage she elopes with him to the Continent, but he wearies of her and deserts her. He perishes in the shipwreck described in Chap. lv.

Steerforth, Mrs., James's mother (see *supra*), an elderly lady, handsome and haughty, entirely devoted to her son until the inevitable clash comes between these two imperious natures.

Stella (Lat. for "Star"), the name under which Sir Philip Sidney, in *Astrophel and Stella*, a series of sonnets, celebrated his only love, the Lady Penelope Devereux. She was a maid when he first met her and a widow before he died, but these sonnets were addressed to her during the period of her married life with Lord Rich.

Stella, a poetical name given by Swift to Miss Esther Johnson. She is thought to have been a natural daughter of Sir William Temple by his housekeeper, Mrs. Johnson, and it was when forming a part of Sir William's household (1688–1694) that Swift met her. That she inspired in him a warm affection is evident by the tone of his *Journal to Stella*, a collection of the letters he wrote to her from London when he was a famous man there. But, for some reason, which has never been satisfactorily explained, he put off marrying her till 1716, and then only went through the forms of a ceremony which was never acknowledged and lived apart from her until her death in 1728.

Who hasn't in his mind an image of Stella? Who does not love her? Fair and tender creature: pure and affectionate heart! Boots it to you, now that you have been at rest for a hundred and twenty years, not divided in death from the cold heart which caused yours, whilst it beat, such faithful pangs of love and grief—boots it to you now, that the whole world loves and deplores you? Scarce any man, I believe, ever thought of that grave, that did not cast a flower of pity on it, and write over it a sweet epitaph. Gentle lady, so lovely, so loving, so unhappy! you have had countless champions; millions of manly hearts mourning for you. From generation to generation we take up the fond tradition of your beauty: we watch and follow your tragedy, your bright morning love and purity, your constancy, your grief, your sweet martyrdom. We know your legend by heart. You are one of the saints of English story.—THACKERAY: *English Humorists.*

Stenio, in George Sand's romance, *Lélia* (1833), a young poet, passionate, romantic, a dreamer of dreams, who falls in love with the titular heroine. Lélia, once deceived, has lost all faith in men, all desire for love. Her sister Pulchérie, a courtesan, has never known love, but only lust. One represents soul without body, the other body without soul. Stenio is intoxicated with the idea that he has conquered Lélia's coldness, but wakes to find that, in hideous irony, she has thrust him into the arms of her sister, who in person exactly resembles her. He falls to the level of the lowest debauchee and, having ruined body and soul, makes away with himself.

Steno, Michel, in Byron's tragedy, *Marino Faliero, the Doge of Venice.* See FALIERO.

Steyne, Marquis of, in Thackeray's *Vanity Fair,* the profligate, cynical, witty, and wicked old nobleman who comes between Becky Sharp and her husband, Rawdon Crawley, and is soundly thrashed by the latter. Although it is generally agreed that he was drawn from a marquis of Hertford, opinions differ as to whether it was the second or the third marquis who furnished the model. The adherents of both candidates for that bad eminence make so excellent a case as to force the conclusion that Thackeray took hints from both: from the elder,—whom Moore called " the hoary old sinner," in his *Two-penny Post-Bag,* whose seduction of Mrs. Massey was a public scandal, and who complaisantly tolerated his own wife's *liaison* with George IV,— and also from the younger, the less notorious but almost equally profligate back of the Regency. A wood-

cut portrait of Lord Steyne which was contained in the first issue of *Vanity Fair,* but immediately suppressed, bears a remarkable likeness to Sir Thomas Laurence's portrait of this third marquis.

Stirling, Peter, hero of a political novel, *The Honorable Peter Sterling* (1895), by Paul Leicester Ford, tracing the career of the better sort of American " boss." Grover Cleveland has been suggested as a possible prototype.

The Honorable Peter Stirling is not a typical boss. Judged by the knowledge of the genus derived from its works, his character is far more ideal than real, but it is so strongly imagined and logically drawn that it satisfies the demand for the appearance of truth in art. . . . The inference from his character and career is not that a boss is a vital necessity, but that he is more than an accident in a great democracy, and that, given a few Stirlings to compete against many Maguires, the name boss and the thing might lose an opprobrious significance.—*N. Y. Nation.*

Storm, John, called by his parishioners in London " Father Storm," hero of Hall Caine's novel, *The Christian* (1897), who on his deathbed marries Glory Quayle.

Strafford, Thomas Wentworth, Earl of (1837), is the hero of Browning's drama, *Strafford.* Its main interest is centered in the character of Strafford and his relation to the king, and the poet has displayed a peculiar sympathy for this proud, sensitive, and impatient man, who recoiled from every proof of his master's treachery to himself, and yet anticipated its worst results in a scarcely interrupted flow of tender, self-sacrificing pity.

Strap, Hugh, in Smollett's *Roderick Random* (1748), a loyal, simple-minded, and disinterested friend and adherent of the graceless hero.

We believe there are few readers who are not disgusted with the miserable reward assigned to Strap in the closing chapter of the novel. Five hundred pounds (scarce the value of the goods he had presented to his master) and the hand of a reclaimed street-walker, even when added to a Highland farm, seem but a poor recompense for his faithful and disinterested attachment."—SIR W. SCOTT.

The *Monthly Magazine* of May, 1809, records the death, at the Lodge, Villiers Walk, Adelphi, of Mr. Hugh Hewson, at the age of eighty-five, and states that he was "the identical Hugh Strap whom Dr. Smollett has rendered so conspicuously interesting," etc. Hewson for over forty years had kept a hair-dresser's shop in the parish of St. Martin's in the Fields. The writer of the notice says, "We understand the deceased left behind him an interlined copy of *Roderick Random*, with comments on some of the passages. According to Nicholls, *Literary Anecdotes*, iii, 465, the original of this character was supposed to be Lewis, a book-binder of Chelsea.—*Notes and Queries*, July 9, 1910.

Strephon, in Sir Philip Sidney's *Arcadia* (1580), a shepherd who makes love to Urania. Since Sidney's time it has become a conventional name for a lover, Chloe being the name of the lady in apposition.

Strong, Dr., in Dickens's *David Copperfield* (1849), master of the school at Canterbury to which David is sent by his aunt. He is an amiable, benevolent, and kindly sort of Casaubon (*q.v.*), and may have suggested that character to George Eliot, for he is engaged on the compilation of a monumental dictionary, which might be completed " in one thousand six hundred and forty-nine years, counting from the doctor's last, or sixty-second, birthday." He has a young wife, Annie, who is devoted to him. Her scapegrace cousin, Jack Maldon, whom the doctor has supported for years, joins with others in an unsuccessful attempt to sow dissension between the pair.

Struldbrugs, in Swift's *Gulliver's Travels*, a race of beings inhabiting Luggnagg who are gifted with immortality, but not with youth, and find a terrible fate in old age and decay. See TITHONUS in vol. II.

Strutt, Lord, in Arbuthnot's *History of John Bull*, (1712), a caricature of the King of Spain and inferentially of the Spanish people. The particular king aimed at is Charles II, who, dying without issue, left his kingdom to Philippe due d'Anson, here called Philip Lord Strutt.

Stryver, C. J. (familiarly known as Bully Stryver), in Dickens's *Tale of Two Cities*, counsel for Charles Darnay in his trial for treason.

He was stout, loud, red, bluff, and free from any drawback of delicacy; had a pushing way of shouldering himself (morally and physically) into companies and conversations, that argued well for his shouldering his way on in life.—Book ii, Chap. 24.

Stuffy, Matthew, in Charles Matthews's farce *At Home* (1818), an amateur actor, loud in comic eulogy of " the immortal Garrick " and his times. He applies to Vellinspeck, a country manager, for a position as prompter, being especially fitted therefore by a cast in his eye which enables him to keep one eye on the actor and another on his book.

Stukeley, Captain, in an anonymous historical tragedy, *The Battle of Alcazar, with the Death of Captain Stukeley* (1594), a marquis of Ireland. Forced by stress of weather to land in Portugal, he finds that King Sebastian had espoused the cause of the exiled Muly Mahomet, King of Barbary, against the latter's uncle, Abdilmec, who has dethroned him. He joins his forces to those of Sebastian. The battle of Alcazar follows. Both the Moorish Kings are slain outright, and Stukeley dies later of his wounds.

Stukely, in Edward Moore's domestic tragedy, *The Gamester* (1753), an unconscionable villain and unblushing hypocrite, who, with the aid of loaded dice and an oily tongue, lures Beverley on to his ruin at the gaming table, and who imposes on his unsuspecting wife as a friend of the family until he makes an attack upon her honor.

Stuyvesant, Peter (1592–1672), the last Dutch governor of New York. He was appointed in 1646 and took his seat next year; conciliated the Indians; arranged a boundary line with the English colonists of Connecticut (1650); dismissed a convention demanding popular reforms (1653); surrendered to the English September, 1664); and, after a short sojourn in the Netherlands, returned and lived on his farm, the Bowerii (Bowery), in New York, until his death. Washington Irving makes delightful fun of him in *Knickerbocker's History of New York* (1809).

Subtle, the titular alchemist in Ben Jonson's comedy, *The Alchemist* (1610), a wily charlatan, who dupes Sir Epicure Mammon and others into the belief that he has discovered the secret of the philosopher's stone. Dryden accused Jonson of having taken Tomkis's comedy of *Albumazar* (*q.v.*) as the "best model" of *The Alchemist*.

> Subtle was got by our Albumazer,
> That Alchemist by this Astrolog.
> *Prologue for revival of Albumazar.*

Summerson, Esther, the heroine of Dickens's *Bleak House*, an orphan niece of Miss Barbery, and the narrator of parts of the story, not entirely unconscious of the facts that she is wise, prudent, pretty, and sweet-tempered, a notable housewife, a self-denying friend, and a universal favorite. She proves to be an illegitimate daughter of Lady Dedlock and Captain Hawdon. Mr. Guppy falls in love with her, proposes, and is rejected. When she loses some of her good looks by smallpox, he is terribly scared lest he be held to his earlier promise. Another suitor is John Jarndyce, and a third Allan Woodcourt, whom she marries. According to Doctor Shelton Mackenzie (*Life of Dickens*, p. 203), this character is supposed to have been drawn from real life, and to have been intended as a portrait of Miss Sophia Iselin, author of a volume of poems published in 1847.

Superman, an imaginary being into whom man may ultimately develop, according to Nietzsche.

In one of his least convincing phrases, Nietzsche had said that just as the ape ultimately produced the man, so should we ultimately produce something higher than the man. The immediate answer of course is sufficiently obvious: the ape did not worry about the man, so why should we worry about the superman? If the superman will come by natural selection, may we leave it to natural selection? If the superman will come by human selection, what sort of superman are we to select? . . . This notion of producing superior human beings by the methods of the studfarm has often been urged, though its difficulties have never been cleared up. . . . The first and most obvious objection to it, of course, is this: that if you are to breed

men as pigs, you require some overseer who is as much more subtle than a man as a man is more subtle than a pig.—G. K. CHESTERTON: *George Bernard Shaw*, p. 204.

Supplehouse, in Anthony Trollope's *Framley Parsonage* (1861), a politician whose ambition runs far ahead of his abilities. It happened that during the Crimean War a portion of the London press had extolled him as the only man who could save the country. Ever since he had been going about swinging his tomahawk against the enemies of himself and the country. In return his country had bestowed upon him a subordinate position. He is ever haunted with the thought, "How can a man born to save a nation and to lead a people be content to fill the chair of an under-secretary?"

Surface, Charles, a young rake in Sheridan's comedy of *The School for Scandal*.

Surface, Joseph, in Sheridan's comedy, *The School for Scandal*, brother of the foregoing, a consummate hypocrite, noted for his "sentiments." He pretends to admire Lady Teazle, and pursues Maria for her fortune.

If that gem, the character of Joseph Surface, was Murphy's, the splendid and more valuable setting was Sheridan's. He took Murphy's Malvil from his lurking-place in the closet, and "dragged the struggling monster into day" upon the stage. That is, he gave interest, life, and action, or, in other words, its dramatic being, to the mere conception and written specimens of a character. This is the merit of Sheridan's comedies, that everything in them *tells;* there is no labor in vain.—HAZLITT: *Comic Writers.*

Surface, Sir Oliver, in Sheridan's comedy, *The School for Scandal*, the uncle of Charles and Joseph Surface.

Susan, heroine of Douglas Jerrold's drama, *Black-eyed Susan, or All in the Downs* (1829), which was suggested by Gay's ballad, *Sweet William's Farewell to Black-eyed Susan*. Captain Crosstree, in the play, attempts to carry off Susan, and William, to save his wife, strikes his superior, is court-martialled, and condemned to death. The Captain, however, acknowledges his fault, and procures a discharge showing that William, when he struck the Captain, was no longer in the king's service.

Susan, Simple, story for children in Miss Edgeworth's *Parent's Assistant.*

A most charming little idyl is that of Simple Susan, who was a real maiden living in the neighborhood of Edgeworthstown. . . . Few among us will not have shared Mr. Edgeworth's partiality for the charming little tale. The children fling their garlands and tie up their violets. Susan bakes her cottage loaves and gathers marigolds for broth, and tends her mother to the distant tune of Philip's pipe coming across the fields. As we read the story again it seems as if we could almost scent the fragrance of the primroses and the double violets, and hear the music sounding above the children's voices, and the bleatings of the lamb, so simply and delightfully is the whole story constructed. Among all Miss Edgeworth's characters few are more familiar to the world than that of Susan's pretty pet lamb.—LADY ANNE THACKERAY RITCHIE.

Svanhild, heroine of Ibsen's *Love Comedy.* The supposed prototype of Svanhild, and also of Ellida in the same author's *Lady from the Sea*, was Camilla Collett (1813-1903), author of *The Prefect's Daughters*, a novel satirizing the conventional ideas on marriage prevalent in contemporary Norway.

There is a story, told by Ibsen himself, that once in Munich, after an evening with the Ibsens, she was being escorted back to her rooms by the dramatist, when she stopped him under a gaslight and asked him point-blank, "Am I Svanhild?" Ibsen parried the question by asking her the name of her street again. "Don't *you* know?" said Camilla, referring back to her question. "Not in the least," answered Ibsen. "However, the landlady in the hotel opposite will take care of you for the night and help you in the morning." And with that he left her.

Svengali, in George du Maurier's novel *Trilby*, a Jew adventurer in Paris, who finds that he can hypnotize Trilby O'Ferral into doing his will in all things, even to singing without knowing a note of music. She becomes a famous vocalist under his influence, but the spell is broken when he dies.

Swan, David, hero of a "Fantasy" by Nathaniel Hawthorne, in *Twice-told Tales* (1837).

The subject is nothing more or less than an hour's sleep by the wayside of a youth while waiting for the coach that is to carry him to Boston. Yet how much of thoughtful and reflective beauty is thrown around it, what strange and airy destinies brush by the youth's unconscious face, how much matter for deep meditation of life and death, the past and future, time and eternity, is called forth by the few incidents in this simple tale!—LONGFELLOW.

Swancourt, Elfrida, heroine of Hardy's novel, *A Pair of Blue Eyes* (1873), who falls in love first with Stephen Smith and next with Henry Knight—marries the wrong lover and dies.

She is as fresh in fiction as she is lovable and natural. With all her complexities of action, she is essentially very simple. She desires to love and to be loved, and, when her father forbids the thought of Stephen Smith, she runs away with him "to make sure," and when afterwards she falls more profoundly in love with Knight, the sense of having first loved some one else oppresses her as a wrong to him, which she longs to have redressed by some former love-affair on his part; she would like to show him how much she could forgive him, but she has nothing to forgive in that way, and this makes it impossible for her to tell of her own former engagement. She has no pride, she has only love; she has no arts save in love, and thrusts herself a helpless victim into the power of the wretched woman, Jethway, whom she had never wronged.— W. D. HOWELLS: *Atlantic Monthly*, October, 1873.

Swat, Akhund of, hero of a humorous poem by G. T. Lanigan. He was a real character. Lanigan assumed hypothetically that he was a governor or ruler of the province of Swat, on the borders of India and Afghanistan. Akhund, however, means a learned man, a doctor, a devotee, a saint. He was the object of pilgrimages and consultations. In 1877 the Ameer of Afghanistan sought his advice as to what course he should take regarding the Russo-Turkish war.

Swiveller, Richard, in Dickens's *The Old Curiosity Shop* (1840), a good-natured, kindly scatter-brain and spendthrift, a cheap swell, at once dirty and smart, gleefully fond of humming dismal airs, with a flowery and even gaudy vocabulary. "What's the odds," he says, apropos of nothing, " so long as the fire of the soul is kindled at the taper of conviviality and the wing of friendship never moults a feather?" In this vocabulary "the rosy" stands for wine, "the balmy" for sleep. At Quilp's request, he was made clerk to Sampson Brass, but, when he was found to be too honest to be managed by Quilp, he lost his situation, fell ill of a fever, was nursed through it by the Marchioness (*q.v.*), and on his recovery married her.

Sycorax, in Shakespeare's comedy, *The Tempest,* a witch, mother of Caliban, who does not appear on the scene but is mentioned in i, 2, and v, i. Ariel had been her servant; to punish his disobedience, she shut him up in a cloven pine, whence after twelve years he was liberated by Prospero.

Synorix, in Tennyson's tragedy of *The Cup* and in other plays based upon this semi-historic personage, an ex-tetrarch of Galatia driven away by his people, who returns with the Roman forces as their treacherous ally. He plots against his successor in the tetrarchy, Sinnatus, unseats and executes him, himself becomes King of Galatia, marries Camma (*q.v.*), the widow of Sinnatus, but he and she die on the wedding-day through the medium of a poisoned cup prepared by Camma.

Syntax, Dr., an amiable, simple-minded, pious, and scholarly cleric, whose adventures are related by William Coombe in three books of octosyllabic verse,—*Dr. Syntax's Tour in Search of the Picturesque* (1812), *Dr. Syntax's Tour in Search of Consolation* (1820), and *Dr. Syntax's Tour in Search of a Wife* (1821). At length he died, and then:

> The village wept, the hamlets round
> Crowded the consecrated ground,
> And waited there to see the end
> Of pastor, teacher, father, friend.

T

Taffy, a familiar name for a Welshman, being simply Davy (short for David) pronounced with an aspiration, as is usual with Welshmen. In George du Maurier's *Trilby,* Taffy is the nickname of Talbot Wynne, a Yorkshire youth of good stature, good family, and unbounded good-nature, who marries Miss Bagot, the sister of Little Billee. Another famous Taffy appears in the ancient nursery jingle which begins

> Taffy was a Welshman,
> Taffy was a thief,
> Taffy came to my house
> And stole a piece of beef.

Talbot, John, first Earl of Shrewsbury (1388–1453), an English general, who was taken prisoner at Patay by Joan of Arc in 1429 and subsequently (1442) raised to the peerage, appears in Shakespeare's historical play *I Henry VI*, and is there anachronistically made Earl of Shrewsbury before the King's coronation. In Act ii, 3, the Countess of Auvergne alludes to the fact that his name was such a terror in France that mothers stilled their babes with it. She expresses surprise at the insignificance of his appearance.

Talleyrand, Prince, French statesman of the Napoleonic era, appears in *A Priest in Spite of Himself*, by Rudyard Kipling, the seventh story in volume *Rewards and Fairies*. Pharaoh Lee tells the children how Talleyrand fled to America after the French Revolution, how he struck up a friendship with him, and how, later, the friendship induced Talleyrand, as Napoleon's minister of finance, to intervene when Pharaoh's ship was conquered and his cargo of tobacco confiscated.

Talus, in Spenser's *Faërie Queene,* a brazen man created by Vulcan to guard the island of Crete, who becomes an attendant upon Artegal.

> [The Puritans] went through the world like Sir Artegal's iron man, Talus, with his flail, crushing and trampling down oppres-

sors, mingling with human beings but having neither part nor lot in human infirmities; insensible to fatigue, to pleasure, and to pain, not to be pierced by any weapon, not to be withstood by any barrier.— MACAULAY: *Essay on Milton.*

Tamar, in W. S. Landor's poem, *Gebir,* the brother of the titular hero, an aspiring shepherd, full of the lust of conquest. A sea-nymph, falling in love with him, carries him off to dwell with her forever beyond the reach of human ambition.

Tamburlaine, hero of Marlowe's *Tamburlaine the Great, or the Scythian Shepherd and the Scourge of God,* a tragedy in verse, acted 1587, printed 1590. Based on the life and death of the historic Timur or Tamerlane, the Tartar conquerer of Asia (1336-1405), it is in two parts, Part I dealing with his exploits, Part II with the death of his consort and himself. Tamburlaine is one of the most terrific figures in literature. He ascends his throne on the necks of prostrate emperors; he harnesses to his chariot relays of kings and princes fattened on raw meat and maddened with pails of muscadel; he kills one of his sons for cowardice; he rips up the flesh of his own arm to teach the others endurance; he burns a city for his consort's funeral; he listens with delight to the cries of ravished virgins and tortured potentates sacrificed for a whim.

Tamerlane (another and more legitimate spelling), the hero of a tragedy by Nicholas Rowe (1702), in which the Asian conqueror is made to typify William III, of England, as Bajazet represents Louis XIV. One of E. A. Poe's early poems took Tamerlane as its titular hero.

Tamora. Queen of the Goths, in *Titus Andronicus.*

Tancred (1050–1112), the hero of the first Crusade, appears in Tasso's *Jerusalem Delivered* (1575), in Sir Walter Scott's *Count Robert of Paris,* and in Rossini's opera *Tancredi* (1813). Tasso follows in outline the facts of history. With Bohemond Tancred landed in Epirus in 1096 and took the oath of allegiance

to the Greek emperor Alexius; he quarrelled with Baldwin for the possession of Tarsus and fought bravely and successfully before Antioch and Jerusalem. After the conquest of Jerusalem, he became Prince of Galilee and later Prince of Antioch. Tasso, still following history, makes "woman's love" his one besetting sin. He loved much and often, his principal flames being Clorinda and Erminia.

Tancred, hero of Disraeli's novel, *Tancred, or the New Crusade* (1847), the heir to a dukedom, who, after sundry adventures in the upper circles of London society, goes out in quest of light to the Holy Land. It is there revealed to him, in a vision, that the regeneration of Christendom must come from a new Anglican Protestantism refined by Judaism.

Tanis, nickname of the heroine of Amélie Rives's novelette, *Tanis the Sangdigger* (1894), a wild, passionate girl of the Southern mountains—a savage nature fighting against its lower impulses when suddenly awakened to spiritual ideas of love.

Tanner, John (*i.e.,* Juan Tenor), in G. B. Shaw's comedy, *Man and Superman* (1903), is a modern Don Juan as conceived by Shavian philosophy. A voluble exponent of Schopenhauer and Nietsche, he is concerned for the future of the race and not for the freedom of his own instincts.

Confronted with the stark problem of the duel of sex, Shaw solved it with the striking conclusion that Man is no longer, like Don Juan, the victor in that duel. Though sharing neither the prejudices of the homoist nor the enthusiasms of the feminist, Shaw found it easy to persuade himself that woman has become dangerous, aggressive, powerful. The rôles established by romantic convention and evidenced in the hackneyed phrase, "Man is the hunter, woman the game," are now reversed: woman takes the initiative in the selection of her mate. Thus is Don Juan reincarnated; once the headlong huntsman, he is now the helpless quarry. *Man and Superman,* in Shaw's own words, is "a stage projection of the tragic-comic love chase of the man by the woman."

Tanqueray, Paulina, heroine of a drama, *The Second Mrs. Tanqueray* (1913), by Arthur W. Pinero.

Dealing in a novel way with an old yet ever recurring and interesting problem,—the woman with a past and her attempted redemption by a man with a future,—it made a more profound impression than any other modern English play, and placed Pinero in the front rank of modern dramatists.—GUSTAV KOBBE, *Forum*, Sept., 1898.

Taper and **Tadpole**, in Disraeli's *Coningsby* and in *Sybil*, political hacks, doing the dirty work of the party, despised yet courted by the wealthy and powerful. Their favorite epigram runs as follows: " To receive £1200 per annum is government; to try to receive £1200 is opposition; to wish to receive £1200 per annum is ambition."

Tappertit, Sim (*i.e.*, **Simon**), in Dickens's novel, *Barnaby Rudge*, the silly and conceited apprentice of Gabriel Varden, in love with his daughter, and hence the bitter enemy of his successful rival, Joe Willet. Though only five feet high, thin-faced, small-eyed, sharp-nosed, he was delighted with his stature and beauty, but especially enraptured with his legs, which were miracles of slimness. His set fancy was that his eyes were irresistible and that their might would subdue the haughtiest beauty.

Tasso, Torquato, the famous Italian poet (1544–95), is the hero of Goethe's drama, *Tasso* (1789), and of Byron's poem, *The Lament of Tasso* (1817). Both poets accept the unverified legend that Tasso was enamoured of Leonora d'Este (sister of his patron, Alfonso, Duke of Ferrara), who was seven years his senior, and Byron makes capital of the undoubted fiction that his seven years' confinement (1579–1586) as a lunatic was due to brotherly resentment. The publication of Tasso's letters by Guasti, in 1853, and, more recently, Angelo Solerti's *Vita di Torquato Tasso* (1895), which is largely drawn from family records, have in a great measure exonerated the duke at the expense of the unhappy poet himself. Briefly, Tasso's intrigues with rival powers—the Medici at Florence, the papal court, and the Holy Office at Bologna—aroused the alarm and suspicion of the duke, whilst his general demeanor and his outbursts of violence and temper compelled, rather than afforded, a pretext for his confinement; and, to quote his own words, " in a fit of madness " he broke out into execrations of the ducal court and family, and of the people of Ferrara. For this offence he was shut up in the Hospital of Sant' Anna.

Tattle, in Congreve's comedy, *Love for Love* (1695), a more egregious sort of Sparkish (*q.v.*), who is described in Act i as " a mixture of lying, foppery, vanity, cowardice, bragging, licentiousness, and ugliness." Though priding himself on his secrecy, he is continually boasting of his amours.

Tearsheet, Doll, in Shakespeare's *II Henry IV*, a woman of low character. In *Henry V*, II, Pistol recommends her to Nym. Prince Hal's remark (*II Henry IV*, II, ii), " This Doll Tearsheet should be some road," has started a conjecture that her name is a misprint or a corruption from Tear-street.

Teazle, Sir Peter, a leading character in Sheridan's comedy, *The School for Scandal* (1777), an old and testy aristocrat, married to a young country girl, whom he is perpetually depreciating to her face for her rustic ways and humble birth, though he really loves her and admires her naïveté and imagined innocence. " I am the sweetest-tempered man alive," he says, with unconscious self-betrayal, " and hate a teasing temper, and so I tell her ladyship a hundred times a day."

Lady Teazle, his wife, is represented at the opening of the play as " a lively and innocent, though imprudent, country girl, transplanted into the midst of all that can bewilder and endanger her, but with still enough of the purity of rural life about her heart to keep the blight of the world from settling upon it permanently." Nevertheless, she manages to get entangled in an affair with the arch-hypocrite Joseph Surface (*q.v.*), from which she emerges with damaged reputation but repentant and reformed.

Tempest, Lady Betty, in Goldsmith's *Citizen of the World*, xxviii (1859), an old maid who, in her brilliant, blooming, but too romantic youth, had turned down all her suitors because none exactly fulfilled her ideals, and so was left to become a wallflower and " a piece of fashionable lumber."

Tempest, Nancy, heroine of Rhoda Broughton's novel, *Nancy*, a romp and a hoyden, who, out of affection for her family and to relieve them in their necessities, has married the elderly Sir Roger Tempest, and learns to love him only after many complications and misunderstandings.

Temple, Charlotte, heroine of a once popular novel by Susanna Haswell Rowson (1790), founded on fact. Her real name was Charlotte Stanley, and she was an English school-girl, induced to come to New York by her betrayer, an English officer, Lieutenant-Colonel Montresor,—the Colonel Montraville of the novel,—and abandoned there. She died after childbirth. There is a monument to her memory over her grave in Trinity Church graveyard, New York City. Colonel Montraville afterward married in New York. By a strange Nemesis, his eldest son became engaged to a girl who turned out to be his own daughter by Charlotte. This part of the story is told in the sequel, *Charlotte's Daughter*, published posthumously.

Temple, Henrietta, titular heroine of a novel (1837) by Benjamin Disraeli. In real life she was Henrietta Villebois, married (1821) to Sir Francis William Sykes of Basildoun, died 1846.

Templeton, Laurence, the pseudonym under which Sir Walter Scott published *Ivanhoe* in the original edition (1820). The preface is initialed L. T., and the dedication by " Laurence Templeton " is to the Rev. Dr. Dryasdust. In a subsequent edition Scott explained that there was " no desire or wish to pass off the supposed Mr. Templeton as a real person. But a kind of continuation of *The Tales of my Landlord*

23

had been recently attempted by a stranger; and it was supposed this Dedicatory Epistle might pass for some imitation of the same kind, and thus putting inquirers upon a false scent, induce them to believe they had before them the work of some new candidate for their favor."

Tennessee's Partner, in a story of that name by Bret Harte (1871), the all-forgiving associate of a scoundrel, known in camp as Tennessee, who runs away with the partner's wife, returns without her, is received back into partnership, is arrested for highway robbery, and hanged, after a vain effort by Partner to bribe the self-constituted court with his entire fortune—"$1700 in coarse gold and a watch."

Tessa, in George Eliot's *Romola*, an innocent Tuscan peasant girl who is bigamously married by Tito Melemma (*q.v.*).

Testy, Timothy, a grouty pessimist, in Beresford's *Miseries of Human Life*.

Teufelsdröckh, Diogenes, Professor of Things in General at Weissnichto in Germany, the feigned author of Carlyle's *Sartor Resartus* (1833–34), which claims to consist only of characteristic passages translated from the original German and held together with a running commentary. Teufelsdröckh (the name means Devil's dung) is described, in Book II, as a foundling who had been brought up by Andreas Futteral, a farmer, and Gretchen his wife, had passed with no special credit through the gymnasium and the university, had studied law and renounced its practice, had lost to a luckier suitor the fair Blumine whom he loved, had plunged into all manner of doubt and despair, and had finally emerged with the conviction that blessedness was better than happiness, and that the idea of his baffled dreams was to be found in the real life around him.

Thaisa, in Shakespeare's *Pericles, Prince of Tyre* (1608), the wife of Pericles and mother of Marina. Dying it was supposed in childbirth, she was cast into the sea, but miraculously revived and became a priestess of Diana at Ephesus.

Thalaba, a famous figure in Oriental mythology, whom Robert Southey took as the hero of his epic, *Thalaba the Destroyer* (1801). He was " father-less, motherless, sisterless, brother-less," for Hodeirah and Zeinab, his parents, had left him orphaned in early youth and before their death all the eight other children had been cut off by the Dom-Danielists (*q.v.*). Even he had almost fallen a victim to an evil spirit sent from Dom-Daniel (see ABDALDAR), but had escaped with Abdaldar's magic ring. Thereupon he set out on his retributive mission as the Destroyer of Dom-Daniel. He successively baffled the stratagems of Lobaba, a sorcerer, and of Mohahreb, another evil spirit, resisted the seductions of the paradise of pleasure, rescued therefrom the maiden Oneiza, whom he married but who died on the bridal night, and finally succumbed to the strategy of Maimana (*q.v.*), recovered his liberty, was befriended by Laila, first in the flesh and when she died, then by her spirit. Under her tutelary guidance he reached Dom-Daniel, slew all the surviving sorcerers, and, having accomplished his mission, was taken up into heaven.

Thekla, in Schiller's drama, *Wallenstein,* daughter of the hero, a lovely and pathetic figure but without any historical justification.

Thelema, Abbey of, in Rabelais's *Gargantua,* an imaginary establishment whose motto, *Fay ce que Vouldras* (old Fr. " Do what you will "), sufficiently illustrates the principles on which it was conducted. Presented by Grangousier to Friar John as a reward for his services in the subjection of Lerné, it was the very reverse of a Catholic religious house, being specially dedicated to luxurious enjoyment, bodily and mental recreation, and intellectual companionship. Religious hypocrites, lawyers, and usurers are excluded, but gallant gentlemen and brilliant ladies are welcomed with effusion. Walter Besant and James Rice in 1878 collaborated on a novel entitled *The Monks of Thelema,* in which a wealthy nineteenth-century idealist, Alan Dunlop, seeks to revive on English soil the Liberty Hall of mediæval French imagination. See RONDELET, MR.

It is always delicate and invidious work to criticise what is meant to be humorous caricature, because one is naturally met with the obvious retort that your practical mind is too dull to appreciate it. Yet we maintain that nineteenth-century caricature should at least have some slight substratum of possibility; and the conditions of the existence of this community of Thelema are simply and glaringly impossible on the face of them. Never would the shrew chaperons of the period so far abdicate their responsibilities and interests as to allow a bevy of beautiful and richly-dowered maidens to live in unrestricted everyday intercourse with a group of gay and fascinating bachelors, some of whom were eminently ineligible.—*Saturday Review,* October 5, 1878.

Thelluson, Hannah, titular heroine of *Hannah* (1871), a novel by Dinah Mulock Craik. On the death of her married sister, the widower, Rev. Bernard Rivers, invites her to take charge of his home and infant daughter. The gentle woman of thirty sees no harm in this arrangement, though it scandalizes the Rivers and their circle. Of course the pair fall in love, and after vainly struggling against fate they marry and defy their worst.

Theobald, Mrs. Jane, heroine of Mrs. Edwards's novel, *Ought we to Visit Her?,* a young girl of Bohemian origin and associations.

The people who will not visit her are the relations of Mr. Theobald, and all the respectable people in Chalkshire, among whom he takes her to live after a free, happy, haphazard life on the Continent. It would be a pity to tell the story, further than to say that the pretty, good-hearted, witty, charming little victim, shunned for no reason by these good people, and deserted by her worthless husband, who takes up an old flirtation with an old reprobate fine lady to beguile the dulness of Chalkshire, comes near being driven into wickedness, but is saved on the way to elopement by one of those sudden fevers which lie in wait in novels, and is reconciled to her husband, and joyfully leaves Chalkshire with him and goes back to their free life on the Continent. Dull respectability and convention are too much for them, and they must fly or be crushed; yet she has done no wrong.— W. D. HOWELLS, in *Atlantic Monthly.*

Theodora, in Disraeli's novel, *Lothair*, a brilliant American woman, a devotee to the cause of Garibaldi and United Italy, with whom Lothair falls platonically in love, and whose influence saves him from the machinations of Catesby and other Roman Catholic friends. She is drawn from a real person (wife of Colonel Chambers, an Englishman), who was in fact the pillar of the Italian cause, for, like the Ayesha of Mahomet, she believed in Garibaldi from the first, encouraged him in his efforts, glorified him in success, consoled him in defeat, and, above all, supplied him with the nerve and sinews of the war on which he had entered. Among Garibaldi's followers she was known as the "Padrona."

Theodora had espoused the cause of Italian freedom with an enthusiasm bordering on frenzy, and was most gallantly seconded by her husband in her endeavors. She was reported in the Italian papers as not being in any one feature like an Englishwoman (which is the highest praise that can be awarded to a woman on the Continent). It is certain that, with her dark, flashing eyes and jet-black hair, she was as unlike as possible to the ordinary British matron. She was far from handsome in countenance, but there was a certain picturesque wildness in her expression which never failed to elicit from strangers the question of "Who is she?" Her dark hair was parted over the forehead and tucked behind her ears, and fell in two thick curls down her neck, in the fashion of Sir Joshua's latest pictures. Her dress was always of the simplest fashion, though made of rich materials. In short, it was impossible for those who had once beheld Theodora ever to forget her.—*Birmingham Post.*

Therese, Madame, in Erckmann-Chatrian's novel of that name, a vivandière of rare elevation of character who is left for dead in the streets of a little village in the Vosges after a fierce conflict in which her soldier comrades are engaged with the Austrian troops and rescued by a philanthropic old doctor from the inhumanity of the villagers and the vengeance of the Austrians.

Theseus, in *A Midsummer Night's Dream* (1594), the Duke of Athens, husband of Hippolyta, before whom, as part of the marriage festivities, is enacted the play within a play of *Pyramus and Thisbe.* They are classical in name only, being in reality romantic mediæval figures. See THESEUS in vol. II.

Theseus is Shakespeare's early ideal of a heroic warrior and man of action. His life is one of splendid achievement and of joy; his love is a kind of happy victory, his marriage a triumph. From early morning, when his hounds—themselves heroic creatures—fill the valley with their "musical confusion," until midnight, when the Athenian clowns end their "very tragical mirth" with a Bergomask dance, Theseus displays his joyous energy and the graciousness of power.—E. DOWDEN: *Shakespeare Primer.*

Thisbe, heroine of the interlude in *A Midsummer Night's Dream.* In classic mythology she is a beautiful maiden of Babylon, beloved by Pyramus, whom she is not allowed to marry. They succeed, however, in communicating with one another through a chink in a wall; whence the amusing episode in Shakespeare's play:

And through wall's chink, poor souls, they
   are content
To whisper.

See PYRAMUS and WALL.

Thornberry, Job, in Beaconsfield's novel, *Endymion* (1880), a political agitator, who is evidently drawn from Richard Cobden.

Mr. Job Thornberry represents Mr. Cobden, whose eloquence is felicitously described in an account of a Corn-law meeting at Manchester. The circumstances of Mr. Thornberry's later life would have perplexed and annoyed his living prototype. Mrs. Thornberry, who is first introduced as a zealous devotee of a Unitarian preacher, joins the Roman communion; and his son, John Hampden Thornberry, puts up portraits of Laud and Strafford over his mantelpiece, and, "embossed in golden letters on a purple ground, the magical word THOROUGH." The same whimsical young gentleman always addresses his father as "Squire," and cultivates an extraordinary passion for game-preserving. Job Thornberry's "intelligence was as clear as ever, and his views on all subjects unchanged; but he was like many other men, governed at home by his affections." . . . The son's name, "Hampden," is perhaps unconsciously suggested by the residence of the Thornberrys at Hurtley, which is identified by description with Great Hampden, an historical house and small hamlet not far from Hughenden. Job's domestic philosophy is an additional illustration of the doctrine of the supremacy of personal motives and influence.—*Saturday Review.*

Thorne, Dr., in Trollope's novel of that name, a physician in the village of Greshambury, an independent, honest gentleman who looks after his niece Mary Thorne, a sweet, modest girl in love with Frank Gresham, whom she eventually marries.

Thornhill, Sir William, in Goldsmith's *Vicar of Wakefield,* a pretended cynic, but really a philanthropist, who assumes the incognito of Mr. Burchell, in order the better to assist the unhappy, the deserving poor, and the oppressed. Hating shams of all sorts, his almost involuntary cry of " Fudge! " at any exhibition of snobbishness or pretension, has become a by-word. He is a constant visitor at the home of Dr. Primrose, the titular vicar, falls in love with and eventually marries one of his daughters, Sophia, and succeeds in saving her sister, Olivia, from undeserved shame, incurred through his own nephew, by proving that what the squire had fancied was a mere mock marriage was in fact a legal one.

Thornhill, Squire, in Goldsmith's *Vicar of Wakefield,* the prodigal and libertine nephew of Sir William Thornhill, who abducts both the vicar's daughters, casts the vicar himself into jail, and imagines that he has betrayed Olivia Primrose, the younger daughter, into a mock marriage, which to his discomfiture turns out to be entirely legal.

Thorpe, Charles, afterward Lord Medway, a leading character in *Quits* (1858), a novel by Baroness Tautphoeus. He is successively the enemy, the reluctant lover, the rejected suitor, and in the end the accepted husband of the heroine, Nora Nixon.

We afterward talked long about *Quits,* and she told me that the character of Thorpe was a favorite bit of work; that she had taken great pains with it, as she wished to produce a typical Englishman of the best class, with all his fine qualities, and the defects inseparable from these qualities; and the most charming arch smile lit up her face as she said, "I must think that I succeeded with Thorpe, for after *Quits* was published I had several very angry letters from some English cousins of mine, any one

of whom might have sat (with some slight changes) for the portrait of Thorpe, and every one of them reproached me in no measured terms for 'putting a fellow into a book.' So you see they fitted the cap upon themselves."—BARONESS TAUTPHOEUS. An interview in *Atlantic Monthly,* July, 1894.

Thorpe, John, in Jane Austen's novel, *Northanger Abbey* (written in 1798), a horsey, slangy undergraduate, vain, boastful, vulgar, who rejoices in flashy clothes and bewilders Catherine Morland by his tall talk. " She had not been brought up to understand the propensities of a rattle, nor to know to how many idle assertions and impudent falsehoods an excess of vanity will lead."

Thoughtless, Betsy, heroine of a novel, *The History of Miss Betsy Thoughtless* (1751), by Mrs. Eliza Haywood, describing the *début* into London society of a giddy and inexperienced but right-minded girl, and the various perils she escaped from the dissolute set amid which she was launched. The novel is chiefly interesting to-day from having furnished hints to Miss Burney for her far superior *Evelina.*

Thule, Princess of. See MACKENZIE, SHEILA.

Thunderer, The, a name bestowed upon *The Times,* in allusion to the vigorous articles contributed to it at one time by Edward Sterling, who possessed a literary style of considerable power.

It appears that the *Times* provided the occasion and even the word. Two women had been bespattered with mud by a horseman riding too close to them, and the *Times* published a harsh reproof of the Duke of Cumberland, the supposed offender. A denial was made on behalf of the duke, and the *Times* recanted, publishing a second article, which began with the words: " When a few days ago we thundered out." That struck the public as the right word for what the *Times* was generally doing in those days, and " The Thunderer " became the *Times's* nickname.

Thundertentronckh, Arminius von, the *nom de plume* under which Matthew Arnold contributed several papers of a satirical character to the pages of *The Pall Mall Gazette*. These, with one or two others originally published in *The Cornhill Magazine*, were republished ln *Friendship's Garland*, which the editor pretended to have woven as a memorial of his dead friend.

Mr. Arnold's "genial and somewhat esoteric philosophy," if I may borrow a phrase applied by Sir George Trevelyan to his uncle, is nowhere more compendiously stated than in *Friendship's Garland*, which appeared in a complete form at the beginning of 1871. The history of this little book is curious. The letters of which it consists were first printed in the *Pall Mall Gazette*, when that journal of many vicissitudes was edited by Mr. Frederick Greenwood. They extend over a period of four years, from 1866 to 1870, dealing chiefly with the victories of Prussia over Austria, and of Germany over France. Attributed to a young Prussian, Arminius von Thunder-ten-Tronckh, whose name is of course taken from *Candide*, they really represent Mr. Arnold's views upon the characteristic deficiencies of his countrymen.—HOWARD PAUL.

Thurio, in *The Two Gentlemen of Verona*, a rival of Valentine in the love of Silvia.

Thurston, Hannah, heroine and title of a novel by Bayard Taylor (1864). At the age of thirty she renounces marriage to take up an ardent advocacy of woman suffrage. She is at the height of her village influence, recognized by all as a woman whom it is possible for men to love, yet with something in her beyond womanhood when she meets her conqueror in Maxwell Woodbury.

Thwackum, Parson Roger, in Fielding's *History of Tom Jones* (1749), a clerical pedagogue, learned, honest, and not unworthy, but intensely selfish and endowed with a furious temper. As to his personal appearance we are told (Bk. iii, Chap. 6), "The pedagogue did in countenance very nearly resemble that gentleman who in the *Harlot's Progress* [by Hogarth] is seen correcting the ladies in Bridewell.

Thyrsis, the name under which Matthew Arnold deplored the death of his friend Arthur Hugh Clough (1819–1861), who died in Florence. *Thyrsis* is a monody or elegy

modelled not on Milton (though the theme suggests *Lycidas* and Edward King), but on Theocritus. Clough, however, had an individuality of his own, and is not likely to become a mere name like the Reverend Mr. King.

Tibbs, Beau, a make-believe dandy and man-about-town in Goldsmith's *Citizen of the World* (1789).

The poor little pinched pretender to fashion, with his tarnished finery and his reed-voiced, simpering helpmate,—with his coffee-house cackle of my Lord Mudler and the Duchess of Piccadilly, and his magnificent promises of turbot and ortolan, which issue pitifully in postponed ox-cheek and bitter beer,—approaches the dimensions of a masterpiece. Charles Lamb, one would think, must have rejoiced over the reckless assurance which expatiates on the charming view of the Thames from the garret of a back-street in the suburbs, which glorifies the "paltry unframed pictures on its walls into essays in the manner of the celebrated Grisoni, and transforms a surly Scotch hag-of-all-work into an old and privileged family servant.—AUSTIN DOBSON: *Eighteenth Century Vignettes.*

Tickler, Timothy, one of the interlocutors in the *Noctes Ambrosianæ* and a frequent contributor under that pseudonym to *Blackwood's Magazine*, was Robert Sym, an Edinburgh lawyer (1750–1854).

Tilburina, in Sheridan's comedy, *The Critic*, the daughter of the governor of Tilbury Fort (hence the name). He is "a plain matter-of-fact man," while his offspring is a love-lorn maiden, full of tears and sighs, raptures and ravings. Both these characters appear in Mr. Puff's tragedy, *The Spanish Armada*, which is supposed to be under rehearsal for critical approval or emendation.

An oyster may be crossed in love, says the gentle Tilburina,—and a drover may be touched on a point of honor, says the Chronicler of the Canongate.—SIR W. SCOTT.

Tim, Tiny, in Dickens's *Christmas Carol*, is the little crippled son of Bob Cratchit. His happy sentiment, "God bless us, every one," is now a household word.

Timias, in Spenser's *Faërie Queene*, the squire to King Arthur, who falls honorably in love with Belphœbe in

---

Book iii, 6, but in Book iv, 7, is discovered by that lady in wanton dalliance with Amoret.

The affection of Timias for Belphœbe is allowed, on all hands, to allude to Sir Walter Raleigh's pretended admiration of Queen Elizabeth; and his disgrace, on account of a less platonic intrigue with the daughter of Sir Nicholas Throgmorton, together with his restoration to favor, are plainly pointed out in the subsequent events. But no commentator has noticed the beautiful insinuation by which the poet points out the error of his friend, and of his friend's wife. Timias finds Amoret in the arms of Corflambo, or sensual passion: he combats the monster unsuccessfully, and wounds the lady in his arms.—SIR W. SCOTT.

Timon, hero of a tragedy by Shakespeare, *Timon of Athens* (1607).

Timon of Athens is the exhibition of a single character in contrasted situations. Timon is rich and generous, which is matter for the first act; his riches and his friends fail him in the second and third acts; he retires to a desert outside the city, curses mankind, and dies, which climax is the theme of the fourth and fifth acts. There is nothing in all Shakespeare's work more stupendous than the colossal figure of Timon, raining his terrible imprecations on the littleness and falsehood of mankind. Yet the play as a whole is unsatisfying, because the cause is inadequate to produce the effect.—WALTER RALEIGH: *Shakespeare,* p. 112.

Tinto, Dick, a "celebrated" painter in Scott's novel, *St. Ronan's Well* (1823), who restores Meg Dods's sign, gilds the bishop's crook, and augments the horrors of the Devil's aspect. He had previously appeared in the introduction to *The Bride of Lammermoor* (1819), as supplying the material for that tale to Peter Pattieson.

Titania, in *A Midsummer Night's Dream* (1592), the Queen of the Fairies and consort of Oberon. In Shakespeare's day the fairies were identified with the classic nymphs, attendants of Diana. Hence Titania, an alternative name for Diana, was selected as the designation for the queen of his midnight sprites. Cf. King James I: "That fourth kind of spirits quhilt by the Gentiles was called Diana and her wandering court, and amongst us called the Phairëe." Tyrwhitt suggests that the progenitors of Oberon and Titania may be found in Chaucer's *Marchantes Tale,* where Pluto is the king of faerie and his queen Proserpina, "who danced and sung about the wall under the laurel in January's garden." But otherwise there is not much resemblance. Knight opines that in Chaucer's *Wife of Bathes Tale,* "Shakespeare found the popular superstition presented in that spirit of gladsome revelry which it was reserved for him to work out in his matchless drama.

"In old days ol King Artour,
Of which that Bretens speken gret honour,
All was this land fulfilled of faërie;
The elfe-queene with her joly compagnie
Danced ful oft in many a grene mede."

May it not be said that Shakespeare took all these ingredients, the popular superstitions, the classic and the current lore concerning Diana, and the brightness and gayety that Chaucer had given to "the elfe-queene," and from them evoked the dainty spirit that the world for evermore knows as "Titania?"

No name, indeed, could have been more appropriate. It embodies rich and complex associations connected with the silver bow, the magic cup, and the triple crown; it embraces in one comprehensive symbol the whole female empire of mystery and night belonging to classical mythology.

Diana, Latona, Hecate, are all goddesses of night, queens of the shadowy world, ruling over its mystic elements and spectral powers. The common name thus awakens recollections of gleaming huntresses in dim and dewy woods, of dark rites and potent incantations under moonlit skies, of strange aërial voyages and ghostly apparitions from the underworld. It was, therefore, of all possible names the one best fitted to designate the queen of the same shadowy empire, with its phantom troops and activities, in the northern mythology. And since Shakespeare, with prescient inspiration, selected it for this purpose, it has naturally come to represent the whole world of fairy beauty, elfin adventure, and goblin sport connected with lunar influences, with enchanted herbs and muttered spells.—THOMAS S. BAYNES.

The Titania of Shakespeare's fairy mythology may thus be regarded as the successor of Diana and other regents of the night belonging to the Greek pantheon.

Titmarsh, Michael Angelo, a pseudonym, or, more specifically, an imaginary character behind which Thackeray, in his early magazine sketches, novels, and burlesques, hid his own personality. Like Michael Angelo, Thackeray was an author artist and had a broken nose. In such portraits as the imaginary Titmarsh drew of himself, he is sketched as a small man with a boyish face.

No doubt my father first made this artist's acquaintance at one of the studios in Paris. Very soon Mr. Titmarsh's criticisms began to appear in various papers and magazines. He visited the salons as well as the exhibitions over here; he drew most of the Christmas books and wrote them too. He had a varied career. One could almost write his life. For a time, as we know, he was an assistant master at Dr. Birch's Academy. He was first cousin to Samuel Titmarsh, of the *Great Hoggarty Diamond;* also he painted in water-colors. To the kingdom of heaven he assuredly belongs! Kindly, humorous, delightful little friend, droll shadow behind which my father loved to shelter himself.—MRS. ANNE THACKERAY RITCHIE: *Introduction to "Yellow Plush Papers," etc.*

Titmouse, Tittlebat, in Samuel Warren's novel, *Ten Thousand a Year,* a vulgar, conceited, ignorant little coxcomb, a linen-draper's assistant, who through a legal technicality wins a fortune of £10,000 a year, but, after a brief career of ostentatious prodigality, is ousted from the estate.

Toby, Uncle. See SHANDY.

Todgers, Mrs. M., in Dickens's *Martin Chuzzlewit,* keeper of a commercial boarding-house in London. She was a rather " bony and hard-featured lady, with a row of curls in front of her head shaped like little barrels of beer, and on the top of it something made of net—you couldn't call it a cap exactly—which looked like a black cobweb." We have it from her own lips, that presiding over such an establishment makes sad havoc with the features. " The gravy alone," as she informed Miss Pecksniff, " is enough to add twenty years to one's age." In her opinion there was no such passion in human nature as the passion for gravy among commercial gentlemen. Neverthe-

less, she owned to feelings of a tender nature for Mr. Pecksniff—unworthy though he was—and befriended his daughter Mercy after her unfortunate marriage with Jonas Chuzzlewit.

Toggenburg, Ritter, hero of a simple and tender ballad by Schiller, telling how the Ritter, on his return from the Holy Wars, whither he had gone to cure himself of a hopeless passion, finds that his lady-love has taken the veil, whereupon he builds himself a hut in sight of the convent, and every day he watches for the time when his beloved shall appear at her window. Finally, one morning, he is found dead, with his eyes still turned toward her casement. The poem was evidently suggested by the mediæval legend of Roland and Hildegunde. See ROLANDSECK in vol. II.

Toinette, in Molière's *Le Malade Imaginaire,* the best of all that author's serving-maids. The embodiment of mirth and vivacity, she brings a breath of fresh air with her whenever she enters the sick-room and lightens it with a gleam of sunshine. She recalls the Dorine of *Tartuffe* and the Nicole of the *Bourgeois Gentilhomme,* but with a more exuberant gayety. It is she who finally rescues her master Argan by proving to him the worthlessness of his wife Béline. Toinette directs her master to stretch himself out as if dead in his easy-chair, and, when Béline appears, Toinette tells her that he has just passed away in her arms.

"Heaven be praised!" exclaims the affectionate wife. "Now I am delivered of a great burden. What use was he when on earth? A man troublesome to all around him,—a dirty, disgusting creature, ever blowing his nose, coughing, or spitting. . . . Since, fortunately, no one knows of his death, let us put him on his bed, and keep the fact concealed till I have done what I want. There are papers and money which I must seize. . . . Come, Toinette, give me the keys."

The defunct man, however, starts to his feet, and the terror-stricken wife flies, never to reappear.

Tolla (an affectionate diminutive of Vittoria), heroine of About's romance of that name (1855), a social satire on the habits of the long descended Roman nobility. The satire is softened, however, by an engaging picture of the simple-minded heroine and by realistic sketches of domestic life in the gloomy interior of a poverty-stricken Roman palace. The story is founded on fact. Vittoria Savorelli was a real person, who loved an Italian prince, was betrayed, and died. Her letters were published in 1841. These About manipulated into a novel, changing her last name to Feraldi, and calling her lover Prince Lello Coromila-Bereghi.

Tom, Uncle, hero of a novel of that name by Harriet Beecher Stowe (1852), which enjoyed a phenomenal popularity in America and in Europe.

Uncle Tom is a paragon of virtue. He is more than mortal in his powers of endurance, in his devotion, in his self-denial, in his Christian profession and practice, and in his abhorrence of spirituous liquors. He is described as a fine, powerful negro, walking through the world with a Bible in his hands and virtuous indignation on his lips, both ready to be called into requisition on the slightest provocation, in season and out of season, at work and at play, by your leave or without it, in sorrow or in joy, for the benefit of his superiors or for the castigation of his equals. He represents in his person the only well-authenticated instance we know, in modern times, of that laudable principle in virtue of which a man presents his left cheek to be smitten after the first has been slapped. The more you "larrup" Uncle Tom the more he blesses you; the greater the bodily agony the more intense becomes his spiritual delight.—*London Times* (1852).

Tommy, Sentimental, in J. M. Barrie's novel of that name (1896), the posthumous son of Thomas Sandys. He begins life as a street urchin. When doubly orphaned by the death of his mother, who had been Jean Myles of Thrums, he and his sister Elspeth are cared for by Aaron Latta, an old lover of his mother. They go to the Hanky School in Thrums. Later Tommy studies for the university, but he allows his imagination to run riot in airy escapades and self-invented love episodes, fails to pass his examination, and is put to work as herdboy on a farm. His history is continued in a sequel, *Tommy and Grizel.*

Tonson, Monsieur, an imaginary character in a farce of that name (1821) by W. T. Moncrief. Jack Ardourly falls in love with a young woman (Adolphine de Courcy) whom he passes in the street, but, not knowing her name or address, he engages Tom King to ferret out both. Tom traces her to the house of a French barber, a refugee named Morbleu, and sends people thither to ask for Mr. Thompson, hoping thus to obtain a clue. Poor Morbleu is driven almost wild assuring his many callers that there is no Monsieur Tonson dwelling in his house. The play is founded upon a prank actually played by an actor named Thomas King, ephemerally famed for his wit, and was made the subject of a poem by John Taylor (1800).

Toots, Mr., in Dickens's *Dombey and Son,* a warm-hearted, simple-minded young person, victim of Dr. Blimber's forcing process, and most lovable of all specimens of arrested development. His energies in school-time are devoted to writing "long letters to himself from persons of distinction, addressed to P. Toots, Esquire, Brighton, Sussex, and preserving them in his desk with great care." Equally innocent and infantile are his attempts to be "fast." He and Feeder, B. A., lock themselves up in the latter's room, and cramming their noses with snuff to enjoy delightful agonies of sneezing, drinking table beer at intervals, feel "all the glories of dissipation." His favorite companion is a prize-fighter (The Chicken), his confidant is Captain Cuttle, to whom he confesses the most intimate details of his hopeless passion for Florence Dombey.

Topsy, in Mrs. Stowe's *Uncle Tom's Cabin* (1852), a little black imp who loves lying for the sake of lying, who is more mischievous than a monkey and in all respects as ignorant. She loses all her individuality by being converted (with miraculous ease) into a commonplace Christian, and ends as missionary to a station in Africa.

Tormes, Lazarillo de, hero of a picaresque romance of that name (1553), by Diego Hurtado de Mendoza. Lazarillo is a street Arab, good-humored and nimble-witted, but absolutely conscienceless, who rises in the world through chicanery and cunning. He learns his first lessons in dissimulation from a rascally blind beggar to whom he acts as guide. Thence he rises to greater frauds and a wider range of crime and adventure, in the service successively of a priest, a country squire starving on his own pride, a retailer of indulgences, a chaplain, and an alguazil. Finally, from the most disgraceful motives, he settles down as a married man, and the unfinished story leaves him town-crier of Toledo.

Mendoza's novel laid the foundation for a classic school of fiction especially national, which, under the name of *gusto picaresco* (the style of roguery), is as well known as any department of Spanish literature, and which was imitated and expanded by Le Sage in *Gil Blas.*

Tory Foxhunter, a character sketched in several numbers of Addison's semi-weekly *Freeholder* (1716), ridiculing with a quiet and urbane humor the bigoted conservatism of the rural squirearchy, who were sworn enemies of the House of Hanover.

The Foxhunter will not allow that there had been any good weather in England since the Revolution. He ridicules travelling abroad, saying " that he scarce ever knew a traveller in his life who had not forsook his principles and lost his hunting-seat." He patronizes an innkeeper whom he describes as " the best Church-of-England man upon the road," whispering, in explanation to the author, that, though boniface had no time to go to church himself, he " had headed a mob at the pulling down of two or three meeting-houses." He characterizes another of his neighbors as " an old fanatical cur," because " we are told in the country that he spoke twice in the Queen's time against taking off the duties upon French claret."

Touchett, Ralph, in Henry James's international novel, *The Portrait of a Lady* (1881), the English cousin and the platonic lover of the New England girl Isabel Light. An invalid, he dies happy in the thought that he has made her happy. In order that she may not be obliged to marry for a support, he had persuaded his father to divide the inheritance that would come to him into two equal parts, one of which went to Isabel. It was for this fortune that Isabel was married by a fortune-hunter whose indifference blasted her life.

Touchstone, the clown in Shakespeare's comedy, *As You Like It.*

He is a rare fellow. He is a mixture of the ancient cynic philosopher with the modern buffoon, and turns folly into wit, and wit into folly, just as the fit takes him. His courtship of Audrey not only throws a degree of ridicule on the state of wedlock itself, but he is equally an enemy to the prejudices of opinion in other respects. The lofty tone of enthusiasm which the Duke and his companions in exile spread over the stillness and solitude of a country life receives a pleasant shock from Touchstone's sceptical determination of the question in his reply to Corin (iii, 2, 14). Zimmerman's celebrated work on *Solitude* discovers only half the sense of this passage.—HAZLITT.

Toussaint l'Ouverture, the negro emancipator of San Domingo from French rule, is the hero of an historical novel, *The Hour and the Man* (1840), by Harriet Martineau. In the uprising of the slaves, August, 1791, Toussaint at first remains loyal to the whites, and even enters the service of the allies of the French king. His mind wavers when the negro convention proclaims the emancipation of his race, and he ends by accepting the leadership of the blacks. From this point the story follows the course of history through his dramatic successes to the tragic end of his extraordinary career.

Traddles, Thomas (better known as **Tommie**), in Dickens's *David Copperfield,* a fellow-pupil with David at Salem House, afterward a barrister and ultimately a judge. In his school days he was " the merriest and most miserable of all the boys." He was always being caned, but found relief in drawing skeletons all over his slate before his eyes were dry. "I used at first to wonder," says Copperfield, "what comfort Traddles found in drawing skeletons, and for some time looked upon him as a sort of hermit who reminded himself by those symbols of mortality that caning couldn't last for ever. But I believe he only did it because they were easy and didn't want any features."

Traffick, Sir Jealous, in Mrs. Centlivre's comedy, *The Busybody* (1709), a wealthy English merchant who unpatriotically imagines that everything Spanish is superior to the English. He is tricked by Charles Gripe, disguised in a Spanish costume as Don Diego Barbinetto, into surrendering the hand of his daughter Isabinda.

Trafford, Geoffrey, hero of Mrs. Alexander's novel, *The Wooing O't* (1873). An aristocratic, cynical, witty, travelled man of the world, who at thirty-two has exhausted its pleasures, and who, though "steady," would "stick at nothing which he wanted very much." He is always a gentleman, however, with infinite depths of possible passion in his dark eyes, so that all women say instinctively to themselves, "How he could love!" Beloved by a legion of women, he never can return their affection until he meets Maggy Grey.

Trajan, hero of a novel of that name (1885), by H. F. Keenan, a young American artist living in Paris at the height of the Second Empire (May, 1870, to May, 1871), and more or less affiliated with the men who afterward were active in the scenes that followed Sedan.

Treherne, Belinda, heroine of W. S. Gilbert's comedy, *Engaged*, played in the original performance (1877) by Miss Marion Terry.

Trelawney, Rose, heroine of a comedy, *Trelawney of the Wells* (1898), by Arthur W. Pinero. An actress engaged to a young English nobleman, she leaves the Sadler's Wells company to visit his home and family. Wearying of the frivolities of aristocratic society she breaks her engage-

ment and returns to the freer life of the stage. Thither her lover follows and becomes an actor in order to win her.

Trelooby, Squire, hero of a farce of that name by Vanbrugh, Congreve, and Walsh (1704), is a squire who comes from Cornwall to London, and meets with substantially the same adventures and misadventures as confounded that gentleman from Limoges, Monsieur de Pourceargnac (*q.v.*), when he left rustic simplicity to come to Paris.

Tremaine, hero of *Tremaine, or the Man of Refinement*, a novel by Robert Plumer Ward, published anonymously in 1825, a refined and amiable sceptic of thirty-eight, a disbeliever in love, in friendship, and in revealed religion, has fled from the hollow world to bury himself in his ancestral estates, and there oscillates between listless indolence and ill-regulated exertion. He is at last redeemed from his various errors through his love for a girl of eighteen, and the influence of her reverend father, a country clergyman.

Trent, Little Nell, an ideal of childish innocence, sweetness, and purity, in Dickens's novel, *The Old Curiosity Shop*, grandchild of the owner of the shop. The old man, obsessed with the idea of making her rich and happy, tempts fortune in the gambling hells, pawns everything, loses everything, and, having been turned into the streets, starts out on weary wanderings with Little Nell as his guide until she dies of weariness and privation.

Triboulet, the historical jester at the courts of Louis XII and Francis I, figures in Rabelais's *Gargantua*, and was taken by Victor Hugo as the hero of his tragedy, *Le Roi S'Amuse.* Hugo's story is sheer fiction, or rather an old legend arbitrarily assigned to Triboulet. Francis I casts lustful eyes upon the jester's daughter Blanche; to save her and wreak vengeance on Francis, Triboulet contrives a plot whereby she shall kill her royal lover and stow his dead body into a sack which Triboulet will find and carry away. In a terrific climax the jester, triumphing over the dead body which he believes to be that of his daughter's seducer, suddenly hears the voice of his light-hearted enemy, and finds that it is his own daughter whose death he has compassed. Verdi turned Hugo's tragedy into the opera *Rigoletto* (1852), choosing for his jester an Italian instead of a Frenchman and changing the daughter's name to Gilda. Tom Taylor, in *The Fool's Revenge* (1859), a drama founded on Hugo, renames the jester and his daughter Bertuccio and Fiordelisa.

Trilby, in Charles Nodier's story of that name (1822), founded on local tradition, a male fairy who attached himself to a Breton fisherman, fell in love with his wife, and performed all sorts of domestic services for her. See O'FERRALL, TRILBY.

Trilby was a name that had long lain *perdu* somewhere at the back of du Maurier's head. He traced it to a story by Charles Nodier. The name Trilby also appears in a poem by Alfred de Musset. And to this name and to the story of a woman which was once told him du Maurier's Trilby owed her birth. "From the moment the name occurred to me," he said, "I was struck with its value. I at once realized that it was a name of great importance. I think I must have felt as happy as Thackeray did when the title of *Vanity Fair* suggested itself to him.— T. MARTIN WOOD: *George du Maurier*, p. 92.

Trim, Corporal, in Sterne's novel of *Tristram Shandy*, servant to Uncle Toby.

Trim, instead of being the opposite, is, in his notions, the duplicate of Uncle Toby. Yet, with an identity of disposition, the character of the common soldier is nicely discriminated from that of the officer. His whole carriage bears traces of the drill-yard, which are wanting in the superior. Under the name of a servant, he is in reality a companion; and he is a delightful mixture of familiarity in the essence and the most deferential respect in forms. Of his simplicity and humanity, it is enough to say that he is worthy to walk behind his master. —ELWIN.

Trissotin, in Molière's comedy, *Las Femmes Savantes*, a poetaster and a self-fancied *bel esprit*, who feigns to be in love with Henriette, although she dislikes him, but gladly retires when her father is reported to be on the verge of bankruptcy. His absurd quarrel with his rival, Vadius, forms a famous episode in the play. In creating the characters of the two rivals Molière was held to have in mind the Abbé Cotin and Ménage. As to the first there can be no doubt. It is even said that in MS. the name appeared as Tricotin, but was afterwards changed. The sonnet and madrigal quoted in the play are taken literally from the *Œuvres Galantes* of the Abbé published in 1663. The Abbé Charles Cotin (1604–1682) was a member of the French Academy and a prolific writer in prose and verse. He had made some veiled attacks upon Molière, but the latter was less moved probably by resentment for the individual than detestation for his kind. He saw in Cotin the embodiment of literary pretentiousness supported on a limited basis of information.

Troilus, son of Priam, king of Troy, hero of Shakespeare's tragedy, *Troilus and Cressida* (1609), and of Chaucer's poem, *Troylus and Cressid*, reproduced from Boccaccio. See this entry in vol. II.

Chaucer's poem was for two centuries the most popular poem in England. In the fifteenth century a Scotch poet, Henryson, wrote a continuation of it. Sixteenth century praises of it abound. "Chaucer," says Sir Philip Sidney, "undoubtedly did excellently in his *Troylus and Cressid*." Lydgate, in his *Troy Book*, when he comes to *Troilus ann Cressida*, at once cites Chaucer's poem as the source of all he has to tell. Shakespeare does not accept the story in the spirit in which Chaucer recounts it. Chaucer's heart was very soft towards women, and he could not harden it enough to represent Cressida faithfully. He is always yearning to excuse her. Even for what he does say he attempts reparation in the *Legend of Good Women*. With all her faults he loved her still, and would fain have been blind to her terrible treason.

Trotwood, Betsy (*i.e.*, **Elizabeth**), in Dickens's *David Copperfield*, a great-aunt of the hero, who kindly welcomes him when he runs away from his cruel stepfather Murdstone. She had been married to a husband younger than herself,—" who was very handsome except in the sense of the homely adage, handsome is that handsome does,"—and, having obtained a separation, resumed her maiden name, bought a cottage on the sea-coast, and there established herself as a single woman with one servant. She is supposed to have been drawn from Miss Mary Strong, who occupied a double-fronted cottage on the sea-front at Broadstairs, now named Dickens House. Copperfield thus describes her:

My aunt was a tall, hard-featured lady, but by no means ill-looking. There was inflexibility in her face, in her voice, in her gait and carriage, but her features were rather handsome than otherwise, though unbending and austere.

Troy, Sergeant Francis, in Thomas Hardy's novel, *Far from the Madding Crowd* (1874), the reputed son of a Weatherby physician, but plausibly suspected to be the illegitimate issue of the late Lord Severn. Articled to an attorney, he enlisted in the dragoons, became particularly expert in fencing and all soldierly exercises, and, returning to Weatherby, married Bathsheba Everdene (*q.v.*). His evil doings and their results form the staple of the plot.

Trulliber, Parson, in Fielding's novel, *The Adventures of Joseph Andrews* (1742), a coarse, brutal, ignorant, and slothful clergyman, who "had a stateliness in his gait when he walked, not unlike that of a goose, only he stalked slower." In mind and manners he forms a striking contrast to the amiable, simple, and devout Parson Adams in the same novel.

Trunnion, Commodore Hawser, in Smollett's *Adventures of Peregrine Pickle*, an eccentric naval veteran, retired from service with honorable scars, but retaining his radical habits. He keeps garrison in his house, which is defended by a ditch crossed by a drawbridge, and he obliges his servants to sleep in hammocks and take turns on watch. See WEMMICK.

Sir Walter thought that Smollet's sailors in *Pickle* "border on caricature." No doubt they do: the eccentricities of Hawser Trunnion, Esq., are exaggerated, and Pipes is less subdued than Rattlin, though always

delightful. But Trunnion absolutely makes one laugh aloud: whether he is criticising the sister of Mr. Gamaliel Pickle in that gentleman's presence at a pothouse; or riding to the altar with his squadron of sailors tacking in an unfavorable gale; or being ran away into a pack of hounds, and clearing a hollow road over a wagoner, who views him with "unspeakable terror and amazement." Mr. Winkle as an equestrian is not more entirely acceptable to the mind than Trunnion. We may speak of "caricature," but if an author can make us sob with laughter, to criticise him solemnly is ungrateful.—ANDREW LANG, *Adventures among Books*, p. 200.

Tubal, in Shakespeare's comedy, *The Merchant of Venice*, a Jew friend of Shylock, appearing only in Act iii, where he alternately exasperates Shylock with reports of his daughter's extravagance and consoles him with news of Antonio's misfortunes.

Tuggs, Simon (self-styled Cymon), in Dickens's *The Tuggs at Ramsgate*, in *Sketches by Boz*, a book-keeper in his father's grocery, who, when the family comes into sudden wealth, apes aristocratic airs and is neatly taken in and swindled by Captain Waters and his wife.

Tulliver, Maggie, heroine of George Eliot's novel, *The Mill on the Floss* (1860). With a warm and yearning heart, overflowing affection, a passionate desire to love and to be loved, she is tortured even in childhood by the sense of her own shortcomings, the pangs of a too tender conscience. As she advances towards maturity the burden and the mystery of existence become more and more inexplicable to her, she gets entangled among the quicksands, and, though she draws back before taking the fatal leap over a moral precipice, it is with such loss of dignity and self-esteem that she welcomes death when it comes through an accident. The story is largely autobiographical. Maggie's childish relations with her brother Tom are evidently a reminiscence of the early life of the author and her brother Isaac—to whom the verses, *Brother and Sister*, are addressed. The alienation of Maggie from her friends and kindred by a single false step has also a parallel in George Eliot's life, her heterodox opinions, and especially her relations with Lewes, whose name she assumed without legal sanction, having severed her from her family and early associates.

> The finest thing in that admirable novel has always been, to our taste, not its portrayal of the young girl's love struggles as regards her lover, but those as regards her brother. The former are fiction,—skilful fiction; but the latter are warm reality, and the merit of the verses is that they are colored from the same source.—HENRY JAMES: *Views and Reviews*, p. 142.

Tulliver, Tom, in George Eliot's novel, *The Mill on the Floss*, the brother of Maggie and her favorite companion in youth. Conceited and hard-headed, though not hard-hearted, he is utterly unable to understand her wayward moods or the lofty ideals that underlie them. As he grows up the estrangement between them grows wider.

> Poor erratic Maggie is worth a hundred of her positive brother, and yet on the very threshold of life she is compelled to accept him as her master. He falls naturally into the man's privilege of always being in the right.—HENRY JAMES: *Views and Reviews*, p. 29.

> The character of Tom is far from being a noble one, but it acquires a certain dignity from its patience, resoluteness, and sense of duty.—LESLIE STEPHEN: *George Eliot*.

Tully-Veolan, in Scott's *Waverley*, perhaps the most celebrated manorhouse in fiction. Scott says he had no particular domicile in view. The peculiarities of the place were common to many old Scotch seats. But Traquair, in Peeblesshire, was probably in his mind.

> Scott's intimate knowledge of the place, his frequent visits to it, and the impression which such a history-haunted pile was likely to make on his imagination, suggest the tolerable certainty of its having at least formed the study for the more finished and bolder-featured picture. The avenue in the novel was undoubtedly modelled from the avenue at Traquair, bating an archway, which Traquair never had. The twin Bears, masses of upright stone battered by the blasts of many winters, still frown on the highway.—W. S. CROCKETT: *The Scott Originals*.

Turcaret, hero and title of a political comedy by Lesage (1708). Turcaret is a burlesque of the financier Samuel Bernard, who had been called in by the Controller, General Desmarest, to regulate the finances of France. This young man, son of a member of the Academy of Painters, raised himself to the highest position in point of wealth and social dignity, and married his daughter to the son of President Molé. His partisans assert that his integrity was equal to his capacity, and that, instead of being the usurer and libertine that Lesage depicts him in *Turcaret*, he devoted all his energies to the service of the state and died almost penniless, it being discovered after his death that he had lent no less than ten million francs to various persons, from whom he had never either asked or received a penny in return.

Turveydrop, Mr., in Dickens's novel, *Bleak House*, a dancing-master and a model of deportment. His imposing outer appearance is inflated from within by nothing more august than the wind of his own self-esteem. Yet he fools the world into acceptance of his fancied superiority. He lived on the earnings of his wife, a meek little dancing-mistress, until she died, when the burden of supporting him was transferred to his son Prince Turveydrop, so named in honor of the Prince Regent, whom the elder Turveydrop adored on account of his deportment.

Twining, Claire, heroine of Edgar Fawcett's novel, *An Ambitious Woman* (1883). She comes from a good old English family on her father's side, but her mother was an American plebeian and vulgarian who married him for his money. After the father's death Claire develops social ambitions. A wealthy schoolgirl friend is her first aid in the struggle for social recognition, a wellborn husband is her second.

Twist, Oliver, hero of Dickens's novel of that name (1837), a nameless orphan born and brought up in a workhouse, whither his mother had come to die, without revealing either her name or his. He startles all bumbledom by asking for more gruel, runs away to London, where he consorts in all innocence with thieves, fences, and prostitutes, is rescued and befriended by the Maylie family, into whose house he had been thrust for burglarious purposes, and finally discovers an aunt in Miss Rose Maylie, an adopted daughter of the house, whose real name, like his own, is Fleming.

Tybalt, in Shakespeare's tragedy, *Romeo and Juliet,* a cousin of Juliet. Mercutio calls him " prince or king of cats " (Act ii, 4), an allusion to the fact that Tybalt, or Tybert, is the name of the cat in *Reynard the Fox.* Fiery and quarrelsome, he forces a quarrel with Romeo and his friends, slays Mercutio, and is himself slain by Romeo (iii, 1).

Tyrrell, Sir James (died 1502), the supposed murderer of the princes in the Tower, appears in that capacity in Shakespeare's play, *Richard III* (Act iv, 3). He was beheaded in 1502 as a co-conspirator with the Earl of Suffolk, and is said to have confessed the murder before his death. The substance of this confession (though the text has not been preserved) forms the basis of the story as we have it in *The History of King Richard III* attributed to Sir Thomas More. The author writes that Sir James was " a brave, handsome man, who deserved a better master, and would have inherited the esteem of all men, had his virtues been as great as his valor."

U

Udolpho, in Anne Radcliffe's romance, *The Mysteries of Udolpho* (1794), a mediæval castle in the Apennines, where during the seventeenth century all sorts of dark dealings with the powers of evil are fabled to have occurred. Emily St. Aubyn, an English girl, is the chief victim of these apparently supernatural agencies. The Chevalier Valencourt, her noble and courageous lover, finally lays the spell, or, rather, exposes the fact that the " mysteries " are all capable of a perfectly natural explanation.

Ugly Duckling, in Andersen's *Fairy Tales,* a cygnet hatched out among a brood of ducklings: mistaken for an uncouth and awkward member of the same species, and persecuted as such until his swanhood is revealed. It is a poetical presentation of Andersen's own tearful youth and finally triumphant maturity. Bismarck read into it an allegory of his own early career. " My mother always thought me an Ugly Duckling," he said.

Ulalume, in Poe's mystic ballad of that name (1849), is plausibly interpreted as a reference to the poet's wife, Virginia Clemm, whom he had buried October, 1848. The hint of a new love had almost effaced her

image, when Psyche—his soul—starts up in alarm to remind him that just a year ago he had buried Ulalume. With the cry that a demon has been tempting him, he dismisses all thoughts of a successor.

Ullin's Daughter, Lord, heroine of a ballad of that name (1803), by Thomas Campbell. She eloped with the chief of Ulva's isle; the fugitives embarked in a row-boat, which capsized (for a storm had arisen), and Lord Ullin from the shore witnessed the catastrophe:

> The waters wild rolled o'er his child,
> And he was left lamenting.

Ulysses, in Shakespeare's *Troilus and Cressida,* the general of the Greek forces before Troy, is a classic outline filled in with Elizabethan feeling. A foil to Troilus, he represents the much-experienced man of the world, possessed of its highest and broadest wisdom, which yet always remains worldly wisdom and never rises into the spiritual contemplation of a Prospero. He sees all the unworthiness of human life, but will use it for high worldly ends; the spirit of irreverence and insubordination in the camp he would restrain by the politic machinery of what he calls

" degree " (I, iii, 75). With right insight Richard Grant White and other critics have seen in this character a portrait of Shakespeare himself in his self-contained maturity, as Romeo represents himself in his passionate boyhood and Hamlet in his self-questioning and self-torturing youth, while Prospero we may imagine is a forecast of his old age. See ODYSSEUS in vol. II.

Shakespeare, acting upon a mere hint, filling up a mere traditionary outline, drew a man of mature years, of wide observation, of profoundest cogitative power, one who knew all the weakness and all the wiles of human nature, and who yet remained with blood unbittered and with soul unsoured— a man who saw through all shams, and fathomed all motives, and who yet was not scornful of his kind, not misanthropic, hardly cynical except in passing moods; and what other man was this than Shakespeare himself? What had he to do when he had passed forty years but to utter his own thoughts when he would find words for the lips of Ulysses?—R. G. WHITE, article *On Reading Shakespeare*, in *Galaxy*, February, 1877.

Ulysses, poem by Tennyson, in which is voiced the eager longing of the heroic spirit for action and adventure, and its contempt for mere sleek comfort and inglorious ease. The immediate source of the poem is a passage in Dante's *Inferno*, xxvi, 90. Ulysses is speaking:

Neither fondness for my son, nor reverence for my aged sire, nor the due love which ought to have gladdened Penelope, could conquer in me the ardor which I had to become experienced in the world, and in human vice and worth. I put out into the deep open sea with but one ship, and with that small company which had not deserted me. . . . I and my companions were old and tardy when we came to that narrow pass where Hercules assigned his landmarks. "O brothers," I said, "who through a hundred thousand dangers have reached the West, deny not to this the brief vigil of your senses that remain, experience of the unpeopled world beyond the sun. Consider your origin, ye were not formed to live like brutes, but to follow virtue and knowledge." . . . Night already saw the other pole with all its stars, and ours so low that it rose not from the ocean floor.

Una, in Spenser's *Faërie Queene,* the type of unity and purity of faith, as Duessa is of duplicity and impurity. Hence Una means Protestantism and Duessa " Papacy," or, more specifi-

cally, Una represents Queen Elizabeth, and Duessa a combination of Mary Tudor and Mary Stuart (see DUESSA). She is the heroine of Canto I. Riding on a white horse and leading a white lamb she appears at the Court of Gloriana praying for a champion who will slay a dragon that holds her parents prisoners. The task is confided to the Red Cross Knight, but Una and he are separated through the wiles of Archimago. She sets out alone, is befriended by a lion who becomes her constant attendant, and finally rejoins the Red Cross Knight. His task accomplished, he is badly wounded. She nurses him back to health and is joined to him in Eden.

Two shall be named pre-eminently dear:—
The gentle Lady married to the Moor,
And heavenly Una with her milk-white
  Lamb.
            WORDSWORTH: *Personal Talk.*

Una is one of the noblest contributions which poetry, whether of ancient or of modern times, has made to its great picture-gallery of characters.—AUBREY DE VERE: *Essays, Chiefly on Poetry,* 1887.

Uncas, a young Indian chief, titular hero of Cooper's novel, *The Last of the Mohicans* (1826). He is the son of Chingachgook, and dies in the effort to rescue Cora Munro from the cruel Magua.

We accept with acquiescence, nay, with admiration, such characters as Magua, Chingachgook, Susquesus, Tamenund, and Canonchet; but when we come to Uncas, in *The Last of the Mohicans,* we pause and shake our heads with incredulous doubt. That a young Indian chief should fall in love with a handsome quadroon like Cora Munro—for she was neither more nor less than that—is natural enough; but that he should manifest his passion with such delicacy and refinement is impossible. We include under one and the same name all the affinities and attractions of sex, but the appetite of the savage differs from the love of the educated and civilized man as much as charcoal differs from the diamond. The sentiment of love, as distinguished from the passion, is one of the last and best results of Christianity and civilization: in no one thing does savage life differ from civilized more than in the relations between man and woman, and in the affections that unite them. Uncas is a graceful and beautiful image; but he is no Indian.—*Atlantic Monthly,* January, 1862.

Have we not had enough of these red Indians—nay, rather too much of them— since the days when Fenimore Cooper, with his pleasant dream of the Last of the Mohicans, deluded our young fancies into believing that the conquering white race had destroyed a transatlantic Arcadia in which the quiet enjoyment of Theocritus's shepherds was combined with the valor of Homer's heroes.—*Saturday Review*, November 10, 1855.

Undine, heroine of a fairy romance of that name (1807), by De la Motte Fouqué,—a water nymph substituted as a changeling for a human infant and brought up by the unsuspecting family. Her putative father is a fisherman living on a peninsula near an enchanted forest. Here she is wooed by Sir Hulbrand. By her marriage she received a soul. When subsequently the knight fell in love with Bertalda, a mortal maiden (who turns out to be the fisherman's real daughter), Undine was snatched away from him by her kinsfolk under the sea. Hulbrand marries Bertalda. On the wedding day she calls for a drink from the well which Undine had covered over to save Hulbrand from the wrath of the water nymphs. Then Undine herself is forced to rise with the upheaving waters, glide into Hulbrand's chamber and kiss him to death. Around his grave there bub- bled a tiny stream. It was Undine herself, who faithful in death as she had been loyal in life, found this opportunity to embrace her knight forever.

Usher, Roderick, hero of a short story, *The Fall of the House of Usher*, by E. A. Poe, included in volume *Tales of the Grotesque and Arabesque* (1840). Roderick and his twin sister, the lady Madeline, were the last scions of an ill-fated family. He himself is a prey to melancholy and morbid fears. His sister dies, apparently, and is buried. He soon realizes that she has been buried alive, but has no strength to go to her assistance, and betrays only a horrified acquiescence when the enshrouded figure of the lady Madeline, bleeding from her efforts at self-release, appears at the door of his room. "For a moment she remained trembling and reeling to and fro upon the threshold—then with a low moaning cry, fell heavily inward upon the person of her brother, and in her violent and now final death agonies, bore him to the floor a corpse, and a victim to the terrors he had anticipated."

V

Valentine, in Shakespeare's *Two Gentlemen of Verona* (1595), one of the titular gentlemen, the other being Protheus. Valentine wooed and married Silvia, daughter of the Duke of Milan, despite the rivalry of Thurio, and Protheus married Julia.

Valentine, in Congreve's *Love for Love*. See LEGEND, VALENTINE.

Valentine, in Goethe's *Faust* (1798), the brother of Margaret. Maddened at her seduction by Faust, he attacks the latter during a serenade and is slain by Mephistopheles.

Valerius, titular hero of a novel (1821), by J. G. Lockhart. The son of a Roman commander in Britain, he is summoned to Rome after his father's death to take possession of the estates to which he has succeeded. He meets a Christian maiden, Athanasia, who converts him and returns with him to Britain as his bride. The time is laid in the reign of Emperor Trojan and the persecution of the Christians forms a part of the historic background.

Valjean, Jean, in Victor Hugo's *Les Misérables*, Part I (1862), a convict who goes through a complete moral renovation. First we have the gradual declension of the innocent son of toil into the depraved and hardened outcast. The saintly charity of Bishop Myriel stirs his deadened conscience and awakens him to the first sense of shame. Nevertheless, the force of habit is still strong. The conversion is premature. Jean cannot resist the temptation of making off with the episcopal plate. When captured and brought back, he is released by the bishop, who quietly observes that he had forgotten the candlesticks. The convict is deeply moved. Not, however, until his evil nature has made one expiring effort in robbing a poor little Savoyard of a five-franc piece do Monseigneur's words and conduct bear their full fruit. The piteous grief of the child shocks the man into full recognition of his wickedness and degradation. The crisis is over and he is reclaimed to virtue. He becomes a wealthy manufacturer, known to the world as M. Madeleine, Mayor of N. sur N., and, best of all, the Elisha upon whom falls the mantle of Monseigneur Myriel when that good man is gathered to his fathers. " Justice " ferrets him out in his disguise, and once more he becomes an outlaw but not an outcast.

Valley of the Shadow of Death, in Bunyan's *Pilgrim's Progress*, Part I, (1678), the valley through which Christian had to pass after his triumph over Apollyon in the Valley of Humiliation. It is described in the language of Jeremiah ii, 6, as a " wilderness, a land of deserts and of pits, a land of drouth and of the shadow of death, a land that no man passeth through, and where no man dwelt." Bunyan adds that the valley was as dark as pitch; that to the right was a deep ditch, to the left a quagmire: that it ran past the very mouth of hell, and that it was infested by hobgoblins, satyrs and dragons.

> Though I walk through the valley of the shadow of death, I will fear no evil: for Thou art with me; Thy rod and Thy staff they comfort me.—*Psalms* xxiii, 4.

Van Bibber, the central figure in a volume of short stories, *Van Bibber and Others* (1890), by Richard Harding Davis. A young New York clubman, moving by birthright among the so-called Four Hundred, he yet has a fondness for bohemian adventures.

Vane, Graham, in Bulwer-Lytton's novel, *The Parisians*, a typical young Englishman, evidently modelled after the author himself in early manhood, who stands serene amid the restless whirl around him,—in dramatic contrast with the priests, atheists, legitimists, Orleanists, millionaire financiers of the Chaussée d'Antin, and the fierce Socialists of Belleville.

Vane, Lady Isabel, heroine of the novel, *East Lynne* (1861), by Mrs. Henry Wood, and of its numerous dramatizations by John Oxenford, J. C. Chute, T. A. Palmer, and others, which have brought fame and fortune to English and American actresses taking the part of Lady Isabel. East Lynne is the name of the ancestral home which Isabel's bankrupt father is compelled to sell just before his death. It is purchased by Archibald Carlyle, who marries the heroine. A rejected suitor, Francis Leveson, foully slanders Carlyle. Isabel, believing he is untrue to her, elopes with Leveson; but, soon repenting, returns, disguised and unrecognized, to her own home, as governess to her own children and to those of Carlyle's second marriage, for he has believed her dead. In the end Carlyle's character is vindicated, Leveson is shown to be a scoundrel, and Isabel dies forgiving and forgiven.

Vanessa, a poetical name given by Dean Swift to Esther Vanhomrigh (1690–1723), a young woman, twenty-five years his junior, who had fallen in love with him and had gone so far as to propose marriage. How Swift received the declaration is told in his poem *Cadenus and Vanessa*. Cadenus is an obvious anagram of *Decanus*, Latin for Dean. Vanessa is more cunningly compounded of *Van*, the first syllable of Vanhomrigh, and *Essa*, diminutive of Esther. See STELLA.

> The loves of Cadenus and Vanessa you may peruse in Cadenus's own poem on the subject, and in poor Vanessa's vehement expostulatory verses and letters to him; she adores him, implores him, admires him, thinks him something god-like, and only prays to be admitted to lie at his feet. As they are bringing him home from church, those divine feet of Dr. Swift's are found pretty often in Vanessa's parlor. He likes to be admired and adored. He finds Miss Vanhomrigh to be a woman of great taste and spirit, and beauty and wit, and a fortune too. He sees her every day; he does not tell Stella about the business: until the impetuous Vanessa becomes too fond of him, until the doctor is quite frightened by the young woman's ardour and confounded by her warmth. He wanted to

24

marry neither of them—that I believe was the truth; but if he had not married Stella, Vanessa would have had him in spite of himself. When he went back to Ireland, his Ariadne, not content to remain in her isle, pursued the fugitive dean. In vain he protested, he vowed, he soothed, and bullied; the news of the dean's marriage with Stella at last came to her, and it killed her—she died of that passion.—THACKERAY: *English Humorists.*

Vanity Fair, in Bunyan's *Pilgrim's Progress,* Part I, a fair so called because it is held in a town that " is lighter than vanity, and also because all that is there sold or that cometh thither is vanity." Bunyan makes an explanatory reference to Psalm lxii, 9, where men of high and low degree are spoken of as " lighter than vanity." He explains that almost 5000 years ago Beelzebub, Apollyon, and Legion, noting that the path to the Celestial City ran through this spot, contrived here to set up a fair. All such merchandise are sold as " houses, lands, trades, places, honors, preferments, titles, countries, kingdoms, lusts, pleasures, and delights of all sorts, as harlots, wives, husbands, children, lives, blood, bodies, souls, silver, gold, pearls, precious stones, and what not." Christian and Faithful, when they reached the city, denounced the fair and told the people there were things in the world of more consequence than money and pleasure. In their turn they were denounced as Bedlamites, were arrested, beaten, and put into a cage. Next day they were taken before Justice Hategood, and Faithful was condemned to be burned at the stake.

Vanna, Monna, titular heroine of a drama (1902), by Maurice Mæterlinck and of an opera founded thereon by Fevrier. The action rakes place in and about Pisa in the later fifteenth century. Prinzivalle, a Florentine mercenary, is besieging the city. A dreamer, a Platonist, a lover of beauty, he had once met and had ever since loved Monna Vanna. She had entirely forgotten him. She is dully content as the wife of Guido Colonna, a commonplace Pisan noble. Prinzivalle agrees to send food to the relief of Pisa on one preposterous condition, that Monna Vanna, clad only in a mantle, should spend the night in his tent. Vanna, determined to save the city at any cost, forces her husband's consent. Prinzivalle loves her too dearly to harm her. He goes back with her to Pisa. Guido cannot believe in the innocence of the pair. He assumes that Vanna has delivered the enemy into his hands and praises her above Lucrece and Judith as a self-immolated heroine. Prinzivalle he condemns to death by torture. Vanna, fully awake now to the difference between the two men, saves Prinzivalle and flees with him.

Varden, Dolly, in Dickens's novel, *Barnaby Rudge* (1841), daughter of Gabriel Varden, locksmith. She was winsome and coquettish, playing fast and loose with the hearts of three admirers, Joe Willett, Hugh of the Maypole Inn, and Simon Tappertit. She dressed in the Watteau style. In 1875–76 a Dolly Varden was the popular name for a vari-colored shirtwaist, and hat imitated from Watteau.

In any just sense there is no heroine in *Barnaby Rudge,* which is a book of more skill and power than any that Dickens had yet written. We may dismiss without self-reproach such a lady-like lay-figure as Emma Haredale, and a goblin effigy like Miss Miggs, and come without delay to Dolly Varden, who, in turn, need hardly delay us longer. She is a cheap little coquette imagined upon the commonest lines, with abundant assertion as to her good looks and graces, but without evidence of the charm that the silliest flirt has in reality. She is nothing and she does nothing; and she cannot be petted and patted by her inventor, with all his fondness, into any semblance of personality.—W. D. HOWELLS: *Heroines of Fiction,* vol. i, p. 136.

Varden, Mrs. Martha, in Dickens's novel, *Barnaby Rudge,* the wife of Gabriel, a lady of uncertain temper, which, " being interpreted, signifies a temper tolerably certain to make everybody more or less uncomfortable. . . . When other people were merry Mrs. Varden was dull, and when other people were dull Mrs. Varden was disposed to be amazingly cheerful."

Varina, a poetical name given by Dean Swift to Miss Jane Waryng, for whom he professed undying affection in his youth and to whom he proposed marriage when a young clergyman of twenty-eight.

Vathek, hero of an Oriental romance (1782) by William Beckford. Historically he was the ninth Abbaside caliph and a grandson of Haroun-al-Raschid. Beckford pictures him as a cruel but magnificent voluptuary, tempted by a diabolical Giaour to the commission of terrible crimes, including apostacy from the Moslem faith. He is finally led to the hall of Eblis, a vast subterranean chamber, where he finds himself a hopeless prisoner forever.

Vaughan, Clara, in Blackmore's romance of that name, is a witness to her father's murder when she is ten years old, and devotes her life to the identification of the murderer. She inherits an abnormal nervous susceptibility.

Vavasour, Mr., in Disraeli's novel, *Tancred,* a hospitable, cheery, and amiable gentleman who was evidently drawn from Richard Monckton Milnes, Lord Houghton. Here is how Disraeli describes him:

With catholic sympathies and an eclectic turn of mind, Mr. Vavasour saw something good in everybody and everything. . . . Vavasour liked to know everybody who was known, and to see everything which ought to be seen. His life was a gyration of energetic curiosity, an insatiable whirl of social celebrity. There was not a congregation of sages and philosophers in any part of Europe which he did not attend as a brother. He was present at the camp of Kalisch in his yeomanry uniform, and assisted at the festivals of Barcelona in an Andalusian jacket. He was everywhere and at everything; he had gone down in a diving-bell and up in a balloon. As for his acquaintances, he was welcomed in every land; his universal sympathies seemed omnipotent. Emperor and king, Jacobin and Carbonari, alike cherished him. He was the steward of Polish balls and the vindicator of Russian humanity; he dined with Louis Philippe and gave dinners to Louis Blanc.

Veal, Mrs., heroine of a hoax by Daniel Defoe, originally published as an introduction to a new edition (1705) of Drelincourt's *Book of Consolations against the Fear of Death;* subsequently issued as a separate brochure under the title *True Relation of the Apparition of One Mrs. Veal.* Drelincourt's publisher, finding his book unsaleable, appealed to Defoe for an introduction. The result was this ghost story, written with such apparent gravity and sincerity, such convincing wealth of detail, that it was accepted as genuine by the public, and awoke Drelincourt's still-born production into vicarious life. The story feigns that Mrs. Veal, on September 8, 1705, the day after her death, appeared to Mrs. Bargrave at Canterbury, and held a long conversation with her on death and immortality.

Veck, Toby, in Dickens's Christmas story, *The Chimes,* a ticket porter nicknamed Trotty from his pace, " which meant speed if it didn't make it." As he trotted on, " he would call out to fast postmen ahead of him to get out of the way, devoutly believing that, in the natural course of things, he must inevitably overtake and run them down." He had a passion for the chime of bells in the church near his station and invested them with a strange and solemn character.

Veiled Prophet of Khorassen. See MOKANNA.

Veneering, Mr. and Mrs. Hamilton, in Dickens's *Our Mutual Friend,* purse-proud parvenus who were tolerated by society on account of their wealth.

Mr. and Mrs. Veneering were bran-new people, in a bran-new house, in a bran-new quarter of London. Everything about the Veneerings was spick and span new. All their furniture was new, all their friends were new, all their servants were new, their plate was new, their carriage was new, their harness was new, their horses were new, their pictures were new, they themselves were new, they were as newly married as was lawfully compatible with their having a bran-new baby.
In the Veneering establishment, from the hall chairs with the new coat of arms, to the grand pianoforte with the new action, and upstairs again to the new fire-escape, all things were in a state of high varnish and polish.—DICKENS: *Our Mutual Friend,* ii (1864).

Venner, Elsie, heroine of a novel (1861) of that name, by O. W. Holmes.

Elsie, a New England girl, is a modern Lamia, whose moral and physical system have absorbed the poison of a rattlesnake that had bitten her mother just prior to her birth. The serpent nature, which overshadows her womanly qualities, expresses itself outwardly in a peculiar undulating walk, in the pattern of her dress, in her habit of coiling and uncoiling a gold chain about her wrist, in the mysterious fascination that dwells within the strange cold glitter of her eyes, compelling involuntary obedience. The story shows the gradual humanizing of Elsie, chiefly through the influence of an absorbing love. But the struggle has been too protracted and too severe. Life perishes with it.

Venus, Mr., in *Our Mutual Friend,* a preserver of animals and birds and an articulator of human bones. Rather against his will, he joins Wegg in his plan of blackmailing Mr. Boffin, but repents and reveals the conspiracy. According to Percy Fitzgerald, the prototype of this character (whose shop was at 42 St. Andrew's Street, London) was introduced to the author by his illustrator, Marcus Stone, after the completion of the first three numbers of *Our Mutual Friend.*

"This original character," writes Mr. Fitzgerald, "excited much attention, and a friend of the great writer, as well as of the present chronicler, passing through this street, was irresistibly attracted by this shop and its contents, kept by one J. Willis. When he next saw Mr. Dickens, he said, 'I am convinced I have found the original of Venus;' on which said Mr. Dickens, 'You are right.'" Any one who then visited the place could recognize the dingy, gloomy interior, the articulated skeleton in the corner, the genial air of thick grime and dust.

Venus of Ille, in Merimée's short story of that name. The basic legend is versified by William Morris in *The Ring given to Venus* in the *Earthly Paradise.* On the day of his nuptials, a bridegroom, in thoughtless sport, placed his spousal ring on a golden statue of Venus. Seeking later to recover it, he found, to his horror, the finger of the image crooked and the ring immovable.

Verges, in Shakespeare's *Much Ado About Nothing* (1600), a blundering constable, fit underling for Dogberry the magistrate.

Dogberry and Verges in this play are inimitable specimens of quaint blundering and misprisions of meaning; and are a standing record of that formal gravity of pretension and total want of common understanding, which Shakespeare no doubt copied from real life, and which in the course of two hundred years appear to have ascended from the lowest to the highest offices in the state.

Verisopht, Lord Frederick, in Dickens's *Nicholas Nickleby* (1838), a young and foolish nobleman under the thumb of Sir Mulberry Hawk, whom eventually he turns against, and who kills him in a duel.

Vernon, Diana, in Scott's novel *Rob Roy* (1818), the brilliant, dashing, and beautiful mistress of Osbaldistone Hall, who by popular acclaim stands peerless among all Scott's heroines. Brought up apart from her sex, she is hoydenish and even boyish in the display of her exuberant spirits, but her excellent natural sense and her maidenly dignity shield her from misunderstanding. Captain Basil Hall thought he had found her original in Jane Anne Craunston, an old Scotch gentlewoman whom, in 1834, he had found nearing her end in a mediæval castle in Styria. She had married its owner, Count Wenzel Purgstall, who had left her a widow in 1812. In youth she had been a friend and confidante of Scott's. Her playful allusions to her independent ways in young womanhood, her fondness for horseback riding, and the fact that Scott had sent her all the *Waverley* novels as they appeared with the single exception of *Rob Roy,* all seemed to confirm the captain's suspicions. (See S. R. CROCKETT: *The Scott Originals.*)

Vernon, Dorothy, heroine of an historical romance, *Dorothy Vernon of Haddon Hall* (1902), by Charles Major. A compound of sweetness and savagery, she is madly in love with Sir John Manners, the son of her father's bitterest enemy, and defies everybody and everything, the proprieties included. She makes all the advances, she lies appallingly; she threatens, bullies, wheedles, and sets two kingdoms by the ears, until she succeeds in having her own way. The story is founded upon fact. Dorothy, the daughter and heiress of Sir George Vernon, eloped with Sir John Manners and became ancestress of the present dukes of Rutland, to whom Haddon Hall in Derbyshire, former seat of the Vernon family, has passed. The door through which Dorothy eloped is still called after her, and the Vernon name is commemorated at Haddon by engravings of their arms.

Vernon, Madame de, in Mme. de Staël's *Delphine* (1803), the intriguing mother of Matilda. In this, the most original and thoroughly finished character in the book, the French public were quick to recognize a caricature of Talleyrand. The feminine Machiavelism, the supreme yet indolent egotism, the cool, systematic dissimulation and passionless dissipation of the character, were all seized upon as so many points of resemblance. Mme. de Staël herself told Sir James Mackintosh the famous *bon-mot* of Talleyrand's: " I understand," he said to her, " that we are both introduced in your book, disguised as women? "

Vidal, Julia, heroine of Adolphe Belot's *Drame de la Rue de la Paix*. Like Fedora in the later play by Sardou, she encourages the devotion of her husband's supposed murderer, Albert Savari, in order to betray him into an avowal of his crime. He does indeed end by confessing, but the motive is less heroic than in the case of Sardou's hero. Savari has killed Maurice because the latter has injured him in some money transaction. The honor of Julia is not concerned, and the questions of casuistry in which Sardou delights have no place in the distress of the heroine. Albert has only to kill himself, and Julia to keep silence, and the curtain falls.

Village Master, The, in Goldsmith's idyllic poem, *The Deserted Village* (1770), an amusing type of the rustic pedagogue, who astonishes the community with " words of learned length and thundering sound,"—

And still they gazed, and still the wonder grew
That one small head could carry all he knew.
The Deserted Village, l. 212.

Irving, in his *Life of Goldsmith*, suggests that the original of this character was Goldsmith's own teacher in the village school at Lissoy, a certain Thomas Byrne (nicknamed Paddy), an old soldier who had seen service, and who consequently may have furnished a hint for the wandering beggar who

Wept o'er his wounds, or tales of sorrow done,
Shouldered his crutch, and showed how fields were won.
The Deserted Village, l. 157.

Village Preacher, The, in Goldsmith's *Deserted Village* (1770), a sketch, exquisite alike in its gentle humor and its immanent pathos, of a Protestant parson in an Irish village. Mrs. Hodgson, Goldsmith's sister, took this to be a portrait of their father; others have identified him as Henry Goldsmith, the brother, and even as the uncle Contarine. They may all have contributed, each a touch, to the fully rounded portrait.

Vincentio, in Shakespeare's comedy, *Measure for Measure* (1603), the Duke of Vienna. Being anxious to learn the truth about the officials that surround him, he delegates his powers for a period to Angelo and feigns to go on a journey, but really disguises himself as Friar Lodowick. Thus he unearths many abuses in his court and unmasks a few hypocrites. He is described as " one that above all other strifes contended especially to know himself."

Vincy, Rosamund, in George Eliot's novel, *Middlemarch* (1871–72), a beautiful young woman who under a veil of perfect delicacy and refinement conceals a selfish, self-occupied, and obstinate spirit. Her marriage to Lydgate is fatal to the development of his higher self. George Eliot is reported to have said that the character which she found most difficult to support was that of Rosamond Vincy.

Rosamund Vincy is a mood of one of the forms of stupidity against which the gods fight in vain. Being utterly incapable of even understanding her husband's aspirations, fixing her mind on the vulgar kind of success, and having the strength of will which comes from an absolute limitation to one aim, she is a most effective torpedo, and paralyses all Lydgate's energies. He is entangled in money difficulties; gives up his aspirations; sinks into a merely popular physician, and is sentenced to die early of diphtheria.—LESLIE STEPHEN: George Eliot.

Viola, heroine of Shakespeare's comedy, *Twelfth Night.* Having been shipwrecked on the coast of Illyria, she assumes male attire to protect herself in this strange country, and under the name of Cesaria enters the service of the duke, with whom she falls deeply in love. Like another and a different John Alden, she is made the confidante of his passion for Olivia and his messenger to her. Olivia, mistaking her sex, falls in her turn in love with Viola.

How careful has Shakespeare been in *Twelfth Night* to preserve the dignity and delicacy of Viola under her disguise! Even when wearing a page's doublet and hose, she is never mixed up with any transaction which the most fastidious mind could regard as leaving a stain on her. She is employed by the Duke on an embassy of love to Olivia, but on an embassy of the most honorable kind. Wycherley borrows Viola [in *The Plain Dealer*] and Viola forthwith becomes a pandar of the basest sort.—MACAULAY, *Essays: Leigh Hunt.*

Violante, one of the heroines of Lord Lytton's *My Novel* (1853).

To the unconscious grace and innate nobility which, rightly or wrongly, we associate with high birth and a long line of ancestors, she adds something of the energy and modest boldness of the Viola in *Twelfth Night,* and possibly Lord Lytton may, with the name, have borrowed from Shakespeare the hint of her relations with L'Estrange. —T. H. S. ESCOTT.

Virginia, heroine of a pastoral romance, *Paul and Virginia* (1788), by Bernardin de St. Pierre. The scene is laid in the island of Port Louis in the Mauritius. Virginia is the daughter of a French widow, Madame La Tour, who had been cast off by the family for marrying beneath her. Paul is the illegitimate son of a woman betrayed by her lover. The children are neighbors; they are brought up in pastoral simplicity and ignorance of the outer world. The boy and girl idyl is rudely interrupted when a letter arrives from Madame La Tour's aunt, who proposes to adopt Virginia if she will come over to France to be educated. So Virginia sails away, leaving Paul disconsolate on the island. Two years pass. Virginia is disowned by the aunt because she will not marry at her dictation. The ship that bears her back to her old home is heralded. Paul in a frenzy of delight rushes down to the shore. A sudden storm arises; the ship goes down in sight of the island. Virginia might have been saved but for the maidenly modesty that made her refuse the proffered assistance of a naked sailor. Her body is washed ashore, and two months later Paul follows her to the grave.

The story has furnished the subject for various musical scores,—notably a three-act opera by Rudolph Kreutzer (1791), a lyrical drama in three acts by Lesueur (1794), and an opera in three acts and seven tableaus (1876), libretto by Michel Carré and Jules Barbier, music by Victor Massé.

Vogler, George Joseph, usually known as Abbé or Abt Vogler (1749–1814), is the subject of Robert Browning's poem, *Abt Vogler,* in *Dramatis Personæ* (1864). He was a German organist, composer, teacher, and inventor, playing on his own instrument, the "orchestrion." The poet puts in his mouth a monologue, taking as its main theme that some soul of permanence lies behind the transitoriness of musical sounds, for the good and the beautiful are lasting, while all negations, such as evil, darkness, ugliness, are non-extant, the shifting shadow cast by the eternal substance.

Volpone, hero of Ben Jonson's comedy, *Volpone, or the Fox* (1605).

Volpone, a miser and sensualist, works on the greed of his acquaintances and, by false reports of his sickness and death, excites their hopes of inheriting his fortune, and lures them into all kind of intolerable knavery. A shameless lawyer, a father who disinherits his son in order to satisfy his own greed, and a wittol who offers his wife in return for an inheritance, are the chief dupes. . . . Nowhere else, unless in Iago, has vice been drawn with such fulness of detail and yet with such consistency as in *Volpone*.—ASHLEY H. THORNDIKE.

Volumnia, in Shakespeare's *Coriolanus*, mother of Coriolanus. See this entry in vol. II.

In Volumnia Shakespeare has given us the portrait of a Roman matron, conceived in the true antique spirit and finished in every part. Although Coriolanus is the hero of the play, yet much of the interest of the action and the final catastrophe turn upon his mother, Volumnia, and the power she exercised over his mind, by which, according to the story, "she saved Rome and lost her son." Her lofty patriotism, her patrician haughtiness, her maternal pride, her eloquence, and her towering spirit are exhibited with the utmost power of effect; yet the truth of female nature is beautifully preserved and the portrait, with all its vigor, is without harshness.—MRS. ANNA B. JAMESON: *Characteristics of Women* (1832).

Vye, Eustacia, heroine of Thomas Hardy's novel, *The Return of the Native* (1878), a beautiful, passionate, discontented woman, " the raw material of a divinity," whose marriage to Clym Yeobright blights his dreams and wrecks his life.

W

Wackles, Mrs., in Dickens's *Old Curiosity Shop*, viii (1840), proprietor of a day school for young ladies at Chelsea; a well-meaning but rather venomous sexagenarian who looked after the corporal punishment and other terrors of the establishment, while the remaining departments were distributed among her three daughters as follows: **Miss Melissa,** English grammar, composition, geography and the use of dumb-bells; **Miss Sophy,** writing, arithmetic, dancing, music and general fascination; **Miss Jane,** needlework, marking and samplery.

Wade, Miss, in Dickens's *Little Dorrit* (1857), a handsome young woman of a sullen and vindictive temper, who fancies herself the object of general persecution. Finding a congenial spirit in Tattycoram (a nickname for Harriet Beadle, adopted child of Mr. Meagles), she enticed her away from the Meagle household, and the two lived together for a while in avowed hatred to all mankind.

Wadman, Widow, in Sterne's novel, *Life and Opinions of Tristram Shandy* (1759), a middle-aged widow, attractive and designing, who seeks to capture Uncle Toby for her second husband. A famous episode is that in which she pretends to have something in her eye and gets the hero of Namur to investigate it. He bends lower and lower as she approaches her face nearer and nearer, but he shrewdly escapes the expected climax of a kiss and a proposal.

Wagg, Mr., in Thackeray's *Pendennis*, a novelist and a professional wit, evidently meant as a caricature of Theodore Hook. Thackeray actually had the audacity to put into Wagg's mouth one of Hook's own jokes. Wagg is made to ask Mrs. Bungay, " Does your cook say he's a Frenchman? " and to reply, when that lady expresses her ignorance, " Because, if he does, he's a-quizzin' yer " (*cuisinier*).

Wagner, Christopher, in the Faust cycle of legends, the famulus or servant apprentice of Faustus. He is introduced into the *Faust* of both Marlowe and Goethe.

The latter makes him the type of the pedant and pedagogue.

He is the Philistine among scholars, the pragmatist, the pedagogue who dwells in the letter and misses the spirit, in whom the love of books degenerates into bibliomania, learning into pedantry, religion into cant, and the eternal longings of the soul after the harmonies of art into mere dilettanteism and connoisseurship. To him the vanity of knowledge can have no meaning, because the chief use of knowledge is to enable him to measure himself with his fellows and find he is a cubit above them. Give him fame, "recognition," and he is happy. To Faust recognition would be useless. A few inches above his fellows places him no nearer to the stars!—WALSH: *Faust, the Legend and the Poem*.

Wakefield, Vicar of. See PRIM-
ROSE, DR. CHARLES.

Wakem, Philip, in George Eliot's
novel, *The Mill on the Floss*, the
crippled son of a lawyer who had
helped to ruin old Mr. Tulliver.
Hence Tom Tulliver, the son, hates
him and all his race, and Maggie is
forced to give up Philip just at the
crisis, when a motherly pity for his
deformity and a keen sympathy with
his high ideals had combined to produce something dangerously akin to
love.

Waldbourg, Count, hero of Kotzebue's melodrama, *Menschenhasz und
Rene* (1787), called *The Stranger* in
the English adaptation (1808) by
Benjamin Thompson. He had married the sixteen-year-old Adelaide,
who eloped with a lover after bearing
him two children. He then wandered
around the world incognito, known
only as the Stranger wherever he
happens to be. She herself, repentant,
discards her lover, and under the
name of Mrs. Haller enters the service
of Countess Wintersen. See HALLER,
MRS.

Waldfried, Heinrich, in Berthold
Auerbach's *Waldfried* (1874), the
head of the Waldfried family, a South
German whose journal forms the
book. An old man who has been
through a great deal and has seen
many changes since 1848, when the
journal begins, he still retains an
enthusiastic temperament, a keen
humor, and a deep fund of pathos.
His account of his wife's death and
his subsequent grief are vividly
affecting.

Wall, in the interlude of *Pyramus
and Thisbe* in *A Midsummer Night's
Dream*, is enacted by Snout, a tinker:

In this same interlude it doth befall,
That I, one Snout by name, present a wall.
                        Act v.

He is thus described in the prologue
to the interlude:

This man with lime and roughcast doth
    present.
Wall, that vile Wall which did these lovers
    sunder;
And through Wall's chink, poor souls, they
    are content
   To whisper. At the which let no man
    wonder.

Wallace, Sir William, the friend of
Robert Bruce and one of the great
national heroes of Scotland, is celebrated in a poetical chronicle, *The
Acts and Deeds of Sir William Wallace*
(*circa* 1460), by the wandering minstrel called Blind Harry. This is
said to have been mainly founded on
a Latin Life of the hero by his school-
fellow, John Blair—

                  The man
That first compild in dyt the Latyne buk
Off Wallace lyff, rycht famous of renoune.

It was republished in 1869.

Wallace is one of the heroes of Jane
Porter's historical novel, *The Scottish
Chiefs* (1809). Infuriated by the
murder of his wife by English soldiers,
he rouses his countrymen against the
English king, Edward I, captures
castles, fights bloody battles, and,
going in disguise as a harper to
Edward's court, assists Bruce to
escape therefrom, and accompanies
him to France to rescue the abducted
Helen Mar.

Walpurga, in Berthold Auerbach's
novel, *On the Heights* (*Auf der Höhe*,
1865), the wet-nurse for the crown
prince, an upright and forthright
German peasant, whose shrewd sayings are the salt of the book. She
rejoins her people laden with presents,
and she and her husband Hansei buy
a farm among their native mountains.
Hither comes the Countess Irma
(*q.v.*), to work out her own salvation
on the heights.

Walter, marquis of Saluzzo, in
Chaucer's *The Clerk's Tale* (1388),
the husband of Griselda (*q.v.*).

Walter, Master, the titular hero of
Knowles's drama, *The Hunchback*.
See JULIA.

Walter of Vanila, in Charles Kingsley's dramatic poem, *The Saint's
Tragedy*, a vassal of the Landgrave
Lewis, representing the healthy animalism of the Teutonic mind, with
its mixture of deep earnestness and
hearty animalism.

Wandering Willie, in Scott's *Redgauntlet*, the blind fiddler, William
Steenson, who tells Darsie Latimer,
as they tramp together across the lea,

the story of Sir Robert Redgauntlet and his son Sir John.

Wangell, Hilda, in Ibsen's drama, *The Master-Builder* (1892), a young girl who tempts Solness, the sexagenarian hero, into a passion that eventually destroys him. She may be taken as a symbol of youth arriving too late within the circle which age has trodden for its steps to walk in, and luring it too rashly by the mirage of happiness into paths no longer within its physical and moral capacity.

Ward, Artemus, " the genial showman," a distinct personality and not a mere pseudonym, invented by Charles Farrar Browne as the pretended author of his works. He is presented to us as a shrewd, course, grasping Yankee, full of humor, both conscious and unconscious, utterly irreverent and always at his ease. With his " wax figgurs " and his kangaroo, " a amoozin little cuss," he passes from State to State and even from America to Europe. He is denounced as " a man of sin " by the Shaker elder; is entertained by the Mormons; is greeted effusively by the Women's Rights females; interviews President Lincoln, beset by " orifice seekers coming down the chimney," and later Albert Edward and Prince Napoleon; listens unconcernedly to Union orators; has his show confiscated by the screaming eagle of the Confederacy; and escapes home to Betsy Jane, the partner of his joys and sorrows, whose relations he is avowedly willing to sacrifice on the altar of his country. There was an American general in the Revolutionary army named Artemas Ward, but he had nothing in common with the showman save his name.

This showman, Artemus, is one of the solidest figures in the gallery of American fiction. To the public for whom Browne wrote he is still a much more real person than is Charles Farrar Browne himself. Certainly there could not be a contrast greater than that between the blatant, vulgar, impudent old buffoon of the book and the quiet, delicate, pensive, sensitive-looking young gentleman of the lecture platform. And yet before he had been speaking five minutes you could understand how and why the creator of Artemus was

his creator.—JULIAN HAWTHORNE and LEONARD LEMON: *American Literature* (1891).

Ward, Rev. John, hero of a novel by Mrs. Margaret C. Deland (1888). A logical Calvinist who believes in all that that term implies and preaches with conviction its sternest doctrines,—election, reprobation, and eternal punishment. His wife, *née* Helen Jaffrey, niece of an easy-going liberal Episcopal, cherishes broad modern views which continually clash with his. The congregation side with the minister, and the domestic circle suffers accordingly.

Any real Calvinist is at this hour rare; one who accepts the full consequences of his faith always has been. John Ward believed in the damnation of the heathen, and more, in the damnation of all who disbelieved in damnation—of all who, to quote one of his elders, were not "grounded on hell." This is also the belief of thousands of to-day, who yet eat, drink, and are merry. John Ward believed, suffered, crucified himself, and fell a martyr to his faith at his own hands, in a fashion logical, but hardly natural.—*N. Y. Nation.*

Wardle, Mr. (of Manor Farm, Dingley Dell), in Dickens's *Pickwick Papers,* friend of Mr. Pickwick and his companions; a stout, hearty, honest old gentleman, who is most happy when he is making others the same.

Wardle, Miss Rachael, sister of the above; a spinster of doubtful age, with dignity in her air, majesty in her eye, and touch-me-not-ishness in her walk. The " too susceptible " Mr. Tupman, falling in love with her, is circumvented by the adroit Mr. Jingle, who elopes with her, but is pursued, overtaken, and induced to relinquish his prize in consideration of a check for a hundred and twenty pounds.

Ware, Thereon, hero of Harold Frederic's novel, *The Damnation of Thereon Ware* (1896). A young Methodist minister in the town of Octavius (identified as Elmira, N. Y.), a married man, detesting " Popery," he has all his views disturbed and distorted by association with one Father Forbes, greatly his superior in learning and intelligence, who shakes his belief in Protestantism without inculcating faith in any other form of Christianity. He falls in love with a Roman Catholic girl, Celia Madden, a great friend of Father Forbes, who toys with him for her own amusement and then throws him over. Maddened with pique, remorse, and shame, he goes on a protracted spree, and is saved by a couple of shrewd sophisticated Methodists, who persuade him to abandon the ministry and go into business.

Waring, titular hero of a poem by Robert Browning, who is identified with Alfred Domett, the poet. Waring is a young man living a secluded life in London. To the world his manners have the reserve of intense pride, but to his few intimates he freely opens his heart, avowing his wild aspirations and his confident belief in his ability to realise them. His boasting is tempered with so much good nature that his friends do not scruple to let him see how ridiculous they deem the contrast between his abilities and his astounding claims. He does not appear to be wounded, yet one night he disappears without a word of farewell.

Browning's poem begins:

"What's become of Waring
    Since he gave us all the slip,
Chose land-travel or sea-faring,
    Boats and chest or staff and scrip,
Rather than pace up and down,
    Any longer, London-town?"

Warner, in Bulwer Lytton's romance, *The Last of the Barons*, a reputed magician in league with Satan, but really a scientific pioneer who invents an embryo steam-engine. The author looked upon this as one of his finest conceptions; Warner's daughter Sybil was another of his favorites.

Warren, Mrs., titular heroine of G. B. Shaw's comedy, *Mrs. Warren's Profession*, is in plain words the keeper of a house of prostitution, who defends her *métier* with cutting sarcasm on modern hypocrisy.

Instead of maintaining an association in the imagination of the spectators between prostitution and fashionable beauty, luxury and refinement, as do *La Dame aux Came-*

lias, The Second Mrs. Tanqueray, Iris Zaza, and countless other plays, *Mrs. Warren's Profession* exhibits the life of the courtesan in all its arid actuality, and inculcates a lesson of the sternest morality.—ARCHIBALD HENDERSON: *George Bernard Shaw*, p. 304.

The play of *Mrs. Warren's Profession* is concerned with a coarse mother and a cold daughter; the mother drives the ordinary and dirty trade of harlotry; the daughter does not know until the end the atrocious origin of all her own comfort and refinement. The daughter, when the discovery is made, freezes up into an iceberg of contempt; which is indeed a very womanly thing to do. The mother explodes into pulverizing cynicism and practicality, which is also very womanly. The dialogue is drastic and sweeping; the daughter says the trade is loathsome; the mother answers that she loathes it herself; that every healthy person does loathe the trade by which she lives.— G. K. CHESTERTON: *George Bernard Shaw*, p. 132.

Warren, Vivie, in George Bernard Shaw's comedy, *Mrs. Warren's Profession*, is the dramatist's conception of "a real modern lady of the governing classes—not the sort of thing that theatrical and critical authorities imagine such a lady to be." He professed himself astonished at William Archer's charge (*Daily News*, June 21, 1902) that Vivie was simply Shaw in petticoats.

One of my female characters, who drinks whiskey and smokes cigars and reads detective stories and regards the fine arts, especially music, as an insufferable and unintelligible waste of time, has been declared by my friend, Mr. William Archer, to be an exact and authentic portrait of myself, on no other grounds in the world except that she is a woman of business and not a creature of romantic impulse.—G. B. SHAW: *Dramatic Opinions*.

Warrington, George, in Thackeray's *Pendennis*, an intimate friend of the titular hero, and eke his guide and philosopher; a warm-hearted, level-headed man, with a rough exterior. In regard to this character Lady Anne Thackeray Ritchie once wrote to an American correspondent: "My father scarcely ever put real people into his books, though he of course found suggestions among the people with whom he was thrown. I have always thought that there was something of himself in Warrington. Perhaps the serious part of his nature was vaguely drawn in that character. There was also a little likeness to his friend Edward Fitzgerald, who always lived a very solitary life." (See *Lippincott's Magazine*.)

One may appeal, however, from Thackeray's daughter to Thackeray himself: When *Pendennis* was published, he sent a copy to one of his intimate friends, George Moreland Crawford, Paris correspondent of the London *Daily News*, who had nursed the novelist through the long and dangerous illness which had nearly interrupted *Pendennis* forever. The copy was accompanied by the following letter:

You will find much to remind you of old talks and faces—of William John O'Connell, Jack Sheehan, and Andrew Archdeckne. There is something of you in Warrington, but he is not fit to hold a candle to you, for, taking you all around, you are the most genuine fellow that ever strayed from a better world into this. You don't smoke, and he is a consumed smoker of tobacco. Bordeaux and port were your favorites at the "Deanery" and the "Garrick," and War, is always guzzling beer. But he has your honesty, and, like you, could not posture if he tried. You have a strong affinity for the Irish. May you some day find an Irish girl to lead you to matrimony! There's no such good wife as a daughter of Erin.

Warrington, therefore, seems to have owed his being to the novelist's acquaintance with Crawford, although there is undoubtedly (and possibly unconsciously) much of Thackeray himself in it,—more, perhaps, than in the character of Pendennis.

Warwick, Diana, heroine of George Meredith's novel, *Diana of the Crossways* (1885). An Irish girl of good family, of unusual wit, beauty, and fascination,—but exuberant, incoherent, unequal,—she makes an unfortunate marriage with Warwick. The uncongenial husband, knowing that he is neither loved nor respected, grows antagonistic, then jealous, and, finding suspicious circumstances in her intimacy with Lord Dannisburg, sues for a divorce. He fails to prove his case. Diana, legally a wife but separated from her husband, maintains herself by her pen, keeps up a charming little house, and draws

about her a brilliant circle of friends. In her personality and her career she is evidently a reminiscence of Lady Caroline Norton, Sheridan's granddaughter, famous for her beauty, her wit, and her independence of conventional opinion.

To construct a character which would fit the known facts; to create a woman dazzling by the brilliancy of her personality, and liable by the very force of the qualities which raised her above the crowd to commit indiscretions unpardonable by the world, was a congenial exercise to his inventive faculty, and the result is a singularly vivid conception, worked out with great literary power. It is to be doubted whether even a poet is a more difficult character for fiction than a witty woman of the world; and amongst all his intellectual and literary feats Mr. Meredith has perhaps never accomplished one more striking than in making us feel that his Diana justified her reputation. He has made her move and speak before us as a living woman, dowered with exceptional gifts of "blood and brains." Of the two the brains "have it" decidedly. She is too much like Charles II in the contrast between her sayings and doings. The latter are almost invariably foolish.—*Saturday Review*, March 21, 1885.

Waters, Esther, heroine and title of a novel (1894) by George Moore. The daughter of a drunkard who neglects his wife, Esther becomes scullery maid in the household of a horse-racing squire, is seduced by a fellow-servant, William Latch, but, pricked by conscience, refuses all proffers of assistance when a son is born, and endures terrible privations to remain respectable and bring up her boy in the right path. Eventually she marries her seducer, now a bookmaker, who keeps a low public house. Untaught, untrained and weakly emotional, she yet remains true to her religious principles, even when circumstances are most unfavorable, and in the end she feels that she has had her own sufficient reward in bringing her son up to man's estate.

Waverley, Captain Edward, titular hero of Scott's historical romance, *Waverley, or 'Tis Sixty Years Since* (1814). He was tall and athletic; "his person promised firmness and agility;" "his blue eye seemed of that kind which melted in love and which kindled in war;" he was handy at "the broadsword and target." But he had no settled convictions; mere chance decided his change from a captain in the king's army to a rebel under Bonnie Prince Charlie, and when he could not win Flora McIvor he subsided cheerfully enough on the more commonplace Rose Bradwardine. Scott himself confessed to his friend Merritt that the Captain was a failure.

"The hero," he says, "is a sneaking piece of imbecility, and if he had married Flora she would have set him up on the chimney-piece as Count Borolaski's wife used to do with him. I am a bad hand at depicting a hero properly so called, and have an unfortunate propensity for the dubious characters of Borderers, buccaneers, Highland robbers, and all others of a Robin Hood description."

Waynefleet, Lady Cicely, heroine of George Bernard Shaw's comedy *Captain Brassbound's Conversion*, a pleasant society lady, frank and naïve, whose predominant impulse is to attribute the best of qualities even to the worst of people, thus converting them for the nonce into the ideal that she conceives.

One of the most living and laughing things that her maker has made. I do not know any stronger way of stating the beauty of the character than by saying that it was written specially for Ellen Terry, and that it is, with Beatrice, one of the very few characters in which the dramatist can claim some part of her triumph.—G. K. CHESTERTON : *George Bernard Shaw.*

Combining, as she does, the temperament of Ellen Terry with the genial esprit of Bernard Shaw, Lady Cicely is a thoroughly delightful and unique type of the eternal feminine.—ARCHIBALD HENDERSON: *George Bernard Shaw,* p. 324.

Wegg, Silas, in Dickens's *Our Mutual Friend* (1864–65), a one-legged rascal who ekes out a living by keeping a stand in Cavendish Square, where he sells fruit, gingerbread, and ballads. Mr. Boffin, in sheer kindness of heart, hires him for two hours every evening to read to him. The rascally Wegg pries around the premises, and, having found a Harmon will of later date than that under which Boffin had taken the Harmon estate, hoped to blackmail Boffin, but was checkmated by the production of a still later will.

Weller, Samuel (better known as Sam; called Samivel by his father), in Dickens's *Pickwick Papers,* an embodiment of London low life in its kindliest and most entertaining form. He is introduced as the Boots in the White Hart Inn, where his high spirits and his unfailing humor so attract Mr. Pickwick that he engages him as valet. Thereafter Sam is a devoted attendant, who remains faithful in every adversity, even sharing his master's imprisonment in the Fleet by having himself arrested for debt. Sam Weller may have flashed upon Dickens in memory of Sam Vale, an actor familiar to him in boyhood. Vale was the Simon Spatterdash of a musical farce, *The Boarding House,* revived in 1822, whose conversation is interlarded with comparisons like, "Come on, as the man said to his tight boot." From the stage Sam Vale carried this trick of speech into private life, and, being a man with a great reputation for humor, both on and off the stage, the latest Sam Valerism would circulate from mouth to mouth. For the rest the name Weller was familiar to Dickens; his mother had a maid called Mary Weller, apothesized in *Pickwick* as Mary the pretty housemaid, to whom Sam writes his famous valentine.

Sam Weller is a monster; monstrous and impossible in two ways: first from within, by the law of his own being, which would not permit such a development as must have produced the creature Dickens has shown us; next from without, the conditions of life would restrain and repress such development, even if the germ of it existed. . . . Yet, monster as he is, how real he seems! he is a living monster; we know him. Sam Weller lives in our memories, a creature of flesh and blood more real than half our acquaintances."—RICHARD GRANT WHITE, in *St. James's Magazine,* August, 1870.

Sam Weller corresponds to no reality. The Londoner born and bred is apt to be the dryest and most uninteresting of beings. All things lost for him the gloss of novelty when he was fifteen years old. He would suit the museum of a *nil admirari* philosopher, as a specimen, shrivelled and adust, of the ultimate result of his principle. But Dickens collected more jokes than all the cabmen in London would utter in a year, and bestowed the whole treasure upon Sam.—PETER BAYNE.

Weller, Tony, in *Pickwick Papers,* the father of Samuel, a coachman of the long-extinct type which drove stages between London and the suburban towns. Tony's provincial end was Dorking. He wore a broad-brimmed hat, top-boots, a great-coat of many capes, and a multitude of waistcoats. Doubtless Dickens found the original in real life, but his imagination may have been stimulated by Washington Irving's description of the type.

He has commonly a broad, full face, curiously mottled with red, as if the blood had been forced by hard feeding into every vessel of the skin; he is swelled into jolly dimensions by frequent potations of malt liquors, and his bulk is still further increased by a multiplicity of coats in which he is buried like a cauliflower, the upper one reaching to his heels. He wears a broad-brimmed, low-crowned hat; a huge roll of colored handkerchiefs around his neck, knowingly knotted and tucked in at the bosom; and has in summertime a large bouquet of flowers in his button-hole,—the present, most probably, of some enamoured country lass. His waistcoat is commonly of some bright color, striped, and his small-clothes extend far below the knees to meet a pair of jockey boots which reach about half-way up his legs.—IRVING: *The Sketch-book, The Stage-Coach.*

Wemmick, in Dickens's novel, *Great Expectations* (1860), cashier to Mr. Jaggers. In the office he is hard, business like, unimaginative. At home he is all imagination. With his own hands he had transformed his little wooden house, which he calls the Castle, into the semblance of a miniature fort. It has a real flagstaff. A plank crossing a ditch four feet wide and two deep represents the drawbridge. Here he lives with his octogenarian father, whom he calls the Aged, and whose daily delight is to fire off the nine o'clock signal gun, mounted in a separate fortress made of lattice-work. There is an evident reminiscence here of Smollett's Commodore Trunnion.

Wenham, in Thackeray's novel, *Vanity Fair,* the Marquis of Steyne's managing man. A mean, despicable creature, he is plausibly believed to have been drawn from the managing man of the third Marquis of Hertford, John Wilson Croker, the Rigby (*q.v.*)

of *Coningsby.* It is said that, when Croker was dead, a mutual friend told Thackeray how Croker had begged his wife to seek out some homeless boys to stay with them from Saturday till Monday. " They will destroy your flower-beds and upset my ink-stands, but we can help them more than they can hurt us." Thackeray choked, and called upon Mrs. Croker and assured her he would never speak ill of her husband again.—LOUIS MELVILLE: *Prototypes of Some of Thackeray's Characters.*

Werner, the name assumed by Kruitzner, Count of Siegendorf, hero of Byron's tragedy, *Werner, or the Inheritance* (1822). Byron avowedly took his plot from *Kruitzner, or the German's Tale,* in the *Canterbury Tales* (vol. III), by the Misses Lee. Harriet Lee, the younger of the sisters, was sole author of *Kruitzner.* Disowned by his father because he has married beneath him, *Kruitzner,* in a moment of desperation, steals a rouleau of gold from the usurping heir, Stralenheim. He confesses to his wife and his son Ulric, but urges in extenuation of his crime that he might have slain the enemy who stood between him and his own. The confession and its plea have an odd issue. Ulric, apparently aghast at his father's guilt, is really spurred on to the greater guilt which his father had avoided. Accident reveals the truth after Kruitzner has regained his ancestral estates, and when Ulric is on the point of marrying the daughter of the dead Siegendorf. Ulric disappears with his father's curse. The curtain descends upon a death-stricken family.

Werther, hero of a novel, *The Sorrows of Werther* (1774), by Wolfgang Goethe. He is a young German student, morbid, over-sensitive, poetical, artistic, who retires into the country for rest and solace. He finds both in his new surroundings. Everything interests him, the children who play around him, the old women who wait upon him, the simple life of his neighbors. He meets Charlotte, wife of his friend Albert. Liking blazes into a terrible passion. He flees back to town. The old life is more loathsome than ever. He wearies of the monotony of conventional society, his pride is hurt by aristocratic pretensions. In vain he returns to the country. The renewal of his acquaintance with Charlotte only accentuates his despair. He ends by shooting himself.

The novel was founded partly upon the story of Goethe's friend, a sentimentalist named Jerusalem, who committed suicide in 1772, and partly by the story of Goethe's own relations with Lotte (*i.e.*, Charlotte) Buff, whom he met (1772), during the interval between her betrothal and her marriage with his friend Kestner and who awoke in him a passion from which he delivered himself by flight.

Western, Sophia, heroine of Fielding's novel *Tom Jones*, who, after a series of misconceptions and misadventures, marries the not entirely worthy hero. She is drawn from the same model as Amelia Booth,—*i.e.*, Fielding's wife. Sophia and Amelia represent Miss Charlotte Cradock before and after she became Mrs. Henry Fielding. Miss Sophia is the model English maid of her period, a little too soft and sweet and yielding for the modern taste, but historically true to the past. A tender heart is conjoined with a cultivated mind; the beauty of her person is an index of the soul that lodges there. She never wavers in her love and reverence for her father, despite all he is and says and does. She does not even ask herself whether he might not more profitably employ his time than in getting drunk every afternoon. She will not marry a man she loathes, but short of that she will obey her father in all things, will submit unquestioningly to his abuse and his punishments.

Western, Squire, in *Tom Jones*, father of the above, an all-too-faithful picture of the English country gentleman of the mid-eighteenth century. Though bred at the university, he talked the broad dialect of Somersetshire, cursed and swore and used foul language in the presence of his womenkind on any provocation, was a cruel tyrant to his daughter Sophia (whom at the same time he idolized), and got drunk every day of his life.

An inimitable picture of ignorance, prejudice, irascibility, and rusticity, united with natural shrewdness, constitutional good humor, and an instinctive affection for his daughter.—SIR WALTER SCOTT.

White Lady of Avenel, in Scott's historical novel, *The Monastery* (1820), a mysterious spirit who watches over the fortunes of the Avenel family, and is "aye seen to yammer [shriek] and wail before ony o' that family dies." Among other "braw services," she rescued Lady Alice's "thick black volume with silver clasps" from the papist hands of Father Philip and Father Eustace, and afterward took Halbert Glendenning into "the bowels of the earth," there to find it lying in a pyramid of fire, yet unconsumed. This is how she describes herself:

Something betwixt heaven and hell,
Neither substance quite or shadow;
Haunting lonely moor and meadow,
Dancing by the haunted spring;
Riding on the whirlwind's wing;
Aping in fantastic fashion
Every change of human passion

She reappears in *The Abbot*, to show her interest in the marriage of Roland Avenel with Catherine Seyton, and "was seen to sport by her haunted well with a zone of gold around her bosom as broad as the baldrick of an earl." (See BANSHEE.)

White, Selma, in Robert Grant's novel, *Unleavened Bread* (1900), a young Western woman, of comparatively humble birth, who sacrifices self-respect and happiness in ceaseless struggle as a soldier climber. She secures a divorce from her first husband, marries an architect from New York, and removes thither, to find that he does not enjoy the social distinction she covets. On his death, she allies herself to a politician whose views of life, though different from hers, are equally meretricious. He becomes Governor and United States Senator, but falls through corrupt practices, carrying her down into the gutter with himself.

Wickfield, Agnes, in Dickens's *David Copperfield* (1849–50), daughter of Mr. Wickfield, a solicitor, and second wife of David. Andersen saw in Mrs. Dickens a likeness to this character. She is more plausibly a portrait of that lady's sister, Georgiana Hogarth.

In Agnes he has painted for us a perfectly unselfish character, living day by day in the lives of others, but accustomed from childhood to a certain self-restraint, which enables her the better to conceal the one attachment of her life under the modest veil of true sisterly affection, to be for years as an adopted sister to the man whom in the secret shrine of her pure heart she worshipped as a lover.—M. E. TOWNSEND: *Great Characters of Fiction*, p. 75.

I had heard many people remark that Agnes in *David Copperfield* was like Dickens's own wife, and, although he may not have chosen her deliberately as a model for Agnes, yet still I can think of no one else in his books so near akin to her in all that is graceful and amiable. Mrs. Dickens had a certain soft womanly repose and reserve about her; but whenever she spoke there came such a light into her large eyes, and such a smile upon her lips, and there was such a charm in the tones of her voice, that henceforth I shall always connect her and Agnes together.—H. C. ANDERSEN: *Autobiography*.

Wild Irish Girl, title of a novel (1806) by Sydney Owenson, Lady Morgan, and nickname of its heroine, Glorvina,—in whom acquaintances of the author detected a clever bit of self-portraiture. She is the last descendant of a line of Connaught princes who for centuries had been at feud with the Sassenach earls that had dispossessed them. The heir to the earldom wooes her in disguise, and wins her after many romantic vicissitudes.

Wild, Jonathan (1682–1725), a famous criminal who was hanged at Tyburn. He is said to have married six wives. He was a receiver of stolen goods, who for a long time, by clever technicalities, evaded the law, and the head of a large corporation of thieves, whom he organized into gangs, each with its allotted sphere of work. An adept in suborning perjury, he could protect the loyal among his followers and crush the disloyal through the constituted legal channels. He is a subsidiary character in Ainsworth's *Jack Sheppard*, the subject of a ballad, *Newgate's Garland*, printed in Swift's *Miscellanies*, and the hero of romances by Defoe and Fielding. The latter, *The History of Johnathan Wild the Great* (1742), departs widely from fact. Fielding makes his hero a dissolute rake of ancient lineage, who achieves the sort of greatness that is measured by success in crime. In his youth he is thrown in with a French gambler, Count La Ruse, and so far betters his master's instructions that the count himself becomes his victim. All goes well with Wild until his marriage with Letitia Snap, a match for himself in deceit and vileness. She betrays him and he perishes on the gallows.

Wildair, Sir Harry, one of Farquhar's best-drawn characters, first introduced in his comedy, *The Constant Couple*, and afterward made the hero of its sequel, *Sir Harry Wildair*. He is the original of all that class of characters who throw the witchery of high birth and splendid manners and reckless dash, good humor, generosity, and gayety over the qualities of the fop, the libertine, and the spendthrift. Farquhar improved upon this first sketch in his *Mirabel*. Sheridan seized the type and made it his own in the still more famous Sir Charles Surface, and it is now a stock character on the stage.

Wilder, in Cooper's romance of the sea, *The Red Rover* (1827), the name assumed by Henry Ark in his effort to capture the famous pirate.

Wildfire, Madge, in Scott's romance, *The Heart of Midlothian* (1818), Meg Murdockson's daughter, driven to insanity by the profligate George Staunton. She is described as " a tall, strapping wench, of eighteen or twenty, dressed fantastically in a sort of blue riding-coat, with tarnished lace; her hair clubbed like that of a man; a Highland bonnet and a bunch of broken feathers: a riding-skirt or petticoat of scarlet camlet embroidered with tarnished flowers. Her features were coarse and masculine, yet, at a little distance, by dint of very bright, wild-looking black eyes, an aquiline nose, and a commanding profile, appeared rather handsome." She derived her nickname from her favorite song, beginning—

I glance like wildfire through country and town.

Coleridge pronounced her the most original of all Scott's characters. Scott himself, in his notes to the novel, says she was modelled (with differences) from Feckless (weakminded) Fannie, a curious, crazed, pathetic figure, who wandered the country far and near about the end of the eighteenth century.

Wildgoose, Geoffrey, hero of a satirical novel, *The Spiritual Quixote* (1772), by Richard Greaves, a not very successful burlesque in the manner of Cervantes. Wildgoose, a young Oxonian, becomes a convert to Methodism, and roams around Gloucestershire and Somerset in company with the cobbler Jeremiah Tugwell.

Wilding, John, in *The Liar* (1761), a farce by Samuel Foote, a young gentleman fresh from Oxford, who has a marvellous faculty for romancing. The original play in Spanish had already been utilized by Corneille in *Le Menteur* and by Steele in his *Lying Lover* (1704).

Wilkins, Peter, hero of *The Life and Adventures of Peter Wilkins, relating chiefly his shipwreck near the South Pole,* etc. (1750). It purported to be written by " R. S., a passenger in the *Hector*," but is now definitely attributed to one Robert Paltock. Like Robinson Crusoe, Wilkins was a voyager shipwrecked on a desolate shore, whereon for a considerable time he dwelt alone. Finally, through a subterranean cavern he passed into a kind of New World, and met with a Gawrey, or Flying Woman, whose life he saved and whom he married. She took him to Nosmnbdsgrsutt, the country of Glumms and Gawreys, or men and women who fly, and a large part of the narrative is devoted to a description of their manners and customs. See YOUWARKEE.

Willet, John, in Dickens's *Barnaby Rudge* (1841), landlord of the Maypole Inn at Chigwell; a burly, large-headed man, with a fat face which betokened profound obstinacy and slowness of apprehension, combined with a very strong reliance on his own merits.

His pig-headedness drives his son Joe to enlist as a soldier; Joe comes back without his right arm, marries Dolly Varden, and succeeds his father as landlord of the Maypole Inn.

William, Sweet. See SUSAN, BLACK-EYED.

Williams, Caleb, in William Godwin's novel of that name (1794), an intelligent young peasant, taken as secretary into the service of Falkland (*q.v.*), the lord of the manor. Partly through inquisitiveness, partly by accident, he discovers the secret of the gloom and mystery hanging round his master. Falkland has committed a murder and allowed an innocent man to suffer the penalty. Finding that Williams knows all, he swears him to secrecy under frightful penalties. Williams's spirit revolts at the servile submission required from him. He escapes from the house. Twice Falkland tracks him down, and has him thrown into prison on a charge of robbery; twice the victim escapes, until, harassed and driven into a corner, he conceives himself absolved from his oath and comes forward as the public accuser of Falkland.

Williams, Slogger, in Thomas Hughes's *Tom Brown at Rugby,* the nickname of the school bully and fistic champion, bested by the hero in a great fight incurred by Tom in defence of his friend Arthur. The account is of quite a professional character. The fight is stopped by the doctor as " The Slogger " is thrown for the third time. Thackeray has a similar episode in *Vanity Fair* (1848), where Cuff, the Cock of the Walk, is reduced to the rank of second Cock by the prowess of the despised " Figs," —*i.e.*, Dobbin.

Willie, Holy, hero of a poem, *Holy Willie's Prayer,* by Robert Burns, a canting hypocrite, recognized as a legitimate caricature of one William Fisher, leading elder in the kirk-session at Kilmarnock, who had publicly denounced the poet for immorality. This precious pharisee was afterward found guilty of embezzling money from the church offerings. He ended his career by dying in a ditch, into which he had fallen when intoxicated.

Wilmot. There are three characters of this name, differentiated as Old Wilmot, Mrs. Wilmot, and Young Wilmot, in George Lillo's tragedy, *Fatal Curiosity* (1736). The story is that of a father and mother reduced to the extremity of want, who murder a visitor to their house for the sake of his casket of jewels, and afterward find the victim was their son. Young Wilmot, returning home after an absence of many years, had been prompted by curiosity to visit his parents incognito, and his mother, in her turn, had the curiosity to examine the stranger's box while he was taking an opportune nap. Lillo found his material in a pamphlet purporting to narrate an episode which happened in 1618 at "Perin," —*i.e.*, Penryn, the scene of the drama. Goethe produced *Fatal Curiosity* at Weimar (excusing himself on the plea that wine-drinkers relish an occasional glass of brandy), and this production suggested to Zacharias Werner his *February 24,* the most successful of all German *Schicksalstragödien* (or *Fate-Tragedies*). See also CHARLOTTE.

Wilson, William, hero of a short story by E. A. Poe. Wilson has an *alter ego* or *doppelgänger,* who pursues him through life and finally kills him in a duel. See JEKYLL, DR.

He [Poe] lived and died a riddle to his friends. Those who had never seen him in a paroxysm could not believe that he was the perverse and vicious person painted in the circulated tales of his erratic doings. To those who had he was two men,—the one an abnormally wicked and profane reprobate, the other a quiet and dignified gentleman. The special moral and mental condition incident to cerebral epilepsy explains these apparent contradictions as felicitously as it elucidates the intellectual and psychical traits of his literature.—FRANCIS GERRY FAIRFIELD: *A Madman of Letters, Scribner's Monthly,* x, p. 696.

Wimble, Will, a member of the fictitious *Spectator Club (q.v.);* said to be intended as a portrait of a Mr. Thomas Morecroft (d. 1741).

Winkelried, Arnold von, an historical character, whom James Montgomery makes the hero of a narrative poem, *Make Way for Liberty.* At the great battle of Sempach, July 9, 1836, which freed Switzerland from the yoke of Austria, the Swiss had failed for a long time to break the serried ranks of the enemy. At last Arnold, commending his wife and children to the care of his comrades, rushed forward, hurled himself upon the Austrian spears, and fell pierced through and through, but not before he had opened a way for his countrymen to follow him to victory.

Winkle, Mr., Senior, in Dickens's *Pickwick Papers,* father of Nathaniel Winkle; an old wharfinger at Birmingham, a man of methodical habits, never committing himself hastily in any affair. He is greatly displeased at his son's marriage to Miss Arabella Allen, but finally forgives him, and admits that the lady is "a very charming little daughter-in-law, after all."

Winkle, Nathaniel, a member of the Corresponding Society of the Pickwick Club, and a cockney pretender to sporting skill.

Winkle, Rip Van, hero and title of a short story (1819), by Washington Irving, adopted from the German legend of Peter Klaus, a goatherd, who fell asleep one day upon the Kyffhäuser Hills and did not wake up till twenty years after, when he returned to his native village to find everything changed and no one who knew him. In Irving's tale the hero is one of the Dutch colonists of New York, who, just before the Revolution, goes to sleep in the Kaatskill, and wakes to find that George Washington has ousted George III and that great changes have occurred in his village and his home. A stage version by Boucicault earned great success through the histrionic genius of Joseph Jefferson.

The first number of the *Sketch-book* contained the tale of Rip Van Winkle, one of the most charming and suggestive of legends, whose hero is an exceedingly pathetic creation. It is indeed a mere sketch, a hint, a suggestion; but the imagination readily completes it. It is the more remarkable and interesting because, although the first American literary creation, it is not in the least characteristic of American life, but, on the contrary, is a quiet and delicate satire on it. The kindly vagabond asserts the charm of loitering idleness in the sweet leisure of woods and fields, against the characteristic American excitement of the overflowing crowd and crushing competition of the city, its tremendous energy, and incessant devotion to money-getting.—CHARLES DUDLEY WARNER: *Washington Irving.*

Winterblossom, Mr. Philip, in Scott's novel, *St. Ronan's Well,* the " man of taste " who presided over the *table d'hôte* at Meg Dod's, and was an influential member of the Committee of Management in the " infant Republic of St. Ronan's Well."

Witches, in Shakespeare's tragedy, *Macbeth,* three figures " so withered and so wild in their attire," who appear before Macbeth and Banquo in Act i, Sc. 1, and make startling prophecies concerning their future destinies. Lamb combats the idea that Shakespeare was indebted for the idea of his " weird sisters " to Middleton's tragedy, *The Witch.*

His witches are distinguished from the witches of Middleton by essential differences. These are creatures to whom man or woman plotting some dire mischief might resort for occasional consultation. Those originate deeds of blood, and begin bad impulses to men. From the moment that their eyes first meet with Macbeth's he is spellbound. That meeting sways his destiny. He can never break the fascination. These witches can hurt the body; those have power over the soul.—*Specimens of Early Dramatic Poetry.*

Witching Hill, an imaginary locality in which E. W. Hornung places eight tales which he has bound together under the general title of *Witching Hill* (1912). Several generations ago, we are told, this estate was the seat of a very wicked nobleman, and the evil he did lives after him. The Hill is cursed. All who come to occupy the suburban villas erected on the subdivided estate succumb to its evil influence. Blameless on arrival, they are speedily moved by an irresistible impulse to deeds of darkness.

Wititterley, Mr. Henry, in Dickens's *Nicholas Nickleby,* a self-important snob, plain in face and manners, but continually boasting of his acquaintance with the aristocracy. His wife, Julia, is a tufthunter as shoddy as himself. The couple are an apparent reminiscence of Beau Tibbs and his wife, but painted with a coarser brush.

Witwould, Sir Wilful, hero of Congreve's comedy, *The Way of the World* (1700), a coxcomb, light-hearted, cynical, and well-bred, who never opens his lips without a compliment, and in his extravagant chatter reaches the utmost heights of folly.

Woffington, Margaret, or **Peg,** in Charles Reade's drama, *Masks and Faces* (1852), afterward turned into the novel, *Peg Woffington,* is the Irish actress of that name (1718-1760), who bewitched the London public and was the mistress of David Garrick before his marriage. Here she is represented as of virginal innocence, beautiful and vivacious, of brilliant wit and of extraordinary mimetic powers. In the greenroom of Covent Garden Theatre she tricks an entire dramatic company by impersonating the tragic actress Anne Bracegirdle. Later, in the studio of James Triplett, who has painted her portrait, she successfully essays a more difficult feat. A party composed of actors and would-be art critics are coming in an unfavorable mood to criticise the painting. She cuts out the painted face, inserts her own in the aperture, and, after the fault-finders have done their worst, confounds them by exploding the truth upon them.

Wolsey, Thomas, Cardinal (1475-1530), a famous English statesman; lord chancellor and prime minister of Henry VIII from 1515 to 1529, when he fell in disgrace with the king and was deprived of his offices. A year later he died. He appears in Shakespeare's *Henry VIII* and is one of the great characters of the play, arrogant, aggressive, tricky, and revengeful when in power, but accepting his fall in a noble and chastened spirit.

Wolsey is drawn with superb power; ambition, fraud, vindictiveness, have made him their own, yet cannot quite ruin a nature possessed of noble qualities. It is hard at first to refuse to Shakespeare the authorship of Wolsey's famous soliloquy in which he bids his greatness farewell (III, ii, 350), but it is certainly Fletcher's.—E. DOWDEN: *Shakespeare Primer.*

Woodhouse, Emma, heroine of Miss Austen's novel, *Emma* (1816), a clever young woman, who exaggerates her own cleverness and meets with disaster in her attempts to marry off her friends to those she considers their proper mates. Finally when she discovers that Harriet Smith, an amiable weakling whom she had designed for Frank Churchill, is secretly in love with her own brother-in-law Knightly, Emma takes alarm, for she realizes that nobody save herself must marry him. Her unconscious admiration for Mr. Knightly's plain common sense, his honesty even in finding fault with her, and his quiet strength of character had changed with her own growth into love. Fortunately, he has been in love with her from the first.

Woodhouse, Mr., in Jane Austen's *Emma*, the father of the titular heroine. He is a valetudinarian, humored by his doctor, but unselfishly and courteously solicitous for others' health besides his own. His daughter has to be watchful lest out of sheer kindness he starve his guests. He chagrins Miss Bates by sending out the asparagus, thinking it not quite dressed. He makes amends with presents of pork, as " a leg of pork boiled delicately with a little turnip is not unwholesome." He is apt to be rather prolix over little Bella's sore throat and his one acrostic; " Kitty, a fair but frozen maid, kindled a flame that I deplore."

Woodville, Elizabeth, Lady Grey, queen of Edward IV, the first English woman who after the conquest was raised from the rank of subject to that of royalty. She was the widow of Sir John Gray when Edward IV, hunting in a forest near Grafton, her father's residence, first caught sight of her. She is introduced in Shakespeare's *Richard III*, and, in Act iv, Sc. iv, entertains a proposal from the enemy of her house for the hand of her daughter Elizabeth, secretly planning, however, to marry her to Richmond in case of the latter's success.

Worm, William, in *A Pair of Blue Eyes* (1873), one of the best-drawn of all Thomas Hardy's rustic characters. He is the Vicar's out-door man, a " poor, wambling creature," as he describes himself, afflicted with perpetual noises in his head, who " hoped Providence would have found it out by this time, living so many years in a parson's family, too, as I have, but 'a don't seem to relieve me. Ay, I be a poor, wambling man, and life's a mere bubble."

Wray, Enoch, hero of Crabbe's poem, *The Village Patriarch* (1738). A centenarian, blind and poor, he is reverenced by the entire neighborhood for his wisdom, meekness and pious resignation.

Wrayburn, Eugene, in Dickens's *Our Mutual Friend,* a briefless barrister who hates his profession, flippant, sarcastic, indolent, alternating from jovial high spirits to gloomy depression. Lizzie Hexam saves his life from the murderous machinations of the jealous schoolmaster, Bradley Headstone, and nurses him tenderly through a long and dangerous illness. He marries her and, transformed by the power of love, develops unsuspected purpose and energy.

Wren, Jenny, in Dickens's novel, *Our Mutual Friend,* an affectionate nickname generally given to Fanny Cleaver, a doll's dress-maker, from her diminutive size and the determined sprightliness with which she meets all misfortune. She supports a good-natured but drunken father known facetiously as Mr. Dolls.

This young lady is the type of a certain class of characters of which Mr. Dickens has made a specialty, and with which he has been accustomed to draw alternate smiles and tears according as he pressed one spring or another. But this is very cheap merriment and very cheap pathos. Miss Jenny Wren is a poor little dwarf, afflicted, as she constantly reiterates, with a "bad back" and "queer legs," who makes dolls' dresses, and is forever pricking at those with whom she converses in the air with her needle, and assuring them that she knows "their tricks and their manners." Like all Mr. Dickens's pathetic characters, she is a little monster.— HENRY JAMES: *Views and Reviews.*

Wronsky, Count Alexis, in Tolstoy's novel, *Anna Karenina*, the lover of the heroine. (See KARENINA.)

Wronsky is described to us by Stiva: he is "one of the finest specimens of the *jeunesse dorée* of St. Petersburg; immensely rich, handsome, aide-de-camp to the emperor, great interest at his back and a good fellow notwithstanding; more than a good fellow, intelligent besides and well read—a man who has a splendid career before him." Let us complete the picture by adding that Wronsky is a powerful man, over thirty, bald at the top of his head, with irreproachable manners, cool and calm, but a little haughty. A hero, one murmurs to oneself,

too much of the Guy Livingstone type, though without the bravado and exaggeration. . . . But Wronsky improves toward the end.—MATTHEW ARNOLD: *Essays in Criticism.* II Series.

Wynne, Hugh, hero of a novel of the American Revolution, *Hugh Wynne, Free Quaker* (1897), by Dr. S. Weir Mitchell. Hugh, who tells his own story, is the son of a Quaker merchant in Philadelphia, sternly set against all youthful folly and against any armed resistance to constituted authority. In his youth, however, he had married a gay, light-hearted, but loving and devoted French girl, whose traits mingle antagonistically with the Quaker inheritance in young Wynne's blood. The latter defies his father, joins the rebels, and rises, after many vicissitudes, to be a brevet lieutenant-colonel on Washington's staff. He loves Darthea Peniston, but this romance is complicated by the fact that she is loved also by his best friend, Jack Warder, and his worst enemy, Arthur Wynne, his own cousin and a plausible villain.

X, Y

Xury, in Defoe's *Robinson Crusoe,* a Moresco boy, servant to Crusoe.

Yahoos, in Swift's *Gulliver's Travels* (1726), a race of beings, human in shape but brutish or worse in spirit. Squalid, screaming, filthy wretches, they evidently represent Swift's idea of what humanity really is beneath its veneer of civilization and under its accidental complement of clothes. Contrasted with them are their masters, the gentle and gracious Houyhnhnms, a race of horses endowed with reason.

Yarico, heroine of the story, *Inkle and Yarico,* told by Richard Steele in the *Spectator,* No. 11 (March 13, 1711), and which he found in Ligon's *History of Barbadoes* (1657).

She was a slave in the West Indies where Ligon himself was her overseer. In 1647 a young Londoner, Thomas Inkle, landed on the island with a party of prospectors, who were

intercepted by the natives. All were slain save Inkle, who was hidden away in the forests and protected by Yarico. Some months later the couple sighted a passing vessel, and escaped on it to the Barbadoes. This was a slave mart. As they neared the port, Inkle's love of gain and habits of civilization resumed their sway. He sold Yarico for a large sum, partly based upon her hope of motherhood. George Colman, the younger, founded a musical drama, *Inkle and Yarico* (1787), on this plot, which had already been utilized by the German Gessner (1762). Rufus Dawes in 1839 published a poem, *Yarico's Lament;* Edward Jerningham another, *The Epistle of Yarico to Inkle* (1766).

Yorick, in Shakespeare's *Hamlet,* is alluded to in Act v, 1, as a former jester at the King of Denmark's court. Hamlet, picking up his skull in the graveyard scene, tells Horatio that he remembered him as "a fellow of infinite jest, of most excellent fancy," and is led on to moralizing on the pathos of life and death.

Laurence Sterne borrows the name for one of his characters in *Tristram Shandy*, a lively, reckless, and humorous parson, whom he represents as of Danish origin and a descendant from Shakespeare's Yorick. Sterne drew this portrait from himself, virtually acknowledging as much when he took it as a pseudonym on the title-page of *A Sentimental Journey* and some volumes of sermons.

Edward Dowden, in his *Shakespeare Primer*, makes a brilliant suggestion: Jaques died, we know not how or when or where; but he came to life again a century later, and appeared in the world as an English clergyman. We need stand in no doubt as to his character, for we all know him under his later name of Laurence Sterne. "Mr. Yorick made a mistake about his family tree; he came not out of the play of *Hamlet*, but out of *As You Like It*. In Arden he wept and moralized over the wounded deer, and at Namport his tears and sentiment gushed forth for the dead donkey."

Youwarkee, heroine of Robert Paltock's *Adventures of Peter Wilkins* (1750). She is a Gawrey, or flying woman, in the imaginary country of Nosmnbdsgrsutt. Wilkins, a ship-wrecked mariner, came upon the lady when she was wounded, nursed her back to health, accompanied her to her people, and married her. The flying apparatus of these people (called a *graundee*) consisted of a natural investment like delicate silk and whalebone, which flew open at pleasure, and thus furnished its possessor with wings or a dress, according to the requirement of the moment. Peter's future wife had been sporting in the air with some other young damsels, one of whom, happening to brush too strongly against her as they stooped among some trees, had occasioned the accident which was the cause of his good fortune.

The book is dedicated to Elizabeth, Countess of Northumberland. The author professes that it was after the pattern of her virtues he drew the "mind" of his Youwarkee.

Now, a sweeter creature is not to be found in books; and she does him immortal honor. She is all tenderness and vivacity; all born good taste and blessed companionship. Her pleasure consists but in his: she prevents all his wishes; has neither prudery nor immodesty; sheds not a tear but from right feeling; is the good of his home, and the grace of his fancy.—LEIGH HUNT.

Z

Zadig, hero of a philosophical romance *Zadig, or Destiny* (1747), by Voltaire. A young Babylonian, full of every virtue, religious without bigotry, profoundly versed in all the learning of his time, intelligent, acute, and clever, his comic misadventures when he seeks to reform the world are pegs for the author's philosophical commentary. In the end he finds that convention and formula are invincible, and that it is impossible to secure any adequate share of even altruistic happiness, by reason of the malice, selfishness, and stupidity of one's neighbors.

Zaïre, heroine and title of a five-act tragedy in verse (1732) by Voltaire. She is a captive among the Turks, born a Christian but brought up as a Mahomedan and now in love with the Moslem prince Orosmanes, who seeks her hand in marriage. At this juncture she is recognized by her father, Lusignan, and her brother, Nerestan, who have come to ransom all Christian captives. They are horrified at the contemplated sacrilege of marriage with an infidel. Zaïre keeps a midnight appointment with Nerestan, and is surprised by Orosmanes, who stabs her in the belief that she is faithless. When he learns that Nerestan is her brother, he stabs himself in turn over her corpse.

Zanga, in Young's tragedy of *The Revenge* (1721), is the Moorish servant of Don Alonzo, a Spaniard of military renown, whom he hates,—vicariously, for that he slew his father in battle, and personally, because he had struck him on the cheek. Swearing endless vengeance, Zanga insidiously separates Alonzo from friend and wife, prompting the execution of the one and the suicide of the other. Then he reveals the truth, exults when his dupe stabs himself, and goes to the scaffold contented with the ruin he has wrought. Zanga was a favorite part of Henry Mossop and John Kemble and was acted by Macready during his first season. (See ABDE-LAZER.)

Zanoni, hero of a novel of that name (1842) by Lord Lytton, a mysterious personage who communicates with spirits, possesses the power of prolonging life, and can produce gold and silver and precious stones from his crucible. After having lived many centuries, he marries an opera-singer, resigning thereby his gifts of supernatural vision and immortality, and perishes during the Reign of Terror.

Zarca, in George Eliot's poem, *The Spanish Gypsy* (1868), the lover of Fedalma.

A vision of no small beauty, the conception of a stalwart chief who distils the cold exultation of his purpose from the utter loneliness and obloquy of his race.—HENRY JAMES: *Views and Reviews.*

Zeluco, hero of a novel of that name (1786), by Dr. John Moore. A Sicilian nobleman, dull of intellect, handsome, profligate, passionate and vindictive, with no virtue save the courage that serves to stimulate his excesses, he passes through an unrestrained boyhood and a youth of dissipation to a manhood of conscienceless pride, lust and cruelty. The boy who in a fit of ill-temper crushes to death a sparrow in his hand, ripens into the man who, in causeless jealousy of his wife, strangles his infant child with the same remorseless fingers. Accidental retribution comes from the fatal stroke of a murderer while Zeluco himself was seeking to crown his infamies with a fearful tragedy.

Zenda, an imaginary castle in the imaginary country of Ruritania, the latter evidently modelled after one or more of the little Balkan kingdoms. Here for three mysterious months an English gentleman, Rudolf Rassendyll, is held captive as an involuntary and unconscious impersonation of the King of Ruritania, and here he wins the heart of the monarch's beautiful cousin.

Zenelophon. (See COPHETUA, KING.)

Zenobia, in *The Blithedale Romance* (1852), by Nathaniel Hawthorne, a brilliant and beautiful woman. She has a dark history, which she would forget in a later love for Hollingsworth. As he is in love with Priscilla, she drowns herself. There are few scenes in literature more realistic than the finding of Zenobia's body, in the dead of the night, drawn from the dark stream, a crooked, stiff shape, and carried to the farm-house, where old women in nightcaps jabber over it. The author doubts whether Zenobia, if she had forseen her appearance after drowning, would ever have committed the act. Hawthorne, in his *American Note-books*, describes a similar scene which happened when he was living at the Old Manse, but the victim here was an ordinary farmer's daughter. To some extent Zenobia was undoubtedly suggested by Margaret Fuller, who was with Hawthorne at Brook Farm, but her traits were probably drawn from various sources.

Zimri, in Dryden's *Absalom and Achitophel,* is a brilliant satire on the second Duke of Buckingham, who had previously caricatured the poet as Bayes (*q.v.*) in *The Rehearsal.* As Zimri conspired against Asa, king of Judah, so Buckingham "formed parties and joined factions" (1 Kings, xvi, 9) against Charles II and his brother James, Duke of York.

Some of the chiefs were princes in the land;
In the first rank of these did Zimri stand.
A man so various that he seemed to be
Not one, but all mankind's epitome;
Stiff in opinions, always in the wrong,
Was everything by starts and nothing long;
But in the course of one revolving moon
Was chymist, fiddler, statesman, and buffoon (l. 545).

Zriny, Nicholas, Count of, a Hungarian patriot (1508–1566), is especially famous for his defence of his castle of Szigeth against the besieging army of Soliman. He was killed in a last desperate sally, the Moslems then stormed the castle, but they had no sooner entered than the powder magazine exploded with terrific violence. This siege cost the invading army the lives of twenty thousand men. Moreover, the sultan himself, who had been in feeble health, three days before the capture of the castle, died of vexation at the repeated failure of his assaults. The story of Zriny, who is sometimes called the Hungarian Leonidas, has afforded a tempting subject to dramatists, but Körner's tragedy (1814) is the only one that has survived. An epic poem called *The Fall of Sigeth* was published in 1651 by Nicholas Zriny, a descendant of the great warrior.

Zuleika, in Byron's *Bride of Abydos* (1813), daughter of Giaffir, the pacha of Abydos. Her love for her cousin Selim is frowned upon by the pacha; the young couple elope and are pursued by Giaffir. Selim is shot, Zuleika dies of a broken heart.

Never was a faultless character more delicately or more justly delineated than that of Lord Byron's Zuleika. Her piety, her intelligence, her strict sense of duty, and her undeviating love of truth, appear to have been originally blended in her mind, rather than inculcated by education. She is always natural, always attractive, always affectionate; and it must be admitted that her affections are not unworthily bestowed.